Fodor's 2011

W9-AFV-790

ARIZONA &
THE GRAND
CANYON

Fodor's Travel Publications   New York, Toronto, London, Sydney, Auckland
www.fodors.com

Be a Fodor's Correspondent

Your opinion matters. It matters to us. It matters to your fellow Fodor's travelers, too. And we'd like to hear it. In fact, we *need* to hear it.

When you share your experiences and opinions, you become an active member of the Fodor's community. That means we'll not only use your feedback to make our books better, but we'll publish your names and comments whenever possible. Throughout our guides, look for "Word of Mouth," excerpts of your unvarnished feedback.

Here's how you can help improve Fodor's for all of us.

Tell us when we're right. We rely on local writers to give you an insider's perspective. But our writers and staff editors—who are the best in the business—depend on you. Your positive feedback is a vote to renew our recommendations for the next edition.

Tell us when we're wrong. We're proud that we update most of our guides every year. But we're not perfect. Things change. Hotels cut services. Museums change hours. Charming cafés lose charm. If our writer didn't quite capture the essence of a place, tell us how you'd do it differently. If any of our descriptions are inaccurate or inadequate, we'll incorporate your changes in the next edition and will correct factual errors at fodors.com *immediately*.

Tell us what to include. You probably have had fantastic travel experiences that aren't yet in Fodor's. Why not share them with a community of like-minded travelers? Maybe you chanced upon a beach or bistro or B&B that you don't want to keep to yourself. Tell us why we should include it. And share your discoveries and experiences with everyone directly at fodors.com. Your input may lead us to add a new listing or highlight a place we cover with a "Highly Recommended" star or with our highest rating, "Fodor's Choice."

Give us your opinion instantly at our feedback center at www.fodors.com/feedback. You may also e-mail editors@fodors.com with the subject line "Arizona Editor." Or send your nominations, comments, and complaints by mail to Arizona Editor, Fodor's, 1745 Broadway, New York, NY 10019.

You and travelers like you are the heart of the Fodor's community. Make our community richer by sharing your experiences. Be a Fodor's correspondent.

Happy Traveling!

Tim Jarrell, Publisher

FODOR'S ARIZONA & THE GRAND CANYON 2011
Editor: Cate Starmer

Editorial Contributors: John Blodgett, Andrew Collins, JoBeth Jamison, Melissa Kim, Cara LaBrie, Mara Levin

Production Editor: Evangelos Vasilakis
Maps & Illustrations: Mark Stroud, David Lindroth, *cartographers*; Bob Blake, Rebecca Baer, *map editors;* William Wu, *information graphics*
Design: Fabrizio La Rocca, *creative director*; Guido Caroti, Siobhan O'Hare, *art directors*; Tina Malaney, Nora Rosansky, Chie Ushio, Jessica Walsh, Ann McBride, *designers*; Melanie Marin, *senior picture editor*
Cover Photo: (Colorado River, Grand Canyon National Park): Marjorie McBride/ Alamy
Production Manager: Steve Slawsky

COPYRIGHT

ISBN 978-1-4000-0484-3

ISSN 1559-6230

SPECIAL SALES

This book is available at special discounts for bulk purchases for sales promotions or premiums. Special editions, including personalized covers, excerpts of existing books, and corporate imprints, can be created in large quantities for special needs. For more information, write to Special Markets/Premium Sales, 1745 Broadway, MD 6-2, New York, New York 10019, or e-mail specialmarkets@randomhouse.com.

AN IMPORTANT TIP & AN INVITATION

Although all prices, opening times, and other details in this book are based on information supplied to us at press time, changes occur all the time in the travel world, and Fodor's cannot accept responsibility for facts that become outdated or for inadvertent errors or omissions. So **always confirm information when it matters**, especially if you're making a detour to visit a specific place. Your experiences—positive and negative— matter to us. If we have missed or misstated something, **please write to us**. We follow up on all suggestions. Contact the Arizona & the Grand Canyon editor at editors@fodors. com or c/o Fodor's at 1745 Broadway, New York, NY 10019.

PRINTED IN CHINA

10 9 8 7 6 5 4 3 2 1

CONTENTS

Fodor's Features

MAPS

ABOUT THIS BOOK

Our Ratings

Sometimes you find terrific travel experiences and sometimes they just find you. But usually the burden is on you to select the right combination of experiences. That's where our ratings come in.

As travelers we've all discovered a place so wonderful that its worthiness is obvious. And sometimes that place is so experiential that superlatives don't do it justice: you just have to be there to know. These sights, properties, and experiences get our highest rating, **Fodor's Choice,** indicated by orange stars throughout this book.

Black stars highlight sights and properties we deem **Highly Recommended,** places that our writers, editors, and readers praise again and again for consistency and excellence.

By default, there's another category: any place we include in this book is by definition worth your time, unless we say otherwise. And we will.

Disagree with any of our choices? Care to nominate a place or suggest that we rate one more highly? Visit our feedback center at www.fodors.com/feedback.

Budget Well

Hotel and restaurant price categories from ¢ to $$$$ are defined in the opening pages of each chapter. For attractions, we always give standard adult admission fees; reductions are usually available for children, students, and senior citizens. Want to pay with plastic? **AE, D, DC, MC, V** following restaurant and hotel listings indicate if American Express, Discover, Diners Club, MasterCard, and Visa are accepted.

Restaurants

Unless we state otherwise, restaurants are open for lunch and dinner daily. We mention dress only when there's a specific requirement and reservations only when they're essential or not accepted—it's always best to book ahead.

Hotels

Hotels have private bath, phone, TV, and air-conditioning and operate on the European Plan (aka EP, meaning without meals), unless we specify that they use the Continental Plan (CP, with a Continental breakfast), Breakfast Plan (BP, with a full breakfast), or Modified American Plan (MAP, with breakfast and dinner) or are all-inclusive (AI, including all meals and most activities). We

always list facilities but not whether you'll be charged an extra fee to use them, so when pricing accommodations, find out what's included.

Listings	
★	Fodor's Choice
★	Highly recommended
⊠	Physical address
✛	Directions or Map coordinates
🕮	Mailing address
☎	Telephone
🖷	Fax
⊕	On the Web
✍	E-mail
🖾	Admission fee
☉	Open/closed times
Ⓜ	Metro stations
⊟	Credit cards
Hotels & Restaurants	
🏨	Hotel
↵	Number of rooms
☕	Facilities
⼌⃝⼌	Meal plans
✕	Restaurant
✑	Reservations
🏛	Dress code
↘	Smoking
🍷	BYOB
Outdoors	
🏌	Golf
⛺	Camping
Other	
♨	Family-friendly
⇒	See also
⊠	Branch address
☞	Take note

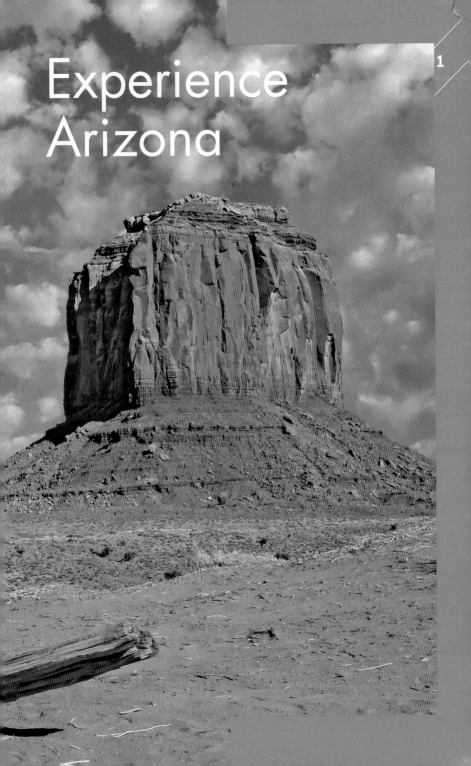

Experience
Arizona

WHAT'S WHERE

The following numbers refer to chapters.

2 Phoenix, Scottsdale, and Tempe. Rising where the Sonoran Desert meets the Superstition Mountains, the Valley of the Sun is filled with resorts and spas, shops and restaurants, more than 200 golf courses, and nearby mountains and trails.

3 Grand Canyon National Park. One of nature's longest-running works in progress, the canyon both exalts and humbles the human spirit. Whether you select the popular South Rim or the remote North Rim, don't just peer over the edge—take the plunge into the canyon on a mule train, on foot, or on a raft trip.

4 North-Central Arizona. Cool, laid-back towns here are as bewitching as the high desert landscape they inhabit. There are quaint escapes such as Prescott and Jerome, New Age Sedona with its red-rock buttes, and the vibrant university town of Flagstaff.

5 Northeast Arizona. This remote area includes the stunning surroundings of Monument Valley. Alongside today's Navajo and Hopi communities, the breathtaking Canyon de Chelly and Navajo National Monument are reminders of how ancient peoples lived with the land.

6 Eastern Arizona. Summer visitors flock to the lush, green White Mountains and the warm colors of the Painted Desert. Nearby Petrified Forest National Park protects trees that stood when dinosaurs walked Earth.

7 Tucson. The history of Arizona begins here, where Hispanic, Anglo, and Native American cultures became intertwined in the 17th century and still are today. Farther out, city slickers enjoy horseback rides at some of the region's many guest ranches, or luxury pampering at world-class spas.

8 Southern Arizona. Splendid mountain and desert scenery evokes the romanticized spirit of the Wild West. Enduring pockets of westward expansion are the largest draw today: infamous Tombstone and the mining boomtown Bisbee.

9 Northwest Arizona and Southeast Nevada. This underexplored corner of Arizona includes Lake Havasu City and its bit of Britannia in the form of London Bridge; old-fashioned Americana around Kingman, a hub on legendary Route 66; and Hoover Dam and Laughlin's casinos, just a short jaunt away in Nevada.

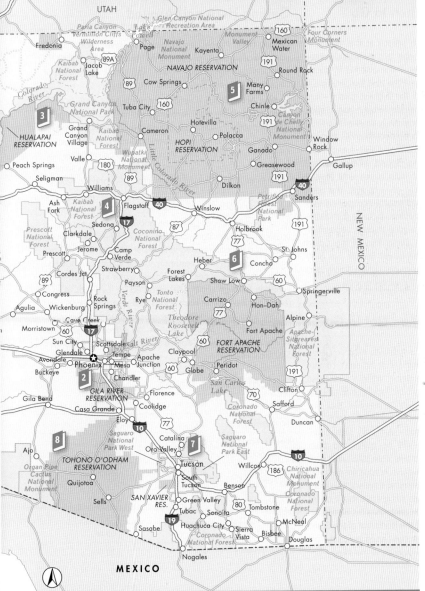

ARIZONA PLANNER

When to Go

High season at the resorts of Phoenix and Tucson is winter, when the snowbirds fly south. Expect the best temperatures—and the highest prices—from December through March, when nearly every weekend is filled with outdoor festivals and the air is scented with orange blossoms. Spring wildflowers are best from March until May. If you're on a budget, the posh desert resorts drop their prices—sometimes by more than half—from June through September. The South Rim of the Grand Canyon and Sedona are busy year-round, but least busy during the winter months.

When Not to Go

For a statewide excursion, keep in mind that Arizona's climate is extreme. While a winter visit might be most comfortable in Phoenix, remember that the Grand Canyon, Flagstaff, and Sedona—Arizona's high country—will be quite cold then. Also take note that areas such as eastern Arizona are designed for summer travelers, thus many shops and restaurants are closed in the winter months. Remember that the North Rim of the Grand Canyon is closed in winter, from mid-October to mid-May.

Getting Here and Around

Getting Here: Phoenix and Tucson have international airports; smaller, regional carriers fly into Flagstaff. Amtrak lines service Flagstaff and Tucson. Car rental is available at airports in Phoenix, Tucson, and Flagstaff.

Getting Around: You'll need a car to properly explore Arizona. Deceptively vast, Arizona is the nation's sixth-largest state at nearly 114,000 square mi. No matter where you start your journey, expect to spend a good portion of your time in the car. Fortunately, Arizona offers an attractive canvas that ranges from desert to forest. It surprises some visitors that the drive from Phoenix to the Grand Canyon takes at least a half day—and that's without stopping or taking side roads. See more driving times below.

Road conditions vary by season and location, so expect anything: you can start your day in 100°F heat in Phoenix and end it in near-freezing temperatures in the Grand Canyon. Be sure to plan accordingly for the weather: if driving in the desert in summer, keep bottled water in the car; in winter in the high country be prepared for icy roads. And remember that violent flash floods and dust storms can pepper the area during the summer monsoons. Storms usually pass quickly. For road information, the Arizona Department of Transportation has a travelers' assistance line. Just dial 511 from any phone.

Typical Travel Times

	Hours by Car	Distance
Phoenix–Flagstaff	2½	145 mi
Phoenix–Grand Canyon South Rim	4½	175 mi
Phoenix–Lake Mead/Hoover Dam	4½	260 mi
Phoenix–Monument Valley	6	275 mi
Phoenix–Yuma	3	185 mi
Tucson–Phoenix	2	120 mi

1

How's the Weather?

Phoenix averages 325 sunny days and 7 inches of precipitation annually. The high mountains see about 25 inches of rain. The Grand Canyon is usually cool at the rim and about 20°F warmer on the floor. The North Rim is generally about 10°F cooler than the South Rim, which is open year-round. Temperatures in valley areas like Phoenix and Tucson average about 60°F to 70°F in the daytime in winter and between 100°F and 115°F in summer. Flagstaff and Sedona stay much cooler, dropping into the 30s and 40s in winter and leveling off at 80°F to 90°F in summer.

What to Pack

Thanks to extreme climates and Western informality, you can go almost anywhere in Arizona in a pair of jeans.

■ Bring layers for trips north or east, particularly when temperatures dip after the sun sets.

■ For formal dining, call ahead for attire requirements. In most places, a shirt and dress slacks will be more than sufficient.

■ Depending on your desired level of activity, you will need to pack different gear: golf shoes, hiking boots, or flip-flops. Most golf courses offer club and golf-cart rentals, but plan on bringing your own shoes. If the slopes are your destination, you can rent all your ski or snowboard gear before hitting the lifts.

■ No matter your plans, be prepared with water, and hats and sunscreen for sun protection. The desert heat can be intense and quite deceptive.

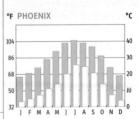

Tribal Lands

Arizona has 22 Native American reservations, each with its own government and culture. Most tribes have Web sites or phone-information lines, and it's best to contact them for information before a trip. Many require a permit for hiking or biking in scenic areas. Always be respectful of individual cultures and traditions.

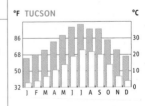

Did You Know . . .

With the exception of the Navajo Nation in the northeast corner of the state, Arizona does not observe daylight saving time. Arizona is in the mountain standard time zone.

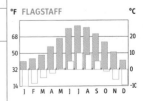

ARIZONA & THE GRAND CANYON TOP ATTRACTIONS

The Grand Canyon

(A) When it comes to visiting Grand Canyon National Park, there are statistics and there are sights, and both are sure to leave you in awe. With an average width of 10 mi, a length of 277 mi, and a depth of 1 mi, the enormity of the canyon is nearly impossible to fathom. You can view the spectacle from the South Rim, but the North Rim is the rim less traveled. Whether exploring the area on foot, by mule, by raft, or by plane, the journey is one worth savoring.

Petrified Forest and the Painted Desert

(B) The Painted Desert takes on hues that range from blood-red to the purest pink throughout the day. View a forest of trees that stood with dinosaurs at the Petrified Forest, as well as ancient dwellings and fossils. The pieces of petrified logs look deceptively like driftwood cast upon an oceanless beach. You can enjoy the entire national park in less than a day and take in a bit of nostalgia with Route 66's vestiges in nearby Holbrook along the way.

Sedona

(C) Loved for its majestic red rocks, its spiritual energy, and its fantastic resorts and spas, Sedona is unlike any other town in America. The fracturing of the western edge of the Colorado Plateau created the red-rock buttes that loom over Sedona, and this landscape has attracted artists, entrepreneurs, and New Age followers from all over who believe the area contains some of Earth's most important vortexes of energy. Take the active route and explore Oak Creek canyon and the surrounding area on foot or by bike or jeep; or indulge in the luxe life at a world-class spa or restaurant.

Scottsdale

(D) The West's most Western town, modern Scottsdale is equal parts kitsch and overt opulence. Resorts, spas, and golf can easily absorb an entire vacation. Stroll through art galleries and Western boutiques in Old Town during the day, and discover chic nightlife and fine cuisine at night. The weekly Art Walk and Frank Lloyd Wright's Taliesin West are a great introduction to Scottsdale's artistic scene. Scottsdale is part of the Valley of the Sun, along with Phoenix, Tempe, and some 20 other communities.

The Heard Museum

(E) One of Phoenix's cultural treasures, the Heard proudly features one of the most comprehensive collections of Native American art in the world. Interactive art-making exhibits are alongside a staggering amount of Southwestern pottery, jewelry, kachinas, and textiles. Plus, the museum gift shop is one of the best places in town to find authentic souvenirs worth cherishing.

Monument Valley

(F) One of the most familiar sights of Arizona—thanks to dozens of Hollywood productions and the keen eye of Ansel Adams—the fantastic sculpted red-sandstone buttes, mesas, and rock formations of Monument Valley Navajo Tribal Park are yet another reminder of the abundance of nature's handiwork in the Grand Canyon State. Take a Navajo-guided tour to appreciate the nuances of the area.

Desert Botanical Garden

(G) While there are stellar museums and preserves across Arizona, none is like the Desert Botanical Garden, 150 acres just outside downtown Phoenix dedicated to the diversity of the desert. With more than 4,000 species of cacti, succulents, trees, and flowers, visitors discover the variety and breadth of this mysterious landscape—all in the comfort of America's fifth-largest city.

QUINTESSENTIAL ARIZONA & THE GRAND CANYON

Road Trips

Arizona is the place to take a road trip. Get in the car, pick a destination, and go take a look. For optimal enjoyment, avoid the interstate highways and take the state routes instead. Stop at every roadside historic marker (well, OK, you can skip some if you want) and at any place with a sign that reads PIE.

Go to Bisbee. Go to Jerome. Go to Oatman. Go to Greer. Travel AZ 260 from Payson to Show Low or historic Route 66 from Ash Fork to Topock; take AZ 60 through the Salt River canyon, or U.S. 191 from Springerville to Clifton; take AZ 88, the Apache Trail, from Apache Junction to Roosevelt Dam.

Wherever you go, roll down the windows, turn up the radio, inhale deeply, and enjoy the ride. Regardless of your destination, the wide-open spaces of Arizona entice and amaze anew with every bend in the road.

Salsa and Margaritas

You're in Arizona, so join the quest to find your favorite salsa and margaritas. No two salsas are the same, and every city and town boasts its own local favorite. Spicy and chunky? Tangy and juicy? Tear-inducing? They run the gamut.

You'll find the flavors change regionally, from mesquite-imbued concoctions in the east, inspired by Tex-Mex cuisine, to fresh-from-the-garden medleys in southern Arizona that are authentically Mexican. In Tucson, check out Café Poca Cosa's salsa, a deep-red blend of garlic, chiles, and tomatoes that's almost decadent. In Phoenix the brave go to Los Dos Molinos, where powerful hatch chiles punctuate every dish.

Perfectly salty-and-sour margaritas can take the sting away from a particularly robust salsa, all while washing down a delightful Mexican feast. Though most tequila is from Mexico, in southern Arizona you can

Arizona is known for its magnificent natural landmarks, its rich history, and its captivating cuisine. Here are some easy ways to get to know the lay of the land and start thinking like an Arizonan.

see the agave plant, which is used to make the liquor.

The Night Sky

Away from the metropolitan areas of the Valley of the Sun (Phoenix, Tempe, Scottsdale, and surrounds) and Tucson, where the by-products of urban life obscure the firmament, the night sky is clear and unpolluted by lights or smog. In December in the desert, the Milky Way stretches like a chiffon scarf across the celestial sphere. Lie on your back on the hood of your car at night, allow your eyes time to adjust to the darkness, and you'll see more stars than you could have possibly imagined.

For a closer look, you can visit Lowell Observatory on Mars Hill, Northern Arizona University (both in Flagstaff) or the Kitt Peak National Observatory in southwest Arizona (outside Tucson) and look at celestial objects through large telescopes.

Rodeo

People take rodeo seriously in Arizona, whether it's a holiday extravaganza like those in Prescott or Payson (which draw top cowboys from around the country), a bull-riding competition at Camp Verde, or a bunch of working cowboys gathered for a team-roping contest in Williams.

These days, particularly with the emergence of bull riding as a stand-alone event—and the crowds often cheer as much for the bulls as the cowboys—rodeos are no longer the hayseed and cowpoke-y events Arizona grandpas might have enjoyed. Rock-and-roll rodeo has arrived and there is frequently live music as well as roping. And other cowboy experiences, like horseback riding and dude ranch stays, are as popular as ever. So, if you see a flyer posted in a shop window advertising a rodeo, take a walk on the wild side and check out the fine arts of riding and roping.

IF YOU LIKE

Hiking

Arizona has a wealth of awe-inspiring natural landmarks. So you can hike in and out, up and down, or around beautiful and varied landscapes, into canyons, to a mountain summit, or just along a meandering trail through a desert or a forest.

Wherever you go, make sure you're well prepared with water, food, a good hat, and a camera to capture your achievement. Be sure you have a decent pair of hiking shoes, and check the weather report first. Storms can roll into the desert quickly (particularly during monsoon season), and you don't want to get caught in a flash flood.

From the long-heralded trails such as **Bright Angel** in the Grand Canyon to iconic **Camelback Mountain** in Phoenix, there's a summit or path in every corner of the state waiting for you.

If waterfalls are your thing, check out **Havasu Canyon**, an 8-mi hike that descends 3,000 feet to splashing pools of turquoise water.

The highest of the four peaks that comprise San Francisco Peaks is **Mount Humphreys,** the ultimate goal for hikers seeking the best view in the state. Timing an ascent can be tricky, though, as the snow doesn't melt until mid-July, and by then the summer rains and lightning come almost daily in the afternoon. Go early in the morning and pay attention to the sky.

For some archaeology with your hiking, **Walnut Canyon National Monument** has a paved and stepped trail descending 185 feet into an island of stone where you can explore prehistoric cliff dwellings. There are steps and handrails, but the climb out is strenuous.

Water Sports

You don't miss the water until it's not there, but Arizonans do their best to ensure that the well doesn't go completely dry. Dams and canal systems help to fill vast reservoirs, and the resulting rivers and lakes provide all manner of water-sport recreation. Of course, this is a state that considers floating in a pool or soaking in a hot tub "water-sport recreation." You can have it easy, you can have it rough, or you can have it fast.

Easy is a week on a **houseboat** on a lake. Houseboats are available for rent on major lakes along the Colorado River, as well as on Lake Powell, Lake Mead, and Lake Havasu. On smaller lakes motorized boats are prohibited, but **kayaks** and **canoes** make for an enjoyable excursion along the pine-covered shorelines. You can even take a rowboat out on Tempe Town Lake, or bake in the sun while taking a lazy float down the Salt River just east of Phoenix.

Rough is a **river raft trip**. There are nearly two dozen commercial rafting companies offering trips as short as three days or as long as three weeks through the Grand Canyon. Options include motorized rafts or dories rowed by Arizona's version of the California surfer—the Colorado River boatman. The Hualapai Tribe, through the Hualapai River Runners headquartered in Peach Springs, offers one-day river trips. Don't let the short duration fool you: the boatmen take you through several rapids, and thrills abound.

Fast involves a **speedboat** and water skis or Jet Skis. Both are popular on major lakes and along the Colorado River. You can go from dam to dam along the Colorado, and on lakes the size of Powell and Mead you can ski until your legs give out.

Desert

Arizona has a desert for you; actually, it has more than one. The trouble is, any desert is inhospitable to life forms unaccustomed to its harsh realities. People die in the desert here every year, from thirst, exposure, and one inexplicable trait—stupidity. Using good sense, you can explore any stretch of desert in April and May and experience a landscape festooned with flowers and blooming cacti.

To experience the desert without running the risk of leaving your bones to bleach in the sun, there are two exceptional alternatives: the **Desert Botanical Garden** in Phoenix is a showcase of the ecology of the desert with more than 4,000 different species of desert flora sustained on 150 acres. A walk through here is wonderfully soothing and extremely educational. You'll be stunned at the variety of color and texture in native desert plants. It's much more than saguaro cactus. Be sure to check out the butterfly exhibit.

There's also the **Arizona-Sonora Desert Museum** in Tucson, which isn't really a museum but a zoo and a botanical garden featuring the animals and plants of the Sonoran Desert. If you want to see a diamondback rattlesnake without jumping out of your shoes, this is the place.

And, of course, there are long drives in which you can see the wide expanses from the comfort of your car. Early spring brings the flaming-red blossoms of the ocotillo and the soft yellow-green branches of the paloverde, and the desert will be carpeted with ephemeral flowers of pink, blue, and yellow.

Along U.S. Highway 93, south of Wikieup in northwest Arizona, you can see the desert in its most abundant display, but there are countless other places, as well.

Native American Culture

John Ford Westerns and the enduring myths of the Wild West pale in comparison to the experience of seeing firsthand the Native American cultures that thrive in Arizona. You can stop at a trading post and see artisans demonstrating their crafts, visit one of Arizona's spectacular Native American museums, or explore an ancient Native American dwelling.

Hubbell Trading Post and **Cameron Trading Post** are on Navajo reservations, while **Keam's Canyon Trading Post** is on the Hopi Reservation. The **Navajo Village Heritage Center** in Page offers an opportunity to understand life on the reservation.

The **Heard Museum,** in Phoenix, houses an impressive array of Native American cultural exhibits and has, quite possibly, the best gift shop in town if you're looking for something truly special and authentic. The **Museum of Northern Arizona,** in Flagstaff, has collections related to the natural and cultural history of the Colorado Plateau, an extensive collection of Navajo rugs, and an authentic Hopi kiva (men's ceremonial chamber). The **Colorado River Museum,** in Bullhead City, focuses on the history of the area and includes information and artifacts pertaining to the Mohave Indians. **Chiricahua Regional Museum and Research Center,** in Willcox, focuses on Apache culture.

The **Montezuma Castle National Monument** is one of the best-preserved prehistoric ruins in North America. **Tuzigoot National Monument** is not as well preserved as Montezuma Castle, but is more impressive in scope. The **Casa Grande National Monument** is a 35-foot-tall structure built by the Hohokam Indians who lived in the area.

TOP EXPERIENCES

Grand Canyon Hiking

You could spend the rest of your life hiking the Grand Canyon and never cover all the trails. There are hiking and walking trails aplenty, for all levels of fitness. Bright Angel Trail is the most famous, but it's tough: with an elevation change of more than 5,000 feet, don't try to hike to the Colorado River and back in one day. Less strenuous is part of the 12-mi Rim Trail, a paved, generally horizontal walk. Other outstanding choices are the South Kaibab Trail and the Hermit Trail. Many short routes lead to epic viewpoints, like the Cape Royal and Roosevelt Point trails on the North Rim.

Jeep Tours

Why drive yourself when open-air four-wheeling is available, complete with guide and driver? Jeep tours abound in the Grand Canyon state, whether it's a rough ride on a Pink Jeep tour in the red rocks of Sedona or a Lavender Jeep tour in historic Bisbee, a weeklong excursion or an afternoon adventure. Some of these companies have special permits that provide access to national forests, and an up-close view of Native American communities.

Colorado River-Rafting

Hiking too boring? Jeep tours not enough? True thrill-seekers take the plunge when they visit Arizona. There are nearly two dozen commercial river-rafting companies in Arizona that offer trips as short as a day or as long as three weeks through the Grand Canyon on the Colorado River. These rough-riding trips are popular with travelers, so be sure to make reservations very early, up to a year in advance.

Personal Pampering

If roughing it in the great outdoors isn't your vacation style, head to one of Arizona's world-class spas for a day of complete relaxation. Enjoy a standard mani-and-pedi afternoon, or further indulge in a specialty treatment, such as a creek-side massage at L'Auberge de Sedona, or a Native American–inspired session at the Golden Door Spa at the Boulders Resort in Carefree. Between sessions be sure to take advantage of relaxation rooms, saunas, and pools. Finish the day with a decadent meal at your resort's restaurant.

Biltmore Golfing

One of Phoenix's most historic hotels is also home to some of the Valley's most heralded golf courses. The Arizona Biltmore, Arizona's first resort, set the standard in 1929. The Biltmore has two 18-hole PGA championship courses, Adobe and Links. Arizona's climate is particularly hospitable to golfers, so green fees are especially pricey in winter and spring. Early risers can find slightly more affordable fees in the wee hours of the morning in summer. Other premier Phoenix-area courses where you can play like a pro include the Phoenician and Troon North.

Native American Traditions

Westerns and the enduring myths of the Wild West don't compare to the experience of seeing firsthand the Native American cultures that thrive in Arizona. In northeast Arizona, you can visit Navajo and Hopi reservations; there are more than 21 tribes in the state today. Stop at a trading post on a reservation to see artisans demonstrating their crafts. Visit one of Arizona's fantastic Native American museums, such as the Heard Museum in Phoenix or the Museum of Northern Arizona in Flagstaff. At spectacular national monuments, such as Montezuma Castle near Camp Verde, visitors can see 600-year-old preserved dwellings.

ARIZONA WITH KIDS

Places that are especially appealing to children are indicated by a rubber-duckie icon (🦆) in the margin.

Choosing a Destination

You can make your trip one for adventure, education, or good ole American play. Stay close to the urban areas surrounding Phoenix or Tucson if you want to revel in **water parks**, swimming pools, and resort children's programs. Travel north to Sedona, where you can see **Snoopy Rock**, before exploring the wonder that is the **Grand Canyon**. If you're looking for an educational journey, don't forget to stop by Phoenix's **Heard Museum** for an introduction to Native American cultures, or spend some quality time in northeast Arizona at **Monument Valley** or **Canyon de Chelly**, also geological marvels.

Choosing a Place to Stay

This is the Old West, after all, and there's a great deal of "roughing it" that you could experience if you're staying at **campsites**, **dude ranches**, or **motels** near the Grand Canyon or northeast Arizona. Don't expect to always have great mobile phone reception or even cable tv. Some motels like Holbrook's **Wigwam** even boast about their lack of technology.

The cities of Arizona, however, have some of the most heralded **resorts** in the world. In Phoenix, check out the **Arizona Grand Resort**, which has an extensive water park. Posh resorts like the **Fairmont Scottsdale Princess** and the **Westin Kierland Resort & Spa** have special kids-only programs that include evening "dive-in" movies and daytime sports and recreation instruction.

Outdoor Activities

With its majestic landscapes and sites that are right out of a Hollywood script, you're going to be spending a lot of your time in Arizona outside. Be sure to take advantage of the national parks' **Junior Ranger Programs**. Of course, there's nothing quite as up close and personal as a mule ride down the **Grand Canyon**, an adventurous rafting trip down the **Colorado River**, or a walk back in time through **Kartchner Caverns State Park**. Let your kids make the most of their digital cameras while they document your journey. If you prefer something slightly less adventurous, be sure to check out **Oak Creek canyon** in Sedona, and cool off at **Slide Rock State Park**. On one of your nights away from the city, take advantage of your location and search for constellations and stargaze.

Indoor Activities

On hot summer days, choose indoor activities for the afternoon, when the sun is at its most intense, and your kids are likely to be their least impatient. This might be a good time to head to downtown Phoenix and check out the **Heard Museum**, the **Phoenix Art Museum**, and the **Arizona Science Center**, all of which are steps away from the city's light-rail system. If you're in the cooler country, take advantage of nighttime programs and events at **Lowell Observatory in Flagstaff**, where you can watch the stars in relative comfort.

Road Trip Tips

Chances are, you'll be exploring most of Arizona by car. There are kid-friendly stops along the way from Phoenix to Sedona or the Grand Canyon, including **Meteor Crater** and **Montezuma Castle**, that can help break up your hours in the car. Children and adults alike can be quite stunned by how quickly Arizona's landscape changes. Your child could start the day in the desert, and wake up from a nap driving through a ponderosa pine winter wonderland in eastern Arizona.

OH STARRY NIGHT

TIPS FOR STARGAZING IN ARIZONA

If your typical view of the night sky consists of a handful of stars dimly twinkling through a hazy, light-polluted sky, get ready for a treat. In most of Arizona, the night sky blazes with starlight—and with a little practice, you can give your family a memorable astronomical tour.

Constellations

Constellations are stories in the sky—many depict animals or figures from Greek mythology. Brush up on a few of these tales before your trip, and you'll be an instant source of nighttime entertainment.

The stars in the Northern Hemisphere appear to rotate around Polaris, the North Star, in fixed positions relative to one another. To get your celestial bearings, first find the bright stars of the Big Dipper. An imaginary line drawn through the two stars that form the outside edge of the cup (away from the handle) will point straight to Polaris (Polaris also serves as the last star in the handle of the Little Dipper). Once you've identified Polaris, you should be able to find the other stars on our chart. Myriad astronomy books and Web sites have additional star charts; *National Geographic* has a cool interactive version with images from the Hubble Space Telescope (⊕ *www.nationalgeographic.com/stars*).

Planets

Stars twinkle, planets don't (because they're so much closer to Earth, the atmosphere doesn't distort their light as much). Planets are also bright, which makes them fairly easy to spot. Unfortunately, we can't show their positions on this star chart, because planets orbit the sun and move in relation to the stars.

The easiest planet to spot is Venus, the brightest object in the night sky besides the moon and the Earth's closest planetary neighbor. Look for it just before sunrise or just after sunset; it'll be near the point where the sun is rising or setting. (Venus and Earth orbit the sun at different speeds; when Venus is moving away from Earth, we see it in the morning, and when it's moving toward us, we see it in the evening.) Like the moon, Venus goes through phases—check it out through a pair of binoculars. You can also spot Mars, Jupiter, Saturn, and Mercury—with or without the aid of binoculars.

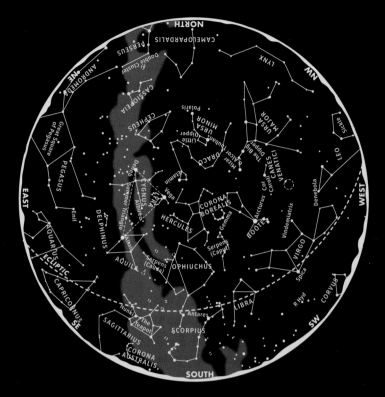

Meteors

It's hard to match the magic of a meteor shower, the natural fireworks display that occurs as Earth passes through a cloud of debris called meteoroids. These pieces of space junk—most the size of a pebble—hit our atmosphere at high speeds, and the intense friction produces brief but brilliant streaks of light. Single meteors are often called "shooting stars" or "falling stars."

Since our planet passes through the same patches of interstellar refuse each year, it's easy to roughly predict when the major meteor showers will occur. Notable ones include the Perseids (mid-August), the Orionids (late October), the Leonids (mid-November), and the Geminids (mid-December). Each shower is named after the point in the sky where meteors appear to originate. If you're not visiting during a shower, don't worry—you can spot individual meteors any time of the year.

Satellites

Right now, according to NASA, there are about 3,000 operative man-made satellites (along with 6,000 pieces of space junk) orbiting the Earth—and you can catch a glimpse of one with a little practice. Satellites look like fast-moving, non-blinking points of light; the best way to spot one is to lie on your back and scan the sky for movement. Be on the lookout for satellites an hour or two before or after sunset (though you may see them at other times as well).

You can take the guesswork out of the search with a few cool online tools (⊕ *www.nasa. gov* or *www.heavens-above.com*). Select your location, and these Web sites will help you predict—down to the minute—when certain objects will be streaking overhead. It's especially worthwhile to use these sites to look for the two brightest satellites: the International Space Station and the space shuttle.

FLAVORS OF ARIZONA

Despite the fact that it has become a culinary melting pot, Arizona has long been lumped into the spicy Southwest category of cuisine. But by pairing all of neighboring and global influences with diverse Native American cultures and regional history and local agriculture, creative chefs and entrepreneurs have started to earn Arizona its own star on the food walk of fame.

The Native Palate

From flash-flood farming in the south to sustained agriculture in the Verde Valley, to livestock ranching in the state's northernmost reaches, Native American food customs are becoming customary off the reservations. Gourds, desert beans, mesquite pods, tree nuts, cactus fruit, agave nectar, and local game like quail and elk are buzzwords on award-winning menus. And Navajo fry bread, a tradition born from the worst of times, is one of the state's most sought-after (and caloric) treats.

Kai, Chandler. Using the Pima word for seed, this elegant and scenery-studded restaurant on the Gila Indian Reservation plants the seeds of blending local food traditions of the Tohono O'odham people with fine dining.

Cameron Trading Post, Cameron. If you're headed to Lake Powell, Monument Valley, or the North Rim, there's no better place to stop and try a Navajo taco, made from fry bread.

Hopi Cultural Center Restaurant, Third Mesa, Hopi Reservation. This is one of the few places to find authentic piki (paper-thin blue-corn bread) and Hopi stew, with lamb, hominy, and chiles.

Spice of Life

Arizona has long been defined by its heat. With a natural affection for everything from Mexican jalapeños to New Mexican

hatch green chiles, local food artists have given recipes ranging from chips and salsa to chicken mole and chilaquiles a most memorable flair.

Café Poca Cosa, Tucson. This hip, family-owned eatery changes its menus daily but consistently maintains its authentic approach to Mexican cuisine.

Los Dos Molinos, Phoenix. For those who like it hot, this is the state's reigning restaurant. Signature dishes like Shrimp Veracruz are drenched in New Mexico red chili.

The Mission, Scottsdale. Try a modern twist on old-school Mexican food like Pollo a la Brasa, chilaquiles, and avocado margaritas.

Fruits of the Desert

Arizona's local-grown wine industry is also not to be overlooked. What began as an experiment in 1973 has become a booming business in southern Arizona's Santa Cruz Valley where the soil is similar to that of Burgundy.

Callaghan Vineyards, Elgin. Producing bold Spanish reds and a delicate white, this southeastern Arizona vineyard and winery has established itself as a favorite on area wine-tasting tours.

Keeling Schaeffer Vineyards, Pearce. Featuring fruity chardonnays, sold-out Grenaches and Syrahs, this vineyard with Mary Jane Colter–inspired architecture offers tastings and tours by appointment only.

Page Springs Cellars, Cornville. Taking a gamble on the Verde Valley's high-desert soil has paid off for winemaker Eric Glomski and his Southern Rhone varietals.

GREAT ITINERARIES

HIGHLIGHTS OF ARIZONA

Arizona is full of history, culture, and awe-inspiring natural landmarks. Here are some suggestions for mixing a road trip with some of the state's top attractions.

PHOENIX AND THE VALLEY OF THE SUN: 1–2 Days

The metropolitan Phoenix area is the best place to begin your trip to Arizona, with a wealth of hotels and resorts. Reserve a day in the Valley and visit the Heard Museum and Desert Botanical Garden. Select one of the area's popular Mexican restaurants for dinner. If time permits, stroll through Old Town Scottsdale's tempting art galleries. Depending on your remaining time in the Valley, you can escape to a spa for a day of pampering, get out your clubs and hit the links, or—if the season is right—catch a major-league baseball spring-training game.

Logistics: Sky Harbor International Airport is located at the center of the city and is 20 minutes away from most of the Valley's major resorts. Plan on driving everywhere in the greater Phoenix area, as public transportation is nearly nonexistent. The Valley of the Sun is a large area, but Phoenix itself is remarkably simple to navigate. Designed on a grid, numbered streets run north–south and named streets (Camelback Road, Glendale Avenue) run east–west. Grand Avenue, running about 20 mi from downtown to Sun City, is the only diagonal. If you need to know which direction you're facing, you can see South Mountain, conveniently looming up in the south, from nearly any point in the city.

GRAND CANYON SOUTH RIM: 1–2 Days

The sight of the Grand Canyon's immense beauty has taken many a visitor's breath away. Whatever you do, though, make sure you catch a sunset or sunrise view of the canyon. A night, or even just dinner, at grand El Tovar Hotel won't disappoint, but book your reservation early (up to six months ahead). Outdoors enthusiasts will want to reserve several days to hike and explore the canyon; less-ambitious travelers can comfortably see the area in one or two days.

Logistics: Arizona is a large state; the drive north from Phoenix to the South Rim of the Grand Canyon will take several hours, so budget at least a half day to make the 225-mi trip. Take Interstate 17 north from Phoenix into Flagstaff. The best way to reach the South Rim of the canyon is via U.S. 180 northwest from Flagstaff. It's best to travel to the canyon from the city during the week—Interstate 17 fills with locals looking to escape the heat on Friday and Saturday. If you have specific plans, whether it's a mule ride and rafting trip or dining and lodging, be sure to book very early for the canyon—reservations are necessary.

RED ROCKS and SPECTACULAR SIGHTS: 3–4 Days

Option 1: Sedona and Surrounding Area

The unusual red-rock formations in Sedona are a key destination for most visitors to Arizona, and it's no wonder. Spend at least a day exploring the town and its beauty, whether on a calm stroll or a thrilling jeep tour. The surrounding area includes Flagstaff, a college town with a love for the outdoors and the stars; Prescott, with its Whiskey Row and

Victorian homes; and Jerome, a charming artists' community that thrives more with every passing year.

Logistics: If possible, visit Sedona midweek, before the city folk fill the streets on the weekend. If Sedona is too pricey for your stay, consider the nearby towns of Flagstaff or Prescott, which have ample motels and budget hotels.

Option 2: Landmarks of Indian Country

The majestic landscapes in Monument Valley and Canyon de Chelly are among the biggest draws to Arizona. Made famous by countless Western movies and famous photographs, the scenes are even more astounding firsthand. This northeast corner of the state is worth several days of exploration. The famous Four Corners, where Arizona, New Mexico, Colorado, and Utah meet, are within a short drive but there is not much to see. For a brief trip, make Monument Valley and Canyon de Chelly the priorities. With added days, you can visit a Native American trading post, Lake Powell and Glen Canyon, and the Four Corners. On your drive toward Interstate 40, be sure to spend an hour or two at Petrified Forest National Park, where you'll see the remains of a prehistoric forest.

Logistics: Approximately 100 mi from Sedona, the fascinating sites of northeast Arizona are a destination unto themselves. Don't be fooled: this is a remote area and will take hours to reach, whether you're coming from Phoenix, Sedona, or the Grand Canyon. Most travelers view this corner of the state as a road trip heaven, as the highways offer one scenic drive after the other. Plan on making one of the main towns—Tuba City, Page, Window Rock—your base, and take day trips

from there. No matter what your itinerary, plan ahead and make reservations early: the best way to see these popular sites is via guided tour.

SCENIC DRIVES and HISTORIC TOWNS: 2–4 Days

Option 1: The White Mountains of Eastern Arizona

If nature walks and hiking are still tops on your itinerary, consider spending a few days in the White Mountains before returning to Phoenix. The breathtaking White Mountains area of eastern Arizona is a favorite for anglers and cross-country skiers. The White Mountains Trails System near Pinetop-Lakeside is considered one of the best in the nation, and can accommodate all fitness levels. Creek-side resorts with private cabins are common in the towns of the White Mountains. Eastern Arizona is primarily a summer destination; many properties close from November to April except for a few ski resort areas.

Logistics: The most scenic route back to Phoenix is via the Salt River canyon on U.S. 60 to Globe. The landscape transforms from ponderosa pine forests to high desert along the journey, marking an ideal transition from one extreme to the other. Or you can travel to Tucson from the White Mountains on one of the most scenic routes in the United States (if a bumpy and wild ride is your style). The Coronado Trail, U.S. 191 from Springerville to Clifton, is one of the world's curviest roads. The trip, which includes steep stretches and plenty of turns, will take at least four hours. Once in Clifton, you can continue south to Willcox, where Interstate 10 will take you to Tucson.

Option 2: Tucson, the Old West, and Historic Sites

If culture and shopping are a bit more attractive, consider spending time in Tucson and visiting its neighboring historic communities. Spend at least a day in Tucson proper, visiting Mission San Xavier del Bac, Saguaro National Park, and the Arizona-Sonora Desert Museum. If hiking is your game, don't miss Sabino Canyon, which offers gorgeous views of the area. With Tucson as your hub, take a day trip just a bit farther south to historic Tombstone and Bisbee. On the way back to the interstate, stop by Kartchner Caverns State Park for a view of the series of spectacular wet caves. Hour-long guided tours are available by reservation; book several months in advance to guarantee entry.

Logistics: Phoenix is two hours away via Interstate 10, a relatively unscenic drive. Casa Grande is the midway point between the two cities, and is a good place to stop for a rest. History buffs may want to stop at Picacho Peak, site of the westernmost battle of the Civil War.

ROAD TRIP TIPS

■ If your budget permits, renting a four-wheel-drive vehicle will allow you to take advantage of side trips to remote areas.

■ Climate extremes, both heat and cold, make Arizona traveling hazardous, so heed the advice of locals. If somebody tells you it's a "little warm" to be poking around in those hills, they're probably correct.

■ Carry plenty of water, and if your vehicle should break down, put the hood up and stay with the vehicle.

■ Arizona's distances can be surprisingly vast. The drive from Phoenix to the Grand Canyon takes at least a half day.

ARIZONA LANDSCAPE ADVENTURES

Arizona's spectacular landscape dominates the eye and floods the senses. No place else in the world has so many unique and bizarre geological features—and the canyons, deserts, and mountains are more than just a backdrop for your journey. To understand and experience the land, you must get outdoors and be willing to accept nature on its own terms. *by Melissa Kim*

ARIZONA'S NATURAL FEATURES

Oak Creek Canyon, near Sedona

The diversity that these regions contain, not just in terrain but in flora and fauna, is unparalleled in the Lower 48. Resourceful plants and animals teach us so much about adapting to our surroundings and learning from nature. Some humans have also learned to survive in these harsh environments, but for most of us even a brief foray into Arizona's landscapes can be an adventure.

Canyons, mountains, and deserts are all closely related in the state's basic regions:

■ The northern section is part of the **Colorado Plateau,** a high-elevation region characterized by glowing red rocks and impossibly graceful slot canyons. It is also home to the Grand Canyon.

■ Along the state's southwestern corridor is the **Basin and Range Province,** where cactus-littered deserts and scrubby valleys rise abruptly to the San Francisco Peaks and Chiracahua Mountains.

■ In between, the **Central Highlands** contain mountain ranges where peaks drop away to canyons and desert grasslands, such as the easily accessible Saguaro National Park and the Arizona-Sonora Desert Museum.

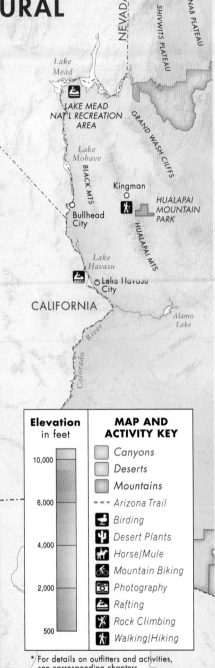

Elevation in feet

10,000

6,000

4,000

2,000

500

MAP AND ACTIVITY KEY

Canyons
Deserts
Mountains
--- Arizona Trail
Birding
Desert Plants
Horse/Mule
Mountain Biking
Photography
Rafting
Rock Climbing
Walking/Hiking

* For details on outfitters and activities, see corresponding chapters.

Lake Powell

Page

Antelope Canyon

MONUMENT VALLEY NAVAJO TRIBAL PARK

Four Corners Nat'l Monument

MONUMENT VALLEY

CHISKA MTS.

KAIBAB PLATEAU

GRAND CANYON NATIONAL PARK

NORTH RIM

BLACK MESA

MARBLE CANYON

ECHO CLIFFS

Colorado River

SOUTH RIM

Grand Canyon

CANYON DE CHELLY NATIONAL MONUMENT

Tusayan Museum

HAVASU CYN.

COCONINO PLATEAU

PAINTED DESERT

NEW MEXICO

Wupatki Nat'l Monument

SAN FRANCISCO PEAKS

Humphreys Peak 12,633ft

SUNSET CRATER VOLCANO NAT'L MONUMENT

Flagstaff

Meteor Crater

PETRIFIED FOREST NATIONAL PARK

Oak Creek Canyon

Sedona

COCONINO NATIONAL FOREST

MOGOLLON PLATEAU

VERDE VALLEY

Prescott

MOGOLLON RIM

Payson

Springerville

Casa Malpais

WHITE MOUNTAINS

SUPERSTITION MOUNTAINS

Arizona Trail

Mt. Baldy 11,404ft

APACHE-SITGREAVES NATIONAL FOREST

Scottsdale

Phoenix

Avondale

Mesa

Desert Botanical Garden

Tempe

Boyce Thompson Southwestern Arboretum

Casa Grande

CABEZA PRIETA NATIONAL WILDLIFE RESERVE

SANTA CATALINA MTS.

GALIURO MTS.

Mount Lemmon

CHIRICAHUA MOUNTAINS

Arizona–Sonora Desert Museum

Tucson

ORGAN PIPE CACTUS NATIONAL MONUMENT

Kit Peak

SAGUARO NATIONAL PARK

CHIRICAHUA NATIONAL MONUMENT

Cochise Stronghold

SULPHUR SPRINGS VALLEY

Tohono O'odham National Cultural Center

Madera Canyon

SONORA

CORONADO NATIONAL FOREST

HUACHUCA MTS.

Ramsey Canyon

Douglas

MEXICO

Nogales

CANYONS

 While the Grand Canyon lives up to its impressive reputation, it is one of many such precious places in Arizona. Each canyon is a unique classroom of geology, where you can see the results of millions of years of shifts in the land.

More than 500 million years ago, a vast sea covered what is now Arizona. Sediments formed in thick layers as the sea rose and fell. Subsequent movement in the earth's crust created mountain ranges and lifted up entire sections of northern Arizona. Erosion and downcutting by rivers created deep canyons, uncovering layers of sandstone, shale, and limestone.

Forces of water and wind work to create some of Arizona's signature landscapes. High-elevation plateaus are continually eroded by rain, ice, rivers and groundwater, chipping and cracking the soft rock to form mesas and buttes, isolated hills or formations with steep sides and flat tops. What's the difference? One general rule of thumb is that a mesa is wider than it is high, while a butte is taller than it is high.

Some Grand Canyon excursions, such as mule tours (top) and rafting (opposite), are so popular they are booked up to a year in advance.

You can get your ecology credits here too. As elevation changes from canyon floor to rim, so do the plants and animals. You can easily pass through four different biomes in a day's hike. Riparian communities on the canyon floor give way to a desert scrub, then to pinyon and Ponderosa pine forests. Where elevation exceeds 8,000 feet, spruce-fir forests make you feel as if you've somehow been transported to Canada.

ANCIENT PEOPLE AND THE LAND

Archaeologists have uncovered artifacts that show that people have lived in the Grand Canyon for at least 4,000 years. Tools, fire pits, cave paintings, and other remains indicate the presence of hunter-gatherers called the Archaic people, descendants of Paleoindians. You can see some "Archaic origami" stick figures on display at the Tusayan Museum at the South Rim.

TOP CANYON EXPERIENCES

WHITEWATER RAFTING
It's the rivers that helped create the canyons, after all, so spending time on the water is to spend time imagining the steady flow that carved out these works of natural art. About two dozen outfitters offer trips on the Colorado River through or near the Grand Canyon. Some sections are quiet and gentle, others rage and roil.

HORSE AND MULE TOURS
The best way to get a sense of the sheer scale of canyons is to be humbled by them—which means that you have to get to the bottom and look up. Hiking can be arduous, so many tour operators and parks offer horse or mule expeditions.

BIRDING
The entire state offers magnificent birding, but two extremes stand out. In the Grand Canyon, you can spot the enormous California condor's nine-foot wingspan since it was re-introduced in the 1990s. In the canyons of Southeast Arizona, birders congregate in summer time to search for tiny hummingbirds.

BEYOND THE GRAND CANYON

In the northeast corner of Arizona, **Canyon de Chelly National Monument**, a National Park on Navajo Tribal Trust Land, rivals the Grand Canyon in natural splendor and can't be beat for cultural significance. People have been in residence here continuously since prehistoric times.

Antelope Canyon, called the world's most photographed slot canyon, is near Page in Northern Arizona. You'll need an authorized guide to hike into this narrow sandstone canyon, which is inside the Navajo Reservation.

Just north of Sedona in North-Central Arizona, **Oak Creek Canyon** is called the Grand Canyon's smaller cousin. You can drive through this canyon and stop in places to take a closer look at the red sandstone cliffs and buttes.

WORTH NOTING
- Canyon X, Northeast Arizona
- Havasu Canyon, Grand Canyon
- Ramsey Canyon, Southern Arizona
- Madera Canyon, Southern Arizona

DESERTS

Deserts are full of mystery, surprises, and stories of plants, animals, and people overcoming odds to survive and flourish. Track down a rare desert bloom, listen to the screech of an owl, or hear the hiss of a rattlesnake and you'll get a sense of the unique beauty and power of the landscape.

Just one of Arizona's claims to nature's hall of fame is as the only state to have all four of the major deserts in the United States within its borders. The Great Basin, the nation's largest cold desert, spills down to touch the northernmost areas of Arizona. In northwest Arizona, low shrubs such as yucca and the Joshua Tree dominate the small Mojave Desert, a hot desert, which has the nation's lowest elevation and highest temperatures. Only a few skinny fingers of the Chihuahan Desert grasslands stretch into the state's southeast corner. Arizona's largest desert, the Sonoran, is unusual with its biseasonal rainfall, mild winters, and subtropical climate that give rise to a diversity rarely seen in a desert environment.

Although deserts may look barren from a distance, a closer look reveals classic saguaros (top) and blooming prickly pear cacti (opposite).

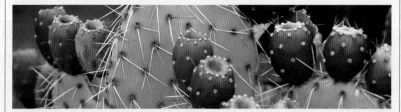

And then there's the Painted Desert, not actually a true desert. In this high, dry region of the Colorado Plateau, colorful layers of sedimentary rocks are buckled and pitched up in grand steps, and carved into canyons and other-worldly rock formations.

ANCIENT PEOPLE AND THE LAND
Thousands of years ago, native people learned to live and thrive in the Sonoran Desert, creating canals to irrigate crops, migrating with the seasons from low valleys to cooler mountains, and harvesting desert plants. Today, the 20,000-plus members of the Tohono O'odham Nation live on more than 2.8 million acres in southwestern Arizona. To see handicrafts by tribal members and sample local food, stop by San Xavier Plaza in Tucson.

TOP DESERT EXPERIENCES

WALKING AND HIKING
Whether you're on a gentle nature stroll or a challenging scramble up a mountain, take the time for a scavenger hunt. Seek out a blooming teddy bear cholla, find a whiptail lizard sunning on a rock, or listen for the howl of a coyote at dusk.

PHOTOGRAPHY
The desert has a singular beauty that changes as the light shifts from scorching midday to shadowy dusk to evocative moonshine. With practice you can learn how to capture the best images of sweeping horizons, wildflowers, horses, cowboys, Monument Valley, and even the wings of a hummingbird.

VIEWING DESERT PLANTS
Throughout the dry desert landscape, hardy succulents—water-retaining plants including cactus—are well-adapted to the extreme conditions. In wild parks and botanical gardens, you can observe bizzare-looking forms like the Joshua Tree as well as the more familiar saguaro, prickly pear, and barrel cactus.

TOP DESTINATIONS

Part zoo, part botanical garden, part natural history museum, the popular **Arizona-Sonora Desert Museum** allows you to sample the wildlife of the Sonoran Desert in downtown Tucson.

If you've got a little more time and energy, head for **Saguaro National Park** near Tucson. Its two districts have wonderful outdoor opportunities. For vistas of abundant cacti, try the Valley View Overlook.

For a true desert wilderness experience, make a trek to **Organ Pipe Cactus National Monument** by heading southwest to the Mexican border, where organ pipe, saguaro, cholla, ocotillo, creosote, and other succulent plants flourish. Hike a trail, bike the 21-mile Ajo Mountain Drive, or camp here for pure serenity.

WORTH NOTING
- Desert Botanical Garden, Phoenix
- Boyce Thompson Arboretum, Phoenix
- Cabeza Prieta National Wildlife Refuge, Southern Arizona
- Petrified Forest National Park, Eastern Arizona

MOUNTAINS

 What goes down, must come up. As Arizona's deserts and canyons were formed, so were mountain ranges. Mountain peaks reaching above 4,000 feet in elevation can be found in all parts of the state except the southwest corner.

Ancient rocky ranges with high meadows and cool alpine lakes, cratered volcanic peaks, and desert mountains that fall away to river gorges in deep canyons—Arizona has it all. The diversity of wildlife is immense and you really can travel from a cactus-covered desert to a snow-covered mountain peak in a day. The same geologic forces that created canyons—tectonic to volcanic to glacial activity—have left the state with mountains both old and young.

The rising and falling of the land created not just ranges but also isolated high-elevation areas in Southern Arizona. Dubbed "sky islands," a collection of 40 forested mountain groups with lush vegetation at the top and their accompanying canyons below is surrounded by deserts or grasslands. The confluence of desert and forest communities has created habitats for rare and endemic

In warm weather, mountains can be cool escapes. Multi-use trails for bikers and hikers criss-cross the area near Sedona (top) and Flagstaff (opposite).

species, and wildlife-watching opportunities are truly unparalleled. And in Eastern Arizona, the pine-covered White Mountains are a cool respite for many outdoor adventures.

ANCIENT PEOPLE AND THE LAND
As Arizona's prehistoric inhabitants evolved from hunting and gathering to agriculture, one group made its home in the forested mountain ranges and nearby valleys: the Mogollon. About 2,000 years ago, early Mogollon people hunted mountain game and gathered fruits, berries, and seeds from alpine meadows and forests to supplement what crops they could grow in the lower valleys. At Casa Malpais, in Springerville, remains of a 16-acre pueblo complex include what is thought to be a Mogollon solstice observatory, built around AD 1200.

TOP MOUNTAIN EXPERIENCES

MOUNTAIN BIKING
You can join a group ride with one of the many biking clubs, take a guided tour, or venture out on your own. Recommended spots include: the Elephant Head Trail in Coronado National Forest, and trails in the Coconino National Forest, between Sedona and Flagstaff.

HIKING THE ARIZONA TRAIL
One of the eleven National Scenic Trails, this long-distance route covers about 800 miles from Mexico to Utah. People commonly take one section at a time. The trail takes you through major mountain ranges, from the Huachucas and Santa Rita in the south, through the Superstition Wilderness and over the San Francisco Peaks.

ROCK CLIMBING
Southern Arizona rock formations and towering cliffs are a great place to learn the basics of climbing. Take a course and start with basic bouldering, then learn how to rope up for multi-pitch climbs. Mount Lemmon and Cochise Stronghold, both near Tucson, are popular climbing spots.

TOP DESTINATIONS

Just north of Flagstaff, the volcanic **San Francisco Peaks** can be experienced by foot, mountain bike, horse, or even ski lift. Humphrey's Peak, the state's highest spot at 12,633 feet, is a rewarding trek for experienced hikers.

Erosion has carved out a "Wonderland of Rocks" at **Chiricahua National Monument** in the southeastern section of the state. A perfect example of a sky island, this is considered one of the most ecologically diverse regions in the entire country.

About 1,000 years ago, a series of violent erruptions formed **Sunset Crater Volcano National Monument** and destroyed plants for five miles. Now, you can hike on a lava flow, climb a cinder cone, and see signs of life regenerating.

WORTH NOTING
- Apache-Sitgreaves National Forest, Eastern Arizona
- White Mountains, Eastern Arizona
- Superstition Wilderness, Phoenix
- Hualapai Mountain Park, Northwest Arizona
- Santa Catalina Mountains, Tucson

DISTINCTIVE ANIMALS OF ARIZONA

❶Coatimundi

These high-energy mammals combine a long ringed tail like a monkey's, a snout like an anteater's, the lumbering walk of a bear, and the mask of a raccoon. Members of the raccoon family, they live in large social groups. Normally tree dwellers, in mountainous southeastern Arizona these nonstop foragers can make dens in caves and crevices.

❷Desert bighorn sheep

Found primarily in the mountains of the Sonoran and Mojave Deserts, the sheep favor steep slopes and canyon walls. Unique padded hooves allow them to grab the surface of the rock. Males use their large curved horns for fighting and to break open cactus, a common food for the large grazers.

❸Elegant trogon

This rare, distinctive bird migrates from Mexico to southeast Arizona's mountains and canyons in the summer. The foot-long birds make their nests in dead or dying sycamore trees in cavities created by woodpeckers. The colorful male has an emerald green back and throat, with a bright red breast and a white breast band.

❹Gila woodpecker

One of the Sonoran Desert's signature species, this woodpecker works away at the saguaro cactus, creating cavities that serve as homes for itself and other animals, including owls, rats, lizards purple martins, and other birds. The very common birds don't hammer just to make holes; they also use sound to mark their territory.

❺Western diamondback rattlesnake

Reptiles are plentiful in all of Arizona's deserts, and while most are fascinating and beautiful, the rattlesnakes can also be very dangerous. The Western Diamondback, with its triangular-shaped head and black and white ringed tail, is active late afternoon and at night, and will strike if it's disturbed. Tread carefully!

DISTINCTIVE PLANTS OF ARIZONA

⑥ Ocotillo
Common in both the Sonoran and Chihuahan Deserts, this tall woody shrub has long, thin, spiny stems that rise up out of a short trunk. Reddish orange flowers bloom at the tips of these stems in spring, providing nectar—and energy—to migrating hummingbirds.

⑦ Ponderosa pine
Forests of these tall stately pines cover high-elevation areas on the Colorado Plateau, and in some cases pure stands stretch for thousands of acres—such as the one from Flagstaff along the Mogollon Rim to the White Mountains. Growing more than 100 feet tall, this tree provides food and shelter to many animals and birds.

⑧ Rocky Mountain iris
There's nothing quite like a mountain meadow in May, when blooming alpine wildflowers herald the season. Among the lupines, paintbrushes, lilies, and poppies, look for the Rocky Mountain iris between 6,000 and 9,000 feet elevation. Growing one or two feet high, the stems produce one to four delicate purple flowers with accents of yellow and white.

⑨ Saguaro cactus
This iconic plant plays such a vital role in the Sonoran Desert, providing food and shelter to bats, bees, and birds. A giant, columnar cactus, with short stout arms that point to the sky, it can grow to be 40 feet tall or higher, with an average life span of 150 years. Its large, creamy white flowers bloom by night in late April and May, harbingers of the red juicy fruit.

⑩ Yellow palo verde (foothill palo verde)
Look for this twiggy, thorny shrub on rocky hillsides. Its green bark contains chlorophyll, so it can still carry on with photosynthesis even when the shrub's leaves drop off during the dry season. The palo verde is the primary nurse plant for the saguaro cactus, providing shade for its seedlings.

A GEOLOGY PRIMER

Left: dramatic spires at the Chiracahuas. Top Right: Rainbow Bridge, the world's longest natural bridge. Lower Right: Monument Valley's Mittens and Merrick Butte.

ARCH This type of opening in a rock wall forms either through erosion, when wind and sand wear away the rock face, or through the freezing action of water. When water enters spaces or joints in a rock and freezes, the expansion of the ice can crack off chunks of rock.

BRIDGE If an opening through a rock is created by water flowing beneath it, it is called a bridge. You can see many natural bridges in Arizona, such as Rainbow Bridge near Lake Powell and Devil's Bridge near Sedona.

BUTTE A butte is what remains when a mesa erodes. You can see good examples of this formation in Monument Valley in Northeast Arizona.

CAVES Natural underground chambers that open to the surface give you an opportunity to descend below the Earth's surface and learn about the forces of heat and water upon rocks and minerals. Kartchner Caverns, south of Tucson, is a living cave where water still flows, dissolving minerals and creating beautiful formations.

MESA A mesa, or hill with a smooth, flat, tablelike top (mesa means "table" in Spanish), is a clear example of how hard rock stands higher and protects the soft rock beneath. A

single mesa may cover hundreds of square miles of land. There are many mesas in the Hopi Reservation, including the villages of First, Second, and Third Mesa.

MONUMENT This general term applies to geologic formations that are much taller than they are wide, or to formations that resemble man-made structures. These are what give Monument Valley its name.

PETRIFIED WOOD If you want to know what the desert of the Southwest used to look like, picture the Florida Everglades populated with giant dragonflies and smaller species of dinosaurs. Arizona's Petrified Forest offers a glimpse of the once lush, tropical world. Stumps and logs from the ancient woodland are now turned to rock because they were immersed in water and sealed away from the air, so normal decay did not occur. Instead, the preserved wood gradually hardened as silica, or sand, filtered into its porous spaces, almost like cement. Erosion was among the geological processes that exposed the wood.

SPIRE As a butte erodes, it may become one or more spires. You can see wonderful examples of these rock formations in Southern Arizona's Chiricahua National Monument.

2

Phoenix, Scottsdale, and Tempe

WORD OF MOUTH

"The Phoenix area is very spread out (think Los Angeles). I'd check out the Heard Museum for sure, and the Orpheum theatre (an art deco theatre that was restored to its original, has tours), and the Phoenix Art Museum (this last also has a decent cafe). I'd second a drive up South Mountain, it really is a nice view."

—ashAZ

WELCOME TO PHOENIX, SCOTTSDALE, AND TEMPE

TOP REASONS TO GO

★ **Resort spas:** With dozens of outstanding desert spas, Phoenix has massaged and wrapped its way to the top of the relaxation destinations list.

★ **Shops and restaurants:** Retail centers Old Town Scottsdale and Fashion Square are another way to retreat and relax in the Valley of the Sun, as well as a melting pot of fine and funky dining establishments.

★ **The Heard Museum:** This small but world-renowned museum elegantly celebrates Native American people, culture, art, and history.

★ **The great outdoors:** Sure there's urban sprawl, but Phoenix also has cool and accessible places to get away from it all, like the Desert Botanical Garden, Papago Park, Tempe Town Lake, and mountain and desert preserves.

★ **Golf:** All year long links lovers can take their pick of top-rated public and private courses—many with incredibly spectacular views.

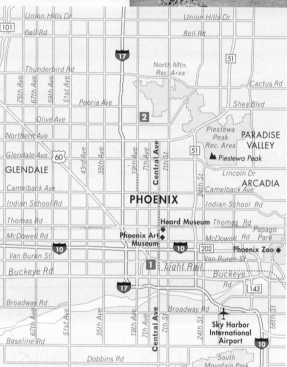

1 Downtown and Central Phoenix. As the site of Arizona's government operations and the state's largest concentration of skyscrapers, this area used to be strictly business. Nowadays it's home to some of the Valley's major museums, performance venues, and sports arenas, plenty of high-rise homeowners, and a light-rail system that's changing the face of the city.

2 Greater Phoenix. Here is an unusual mix of attractions ranging from hip, historic neighborhoods to acres of mountain preserves, cultural and ethnic centers, and corridors of modern commercial enterprise. Hike a couple of peaks, peek at the animals in the Phoenix Zoo, zoom on over to the Phoenix Art and Heard museums, and then relax at a luxury mountainside resort—all in one day.

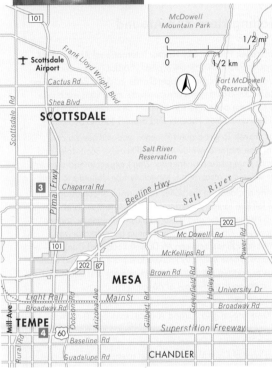

GETTING ORIENTED

It can be useful to think of Phoenix as a flower with petals (other communities) growing in every direction from the bud of Sky Harbor Airport. The East Valley includes Scottsdale, Paradise Valley, Ahwatukee, Tempe, Mesa, Fountain Hills, and Apache Junction. To the southeast are Chandler and Gilbert. The West Valley includes Glendale, Sun City, Peoria, and Litchfield Park. Central Avenue, which runs north and south through the heart of downtown Phoenix, is the city's east–west dividing line. Everything east of Central is considered the East Valley and everything west of Central is the West Valley. Phoenix has grown around what was once a cluster of independent towns in Maricopa County, but the gaps between communities that were open desert space just a few short years ago have begun to close in and blend the entire Valley into one large, sprawling community.

3 Scottsdale. Once an upscale Phoenix sibling, it now flies solo as a top American destination. A bastion of high-end and specialty shopping, historic sites, elite resorts, restaurants, spas, and golf greens next to desert views, Scottsdale can easily absorb an entire vacation.

4 Tempe and around. The home of Arizona State University and a creative melting pot of residents, Tempe is equal parts party and performance, especially along its main artery, Mill Avenue, where commerce and culture collide.

PHOENIX, SCOTTSDALE, AND TEMPE PLANNER

How's the Weather?

It's a common misconception that Phoenix forever hovers around 100°F. That may hold true from May to October, but the winter months have been known to push the mercury down to 35°F. The city also has experienced consecutive days of nonstop rain. Such instances are rare, but it's good to be prepared and check weather reports before you pack.

Arizona can get pretty darn hot in summer, so plan your outdoor activities for the cooler parts of the day and save the air-conditioned stuff for when it's needed: the Heard Museum is not only a must-see, it's also inside, as are the nearby Phoenix Art Museum and many other popular attractions.

Visitor Information

Most Valley cities have tourism centers where you can get maps or excursion suggestions, such as **Greater Phoenix Convention & Visitors Bureau** (☎ 877/225–5749 or 602/254–6500 ⊕ www.phoenixcvb.com) and **Scottsdale Convention & Visitors Bureau** (☎ 800/782–1117 ☎ 480/421–1004 ⊕ www.scottsdalecvb.com).

Getting Here and Around

Air Travel: Phoenix **Sky Harbor International Airport (PHX** ☎ 602/273–3300 ⊕ www.phxskyharbor.com) is served by most major airlines. **SuperShuttle** (☎ 602/244–9000 or 800/258–3826 ⊕ www.supershuttle.com) vans each take up to seven passengers to different destinations. Fares are $13 to downtown Phoenix and around $20 to Scottsdale.

Car Travel: To get around Phoenix, you will need a car. Only the major downtown areas (Phoenix, Scottsdale, and Tempe) are pedestrian-friendly. Don't expect to nab a rental car without a reservation, especially from January to April.

Many accidents in the Valley are a result of confusion in the left-turn lanes. Weekdays from 6 AM to 9 AM and 4 PM to 6 PM the center and left-turn lanes on the major surface arteries of 7th Street and 7th Avenue become one-way traffic-flow lanes between McDowell Road and Dunlap Avenue. These specially marked lanes are dedicated mornings to north–south traffic (into downtown) and afternoons to south–north traffic (out of downtown).

Roads in Phoenix and its suburbs are laid out on an 800-square-mi grid. Grand Avenue, running 20 mi from downtown to Sun City, is the only diagonal. Central Avenue is the main north–south grid axis: all roads parallel to and west of Central are numbered avenues; all roads parallel to and east of Central are numbered streets. The numbering begins at Central and increases in each direction.

Public Transportation Travel: The Valley's light-rail system is convenient for exploring the downtown Phoenix museums or near Arizona State University. Fares are $3.50/day and multiday passes are available. Phoenix runs a free Downtown Area Shuttle (DASH), and Tempe operates the Free Local Area Shuttle (FLASH). **Valley Metro** (☎ 602/253–5000 ⊕ www.valleymetro.org) has more info.

Taxi Travel: Taxi fares are unregulated in Phoenix, except at the airport. The 800-square-mi metro area is so large that one-way fares in excess of $50 are not uncommon. Except within a compact area, travel by taxi is not recommended. Taxis charge about $3 for the first mile and $2 per mile thereafter, not including tips. Try **Checker/Yellow Cab** (☎ 602/252–5252 ⊕ www.aaayellowaz.com) or **Courier Cab** (☎ 602/232–2222).

Making the Most of Your Time

Three to five days is an optimal amount of time to spend in Phoenix if you want to relax, get outside to hike or golf, and see the main sites like the Heard Museum and Scottsdale. Extra time will allow you to make some interesting side trips to nearby places like Arcosanti, Wickenburg, Cave Creek, and Carefree.

Remember that the Valley of the Sun is sprawling, so planning ahead will help you save time and gas. If you're heading to the Heard Museum downtown, for instance, you might want to visit the nearby Arizona Science Center and/or the Phoenix Art Museum, too, both of which are close to the light-rail line. If you're going to Taliesin West, do so before or after spending time in Scottsdale.

Phoenix to Grand Canyon Timing Tip

If you're driving to the Grand Canyon from Phoenix, allow at least two full days, with a minimum drive time of four hours each way. You can always anticipate slow-moving traffic on Interstate 17, but in the afternoon and evening on Friday and Sunday lengthy standstills are almost guaranteed, something to remember if your plans involve getting back to Sky Harbor Airport to catch a flight out.

Orientation Tours

If you'd like a break from driving, consider a tour to see the Valley's top attractions. Reservations are a must all year.

Gray Line Tours (☎ *602/437–3484* or *800/777–3484* ⊕ *www.graylinephoenix.com*) gives seasonal, three-hour narrated tours including downtown Phoenix, the Arizona Biltmore hotel, Camelback Mountain, Papago Park, and Scottsdale's Old Town; the price is about $62.

Open Road Tours (☎ *602/997–6474* or *800/766–7117* ⊕ *www.openroadtours.com*) offers excursions to Sedona and the Grand Canyon, Phoenix city tours, and Native American–culture trips to the Salt River Pima–Maricopa Indian Reservation. Local tours cost about $59.

Vaughan's Southwest Custom Tours (☎ *602/971–1381* or *800/513–1381* ⊕ *www.southwesttours.com*) gives a 4½-hour city tour for 11 or fewer passengers in custom vans, stopping at the Pueblo Grande Museum, the Arizona Biltmore, and the state capitol for $50. Vaughan's will also take you east to the Apache Trail.

Festivals and Events

Jan. **Waste Management Phoenix Open.** Formerly the Phoenix Open (and most recently the FBR Open), this golf tournament is the "Greatest Show on Grass." ☎ *602/870–0163* ⊕ *www.wastemanagement phoenixopen.com.*

Fabulous car auctions including **Barrett-Jackson** attract thousands each year ☎ *480/663–6255* ⊕ *www. barrett-jackson.com.*

Feb. The Heard Museum hosts the spectacular **Annual World Hoop Dance Championship**, with traditional music and costumes. ☎ *602/252–8848* ⊕ *www.heard.org.*

Mar. **Indian Fair & Market.** More than 600 Native American artists and artisans are showcased at the Heard Museum. ☎ *602/252–8848* ⊕ *www.heard.org.*

Tempe Music Festival. Top acts from a variety of genres perform on multiple stages in Tempe. ☎ *480/970–3378* ⊕ *www. tempemusticfestival.com.*

The Parada del Sol Parade and Rodeo. "The World's Largest Horse Drawn Parade," features cowboys, cowgirls, horses, and floats. ☎ *480/990–3179* ⊕ *www. paradadelsol.org.*

Scottsdale Arts Festival. This is jam-packed with arts and crafts—and music. ☎ *480/994–2787* ⊕ *www. scottsdaleperformingarts.org.*

SPA TIME IN ARIZONA: SAY AHHH

OK, so you came, you saw, you shopped, you dined, you recreated. Now it's time for some rest and relaxation at one, or even several, of the *many* area spas. Arizona's own approach to pampered repose is world-renowned and worth exploring with all of your senses.

Above: Royal Palms couples massage. Upper right: A water retreat at Sanctuary Camelback Mountain. Lower right: Moroccan-inspired treatment room in Joya Spa at Montelucia Resort

Whether you're looking for a simple massage or an entire lifestyle change, Arizona rubs just about everyone the right way—from exclusive "immersion environments" of remote destination spas, to more accessible and affordable resort and day spas around the state. Each has its own signature style and blend of services, including purely local luxury at Sanctuary Spa on Camelback Mountain. In the midst of the Southwest's deserts and cities, you are sure to find spa menus boasting treatments and treats from around the world: Swedish and Japanese massage, French manicures and Vichy showers, Turkish-style baths, ayurvedic practices from India, California cuisine, and mood music from the Middle East and New Mexico.

A HISTORY OF HEALING

Arizona's hot, arid climate was considered a cure-all for respiratory ailments and joint pain. The East Coast power elite (Astors, Vanderbilts, and Rockefellers, to name a few) who grew sick of brutal winters and humid summers made a second home out of local resorts and spas. The hospitality industry has been striving to meet high standards for rejuvenation and health ever since.

RULES TO RELAX BY

Observing simple spa rules can ensure ultimate spa satisfaction versus an uncomfortable experience. First, decide on a budget beforehand and research spa menus; many are available online. Plan on a 15%–20% gratuity (cash preferred) for each treatment. Second, book at least a week ahead, longer for the most popular spas like Sanctuary Camelback Mountain in Phoenix's Paradise Valley. Third, check in at least 20 minutes prior to your first treatment. The earlier you arrive, the longer you can enjoy the spa's gratis amenities, like relaxation areas, pools, and steam rooms.

DAY OR DESTINATION?

Day spas are just that. They keep daytime hours and offer luxury treatments, but not long-term wellness programs. Destination spas, like Mii amo at Sedona's Enchantment Resort and Tucson's exclusive Canyon Ranch, have "immersion environments" with on-site accommodations and curricula designed for an inner- and outer-body overhaul. Most resort spas operate like day spas and do not require an overnight stay; however, hotel guests take precedence when it comes to booking.

LOCAL LURE AND LORE

A few spas are sanctioned to offer the innovative treatments and environments inspired by the traditions of local Native American tribes. Just south of Phoenix,

Aji Spa at the Sheraton Wild Horse Pass Resort draws on the surrounding Pima and Maricopa communities to create unique experiences. Many of their treatments employ time-honored healing methods, approved by tribal elders. Tribal practitioners administer the treatments with culturally significant, locally grown ingredients.

A TOUCH OF ROMANCE

If an indulgent spa visit is your ideal romantic getaway, pick a place that truly specializes in making it special. Most spa menus include a couples massage, but some focus on creating an entire experience for pairs. Alvadora in Phoenix offers frequent romance packages (and discounted rates during the hot summer months) along with twosome-oriented treatments and amenities, while Joya in Paradise Valley offers a specially outfitted couples' day suite.

TASTE TREATMENT

If you are focusing on a detoxifying spa experience, the last thing you want to do is replenish with unsavory elements. Camelback Inn in Scottsdale, Sheraton Wild Horse Pass Resort in Chandler, and Mii amo at Enchantment Resort in Sedona have restaurants or cafés that specialize in "spa cuisine," often surprisingly delicious, health-conscious dishes made with locally grown ingredients. Good for you and the planet.

VALLEY OF THE SUN GOLF: DRIVING AMBITION

Itching to get into the swing of things? Hoping to partake in some coursework? Looking to get linked in? In other words, would you rather be golfing? You're in the right place. Despite the dry climate this place is a gold mine of lush greens and far-reaching fairways.

Above: It's easy to find greens in the Valley of the Sun. Upper right: Tournament Players Club (TPC) at the Fairmont Scottsdale Princess Resort. Lower right: The setting at the Boulders Resort.

Golf is one of Arizona's leading draws for locals and visitors from around the world. Big, professional courses mean big business in the Valley of the Sun, evidenced by the more than 200 courses that consume much of the area and surround some of its finest resorts, locally based golf companies such as Ping and Dixon, and by the Phoenix Open—an annual world-class tournament and weeklong party that takes place in north Scottsdale at the renowned Tournament Players Club (TPC). That may sound intimidating, but consider it an invitation. Whether you're an amateur or an ace, and whether you're looking out for pars, your pocketbook, or just a pretty place to play a round, there is something for all ranges here.

TEE TIME TIP

Book online. Most courses are connected to reservation services that book tee times online, up to a week in advance. Get availability, pricing, and discounted tee time information by logging on to an individual course's Web site. Municipal courses can also be booked online, many at ⊕ www.phoenix.gov/sports/golf.html or visit ⊕ www.thegolfcourses.net and search Phoenix or Scottsdale for links to all the Valley's links.

PLAN AHEAD

Call well ahead for tee times during the cooler months from January to April, especially for popular courses. In summer, it's not uncommon to schedule a round before dawn. If you are booking a room at a resort with a course, be sure to book your tee time then also. Last minute tee times are often sometimes available through online reservation services, depending on the season.

PERFECT YOUR GOLF SWING

Feel like you need to swing like a pro before you take on the Valley of the Sun's premier golf courses? Troon North has a solution: the **Callaway Golf Performance Center** (☎ 480/585–5300 ⊕ *www. troonnorthgolf.com*) is a state-of-the-art facility that analyzes your swing and fits your clubs with 3-D imagery and software designed by the experts at Callaway. Golf greats like Tiger Woods and Phil Mickelson use similar technologies to perfect their games—why shouldn't you? With only 10 such facilities in the country, it's definitely worth checking out.

SAVINGS TIPS

Encanto Park and Papago Golf Course are just some of the city and public courses that are a great value. Check course Web sites for discounts before making your reservations. Some golf courses offer a discounted twilight rate—and the weather is often much more amenable at this time of day. Fees drop

dramatically in summer but remember that afternoon heat can be sweltering.

"GREENER" GREENS

Short of creating sand and cactus courses, desert golf facilities are hard-pressed to answer the eco-friendly call, but some are making strides in chipping away their carbon cleat print. Most courses now use reclaimed water and are experimenting with low-water grasses. In 2009, Arizona Biltmore Country Club hosted the state's first carbon-neutral golf event. Arizona State University's Karsten Golf Course recently signed a deal with a company that manufactures high-performance recyclable golf balls, made from recycled materials.

GROUPS TO GUIDE YOU

Package deals abound at resorts as well as through booking agencies like **Scottsdale Golf Adventures** (☎ 800/398–8100 ⊕ *www.scottsdalegolfadventures.com*), who will plan and schedule a nonstop golf holiday for you.If you're looking for a little more pampering, try **Scottsdale Swing** (☎ 888/807–9464 ⊕ *www. scottsdaleswing.com*), who will arrange a complete golf holiday, including access to the area's best night clubs. For a copy of the *Arizona Golf Guide*, contact the **Arizona Golf Association** (☎ 602/944–3035 or 800/458–8484 ⊕ *www.azgolf.org*).

VALLEY OF THE SUN FOOD

Arizona is still the state that people think of for cowboys, cactus, and "It's a dry heat," but many have thought of it as an endless possibility for creating another timeless icon: cuisine. As Old West staples get global updates, food is making lasting memories.

Above: Modern interpretations of tacos in endless varieties. Top Right: Table-side guacamole is made to taste at The Mission in Scottsdale. Lower right: A Navajo taco, made with fry bread.

When the Valley's culinary innovators pull together their creations, they certainly practice safe cooking, but figuratively speaking, the gloves are off. Building on signature Sonoran Desert fruits and flavors, chefs began experimenting outside the Tex-Mex box. For example, Vincent Guerithault of Vincent on Camelback combined his background in haute French cuisine with his Southwestern foreground. Matt Carter of Scottsdale's Latin-inspired Mission had a private aptitude for roasting meats and a desire to make it public. Chandler's Kai creators wanted a sustainable restaurant reflecting the culinary lore of the surrounding Indian reservations. All good food has a history and Arizona's leading chefs are pulling from it to make their own.

FRESH AIR FARE

At April's Arizona food innovation at the Great Arizona Picnic during the **Scottsdale Culinary Festival** (*www. scottsdaleculinaryfestival. org*) sample creations from more than 50 restaurants.

Visit the **Camelback Market** Saturdays, October to May, for fine wines, fresh produce, grilled meats, crepes, paninis, pizza, and pastry.

TAKE IT SLOW

Slow-roasted pork is a Southwestern specialty that few have mastered like Valley venues have. **Barrio Cafe**'s citrus-marinated *cochinita pibil*is pork slow-roasted for 12 hours and served with spicy red pepper and sour orange seasoning. The melt-in-your-mouth red chile carne *adovada* at **Dick's Hideaway** *6008 N. 16th St., Central Phoenix* ☎ *602/265-5886* ⊕ *www.burningembersphoenix.com*) takes days to prepare but is usually consumed in heaven-sent minutes, while the pork shoulder at **The Mission** makes for delicious tacos.

NATIVE SUN

Native American traditions also play a strong role in the local cuisine scene. **Kai** uses locally grown, customary tribal ingredients, including native seeds, agave sap, and saguaro blossom syrup in its organic entrées. Places like **Fry Bread House** bank on the less healthful but totally tasty traditions of fry bread and Navajo tacos.

STEAK OUT

While many restaurateurs spent years trying to break the meat-and-potatoes mold, some recognized it as an enduring dining genre and sought to reinvent the concept. For a classic spin try **Durants**, while many of the area's resorts bid adieu to former fine dining establishments to welcome modern spins on the American steak house. **Bourbon Steak**

and **BLT Steak** offer pricey but exquisite à la carte menus featuring regional grass-fed and Kobe beef.

WINE AND DINE

Lighter, shared fare is popular among the jet set who want to see, be seen, drink, and eat a little—but not too much. Wine bars draw the happy-hour crowd and keep them through dinner with delicious tapas-style noshes. Try bruschetta at **Postino Winecafe**, panini at **Bomberos Café & Wine Bar**, or the savory chickpeas and spinach at **Lola Tapas**, where white and red sangria reign supreme.

ROLLING IN DOUGH

Fresh-baked bread products have become a vital part of some of the most successful menus. It may be safe to say that **La Grande Orange** now *owns* the English muffin with their version, made on-site at LGO daily. The bread-infused menu at **My Florist Café** (⊠ *534 W. McDowell Rd., Downtown Phoenix* ☎ *602/254–0333* ⊕ *www.myfloristcafe.com*) is supplied by the acclaimed Willo Bakery, right next door. And there are a least a bakers-dozen delicious reasons that area eateries (including LGO) clamor to serve the fresh baked and caked goods of **Tammie Coe Cakes & MJ Bread** (⊠ *4410 N. 40th St., Central Phoenix* ☎ *602/840–6765* ⊕ *www.tammiecoecakes.com*).

SCOTTSDALE SHOPPING

Above: Biltmore Fashion Park is an upscale mall in an open-air setting. Top Right: Art at the Wilde Meyer Galleries.

Despite its origins as a livestock town, Scottsdale has steadily evolved from a sow's ear into a silk purse. Once a sleepy suburb of Phoenix, it has become a high-end shopping mecca—so renowned that glossy magazine ads now read: Paris, London, New York, Scottsdale.

When life gives you heat, become the hottest thing around. It's not Scottsdale's motto, but it should be. Not only has it built a reputation as one of the world's spending hot spots, it has made year-round vacation destinations out of trendy, temperature-controlled malls, marketplaces, and upscale plazas, exclusive department stores and chic boutiques that are powerful magnets for old and new money, celebrities, and the diva in us all. But Scottsdale hasn't completely glossed over its rustic, cowboy beginnings and compelling heritage. In addition to finding the latest fashions, you can also find authentic Western wear; traditional Native American rugs and jewelry; Arizona novelties; fine art of every genre and medium; and historic mementos in the area's many galleries, museums, mom-and-pop shops, and specialty stores.

BEST TIME TO GO

During the summer months, your most comfortable shopping bets are the malls and centers with ample air-conditioning such as **Scottsdale Fashion Square**. The rest of the year Old Town is a great neighborhood to shop and stroll, especially during **Art Walk**, every Thursday 7–9 PM year-round in the galleries and shops of Marshall Way and Main Street Arts Districts.

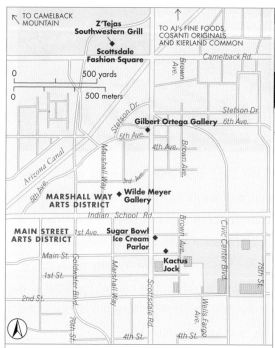

TOP FINDS

Local arts and crafts:
For paintings and more inspired by the beauty of the Southwest, explore **Wilde Myer Galleries**. Old Town Scottsdale is a good place for Native American finds, including the many locations of **Gilbert Ortega Indian Jewelry and Gallery**. Just north of the hustle and bustle of Scottsdale Fashion Square sits the tranquil, shaded property of the **Cosanti Originals** where the signature ceramic and bronze wind-bells of renowned architect Paolo Soleri are made and sold.

Edible goods: Shopping for a foodie? Heat things up with Goldwater's salsa and Arizona Gunslinger hot sauce products. **AJ's Fine Foods** is a great place for local tastes; **Kactus Jock** has nonedible souvenirs, too.

Signature style: Bola ties are the official neckwear of Arizona. Crafted from braided leather, metal tips, and a securing ornament, these ties have long been a craft of the Hopi, Navajo, and Zuni Indian tribes and are found in shops and galleries throughout Old Town.

QUICK BITES/REFUELING

For Kierland Commons shoppers, stop at **Chloe's Corner** (✉ 15215 N. Kierland Blvd., #190North Scottsdale ☎ 480/998-0202 ⊕ www.chloescorner.com) for a light but filling bite, with gourmet sandwiches, salads, baked goods, and milk shakes.

The **Sugar Bowl Ice Cream Parlor** (✉ 4005 N. Scottsdale Rd., Old Town ☎ 480/946-0051 ⊕ www.sugarbowlscottsdale.com) transports you back in time to a 1950s malt shop, complete with great burgers and lots of yummy ice-cream confections.

Z'Tejas Southwestern Grill (✉ 7014 E. Camelback Rd.,, Old TownScottsdale ☎ 480/946-4171 ⊕ www.ztejas.com) is conveniently located in Scottsdale Fashion Square and offers tasty food portions and ample margaritas to soothe the shopping beast.

Updated by
Cara LaBrie

The Valley of the Sun, otherwise known as metro Phoenix (i.e., Phoenix and all its suburbs, including Tempe and Scottsdale), is named for its 325-plus days of sunshine each year. Although many come to Phoenix for the golf and the weather, the Valley has much to offer by way of shopping, outdoor activities, and nightlife. The best of the latter is in Scottsdale and the East Valley with their hip dance clubs, old-time saloons, and upscale wine bars.

The Valley marks the northern tip of the Sonoran Desert, a prehistoric seabed that extends into northwestern Mexico with a landscape offering much more than just cacti. Paloverde and mesquite trees, creosote bushes, brittle bush, and agave dot the land, which is accustomed to being scorched by temperatures in excess of 100°F for weeks at a time. Late summer brings precious rain as monsoon storms illuminate the sky with lightning shows and the desert exudes the scent of creosote. Spring sets the Valley blooming, and the giant saguaros are crowned in white flowers for a short time in May—in the evening and cool early mornings—and masses of vibrant wildflowers fill desert crevices and span mountain landscapes.

EXPLORING

DOWNTOWN AND CENTRAL PHOENIX

Changes in the Valley over the past two decades have meant the emergence of a real downtown in Phoenix, where people hang out: there are apartments and loft spaces, cultural and sports facilities—including Jefferson Street's Chase Field (formerly known as Bank One Ballpark and still affectionately referred to by many locals as BOB) and US Airways Center, and large areas for conventions and trade shows. It has retained a mix of past and present, too, as restored homes in Heritage Square,

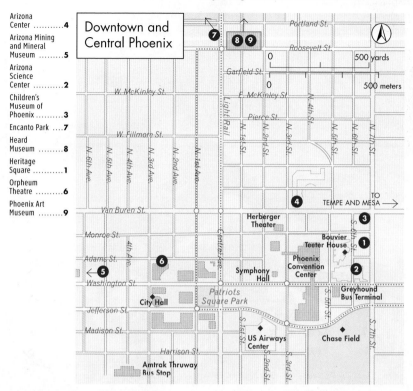

from the original townsite, give an idea of how far the city has come since its inception around the turn of the 20th century. Many locals refer to parts of downtown, particularly around the sports venues, as Copper Square.

GETTING HERE AND AROUND
There are lots of parking options downtown, and they're listed on the free map provided by Downtown Phoenix Partnership, available in many local restaurants (⊕ *www.downtownphoenix.com*). Many downtown sites are served by the light-rail system or DASH (Downtown Area Shuttle), a free bus service.

TIMING
Artlink's First Fridays & Art Detour is an excellent way to check out the Phoenix arts scene: galleries stay open late and crowds converge to view the work of emerging and established artists, listen to live music, and see impromptu street performances on the first Friday of every month. ☏ *602/256–7539* ⊕ *www.artlinkphoenix.com*.

Numbers in the margin correspond to numbers on the Downtown and Central Phoenix map.

TOP ATTRACTIONS

❸ **Children's Museum of Phoenix.** The Children's Museum of Phoenix is a playground for kids of all ages, featuring hands-on exhibits where children learn by playing. Venture through the "noodle forest," relax in the book loft, or get a crash course in economics by role-playing at the

on-site market. ✉ *215 N. 7th St., Downtown Phoenix* ☎ *602/253–0501* ⊕ *www.childrensmuseumofphoenix.org* 💲 *$9; free on 1st Fri. evenings* ⏱ *Tues.–Sun. 9* AM–*4* PM, *Fri. 6–10* PM *for 1st Fri.*

8 **Heard Museum.** Pioneer settlers Dwight and Maie Heard built a Spanish colonial–style building on their property to house their collection of Southwestern art. Today the staggering collection includes such exhibits as a Navajo hogan, an Apache wickiup (a temporary Native American structure, similar to a lean-to, constructed from branches, twigs, and leaves, sometimes covered with hides), and rooms filled with art, pottery, jewelry, kachinas, and textiles. The Heard also actively supports contemporary Indian artists and displays their work. Their fabulous signature cultural exhibition is "Home: Native People in the Southwest." Annual events include the World Championship Hoop Dance Contest in February and the Guild Indian Fair & Market in March. Children enjoy the interactive art-making exhibits. ■ **TIP→ The museum also has an incredible gift shop with authentic, high-quality goods purchased directly from Native American artists.** There's a museum satellite branch in Scottsdale that has rotating exhibits. ✉ *2301 N. Central Ave., Central Phoenix* ☎ *602/252–8848* ⊕ *www.heard.org* 💲 *$12* ⏱ *Mon.– Sat. 9:30–5, Sun. 11–5* ✉ *Heard Museum North: 32633 N. Scottsdale Rd., North Scottsdale, Scottsdale* ☎ *480/488–9817* 💲 *$5* ⏱ *Mon.–Sat. 10–5, Sun. 11–5.*

Fodor's Choice
★

1 **Heritage Square.** In a park-like setting from 5th to 7th streets between Monroe and Adams streets, this city-owned block contains the only remaining houses from the original Phoenix townsite. On the south side of the square, along Adams Street, stand several houses built between 1899 and 1901. The Bouvier Teeter House has a Victorian-style tearoom, and the Thomas House and Baird Machine Shop are now Pizzeria Bianco, one of the area's most popular eateries. **The one-story brick Stevens House holds the Arizona Doll and Toy Museum** (✉ *602 E. Adams St., Downtown Phoenix* ☎ *602/253–9337* 💲 *$3* ⏱ *Tues.–Sat. 10–4, Sun. noon–4. Closed Mon. and Aug.*). **Rosson House, an 1895 Victorian in the Queen Anne style, is the queen of Heritage Square. Built by a physician who served a brief term as mayor, it's the sole survivor among fewer than two dozen Victorians erected in Phoenix. It was bought and restored by the city in 1974.** ✉ *6th and Monroe Sts., Downtown Phoenix* ☎ *602/262–5070* ⊕ *www.rossonhousemuseum. org* 💲 *$5* ⏱ *Wed.–Sat. 10–3:30, Sun. noon–3:30.*

9 **Phoenix Art Museum.** This museum is one of the most visually appealing pieces of architecture in the Southwest. Basking in natural light, the museum makes great use of its modern, open space by tastefully fitting more than 17,000 works of art from all over the world—including sculptures by Frederic Remington and paintings by Georgia O'Keeffe, Thomas Moran, and Maxfield Parrish—within its soaring concrete walls. The museum hosts more than 20 significant exhibitions annually. Complete your tour with lunch at Arcadia Farms, the in-house café that serves some of the best homemade fare in town. ✉ *1625 N. Central Ave., Central Phoenix* ☎ *602/257–1222* ⊕ *www.phxart.org* 💲 *$10; free Wed. 3–9* PM *and on 1st Fri. evenings* ⏱ *Thurs.–Sat. 10–5, Wed. 10–9, Sun. noon–5; 1st Fri. evenings 6–10.*

WORTH NOTING

④ **Arizona Center.** Amid dramatic fountains, sunken gardens, and towering palm trees stands this two-tier, open-air structure: downtown's most attractive shopping venue. The center has about 50 shops and restaurants, open-air vendors, a large sports bar, and a multiplex cinema. ⊠ *400 E. Van Buren St., Downtown Phoenix* ☎ *602/271–4000* ⊕ *www.arizonacenter.com.*

WORD OF MOUTH

"I really enjoyed a visit to the Desert Botanical Garden in Phoenix when I visited Arizona. There is a special sculpture exhibit (separate admission) and they have concerts on Sundays."   —dsgmi

⑤ **Arizona Mining and Mineral Museum.** Arizona's phenomenal wealth and progress have had a lot to do with what lies beneath the actual land, namely the copper, gold, silver, and other earthbound deposits. This museum offers a mother lode of information and features more than 3,000 rocks, minerals, fossils, and mining equipment, including a 43-foot-tall Boras mine head frame and an 1882 baby-gauge steam train locomotive. ⊠ *1502 W. Washington, Downtown Phoenix* ☎ *602/771–1611* ⊕ *www.admmr.state.az.us* 🖾 *$2* ⊙ *Weekdays 8–5, Sat. 11–4.*

② **Arizona Science Center.** With more than 300 hands-on exhibits, this is
☾ the venue for science-related exploration. You can pilot a simulated
★ airplane flight, travel through the human body, navigate your way through the solar system in the Dorrance Planetarium, and watch a movie in the giant, five-story IMAX theater. ⊠ *600 E. Washington St., Downtown Phoenix* ☎ *602/716–2000* ⊕ *www.azscience.org* 🖾 *Museum $12; combination museum, IMAX, and planetarium $28* ⊙ *Daily 10–5.*

⑦ **Encanto Park.** Urban Encanto (Spanish for "enchanted") Park covers 222
☾ acres at the heart of one of Phoenix's oldest residential neighborhoods. There are many attractions, including picnic areas, a lagoon where you can paddleboat and canoe, a municipal swimming pool, a nature trail, **Enchanted Island** amusement park (⊕ *www.enchantedisland.com*), fishing in the park's lake, and two public golf courses. ⊠ *1202 W. Encanto Blvd., Central Phoenix* ☎ *602/261–8993 or 602/254–1200* ⊕ *phoenix.gov/parks/encanto.html* 🖾 *Park free, Enchanted Island rides $1.10 each* ⊙ *Park daily 6–midnight; Enchanted Island hrs vary by season and weather.*

QUICK BITES

SWITCH (⊠ *2603 N. Central Ave., Downtown Phoenix* ☎ *602/264–2295* ⊕ www.switchofarizona.com) is a cool way to beat the summer heat. The unique menu features fresh sandwiches, healthful salads, a fabulous cheese platter, gourmet burgers, steaks, seafood, baked goods, and crepes, in a sleek, modern setting with couch conversation pits and one of downtown's best patios, free from direct sunlight and traffic noise.

GREATER PHOENIX

While suburban towns are popping up all around Phoenix, the city's core neighborhoods just outside downtown Phoenix maintain the majority of their history and appeal. There are options aplenty to take you out hiking in the hills, or inside to some interesting cultural sites.

2

TOP ATTRACTIONS

⑮ **Desert Botanical Garden.** Opened in 1939 to conserve and showcase the ecology of the desert, these 150 acres contain more than 4,000 different species of cacti, succulents, trees, and flowers. A stroll along the **Fodor's Choice** 0.5-mi-long "Plants and People of the Sonoran Desert" trail is a fascinating lesson in environmental adaptations; children enjoy playing the ★ self-guiding game "Desert Detective." Specialized tours are available at an extra cost; check online for times and prices. ■ TIP➔ The Desert Botanical Garden stays open late, to 8 PM year-round, and it's particularly lovely when lighted by the setting sun or by moonlight, so you can plan for a cool, late visit after a full day of activities. ⊠ *1201 N. Galvin Pkwy., Papago Salado* ☎ *480/941–1225* ⊕ *www.dbg.org* ☒ *$15* ⊗ *Oct.–May, daily 8–8; June–Sept., daily 7–8.*

⑯ **Hall of Flame.** Retired firefighters lead tours through more than 100 restored fire engines and tell harrowing tales of the "world's most dangerous profession." The museum has the world's largest collection of firefighting equipment, and children can climb on a 1916 engine, operate alarm systems, and learn fire safety lessons from the pros. Helmets, badges, and other firefighting-related articles dating from as far back as 1725 are on display. ⊠ *6101 E. Van Buren St., Papago Salado* ☎ *602/275–3473* ⊕ *www.hallofflame.org* ☒ *$6* ⊗ *Mon.–Sat. 9–5, Sun. noon–4.*

⑲ **Huhugam Heritage Center.** Built to harmonize with the land, the Huhugam ★ Heritage Center mixes cool modern architecture with red earth, and as a whole is an impressive new way of looking at the past. Named for the tribe from which the modern-day Akimel O'odham (Pima) and Pee Posh (Maricopa) tribes descended, the small museum and education center is a celebration and collection of arts, culture, and history of the native people of the Gila River. It's about a 45-minute drive from downtown Phoenix and worthwhile for those interested in Native American culture. ⊠ *4759 N. Maricopa Rd., Gila River Indian Community, Chandler* ☎ *520/796–3500* ⊕ *www.huhugam.com* ☒ *$5* ⊗ *Wed.–Fri. 10–4.*

⑩ **Musical Instrument Museum (MIM).** With more than 10,000 instruments and artifacts from across the globe, the museum offers a rare display of music and instruments going back hundreds of years. Special galleries highlight video demonstrations as well as audio tracks that showcase the sounds that instruments, both primitive and contemporary, create. Among the museum's dazzling array of instruments are the piano on which John Lennon composed "Imagine," and the first Steinway piano. ⊠ *4725 E. Mayo Blvd. North Phoenix* ☎ *480/478–6000* ⊕ *themim.org* ☒ *$15* ⊗ *Sun.–Wed. 9–5, Thurs.–Fri. 9–9, Sat. 9–5.*

⑫ **Mystery Castle.** At the foot of South Mountain lies a curious dwelling built from desert rocks by Boyce Gulley, who came to Arizona to cure ★ his tuberculosis. Full of fascinating oddities, the castle has 18 rooms

Phoenix History: A City Grows in the Desert

As the Hohokam (the name comes from the Piman word for "people who have gone before") discovered 2,300 years ago, the miracle of water in the desert can be augmented by human hands. Having migrated from northwestern Mexico, Hohokam cultivated cotton, corn, and beans in tilled, rowed, and irrigated fields for about 1,700 years, establishing more than 300 mi of canals—an engineering phenomenon when you consider the limited technology available. They constructed a great town upon whose ruins modern Phoenix is built, and then vanished. Drought, long winters, and other causes are suggested for their disappearance.

MODERN BEGINNINGS

From the time the Hohokam left until the Civil War, the once fertile Salt River valley lay forgotten, used only by occasional small bands of Pima and Maricopa Indians. Then in 1865 the U.S. Army established Fort McDowell in the mountains to the east, where the Verde River flows into the Salt River. To feed the men and the horses stationed there, a former Confederate Army officer reopened the Hohokam canals in 1867. Within a year, fields bright with barley and pumpkins earned the area the name Pumpkinville. By 1870 the 300 residents had decided that their new city would arise from the ancient Hohokam site, just as the mythical phoenix rose from its own ashes.

A CITY ON THE RISE

Phoenix would grow indeed. Within 20 years it had become large enough—its population was about 3,000—to wrest the title of territorial capital from Prescott. By 1912, when Arizona was admitted as the 48th state, the area,

irrigated by the brand-new Roosevelt Dam and Salt River Project, had a burgeoning cotton industry. Copper was mined elsewhere but traded in Phoenix, and cattle were raised elsewhere but slaughtered and packed here in the largest stockyards outside of Chicago.

Meanwhile, the climate, so long a crippling liability, became an asset. Desert air was the prescribed therapy for the respiratory ills rampant in the sooty, factory-filled East; Scottsdale began in 1901 as "30-odd tents and a half dozen adobe houses" put up by health seekers. By 1930 travelers looking for warm winter recreation as well as rejuvenating aridity filled the elegant Crowne Plaza San Marcos hotel and Arizona Biltmore, the first of the many luxury retreats for which the area is now known worldwide. The 1950s brought residential air-conditioning, an invention that made the summers bearable for the growing workforce of the burgeoning technology industry.

PHOENIX TODAY

The Valley is very much a work still in progress, and historians are quick to point out that never in the world's history has a metropolis grown from "nothing" to attain the status of Phoenix in such a short period of time. At the heart of all the bustle, though, is a way of life that keeps its own pace: Phoenix is one of the world's largest small towns—where people dress informally and where the rugged, Old West spirit lives on in many of the Valley's nooks and crannies despite the sprawling growth. And if summer heat can be overwhelming, at least it has the restorative effect of slowing things down to an enjoyable pace.

2

with 13 fireplaces, a downstairs grotto tavern, a roll-away bed with a mining railcar as its frame, and some original pieces of Frank Lloyd Wright–designed furniture. The pump organ belonged to Elsie, the "Widow of Tombstone," who buried six husbands under suspicious circumstances. ⊠ *800 E. Mineral Rd., South Phoenix* ☏ *602/268–1581* ⊠ *$5* ⊙ *Oct.–May, Thurs.–Sun. 11–4. Call to confirm hrs.*

⓮ **Pueblo Grande Museum and Cultural Park.** Phoenix's only national land-
ⓒ mark, this park was once the site of a 500-acre Hohokam village sup-
Fodor'sChoice porting about 1,000 people and containing homes, storage rooms,
★ cemeteries, and ball courts. Three exhibition galleries hold displays on the Hohokam culture and archaeological methods. View the 10-minute orientation video before heading out on the 0.5-mi Ruin Trail past exca-vated sites that give a hint of Hohokam savvy: there's a building whose corner doorway was perfectly placed for watching the summer-solstice sunrise. Children particularly like the hands-on, interactive learning center. Guided tours by appointment only. ⊠ *4619 E. Washington St., Papago Salado* ☏ *602/495–0901* ⊕ *www.pueblogrande.com* ⊠ *$6* ⊙ *Oct.–Apr., Mon.–Sat. 9–4:45, Sun. 1–4:45; May–Sept., Tues.–Sat. 9–4:45 (closed Sun. and Mon.).*

WORTH NOTING

⓲ **Papago Park.** An amalgam of hilly desert terrain, streams, and lagoons,
ⓒ this park has picnic ramadas (shaded, open-air shelters), a golf course, a playground, hiking and biking trails, and even largemouth bass and trout fishing. (An urban fishing license is required for anglers age 15 and over. Visit ⊕ *www.azgfd.gov* for more information.) The hike up to landmark **Hole-in-the-Rock**—a natural observatory used by the native Hohokam to devise a calendar system—is steep and rocky, and a much easier climb up than down. **Governor Hunt's Tomb,** the white pyramid at the top of Ramada 16, commemorates the former Arizona leader and provides a lovely view. ⊠ *625 N. Galvin Pkwy., Papago Salado* ☏ *602/262–4881* ⊕ *www.papagosalado.org* ⊠ *Free* ⊙ *Daily 5 AM–11 PM.*

⓱ **Phoenix Zoo.** Four designated trails wind through this 125-acre zoo, rep-
ⓒ licating such habitats as an African savanna and a tropical rain forest. Meerkats, warthogs, desert bighorn sheep, and the endangered Arabian oryx are among the unusual sights. The Forest of Uco is home to the endangered spectacled bear from South America. Harmony Farm on the Discovery Trail introduces youngsters to small mammals, and a stop at the Big Red Barn provides a chance to groom a horse or milk a cow. The Butterfly Pavilion is also enchanting. The 30-minute narrated safari train tour costs $3 and provides a good orientation to the park. ■**TIP→** **In December the zoo stays open late (6–10 PM) for the popular "ZooLights" exhibit that transforms the area into an enchanted forest of more than 225 million twinkling lights, many in the shape of the zoo's residents.** Starry Safari Friday Nights in summer are fun, too. ⊠ *455 N. Galvin Pkwy., Papago Salado* ☏ *602/273–1341* ⊕ *www.phoenixzoo.org* ⊠ *$16* ⊙ *Hrs vary by month and weather. Check Web site for more details. Gener-ally, Oct.–May, daily 9–4; June–Sept., daily 7–2. ZooLights extends holiday hrs until 10.*

⓫ ☾ ★ **Shemer Arts Center.** Near the Phoenician resort, the Shemer Arts Center features revolving exhibits of current Arizona artists who have agreed to donate one of their pieces to the center's permanent collection. The collection is largely contemporary, and exhibits change every month or so in this former residence. ⊠ *5005 E. Camelback Rd., Camelback Corridor* ☎ *602/262–4727* ⊕ *www.phoenix.gov/shemer* ⌦ *Free* ☾ *Tues.–Thurs. 12:30–8:30, Fri. 12:30–5:30, Sat. 9:30–12:30.*

⓭ ☾ ★ **South Mountain Park.** This desert wonderland, the world's largest city park (almost 17,000 acres), offers a wilderness of mountain-desert trails for hikers, bikers, and horseback riders—and a great place to view sunsets. The Environmental Center has a model of the park as well as displays detailing its history, from the time of the ancient Hohokam people to gold seekers. Roads climb past picnic ramadas constructed by the Civilian Conservation Corps, winding through desert flora to the trailheads. Look for ancient petroglyphs, try to spot a desert cottontail rabbit or chuckwalla lizard, or simply stroll among the desert vegetation. Maps of all scenic drives as well as hiking, mountain biking, and horseback trails are available at the Gatehouse Entrance just inside the park boundary (⇨ *also see Sports and the Outdoors below).* ⊠ *10919 S. Central Ave., South Phoenix* ☎ *602/495–0222* ⊕ *www.phoenix.gov/parks* ⌦ *Free* ☾ *Daily 4:30 AM–10:30 PM; Environmental Education Center: Fri.–Sat. 9–3.*

> **PAPAGO SALADO**
>
> The word Papago, meaning "bean eater," was a name given by 16th-century Spanish explorers to the Hohokam, a vanished native people of the Phoenix area. Farmers of the desert, the Hohokam lived in central Arizona from about AD 1 to 1450, when their civilization abandoned the Salt River (Rio Salado) valley, leaving behind the remnants of their villages and also a complex system of irrigation canals.

SCOTTSDALE

Nationally known art galleries, souvenir shops, and funky Old Town fill downtown Scottsdale—the third-largest artist community in the United States. Fifth Avenue is known for shopping and Native American jewelry and crafts stores, while Main Street and Marshall Way are home to the international art set with galleries and interior-design shops.

GETTING HERE AND AROUND   Although your tour of downtown can easily be completed on foot, the **Ollie the Trolley** service operates a trolley with regular service through Scottsdale (☎ *480/970–8130* ⊕ *www.olliethetrolley.net).*

TIMING   If you have limited time in the area, spend a half day in downtown Scottsdale and the rest of the day at Taliesin West.

Art Walk (⊕ *www.scottsdalegalleries.com),* every Thursday 7–9 PM year-round (except Thanksgiving), is perfect for checking out the Scottsdale galleries: locals and tourists browse Main Street and Marshall Way, the two major gallery strips, and there's a party atmosphere.

Numbers in the margin correspond to numbers on the Scottsdale map.

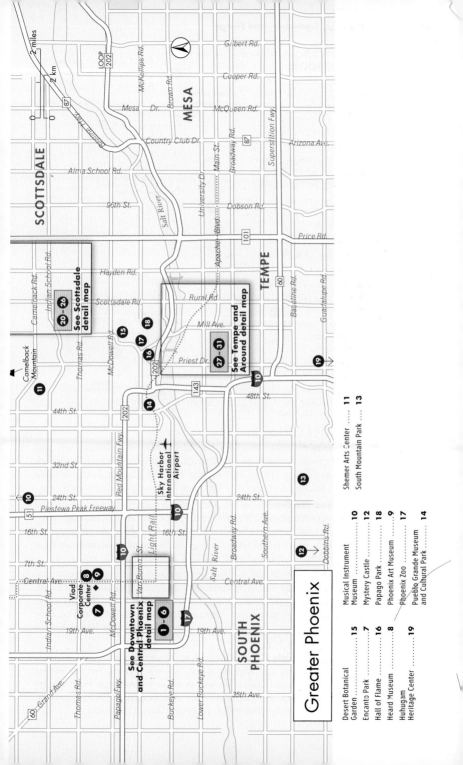

Greater Phoenix

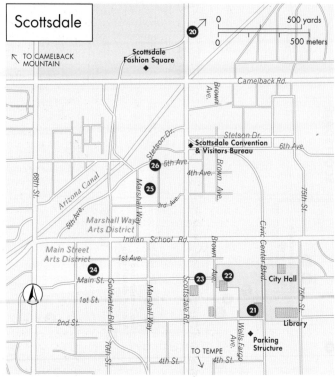

TOP ATTRACTIONS

26 **5th Avenue.** Whether you seek handmade Native American arts and crafts, casual clothing, or cacti, you'll find it here—at such landmark shops as Gilbert Ortega and Kactus Jock. ⊠ *5th Ave. between Civic Center Rd. and Stetson Dr., Old Town* ⊕ *www.scottsdale5thave.org.*

24 **Main Street Arts District.** Gallery after gallery displays artwork in myriad
★ styles—contemporary, Western realism, Native American, and traditional. Several antiques shops are also here; specialties include porcelain and china, jewelry, and Oriental rugs. ⊠ *Bounded by Main St. and 1st Ave., Scottsdale Rd. and 69th St., Old Town.*

25 **Marshall Way Arts District.** Galleries that exhibit predominantly contemporary art line the blocks of Marshall Way north of Indian School Road, and upscale gift and jewelry stores can be found here, too. Farther north on Marshall Way across 3rd Avenue are more art galleries and creative stores with a Southwestern flair. ⊠ *Marshall Way from Indian School Rd. to 5th Ave., Old Town.*

23 **Old Town Scottsdale.** "The West's Most Western Town," this area has rustic storefronts and wooden sidewalks; it's touristy, but the closest you'll come to experiencing life here as it was 80 years ago. High-quality jewelry, pots, and Mexican imports are sold alongside kitschy souvenirs. ⊠ *Main St. from Scottsdale Rd. to Brown Ave., Old Town.*

② Taliesin West. Ten years after visiting Arizona in 1927 to consult on
Fodor's Choice designs for the Biltmore hotel, architect Frank Lloyd Wright chose 600
★ acres of rugged Sonoran Desert at the foothills of the McDowell Mountains as the site for his permanent winter residence. Today the site is a
National Historic Landmark and still an active community of students
and architects. Wright and apprentices constructed a desert camp here
using organic architecture to integrate the buildings with their natural
surroundings. In addition to the living quarters, drafting studio, and
small apartments of the Apprentice Court, Taliesin West has two the-
aters, a music pavilion, and the Sun Trap—sleeping spaces surrounding
an open patio and fireplace. Five guided tours are offered, ranging from
a one-hour "panorama" tour to a three-hour behind-the-scenes tour,
with other tours offered seasonally; all visitors must be accompanied by
a guide. ■ TIP→ Wear comfortable shoes for walking. The half-hour drive
from downtown Scottsdale is very worthwhile. Drive north on the 101
Freeway to Frank Lloyd Wright Boulevard. Follow Frank Lloyd Wright
Boulevard for a few miles to the entrance at the corner of Cactus Road.
✉ *12621 Frank Lloyd Wright Blvd., North Scottsdale* ☎ *480/860–2700*
⊕ *www.franklloydwright.org* ✈ *$27–$60* ⊙ *Daily 9–4, with evening
tours most days. Call to confirm.*

WORTH NOTING

② Scottsdale Center for the Peforming Arts. Galleries within this cultural and
entertainment complex rotate exhibits frequently, but they typically
emphasize contemporary art and artists. You might be able to catch a
comical, interactive performance of the long-running "Late Night Cat-
echism," or an installation of modern dance. The acclaimed Scottsdale
Arts Festival is held annually in March. **SMoCA, the Scottsdale Museum
of Contemporary Art** (✉ *7374 E. 2nd St., Old Town* ☎ *480/994–2787*
⊕ *www.smoca.org* ✈ *$7, free Thurs.* ⊙ *Hrs vary*), a **"museum without
walls,"** is on-site, and there's also a good museum store for unusual
jewelry and stationery, posters, and art books. New installations are
planned every few months, with an emphasis on contemporary art,
architecture, and design. Free docent-led tours are conducted on Thursday at 1:30. Kids can visit the Young at Art gallery. ✉ *7380 E. 2nd
St., Old Town* ☎ *480/994–2787* ⊕ *www.scottsdaleperformingarts.org*
✈ *Free* ⊙ *Call for performance info.*

② Scottsdale Historical Museum. Scottsdale's first schoolhouse, this redbrick
building houses a reconstruction of the 1910 schoolroom, as well as
photographs, original furniture from the city's founding fathers, and
displays of other treasures from Scottsdale's early days. ✉ *7333 Scottsdale Mall, Old Town* ☎ *480/945–4499* ⊕ *www.scottsdalemuseum.com*
✈ *Free* ⊙ *Oct.–May, Wed.–Sun. 10–5; June–Sept., Wed.–Sun. 10–2.*

TEMPE AND AROUND

Tempe is the home of Arizona State University's main campus and
a thriving student population. A 20-minute drive from Phoenix, the
tree- and brick-lined Mill Avenue is the main drag, filled with student
hangouts, bookstores, boutiques, eateries, and a repertory movie house.
There are always things to do or see, and plenty of music venues and

Frank Lloyd Wright's Taliesen West

More than just an artist's retreat and workshop, Taliesin West and the surrounding desert still inspire both visitors and architects who study here. Frank Lloyd Wright once said "The desert abhors the straight, hard line." Though much of Wright's most famed work is based on such lines, this sprawling compound takes its environment into consideration like few desert structures do. Taliesin West mirrors the jagged shapes and earthen colors of its mountain backdrop and desert surroundings. Even Wright's interior pieces of "origami" furniture assume the mountain's unpredictable shapes.

ARIZONA INSPIRATION

Wright first came to Phoenix from Wisconsin in 1927 to act as a consultant to architect Albert Chase McArthur on the now famed Arizona Biltmore. Later Wright was also hired to design a new hotel in what is currently Phoenix South Mountain Park. Wright and his working entourage returned to the Valley and, instead of residing in apartments, they built a camp of asymmetrical cabins with canvas roofs that maximized but pleasantly diffused light, and blended into the rugged mountain backdrop.

When the hotel project failed due to the stock market crash of 1929, Wright and his crew returned to Taliesin, his Wisconsin home and site of his architectural fellowship, and the camp was disassembled and carted away. But the concept of his humble worker village would remain in Wright's creative consciousness and a decade later the renowned architect found an appropriate plot of land north of Scottsdale.

NATURAL CONSTRUCTION

Built upon foundations of caliche, known as nature's own concrete, and painted in crimson and amber hues that highlight the "desert masonry," the buildings seem to adhere naturally to the landscape. The asymmetrical roofs resemble those of Wright's South Mountain camp and were covered with canvas for many years before Wright added glass. Supported by painted-steel-and-redwood beams, they face the sun-filled sky like the hard shell of a desert animal that seems to be comfortable here despite all the odds against its survival.

ARCHITECTURAL LEGACY

The over 70-year-old property and its structures, which Wright envisioned as a "little fleet of ships," are perhaps some of the best non-native examples of organic architecture. They also serve as desert building blocks for future generations of Wright protégés—some perhaps schooled on these very grounds—to balance man and Mother Nature.

WORD OF MOUTH

Travelers at Fodors.com recommend the following tours and tips for your visit:

"The 90 minute tour [was] a great introduction to Wright's life, architectural philosophy and school, and to the desert landscape."   —sms73

"I highly recommend reading *Loving Frank* [by Nancy Horan] to gain insight into this man."   —DebitNM

"If they are offering a night tour, take that one. The place is magical at night and you can get a glimpse of what it was like when the complex was WAY out in the desert all alone."   —starrs

Taliesin West was Frank Lloyd Wright's winter residence. The original Taliesin in Wisconsin was his summer home.

fun, casual dining spots. This is one part of town where the locals actually hang out, stroll, and sit at the outdoor cafés.

The inverted pyramid that is Tempe City Hall, on 5th Street, one block east of Mill Avenue, was constructed by local architects Rolf Osland and Michael Goodwin not just to win design awards (which they have), but also to shield city workers from the desert sun. The pyramid is built mainly of bronzed glass and stainless steel, and the point disappears in a sunken courtyard lushly landscaped with jacaranda, ivy, and flowers, out of which the pyramid widens to the sky: stand underneath and gaze up for a weird fish-eye perspective.

The banks of the Rio Salado in Tempe are the site of a new commercial and entertainment district, and Tempe Town Lake—a 2-mi-long waterway created by inflatable dams in a flood control channel—which is open for boating. There are biking and jogging paths on the perimeter.

GETTING HERE AND AROUND Street parking is hard to find, especially amid all the construction, but you can park in the public garage at Hayden Square, just north of 5th Street and west of Mill Avenue. Get your ticket stamped by a local merchant to avoid paying parking fees. The FLASH (Free Local Area Shuttle) (☎ 602/253–5000) does a loop around Arizona State University, with stops at Mill Avenue and Sun Devil Stadium. Light-rail also stops at 3rd Street and Mill Avenue.

TIMING The **Tempe Festival of the Arts** (⊕ www.tempefestivalofthearts.com) on Mill Avenue is held twice a year in early December and March–April; it has all sorts of interesting arts and crafts.

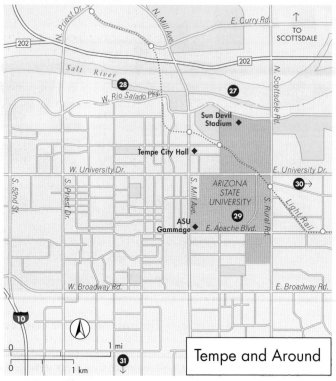

Numbers in the text correspond to numbers on the Tempe and Around map.

EXPLORING

29 **Arizona State University.** What began as the Tempe Normal School for Teachers—in 1886 a four-room redbrick building and 20-acre cow pasture—is now the 750-acre Tempe campus of ASU, the largest university in the Southwest. The university now has four campuses located across the Valley. **The ASU Memorial Union (⊠ 1290 S. Normal Ave. ☎ 480/965–5728) has maps of a self-guided walking tour of the Tempe campus—it's a long walk from Mill Avenue, so you might opt for the short version suggested here.** You'll wind past public art and innovative architecture—including a music building that bears a strong resemblance to a wedding cake, designed by Taliesin students to echo Frank Lloyd Wright's Gammage Auditorium, and a law library shaped like an open book—and end up at the 71,706-seat **Sun Devil Stadium** (⊠ ASU Campus, 5th St. ☎ 480/965–9011), home to the school's Sun Devils. One of the most outstanding stadiums in the country, it has a spectacular setting. It's literally carved out of a mountain and cradled between the Tempe buttes. **While touring the west end of campus, stop into the Arizona State University Art Museum** (⊠ Mill Ave. and 10th St. ☎ 480/965–2787 ⊕ www.asuartmuseum.asu.edu ⊠ Free ☉ Sept.–Apr., Tues. 11–8,

Wed.–Sat. 11–5; May–Aug., Tues.–Sat. 11–5). It's in the gray-purple stucco Nelson Fine Arts Center, just north of Gammage Auditorium. For a relatively small museum, it has an extensive collection, including 19th- and 20th-century painting and sculpture by masters such as Winslow Homer, Edward Hopper, Georgia O'Keeffe, and Rockwell Kent. Works by faculty and student artists are also on display, and there's a gift shop. In Matthews Hall, the Northlight Gallery (⊠ *Matthews Hall, Mill Ave. and 10th St.* ☎ *480/965–6517* ⊕ *art.asu.edu/gallery/northlight/* 🖼 *Free* ☉ *Tues.–Thurs. 10:30–4:30, Closed Mon., Fri.–Sat.*) exhibits works by both renowned and emerging photographers.

30 **Arizona Museum of Natural History.** Kids young and old get a thrill out of the largest collection of dinosaur fossils in the state at this large museum where you can also pan for gold and see changing exhibits from around the world. ⊠ *53 N. Macdonald St., Mesa* ☎ *480/644–2230* ⊕ *www. azmnh.org* 🖼 *$10* ☉ *Tues.–Fri. 10–5, Sat. 11–5, Sun. 1–5.*

31 **Arizona Sealife Aquarium.** For up-close views of some 5,000 creatures including sharks, sting rays, eels, and a giant octopus, head straight to this underwater menagerie in Tempe. You can walk through a 360-degree viewing tunnel in a 165,000-gallon tank that is the first of its kind. Who says there's no water in the desert? ⊠ *Arizona Mills, 5000 Arizona Mills Circle, Tempe* ☎ *480/478–7600* ⊕ *www.sealifeus. com/phoenix* 🖼 *$18.50* ☉ *Mon.–Sat. 10–9, Sun. 10–7.*

28 **Tempe Center for the Arts.** This small, architecturally interesting arts center at the edge of Tempe Town Lake has become a great source of local pride since it opened in 2007. Visual art, music, theater, and dance, featuring local, regional, and international talent are showcased in a state-of-the-art, 600-seat proscenium theater, a 200-seat studio theater, and a 3,500 square-foot gallery. ⊠ *700 W. Rio Salado Pkwy.* ☎ *480/350–2822* ⊕ *www.tempe.gov/arts.*

27 **Tempe Town Lake.** The man-made Town Lake has turned downtown Tempe into a commercial and urban-living hot spot, and attracts college students and Valley residents of all ages. Little ones enjoy the Splash Playground, and fishermen appreciate the rainbow trout–stocked lake. **Rio Lago Cruises** rents boats and has a selection of short cruise options. ⊠ *80 W. Rio Salado Pkwy., between Mill and Rural Aves. north of Arizona State University* ☎ *480/350–8625 or 480/517–4050* ⊕ *www. riolagocruise.com.*

SPORTS AND THE OUTDOORS

The mountains surrounding the Valley of the Sun are among its greatest assets, and outdoors enthusiasts have plenty of options within the city limits to pursue hiking, bird-watching, or mountain-biking passions. Piestewa (formerly Squaw) Peak, north of downtown, is popular with hikers, and Camelback Mountain and the Papago Peaks are landmarks between Phoenix and Scottsdale. South of downtown are the much less lofty peaks of South Mountain Park, which separates the Valley from the rest of the Sonoran Desert. East of the city, beyond Tempe and Mesa, the peaks of the Superstition Mountains—named for their eerie way of seeming just a few miles away—are the first of a range that stretches all the way into New Mexico.

Central Arizona's dry desert heat imposes particular restraints on outdoor endeavors—even in winter hikers and cyclists should wear lightweight opaque clothing, a hat or visor, and high-UV-rated sunglasses, and should carry a quart of water for each hour of activity. The intensity of the sun makes strong sunscreen (SPF 15 or higher) a must, and don't forget to apply it to your hands and feet. ■TIP➔ From May 1 to October 1 you shouldn't jog or hike from one hour after sunrise until a half hour before sunset. During these times the air is so hot and dry that your body will lose moisture at a dangerous, potentially lethal rate. And keep your eyes peeled in natural desert areas; rattlesnakes and scorpions could be on the prowl.

BALLOONING

A sunrise or sunset hot-air-balloon ascent is a remarkable desert sightseeing experience. The average fee—there are more than three dozen Valley companies to choose from—is $150 per person, and hotel pickup is usually included. Since flight paths and landing sites vary with wind speeds and directions, a roving land crew follows each balloon in flight. Time in the air is generally between 1 and 1½ hours, but allow 3 hours for the total excursion.

Adventures Out West and Unicorn Balloon Company (☎ *480/991–3666 or 800/755–0935* ⊕ *www.adventuresoutwest.com*) has horseback riding, jeep tours, and hot-air-balloon flights that conclude with complimentary champagne, a flight certificate, and video. The **Hot Air Balloon Company** (☎ *623/847–1511 or 800/843–5987* ⊕ *www.arizonaballooning. com*) offers private and group sunrise and sunset flights with sparkling beverages and fresh pastries served on touchdown. **Hot Air Expeditions** (☎ *480/502–6999 or 800/831–7610* ⊕ *www.hotairexpeditions.com*) is the best ballooning in Phoenix. Flights are long, the staff is charming, and the gourmet snacks, catered by the acclaimed Vincent restaurant, are out of this world.

BICYCLING

There are plenty of gorgeous areas for biking in the Phoenix area, but riding in the streets isn't recommended, as there are few adequate bike lanes in the city. **Phoenix Parks and Recreation** (☎ *602/262–6861* ⊕ *www. ci.phoenix.az.us/parks*) has detailed maps of Valley bike paths. Note that the desert climate can be tough on cyclists, so make sure you're prepared with lots of water.

Pinnacle Peak (✉ *26802 N. 102nd Way, 25 mi northeast of downtown Phoenix, Scottsdale* ☎ *480/312–0990* ⊕ *scottsdaleaz.gov/parks*) is a popular place to take bikes for the ride north to Carefree and Cave Creek, or east and south over the mountain pass and down to the Verde River, toward Fountain Hills. **Scottsdale's Indian Bend Wash** (✉ *Along Hayden Rd. from Shea Blvd. south to Indian School Rd., Scottsdale* ☎ *480/312–7275* ⊕ *scottsdaleaz.gov/parks*) has paths suitable for bikes winding among its golf courses and ponds.

★ **South Mountain Park** *(see above)* is the prime site for mountain bikers, with its 40-plus mi of trails—some of them with challenging ascents

BASEBALL'S SPRING TRAINING

For dyed-in-the-wool baseball fans there's no better place than the Valley of the Sun. Baseball has become nearly a year-round activity in the Phoenix area, beginning with spring training in late February and continuing through the Arizona Fall League championships in mid-November.

SPRING

Today the Cactus League consists of 14 major-league teams (12 in the Valley and two in Tucson). Ticket prices are reasonable, around $7 to $8 for bleacher seats to $15 to $30 for reserved seats. Many stadiums have lawn-seating areas in the outfield, where you can spread a blanket and bring a picnic. Cactus League stadiums are more intimate than big-league parks, and players often come right up to the stands to say hello and to sign autographs.

Tickets for some teams go on sale as early as December. Brochures listing game schedules and ticket information are available from the **Cactus League's** Web site (⊕ *www. cactusleague.com*).

SUMMER

During the regular major-league season the hometown Arizona Diamondbacks (⊕ *www.azdiamondbacks.com*) play on natural grass at Chase Field in the heart of downtown Phoenix (the team does spring training in Tucson). The stadium is a technological wonder; if the weather's a little too warm outside, they close the roof, turn on the gigantic air-conditioners, and keep you cool while you enjoy the game. You can tour the stadium except on afternoon-game days and holidays.

FALL

At the conclusion of the regular season the Arizona Fall League runs until the week before Thanksgiving. Each major-league team sends six of its most talented young prospects to compete with other young promising players—180 players in all. There are six teams in the league, broken down into two divisions. It's a great way to see future Hall of Famers in their early years. Tickets for Fall League games are $6.

Call **Scottsdale Stadium** (☎ *480/312–2586*), one of the league's host sites, for ticket information.

and all of them quiet and scenic. **Tempe Town Lake** (⊠ *Southwest corner of Mill Ave. and Washington St., Tempe* ☎ *480/350–8625* ⊕ *tempe.gov/ lake*) has 5 mi of paths for skating, running, bicycling, and walking. **Trail 100** (⊠ *Enter at Dreamy Draw park, just east of the intersection of Northern Ave. and 16th St. North Central Phoenix* ☎ *602/262–6696* ⊕ *phoenix.gov/parks*) runs throughout the Phoenix Mountain preserve; it's just the thing for mountain bikers.

OUTFITTERS AND EXPEDITIONS   **ABC/Desert Biking Adventures** (☎ *602/320–4602 or 888/249–2453* ⊕ *www. desertbikingadventures.com*) offers two-, three-, and four-hour mountain-biking excursions through the McDowell Mountains and the Sonoran Desert. **AOA Adventures** (☎ *480/945–2881 or 866/455–1601* ⊕ *www. aoa-adventures.com*) leads half-day, full-day, and multiple-day adventures, with their extremely knowledgeable and personable staff. **Wheels**

N' Gear (✉ *16447 N. 91st St., North Scottsdale, Scottsdale* ☎ *480/945–2881*) rents bikes by the day or the week.

FOUR-WHEELING

Taking a jeep through the backcountry has become a popular way to experience the desert's saguaro-covered mountains and curious rock formations. Prices start at around $100 per person.

Arrowhead Desert Jeep Tours (*Phoenix* ☎ *602/942–3361* ⊕ *www. azdeserttours.com*) offers gold panning on a private claim, cookouts, cattle drives, river crossings, and Native American dance demonstrations. **Desert Dog Hummer Adventures** (☎ *480/837–3966* ⊕ *www. azadventures.com*) heads out on half- and full-day Humvee tours to the Four Peaks Wilderness Area in Tonto National Forest and the Sonoran Desert. U-Drive desert cars and ATV tours are also available. **Desert Storm Hummer Tours** (☎ *480/922–0020 or 866/374–8637* ⊕ *www.dshummer.com*) conducts four-hour nature tours, climbing 4,000 feet up the rugged trails of Tonto National Forest via Hummer. **Wayward Wind Tours** (☎ *602/867–7825 or 800/804–0480* ⊕ *www. waywardwindtours.com*) ventures down to the Verde River on its own trail and offers wilderness cookouts for large groups. **Wild West Jeep Tours** (☎ *480/922–0144* ⊕ *www.wildwestjeeptours.com*) has special permits that allow it to conduct four-wheeler excursions in the Tonto National Forest and to visit thousand-year-old Indian sites listed on the National Register of Historic Places.

GOLF

Arizona has more golf courses per capita than any other state west of the Mississippi River, making it one of the most popular golf destinations in the United States. The sport is also one of Arizona's major industries, and the green fee can run from $35 at a public course to more than $500 at some of Arizona's premier golfing spots. New courses seem to pop up routinely: there are more than 200 in the Valley (some lighted at night), and the PGA's Southwest section has its headquarters here.

MUNICIPAL
COURSES
Fodor's Choice
★

ASU Karsten Golf Course (✉ *1125 E. Rio Salado Pkwy., Tempe* ☎ *480/921–8070* ⊕ *www.asukarsten.com* ⅃ *18 holes. 4765–7002 yds (4 sets of tees). Par 70. Slope 132. Green Fee: $40–$108* ☞ *Facilities: Driving range, putting green, golf carts, rental clubs, pro shop, lessons, restaurant, bar*) is the Arizona State University 18-hole golf course where NCAA champions train.

Encanto Park (✉ *2775 N. 15th Ave., Central Phoenix* ☎ *602/253–3963* ⊕ *phoenix.gov/sports* ⅃ *18 holes. 5737–6361 yds. Par 70. Slope 120/113. Green Fee: $24–$46* ☞ *Facilities: Driving range, putting green, golf carts, rental clubs, pro shop, restaurant, bar*) has attractive, affordable public 9- and 18-hole courses.

Papago Golf Course (✉ *5595 E. Moreland St., Papago Salado* ☎ *602/275–8428* ⊕ *phoenix.gov/sports/papago.html* ⅃ *18 holes. 5434/7333 yds. Par 72. Slope 125/128. Green Fee: $44–$99* ☞ *Facilities: Driving range, putting green, golf carts, rental clubs, pro shop, restaurant, bar*) is a low-priced 18 holes and Phoenix's best municipal course.

2

PUBLIC
COURSES
Fodor's Choice
★   **Gold Canyon Golf Club** (✉ *6100 S. King's Ranch Rd., Gold Canyon* ☎ *480/982–9090 or 800/827–5281* ⊕ *www.gcgr.com* ⚑ *Dinosaur Mountain: 18 holes. 4921–6584 yds. Par 72. Slope 115–140. Green Fee: $75–$125. Sidewinder: 18 holes. 4534–6481 yds. Par 72. Slope 124–133. Green Fee: $49–$79* ☞ *Facilities: Driving range, putting green, golf carts, rental clubs, pro shop, lessons, restaurant, bar*), near Apache Junction in the East Valley, offers fantastic views of the Superstition Mountains and challenging golf.

★   **Grayhawk Country Club** (✉ *8620 E. Thompson Peak Pkwy., North Scottsdale, Scottsdale* ☎ *480/502–1800* ⊕ *www.grayhawk.com* ⚑ *Talon: 18 holes. 6973–7135 yds. Par 72. Slope 120/143. Raptor: 18 holes. 5309–7135 yds. Par 72. Slope 127/143. Green Fee: $155–$225* ☞ *Facilities: Driving range, putting green, golf carts, rental clubs, pro shop, lessons, restaurant, bar*), a 36-hole course, has beautiful mountain views. In summer the green fee is much lower.

Hillcrest Golf Club (✉ *20002 Star Ridge Dr., Sun City West* ☎ *623/584–1500* ⊕ *www.hillcrestgolfclub.com* ⚑ *18 holes. 5512–7002 yds. Par 70. Slope 120–126. Green Fee: $34–$52* ☞ *Facilities: Driving range, putting green, golf carts, rental clubs, pro shop, lessons, restaurant, bar*) is the best course in the Sun Cities development, with 18 holes on 179 acres of well-designed turf.

Raven Golf Club at South Mountain (✉ *3636 E. Baseline Rd., South Phoenix* ☎ *602/243–3636* ⊕ *www.ravenatsouthmountain.com* ⚑ *18 holes. 5759–7078 yds. Par 72. Slope 119–130. Green Fee: $49–$180* ☞ *Facilities: Driving range, putting green, golf carts, rental clubs, pro shop, lessons, restaurant, bar*) has thousands of Aleppo pines and Lombardy poplars, making it a cool, shady 18-hole haven for summertime golfers. Call or visit the Web site for other Raven golf properties.

SunRidge Canyon (✉ *13100 N. SunRidge Dr., Fountain Hills* ☎ *480/837–5100* ⊕ *www.sunridgegolf.com* ⚑ *18 holes. 4689–6823 yds. Par 72. Slope 119–142. Green Fee: $60–$190* ☞ *Facilities: Driving range, putting green, golf carts, rental clubs, pro shop, lessons, restaurant, bar*), east of Scottsdale, is a great 18-hole course for both the low handicapper and those who score above 100. The incredible mountain views are almost distracting.

Fodor's Choice
★   **Troon North** (✉ *10320 E. Dynamite Blvd., North Scottsdale, Scottsdale* ☎ *480/585–7700* ⊕ *www.troonnorthgolf.com* ⚑ *Monument: 18 holes. 5099–7070 yds. Par 72. Slope 118–147. Pinnacle: 18 holes. 4883–7025 yds. Par 71. Slope 116–147. Green Fee: $215–$295* ☞ *Facilities: Driving range, putting green, golf carts, rental clubs, pro shop, lessons, restaurant, bar*) is a challenge for the length alone (7,025 yards). The million-dollar views add to the experience at this perfectly maintained 36-hole course.

RESORT
COURSES
Arizona Biltmore Country Club (✉ *Arizona Biltmore Resort & Spa, 24th St. and Missouri Ave., Camelback Corridor* ☎ *602/955–9655* ⊕ *www.arizonabiltmore.com* ⚑ *Adobe: 18 holes. 5417–6428 yds. Par 71. Slope 119–123. Links: 18 holes. 4747–6300 yds. Par 71. Slope 110–125. Green Fee: $49–$185* ☞ *Facilities: Driving range, putting green, golf carts, rental clubs, pro shop, lessons, restaurant, bar*), the granddaddy

The Valley of the Sun is a popular destination for golfing with more than 200 courses in the area.

of Valley golf courses, has two 18-hole PGA championship courses, lessons, and clinics.

Lookout Mountain Golf Club (⊠ *Pointe Hilton at Tapatio Cliffs, 1111 N. 7th St., North Central Phoenix* ☎ *602/866–6356* ⊕ *www.pointehilton.com* ⅄ *18 holes. 4557–6535 yds. Par 71. Slope 113–135. Green Fee: $79–$149 ☞ Facilities: Driving range, putting green, golf carts, rental clubs, pro shop, lessons, restaurant, bar*) has one 18-hole, par-71 course.

Marriott's Camelback Golf Club (⊠ *Marriott's Camelback Inn, 7847 N. Mockingbird La., Paradise Valley* ☎ *480/596–7050* ⊕ *www.camelbackinn.com* ⅄ *Padre: 18 holes. 6903 yds. Par 72. Slope 125. Indian Bend: 18 holes. 7014 yds. Par 72. Slope 122. Green Fee: $59–$149 ☞ Facilities: Driving range, putting green, golf carts, rental clubs, pro shop, lessons, restaurant, bar*) has two 18-hole courses. Summer twilight green fee is $40.

Ocotillo Golf Resort (⊠ *3751 S. Clubhouse Dr., Chandler* ☎ *480/917–6660* ⊕ *www.ocotillogolf.com* ⅄ *Blue/Gold: 18 holes. 5128–7016 yds. Par 72. Slope 124–133. White/Gold: 18 holes. 5124–6804 yds. Par 70. Slope 118–128. Blue/White: 18 holes. 5134–6782 yds. Par 71. Slope 117–133. Green Fee: $35–$115 ☞ Facilities: Driving range, putting green, golf carts, rental clubs, pro shop, lessons, restaurant, bar*) is designed around 95 acres of man-made lakes; there's water in play on nearly all 27 holes. Summer twilight green fee is $35.

★ **The Phoenician Golf Club** (⊠ *The Phoenician, 6000 E. Camelback Rd., Camelback Corridor* ☎ *480/423–2449* ⊕ *www.thephoenician.com* ⅄ *Canyon/Oasis: 18 holes. 4871–6258 yds. Par 70. Slope 111–130. Desert/Canyon: 18 holes. 4777–6068 yds. Par 70. Slope 114–131. Oasis/Desert: 18 holes. 5024–6310 yds. Par 70. Slope 113–130. Green Fee:*

$35–$200 ☞ *Facilities: Driving range, putting green, golf carts, rental clubs, pro shop, lessons, restaurant, bar*) has a 27-hole course. Summer fees after 11 AM start at $35.

★ **Tournament Players Club of Scottsdale** (⊠ *Fairmont Scottsdale Princess Resort, 17020 N. Hayden Rd., North Scottsdale, Scottsdale* ☎ *480/585–4334 or 888/400–4001* ⊕ *www.tpc.com* ⸡ *Stadium: 18 holes. 5567–7216 yds. Par 71. Slope 124–141. Champions: 18 holes. 5342–7115 yds. Par 71. Slope 120–139. Green Fee: $49–$243* ☞ *Facilities: Driving range, putting green, golf carts, rental clubs, pro shop, lessons, restaurant, bar*), a 36-hole course by Tom Weiskopf and Jay Morrish, is the site of the PGA Waste Management Phoenix Open, which takes place in January.

Wigwam Golf and Country Club (⊠ *Wigwam Resort, 300 Wigwam Blvd., Litchfield Park* ☎ *623/935–3811* ⊕ *www.wigwamresort.com* ⸡ *Blue: 18 holes. 4791–6000 yds. Par 70. Slope 113–123. Gold: 18 holes. 5885–7430 yds. Par 72. Slope 125–135. Red: 18 holes. 5806–6852 yds. Par 72. Slope 118–126. Green Fee: $64–$172* ☞ *Facilities: Driving range, putting green, golf carts, rental clubs, pro shop, lessons, restaurant, bar*) is the home of the famous Gold Course, as well as two other 18-hole courses.

HIKING

One of the best ways to see the beauty of the Valley of the Sun is from above, so hikers of all calibers seek a vantage point in the mountains surrounding the flat Valley.

The Phoenix Mountain Preserve Council administers the city's **Phoenix Mountain Preserve System** (☎ *602/390–6086* ⊕ *www.phoenixmountains. org*), a series of mountainous regions that surround the city. The group has its own park rangers who can help plan your hikes. It also publishes a book, *Day Hikes and Trail Rides in and around Phoenix.* ■TIP➜ No matter the season, be sure to bring sunscreen, a hat, plenty of water, and a camera to capture a dazzling sunset. It's always a good idea to tell someone where you'll be and when you plan to return.

★ **Camelback Mountain and Echo Canyon Recreation Area** (⊠ *Tatum Blvd. and McDonald Dr., Paradise Valley* ☎ *602/256–3220 Phoenix Parks & Recreation Dept.*) has intermediate to difficult hikes up the Valley's most outstanding central landmark.

♨ **The Papago Peaks** (⊠ *Van Buren St. and Galvin Pkwy., Papago Salado* ☎ *602/261–8318 Phoenix Parks & Recreation Dept. Eastern and Central District*) were sacred sites for the Tohono O'odham. The soft-sandstone peaks contain accessible caves, some petroglyphs, and splendid views of much of the Valley. This is a good spot for family hikes.

Piestewa Peak (⊠ *2701 E. Piestewa Peak Dr., North Central Phoenix* ☎ *602/262–7901 North Mountain Preserves Ranger Station*), just north of Lincoln Drive, has a series of trails for all levels of hikers. It's a great place to get views of downtown. Allow about 1½ hours for each direction. **Pinnacle Peak Trail** (⊠ *26802 N. 102nd Way, 1 mi south of Dynamite and Alma School Rds., North Scottsdale, Scottsdale* ☎ *480/312–0990*) is a well-maintained trail offering a moderately challenging 3.5-mi round-trip hike—or a horseback experience for those who care to round up a horse at the local stables. Interpretive programs and trail signs along the way describe the geology, flora, fauna, and cultural history of the area. **Lost Dog Wash Trail** (⊠ *12601 N. 124th St., north of Shea Blvd., North Scottsdale, Scottsdale ⊕ www.scottsdaleaz.gov/ preserve ☎ 480/312–7013*), part of the continually expanding **McDowell-Sonoran Preserve** (⊕ *www.mcdowellsonoran.org*), is a mostly gentle 4.5-mi round trip that will get you away from the bustle of the city in a hurry. The trailhead has restrooms and a map that shows a series of trails for varying skill levels.

★ **South Mountain Park** (⊠ *10919 S. Central Ave., South Phoenix ☎ 602/495– 0222*) is the jewel of the city's mountain park preserves. Its mountains and arroyos contain more than 60 mi of marked and maintained trails— all open to hikers, horseback riders, and mountain bikers. It also has three car-accessible lookout points, with 65-mi views. Rangers can help you plan hikes to view some of the 200 petroglyph sites.

☪ **Waterfall Trail** (⊠ *13025 N. White Tank Mountain Rd., Waddell ☎ 623/935–2505*) is a short and easy trail. Part of the 25 mi of trails available at the White Tanks Regional Park, it's kid-friendly, and strollers and wheelchairs roll along easily to Petroglyph Plaza, which boasts 1,500-year-old boulder carvings—dozens are in clear view from the trail. From there the trail takes a rockier but manageable course to a waterfall, which, depending on area rainfall, can be cascading, creeping, or completely dry. Stop at the visitor center to view desert reptiles such as the king snake and a gopher snake in the aquariums.

OUTFITTERS AND EXPEDITIONS The wonderful folks at **AOA Adventures** (☎ *480/945–2881 or 866/455– 1601 ⊕ www.aoa-adventures.com*) cater to hikers at different levels of expertise on their half-day, full-day, and multiple-day hikes. The guides are extremely knowledgeable about local flora and fauna.

HORSEBACK RIDING

More than two-dozen stables and equestrian-tour outfitters in the Valley attest to the saddle's enduring importance in Arizona—even in this auto-dominated metropolis. Stables offer rides for an hour, a whole day, and even some overnight adventures. Some local resorts can arrange for lessons on-site or at nearby stables.

Arizona Cowboy College (⊠ *30208 N. 152nd St., North Scottsdale, Scottsdale ☎ 480/471–3151 or 888/330–8070 ⊕ www.cowboycollege.com*) has wranglers who will teach you everything you need to know about ridin', ropin', and ranchin'.

MacDonald's Ranch (⊠ *26540 N. Scottsdale Rd., North Scottsdale, Scottsdale ☎ 480/585–0239 ⊕ www.macdonaldsranch.com*) offers one- and two-hour trail rides and guided breakfast, lunch, and dinner rides through desert foothills above Scottsdale.

★ **OK Corral & Stable** (⊠ *2655 E. Whiteley St., Apache Junction ☎ 480/982– 4040 ⊕ www.okcorrals.com*) offers one-, two-, and four-hour horseback trail rides and steak cookouts as well as one- to five-day horse-packing trips. Ron Feldman, an authority on the history and secrets of the Lost Dutchman Mine, is the guide for historical pack trips through the Superstition Mountains.

Ponderosa Stables (⊠ *10919 S. Central Ave., South Phoenix* ☎ *602/268–1261* ⊕ *www.arizona-horses.com*) lets you enjoy your South Mountain experience from a higher perch. Consider renting horses at this nearby stable. This private company rents its land from the city of Phoenix, and will take you on an excursion, or send you on one of your own. Rentals cost $30 per person, per hour.

RAFTING

Cimarron River Co. (☎ *480/994–1199* ⊕ *www.cimarrontours.com*) arranges half-day float trips down the Salt and Verde rivers; trips cost about $45 per person. **Desert Voyagers** (☎ *480/998–7238* ⊕ *www.desertvoyagers. com*) specializes in raft and kayak trips.

SAILPLANING–SOARING

Turf Soaring School (⊠ *8700 W. Carefree Hwy., Carefree* ☎ *602/439–3621* ⊕ *www.turfsoaring.com*) gives scenic sailplane rides that last from 20 to 30 minutes. Costs are from $109 per person.

TENNIS

With all the blue sky and sunshine in the Valley, it's a perfect place to play tennis or watch the pros. The Surprise Tennis and Racquet Complex, a public facility in Surprise, is the place to watch big-time tournaments such as the Fed Cup. Most major resorts, such as the Radisson, Phoenician, Wigwam, Fairmont Princess, and JW Marriott Desert Ridge (and many smaller properties), have tennis courts. Granted, tennis plays second fiddle to golf here—but many of the larger resorts offer package tennis deals. If you're not staying at a resort, there are more than 60 public facilities in the area.

Kiwanis Park Recreation Center (⊠ *6111 S. All America Way, Tempe* ☎ *480/350–5201* ⊕ *www.tempe.gov/kiwanis*) has 15 lighted premier-surface courts (all for same-day or one-day-advance reserve). **Mountain View Tennis Center** (⊠ *1104 E. Grovers Ave., North Central Phoenix* ☎ *602/534–2500* ⊕ *www.phoenix.gov/sports*), just north of Bell Road, has 20 lighted courts and group lessons. Court fees are $1.50 per person for 90 minutes. **Phoenix Tennis Center** (⊠ *6330 N. 21st Ave., West Phoenix* ☎ *602/249–3712* ⊕ *www.phoenix.gov/sports*) is a city facility with 22 lighted hard courts. **Scottsdale Ranch Park** (⊠ *10400 E. Via Linda, North Scottsdale* ☎ *480/312–7774* ⊕ *www.scottsdaleaz.gov/ parks*) is a city facility with 12 lighted courts. Lessons are available. **Surprise Tennis and Racquet Complex** (⊠ *14469 W. Paradise La., Surprise* ☎ *623/222–2400* ⊕ *www.surpriseaz.com/tennis*) features 25 public courts where you can play for 90 minutes on their state-of-the-art lighted courts for only $4.

TOURS

Arizona Outback Adventures (☎ *480/945–2881 or 866/455–1601* ⊕ *www. aoa-adventures.com*) leads hiking, biking, and rafting tours around the state.

TUBING

The Valley may not be known for its wealth of water, but locals manage to make the most of what there is. A popular summer stop is the northeast side of the Salt River, where sun worshippers can rent an inner tube and float down the river for an afternoon. Tubing season runs from May to September. Several Valley outfitters rent tubes. Make sure you bring lots of sunscreen, a hat, water—and a rope for attaching your cooler to a tube.

Salt River Recreation (✉ *Usery Pass and Power Rds., Mesa* ☎ *480/984–3305* ⊕ *www.saltrivertubing.com*), offers shuttle-bus service to and from your starting point and rents tubes for $15 (cash only) for the day.

WHERE TO EAT

Phoenix and its surroundings have metamorphosed into a melting pot for every type of cuisine imaginable, from northern to Tuscan Italian; from mom-and-pop to Mexico City Mexican; from low-key Cuban to high-end French- and Greek-inspired Southwestern; from Japanese- and Spanish-style tapas to kosher food and American classics with subtle ethnic twists.

Just as the Valley of the Sun has attracted visitors from around the world, it has also been attracting a record number of worldly residents. Fortunately for everyone, many of those people are skilled chefs and/or restaurateurs who have opted to share their gifts with the public.

Eateries like La Grande Orange grocery are revolutionizing Phoenix's "fast-food" concept with gourmet pay-and-take meals, while tapas-style restaurants like Lola are usurping the traditional sit-down dinner by offering mouthwatering mini-entrées in a casually hip, community-oriented atmosphere. Four-star cuisine, some concocted by celebrity chefs, also awaits all over the Valley, from Kai in Chandler to Scottsdale's Bourbon Steak, along with Binkley's and Café Bink in Carefree. Dotted with massive strip malls, Phoenix outskirts are becoming a haven of corporate eateries, but don't worry, there's plenty of divine, independent dining for all tastes and all trends in between.

Many of the best restaurants in the Valley are in resorts, camouflaged behind courtyard walls, or tucked away in shopping malls. Newer, upscale eateries are clustered along Camelback Corridor—a veritable restaurant row, running west to east from Phoenix to Scottsdale—and in Scottsdale itself. Great Mexican food can be found throughout the Valley, but the most authentic spots are in the neighborhoods of north-central and south Phoenix.

PLANNING INFORMATION

Restaurants change hours, locations, chefs, prices, and menus frequently, so it's best to call ahead to confirm. Show up without a reservation during tourist season (October through mid-May), and you may have to head for a fast-food drive-through window to avoid a two-hour wait for a table. All listed restaurants are open for lunch and dinner unless otherwise specified.

WHAT IT COSTS				
¢	$	$$	$$$	$$$$
AT DINNER under $8	$8–$12	$13–$20	$21–$30	over $30

Prices are per person for a main course. The final tab will include sales tax of 8.3% in Phoenix, 7.95% in Scottsdale, and 8.1% in Tempe.

Use the coordinate (✛ B2) at the end of each listing to locate a site on the corresponding map.

DOWNTOWN AND CENTRAL PHOENIX

CENTRAL PHOENIX

$$ ✕ **Baby Kay's**. Named for the Louisiana native who brought her know-
CAJUN   how and love for creole creations to the Valley, Baby Kay's is one of the few Phoenix places specializing in Cajun cuisine. You'll find authentic takes on red beans and rice, gumbo, jambalaya, po'boys, catfish, and the house specialty: spicy crawfish stew étouffée. Baby Kay sold the restaurant in 2006, but her piquant spirit rolls on. Worthwhile extras include the green-olive coleslaw. For the cholesterol conscious, grilled items and spring salads with creole vinaigrette will do in a pinch. ✉ *2119 E. Camelback Rd., Town and Country Shopping Center, Central Phoenix* ☎ *602/955–0011* ⊕ *www.babykayscajunkitchen.com* ⊟ *AE, MC, V* ☺ *Closed Sun.* ✛ *C4.*

$$ ✕ **Barrio Cafe**. Owners Wendy Gruber and Silvana Salcido Esparza have
MEXICAN taken Mexican cuisine to a new level. Expect guacamole made to order at your table and modern Mexican specialties such as *cochinita pibil*, 12-hour slow-roasted pork with red achiote and sour orange, and *chiles en Nogada*, a delicious traditional dish from central Mexico featuring a spicy poblano pepper stuffed with fruit, chicken, and raisins. The flavor-packed food consistently draws packs of people, but you can drink in the intimate atmosphere—and a specialty margarita or *aqua fresca* (fruit water)—while you wait for a table. ✉ *2814 N. 16th St., Central Phoenix* ☎ *602/636–0240* ⊕ *www.barriocafe.com* ⌦ *Reservations not accepted* ⊟ *AE, MC, V* ☺ *Closed Mon.* ✛ *C4.*

$$ ✕ **Chelsea's Kitchen**. With its hip, Pacific Northwest–chic interior and a
AMERICAN patio that feels more like a secret garden, Chelsea's Kitchen can easily
Fodor's Choice make you forget you're dining in the desert. This casually sophisti-
★ cated establishment insists on the freshest ingredients (especially fish), used with equally fresh and flavorful ideas that complement the restaurant's cool but comfortable style. Specials change frequently, and are always worth steering away from the menu, but regulars love the shrimp ceviche, burgers, signature tacos with tortillas and corn chips made on-site, and red velvet cake for dessert. On Sunday brunch is served 10–3. ✉ *5040 N. 40th St., Central Phoenix* ☎ *602/957–2555* ⊕ *www.chelseaskitchenaz.com* ⊟ *AE, MC, V* ✛ *D4.*

$$$ ✕ **Coup Des Tartes**. Tables are scattered among three small rooms and an
FRENCH enclosed patio of a charming old house at this country French restaurant. It's BYOB, and there's an $8 corkage fee, but all's forgiven when you taste the delicate cuisine prepared in the tiny kitchen. The menu

BEST BETS FOR PHOENIX, SCOTTSDALE, AND TEMPE DINING

With hundreds of restaurants to choose from, how will you decide where to eat? Fodor's writers and editors have selected their favorite restaurants by price, cuisine, and experience in the Best Bets lists *below*. In the first column, Fodor's Choice properties represent the "best of the best" in every price category. You can also find specific details about a restaurant in the full reviews, listed by neighborhood then alphabetically in the following pages.

Fodor's Choice ★

Chelsea's Kitchen, p. 79
Christopher's, p. 86
FEZ, p. 81
Kai, p. 96
La Grande Orange, p. 84
Matt's Big Breakfast p. 85
The Mission, p. 95
Noca, p. 87
Pane Bianco, p. 84
Pepe's Taco Villa, p. 85
Rancho Pinot Grill, p. 93
Scratch Pastries, p. 93
T. Cook's at the Royal Palms, p. 87
Via Delosantos, p. 90

Best by Price

¢

Carolina's, p. 89

Fry Bread House, p. 81
La Grande Orange, p. 84

$

Kashman's Place, p. 137
Mrs. White's Golden Rule Café, p. 85
Pane Bianco, p. 84
Pepe's Taco Villa, p. 85

$$

L'Ecole, p. 92
Via Delosantos, p. 90

$$$

Rancho Pinot Grill, p. 93

$$$$

Binkley's, p. 137
Bourbon Steak, p. 94
Kai, p. 96

Best by Cuisine

BEST LOCAL EATS

La Grande Orange, p. 84
Mrs. White's Golden Rule Café, p. 85
Via Delosantos, p. 90

BEST MARGARITAS

Los Dos Molinos, p. 91
Pepe's Taco Villa, p. 85
Via Delosantos, p. 90

Best by Experience

BEST BREAKFAST

La Grande Orange, p. 84
Matt's Big Breakfast, p. 85

BEST HOTEL DINING

Bourbon Steak at the Fairmont Scottsdale Princess, p. 94
Kai at Sheraton Wild Horse Pass Resort, p. 96
T. Cook's at the Royal Palms, p. 87

BEST PATIO WINING AND DINING

Chelsea's Kitchen, p. 79
elements, p. 91
House of Tricks, p. 97
Olive & Ivy, p. 93

BEST SPECIAL OCCASION

Binkley's, p. 137
Kai, p. 96
T. Cook's at the Royal Palms, p. 87

BEST SUNDAY BRUNCH

Bistro 24, p. 86
Bourbon Steak, p. 94
Lon's at the Hermosa, p. 91
The Mission, p. 95

GREAT VIEW

elements, p. 91
Lon's at the Hermosa, p. 91
T. Cook's at the Royal Palms, p. 87

2

changes seasonally, but if you're lucky it will feature the utterly unforgettable Moroccan-inspired lamb shank with harissa-spiced ragout, the pork tenderloin with pineapple maple glaze, or the citrus fettuccine. The banana brûlée tarte is their signature dessert, but seasonal offerings like the four-berry tarte remind mouths why they put the mind through all the guilt. ☒ *4626 N. 16th St., Central Phoenix* ☎ *602/212–1082* ⊕ *www.nicetarts.com* ⇗ *Reservations essential* ▭ *AE, D, MC, V* 🍴 *BYOB* ☼ *Closed Sun. and Mon. No lunch* ✛ *C4.*

$$$$ ✕ **Durant's Fine Foods.** Durant's has endured since 1950 in the same loca-
STEAK   tion with the same menu and even many of the original waitstaff, making it one of Phoenix's legendary eating establishments. Supreme steaks, chops, and fresh seafood, including Florida stone crab and oysters Rockefeller, dominate here; when the restaurant once tried to update its menu, regulars protested so furiously the idea was shelved. Durant's is not à la carte, like many Valley steak houses, which means their entrée prices include soup or salad and a side dish. Those in the know enter through the kitchen door and frequent the Rat Pack–style bar for jumbo martinis fit for ol' Blue Eyes himself. ☒ *2611 N. Central Ave., at Virginia, Central Phoenix* ☎ *602/264–5967* ⊕ *www.durantsfinefoods. com* ▭ *AE, D, DC, MC, V* ✛ *B5.*

$$ ✕ **FEZ.** From its sleek interior to its central location and diverse clien-
ECLECTIC   tele, right down to its affordable lunch, happy hour, dinner, Sunday
Fodor'sChoice   brunch, and late-night menus, FEZ covers everything. "American fare
★   with a Moroccan flair" means bold culinary leaps, with choices like the FEZ Burger, *kisras* (flat-bread pizza), and the signature crispy rosemary pomegranate chicken—but it all lands safely on the taste buds. Potables include specialty martinis and margaritas and a formidable wine list. ☒ *3815 N. Central Ave., Central Phoenix* ☎ *602/287–8700* ⊕ *www. fezoncentral.com* ▭ *AE, MC, V* ✛ *B4.*

¢ ✕ **Fry Bread House.** Indian fry bread, a specialty of the Native American
SOUTHWESTERN   culture, is a delicious treat—pillows of deep-fried dough topped with sweet or savory toppings and folded in half. Local fry-bread fanatics get their fix from chef-owner Cecelia Miller of the Tohono O'odham nation. Choose from culture-crossing combinations like savory shredded chili beef with cheese, beans, green chiles, veggies, and sour cream, or try the sweeter synthesis of honey and sugar, or chocolate with butter. ☒ *4140 N. 7th Ave., Central Phoenix* ☎ *602/351–2345* ▭ *D, MC, V* ☼ *Closed Sun.* ✛ *B4.*

$ ✕ **Honey Bear's BBQ.** Honey Bear's motto—"You don't need no teeth to eat
SOUTHERN   our meat"—may fall short on grammar, but this place isn't packed with folks looking to improve their language skills. In 1986 childhood friends Mark Smith and Gary Clark expanded from a catering business to their first wildly successful Honey Bear's restaurant on East Van Buren Street; today they are in demand all across the Valley. This is Tennessee-style barbecue, which means smoky baby back ribs basted in a tangy sauce. The sausage-enhanced "cowbro" beans and scallion-studded potato salad are great sides, and, teeth or no teeth, finishing off with a no-frills but tasty piece of sweet-potato pie will put a smile on your face. All locations feel like neighborhood joints; there's another branch at 7670 South Priest Drive in Tempe. ☒ *2824 N. Central., Central Phoenix* ☎ *602/279–7911*

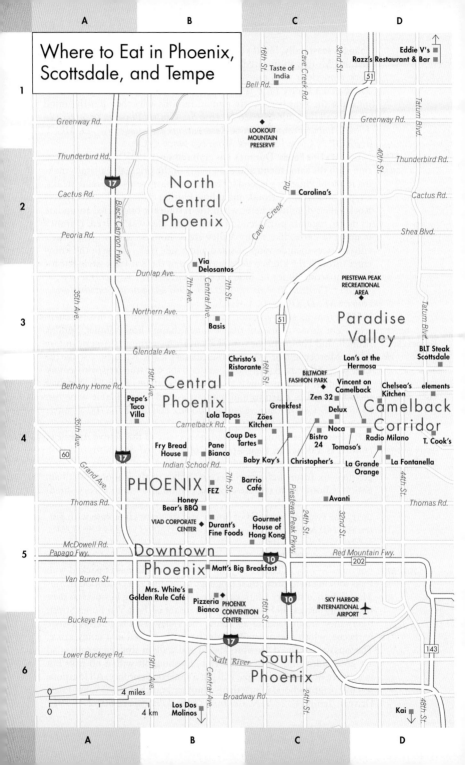

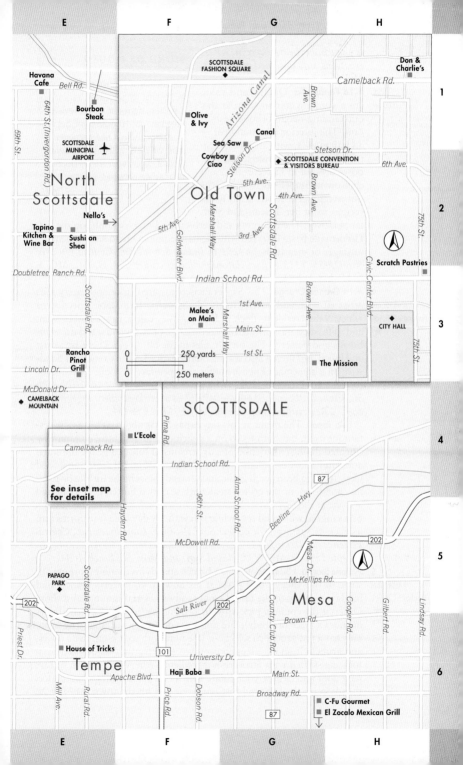

⊕ *www.honeybearsbbq.com* ⚲ *Reservations not accepted* ⊟ *AE, D, MC, V* ✛ *B5.*

$$$
ITALIAN
✕ **La Fontanella.** Quality and value are a winning combination at this outstanding neighborhood restaurant. The interior is reminiscent of an Italian villa, with antiques, crisp table linens, fresh flowers, and windows dressed in lace curtains, and chef-owner Isabelle Bertuccio turns out magnificent food, often using recipes from her Tuscan and Sicilian relatives. The escargots and herb-crusted rack of lamb top the list. Homemade pasta is served with Sicilian semolina bread and homemade sausages or meatballs. ⊠ *4231 E. Indian School Rd., Central Phoenix* ☎ *602/955–1213* ⊕ *www.lafontanellaphx.com* ⊟ *AE, D, DC, MC, V* ⊘ *No lunch* ✛ *D4.*

¢
AMERICAN
Fodor's Choice
★
✕ **La Grande Orange.** This San Francisco–inspired store and eatery sells artisanal nosh and novelty items, along with a formidable selection of wines. Valley residents flock to LGO, as they call it, to see and be seen, and to feast on mouthwatering sandwiches, pizzas, salads, and decadent breads and desserts. The small tables inside fill up quickly at breakfast and lunch, but there's also seating on the patio. Try the Commuter Sandwich on a homemade English muffin, the open-faced Croque Madame, or the delicious French pancakes with a sweet Spanish latte. ⊠ *4410 N. 40th St., Central Phoenix* ☎ *602/840–7777* ⊕ *www.lagrandeorangegrocery.com* ⚲ *Reservations not accepted* ⊟ *AE, MC, V* ✛ *D4.*

$
SPANISH
✕ **Lola Tapas.** The menu at this tiny tapas bar is about as big as the restaurant itself, but both focus on a delicious and delightful community-oriented dining experience. Steady streams of folks come for the snug, ambient Latin atmosphere and the sensible portions of sensational food like garbanzo beans with garlic and sautéed spinach, the tortilla *de patatas* (potatoes), or the grilled steak with seasoned butter. If you can find a space at the tiny bar in back, settle in with what may be the Valley's best sangria, white and red, while you wait. By day Lola transforms into a delicious Spanish-style coffeehouse. ⊠ *800 E. Camelback Rd., Central Phoenix* ☎ *602/265–4519* ⊕ *www.lolatapas.com* ⚲ *Reservations not accepted* ⊟ *AE, MC, V* ⊘ *Closed Sun. and Mon. No lunch* ✛ *B4.*

$
AMERICAN
Fodor's Choice
★
✕ **Pane Bianco.** Chef-owner Chris Bianco spends his evenings turning out some of the Valley's best pizza at his downtown Pizzeria Bianco, and his days creating to-die-for take-out sandwiches at this minimalist shop. Order at the counter, pick up your brown-bagged meal (which always includes a piece of candy), and dine outside at a picnic table. The menu only has a few sandwich selections (the tuna with red onion, gaeta olives, and arugula is an excellent choice), but each features wood-fired-oven focaccia stuffed with farm-fresh ingredients. Afterward, pop in to Lux next door and cleanse your palate with a cup of the Valley's best coffee, then hop on the light-rail just out front and hit the town. ⊠ *4404 N.*

Central Ave., Central Phoenix ☎ *602/234–2100* ⊕ *www.pizzeriabianco. com* ⊟ *AE, MC, V* ⊗ *Closed Sun. and Mon. No dinner* ✛ *B4.*

$ ✗ **Pepe's Taco Villa.** The neighborhood's not fancy, and neither is this
MEXICAN   restaurant, but in a town with a lot of gringo-ized south-of-the-border
Fodor's Choice   fare, this is the real friendly, real deal. Tacos *rancheros*—spicy, shred-
★   ded pork pungently lathered with adobo paste—are a dream. So are
the green-corn tamales and authentic imported *machacado* (air-dried
beef). The chiles rellenos may be the best in the state. All are perfect with a margarita from the full bar. Don't leave without trying the
sensational mole, a rich sauce fashioned from chiles and chocolate.
⊠ *2108 W. Camelback Rd., Central Phoenix* ☎ *602/242–0379* ⊕ *www.
pepestacovilla.com* ⊟ *AE, D, MC, V* ⊗ *Closed Tues.* ✛ *A4.*

$$$ ✗ **Radio Milano.** One of the many eateries conceived by the wildly suc-
ITALIAN   cessful team behind La Grande Orange (LGO), Radio Milano is a
ℭ   sleek and casual Italian-inspired experience with simple, but simply
fantastic food. Radio serves unusual but tasty fare like Italian fresh-fish
sashimi, deviled eggs, and celery Caesar salad for starters, and simple
but standout pasta dishes and entrées like handmade pappardelle with
goat cheese, corn, asparagus, and tomatoes, and pork roast "prime
rib" with baby spinach and potato. Kids eat free noodles, meatballs,
and minipizza until 7 PM. Adults will enjoy a small but great selection
of wine and beer along with cool, crisp Italian-inspired cocktails like
blood-orange champagne or limoncello. Leave room for the olive-oil
cake. ⊠ *3950 E. Campbell Ave., Central Phoenix* ☎ *602/956–6600*
⊕ *www.radiomilanobar.com* ⊟ *AE, MC, V* ✛ *D4.*

DOWNTOWN PHOENIX

$ ✗ **Gourmet House of Hong Kong.** Traditional Chinatown specialties like
CHINESE   *chow fun* (thick rice noodles) are excellent at this simple, diner-style
place: try the assorted-meat version, with chicken, shrimp, pork,
and squid. Dishes with black-bean sauce are among the menu's best.
Delights such as five-flavor frogs' legs, duck feet with greens, and
beef tripe casserole are offered, if you're feeling adventurous. ⊠ *1438
E. McDowell Rd., Downtown Phoenix* ☎ *602/253–4859* ⊕ *www.
gourmethouseofhongkong.com* ⊟ *D, DC, MC, V* ✛ *C5.*

¢   ✗ **Matt's Big Breakfast.** Breakfast is back, thanks to Matt Pool and his
AMERICAN   wife Erenia. Fresh, filling, and simply fantastic, the food at this itty-
Fodor's Choice   bitty, retro hip diner is a great way to start any day, especially when
★   you have time to walk or sleep it off afterward. Ingredients like hearty
bacon strips, jams, and whole-grain breads come from local sources, and
each one is of the highest quality. Build your own omelet with a side of
crispy hash browns or indulge in a Belgian waffle, but let it be known
that Matt's fat pancakes are legendary. Lunch options include sand-
wiches and chili, or breakfast, again. Be prepared to wait, or call ahead
for takeout. ⊠ *801 North 1st St.Downtown Phoenix* ☎ *602/254–1074*
⊕ *www.mattsbigbreakfast.com* ⊴ *Reservations not accepted* ⊟ *AE, MC,
V* ⊗ *Closed Mon. No dinner* ✛ *B5.*

$ ✗ **Mrs. White's Golden Rule Café.** This lunch spot, located in a plain
SOUTHERN   yellow building downtown, has been the best place in town for true
Southern cooking for decades. The humble lunch counter and few sur-
rounding tables are the setting in which to enjoy rich entrées—from

fried chicken to catfish and pork chops. Each of the six entrées comes with corn bread and peach cobbler, all of which fill not just the belly but also the soul. ✉ *808 E. Jefferson St., Downtown Phoenix* ☎ *602/262–9256* ⊕ *www.mrs-whitesgoldenrulecafe.com* ⌂ *Reservations not accepted* ▭ *No credit cards* ☉ *Closed Sun. No dinner* ✛ *B5.*

$ ✗ **Pizzeria Bianco.** Brooklyn native
PIZZA   Chris Bianco makes pizza with a passion in this small establishment on Heritage Square. His wood-fired-oven thin-crust creations incorporate the finest and freshest ingredients including homemade mozzarella cheese. The brick oven was imported from Italy. Bar Bianco next door is a good place to relax with a beverage while you wait for your table. ■ TIP➔ Arrive a few minutes before they open at 5 PM to avoid the long wait, especially on Friday and Saturday nights. ✉ *623 E. Adams St., Downtown Phoenix* ☎ *602/258–8300* ⊕ *www.pizzeriabianco.com* ▭ *AE, MC, V* ☉ *Closed Sun. and Mon. No lunch* ✛ *B5.*

GREATER PHOENIX

CAMELBACK CORRIDOR

$$$$ ✗ **Bistro 24.** Smart and stylish, with impeccable service, the Ritz's Bistro
FRENCH   24 has a parquet floor, colorful murals, an elegant bar, and an outdoor patio. Take a break from shopping at the nearby Biltmore Fashion Park and enjoy the largest Cobb salad in town. For dinner, try classic French steak *au poivre* with *frites*, grilled fish, or sushi. Happy hour is every day 5–7 in the bar. Sunday brunch is a local favorite. ✉ *Ritz-Carlton Hotel, 2401 E. Camelback Rd., Camelback Corridor* ☎ *602/952–2424* ⊕ *www.ritzcarlton.com* ▭ *AE, D, DC, MC, V* ☉ *No dinner Sun. and Mon.* ✛ *C4.*

$$$ ✗ **Christopher's.** Upon total renovation of the Biltmore Fashion Park,
FRENCH   Chef Christopher Gross and wife Paola took their wildly successful
Fodor'sChoice   Fermier Brasserie and Wine Bar from one end of the complex and rein-
★   vented it on the other in 2008. New, incredibly hip, and even better than their last incarnation, Christopher's delivers casual, contemporary elegance with a social, exhibition-kitchen bar, an open dining area, a private table, and an intimate lounge. The menu ranges from good-value wood-fired-oven pizzas and outstanding burgers and creative bar nosh to the pricier French inspirations. Gross is famous for dishes like the smoked truffle-infused filet mignon and stunning new masterpieces. Don't forget the Gruyère mashed potatoes on the side, and the Grande Marnier soufflé to finish. ✉ *Biltmore Fashion Park, 2502 E. Camelback Rd., Camelback Corridor* ☎ *602/522–2344* ⊕ *www.chirstophersaz.com* ▭ *AE, MC, V* ✛ *C4.*

2

$ ✕ **Delux.** Cool tones of blue and gray are accented by a granite-topped
AMERICAN bar and a long candlelit communal table in the center of this small, hipster burger joint. Delux serves delicious salads, sandwiches, and burgers made with all-natural Harris Ranch beef—try the Delux Burger, with Maytag blue and Gruyère cheeses and caramelized onions. Sweet-potato or regular, crispy fries arrive in a fun mini shopping cart. Open every night until 2 AM, this is a great place to grab a late-night bite. Leave room for something cool and creamy at the Gelato Spot across the parking lot. ⊠ *3146 E. Camelback Rd., Camelback Corridor* ☎ *602/522–2288* ⊕ *www.deluxburger.com* ♨ *Reservations not accepted* ⊟ *AE, D, DC, MC, V* ✛ *C4.*

$$$ ✕ **Greekfest.** This informal but elegant restaurant is lovingly decorated
GREEK with whitewashed walls, hardwood floors, and imported Greek artifacts. Search the menu's two pages of appetizers for *taramosalata* (caviar blended with lemon and olive oil) and *saganaki* (cheese flamed with brandy and extinguished with a squirt of lemon). The *moussaka* (lamb casserole) is wonderful, and don't forget dessert (try *galaktoboureko,* warm custard pie baked in phyllo). If all you seek is a sweet treat and some genuine Greek coffee, visit the adjoining Cafestia European dessert and coffeehouse. ⊠ *1940 E. Camelback Rd., Camelback Corridor* ☎ *602/265–2990* ⊕ *www.thegreekfest.com* ⊟ *AE, D, DC, MC, V* ☾ *Closed Sun.* ✛ *C4.*

$$$ ✕ **Noca.** This small, hidden strip-mall establishment quickly became a
AMERICAN Valley favorite. Not only is it a fun place to see, be seen, and to sample
Fodor'sChoice everything, owner Eliot Wexler also wants to see everyone happy. The
★ waitstaff are veteran fine-dining servers, and the chefs manage to turn even cotton candy into a culinary work of art. Different nights of the week offer daily specials like the lauded Japanese Wagyu cheesesteak with Kobe beef on Thursday and a fried chicken dinner on Sunday. For starters, try their bacon and eggs (crispy poached egg with pork-belly confit, onion jam, and maple syrup) or the duck confit with a huckleberry waffle, dates, and vinaigrette. Sound a lot like breakfast? Wait until you try the doughnut holes for dessert. ⊠ *3118 E. Camelback Rd., Camelback Corridor* ☎ *602/956–6622* ⊕ *www.restaurantnoca. com* ⊟ *AE, MC, V* ☾ *No lunch* ✛ *C4.*

$$$$ ✕ **T. Cook's at the Royal Palms.** One of the finest restaurants in the Valley, T.
MEDITERRANEAN Cook's oozes romance, from the floor-to-ceiling windows with dramatic
Fodor'sChoice views of Camelback Mountain to its 1930s-style Spanish-colonial archi-
★ tecture and decor. The Mediterranean-influenced menu includes grilled "fireplace" fare like bone-in beef short rib with carrot risotto cake, paella, and a changing variety of enticing entrées. Desserts and pastries are works of art. For special-occasion meals, call on the services of the resort's Director of Romance. ⊠ *Royal Palms Resort & Spa, 5200 E. Camelback Rd., Camelback Corridor* ☎ *602/840–3610* ⊕ *www.royalpalmshotel.com* ♨ *Reservations essential* ⊟ *AE, D, DC, MC, V* ✛ *D4.*

$$$ ✕ **Tomaso's.** In a town where restaurants can come and go almost over-
ITALIAN night, Tomaso's has been a favorite since 1977, and for good reason. Chef Tomaso Maggiore learned to cook at the family's restaurant in Palermo, Sicily, and honed his skills at the Culinary Institute of Rome. The result is authentic Italian cuisine that's consistently well prepared

Many restaurants are tucked into strip malls, but some resorts have great restaurants, like T. Cook's at the Royal Palms.

and delicious. The house specialty, osso buco (braised veal shank), is outstanding. Other notables include risotto and cannelloni. The Phoenix location has long been an unpretentious favorite, nestled into the northeast corner of a small, upscale shopping center in the heart of Camelback Corridor. Meanwhile, the elegant but enormous Chandler location at 7341 North Ray Road is all about the party, with a large main dining room and lounge as well as a number of private rooms that accommodate parties of 10 to 120. ✉ *3225 E. Camelback Rd., Camelback Corridor* ☎ *602/956–0836* ⊕ *www.tomasos.com* ▭ *AE, D, DC, MC, V* ☺ *Closed Sun. No lunch weekends* ✛ *D4.*

$$$$ ✕ **Vincent on Camelback.** Chef Guerithault is best known for creating
SOUTHWESTERN French food with a Southwestern touch. You can make a meal of his famous appetizers: corn ravioli with white-truffle oil, or shrimp beignets with lavender dressing. The dessert menu overflows with intoxicating soufflés. The multiroom interior is intimate and elegant, but the service can be gruff. Better known among locals is the market held in the parking lot on Saturday during the cooler months. ✉ *3930 E. Camelback Rd., Camelback Corridor* ☎ *602/224–0225* ⊕ *www.vincentsoncamelback. com* ✑ *Reservations essential* ▭ *AE, D, DC, MC, V* ☺ *Closed Sun. No lunch Sat.* ✛ *D4.*

$$ ✕ **Zen 32.** In the ebb and flow of central Phoenix, Zen 32 has managed
SEAFOOD to stay afloat while just about every other sushi restaurant has sunk—the convenient location, casually chic atmosphere, and consistently creative rolls make it easy to understand why. The soft-shell crab, rainbow, and caterpillar rolls, and the succulent citrus yellowtail are favorites from the sushi menu, while the grill produces plenty of tasty nonfish fare. The covered patio faces the zoom and vroom of 32nd Street, but the soothing

The Phoenix area dining scene is hot, and not just because of the many spicy Southwestern and Mexican ingredients.

mist and meditation music create a tranquil, yes, even Zen-like atmosphere. ⊠ *3160 E. Camelback Rd., Camelback Corridor* ☎ *602/954–8700* ⊕ *www.zen32.com* ⊟ *AE, MC, V* ⊗ *No lunch weekends* ✣ *C4.*

NORTH CENTRAL PHOENIX

$$
AMERICAN
Fodor's Choice
★

✕ **Basis.** Fortunately, enough people have known about this little strip-mall secret to keep it going since 2003, but it's high time the gossip got out. In a bright, contemporary and tasteful space the menu is a great mix of American creations with a splash of Southwestern and Cajun accents, including crisp calamari with vinaigrette, seared (to perfection) ahi tuna salad, a shrimp po'boy sandwich with chipotle aioli, blackened jumbo scallops and tenderloin medallions, or Basis mac and cheese. The staff is friendly, knowledgeable, and adept at pairing the perfect wine from their distinctive selection with their unusual dishes. Leave room for the guajillo squash flan or an ancho-chile brownie. ⊠ *410 E. Thunderbird Rd., North Central Phoenix* ☎ *602/843–3689* ⊕ *www.basisnewamerican.com* ⊟ *AE, MC, V* ✣ *B3.*

¢
MEXICAN

✕ **Carolina's.** This small, nondescript restaurant in north-central Phoenix makes the most delicious, thin-as-air flour tortillas imaginable. In-the-know locals have been lining up at Carolina's for years to partake of the homey, inexpensive Mexican food, so it makes sense that she expanded from the original downtown location to let a little more of the Valley in on the action. The tacos, tamales, burritos, flautas, and enchiladas are served on paper plates. You can buy tortillas to take away, but good luck getting home with a full bag. Note that they close for dinner early: on weekdays at 7:30 PM and Sat. at 6 PM. There are also branches in south Phoenix at 1202 East Mohave Street and one in Peoria. ⊠ *2126 E. Cactus Rd.,*

North Central Phoenix ☎ *602/252–1503* ⊕ *www.carolinasmex.com* ➡ *AE, D, DC, MC, V* ⊘ *No dinner on Sun.* ✢ *C2.*

$$
ITALIAN
✕ **Christo's Ristorante**. Don't judge this book by its cover. Cozy and unassuming in a Phoenix strip mall, Christo's keeps its tables filled with loyal customers who enjoy fine Italian cuisine. Attentive servers ensure that your water glass never empties, and folks rave about the fresh seafood dishes, the roasted rack of lamb, the veal, and the delicious pasta dishes. Start with the delicious, panfried calamari. Dinner's main courses come with soup and salad. Before or after dinner, enjoy a cocktail in the piano bar or spend your evening snacking to the music from the bar menu. ✉ *6327 N. 7th St., North Central Phoenix* ☎ *602/264–1784* ⊕ *www.christos1.com* ➡ *AE, D, DC, MC, V* ⊘ *Closed Sun.* ✢ *B3.*

> ## CAMELBACK MARKET
>
> On Saturday from 9 AM to 1 PM, October through May, some of the Valley's tastiest creations, from crepes to paella to panini, can be found in the parking lot of Vincent on Camelback (⊕ *www.vincentsoncamelback.com*), at the **Camelback Market**. Overseen by the restaurant, young Vincent protégés cook up custom orders and people are encouraged to "custom tip" into jars labeled with creative causes such as "Saving for MIT" or "Honeymoon Fund." The market also features a wine vendor and sellers of independent culinary curios like fresh pesto, honey, jam, and wines.

$$
INDIAN
✕ **Taste of India**. This perennial favorite in the Valley specializes in northern Indian cuisine. Breads here—*bhatura, naan, paratha*—are superb, and vegetarians enjoy wonderful meatless specialties, including the eggplant-based *benghan bhartha* and *bhindi masala*, a tempting okra dish. Just about every spice in the rack is used for the lamb and chicken dishes, so be prepared to guzzle extra water—or an English beer. If your server says that a dish is spicy, *trust them.* ✉ *1609 E. Bell Rd., Suite B4, North Central Phoenix* ☎ *602/788–3190* ⊕ *www.tasteofindiaaz.com* ➡ *AE, MC, V* ✢ *C1.*

$$
MEXICAN
Fodor's Choice
★
✕ **Via Delosantos**. The family-owned restaurant looks a little rough around the edges outside, but it's what's inside that counts—an accommodating staff, an enormous and authentic Mexican menu, and one of the best-tasting and best-priced house margaritas in town. Entrées are ample, and include more than just tired combinations of beef, beans, and cheese. Try the fajitas *calabacitas* with a yellow- and green-squash succotash; or the delicious chicken *delosantos*, a cheesy chicken breast and tortilla concoction. Expect to wait on weekends, either at the bar or outside, but the experience will be worth it. ✉ *9120 N. Central Ave., North Central Phoenix* ☎ *602/997–6239* ⌂ *Reservations not accepted* ➡ *AE, D, DC, MC, V* ✢ *B3.*

PARADISE VALLEY

$$$$
STEAK
✕ **BLT Steak Scottsdale**. Chef Laurent Tourondel's mini-empire includes this stylish 300-seater, merging signature dishes from the brand, such as hot popovers laced with Gruyère, Kobe, and American Wagyu beef, with distinctive nods to its desert setting such as reclaimed mesquite wood floors. A knowledgeable waitstaff offer suggestions for pairing steaks

2

with sauces (including red wine and mustard), picking sides (including stuffed mushroom caps and poached green beans), and deciding on a potato dish (a retro favorite: candied sweet potatoes). The house specialty, "Cowboy Steak," is 26 ounces of mesquite-smoked rib eye rubbed with chiles, coriander, cumin, smoked paprika, and brown sugar. Choose from inspired desserts with deceptively modest names such as warm chocolate tart. ⊠ *5402 E. Lincoln Dr. at Camelback Inn, Paradise Valley* ☎ *480/905–7979* ⊕ *www.bltscottsdale.com* ⊟ *AE, MC, V.* ✛ *D3*

$$$$
ECLECTIC

✕ **elements.** Perched on the side of Camelback Mountain at the Sanctuary resort, this stylish modern restaurant offers breathtaking desert-sunset and city-light views. There's a cordial community table where you can sit and order such appetizers as the trilogy of duck, wild escargot wontons, and fried calamari with miso-scallion vinaigrette. Seasonal specials and entrées are excellent; among the best is the bacon-wrapped fillet of beef with blue cheese and merlot demi-glace. ⊠ *Sanctuary Camelback Mountain, 5700 E. McDonald Dr., Paradise Valley* ☎ *480/607–2300* ⊕ *www.sanctuaryoncamelback.com* ⊜ *Reservations essential* ⊟ *AE, D, DC, MC, V* ✛ *D4.*

$$$
AMERICAN

✕ **Lon's at the Hermosa.** In an adobe hacienda hand-built by cowboy artist Lon Megargee, this romantic spot has sweeping vistas of Camelback Mountain and the perfect patio for after-dinner drinks under the stars. Megargee's art and cowboy memorabilia decorate the dining room, while Chef Michael Rusconi's creations decorate the tables. The menu changes seasonally, but includes appetizers like short ribs. Wood-grilled, melt-in-your-mouth filet mignon over Gorgonzola mashed potatoes, and more-exotic dishes like cactus pear–lacquered duck breast are main-course options. Phoenicians love the Sunday brunch. ⊠ *Hermosa Inn, 5532 N. Palo Cristi Dr., Paradise Valley* ☎ *602/955–7878* ⊕ *www.lons. com* ⊟ *AE, D, DC, MC, V* ☽ *No lunch Sat.* ✛ *D3.*

SOUTH PHOENIX

$
MEXICAN

✕ **Los Dos Molinos.** In a hacienda that belonged to silent-era movie star Tom Mix, this fun restaurant focuses on New Mexican–style Mexican food. That means *hot.* New Mexico chiles form the backbone and fiery breath of the dishes, and the green-chile enchilada and beef taco are potentially lethal. The red salsa and enchiladas with egg on top are excellent, as is the popular shrimp Veracruz with red chile sauce. This adobe building is in a largely Hispanic neighborhood in the South Mountain foothills, and features a funky courtyard where you can sip potent margaritas while waiting for a table. Fodors.com users agree that this is a must-do dining experience if you want true New Mexican–style food, but be prepared to swig lots of water. ⊠ *8646 S. Central Ave., South Phoenix* ☎ *602/243–9113* ⊕ *www.losdosmolinosaz.com* ⊜ *Reservations not accepted* ⊟ *AE, D, DC, MC, V* ☽ *Closed Sun. and Mon.* ✛ *B6.*

SCOTTSDALE

CENTRAL SCOTTSDALE

$$$
STEAK

✕ **Don & Charlie's.** Attention sports fans! This hangout is a favorite with major-leaguers in town for spring training, playoff, or Superbowl games. A venerable chophouse, D&C specializes in "American comforts" with

WHERE TO REFUEL AROUND TOWN

Here are the most popular reliable chain restaurants, particularly for large groups (and large portions):

Elephant Bar. The predominantly Pacific Rim, elephant-size menu at this large chain offers some pleasant Cajun (catfish and jambalaya) and plain old American (New York steak, lemon herb chicken) entrées. Pacific Rim specialties include Miso Yaki fire-grilled salmon and the delicious pan-Asian vegetable and noodle soup with teriyaki chicken skewers. ⊕ www.elephantbar.com

Garduño's. This gargantuan Mexican restaurant has several equally ample locations in the area. Try the unusually good green-chile clam chowder or the fresh guacamole made table-side for starters, and experience a grilled chimichanga or fajitas for a main course. ⊕ www.gardunosrestaurants.com

Morton's of Chicago. The Windy City chain is famous for exceptional service, immense steaks, and entertaining presentations. Its business-formal atmosphere, menus, and operations are replicated at the Camelback Road and north Scottsdale locations. The monstrous 24-ounce porterhouse or 14-ounce double-cut fillet can satisfy the hungriest cowpoke. ⊕ www.mortons.com

Nello's. Leave it to two brothers from Chicago to come up with the motto "In Crust We Trust," and Nello's excels in both thin-crust and deep-dish pies at the five Valley locations. Try traditional varieties heaped with homemade sausage and mushrooms, or go vegetarian with the spinach pie. Pasta entrées are very good, too, and the family-style salads are inventive and fresh. ⊕ www.nellosscottsdale.com

Oregano's. Huge portions are an understatement at this eight-branch casual Chicago-theme eatery. Come hungry and feast on tasty baked sandwiches, pizza (deep-dish, thin crust, or stuffed), and pasta dishes. The young, friendly staff and kitschy 1950s decor create a fun and comfortable, family-friendly vibe. ⊕ www.oreganos.com

Zoe's Kitchen. Cool, clean, fast, inexpensive, and nutritious, this national chain is great for a light but filling, Greek-inspired meal without the guilt. Each location is uniform in its bright, modern cafeteria-like setting, where first you order, then you sit. Make sure to try the Greek chicken pita or Greek salad, and the coleslaw with feta cheese. ⊕ www.zoeskitchen.com

prime-grade steak and sports memorabilia—the walls are covered with pictures, autographs, and uniforms. The spacious and Cheers-like interior; friendly staff; and New York sirloin, prime rib, and double-thick lamb chops are a hit. Sides include au gratin potatoes and creamed spinach. ⊠ *7501 E. Camelback Rd., Central Scottsdale* ☎ *480/990–0900* ⊕ *www.donandcharlies.com* ⊟ *AE, D, DC, MC, V* ☉ *No lunch* ✣ *H1.*

$$

FRENCH ✕ **L'Ecole.** You won't regret putting yourself in the talented hands of the student chefs at the Valley's premier cooking academy. Choose from an extensive list of French-inspired entrées or the four-course prix-fixe menu, available for lunch ($30) and dinner ($35). The fine-dining atmosphere is designed to give students (who fill each restaurant position) and customers the impression of the real thing, which is why customers keep coming back. The menu changes seasonally, but expect inventive appetizers such as lobster gratin, stuffed rabbit saddle, ricotta gnocchi, and entrées such as filet mignon. ⊠ *Scottsdale Culinary Institute, 8100 E. Camelback Rd., Central Scottsdale* ☏ *480/425–3111* ⊕ *www.dinewithsci.com* ⌕ *Reservations essential* ▭ *AE, D, DC, MC, V* ⊙ *Closed weekends* ✛ *F4.*

$$
MEDITERRANEAN
✕ **Olive & Ivy.** Tucked into the south side of the high-traffic, high-priced Scottsdale waterfront complex, Olive & Ivy is a pleasant surprise. By day the light comes from the wall of windows that look out onto the ample patio with cozy couches and fire pits, as well as the man-made waterway for which the complex is named. By night the giant space becomes intimate with dim, designer lighting. A full dinner menu, featuring a mix of fish and meat creations with Italian and Mediterranean twists like white-shrimp risotto and veal and spinach ravioli, is available, but the delicious variety of appetizers, like bacon-wrapped Medjoul dates, beet salad with goat-cheese dressing, and flat breads make for a good meal. Wash them down with something from their ample wine list or one of their unique, not-too-sweet peach hibiscus margaritas. ⊠ *7135 E. Camelback Rd., Suite 195, Central Scottsdale* ☏ *480/715–2200* ⊕ *www.foxrc.com/olive_ivy.html* ⌕ *Reservations not accepted* ▭ *AE, D, DC, MC, V* ✛ *F1.*

$$$
ECLECTIC
Fodor's Choice
★
✕ **Rancho Pinot Grill.** The attention to quality paid by the husband-and-wife proprietors here—he manages, she cooks—has made this one of the town's most lauded dining spots. The ambivalent minimalist cowboy decor and almost secret-handshake location are completely forgotten upon the first bite of food and replaced with taste-bud heaven. Chef Chrysa Robertson's inventive menu changes daily, depending on what's fresh. If you're lucky, you'll get a crack at the flatiron steak with arugula and salsa verde, the succulent short ribs with posole-style hominy and cojita cheese, or Nonni's Sunday chicken with toasted polenta. Organic and locally grown and raised ingredients are used whenever possible, which is just another reason why you'll want to return as many times as possible. ⊠ *6208 N. Scottsdale Rd., northwest of Trader Joe's in Lincoln Village Shops, Central Scottsdale* ☏ *480/367–8030* ⊕ *www.ranchopinot.com* ▭ *AE, D, DC, MC, V* ⊙ *Closed Sun. and Mon. mid-May–Nov. No lunch* ✛ *E3.*

$$
CAFÉ
Fodor's Choice
★
✕ **Scratch Pastries.** Duc and Noelle Liao are a model couple, literally. The two met in Paris where Duc worked as a fashion photographer and Noelle as a model. Now, the two are the hottest pair in pastry making. A graduate of Le Cordon Bleu, Duc Liao conjures up sublime creations, both salty and sweet, from a savory duck-breast sandwich and a mouth-watering mushroom quiche to perfectly flaky croissants and a delicately sweet, parfaitlike mont blanc dessert. Don't let the pastry shop's location in a strip mall fool you; this is a flavor trip all the way to France. Expect crowds during peak lunch hours. ⊠ *7620 E. Indian School Rd., Suite 103, Central Scottsdale* ☏ *480/947–0057* ⊕ *www.scratchpastries.com* ⌕ *Reservations not accepted* ▭ *AE, MC, V* ✛ *H3.*

NORTH SCOTTSDALE

$$$$
STEAK
✕**Bourbon Steak.** Formerly the site of the once-renowned Marquesa restaurant, this upscale steak restaurant run by top-rated chef Michael Mina has been living up to the royal reputation of the Scottsdale Princess. Its severe but stunning stone-and-glass entry lets people know that they are in for something serious—seriously good. Its modern elegance is as tasty to the eyes as the food is to the palate. Select from American-grade or Japanese Kobe beef but be prepared for the prices—including one $150 steak. The flaming doughnuts Foster makes a perfect finish to a fine meal. Sunday brunch is also popular. ✉ *Fairmont Scottsdale Princess Resort, 7575 E. Princess Dr., North Scottsdale* ☎ *480/585–4848* ⊕ *www.fairmont.com/scottsdale* ⚓ *Reservations essential* ▭ *AE, D, DC, MC, V* ☉ *Closed Mon. and Tues. No dinner Sun. No lunch* ✛ *E1.*

$$$
AMERICAN
✕**Eddie V's.** The DC Ranch area is booming with great restaurants to keep the North Valley locals happy, including this one. By night Eddie V's appears almost too sophisticated for its upscale-mall location. Sleek lighting filters through massive panes of tinted glass, revealing an elegant, contemporary interior clad in crisp linens. Specializing in fresh seafood done right (try the Hong Kong–style Chilean sea bass or the broiled scallops), grilled meats, and fine wines, the place is great for fine dining. But with its inviting bar and lounge area and succulent appetizers like kung pao–style calamari and a variety of fresh oysters, Eddie's is also enormously popular (and slightly more affordable) as a happy-hour spot. ✉ *20715 N. Pima Rd., Suite F1, North Scottsdale* ☎ *480/538–8468* ⊕ *www.eddiev.com* ▭ *AE, D, DC, MC, V* ✛ *D1.*

$$
LATIN AMERICAN
✕**Havana Cafe.** Tapas are marvelous at this local chain of cozy Cuban-style cantinas. The rich, toucan- and banana-inspired café atmosphere allows guests to step into a tropical, culinary vacation. While sampling authentic Cuban creations like shrimp pancakes, ham and chicken croquettes, Cuban tamales, and paella heaped with a whole Maine lobster, diners can shed the stresses of an arid metropolis. New Puerto Rican menu items include stuffed green plantains and plantains with pork cracklings. There's something special for vegetarians, too: *cho cho*, a fresh chayote squash stuffed with loads of veggies and topped with a Jamaican curry sauce, and the new rice with pigeon peas. There's another location on Camelback Road in Phoenix. ✉ *6245 E. Bell Rd., North Scottsdale* ☎ *480/991–1496* ⊕ *www.havanacafe-az.com* ▭ *AE, D, DC, MC, V* ☉ *No lunch Sun.* ✛ *E1.*

$$$
ECLECTIC
✕**Razz's Restaurant and Bar.** There's no telling what part of the globe chef-proprietor and maestro of fusion Erasmo "Razz" Kamnitzer will use for culinary inspiration on any given day, but his creations give dormant taste buds a wake-up call: black-bean paella is a twist on a Spanish theme; South American bouillabaisse is a fragrant fish stew stocked with veggies; and *bah mie goreng* teams noodles with fish, meat, and vegetables, perked up with dried cranberries and almonds. Count on it—Razz'll dazzle. ✉ *10315 N. Scottsdale Rd., North Scottsdale* ☎ *480/905–1308* ⊕ *www.razzrestaurant.com* ▭ *AE, D, DC, MC, V* ☉ *Closed Sun. and Mon. and June–Aug. No lunch* ✛ *D1.*

$$
JAPANESE
✕**Sushi on Shea.** You may be in the middle of the desert, but the sushi here will make you think you're at the ocean's edge. Fresh yellowtail,

toro, shrimp, scallops, freshwater eel, and even monkfish liver pâté are among the long list of delights. *Nabemono* (hot pot or meals-in-a-bowl) are prepared at your table. The best dish? Maybe it's the *una-ju* (broiled freshwater eel with a sublime smoky scent) served over sweet rice. The fact that some people believe eel is an aphrodisiac only adds to its charm. The bento box is a good way to sample a variety of menu offerings. ✉ *7000 E. Shea Blvd., North Scottsdale* ☎ *480/483–7799* ⊕ *www.sushionshea.com* ▭ *AE, D, DC, MC, V* ✛ *E2.*

OLD TOWN

$$$ ╳ **Cowboy Ciao.** Looking for a culinary kick in Old Town Scottsdale? This
ECLECTIC kitchen, clad in pleasing cowboy cupid murals, weds Southwestern fare and Italian flair, and it's no shotgun wedding. The menu changes frequently, but offers standby favorites such as espresso-rubbed filet mignon and slow-roasted short ribs. The bread pudding creations are must-tries. The wine list represents more than 40 countries and features 225 grape varietals. Too much to choose from? Ask for the *Nifty Fifty,* a one-page list of guest favorites. ✉ *7133 E. Stetson Dr., Old Town* ☎ *480/946–3111* ⊕ *www.cowboyciao.com* ▭ *AE, D, DC, MC, V* ✛ *G2.*

$$ ╳ **Malee's on Main.** This cozy but fashionable, casual eatery in the heart
THAI of Scottsdale's Main Street Arts District serves sophisticated, Thai-inspired fare. Try the best-selling, crispy *pla:* flash-fried whitefish fillets with fresh cilantro and sweet jalapeño garlic sauce. The spicy garlic sautéed spinach is a must, along with curries made to order with tofu, chicken, beef, pork, or seafood. You specify the spiciness—from mild to flaming—but even "mild" dishes have a bite. ✉ *7131 E. Main St., Old Town* ☎ *480/947–6042* ⊕ *www.maleesthaibistro.com* ⌂ *Reservations essential* ▭ *AE, DC, MC, V* ✛ *F3.*

$$$ ╳ **The Mission.** Not only will the food take your taste buds to new levels,
SOUTHWESTERN the dark and sophisticated space is also adjacent to an historic Catholic
Fodor'sChoice mission. Whether the savvy staff is explaining Spanish phrases on the
★ menu or guiding you through the intricacies of tequila tasting, it's clear they like this place as much as the customers. Sit at the elegant bar or fireside on the patio and enjoy an avocado margarita with supreme starters or sides like table-side-crafted guacamole; Mission fries with lemon, chile, and cumin; or grits with chipotle and honey. House favorites include the pecan- and mesquite-grilled pork shoulder, grass-fed Uruguayan rib eye, and scallops with smoked tomato and Serrano ham. The weekend brunch menu alone could keep this place afloat with its *pollo a la brasa y waffles* (chicken waffles) and bacon-infused maple syrup, *chilaquiles* (like a spicy Spanish lasagna), and outstanding corn-and-crab pancakes with smoked Oaxacan pasilla crema. ✉ *3815 N. Brown Ave., Old Town* ☎ *480/636–5005* ⊕ *www.themissionaz.com* ▭ *AE, MC, V* ✛ *G3.*

TEMPE AND AROUND

CHANDLER

$$ ╳ **C-Fu Gourmet.** This is serious Chinese food, the kind you'd expect to
CHINESE find on Mott Street in New York City's Chinatown or Grant Avenue in San Francisco. The large restaurant is generally loud and chaotic,

but there's a good reason why tons of Valley residents will endure long drives and wait times to be part of it. C-Fu's specialty is fish, and you can watch several species swimming around the big holding tanks. Shrimp are fished out of the tank, steamed, and bathed in a potent garlic sauce. Clams in black-bean sauce and tilapia in a ginger-scallion sauce also hit all the right buttons. If you don't find what you're looking for on the menu, tell them what you want and they'll make it. There's a daily dim sum brunch, too. ⊠ *2051 W. Warner Rd., Chandler* ☎ *480/899–3888* ⊕ *www. cfugourmet.com* ⊟ *AE, D, DC, MC, V* ✢ *G6.*

WORD OF MOUTH

"If you want a really high end place or are a "foodie" then I would highly recommend Kai. It is fully owned by the two Indian tribes and the menu features several native dishes. My ideal meal at Kai is the winter squash puree to start off, then the lobster appetizer, then either the buffalo tenderloin or the veal rib eye for the entree." —Bill_H

$$ ⨉ **El Zocalo Mexican Grill.** A positively *caliente* experience in El Zocalo

MEXICAN might be one of the key reasons to put Chandler on your map. With high ceilings, plenty of open space, and a modern twist, El Zocalo is a far cry from the typical Mexican cantina. Enjoy a huge selection of Mexico's finest tequilas and sip on Spanish wines while savoring some authentic Mexican fare out on the inviting, courtyard-style patio. As the night marches on, push your table aside and put on your dancing shoes for some fantastic salsa music performed live by a top-notch local band. ⊠ *28 S. San Marcos Pl., Chandler* ☎ *480/722–0303* ⊕ *www.elzocalo. com* ⊟ *AE, D, DC, MC, V* ☉ *Closed Sun. and Mon.* ✢ *G6.*

$$$$ ⨉ **Kai.** Innovative Southwestern cuisine at the prestigious and award-

SOUTHWESTERN wining, yet oddly earthy Kai ("seed" in the Pima language) uses indig-

Fodor's Choice enous ingredients from local tribal farms. The seasonal menu reflects

★ the restaurant's natural setting on the Gila River Indian Community. Standout appetizers include lobster tail on Indian fry bread and sea urchin in piquillo pepper fondue. Entrées like loin of Rocky Mountain elk with pumpkin, and the Cheyenne River buffalo tenderloin are excellent. The restaurant is adorned with Native American artifacts and has huge windows that showcase gorgeous mountain and desert views. ⊠ *Sheraton Wild Horse Pass Resort & Spa, 5594 W. Wild Horse Pass Blvd., Chandler* ☎ *602/225–0100* ⊕ *www.wildhorsepassresort. com* ⌕ *Reservations essential* 🏠 *Jacket required* ⊟ *AE, D, DC, MC, V* ☉ *Closed Sun. and Mon.* ✢ *D6.*

TEMPE

$ ⨉ **Haji Baba.** This casual Tempe treasure is a local, hole-in-the-wall Mid-

MIDDLE EASTERN dle Eastern favorite that gets consistent rave reviews. The reasonably priced menu includes hummus, *labni* (fresh cheese made from yogurt), fabulous falafel gyros, shawarma, and kebab plates, all served up by a friendly and efficient staff. The adjoining store stocks an ample selection of imported Middle Eastern, Mediterranean, Indian, and European foods including everything from delicious cured olives, fava beans, and grape leaves to chocolate-covered halvah bars, rose water, and countless other hard-to-find specialties. ⊠ *1513 E. Apache Blvd., Tempe*

☎ *480/894–1905* ⊕ *www.haji-baba.com* 🥢 *Reservations not accepted* 🟰 *AE, D, MC, V* ☽ *Takeout only on Sun.* ✛ *F6.*

$$$ ╳ **House of Tricks.** There's nothing up the sleeves of Robert and Robin
ECLECTIC Trick, who work magic on the ever-changing eclectic menu that empha-
sizes the freshest available seafood, poultry, and fine meats, as well
as vegetarian selections, keeping up with the changing tastes of ASU
attendees and visitors. One of the Valley's most unusual dining venues,
the restaurant encompasses a completely charming 1920s home and a
separate brick- and adobe-style house originally built in 1903, adjoined
by an intimate wooden deck and outdoor patio shaded by a canopy of
grapevines and trees. Dinner serves up entrées like cider-roasted chicken
on chorizo corn-bread stuffing. At lunch you can't go wrong with the
quiche of the day. ✉ *114 E. 7th St., Tempe* ☎ *480/968–1114* ⊕ *www.*
houseoftricks.com 🟰 *AE, D, MC, V* ☽ *Closed Sun.* ✛ *E6.*

WHERE TO STAY

The Valley of the Sun now offers locals and visitors some of the country's
best choices when it comes to funky, high-fashion accommodations.

Developers and hoteliers have taken advantage of the Valley's wide-
open spaces to introduce super-size, luxury resorts like the Westin
Kierland and the JW Marriott Desert Ridge Resort offering everything
from their own golf courses and water parks to four-star restaurants
and shopping villages. Places like the retro-hip Hotel Valley Ho, the
Hollywood-chic Hotel Theodore, and the sleek, mountainside Sanctu-
ary have brought Arizona to the forefront of luxury-hotel style. Regal
resorts like the Phoenician, the Four Seasons, the romantic Royal Palms
Resort, and the new Spanish-inspired Intercontinental Montelucia keep
lodging grounded in traditional, unsurpassed elegance, while plenty of
boutique and business hotels keep it grounded in price.

Downtown Phoenix properties tend to be the business hotels, close to
the heart of the city and the convention centers—and often closer to the
average vacationer's budget. Many properties here cater to corporate
travelers during the week but lower their rates on weekends to entice
leisure travelers, so ask about weekend specials when making reserva-
tions. With more than 55,000 hotel rooms in the metro area, you can
take your pick of anything from a luxurious resort to a guest ranch to
an extended-stay hotel. For a true Western experience, guest-ranch ter-
ritory is 70 mi northwest, in the town of Wickenburg.

PLANNING INFORMATION

Many people flee snow and ice to bask in the warmth of the Valley,
so winter is the high season, peaking from January through March.
Summer season—mid-May through the end of September—is giveaway
time, when a night at a resort often goes for half of the winter price, but
be forewarned: in the height of summer it can be too hot to do anything
outside your air-conditioned room.

BEST BETS FOR PHOENIX, SCOTTSDALE, AND TEMPE LODGING

Fodor's offers a selective listing of lodging at every price range, from the city's best budget motel to its most sophisticated luxury hotel. Here we've compiled our top picks by price and experience. The very best properties—those that provide a particularly remarkable experience in their price range—are designated with the Fodor's Choice logo.

WHAT IT COSTS					
	¢	$	$$	$$$	$$$$
FOR 2 PEOPLE	under $100	$100–$150	$151–$225	$226–$350	over $350

Prices are for a standard double in high season.

Use the coordinate (✛ B2) at the end of each listing to locate a site on the corresponding map.

DOWNTOWN AND CENTRAL PHOENIX

CENTRAL PHOENIX

$$$ ⊞ **Hilton Suites.** This practical hotel is a model of excellent design within tight limits. It sits off Central Avenue, 2 mi north of downtown amid a cluster of office towers. The marble-floor, pillared lobby opens into an 11-story atrium with palm trees, natural boulder fountains, glass elevators, and a lantern-lighted café. The hotel offers a full breakfast, and if you're up for more than a drink at the inviting lounge bar or dinner at the on-site chain restaurant, you can take the free shuttle service to other area eats and attractions. **Pros:** spacious rooms with flat-screen TVs; great business amenities; nicest and largest hotel serving this pocket of central Phoenix; close to light-rail. **Cons:** expensive parking. ⊠ *10 E. Thomas Rd., Central Phoenix* ☎ *602/222–1111* ⊕ *www.phoenixsuites.hilton.com* ⥰ *226 suites* ⸝ *In-room: a/c, Internet, Wi-Fi. In-hotel: restaurant, room service, bar, pool, gym, laundry facilities, laundry service, Wi-Fi hotspot, parking (paid), some pets allowed* ⊟ *AE, D, DC, MC, V* ⦿*|BP* ✛ *B5.*

DOWNTOWN PHOENIX

$$ ⊞ **Hotel San Carlos.** Built in 1927 in an Italian Renaissance design, the seven-story San Carlos is the only historic hotel still operating in downtown Phoenix. Among other distinctions, it was the Southwest's first air-conditioned hotel, and suites bear the names of such movie-star guests as Marilyn Monroe and Spencer Tracy. Big-band music, wall tapestries, Austrian crystal chandeliers, shiny copper elevators, and an accommodating staff transport you to a more genteel era. Updated rooms are snug by modern standards but have attractive period furnishings. An off-site fitness center accommodates guests for a small fee. **Pros:** a distinctive, character-filled spot for a downtown stay. **Cons:** old-time charm may not translate well to those used to modern spaciousness and amenities. ⊠ *202 N. Central Ave., Downtown Phoenix* ☎ *602/253–4121 or 866/253–4121* ⊕ *www.hotelsancarlos.com* ⥰ *109 rooms, 12 suites* ⸝ *In-room: a/c, Wi-Fi. In-hotel: restaurant, room service, pool, laundry service, Wi-Fi hotspot, parking (paid)* ⊟ *AE, D, DC, MC, V* ✛ *B5.*

$$$ ⊞ **Hyatt Regency Phoenix.** This convention-oriented hotel efficiently handles the arrival and departure of hundreds of business travelers each day. The seven-story atrium has huge sculptures, colorful tapestries, potted plants, and comfortable seating areas. The revolving Compass restaurant has panoramic views of the Phoenix area. Rooms

Where to Stay in Phoenix, Scottsdale, and Tempe

A   **B**   **C**   **D**

16th St.
Cave Creek Rd.
32nd St.
Tatum Blvd.

Bell Rd.

Greenway Rd.

LOOKOUT MOUNTAIN PRESERVE

Greenway Rd.

Thunderbird Rd.

40th St.

Thunderbird Rd.

North Central Phoenix

Cactus Rd.

Cactus Rd.

Peoria Rd.

Shea Blvd.

Black Canyon Fwy.

35th Ave.

Dunlap Ave.

7th St.

Cave Creek Rd.

PIESTEWA PEAK RECREATIONAL AREA

7th Ave.

Central Ave.

Northern Ave.

Best Western Inn Suites Hotel

Paradise Valley

Tatum Blvd.

Pointe Hilton at Piestewa Peak

JW Marriott's Camelback Inn

Glendale Ave.

19th Ave.

Central Phoenix

16th St.

Intercontinental Montelucia Resort & Spa

Bethany Home Rd.

BILTMORE FASHION PARK

Arizona Biltmore

Hermosa Inn

Sanctuary on Camelback Mountain

Courtyard Phoenix Camelback

Camelback Rd.

The Ritz-Carlton

Camelback Corridor

35th Ave.

60

17

Homewood Suites

Phoenix Inn Suites

Hotel Highland

44th St.

Royal Palms Resort & Spa

Indian School Rd.

PHOENIX

Grand Ave.

Wigwam Resort

Hilton Suites

Piestewa Peak Pkwy.

Thomas Rd.

24th St.

32nd St.

Thomas Rd.

VIAD CORPORATE CENTER

7th St.

Papago Fwy.

Downtown Phoenix

McDowell Rd.

10

Red Mountain Fwy.

202

Van Buren St.

Hotel San Carlos

Wyndham Phoenix

10

SKY HARBOR INTERNATIONAL AIRPORT

Hyatt Regency Phoenix

PHOENIX CONVENTION CENTER

16th St.

Buckeye Rd.

143

Lower Buckeye Rd.

19th Ave.

Central Ave.

17

Salt River

24th St.

48th St.

South Phoenix

Broadway Rd.

The Buttes Marriot Resort

Sheraton Wild Horse Pass Resort & Spa ↓

Arizona Grand Resort ↓

A   **B**   **C**   **D**

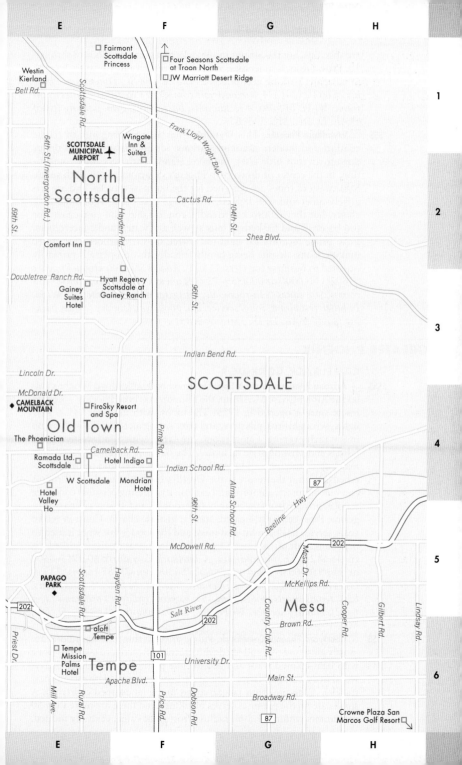

are spacious, but the atrium roof blocks east views on Floors 8 through 10. **Pros:** business amenities; views from restaurant. **Cons:** tricky area to navigate; parking gets pricey. ⊠ *122 N. 2nd St., Downtown Phoenix* 🕾 *602/252–1234* ⊕ *www.hyatt.com* ⤳ *693 rooms, 14 suites* ⚷ *In-room: Wi-Fi. In-hotel: 4 restaurants, bars, pools, gym, parking (paid)* ⊟ *AE, D, DC, MC, V* ✛ *B5.*

$$$ 🔝 **Wyndham Phoenix.** This Wyndham has an appealing mix of classic comfort and modern accommodations. Ideally situated for all things downtown (but little else), the hotel stands, with very little competition, in the center of downtown Phoenix. Spacious rooms with subtle Southwestern tones are designed for the business traveler, and are relatively quiet and well lighted, with large desks and ergonomic desk chairs, but they're also kid-friendly, comfortable, and convenient for pro baseball and basketball fans as well as theater- and concertgoers. **Pros:** prime location for light-rail travel; on-site Starbucks for coffee junkies. **Cons:** despite being family-friendly, this property is primarily oriented to business travelers. ⊠ *50 E. Adams St., Downtown Phoenix* 🕾 *602/333–0000 or 800/359–7253* ⊕ *www.wyndhamphx.com* ⤳ *532 rooms, 108 suites* ⚷ *In-room: a/c, refrigerator (some), Internet, Wi-Fi. In-hotel: restaurant, room service, bar, pool, gym, laundry service, parking (paid)* ⊟ *AE, D, DC, MC, V* ✛ *B5.*

GREATER PHOENIX

CAMELBACK CORRIDOR

$$$$ 🔝 **Arizona Biltmore Resort & Spa.** Designed by Frank Lloyd Wright's colleague Albert Chase McArthur, the Biltmore has been Phoenix's premier resort since it opened in 1929. The lobby, with its stained-glass skylights, wrought-iron pilasters, and cozy sitting alcoves, fills with piano music each evening. Guest rooms are large, with Southwestern-print fabrics and Mission-style furniture. The Biltmore sits on 39 impeccably manicured acres of cool fountains, open walkways, and colorful flowerbeds. Within the resort is the Ocatilla boutique hotel—120 rooms combine intimacy, comfort, and exclusivity, offering personal concierge service, privacy from the main hotel grounds, and all-day culinary programs. **Pros:** centrally located; stately; historic charm. **Cons:** in recent years service has been hit-and-miss, and the food is not what it used to be; young staff often is not adept at meeting needs of distinguished clientele. ⊠ *2400 E. Missouri Ave., Camelback Corridor* 🕾 *602/955–6600 or 800/950–0086* ⊕ *www.arizonabiltmore.com* ⤳ *787 rooms, 72 villas* ⚷ *In-room: a/c, safe, refrigerator, Internet. In-hotel: 5 restaurants, bars, tennis courts, pools, gym, spa, bicycles, children's programs (ages 6–12), laundry service, Wi-Fi hotspot, parking (paid)* ⊟ *AE, D, DC, MC, V* ✛ *C4.*

$$ 🔝 **Courtyard Phoenix Camelback.** Public areas in this four-story hotel are mostly glass and tile, and filled with greenery. Rooms are tastefully done with light-colored walls and accents like plush down bedding, cherry-wood armoires, and large, pullout desks to accommodate the business traveler. A lap pool and Jacuzzi await in the landscaped courtyard. A small café on the premises serves breakfast, and there are more than 50 restaurants within a 1.5-mi radius. **Pros:** great value; centrally located.

Cons: tucked into a strip mall–looking property, it can be hard to find; rooms facing parking garage may be noisy. ⊠ *2101 E. Camelback Rd., Camelback Corridor* ☎ *602/955–5200 or 800/321–2211* ⊕ *www. camelbackcourtyard.com* ⬦ *155 rooms, 12 suites* ⬦ *In-room: a/c, refrigerator (some), Internet. In-hotel: restaurant, pool, gym, laundry facilities, laundry service, parking (free)* ⊟ *AE, D, DC, MC, V* ⊹ *C4.*

$$ ⬚ **Homewood Suites Phoenix–Biltmore.** This all-suites chain is a major value, especially considering its location in the heart of the upscale Biltmore district and Camelback Corridor. Suites have a spacious living and working area with a sleeper sofa and one or two separate bedrooms; each has a full kitchen. Every Monday to Thursday evening there is a complementary "Welcome Home" reception featuring anything from a taco bar to baked potatoes with all the trimmings. Guests also get free passes to a nearby fitness club, free breakfast, and transportation within a 5-mi radius of the hotel. **Pros:** great location; within walking distance of Trader Joe's, where you can stock your kitchen. **Cons:** you get what you pay for with the free food. ⊠ *2001 E. Highland Ave., Camelback Corridor* ☎ *602/508–0937* ⊕ *www.homewoodsuites.hilton.com* ⬦ *124 suites* ⬦ *In-room: a/c, kitchen, Wi-Fi. In-hotel: pool, gym, laundry facilities, laundry service, Wi-Fi hotspot* ⊟ *AE, D, DC, MC, V* ⦿ *BP* ⊹ *C4.*

$$ ⬚ **Hotel Highland.** Conveniently located and remodeled in 2008, this four-story hotel one block off Camelback Road is a heck of a deal. Done in subtle Southwestern hues, rooms are designed for the business traveler and are spacious, cool, and comfortable. Local calls and Wi-Fi are free, and several rooms have jetted tubs. **Pros:** great value; central location; friendly staff. **Cons:** though gated, the pool area is exposed to the parking lot and street. ⊠ *2310 E. Highland Ave., Camelback Corridor* ☎ *602/956–5221 or 800/956–5221* ⊕ *www.hotelhighland.us.com* ⬦ *120 rooms* ⬦ *In-room: a/c, refrigerator, Wi-Fi. In-hotel: restaurant, room service, bar, pool, gym, laundry facilities, Wi-Fi hotspot* ⊟ *AE, D, DC, MC, V* ⦿ *CP* ⊹ *C4.*

$$$$ ⬚ **The Ritz-Carlton, Phoenix.** Behind the sand-color facade and out-of-place architecture hides a graceful luxury hotel known for impeccable service. The lobby and public rooms are elegantly inviting, decorated with 18th- and 19th-century European paintings. Guest rooms and suites are spacious enclaves of luxury with premium mattresses and pillows, Egyptian-cotton sheets, and downy duvets that are even more inviting after the nightly turndown service, complete with fine chocolate. The staff is conscientious and attentive, and the central location means dining, shopping, and entertainment are within strolling distance. Mountain and city vistas can be appreciated from the second-floor terrace, where there is also a heated pool. **Pros:** impeccable service; a walkway (under Camelback Road) gives guests easy access to Biltmore Fashion Park. **Cons:** right on the corner of one of the busiest intersections in town, so expect noise and exhaust when patio dining. ⊠ *2401 E. Camelback Rd., Camelback Corridor* ☎ *602/468–0700 or 800/241-3333* ⊕ *www.ritzcarlton.com/ hotels/phoenix* ⬦ *267 rooms, 14 suites* ⬦ *In-room: a/c, safe, refrigerator, Internet, Wi-Fi. In-hotel: restaurant, room service, bar, pool, gym, children's programs (ages 5–12), laundry service, Wi-Fi hotspot, parking (paid)* ⊟ *AE, D, DC, MC, V* ⊹ *C4.*

RESORTS IN PHOENIX, SCOTTSDALE, AND TEMPE

Hotel Name	Worth Noting	Location	Rooms	Restaurants	Bars	Pools	Spa	Golf Courses	Shopping	Near Major Venues
★ Arizona Biltmore	Quiet and sophisticated	Camelback Corridor	811	4	2	8	yes	2	yes	
Arizona Grand Resort	Great for families	South Phoenix	640	6	4	7		1	yes	yes
Best Western Inn Suites	Well priced, convenient north-central location	North Central Phoenix	109			1			yes	
Buttes Marriott Resort	Hillside resort near ASU	Tempe	353	2	3	1	yes		yes	yes
Comfort Inn	Affordable Scottsdale location	North Scottsdale	124			1			yes	
Courtyard Phoenix Camelback	Great location, Marriott amenities	Camelback Corridor	167	1	2	1			yes	
Crowne Plaza San Marcos Golf Resort	Historic golf resort	Chandler	295	2	2	1	yes	1	yes	
Fairmont Scottsdale Princess	Home of TPC golf course and 6,300-seat tennis stadium	North Scottsdale	651	5	6	5	yes	2	Yes	yes
★ FireSky Resort & Spa	Unique, upscale family fun	Central Scottsdale	204	1	2	3	yes		Yes	yes
★ Four Seasons at Troon North	Remote but luxurious desert mountain getaway	North Scottsdale	232	3	1	3	yes	1		
Gainey Suites Hotel	Chic boutique hotel	North Scottsdale	162			1			Yes	
Hermosa Inn	A cozy getaway	Paradise Valley	35	1	1	1			Yes	

	Hilton Suites	Comfortable, central location	Central Phoenix	226	1	1	1			Yes	yes
	Homewood Suites Phoenix-Biltmore	Residential living, great location	Camelback Corridor	124	1	1	1			Yes	yes
★	JW Marriott Desert Ridge	Desert setting filled with water features	North Central Phoenix	950	9	5	5	yes	2	Yes	yes
	Hotel Theodore	Hollywood Haute Hotel	Central Scottsdale	194	1	3	1	yes		Yes	yes
★	Phoenician	Luxury with a fabulous location	Central Scottsdale	755	6	2	10		3	Yes	yes
	Hotel Highland	Great location	Camelback Corridor	120	1	1	1			Yes	
	Pointe Hilton at Piestewa Peak	Unique, inner-city mountain resort	North Central Phoenix	562	3	3	2	yes		Yes	
	Ritz-Carlton, Phoenix	In the heart of the Valley, across from Biltmore Fashion Park	Camelback Corridor	281	1	1	1			Yes	
★	Royal Palms Resort & Spa	Gorgeous foothill location	Camelback Corridor	182	1	1	1	yes		Yes	
★	Sanctuary Camelback Mountain	Modern amenities, spectacular views	Paradise Valley	98	1	1	3	yes		Yes	
	Sheraton Wild Horse Pass Resort & Spa	Award-winning accommodations and dining	Chandler	500	4	3	4	yes	2	Yes	yes
★	Westin Kierland Resort & Spa	Central to fine shopping and dining	North Scottsdale	827	8	6	4	yes	1	Yes	yes
	Wigwam Resort	Historic West Valley charm	Litchfield Park	331	2	2	2	yes	3		yes
	Wingate Inn & Suites	Scottsdale Airpark convenience, class, and comfort	North Scottsdale	117	1	1	1				yes
	Wyndham Phoenix	Prime downtown location	Downtown Phoenix	640	1	1	1			Yes	yes
	W Scottsdale	Modern Scottsdale Hot Spot	Camelback Corridor	224	1	3	1	yes		Yes	yes

$$$$
Fodor's Choice
★

Royal Palms Resort & Spa. Once the home of Cunard Steamship executive Delos T. Cooke, this Mediterranean-style resort has a stately row of the namesake palms at its entrance, courtyards with fountains, and individually designed rooms. Deluxe suites, casitas, and villas are all different, though they follow one of three elegant styles—trompe-l'oeil, romantic retreat, or Spanish colonial. The restaurant, T. Cook's, is renowned, and the open-air Alvadora Spa seems like it has every imaginable amenity, including an outdoor rain shower. **Pros:** a favorite among Fodors.com users in search of romantic getaways; houses a cozy cigar lounge. **Cons:** expensive. ✉ 5200 E. Camelback Rd., Camelback Corridor ☎ 602/840–3610 or 800/672–6011 ⊕ www.royalpalmshotel.com ↝ 43 rooms, 27 suites, 44 casitas, 5 villas ☐ In-room: a/c, safe, refrigerator, Internet, Wi-Fi. In-hotel: restaurant, room service, bar, pool, gym, spa, bicycles, laundry service, parking (paid) ☐ AE, D, DC, MC, V ✛ D4.

$$$$ **W Scottsdale.** If you'd like to hang your hat somewhere modern, hip, and downright fabulous, look no further. A taste of youthful but sophisticated New York elegance, this hot spot hotel, located in the heart of Scottsdale's shopping and social scene, caters to the wants and needs of the fashionable but fickle traveler with "Whatever/Whenever" service that provides guests with anything they want ("as long as it's legal!"). Live like a celebrity in the variety of top-notch bars and lounges, including the Living Room Lounge and Roku, the property's fine-dining sushi restaurant; or lie low with stunning mountain views at Wet, the exclusive pool and waterside experience—all things that make this a metropolitan desert oasis. **Pros:** unpretentious elegance right across from Scottsdale Fashion Square. **Cons:** decor can be an acquired taste for some; the staff's mandatory use of words that begin with "W" is annoying. ✉ 7277 E. Camelback Rd., Camelback Corridor ☎ 480/970–2100 ⊕ www.whotels.com/scottsdale ↝ 197 rooms, 27 suites ☐ In-room: a/c, safe, refrigerator, Internet, Wi-Fi. In-hotel: restaurant, room service, bars, pool, gym, spa, laundry service, Wi-Fi hotspot, parking (paid) ☐ AE, D, DC, MC, V ✛ E4.

LITCHFIELD PARK

$$$ **Wigwam Resort.** Built in 1918 as a retreat for executives of the Goodyear Company, the Wigwam has a long and storied history. The resort maintains its historical character while delivering a modern-day, first-class luxury experience. The property, which can be accessed by chauffeured golf carts, is stunning, and features great golf and a true Old West experience that puts less of an emphasis on "old." **Pros:** as part of Starwood's Luxury Collection, the Wigwam's standards are higher than they've ever been. **Cons:** historical properties will always have antiquated elements that don't meet every expectation. ✉ 300 Wigwam Blvd., Litchfield Park ☎ 623/935–3811 or 800/327–0396 ⊕ www.wigwamresort.

com 🛏 *259 rooms, 72 suites* 👪 *In-room: a/c, safe, refrigerator (some), Internet. In-hotel: 3 restaurants, bars, golf courses, tennis courts, pools, gym, spa, children's programs (ages 6–12), parking (free)* ⊟ *AE, D, DC, MC, V* ✛ *A4.*

NORTH CENTRAL PHOENIX

$ ▦ **Best Western Inn Suites.** Just north of the Pointe Hilton, this affordable all-suites hotel is often overlooked as an option in the neighborhood, but it has the same proximity to everything as the Hilton, including great recreation areas (Piestewa Peak Mountain Preserve); great dining options (Via Delosantos and Lola Tapas are all nearby); and it's less than 1 mi from AZ 51, which offers quick and easy access to major freeways, Valley shopping, and Sky Harbor Airport. Pillow-top mattresses and upgraded furnishings are recent additions. **Pros:** the price is right, especially for the area. **Cons:** underwhelming staff etiquette. ✉ *1615 E. Northern Ave., North Central Phoenix* ☎ *602/997–6285* ⊕ *www.bwsuite.com* 🛏 *77 rooms, 32 2-room suites* 👪 *In-room: Internet, Wi-Fi. In-hotel: pool, gym, laundry service, Wi-Fi hotspot, parking (free), some pets allowed* ⊟ *AE, D, DC, MC, V* ✛ *C3.*

$$$$ ▦ **JW Marriott Desert Ridge Resort & Spa.** Arizona's largest resort has an
🄲 immense entryway with floor-to-ceiling windows that allow the sand-
Fodor'sChoice stone lobby, the Sonoran Desert, and the resort's amazing water features
★ to meld together in a single prospect. This sprawling and busy property includes 4 acres of water fun with a popular "lazy river," where you can flop on an inner tube and float the day away. Young 'uns love the Kokopelli Kids program, while adults can rejuvenate at Revive Spa or tee off at the on-site golf courses. Each elegantly decorated room has a balcony or patio. **Pros:** perfect for luxuriating with family or groups. **Cons:** a bit impersonal for the price tag; not ideal for cozy getaways. ✉ *5350 E. Marriott Dr., North Central Phoenix* ☎ *480/293–5000 or 800/835–6206* ⊕ *www.jwdesertridgeresort.com* 🛏 *869 rooms, 81 suites* 👪 *In-room: a/c, safe, refrigerator (some), Internet. In-hotel: 9 restaurants, room service, bars, golf courses, tennis courts, pools, spa, bicycles, children's programs (ages 4–12), Wi-Fi hotspot* ⊟ *AE, D, DC, MC, V* ✛ *F1.*

$$ ▦ **Pointe Hilton at Piestewa Peak.** The highlight of this family-oriented
🄲 Hilton is the 9-acre recreation area Hole-in-the-Wall River Ranch. It has swimming pools with waterfalls, a 130-foot waterslide, and a 1,000-foot "river" that winds past a miniature golf course, tennis courts, and artificial buttes. Accommodations in the newly updated stucco buildings vary from standard two-room suites to a grand three-bedroom house; all have balconies. It is also adjacent to the very busy AZ 51, though it manages to filter out most freeway noise. Kids can enjoy the "Coyote Camp" youth programs while adults take in area golf and the Tocasierra Spa. **Pros:** adjacent to the Phoenix Mountain Preserve, making it an ideal base for hiking and biking trips; great summer deals. **Cons:** often seems to be operating at half-staff. ✉ *7677 N. 16th St., North Central Phoenix* ☎ *602/997–2626 or 800/876–4683* ⊕ *www.pointehilton.com* 🛏 *431 suites, 130 casitas, 1 house* 👪 *In-room: a/c, kitchen (some), refrigerator (some), Wi-Fi. In-hotel: 3 restaurants, bars, tennis courts, pools, gym, spa, bicycles, children's programs (ages 6–12), parking (free)* ⊟ *AE, D, MC, V* ✛ *C3.*

PARADISE VALLEY

$$$ ⌐⌐ **Hermosa Inn.** This boutique hotel's ranch-style lodge was the home and studio of cowboy artist Lon Megargee in the 1930s; today the adobe structure houses Lon's at the Hermosa, justly popular for its New American cuisine. Villas as big as private homes and individually decorated casitas hold an enviable collection of Western art. The Hermosa, on 6 acres of lushly landscaped desert, is a blessedly peaceful alternative to some of the larger resorts. **Pros:** luxurious but cozy; flat-screen TVs. **Cons:** inconsistent housekeeping service. ⌐ *5532 N. Palo Cristi Rd., Paradise Valley* ☎ *602/955–8614 or 800/241–1210* ⊕ *www.hermosainn.com* ⊅ *4 villas, 3 haciendas, 11 casitas, 17 ranchos* ⟁ *In-room: a/c, kitchen (some), refrigerator (some), Wi-Fi. In-hotel: restaurant, bar, pool, Wi-Fi hotspot, parking (free), some pets allowed* ⊟ *AE, D, DC, MC, V* ⟟⊙⟟ *CP* ✛ *C4.*

$$$ ⌐⌐ **Intercontinental Montelucia Resort & Spa.** This luxury resort brings a touch of the Mediterranean to Paradise Valley with its exquisite dark furnishings and light stone work, its impeccable Joya Spa, its pool pavilion, and a Spanish-inspired wedding chapel. Spacious rooms feature sunken tubs, large balconies, feather beds, and handmade Moroccan light fixtures. The hotel's restaurant, Prado, has a superb mix of Spanish and Mediterranean cuisine, while the Kasbah patio is another heavenly place to watch the Paradise Valley sunsets. **Pros:** inner-city getaway with stellar sunset views and a new approach to luxury. **Cons:** while the grounds are beautiful, the layout is boxy, awkward, and confusing; fee to rent cabanas ⌐ *4949 E. Lincoln Dr., Paradise Valley* ☎ *480/627–3200 or 800/245–2051* ⊕ *www. icmontelucia.com* ⊅ *252 guest rooms, 41 suites* ⟁ *In-room: a/c, kitchen (some), refrigerator (some), Internet, Wi-Fi. In-hotel: 5 restaurants, room service, bar, tennis courts, pools, gym, spa, Wi-Fi hotspot, parking (free), some pets allowed* ⊟ *AE, D, DC, MC, V* ✛ *D4.*

$$$$ ⌐⌐ **JW Marriott Camelback Inn Resort, Golf Club & Spa.** The inn's true Western integrity lives on in noteworthy harmony with haute contemporary style. Built on 125 acres in the mid-1930s and gorgeously renovated to keep the cowboy character, the hacienda-style resort remains top-notch. Grounds are gloriously adorned with stunning cacti and desert flowers. Rooms are spacious and elegant, with luxury amenities, and seven suites have private swimming pools. **Pros:** a specialty restaurant (BLT Steak); a world-class spa and golf course; upscale retail space; stunning place to catch a sunset. **Cons:** a bit formal and stuffy. ⌐ *5402 E. Lincoln Dr., Paradise Valley* ☎ *480/948–1700 or 800/242–2635* ⊕ *www. camelbackinn.com* ⊅ *453 rooms, 18 suites* ⟁ *In-room: a/c, kitchen (some), Internet, Wi-Fi. In-hotel: 6 restaurants, bar, golf courses, tennis courts, pools, spa, children's programs (ages 5–12), Wi-Fi hotspot, parking (free)* ⊟ *AE, D, DC, MC, V* ✛ *D3.*

$$$$ ⌐⌐ **Sanctuary Camelback Mountain.** This luxurious boutique hotel is the
Fodor's Choice   only resort on the north slope of Camelback Mountain. Secluded moun-
★   tain casitas are painted in desert hues and feature breathtaking views of Paradise Valley. Chic spa casitas surround the pool and are outfitted with contemporary furnishings and private patios. Bathrooms are travertine marble with elegant sinks and roomy tubs. For those who enjoy going *eau* and even *au naturel*, some suites have outdoor tubs.

2

An infinity-edge pool, Zen meditation garden, and Asian-inspired Sanctuary Spa make this a haven for relaxation. The hotel's restaurant, elements, is the hot spot for cocktails at sunset and award-winning cuisine. **Pros:** inner-city getaway with mountain seclusion; unparalleled views of Camelback's Praying Monk Rock. **Cons:** it can be hard to find your room on the sprawling property; walking between buildings can mean conquering slopes or flights of stairs. ⊠ *5700 E. McDonald Dr., Paradise Valley* ☎ *480/948–2100 or 800/245–2051* ⊕ *www.sanctuaryoncamelback.com* ⇨ *53 casitas, 52 suites* ⌂ *In-room: a/c, kitchen (some), refrigerator (some), Internet, Wi-Fi. In-hotel: restaurant, room service, bar, tennis courts, pools, gym, spa, Wi-Fi hotspot, parking (free)* ⊟ *AE, D, DC, MC, V* ✛ *D4.*

SOUTH PHOENIX

$$$–$$$$ ⊡ **Arizona Grand Resort.** This beautifully all-suites resort next to South Mountain Park is home to Oasis, one of the largest water parks in the country, and one of the Valley's more challenging golf courses. Modern but warm, it's a good match in a place called the Valley of the Sun. Fitting for families, this massive property feels like a true getaway, even though it sits just off Interstate 10. Enjoy a four-story sports center, a spa, multiple restaurants, tennis, horseback riding, and mountain biking. **Pros:** great family or large-group location; nicely upgraded rooms. **Cons:** huge property can overwhelm. ⊠ *8000 S. Arizona Grand Pkwy., South Phoenix* ☎ *602/438–9000 or 877/800–4888* ⊕ *www.arizonagrandresort.com* ⇨ *640 suites* ⌂ *In-room: a/c, refrigerator, Wi-Fi. In-hotel: 6 restaurants, room service, bars, golf course, tennis courts, pools, gym, spa, bicycles, laundry facilities, Wi-Fi hotspot, parking (free)* ⊟ *AE, D, DC, MC, V* ✛ *D6.*

Fodor's Choice ★ (margin icons)
⟳ (margin icon)

SCOTTSDALE

CENTRAL SCOTTSDALE

$$$–$$$$ ⊡ **FireSky Resort & Spa.** FireSky was built on the belief that a hotel should "relieve travelers of their insecurity and loneliness." This boutique resort achieves that by providing an elegant, intimate, eco- and family-friendly environment. Attentive staff focus on even the smallest details—personal and professional—to anticipate and alleviate worries. Rooms are done in pleasing contemporary Western decor, and have crisp linens, cozy bathrobes, and brand-name bath amenities. Jurlique, the full-service European spa, offers massages and treatments that the muscles will remember fondly. A hosted wine reception is offered to guests nightly. Soothe your soul and your *soles* in the luxurious sand-bottom pool. Kids are welcomed with special "KimptonKids" guest kits. **Pros:** the lavish pool and lounge area are considered among the area's nicest; organic food offerings; designer in-room recycling bins; pet-friendly; special rooms for tall people. **Cons:** rooms with parking-lot view are disappointing for the price tag—ask for a pool room. ⊠ *4925 N. Scottsdale Rd., Central Scottsdale* ☎ *480/945–7666 or 800/528–7867* ⊕ *www.fireskyresort.com* ⇨ *196 rooms, 8 suites* ⌂ *In-room: a/c, refrigerator (some), Wi-Fi. In-hotel: restaurant, bars,*

Fodor's Choice ★ (margin icons)
⟳ (margin icon)

pools, Internet terminal, Wi-Fi hotspot, some pets allowed ▤ *AE, D, DC, MC, V* ✣ *E4.*

$$ 🖵 **Hotel Indigo.** This Scottsdale spot is perfect for what it is: simple, modern, and, most of all, centrally located. Eclectic rooms are colorfully accented with clean lines, plasma-screen TVs, and exceptionally comfy beds. Suites feature entire walls covered with images of Arizona's spectacular slot canyons. Large, natural-stone showers feature Aveda products. The Golden Bean café serves Starbucks coffee, and the Phi Bar offers a nice selection of wine and beer. **Pros:** great value; ideal Scottsdale location; pet-friendly. **Cons:** walls aren't thick enough to block out the Top 40 music piped through the entryway. ⊠ *4415 N. Civic Center Plaza, Central Scottsdale* ☎ *480/941–9400* ⊕ *www.ichotelsgroup.com* ⤴ *117 rooms, 9 suites* ⌂ *In-room: a/c, safe, refrigerator (some), Internet, Wi-Fi. In-hotel: restaurant, bar, pool, gym, laundry service, parking (free)* ▤ *AE, D, DC, MC, V* ✣ *F4.*

$$$$ 🖵 **Hotel Theodore.** Formerly the Mondrian hotel, this urban resort is a

Fodor's Choice museum of modern art. Surrounded by lush landscaping, the property

★ features two oasis-worthy pools. Outfitted with fireplaces, sofas, and televisions, the poolside cabanas could tempt travelers to shed their sightseeing ambitions. Modern-style rooms include 42-inch plasma TVs, entertainment centers with iPod connections, and comfy beds with down comforters and pillows. Indulge in an Italian meal at Cielo, then redeem yourself with the fitness center or on-site Agua Spa. **Pros:** great location for shopping, entertainment, and Valley activities; modern property in every way. **Cons:** decor is not for everyone, so check pictures online before booking. ⊠ *7353 E. Indian School Rd., Central Scottsdale* ☎ *480/308–1100 or 800/697–1791* ⊕ *hoteltheodore.com* ⤴ *177 rooms, 15 suites, 2 apartments* ⌂ *In-room: a/c, safe, refrigerator, Internet, Wi-Fi. In-hotel: restaurant, room service, bar, pool, gym, spa, laundry service, parking (free)* ▤ *AE, D, DC, MC, V* ✣ *F4.*

$$$$ 🖵 **The Phoenician.** In a town where luxurious, expensive resorts are the

ↄ rule, the Phoenician still stands apart, primarily in the realm of service. The gilded, marbled lobby with towering fountains is the backdrop for a $25 million fine-art collection. Large rooms in the main building and outlying casitas are decorated with elegant 1960s furniture and have private patios and oversize marble bathrooms. There's a secluded tennis garden and 27 holes of premier golf. The Centre for Well Being Spa has a meditation atrium and a pool lined with mother-of-pearl tiles, where you can drift off to another world. Afterward, you can take in a sophisticated afternoon tea or dinner at J&G Steakhouse. **Pros:** you get what you pay for in terms of luxury; highest industry standards. **Cons:** high prices, even in the off-season; not a laid-back resort experience. ⊠ *6000 E. Camelback Rd., Central Scottsdale* ☎ *480/941–8200 or 800/888–8234* ⊕ *www.thephoenician.com* ⤴ *647 rooms, 108 suites* ⌂ *In-room: a/c, safe, refrigerator (some), Internet, Wi-Fi. In-hotel: 7 restaurants, room service, bars, golf courses, tennis courts, pools, gym, children's programs (ages 5–12), Wi-Fi hotspot, parking (free)* ▤ *AE, D, DC, MC, V* ✣ *E4.*

NORTH SCOTTSDALE

$ 🖼 **Comfort Inn.** This may be one of the nicest Comfort Inns you'll ever lay eyes on, and it's in a quiet, upscale north Scottsdale neighborhood along the Scottsdale Road corridor. The three-story glass entryway is bright and welcoming. Rooms are utilitarian but moderately updated, clean, and have free HBO. There are trendy restaurants and shopping opportunities within easy walking distance, making this a comfortable, affordable, and family-friendly alternative. **Pros:** quiet; perfect for the price in this area. **Cons:** while rooms are predictable for a Comfort Inn, the service can vary greatly. ⊠ *7350 E. Gold Dust Rd., at Scottsdale Rd., North Scottsdale* ☎ *480/596–6559 or 888/296–9776* ⊕ *www.comfortinnscottsdale.com* ⊃ *123 rooms, 1 suite* ⌂ *In-room: a/c, refrigerator, Wi-Fi. In-hotel: pool, gym, Wi-Fi hotspot, parking (free)* ⊟ *AE, D, DC, MC, V* 🍴 *CP* ✛ *E2.*

$$$$ 🖼 **Fairmont Scottsdale Princess.** Home of the Tournament Players Club Stadium golf course and the Phoenix Open, this resort covers 450 breathtakingly landscaped acres of desert. Willow Stream Spa, one of the top spa spots in the country, has a dramatic rooftop pool, and kids love the fishing pond and waterslides. Renovated rooms are done in a chic blend of contemporary styles, as are the Fairmont Gold hotel-within-a-hotel boutique rooms. Service is what you'd expect at a resort of this caliber: excellent and unobtrusive. Home to the acclaimed Bourbon Steak restaurant. **Pros:** upscale favorite, especially with families; extras like in-room espresso machines; close to shopping. **Cons:** Mission-meets-modern decor doesn't work with the exterior of the resort. ⊠ *7575 E. Princess Dr., North Scottsdale* ☎ *480/585–4848 or 800/344–4758* ⊕ *www.fairmont.com/scottsdale* ⊃ *513 rooms, 119 casitas, 72 villas, 2 suites* ⌂ *In-room: a/c, safe, Wi-Fi. In-hotel: 5 restaurants, bars, golf courses, tennis courts, pools, gym, spa, children's programs (ages 6–16), parking (free), some pets allowed* ⊟ *AE, D, DC, MC, V* ✛ *E1.*

$$$$ 🖼 **Four Seasons Scottsdale at Troon North.** This is a logical choice for serious golfers, as it's adjacent to two Troon North premier courses, whose guests receive preferential tee times and free shuttle service. The resort is tucked in the shadows of Pinnacle Peak, near the popular hiking trail. Large, casita-style rooms have separate sitting and sleeping areas as well as outdoor garden showers, fireplaces, and balconies or patios. Suites come with telescopes and star charts. Talavera, the hotel's main restaurant, is elegant and accommodating. **Pros:** while developments are breathing down its neck, this resort remains a true, remote desert oasis. **Cons:** far from everything. ⊠ *10600 E. Crescent Moon Dr., North Scottsdale* ☎ *480/515–5700 or 888/207–9696* ⊕ *www.fourseasons.com/scottsdale* ⊃ *210 rooms, 22 suites* ⌂ *In-room: a/c, safe, refrigerator (some), Internet, Wi-Fi. In-hotel: 3 restaurants, bar, golf course, tennis courts, pools, gym, spa, children's programs (ages 5–12), laundry service, parking (free)* ⊟ *AE, D, DC, MC, V* ✛ *F1.*

Fodor'sChoice ★

$$$ 🖼 **Gainey Suites Hotel.** This independently owned and completely remodeled boutique hotel is a rare find for both amenities and price. Floor plans vary from studios to two-bedroom suites that sleep eight, all with fully equipped kitchens and flat-panel wide-screen TVs. Cozy conversation areas in the lobby and an evening hors-d'oeuvres reception

Royal Palms Resort & Spa

Arizona Grand Resort

Sanctuary on Camelback Mountain

The Westin Kierland Resort & Spa

JW Marriott Desert Ridge Resort & Spa

Four Seasons Scottsdale at Troon North

create a warm atmosphere. The hotel is directly adjacent to the Gainey Village development, with boutique shopping and upscale dining, as well as a spa. **Pros:** hotel layout, price, and inclusive breakfast buffet are ideal for families and groups. **Cons:** comfortable but fairly generic decor; not ideal for a romantic getaway. ⊠ *7300 E. Gainey Suites Dr., North Scottsdale* ☏ *480/922–6969 or 800/970–4666* ⊕ *www.gaineysuiteshotel.com* ⇱ *162 suites* ⓖ *In-room: a/c, kitchen, refrigerator, Internet, Wi-Fi. In-hotel: pool, gym, laundry facilities, Wi-Fi hotspot* ▤ *AE, D, MC, V* ⏐◯⏐ *CP* ✣ *E3.*

$$$$ ▥ **Hyatt Regency Scottsdale at Gainey Ranch.** When you stay here, it's
ⓒ easy to imagine that you're relaxing at an ocean-side resort instead of in the desert. Shaded by towering palms and with manicured gardens and paths, the property has water everywhere—a large pool area has a beach, a three-story waterslide, waterfalls, and a lagoon. The two-story lobby, filled with Native American art, opens to outdoor conversation areas where fires burn in stone fireplaces on cool nights. Large, updated rooms have balconies or patios and 37-inch LCD TVs. Three golf courses at nearby Gainey Ranch Golf Club will suit any duffer's fancy. Spa Avania aims to soothe the soul, while kids get their kicks at Camp Hyatt. **Pros:** lots of pools for all; oasis atmosphere; best Sunday brunch in town. **Cons:** if you're early to bed, avoid a room near the lobby. ⊠ *7500 E. Doubletree Ranch Rd., North Scottsdale* ☏ *480/444–1234 or 800/233–1234* ⊕ *www.scottsdale.hyatt.com* ⇱ *461 rooms, 7 casitas, 22 suites* ⓖ *In-room: a/c, Internet, Wi-Fi. In-hotel: 4 restaurants, bars, golf courses, tennis courts, pools, gym, spa, bicycles, children's programs (ages 3–12), parking (free)* ▤ *AE, D, DC, MC, V* ✣ *F2.*

$$$$ ▥ **Westin Kierland Resort & Spa.** Original artwork by Arizona artists is
ⓒ displayed throughout the Westin Kierland, and the spacious rooms all
Fodor's Choice have balconies or patios with views of the mountains or the resort's
★ water park and tubing river, where kids can enjoy programs like "Club Teen." Kierland Commons, within walking distance, is a planned village of upscale specialty boutiques and restaurants. A new leisure center specifically accommodates nonbusiness travelers. Of the eight restaurants, Deseo is the star, presided over by well-known chef Douglas Rodriguez, regarded as the inventor of Nuevo Latino cuisine. **Pros:** bagpipers stroll around the courtyard at sunset; amazing beds and bedding; organic superfood menu; programs for kids' photography and scuba certification. **Cons:** bagpipers; both Internet access and customer service can be unreliable. ⊠ *6902 E. Greenway Pkwy., North Scottsdale* ☏ *480/624–1000* ⊕ *www.kierlandresort.com* ⇱ *732 rooms, 55 suites, 32 casitas* ⓖ *In-room: a/c, refrigerator (some), Internet, Wi-Fi. In-hotel: 8 restaurants, bars, golf courses, tennis courts, pools, gym, spa, children's programs (ages 4–17), Wi-Fi hotspot, parking (free)* ▤ *AE, D, DC, MC, V* ✣ *E1.*

$$$ ▥ **Wingate Inn & Suites–Scottsdale.** Located right off the 101 Freeway, in the Scottsdale Airpark, this affordable hotel is an ideal base of operations. Cool and modern throughout, it has clean, simply decorated rooms. A beautiful pool and waterfall are great for escaping the summer heat. Fill up on the complimentary breakfast before strolling around Taliesin West. **Pros:** clean and spacious rooms; comfortable beds; good price for

2

location. **Cons:** convenient Airpark and freeway location; more practical than perfect. ⊠ *14255 N. 87th St., North Scottsdale* ☎ *480/922–6500 or 877/570–6500* ⊕ *www.scottsdalewingate.com* ⌧ *82 rooms, 35 suites* ⌂ *In-room: refrigerator, Internet, Wi-Fi. In-hotel: pool, gym, laundry service, parking (free)* ▤ *AE, D, DC, MC, V* ⊹ *F2.*

OLD TOWN

$$$ ⊡ **Hotel Valley Ho.** One of Scottsdale's hot-spot hotels is actually one of its oldest. Originally opened in 1956, it was a hangout for celebrities, including Natalie Wood, Robert Wagner, and Tony Curtis. In 2001 the hotel was restored to its former '50s fabulousness—complete with Trader Vic's, the hotel's original restaurant and lounge with legendary cocktails. A large pool is at the heart of this Frank Lloyd Wright–inspired hotel surrounded by lush landscaping and an outdoor grill and dining area. A 6,000-square-foot spa, a fitness center, and 10,000 square feet of meeting space have been added as well as the Tower, which houses 35 residential suites. **Pros:** retro decor; great history; hip, youthful style. **Cons:** the busy location and retro-hip decor are not for everyone, so check pictures online before booking. ⊠ *6850 E. Main St., Old Town* ☎ *480/248–2000* ⊕ *www.hotelvalleyho.com* ⌧ *190 rooms, 35 condo (tower) suites, 4 terrace suites, 2 executive suites* ⌂ *In-room: a/c, Internet, Wi-Fi. In-hotel: 3 restaurants, bars, pool, gym, spa, Wi-Fi hotspot* ▤ *AE, D, DC, MC, V* ⊹ *E4.*

$ ⊡ **Ramada Limited Scottsdale.** There are two attractive things about this exterior-corridor, three-story motel: the location, which is within walking distance of Scottsdale's Old Town, and the price, which includes complimentary Continental breakfast. The simple but clean rooms have standard, serviceable furnishings. **Pros:** great price; great location in the heart of Scottsdale. **Cons:** rooms are dated; pool noise and busy street noise can be heard in rooms. ⊠ *6935 E. 5th Ave., Old Town* ☎ *480/994–9461 or 800/528–7396* ⊕ *www.ramadascottsdale. com* ⌧ *92 rooms* ⌂ *In-room: a/c, refrigerator, Wi-Fi. In-hotel: pool, gym, laundry facilities, parking (free), some pets allowed* ▤ *AE, D, DC, MC, V* ⎮◎⎮ *CP* ⊹ *E4.*

TEMPE AND AROUND

CHANDLER

¢ ⊡ **Crowne Plaza San Marcos Golf Resort.** When it opened in 1912 the
⟳ San Marcos was the first golf resort in Arizona, and it's still one of the state's most treasured landmarks. The palm-studded, Mission-style San Marcos has undergone luxury upgrades, while maintaining its historic beauty and charm: the Images day spa and restyled rooms with pillow-top mattresses, high-thread-count sheets, and down-filled duvets. Each room and suite has either a balcony or patio, and the quiet, single-level golf-course casitas offer patios with "*Fore!*-star" views. **Pros:** a diamond in the Valley's remote rough. **Cons:** far from the central Valley; despite its name, it is less a resort and more a conference-oriented hotel. ⊠ *1 San Marcos Pl., Chandler* ☎ *480/812–0900* ⊕ *www.sanmarcosresort. com* ⌧ *238 rooms, 45 casitas, 12 suites* ⌂ *In-room: a/c, Internet, Wi-Fi*

(some). In-hotel: 2 restaurants, room service, bars, golf course, pools, spa, parking (free) ▭ *AE, D, DC, MC, V* ✛ *H6.*

$$$$ ⛑ **Sheraton Wild Horse Pass Resort & Spa.** On the grounds of the Gila River Indian community, 11 mi south of Sky Harbor Airport, the culture and heritage of the Pima and Maricopa tribes are reflected in every aspect of this property. Guest rooms are detailed with Native American art and textiles (but also have flat-screen TVs), and Kai Restaurant combines Southwestern and Native American culinary traditions. Families enjoy the Koli Center for on-site equestrian activities and the kids-oriented activity pool. A 2.5-mi replica of the Gila River meanders through the property; you can take a boat to the Whirlwind Golf Clubhouse, the nearby Wild Horse Pass Casino, or Rawhide Western Town. Keep your eyes open for the wild horses for which the resort is named—or keep them comfortably closed at the Aji Spa. **Pros:** great views and service; ideal for families and older travelers looking to escape urban chaos. **Cons:** conferences can sometimes overrun the place; so spread out it requires a lot of walking. ⊠ *5594 W. Wild Horse Pass Blvd., Chandler* ☎ *602/225–0100 or 800/325–3535* ⊕ *www.wildhorsepassresort.com* ⤲ *474 rooms, 26 suites* ⌂ *In-room: a/c, safe, refrigerator (some), Internet. In-hotel: 4 restaurants, bars, golf courses, tennis courts, pools, gym, spa, laundry service, Wi-Fi hotspot, parking (free)* ▭ *AE, D, DC, MC, V* ✛ *C6.*

TEMPE

$$ ⛑ **aloft Tempe.** True to its name, this hip hotel, located right on Tempe's Rio Salado waterfront, features loft-inspired design, with modern, minimalist decor. Bright, flashy, and fun, aloft is unlike anything the Valley has seen. It seeks to create a social experience for travelers, pulling them out into community areas where "energy flows" instead of encouraging them to hole up in their rooms. Built with the intention of getting guests to socialize, the modern European-style rooms are small, affording views of Tempe Town Lake on the south side. Bathrooms are also stylish but utilitarian. **Pros:** 42-inch LCD TVs, eco-friendly, highly social; adjacent to Town Lake and ASU action. **Cons:** adjacent to Town Lake and ASU action; social lodging experience not for everyone. ⊠ *951 E. Playa Del Norte Dr., Tempe* ☎ *480/621–3300 or 888/867–7492* ⊕ *www.starwoodhotels.com/alofthotels* ⤲ *136 rooms* ⌂ *In-room: a/c, refrigerator, Internet, Wi-Fi. In-hotel: 2 restaurants, bar, pool, gym, Wi-Fi hotspot, parking (free)* ▭ *AE, D, DC, MC, V* ✛ *E6.*

$$$ ⛑ **The Buttes Marriott Resort.** Two miles east of Sky Harbor Airport, nestled in among desert buttes at Interstate 10 and U.S. 60, this hotel joins dramatic architecture (the lobby's back wall is the volcanic rock itself) and classic Southwest design (pine and saguaro-rib furniture, works by major regional artists) with stunning Valley views. Purchased and completely renovated by Marriott, the Buttes has reemerged as a beacon on the hill, and now includes the Naranda "Revive" spa facility. "Radial" rooms are the largest; inside rooms face the huge free-form pools with waterfall, hot tubs, and a poolside cantina. The Top of the Rock restaurant is elegant. Kids can enjoy the new waterslide and summer activities. **Pros:** beautiful, centrally located Tempe property; great beds; sand volleyball; friendly service. **Cons:** "city views" also include freeway and parking-lot views. ⊠ *2000 Westcourt Way, Tempe* ☎ *602/225–9000* *or 888/867–7492 ⊕ www.marriott.com ⟿ 345 rooms, 9 suites ⌂ In-room: refrigerator (some), Wi-Fi. In-hotel: a/c, 4 restaurants, bars, tennis courts, pool, gym, spa, laundry service, Wi-Fi hotspot, parking (free) ⊟ AE, D, DC, MC, V ⊕ D6.*

$$$ ⊡ **Tempe Mission Palms Hotel.** A handsome, casual lobby and an energetic young staff set the tone at this three-story courtyard hotel. Rooms are Southwestern in style and quite comfortable. Between the Arizona State University campus and Old Town Tempe, this is a convenient place to stay if you're attending ASU sports events, and Harry's Place becomes a lively sports lounge at game time. **Pros:** nice hotel with friendly service and a rooftop pool; right at the center of ASU and Mill Avenue activity. **Cons:** all that activity can be bad for light sleepers. ⊠ *60 E. 5th St., Tempe* ☎ *480/894–1400 or 800/547–8705* ⊕ *www.missionpalms.com* ⟿ *297 rooms, 6 suites ⌂ In-room: a/c, refrigerator (some), Internet, Wi-Fi. In-hotel: restaurant, room service, bar, tennis courts, pool, gym, Wi-Fi hotspot, parking (free) ⊟ AE, D, DC, MC, V ⊕ E6.*

SHOPPING

Since its resorts began multiplying in the 1930s and '40s, Phoenix has acquired many high-fashion clothiers and leisure-wear boutiques, but you can still find the Western clothes that in many parts of town still dominate the fashion. Jeans and boots, cotton shirts and dresses, 10-gallon hats, and bola ties (the state's official neckwear) are still the staples. On the scene as well are the arts of the Southwest's true natives—Navajo weavers, sand painters, and silversmiths; Hopi weavers and kachina-doll carvers; Pima and Tohono O'odham (Papago) basket makers and potters; and many more. Inspired by the region's rich cultural traditions, contemporary artists have flourished here, making Phoenix—particularly Scottsdale, a city with more art galleries than gas stations—one of the Southwest's largest art centers alongside Santa Fe, New Mexico.

Today's shoppers find the best of the old and the new—all presented with Southwestern style. Upscale stores, one-of-a-kind shops, and outlet malls sell the latest fashions, cowboy collectibles, handwoven rugs, traditional Mexican folk art, and contemporary turquoise jewelry.

Most of the Valley's power shopping is concentrated in central Phoenix, downtown Scottsdale, and the Kierland area in north Scottsdale, but auctions and antiques shops cluster in odd places—and as treasure hunters know, you've always got to keep your eyes open.

SHOPPING CENTERS

Although some of Phoenix's malls are gorgeously landscaped outdoor areas, most, like Scottsdale Fashion Square, are indoor complexes. Cool stores with icy air-conditioning can be just the ticket for relief from the midday desert heat.

Arizona Mills (⊠ *5000 Arizona Mills Circle, I–10 and Baseline Rd., Tempe* ☎ *480/491–9700* ⊕ *www.arizonamills.com*), a mammoth "value-oriented retail and entertainment mega mall," features more than 175 outlet stores and sideshows, including Off 5th–Saks Fifth Avenue, and Last

Call from Neiman Marcus. When you tire of bargain hunting, relax in the food court, cinemas, or faux rain forest.

★ **Biltmore Fashion Park** (⊠ *24th St. and Camelback Rd., Camelback Corridor* ☎ *602/955–8400* ⊕ *www.shopbiltmore.com*) has a posh, parklike setting. Macy's, Saks Fifth Avenue, and Borders are the anchors for more than 70 stores and upscale boutiques such as Cornelia Park. It's accessible from the Camelback Esplanade and the Ritz Carlton by a pedestrian tunnel that runs beneath Camelback Road.

The Borgata (⊠ *6166 N. Scottsdale Rd., Paradise Valley* ☎ *602/953–6311* ⊕ *www.borgata.com*), an outdoor re-creation of the Italian village of San Gimignano, with courtyards, stone walls, turrets, and fountains, is a lovely setting for browsing upscale boutiques or just sitting at an outdoor café.

Chandler Fashion Center (⊠ *3111 W. Chandler Blvd., Chandler* ☎ *480/812–8488* ⊕ *www.chandlermall.com*) features anchor stores Nordstrom, Dillard's, Macy's, and Sears, along with more than 180 other national retail chains such as Coach, Pottery Barn, and Cheesecake Factory.

Cofco Chinese Cultural Center (⊠ *668 N. 44th St., South Phoenix* ☎ *602/273–7268* ⊕ *www.phxchinatown.com*) is adorned with replicas of pagodas, statues, and traditional Chinese gardens. It's the place to find Asian restaurants, gift shops, and the Super L, a huge Asian grocery store. Take a stroll through the market's fish department—you'll forget you're in the desert.

Kierland Commons (⊠ *Greenway Pkwy. at Scottsdale Rd., North Scottsdale, Scottsdale* ☎ *480/348–1577* ⊕ *www.kierlandcommons.com*), next to the Westin Kierland Resort, is one of the city's newest shopping areas. "Urban village" is the catchphrase for this outdoor pedestrian mall with restaurants and upscale chain retailers, among them J. Crew and Tommy Bahama.

★ **Mill Avenue Shops** (⊠ *Mill Ave. between Rio Salado Pkwy. and University Dr., Tempe* ☎ *480/921–2300* ⊕ *www.millavenue.com*), named for the landmark Hayden Flour Mill, is an increasingly commercial and construction-laden area, but it's still a fun-filled walk-and-shop experience. Directly west of the Arizona State University campus, Mill Avenue is an active melting pot of students, artists, residents, and tourists. Shops include some locally owned stores, mid-range chains, and countless bars and restaurants. The Valley Art Theater is a Mill Avenue institution and Tempe's home of indie cinema. Twice a year (in early December and March/April), the Mill Avenue area is the place to find indie arts and crafts when it hosts the Tempe Festival of the Arts.

Fodor's Choice **Old Town Scottsdale** (⊠ *Between Goldwater Blvd., Brown Ave., 5th Ave.* ★ *and 3rd St., Old Town, Scottsdale*) is the place to go for authentic Southwest-inspired gifts, clothing, art, and artifacts. Despite its massive modern neighbors, this area and its merchants have long respected and maintained the single-level brick storefronts that embody Scottsdale's upscale cow-town charm. More than 100 businesses meet just about any aesthetic want or need, including Gilbert Ortega, one of the premier places for fine Native American jewelry and art. Some of Scottsdale's best restaurants are also found in this pleasing maze of merchandizing.

★ **Scottsdale Fashion Square** (✉ *Scottsdale and Camelback Rds., Camelback Corridor, Scottsdale* ☎ *480/941–2140* ⊕ *www.fashionsquare.com*) has a retractable roof and many specialty shops unique to Arizona. There are also Barney's, Nordstrom, Dillard's, Neiman Marcus, Macy's, Juicy Couture, Louis Vuitton, Tiffany, Cartier, and Gucci. A huge food court, restaurants, and a cineplex complete the picture.

★ **The Shops Gainey Village** (✉ *8787 N. Scottsdale Rd., North Scottsdale-Scottsdale* ☎ *480/458–8064* ⊕ *www.theshopsgaineyvillage*), near historic Gainey Ranch, makes for stiff shopping competition in the area. Composed primarily of upscale boutiques, this stylish strip mall also features fine dining at hot spots like Bloom and Thai Foon and nosh spots like Paradise Bakery, the Coffee Bean, and Pei Wei Asian Café.

OPEN-AIR MARKETS

It can be a real treat to visit a farmers' market even if you're not a local doing grocery shopping. Phoenix markets often feature funky tortillas and Mexican wares, so you can sample some goodies and maybe find some presents to take home. Two of metropolitan Phoenix's best markets are in the tiny town of Guadalupe, which centers around Interstate 10, Baseline Road, and Warner Road. Take Interstate 10 south to Baseline Road, go east 0.5 mi, and turn south on Avenida del Yaqui to find open-air vegetable stalls, roadside fruit stands, and tidy houses covered in flowering vines. A conversational knowledge of Spanish will aid you in shopping. To find the fresh wares of a Valley farmers' market, visit ⊕ *www.arizonafarmersmarkets.com*, a comprehensive calendar listing started and maintained by longtime market coordinators Dee and John Logan.

Guadalupe Farmer's Market (✉ *9210 S. Avenida del Yaqui, Guadalupe* ☎ *480/730–1945*) has all the fresh ingredients you'd find in a rural Mexican market—tomatillos, varieties of chile peppers, fresh-ground masa (cornmeal) for tortillas, spices like cumin and cilantro, and on and on. It's open every day year-round: 9 AM–6 PM in fall, winter, and spring; to 7 PM in summer; and to 5 PM Sunday.

Mercado Mexico (✉ *8212 S. Avenida del Yaqui, Guadalupe* ☎ *480/831–5925*) carries ceramics, paper-, tin-, and lacquerware, all at unbeatable prices. Stock up 10 AM–6 PM daily, year-round.

SPECIALTY SHOPS

ANTIQUES AND COLLECTIBLES

The central-Phoenix corridor, between 7th Street and 7th Avenue, has many antiques stores. Most shops sit north of Thomas and south of Camelback. Prices, though reasonable, are firm at most shops. A surprise to many visitors is the Old Town district of suburban Glendale, with more than 80 antiques and collectibles shops nestled around historic Old Towne and Catlin Court, which are listed on the National Register of Historic Places.

Antique Centre (✉ *2012 N. Scottsdale Rd., Central Scottsdale, Scottsdale* ☎ *480/675–9500*) has a hodgepodge of collectibles and trinkets. The

The Southwest continues to inspire contemporary artists. You can see some pieces yourself at the Wilde Meyer Galleries.

Glendale Old Towne & Catlin Court (⊠ *59th and Glendale Aves., Glendale*) antiques district has a plethora of shops and restaurants in colorful, century-old bungalows. Stop in at antiques-filled Aunt Pittypat's Kitchen for breakfast or lunch, or have a cup of tea at the Spicery, which is in an 1895 Victorian home.

ARTS AND CRAFTS

Art One (⊠ *4120 N. Marshall Way, Old Town, Scottsdale* ☎ *480/946–5076* ⊕ *www.artonegalleryinc.com*) carries works by students as well as local and emerging artists.

Fodor's Choice
★ **Cosanti Originals** (⊠ *6433 Doubletree Ranch Rd., Paradise Valley* ☎ *800/752–3187* ⊕ *www.cosanti.com*) is the studio where architect Paolo Soleri's famous bronze and ceramic wind chimes are made and sold. You can watch the craftspeople at work, then pick out your own—prices are surprisingly reasonable.

Drumbeat Indian Arts (⊠ *4143 N. 16th St., Central Phoenix* ☎ *602/266–4823* ⊕ *www.drumbeatindianarts.com*) is a small, interesting shop specializing in Native American music, movies, books, drums, and crafts supplies. If you're lucky, you might find authentic fry bread and Navajo tacos being cooked in the parking lot on weekends.

Gilbert Ortega Indian Jewelry and Gallery (⊠ *7155 E. 5th Ave., Old Town, Scottsdale* ☎ *480/941–9281*) has many Native-American shops throughout Scottsdale. Prices are steep.

★ **The Heard Museum Shop** (⊠ *2301 N. Central Ave., Downtown Phoenix* ☎ *602/252–8344* ⊕ *www.heard.org*) is hands-down the best place in town for Southwestern Native American and other crafts, both traditional and modern. Prices tend to be high, but quality is assured, with many one-of-a-kind items among the collection of rugs, kachina dolls, pottery, and other crafts; there's also a wide selection of lower-priced gifts.

Trailside Galleries (⊠ *7330 Scottsdale Mall, Old Town, Scottsdale* ☎ *480/945–7751* ⊕ *www.trailsidegalleries.com*) has been showcasing works by members of the Cowboy Artists of America for more than 40 years, and specializes in traditional American paintings and sculptures.

Fodor's Choice ★ **Wilde Meyer Galleries** (⊠ *4142 N. Marshall Way, Old Town, Scottsdale* ☎ *480/945–2323* ⊠ *Colores by Wilde Meyer, 7100 E. Main St., Old Town, Scottsdale* ☎ *480/947–1489* ⊕ *www.wildemeyer.com*) has two locations around the Valley of the Sun and another in Tucson; it's the place to go for the true colors of the Southwest. In addition to one-of-a-kind paintings, the galleries also feature rustic, fine-art imports from around the state and the world, including furniture, sculptures, and jewelry. Look for Linda Carter Holman's "Latin Ladies" paintings and works by Scottsdale's own Sherri Belassen, whose unique cowboys and cattle will leave you with a colorful new Western perspective.

BOOKS

The major U.S. chains—Barnes & Noble and Borders—are represented in the Valley, but there are still some interesting independents.

Fodor's Choice ★ **Changing Hands Bookstore** (⊠ *6428 S. McClintock Dr., Tempe* ☎ *480/730–0205* ⊕ *www.changinghandstempe.com*) has a large selection of new and used books.

Guidon Scottsdale (⊠ *7117 W. Main St., Old Town, Scottsdale* ☎ *480/945–8811* ⊕ *www.guidon.com*), a small, independent bookshop in Scottsdale's art district, specializes in out-of-print and hard-to-find Western fiction and nonfiction titles.

FOOD AND WINE SHOPS

★ **AJ's Fine Foods** (⊠ *5017 N. Central Ave., North Central Phoenix* ☎ *602/230–7015* ⊠ *7141 E. Lincoln Dr., North Scottsdale* ☎ *480/998–0052* ⊠ *7131 W. Ray Rd., Chandler* ☎ *480/705–0011* ⊠ *20050 N. 67th Ave., Glendale* ☎ *623/537–2310* ⊠ *15031 Thompson Peak Pkwy., North Scottsdale* ☎ *480/314–6500* ⊕ *www.ajsfinefoods.com*) is the Valley's grandest upscale grocery store and a great place to fill your basket with exclusive local creations ranging from Goldwater's salsas and sauces—created by the daughters of the late senator Barry Goldwater—to Sada's Pepper Melody and Rene's Desert Rub spice mixes. It's possible to spend hours at any of the 13 identical Valley locations, and it's also possible to spend far more money than you would at an average grocery store, but the vast inventory of unusual products not found together anywhere else and the first-class, one-stop shopping experience make it all worthwhile. The wine selection is among the best in town, and the sommelier-quality staff will gladly offer suggestions. Be sure to partake of the fresh, chef-prepared food offerings, like homemade soups, salad, pizza, specialty sandwiches, and gourmet take-out entrées from the bistro.

★ **Sportsman's Fine Wine & Spirits** (⊠ *3205 E. Camelback Rd., Paradise Valley* ☎ *602/955–9463* ⊠ *10893 N. Scottsdale Rd., North Scottsdale* ☎ *480/948–0520* ⊕ *www.sportsmans4wine.com*) is the place to go to "lift your spirits." Sportsman's stocks fine wines and rare beverage finds from both local and international sources. They also sell cheeses and other delicious wine accompaniments including panini sandwiches, roasted garlic, hummus, bruschetta, baked feta, and warm pretzels.

GIFTS

Kactus Jock is a somewhat kitschy Arizona souvenir store, with food, t-shirts, and some art. ⊠ 7233 E. Main St., Old Town ☎ 480/945–3380 ⊕ www.kactusjock.com

VINTAGE CLOTHING AND FURNITURE

In certain parts of the Valley "old" is the new "new." The Melrose District, on 7th Avenue between Indian School and Camelback roads in central Phoenix, is banking on its Old Phoenix charm in a slow but steady race to become the next hip historic neighborhood. New faces on old buildings are the perfect welcome mat for progress with forthcoming lofts, condos, eateries, and big plans for public art, but the overall charm is anchored by its variety of vintage stores. Open hours are generally 11–6, and many stores are closed Monday and Tuesday.

Home Again (⊠ 4302 N. 7th Ave., North Central Phoenix ☎ 602/424–0488) is a down-home store that buys and sells vintage and modern home furnishings and antiques. A registered antiques dealer, Home Again welcomes dealers.

Melrose Vintage (⊠ 4238 N. 7th Ave., North Central Phoenix ☎ 602/636–0300) has a cheerful, dollhouse-like yellow exterior, and that's not the only thing that makes it memorable. The no-nonsense staff knows its stuff, which includes tasteful and fun low- to high-end shabby-chic furnishings—everything from ribbon to armoires.

Phoenix Metro Retro (⊠ 5102 N. Central Ave., North Central Phoenix ☎ 602/279–0702 ⊕ www.phoenixmetroretro.com) is a vintage, midcentury, and modern furniture store. Cool and inviting, Metro Retro aptly exhibits the talent and time it takes for people like owner Carl Reese to find those "perfect" pieces for your purchasing pleasure.

Vintage Solutions (⊠ 3604 N. 16th St., North Central Phoenix ☎ 602/604–1831) is the place for sweet deals on deco and midcentury furniture, collectibles, and accessories that stand the test of time. A local newspaper recently called the owners and operators of Vintage Solutions "eagle-eye tchotchke aficionados who know a good deal when they see one, and aren't above passing their savings on to you."

NIGHTLIFE AND THE ARTS

Over the past decade the Valley of the Sun has gone from a "cow town" to "now town," and the nightlife and culture options are no exception. Downtown Phoenix and Scottsdale are especially packed with entertainment choices.

Frank Lloyd Wright's architectural legacy in the Valley of the Sun includes ASU Gammage Auditorium in Tempe.

THE ARTS

For weekly listings of theater, arts, and music, check out Thursday's *Arizona Republic,* pick up a free issue of the independent weekly *New Times,* or check out *Where Phoenix/Scottsdale Magazine,* available free in most hotels. Good online sources of information on events in the Valley are the *Arizona Republic* Web site (⊕ *www.azcentral.com*) and ⊕ *www.showup.com*. Both have extensive nightlife and arts listings; ShowUp has some good last-minute deals on performances.

TICKETS **Arizona State University Public Events Box Office** (☎ *480/965–6447* ⊕ *www. herbergercollege.asu.edu/calendar*) sells tickets for ASU events. **Tickets.com** (⊕ *www.tickets.com*) sells tickets for ASU Public Events at ASU Gammage Auditorium and Kerr Cultural Center. **Ticketmaster** (☎ *480/784–4444* ⊕ *www.ticketmaster.com*) sells tickets for nearly every event in the Valley and has outlets at Fry's and Macy's stores.

MAJOR PERFORMANCE VENUES

To feed its growing tourism industry Phoenix has cooked up enticing entertainment venues that attract everything from major-league sporting events to the hottest music acts and the most raved-about theater productions.

PHOENIX The **Celebrity Theatre** (⊠ *440 N. 32nd St., Airport* ☎ *602/267–1600* ⊕ *www.celebritytheatre.com*) is a 2,600-seat theater-in-the-round hosting concerts and other live performances.

Cricket Pavilion (⊠ *2121 N. 83rd Ave., West Phoenix* ☎ *602/254–7200* ⊕ *www.cricket-pavilion.com*) is an outdoor amphitheater that books major live concerts.

The **Dodge Theatre** (✉ *400 W. Washington St., Downtown Phoenix* ☎ *602/379–2800* ⊕ *www.dodgetheatre.com*) is Phoenix's high-tech, state-of-the-art entertainment venue. The space morphs from an intimate Broadway stage setup to a concert hall seating 5,000. There are great views from almost every seat.

Herberger Theater Center (✉ *222 E. Monroe St., Downtown Phoenix* ☎ *602/254–7399* ⊕ *www.herbergertheater.org*) is the permanent home of the Arizona Theatre Company and Actors Theatre of Phoenix; it also hosts performances of visiting dance troupes, orchestras, and Broadway shows.

Mesa Arts Center (✉ *1 E. Main St., Mesa* ☎ *480/644–6500* ⊕ *www. mesaartscenter.com*) has risen to the demand for culture and creative art and is fast becoming one of the Valley's top destinations for exhibits, visual-art performances, and A-list concerts.

The Spanish-colonial **Orpheum Theatre** (✉ *203 W. Adams St., Downtown Phoenix* ☎ *602/534–5600, 602/262–7272 box office* ⊕ *www. friendsoftheorpheumtheatre.org*), built in 1927 and renovated throughout the '90s, is a glamorous theater showcasing the Arizona Ballet, children's theater, and film festivals.

Facing the Herberger Theater is **Symphony Hall** (✉ *225 E. Adams St., Downtown Phoenix* ☎ *602/495–1999 or 800/776–9080* ⊕ *www. phoenixsymphony.org*), home of the Phoenix Symphony and Arizona Opera.

SCOTTSDALE **Kerr Cultural Center** (✉ *6110 N. Scottsdale Rd., Central Scottsdale, Scottsdale* ☎ *480/596–2660* ⊕ *www.asukerr.com*) showcases smaller theater and dance performances.

Scottsdale Center for the Performing Arts hosts cultural events on the Scottsdale Mall as well as year-round performances in two intimate theater settings. ✉ *7380 E. 2nd St, Old Town, Scottsdale* ☎ *480/994–2787* ⊕ *www.scottsdaleperformingarts.org.*

TEMPE Frank Lloyd Wright designed the **ASU Gammage Auditorium** (✉ *Arizona State University, Mill Ave. at Apache Blvd., Tempe* ☎ *480/965–3434* ⊕ *www.asugammage.com*), which presents more Broadway shows outside the Big Apple than any other venue in the nation.

The Chandler Center for the Arts (✉ *250 N. Arizona Ave., Chandler* ☎ *480/ 782–2680* ⊕ *www.chandlercenter.org*), features some of the nation's most popular touring performances for families and children.

Herberger College of Fine Arts at Arizona State University (✉ *Arizona State University, Mill Ave. at Apache Blvd., Tempe* ☎ *480/965–6447* ⊕ *www. herbergercollege.asu.edu*) includes Katzin Concert Hall, Lyceum Theatre, Galvin Playhouse, and the Evelyn Smith Music Theatre and Organ Hall, which houses an 1,800-pipe Fritts Organ. Numerous performances are offered during the school year, from September through April, and many are free.

CLASSICAL MUSIC

Arizona Opera (✉ *4600 N. 12th St., Downtown Phoenix* ☎ *602/266–7464* ⊕ *www.azopera.com*) stages an opera season in both Tucson and Phoenix. The Phoenix season runs from October to March at Symphony Hall.

Phoenix Symphony Orchestra (✉ *1 N. 1st St., Downtown Phoenix* ☎ *602/495–1999 or 800/776–9080* ⊕ *www.phoenixsymphony.org*) is the resident company at Symphony Hall. Its season, which runs September through May, includes orchestral works from classical and contemporary composers, a chamber series, composer festivals, and outdoor pops concerts.

EXPERIENCE THE WILD WEST

In addition to the state and county fairs, and some seasonal shows, there are several places in and around Phoenix to get a taste of what the West was like way back when. Rawhide and the Rockin' R Ranch, closer to town, are more kid-friendly, while Pioneer Living History Village and Goldfield Ghost Town *(see Apache Trail)* are more sedate, with a stronger emphasis on authentic historic buildings.

DANCE

Ballet Arizona (☎ *602/381–1096* ⊕ *www.balletaz.org*), the state's professional ballet company, presents a full season of classical and contemporary works (including pieces commissioned for the company) in Tucson and Phoenix, where it performs at the Orpheum Theater, downtown. The season runs from October through May.

THEATER

Actors Theatre of Phoenix (☎ *602/253–6701* ⊕ *www.atphx.org*) is the resident theater troupe at the Herberger Theater Center. It presents a full season of drama, comedy, and musical productions from September through May.

Arizona Theatre Company (☎ *602/256–6995* ⊕ *www.aztheatreco.org*) is based in Tuscon but also performs at the Herberger Theater Center. Productions, held from September through June, range from classic dramas to musicals and new works by emerging playwrights.

Black Theater Troupe (☎ *602/258–8128* ⊕ *www.blacktheatretroupe.org*) presents original and contemporary dramas and musical revues, as well as adventurous adaptations, between September and May.

ᙰ **Childsplay** (✉ *900 S. Mitchell Dr., Tempe* ☎ *480/921–5700* ⊕ *www.childsplayaz.org*) is the state's theater company for young audiences and families, which runs during the school year. Rotating through many a venue, these players deliver high-energy performances.

ᙰ **Great Arizona Puppet Theatre** (✉ *302 W. Latham St., Downtown Phoenix* ☎ *602/262–2050* ⊕ *www.azpuppets.org*), which performs in a historic building featuring lots of theater and exhibit space, mounts a yearlong cycle of inventive puppet productions that change frequently.

Phoenix Theatre (✉ *100 E. McDowell Rd., Downtown Phoenix* ☎ *602/254–2151* ⊕ *www.phxtheatre.org*), across the courtyard from the Phoenix Art Museum, stages musical and dramatic performances as well as productions for children by the Cookie Company.

Rawhide Western Town, or another wild west show with dinner, is a great recipe for family fun.

WILD WEST SHOWS

Fodor's Choice

Rawhide Western Town and Steakhouse at Wild Horse Pass (✉ *5700 W. North Loop Rd., Gila River Indian Community, Chandler* ☎ *480/502–5600* ⊕ *www.rawhide.com*), a Valley favorite for more than four decades, calls the 2,400-acre master-planned Wild Horse Pass Development in the Gila River Indian Community home. Featuring its legendary steak house and saloon, Main Street and all of its retail shops, and the Six Gun Theater, Rawhide is the kitschiest place in town to experience the Old West. Enjoy canal rides along the Gila River Riverwalk, train rides, and a Native American village honoring the history and culture of the Akimel O'othom and Pee Posh tribes. Immerse yourself into the Wild West, where you can watch a stunt show featuring gunslingers, have a fellow guest arrested and tossed in jail, or watch trick roping performed by the pros.

Rockin' R Ranch (✉ *6136 E. Baseline Rd., Mesa* ☎ *480/832–1539* ⊕ *www. rockinr.net*) includes a petting zoo, a reenactment of a Wild West shoot-out, and—the main attraction—a nightly cookout with a Western stage show. Pan for gold or take a wagon ride until the "vittles" are served, followed by music and entertainment.

NIGHTLIFE

From brewpubs, sports bars, and coffeehouses to dance clubs, mega-concerts, and country venues, the Valley of the Sun offers nightlife of all types. Nightclubs, comedy clubs, upscale lounges, and wine bars abound in downtown Phoenix, along Camelback Road in north-central Phoenix, and in Scottsdale and Tempe, as well as the other suburbs.

Among music and dancing styles, country-and-western has the longest tradition here. Jazz venues, rock clubs, and hotel lounges are also numerous and varied. Phoenix continues to get hipper and more cosmopolitan, so behind the bar you're just as likely to find a mixologist as a bartender. There are also more than 30 gay and lesbian bars, primarily on 7th Avenue, 7th Street, and the stretch of Camelback Road between the two.

You can find listings and reviews in the *New Times* free weekly newspaper, distributed Wednesday, "The Rep Entertainment Guide" of the *Arizona Republic,* or online at ⊕ *www.azcentral.com*, the paper's Web site. The local gay scene is covered in *Echo Magazine,* which you can pick up all over town.

BARS AND LOUNGES

PHOENIX **Bomberos Café & Wine Bar** (✉ *8801 N. Central Ave., North Central Phoenix* ☎ *602/687–8466* ⊕ *www.bomberoswinebar.com*) occupies a former firehouse. This little neighborhood ember burns bright with its pleasant outdoor patio, delectable paninis and bruschetta, rich desserts, Illy coffees, and a rich selection of unique and flavorful world wines.

Fez On Central (✉ *3815 N. Central Ave., Central Phoenix* ☎ *602/287–8700* ⊕ *www.fezoncentral.com*) is a stylish restaurant by day and a gay-friendly, hip hot spot by night. The sleek interior and fancy drinks make you feel uptown, while the happy-hour prices and location keep this place grounded.

★ **Jade Bar** (✉ *5700 E. McDonald Dr., Sanctuary Camelback Mountain resort, Paradise Valley* ☎ *480/948–2100* ⊕ *www.sanctuaryoncamelback. com*) has spectacular views of Paradise Valley and Camelback Mountain; an upscale, modern bar lined with windows; and a relaxing fireplace-lighted patio.

Majerle's Sports Grill (✉ *24 N. 2nd St., Downtown Phoenix* ☎ *602/253–9004* ✉ *3095 W. Chandler Blvd., Chandler* ☎ *480/899–7999*) ⊕ *www. majerles.com*), operated by former Suns basketball player Dan Majerle, offers a comprehensive menu for pre- and post-game celebrations as well as some of the best people-watching potential in town.

Postino Winecafe (✉ *3939 E. Campbell Ave., Camelback Corridor* ☎ *602/852–3939* ⊕ *www.postinowinecafe.com*) and (✉ *5144 N. Central Ave., North Central Phoenix* ☎ *602/274–5144*) has grown from a small neighborhood haunt into two separate destinations in the central part of Phoenix. More than 40 wines are poured by the glass. Order a few grazing items off the appetizer menu (the bruschetta is unmatched by any in the Valley) and settle in, or carry out a bottle of wine, hunk of cheese, and loaf of bread for a twilight picnic.

Next to two of the Valley's major sports complexes and inside a historic home, the **Rose & Crown** (✉ *628 E. Adams St., at 7th St., Downtown Phoenix* ☎ *602/256–0223* ⊕ *www.theroseandcrownpub.net*) serves hearty, traditional, English pub grub—fish-and-chips, bangers and mash, and shepherd's pie—with equally hearty beers to wash it down. Expect a wait on game and special-event nights.

Seamus McCaffrey's Irish Pub (✉ *18 W. Monroe St., Downtown Phoenix* ☎ *602/253–6081* ⊕ *www.seamusmccaffreys.com*) is a fun and friendly place to enjoy one of the dozen European brews on draft. A small kitchen turns out traditional Irish fare.

SCOTTSDALE **AZ88** (✉ *7353 Scottsdale Mall, Scottsdale Civic Center, Old Town, Scottsdale* ☎ *480/994–5576* ⊕ *www.az88.com*) is great for feasting on huge portions of great food and lavish quantities of liquor, but also for feasting your eyes on the fabulous people who flock here on weekend nights to see and be seen. It's a great stop before and after an Old Town event or a night of partying, Scottsdale style.

Kazimierz World Wine Bar (✉ *7137 E. Stetson Dr., Old Town, Scottsdale* ☎ *480/946–3004* ⊕ *www.kazbar.net*) is entered through a door marked THE TRUTH IS INSIDE, beyond which lies a dark, cavelike wine bar with comfy chairs and good music.

The Salty Senorita (✉ *336 N. Scottsdale Rd., Old Town, Scottsdale* ☎ *480/946–7258* ⊕ *www.saltysenorita.com*) is known more for its extensive margarita selection and lively patio crowd than for its food. The restaurant-bar touts 51 different margaritas—with some recipes so secret they won't tell you what goes in them. Try the El Presidente or the Chupacabra.

TEMPE AND **Casey Moore's Oyster House** (✉ *850 S. Ash Ave., Tempe* ☎ *480/968–9935*
AROUND ⊕ *www.caseymoores.com*) is a laid-back institution where rockers, hippies, and families come together in a 1910 house rumored to be haunted by ghosts. Enjoy 28 beers on tap and fresh oysters at this Irish pub–style favorite.

Dos Gringos Trailer Park (✉ *1001 E. 8th St., Tempe* ☎ *480/968–7879* ✉ *4209 N. Craftsman Ct., Old Town, Scottsdale* ☎ *480/423–3800* ⊕ *www.dosgringosaz.com*) is a kitschy indoor-outdoor cantina that will remind you of trips over the Mexican border, or at least spring break. Crowds (mostly college students and twentysomethings) swig margaritas and beer in a multilevel courtyard surrounded by TVs and limestone fountains.

The Monastery Too (✉ *4810 E. McKellips, Mesa* ☎ *480/474–4477* ⊕ *www.realfunbar.com*) is a casual beer and wine pub where you grill your own burgers and nosh on picnic food. You can play horseshoes, chess, or volleyball.

BLUES, JAZZ, AND ROCK

Fodor'sChoice **Char's Has the Blues** (✉ *4631 N. 7th Ave., Central Phoenix* ☎ *602/230–*
★ *0205* ⊕ *www.charshastheblues.com*) is one of the Valley's top blues clubs, with nightly bands.

Marquee Theatre (✉ *730 N. Mill Ave., Tempe* ☎ *480/829–0607* ⊕ *www.luckymanonline.com*) hosts mainly headlining rock-and-roll entertainers.

★ **Rhythm Room** (✉ *1019 E. Indian School Rd., Central Phoenix* ☎ *602/265–4842* ⊕ *www.rhythmroom.com*) attracts excellent local and national rock artists, as well as blues, seven nights a week. The perfect sidekick, Rack Shack Blues BBQ, in the parking lot, cooks up good barbecue Wednesday through Saturday evenings.

CASINOS

There are casinos on Indian reservations around the Valley of the Sun. Compared with Las Vegas, they offer smaller venues and a low-key atmosphere. The casinos follow Arizona gaming law, such as no betting cash—chips only.

Casino Arizona at Indian Bend (✉ *9700 E. Indian Bend Rd., North ScottsdaleScottsdale* ☎ *480/850–7777* ⊕ *www.casinoaz.com*) draws locals for blackjack, poker, keno, more than 200 slot machines, and an off-track-betting room that has wide-screen TVs.

Casino Arizona at Salt River (✉ *524 N. 92nd St., Scottsdale* ☎ *480/850–7777; 480/850–7790 for free transportation* ⊕ *www.casinoaz.com*) is the largest casino in the area, with five restaurants, four lounges, a sports bar, a 250-seat theater featuring live performances, two large blackjack rooms, and a keno parlor. There's live music and dancing most nights.

Fort McDowell Casino (✉ *AZ 87 at Fort McDowell Rd., Fountain Hills* ☎ *800/843–3678* ⊕ *www.fortmcdowellcasino.com*) is popular with the resort crowd. In addition to the cards, slot machines, bingo hall, and keno games, off-track greyhound wagering takes place in a classy mahogany room with 18 giant video screens. Take advantage of the free Valley-wide shuttle.

Gila River Casino Wild Horse Pass (✉ *5550 W. Wild Horse Pass, Chandler* ☎ *800/946–4452* ⊕ *www.wingilariver.com*), as part of the Wild Horse Pass Resort & Spa, includes 500 slots, live poker, blackjack, keno, and complimentary soft drinks.

COFFEEHOUSES

Gold Bar Espresso (✉ *3141 S. McClintock Dr., Suite 6, Tempe* ☎ *480/839–3082* ⊕ *www.goldbarespresso.org*) is an inviting coffeehouse decorated with funky antiques. The coffee is first-rate, and there's live jazz on weekends.

★ **Lux Coffee Bar** (✉ *4404 N. Central, Downtown Phoenix* ☎ *602/696–9976* ⊕ *www.luxcoffee.com*), with local art and retro furniture, is an eclectic gathering place where artists, architects, and downtown businesspeople enjoy excellent classic European espresso drinks.

Paisley Violin European Cafe (✉ *1030 N.W. Grand Ave., Downtown Phoenix* ☎ *602/254–7843* ⊕ *www.thepaisley.com*) is an offbeat, beatnik coffeehouse–café with live local music Wednesday through Saturday nights. Nosh on Mediterranean food and sip a cappuccino amid local art and mismatched furniture. This is a good place to start and finish visiting art galleries on First Fridays.

COMEDY

The Comedy Spot (✉ *7117 E. 3rd Ave., Old Town, Scottsdale* ☎ *480/945–4422* ⊕ *www.thecomedyspot.net*) features local and national stand-up talent. They also offer classes for wannabe comedians on Sunday.

The Tempe Improv (✉ *930 E. University Dr., Tempe* ☎ *480/921–9877* ⊕ *www.tempeimprov.com*), part of a national chain, showcases better-known headliners from Thursday to Sunday. Get there early for good seats.

Theater 168 (✉ *7117 E. McDowell Rd., Scottsdale* ☎ *480/423–0120* ⊕ *www.theater168.com*) has clean, family-friendly comedy shows performed by Jester'Z Improvisational Troupe on Thursday, Friday, and Saturday nights at 8 PM.

COUNTRY AND WESTERN

★ **Greasewood Flat** (✉ *27535 N. Alma School Pkwy., North Scottsdale-Scottsdale* ☎ *480/585–9430* ⊕ *www.greasewoodflat.net*) isn't fancy; in fact, it's downright ramshackle, but the burgers are delicious and the crowds friendly. There's a dance floor with live music Thursday through Sunday. In winter, wear jeans and a jacket, since everything is outside; to keep warm, folks congregate around fires burning in halved oil drums.

Handlebar-J (✉ *7116 E. Becker La., Central ScottsdaleScottsdale* ☎ *480/948–0110* ⊕ *www.handlebarj.com*) is a lively restaurant and bar with a Western line-dancing, 10-gallon-hat–wearing crowd.

DANCE CLUBS

★ **Axis/Radius** (✉ *7340 E. Indian Plaza Rd., Central ScottsdaleScottsdale* ☎ *480/970–1112* ⊕ *www.axis-radius.com*) is the dress-to-impress locale where you can party at side-by-side clubs connected by a glass catwalk.

Cherry Lounge & Pit (✉ *411 S. Mill Ave., Tempe* ☎ *480298–1384* ⊕ *www.thecherryloungeaz.com*) is considered by locals to be the best dance club in the Valley. The fact that it is equipped with plenty of patron-accessible dance poles and that free pole-dancing lessons are offered during nonpeak hours probably give it a leg up.

Myst (✉ *7340 E. Shoeman La., Old Town, Scottsdale* ☎ *480/970–5000* ⊕ *www.mystaz.com*) is an ultraswanky dance club where you can sip cocktails in a sunken lounge or hang out at the white-hot Milk Bar adorned with white-leather seating and an all-white bar. Upstairs is the private VIP lounge, complete with skyboxes overlooking the dance floor.

GAY AND LESBIAN BARS

★ **Amsterdam** (✉ *718 N. Central Ave., Downtown Phoenix* ☎ *602/258–6122* ⊕ *www.amsterdambar.com*) attracts a young crowd that wants to see and be seen; it's where Phoenix's beautiful gay people hang out.

B.S. West (✉ *7125 E. 5th Ave., Old Town, Scottsdale* ☎ *480/945–9028* ⊕ *www.bswest.com*) is tucked behind a shopping center on Scottsdale's main shopping drag and draws a stylish, well-heeled crowd.

Cash Inn Country (✉ *2140 E. McDowell Rd., Downtown Phoenix* ☎ *602/244–9943* ⊕ *www.cashinncountry.net*) has an eclectic clientele of women and features music just as diverse, from Latin to country.

Charlie's (✉ *727 W. Camelback Rd., Central Phoenix* ☎ *602/265–0224* ⊕ *www.charliesphoenix.com*), a longtime favorite of local gay men, has a country-western look (cowboy hats are the accessory of choice) and friendly staff.

MICROBREWERIES

★ **Four Peaks Brewing Company** (✉ *1340 E. 8th St., Tempe* ☎ *480/303–9967* ⊕ *www.fourpeaks.com*) is the former redbrick home of Bordens Creamery. Ten different brews are on tap, and pub grub, pizza, and burgers fill the menu.

Rock Bottom Brewery (✉ *8668 E. Shea Blvd., North Scottsdale* ☎ *480/998–7777* ✉ *21001 N. Tatum Blvd., Desert Ridge Mall, North Central Phoenix* ☎ *480/513–9125* ⊕ *www.rockbottom.com*) has beer brewed on the premises and tasty pub grub—start with the giant soft pretzels served with spicy spinach dip. Watch out: the bill tends to rack up quickly.

San Tan Brewing Company (✉ *8 San Marcos Pl., Chandler* ☎ *480/917–8700* ⊕ *www.santanbrewing.com*) combines good food with great beer and an energetic pub atmosphere without the tired, hole-in-the-wall or overly commercial feel. Wash down some raspberry mushrooms and a stuffed burger with a San Tan IPA.

Sonora Brewhouse (✉ *322 E. Camelback Rd., Central Phoenix* ☎ *602/279–8909* ⊕ *www.sonorabrewhouse.com*) is a great hangout with mediocre pub grub and outstanding locally crafted brews like Light Cream Ale, Trooper IPA, and Brewer's Den Hefeweizen, one of the Valley's best.

SPAS

There's no better place for relaxation than at one of Phoenix's rejuvenating resort spas. Many feature Native American–inspired treatments and use indigenous ingredients such as agave and desert clay.

★ **Aji Spa at the Sheraton Wild Horse Pass Resort & Spa**. A gem on the grounds of the Gila River Indian community, Aji incorporates its Native American surroundings into every aspect of the spa, from the name ("Aji" is Pima for sanctuary) to its Sonoran design and treatments. The Bahn or Blue Coyote Wrap ($195–$215 for 80 minutes) begins with a dry-brush exfoliation and an application of Azulene mud, and culminates with a cedar–sage oil massage. For the true local feel, try the Pima Medicine massage, which includes ancient Indian healing techniques. ($145–$165). Massages start at 50 minutes for $125. ✉ *Sheraton Wild Horse Pass Resort & Spa, 5594 W. Wild Horse Pass Blvd., Chandler* ☎ *602/225–0100* ⊕ *www.wildhorsepassresort.com*.

Alvadora at the Royal Palms Resort & Spa. Romance is not limited to the restaurant and rooms here. Alvadora offers treatments that incorporate herbs, flowers, oils, and minerals indigenous to the Mediterranean, like the Royal Body Polish, which sloughs off the old and enhances new, soft skin ($145). The massage menu ranges from a 60-minute classic ($145) to couples' massage sessions ($290–$410) and the controversial Watsu (aqua shiatsu) ($145 for 60 minutes). Spa use for nonresort guests is only Sunday through Thursday, and requires purchase of a spa package. ✉ *5200 E. Camelback Rd., Camelback Corridor* ☎ *602/840–3610 or 800/672–6011* ⊕ *www.royalpalmshotel.com*.

Four Seasons Troon North. The elegant Spa at Four Seasons Troon North is a moderate little bit of heaven hidden in the serene foothills of the Sonoran Desert. The list of massages seems endless, and includes an 80-minute moonlight balcony massage ($220–$370). Body treatments range from $95 to $310. Try the Golfers' Massage in which muscles are kneaded with warmed golf balls ($155–$210). ✉ *10600 E. Crescent Moon Dr., North ScottsdaleScottsdale* ☎ *480/515–5700 or 888/207–9696* ⊕ *www.fourseasons.com/scottsdale*.

Golden Door Spa at the Boulders Resort. If you're seeking the serenity of the desert, this is the place. Influenced by Asian and Native American cultures, the soothing Southwestern spa is divided into two wings—east for relaxation and west for activity, which includes a movement studio for Pilates, tai chi, and yoga. Try a Native American–inspired treatment like the Turquoise Wrap ($215), which includes a Hopi blue-cornmeal body scrub and a turquoise clay wrap; surrender to an Asian-inspired 50-minute shiatsu massage ($225); or take a walk through the Hopi-inspired path-to-tranquillity labyrinth. ⊠ *34631 N. Tom Darlington Dr., Carefree* ☎ *480/488–9009 or 800/553–1717* ⊕ *www.goldendoor.com/boulders.*

★ **Joya Spa at Montelucia Resort.** This new, two-story spa offers a stairway to the heavens. Everything here is meticulously handcrafted, handpicked, or hand-placed to summon the healing spirits. Enjoy the Eastern body hammam experience with any treatment ($45) or the signature 90-minute Joyambrosia using organic moon-kissed oils, citrus, spices, and mint ($165–$245). The amazing Couples' Romance Journey is a 4-hour session that will feel like 24 ($995–$1,195). ⊠ *4949 E. Lincoln Dr., Paradise Valley* ☎ *480/627–3200 or 800/245–2051* ⊕ *www.joyaspa.com.*

Jurlique Spa at FireSky Resort and Spa. With its unforgettably elegant and relaxing interior, Jurlique focuses on repairing and restoring from within by relying on plant science and a combination of Eastern and Western spa philosophies. Try a 90-minute Zen Harmony facial or any 90-minute massage for $170–$190. Spa packages range from 1½ to 6½ hours and cost $140 to $590. The herbal water therapies are heaven "scent," as are the all-natural Jurlique products. ⊠ *4925 N. Scottsdale Rd., Central ScottsdaleScottsdale* ☎ *480/945–7666 or 800/528–7867* ⊕ *www.fireskyresort.com.*

Revive Spa at JW Marriott Desert Ridge Resort. A huge, two-story temple devoted to the health and healing of the human body, Revive at Desert Ridge features 41 luxury treatment rooms, an Olympic-size swimming pool, private balconies for outdoor massages, indoor relaxation rooms with fireplaces, outdoor celestial showers, a healthful bistro, a fitness center, and a full salon. A pumpkin-enzyme peeling mask is just $20; a caviar facial is $195. Massages range from $125 to $190 and body treatments from $130 to $225. ⊠ *5350 E. Marriott Dr., North Central Phoenix* ☎ *480/293–5000 or 800/835–6206* ⊕ *spa.jwdesertridgeresort.com.*

Fodor'sChoice **Sanctuary Spa at Sanctuary Camelback Mountain.** This sleek Zen-like spa
★ has 12 Asian-inspired indoor-outdoor treatment rooms nestled against Camelback Mountain. For a more intimate experience, indulge in the privacy of the couple's suite or the stone-walled Sanctum hideaway. A meditation garden is the perfect place to reflect and relax; for a longer experience consider a four-day Satori Wellness retreat. Try a Watsu in-water body massage ($150–$210), a transporting 30-minute Thai Foot Reflexology massage ($95–$170), or a Bamboo Lemongrass Scrub ($90–$210). A 60-minute massage starts at $150. ⊠ *5700 E. McDonald Dr., Paradise Valley* ☎ *480/948–2100 or 800/245–2051* ⊕ *www.sanctuaryoncamelback.com.*

The Spa at JW Marriott's Camelback Inn. One of the Valley's most popular spas blends Mediterranean and desert themes. Aches and pains will melt away with the 60-minute Native Hot Stone Massage (starts at $135); the Sonoran Rose Facial is two treatments in one, and incorporates the hands and arms ($145). A Thai Table Massage incorporates yoga and compressions to increase energy flow ($140). ✉ *5402 E. Lincoln Dr., Paradise Valley* ☎ *480/948–1700 or 800/242–2635* ⊕ *www.camelbackinn.com.*

Spa Avania at the Hyatt Regency Scottsdale at Gainey Ranch. Spa Avania's claim to fame is that it's "the first complete spa experience choreographed to your body's perfect timing." The gorgeous stone-tiled spa seeks to cleanse the body of unnatural stimuli and give equilibrium through the senses, the way nature intended. Specialty treatments include a 30-minute blackberry-balm hand massage ($80), golfer massage ($165), and couples' massage ($405–$525). Two- to four-hour spa packages range from $289 to $555. ✉ *7500 E. Doubletree Ranch Rd., North ScottsdaleScottsdale* ☎ *480/444–1234 or 800/233–1234* ⊕ *www.scottsdale.hyatt.com.*

VH Spa at the Hotel Valley Ho. After seeing the rebirth of the Hotel Valley Ho, guests should feel comfortable entrusting renovation of the body and soul to the hip, colored-glass VH (Vitality Health) Spa. Get a popular 60-minute poolside cabana massage ($155), or go full spa with the unique Red Flower Hammam Full-Body Treatment Massage, a Turkish-inspired detoxification that scrubs the skin with coffee, olive stones, and fresh lemon ($185), or consult for a better body through Tibetan technique ($250). ✉ *6850 E. Main St., Old TownScottsdale* ☎ *480/248–2000* ⊕ *www.hotelvalleyho.com.*

Willow Stream Spa at the Fairmont Scottsdale Princess. This is one of the Valley's most elaborate spas. Inspired by Havasu Canyon, a hidden oasis in the Grand Canyon, there's water everywhere. A 60-minute massage starts at about $160 or you can splurge for the two-hour Havasupai Body Treatment ($319), under waterfalls of varying pressure. ✉ *Fairmont Scottsdale Princess Resort, 7575 E. Princess Dr., North ScottsdaleScottsdale* ☎ *480/585–4848* ⊕ *www.willowstream.com.*

SIDE TRIPS NEAR PHOENIX

The following sights are within a 1- to 1½-hour drive of Phoenix. To the north, the thriving artist communities of Carefree and Cave Creek are popular Western attractions. Arcosanti and Wickenburg are half- or full-day trips from Phoenix. Stop along the way to visit the petroglyphs of Deer Valley Rock Art Center and the reenactments of Arizona territorial life at the Pioneer Living History Village. You also might consider Lake Pleasant, Arcosanti, and Wickenburg as stopovers on the way to or from Flagstaff, Prescott, or Sedona.

South of Phoenix, an hour's drive takes you back to prehistoric times and the site of Arizona's first known civilization at Casa Grande Ruins National Monument, a vivid reminder of the Hohokam who began farming this area more than 1,500 years ago.

DEER VALLEY ROCK ART CENTER

15 mi north of downtown Phoenix.

GETTING HERE AND AROUND

Take Interstate 17 north from Phoenix for 15 mi, exit at West Deer Valley Road, and drive 2 mi west.

EXPLORING

Deer Valley Rock Art Center has the largest concentration of ancient petroglyphs in the metropolitan Phoenix area. Some 1,500 of the cryptic symbols are here, left behind by Native American cultures that lived in the Valley (or passed through) during the last 1,000 years. After watching a video about the petroglyphs, pick up a pair of binoculars ($1) and an informative trail map and set out on the 0.25-mi path. Telescopes point to some of the most skillful petroglyphs; they range from human and animal forms to more abstract figures. *Also see Petroglyphs CloseUp box in Eastern Arizona.* ⊠ *3711 W. Deer Valley Rd., North Central Phoenix* ☎ *623/582–8007* ⊕ *http://dvrac.asu.edu* ⊠ *$7* ⊙ *May–Sept., Tues.–Sun. 8–2; Oct.–Apr., Tues.–Sat. 9–5, Sun. noon–5.*

PIONEER LIVING HISTORY VILLAGE

25 mi north of downtown Phoenix.

GETTING HERE AND AROUND

Take Interstate 17 north from downtown Phoenix 25 mi. Just north of Carefree Highway (AZ 74), take Exit 225, turn left on Pioneer Road to entrance.

EXPLORING

↻ The **Pioneer Living History Museum** contains 28 original and reconstructed buildings from throughout territorial Arizona. Costumed guides filter through the bank, schoolhouse, and print shop, as well as the Pioneer Opera House, where classic melodramas are performed daily. It's popular with the grade-school field-trip set, and it's your lucky day if you can tag along for their tour of the site—particularly when John the Blacksmith forges, smelts, and answers sixth-graders' questions that adults are too know-it-all to ask. ⊠ *3901 W. Pioneer Rd., Pioneer* ☎ *623/465–1052* ⊕ *www.pioneer-arizona.com* ⊠ *$7* ⊙ *Oct.–May, Wed.–Sun. 9–4; June–Sept., Wed.–Sun. 8–2.*

CAVE CREEK AND CAREFREE

30 mi north of downtown Phoenix.

Some 30 mi north of Phoenix, resting high in the Sonoran Desert at an elevation of 2,500 feet, the towns of Cave Creek and Carefree look back to a lifestyle far different from that of their more populous neighbors to the south.

Cave Creek got its start with the discovery of gold in the region. When the mines and claims "played out," the cattlemen arrived, and the sounds of horse hooves and lowing cattle replaced those of miners' picks. The area grew slowly and independently from Phoenix to the south, until a paved road connected the two in 1952. Today the mile-

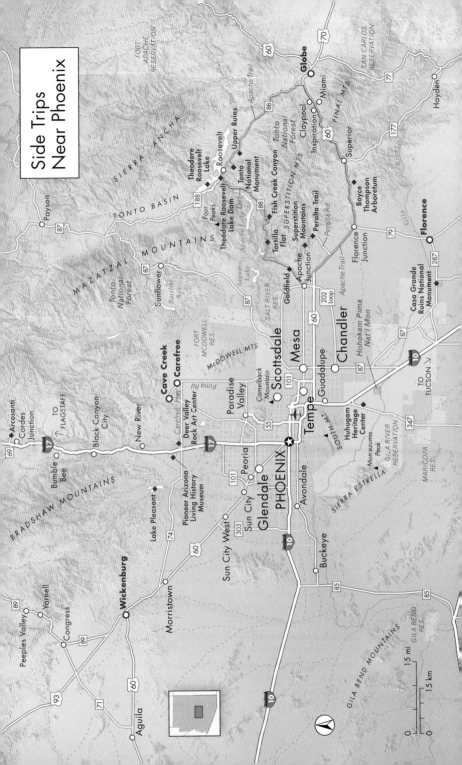

Side Trips
Near Phoenix

long main stretch of town on Cave Creek Road is a great spot to have some hot chili and cold beer, try on Western duds, or learn the two-step in a "cowboy" bar. You're likely to run into folks dressed in cowboy hats, boots, and bold belt buckles. Horseback riders and horse-drawn wagons have the right of way here, and the 25 MPH speed limit is strictly enforced by county deputies. You can amble up the hill and rent a horse for a trip into the Tonto

National Forest in search of some long-forgotten native petroglyphs or take a jeep tour out to the forest.

Just about the time the dirt-road era ended in Cave Creek, planners were sketching out a new community, which became neighboring Carefree. The world's largest sundial, at the town's center, is surrounded by crafts shops, galleries, artists' workshops, and cafés. Today Cave Creek and Carefree sit cheek by jowl—but the former has beans, beef, biscuits, and beer, while the latter discreetly orders up a notch or two.

GETTING HERE AND AROUND

Follow Interstate 17 north of downtown Phoenix for 15 mi. Exit at Carefree Highway (AZ 74) and turn right, then go 12 mi. Turn left onto Cave Creek Road and go 3 mi to downtown Cave Creek, then another 4 mi on Cave Creek Road to Carefree. Pick up maps and information about the area at the Chamber of Commerce.

ESSENTIALS

Visitor Info Carefree–Cave Creek Chamber of Commerce. ⊠ 748 Easy St., No. 9, Carefree ☎ 480/488–3381 ⊕ www.carefreecavecreek.org ☽ Weekdays 8–4.

EXPLORING

Exhibits at the **Cave Creek Museum** depict pioneer living, mining, and ranching. See the last original 1920s tuberculosis cabin and a collection of Indian artifacts from the Hohokam and Yavapai tribes. ⊠ 6140 E. Skyline Dr., Cave Creek ☎ 480/488–2764 ⊕ www.cavecreekmuseum.org ⌑ $3 ☽ Oct.–May, Wed., Thurs., and weekends 1–4:30, Fri. 10–4:30.

☾ Pseudo-Western **Frontier Town** (⊠ 6245 E. Cave Creek Rd., Cave Creek ⊕ www.frontiertownaz.com) has wooden sidewalks, ramshackle buildings, and souvenir shops. **Grab a sandwich and a bottle of Cave Creek Chili Beer—with a real chile pepper in each bottle—at Silver Spur** (⊠ 6245 E. Cave Creek Rd., Cave Creek ☎ 480/488–3317 ⊕ www.silverspoonsaloon.com).

The **Heard Museum North**, a satellite of the big Heard in downtown Phoenix, has one gallery with its own small, permanent collection of Native American art. It also hosts two rotating exhibits during the year. The gift shop is well stocked with expensive, high-quality items. ⊠ 32633 N. Scottsdale Rd., at Carefree Hwy., Scottsdale ☎ 480/488–9817 ⊕ www.heard.org ⌑ $5 ☽ Mon.–Sat. 10–5, Sun. 11–5.

2

Bakery Café at el Pedregal Marketplace (⊠ *34505 N. Scottsdale Rd., at Carefree Hwy., Carefree* ☎ *480/488–4100*), adjacent to the Boulders Resort and not far from the Heard Museum North, is a good place to pick up a breakfast or lunch of fresh-baked goods or to take a shopping break with a sandwich and a cool drink.

SPORTS AND THE OUTDOORS

HORSEBACK
RIDING

Spur Cross Stable (⊠ *44029 Spur Cross Rd., Cave Creek* ☎ *480/488–9117 or 800/758–9530* ⊕ *www.horsebackarizona.com*) has well-cared-for horses that will take you on one- to seven-hour rides to the high Sonoran Desert of the Spur Cross Preserve and the Tonto National Forest. Some rides include visits to petroglyph sites and a saddlebag lunch.

TENNIS AND
GOLF

The **Boulders Resort Golf Club** (⊠ *The Boulders, 34631 N. Tom Darlington Dr., Carefree* ☎ *480/488–9028 or 866/397–6520* ⊕ *www.theboulders. com* ⅃. *North Course: 18 holes. 4900–6811 yds. Par 72. Slope 115–137. South Course: 18 holes. 4716–6726 yds. Par 71. Slope 117–140. Green Fee: $75–$250* ☞ *Facilities: Driving range, putting green, golf carts, rental clubs, pro shop, lessons, restaurant, bar*) has two championship 18-hole, par-72 courses, and eight tennis courts.

WHERE TO EAT

$$$$
AMERICAN

✕**Binkley's Restaurant.** This upscale, casual restaurant is a diamond in the Valley's last bit of rough. In a town of cowboy bars and gut bombs, chef Kevin Binkley makes a world-class impression with tasting menus featuring delicate portions of such dishes as black-truffle whipped potatoes, *loupe de mer* (Seabass) with coconut quinoa and grapefruit hollandaise, and red-wine-poached filet mignon. For something a little more casual and inexpensive, try Café Bink at 36899 North Tom Darlington Drive in Carefree. ⊠ *6920 E. Cave Creek Rd., Cave Creek* ☎ *480/437–1072* ⊕ *www.binkleysrestaurant.com* ▭ *AE, D, DC, MC, V.*

$
CAFÉ

✕**Cave Creek Coffee Company & Wine Bar.** The eating, drinking, and live entertainment are so great here that even Phoenician homebodies have been known to make the out-of-the-way journey. Some of acoustic music's finest artists perform at this peaceful, first-rate venue, which claims to be Arizona's version of Austin City Limits. The eclectic menu offers breakfast burritos, artisanal sandwiches, salads, pizzas, antipasti, and sweets. ⊠ *6033 E. Cave Creek Rd., Cave Creek* ☎ *480/488–0603* ⊕ *www.cavecreekcoffee.com* ▭ *AE, D, DC, MC, V.*

$$
AMERICAN

✕**Horny Toad Restaurant.** The Horny Toad is a rustic spot for barbecued pork ribs and steak, but the real star is the fried chicken. The quirky menu features a range of fare from soup "de joor" to Icelandic cod and carne asada. ⊠ *6738 E. Cave Creek Rd., Cave Creek* ☎ *480/488–9542* ⊕ *www.thehornytoad.com* ▭ *AE, D, DC, MC, V.*

$
AMERICAN

✕**Kashman's Place.** This local duo of Jewish delis came all the way from Brooklyn, and brought a wealth of other influences with it. Nancy and Steve Kashman's sumptuous omelets with crisp home fries, creatively blended salads, and piled-high sandwiches (like the Pennsylvania baked ham and Brie with champagne mustard on baguette) cater to a large following of locals and Fodors.com fans. Everything is deliciously fresh, and portions are generous. New York bagels (including the not-so-traditional multigrain, protein "power" bagel) are done the authentic way—boiled and baked on the premises using filtered water duplicated from New York City water samples. The matzo-ball soup is award-winning. Expect lines on weekends. There's another location at 32531 N. Scottsdale Road. ⊠ *23425 N. Scottsdale Rd., at Ashler Hills,* ☎ *480/488–5274* ⊕ *www.kashmansplace.net* ⊟ *AE, D, DC, MC, V* ☉ *No dinner.*

$$$
AMERICAN

✕ **Tonto Bar & Grill at Rancho Manana**. Old West ambience oozes from every corner of the Tonto Bar & Grill, from the hand-carved ceiling beams to the *latilla* (stick)-covered patios with views of the pristine Sonoran Desert. Try the cowboy Cobb salad or the Tonto burger piled with fried onions and Tillamook cheddar for lunch; lamb chops with leek fondue or grilled grouper with orange-tomato salsa are good choices at dinner. ⊠ *5736 E. Rancho Manana Blvd., Cave Creek* ☎ *480/488–0698* ⊕ *www.tontobarandgrill.com* ⊟ *AE, D, DC, MC, V.*

WHERE TO STAY

$$$
Fodor's Choice
★

🖼 **The Boulders Resort and Golden Door Spa**. One of the country's top resorts—and one of the few with an all-organic approach—hides amid hill-size, 12-million-year-old granite boulders and the lush Sonoran Desert. Casitas snuggled against the rocks have exposed log-beam ceilings and curved, pueblo-style half walls. Each has a patio with a view, a wood-burning fireplace, and a spacious bathroom with deep soaking tub. An upscale mall, el Pedregal Marketplace, adjoins the resort, and there are two golf courses. The Golden Door spa is one of the best in the state. **Pros:** remote desert getaway; also in the center of Cave Creek and Carefree shopping, events, and activities. **Cons:** on-site dining is priced above average; minimum 45-minute drive to Phoenix attractions. ⊠ *34631 N. Tom Darlington Dr., Carefree* ☎ *480/488–9009 or 800/553–1717* ⊕ *www.theboulders.com* 📱 *160 casitas, 60 villas and haciendas* ♿ *In-room: safe, kitchen (some), refrigerator, Internet, Wi-Fi. In-hotel: 5 restaurants, room service, golf courses, tennis courts, pools, gym, spa, parking (free)* ⊟ *AE, D, DC, MC, V.*

$

🖼 **Cave Creek Tumbleweed Hotel**. Innkeepers Gary and Jeri Rust have kept the 1950s flavor of this Western hotel intact. There's a fireplace in the lobby and a quiet pool outside. Red-and-tan rooms have Southwestern and cowboy accents, giving it a perfectly quaint Cave Creek atmosphere. The hotel is a short walk from restaurants and shops in town. **Pros:** a true Old West experience; quite affordable compared to the very pricey area competition. **Cons:** sparse accommodations; far drive from Phoenix and Scottsdale activities. ⊠ *6333 E. Cave Creek Rd., Cave Creek* ☎ *480/488–3668* ⊕ *www.tumbleweedhotel.com* 📱 *32 rooms, 8 casitas* ♿ *In-room: kitchen (some). In-hotel: pool* ⊟ *AE, MC, V.*

SHOPPING

Cave Creek and Carefree have a thriving arts community, with hundreds of artists and dozens of galleries. **El Pedregal** (⊠ *34505 N. Scottsdale Rd., at Carefree Hwy., Carefree* ☎ *480/488–1072*) is a two-tier shopping plaza at the foot of a 250-foot boulder formation. In spring and summer there are open-air Thursday-night concerts in the courtyard amphitheater. In addition to its posh boutiques and specialty stores, el Pedregal is home to some of the finest art galleries in the area. **Spanish Village**

The Boulders Resort and Golden Door Spa

Rancho de los Caballeros

(⊠ *7208 E. Ho Rd., Ho and Hum Rds., Carefree* ☎ *480/488–0350*) is an outdoor shopping area complete with bell tower, fountains, courtyards, and winding alleyways. You can while away an afternoon browsing 30 shops, then contemplate dinner at one of several casual restaurants.

NIGHTLIFE

Watch real cowboys and cowgirls two-step to live music at **Buffalo Chip Saloon** (⊠ *6811 E. Cave Creek Rd., Cave Creek* ☎ *480/488–9118* ⊕ *www.buffalochipsaloon.com*), where you can also gorge on mesquite-grilled chicken and buffalo chips—hot, homemade potato chips. Reservations are suggested for the all-you-can-eat Friday-night fish fry that draws crowds. There's live music and dancing Thursday through Saturday. At **Silver Spur Saloon** (⊠ *6245 E. Cave Creek Rd., Cave Creek* ☎ *480/488–3317*) you can enjoy live music on weekends. **Harold's Cave Creek Corral** (⊠ *6895 E. Cave Creek Rd., Cave Creek* ☎ *480/488–1906* ⊕ *www.haroldscorral.com*) is just across the dirt parking lot from the Buffalo Chip Saloon. Harold's has two full bars, a huge dance floor with live bands on weekends, a game room, 15 TVs, and a restaurant—serving some of the best ribs in the Valley.

WICKENBURG

70 mi northwest of downtown Phoenix.

This town, land of guest ranches and tall tales, is named for Henry Wickenburg, whose nearby Vulture Mine was the richest gold strike in the Arizona Territory. In the late 1800s Wickenburg was a booming mining town on the banks of the Hassayampa River, with a seemingly endless supply of gold, copper, and silver. Nowadays Wickenburg's Old West history attracts visitors to its sleepy downtown and Western museum. There's a group of good antiques shops, most of which are on Tegner and Frontier streets.

GETTING HERE AND AROUND

Follow Interstate 17 north from Phoenix for about 15 mi to the Carefree Highway (AZ 74) junction. About 30 mi west on AZ 74, take U.S. 89/93 north and go another 10 mi to Wickenburg.

Maps for self-guided walking tours of the town's historic buildings are available at the Wickenburg Chamber of Commerce, in the town's old Santa Fe Depot.

ESSENTIALS

Visitor Info Wickenburg Chamber of Commerce (⊠ *216 N. Frontier St.* ☎ *928/684–5479 or 800/942–5242* ⊕ *www.wickenburgchamber.com*)

EXPLORING

On the northeast corner of Wickenburg Way and Tegner Street, check out the **Jail Tree**, to which prisoners were chained, the desert heat sometimes finishing them off before their sentences were served.

☼ The **Desert Caballeros Western Museum** has one of the best collections of Western art in the nation, with paintings and sculpture by Remington, Bierstadt, Joe Beeler (founder of the Cowboy Artists of America), and others. Kids enjoy the re-creation of a turn-of-the-20th-century Main

Street that includes a general store, period clothing, and a large collection of cowboy gear. ✉ *21 N. Frontier St.* ☎ *928/684–2272* 🌐 *www.westernmuseum.org* 🎟 *$7.50* ⏲ *Mon.–Sat. 10–5, Sun. noon–4.*

2

The self-guided trails of **Hassayampa River Preserve** wind through lush cottonwood-willow forests, mesquite trees, and around a 4-acre, spring-fed pond and marsh habitat. Waterfowl, herons, and Arizona's rarest raptors shelter here. ✉ *3 mi southeast of Wickenburg on U.S. 60* ☎ *928/684–2772* 🎟 *$5* ⏲ *Mid-Sept.–mid-May, Wed.–Sun. 8–5; summer hrs vary depending on fire danger and weather. Call to confirm.*

Robson's Mining World is a replica of a 19th-century mining town that has the world's largest collection of antique mining equipment, the Nellie Meda gold mine, more than 30 buildings, a restaurant, a saloon, and a general store. Visitors can stay at the old mining hotel, which has 26 simple rooms. Attractions include hanging out in town, panning for gold, or hiking in the desert or the nearby Harcuvar Mountains. The restaurant serves juicy prime rib and a miners' pie filled with meat, potatoes, and vegetables and baked in pastry. ✉ *Milepost 90, 29 mi west of Wickenburg on U.S. 60 to AZ 71, Box 3465, Wickenburg* ☎ *928/415–0983* 🌐 *www.robsonsminingworld.com* ⏲ *Call for reservations.*

The **Vulture Mine** was once the largest producing gold mine in Arizona, though its vein has long since run out. A small town originally grew up around the mine, but the only things left today are a few storage buildings and a home where caretakers live. The self-guided tour through this "ghost town" wanders past mining memorabilia; old buildings including bunkhouses, the jail, and a blacksmith shop; the mine shaft itself; and the infamous hanging tree, where more than a dozen ore thieves (high graders) were hanged. **■ TIP→ Vulture Mine offers no protective safeguards for its aged buildings, shafts, and equipment. Wander at your own risk and keep an eye on children.** Head west from Wickenburg on U.S. 60 for about 6 mi, then turn left onto Vulture Mine Road and travel 12 mi to the mine at the end of the pavement. ✉ *Vulture Mine Rd., Vulture Mine* ☎ *602/859–2743* 🎟 *$10* ⏲ *Sept.–Apr., daily 8–4.*

WHERE TO EAT AND STAY

$ MEXICAN ✕ **Anita's Cocina.** Reliable Tex-Mex fare is served at Anita's. The fresh tamales are tasty for lunch or dinner. And if you're not in the mood for Mexican, fret not; Anita's also has pizza. Try a fruit burrito for dessert. ✉ *57 N. Valentine St.* ☎ *928/684–5777* 🌐 *www.anitascorp.com* 💳 *MC, V.*

$$$$ 🏨 **Kay El Bar Ranch.** On the National Register of Historic Places, this remote guest ranch is personable and low-key. Some of the biggest mesquite trees in Arizona shade the lodge, a family cottage with private patio (built in 1914), two separate casitas, and a charming adobe cookhouse. In the evening everyone gathers in the living room by the stone fireplace for cocktails and homemade hors d'oeuvres. **Pros:** one of the few remaining true Arizona dude ranch experiences; price includes meals and horseback riding. **Cons:** only open six months out of the year. ✉ *37500 S. Rincon Rd.* 📫 *Box 2480, 85358* ☎ *928/684–7593 or 800/684–7583* 🌐 *www.kayelbar.com* 🛏 *8 rooms, 1 house, 2 casitas* 👍 *In-room: no phone, no TV. In-hotel: restaurant, pool* 💳 *MC, V* ⏲ *Closed May–mid-Oct.* 🍽 *FAP.*

$$$$ 🖼 **Rancho de los Caballeros.** This 20,000-acre property combines the guest-
🕘   ranch experience with first-class amenities. Meals are served in the lodge's
Fodor's Choice   bright, festive dining room, and everyone is asked to dress for each night's
★   sit-down dinner. Rooms are spacious and done in low-key Southwestern
style. Some contain two queen-size beds and can be creatively configured
through a system of adjoining doors to annex separate living rooms or
sleeping quarters for children. Activities ranging from skeet shooting to
horseback riding are available. The Los Caballeros Golf Club course is
considered one of the country's top resort courses. **Pros:** large rooms,
casitas, and suites; abundant activity roster; a great place for family gath-
erings. **Cons:** remote location; long hikes to rooms. ✉ *1551 S. Vulture
Mine Rd.* 🕾 *928/684–5484 or 800/684–5030* ⊕ *www.sunc.com* ↘ *79
rooms* ♿ *In-room: Internet. In-hotel: restaurant, bar, golf course, tennis
courts, pool, spa, bicycles, children's programs (ages 5–12), Wi-Fi hotspot*
⊟ *MC, V* ☽ *Closed mid-May–early Oct.* ⏉ *BP.*

NIGHTLIFE

The **Rancher Bar** (✉ *910 W. Wickenburg Way* 🕾 *928/684–5957*) is a
modern-day saloon where real live wranglers and cowboys meet up to
shoot some pool, and the breeze, after a hard day's work.

ARCOSANTI

65 mi north of downtown Phoenix.

GETTING HERE AND AROUND

From Phoenix, take Interstate 17 north 65 mi to Exit 262 (Condes Junction). Follow the partly paved road 2.5 mi northeast to the community.

EXPLORING

The evolving complex and community of **Arcosanti** was masterminded
by Italian architect Paolo Soleri to be a self-sustaining habitat in which
architecture and ecology function in symbiosis. Building began in 1970,
but Arcosanti is a bit tired-looking these days and hasn't quite achieved
Soleri's original vision. It's still worth a stop to take a tour, have a bite
at the café, and purchase one of the hand-cast bronze wind-bells made
at the site. 🕾 *928/632–7135* ⊕ *www.arcosanti.org* 🎫 *Tour $10* ☽ *Daily
9–5; tours hourly 10–4.*

CASA GRANDE RUINS NATIONAL MONUMENT

36 mi southeast of downtown Phoenix.

GETTING HERE AND AROUND

Take U.S. 60 east (Superstition Freeway) to Florence Junction (U.S. 60
and AZ 89), and head south 16 mi on AZ 89 to Florence. Casa Grande is
9 mi west of Florence on AZ 287 or, from Interstate 10, 16 mi east on AZ
387 and AZ 87. Note: follow signs to ruins, not to town of Casa Grande.
When leaving the ruins, take AZ 87 north 35 mi back to U.S. 60.

EXPLORING

The **Casa Grande Ruins National Monument**, whose original purpose still
eludes archaeologists, was unknown to European explorers until Father
Kino, a Jesuit missionary, first recorded the site's existence in 1694. The

area was set aside as federal land in 1892 and named a national monument in 1918. Although only a few prehistoric sites can be viewed, more than 60 are in the monument area, including the 35-foot-tall—that's four stories—Casa Grande (Big House). The tallest Hohokam building known, Casa Grande was built in the early 14th century and is believed by some to have been an ancient astronomical observatory or a center of government, religion, trade, or education. Allow an hour to explore the site, longer if park rangers are giving a talk or leading a tour. On your way out, cross the parking lot by the covered picnic grounds and climb the platform for a view of a ball court and two platform mounds, said to date from the 1100s. ⊠ *1100 W. Ruins Dr., Coolidge* ☎ *520/723–3172* ⊕ *www.nps.gov/cagr* ⊠ *$5* ⊙ *Daily 8–5.*

THE APACHE TRAIL

Fodor's Choice ★ President Theodore Roosevelt called this 150-mi drive "the most awe-inspiring and most sublimely beautiful panorama nature ever created." A stretch of winding highway, the AZ 188 portion of the Apache Trail closely follows the route forged through wilderness in 1906 to move construction supplies for building the Roosevelt Dam, which lies at the northernmost part of the loop.

PLANNING YOUR TIME
Although the drive itself can be completed in one day, it's advisable to spend a night in Globe, continuing the loop back to Phoenix the following day.

GETTING HERE AND AROUND
From the town of Apache Junction you can choose to drive the trail in either direction; there are advantages to both. If you begin the loop going clockwise—heading eastward on AZ 188 to the Superstition Mountains, the Peralta Trail, Boyce Thompson Arboretum, Globe, Tonto National Monument, Theodore Roosevelt Lake Reservoir & Dam, and Tortilla Flat—your drive may be more relaxing; you'll be on the farthest side of this narrow dirt road some refer to as the "white-knuckle route," with its switchbacks and drop-offs straight down into spectacular Fish Creek Canyon. ■TIP➡ This 42-mi section of the drive is not for anyone afraid of heights. But if you follow the route counterclockwise—continuing on U.S. 60 past the town of Apache Junction—you'll be able to appreciate each attraction better.

SUPERSTITION MOUNTAINS

30 mi east of downtown Phoenix.

GETTING HERE AND AROUND
From Phoenix, take Interstate 10 and then U.S. 60 (the Superstition Freeway) east through the suburbs of Tempe, Mesa, and Apache Junction.

EXPLORING
As the Phoenix metro area gives way to cactus- and creosote-dotted desert, the massive escarpment of the **Superstition Mountains** heaves into view and slides by to the north. The Superstitions are supposedly where

the legendary Lost Dutchman Mine is, the location—not to mention the existence—of which has been hotly debated since pioneer days.

ⓒ The best place to learn about the "Dutchman" Jacob Waltz and the Lost Dutchman Mine is at **Superstition Mountain Museum** (⊠ *4087 N. Apache Trail, AZ 188, Junction* ☎ *480/983–4888* ⊕ *www. superstitionmountainmuseum.org* ⊠ *$5* ⊙ *Daily 9–4*). The museum exhibits include a collection of mining tools, historical maps, and artifacts relating to the "gold" age of the Superstition Mountains.

ⓒ Goldfield became an instant city of about 4,000 residents after a gold strike in 1892; the town dried up five years later when the gold mine flooded. Today the **Goldfield Ghost Town** (⊠ *4650 N. Mammoth Mine Rd., 4 mi northeast of Apache Junction on AZ 188, Goldfield* ☎ *480/983–0333* ⊕ *www.goldfieldghosttown.com*) **is an interesting place to grab a cool drink,** pan for gold, go for a mine tour, or take a desert jeep ride or horseback tour of the area. The ghost town's shops are open daily 10–5, the saloon daily 11–9, and gunfights are held hourly noon–4 on weekends.

PERALTA TRAIL

25 mi east of downtown Phoenix.

GETTING HERE AND AROUND

About 11.5 mi southeast of Apache Junction, off U.S. 60, take Peralta Trail Road, just past King's Ranch Road, an 8-mi, rough gravel road that leads to the start of the Peralta Trail.

EXPLORING

The 4-mi round-trip **Peralta Trail** winds 1,400 feet up a small valley for a spectacular view of **Weaver's Needle,** a monolithic rock formation that is one of Arizona's more famous sights. Allow a few hours for this rugged and challenging hike, bring plenty of water, sunscreen, a hat, and a snack or lunch, and don't hike it in the middle of the day in summer.

BOYCE THOMPSON ARBORETUM

60 mi east of downtown Phoenix

GETTING HERE AND AROUND

From Florence Junction, take U.S. 60 east for 12 mi.

EXPLORING

★ At the foot of Picketpost Mountain in Superior, the **Boyce Thompson Arboretum** is often called an oasis in the desert: the arid rocky expanse gives way to lush riparian glades home to 3,200 different desert plants and more than 230 bird and 72 terrestrial species. The arboretum offers a living album of the world's desert and semiarid region plants, including exotic species such as Canary Islands date palms and Australian eucalyptus. Trails offer breathtaking scenery in the gardens and the exhibits, especially during the spring wildflower season. A variety of tours are offered year-round. Benches with built-in misters offer relief from the heat. Bring along a picnic and enjoy the beauty. ⊠ *37615*

U.S. 60, Superior ☎ *520/689–2811* ⊕ *www.ag.arizona.edu/bta* 🖾 *$7.50* ⊙ *May–Aug., daily 6–3; Sept.–Apr., daily 8–4.*

EN
ROUTE
A few miles past the arboretum, **Superior** is the first of several modest mining towns and the launching point for a dramatic winding ascent through the Mescals to a 4,195-foot pass that affords panoramic views of this copper-rich range and its huge, dormant, open-pit mines. Collectors will want to watch for antiques shops, but be forewarned that quality varies considerably. A gradual descent will take you into **Miami** and **Claypool,** once-thriving boomtowns that have carried on quietly since major-corporation mining ground to a halt in the '70s. Working-class buildings are dwarfed by the mountainous piles of copper tailings. At a stoplight in Claypool AZ 188 splits off northward to the Apache Trail, but continue on U.S. 60 another 3 mi to Globe.

GLOBE

90 mi east of downtown Phoenix, 51 mi east of Apache Junction, 25 mi east of Superior, and 3 mi east of Claypool's AZ 188 turnoff.

In the southern reaches of Tonto National Forest, Globe is the most cosmopolitan of the area's mining towns. Initially, it was gold and silver that brought miners here—the city allegedly got its name from a large, circular boulder of silver, with lines like continents, found by prospectors—although the region is now known for North America's richest copper deposits. ■TIP→ If you're driving the Apache Trail loop, stop in Globe to fill up the tank; it's the last chance to gas up until looping all the way back to U.S. 60 at Apache Junction. Globe is worth more than a quick pit stop, though; its charm is its lack of prestige—and, in some cases, modernity.

GETTING HERE AND AROUND

Globe is at the intersection of U.S. 60 and AZ 188. At the Globe Chamber of Commerce, you can pick up brochures detailing the self-guided Historic Downtown Walking Tour.

ESSENTIALS

Visitor Info Globe Chamber of Commerce (✉ *1360 N. Broad St., 1.25 mi north of downtown on U.S. 60* ☎ *928/425–4495 or 800/804–5623* ⊕ *www.globemiamichamber.com*).

EXPLORING

At the **Gila County Historical Museum** (✉ *1330 N. Broad St.* ☎ *928/425–7385* 🖾 *Free* ⊙ *Mon.–Sat. 9–4*), you can see the collection of memorabilia from the area's mining days.

The late-19th-century Gila County Courthouse houses the free **Cobre Valley Center for the Arts** (✉ *101 N. Broad St.* ☎ *928/425–0884* ⊕ *www. cvarts.org* ⊙ *Mon.–Sat. 10–4*) and showcases works by local artists.

For a step 800 years back in time, tour the 2 acres of the excavated Salado Indian site at the **Besh-Ba-Gowah Archaeological Park** on the southeastern side of town. After a trip through the small museum and a video introduction, enter the area full of remnants of more than 200 rooms occupied here by the Salado during the 13th and 14th centuries.

Public areas include the central plaza (also the principal burial ground), roasting pits, and open patios. Besh-Ba-Gowah is a name given by the Apaches, who, arriving in the 17th century, found the pueblo abandoned, and moved in—loosely translated, the name means "metal camp," and remains left on the site point to it as part of an extensive commerce and trading network. ⊠ *150 N. Pine St.* ☎ *928/425–0320 or 800/804–5623* 🗎 *$4* ⊙ *Daily 9–5.*

WHERE TO EAT AND STAY

$

MEXICAN

✕ **Chalo's.** This roadside spot offers top-notch Mexican and Tex-Mex food for a slightly different flavor than your average Mexican plate. Chalo's specialty is using green chiles. Fortunately, you can request mild or spicy versions of green-chile enchiladas, burros, and practically anything else on the menu. Be sure to ask for water. Try the savory stuffed sopaipillas, filled with pork and beef, beans, and red or green chiles. It's a favorite among locals, so plan for an early lunch or dinner to avoid a wait. ⊠ *902 E. Ash St.* ☎ *928/425–0515* ⊕ *www.chalos.com* ⊟ *AE, D, MC, V.*

¢–$

▣ **Noftsger Hill Inn.** Built in 1907, this B&B was originally the North Globe Schoolhouse; now classrooms serve as guest rooms, filled with mining-era antiques and affording fantastic views of the Pinal Mountains and historic Old Dominion Mine. All rooms have private baths; one has air-conditioning, and the rest have evaporative coolers, which work well at this higher elevation. You can walk off "miner-size" breakfasts on the enjoyable hike through the scenic Copper Hills behind the old school. **Pros:** giant windows offer pleasant natural light; many rooms have original classroom chalkboards devoted to guest comments. **Cons:** the spacious, former-schoolhouse rooms aren't exactly cozy. ⊠ *425 North St.* ☎ *928/425–2260 or 877/780–2479* ⊕ *www. noftsgerhillinn.com* 🛏 *6 rooms* ⌂ *In-room: no a/c (some), no TV (some)* ⊟ *MC, V* ⊙ *BP.*

SHOPPING

Broad Street, Globe's main drag, is lined with antiques and gift shops. On Ash, between Hill and South East streets, **Copper City Rock Shop** (⊠ *566 Ash St.* ☎ *928/425–7885*) specializes in mineral products, many from Arizona. **Past Times** (⊠ *150 W. Mesquite* ☎ *928/425–2220*) carries antique furniture and accessories, including vintage glassware and kitchen items. **True Blue Jewelry** (⊠ *200 N. Willow St.* ☎ *888/425–7698* ⊕ *www.truebluejewelry.com*) carries high-quality jewelry made with turquoise supplied by Globe's Sleeping Beauty Mine. Ask to watch the five-minute video about turquoise mining and preparing it for use.

NIGHTLIFE

Run by the San Carlos Apache tribe, **Apache Gold** (⊠ *U.S. 70, 5 mi east of Globe* ☎ *800/272–2438* ⊕ *www.apachegoldcasinoresort.com*) has more than 500 slots, blackjack, keno, bingo, and video and live poker. Call about the free shuttle from most of Globe's hotels and motels. The Apache Grill Restaurant offers gourmet dishes, and the Wickiup Buffet serves authentic Apache and Southwestern cuisine.

CLOSE UP

The Lost Dutchman Mine

Not much is known about Jacob "the Dutchman" Waltz, except that he was born around 1808 in Germany (he was "Deutsch," not "Dutch") and emigrated to the United States, where he spent several years at mining camps in the Southeast, in the West, and finally in Arizona. There's documentation that he did indeed have access to a large quantity of gold, though he never registered a claim for the mine that was attributed to him.

GOLDEN RUMORS

In 1868 Waltz appeared in the newly developing community of Pumpkinville, soon to become Phoenix. He kept to himself on his 160-acre homestead on the bank of the Salt River. From time to time he would disappear for a few weeks and return with enough high-quality ore to keep him in a wonderful fashion. Soon word was out that "Crazy Jake" had a vast gold mine in the Superstition Mountains, east of the city near the Apache Trail.

At the same time, stories about a wealthy gold mine discovered by the Peralta family of Mexico were circulating. Local Apaches raided the mine, which was near their sacred Thunder Mountain. In what became known as the Peralta Massacre, the Peraltas and more than 100 people working for them at the mine were killed. Rumors soon spread that Waltz had saved the life of a young Mexican who was part of Peralta's group—one of few who had escaped—and was shown the Peralta's mine as a reward.

SEARCHING THE SUPERSTITIONS

As the legend of the Dutchman's mine grew, many opportunists attempted to follow Waltz into the Superstition Mountains. A crack marksman, Waltz quickly discouraged several who tried to track him. The flow of gold continued for several years.

In 1891 the Salt River flooded, badly damaging Waltz's home. When the floodwaters receded, neighbors found Waltz there in a weakened condition. He was taken to the nearby home and boardinghouse of Julia Thomas, who nursed the Dutchman for months. When his death was imminent, he reportedly gave Julia the directions to his mine.

Julia and another boarder searched for the mine fruitlessly. In her later years she sold maps to the treasure, based upon her recollections of Waltz's description. Thousands have searched for the lost mine, many losing their lives in the process—either to the brutality of fellow searchers or that of the rugged desert—and more than a century later gold seekers are still trying to connect the pieces of the puzzle.

THE LEGEND TODAY

There's no doubt that the Dutchman had a source of extremely rich gold ore. But was it in the Superstition Mountains, nearby Goldfields, or maybe even in the Four Peaks region? Wherever it was, it's still hidden. Perhaps the best-researched books on the subject are T. E. Glover's *The Lost Dutchman Mine of Jacob Waltz* and the companion book *The Holmes Manuscript*. Ron Feldman of OK Corral (☎ 480/982–4040 ⊕ www.okcorrals. com) in Apache Junction has become an expert on the subject during his 30-plus years in the region. He leads adventurers on pack trips into the mysterious mountains to relive the lore and legends.

Hikers in the Superstition mountains—perhaps searching for the riches of the Lost Dutchman Mine

EN ROUTE At the stoplight 3 mi south of Globe on U.S. 60, AZ 188 splits off to the northwest. About 25 mi later on AZ 188, heading toward the Tonto National Monument, you'll see towering quartzite cliffs about 2 mi away—look up and to the left for the 40-room **Upper Ruins,** 14th-century condos left behind by the Salado people. They can't be seen from within the national monument, so make sure you've got binoculars.

TONTO NATIONAL MONUMENT

30 mi northeast of the intersection of U.S. 60 and AZ 188.

GETTING HERE AND AROUND

Tonto National Monument is located off AZ 188, approximately 25 miles north of U.S. 60. It's about a two-hour drive from the Phoenix area. If you feel like a real journey, take AZ 88, otherwise known as the Apache Trail, to Tonto National Monument. Almost half of the 47-mi trail is gravel, so be prepared for a very long and bumpy ride.

Tonto National Monument has a well-preserved complex of 13th-century Salado cliff dwellings. There's a self-guided walking tour of the Lower Cliff Dwellings, but if you can, take a ranger-led tour of the 40-room Upper Cliff Dwellings, offered on selected mornings from November to April. Tour reservations are required and should be made as far as a month in advance. ⊠ *AZ 188, Roosevelt* ✆ *HC 02, Box 4602, 85545* ☎ *928/467–2241* ⊕ *www.nps.gov/tont* 🖃 *$3* ☉ *Daily 8–5.*

THEODORE ROOSEVELT LAKE RESERVOIR AND DAM

5 mi northwest of Tonto National Monument on AZ 188.

Flanked by the desolate Mazatzal and Sierra Anchas mountain ranges, **Theodore Roosevelt Lake Reservoir & Dam** is an aquatic recreational area—a favorite with bass anglers, water-skiers, and boaters. This is the largest masonry dam on the planet, and the massive bridge is the longest two-lane, single-span, steel-arch bridge in the nation.

EN ROUTE
Past the reservoir, AZ 188 turns west and becomes a meandering dirt road, eventually winding its way back to Apache Junction via the magnificent, bronze-hued volcanic cliff walls of **Fish Creek Canyon**, with views of the sparkling lakes, towering saguaros, and, in the springtime, vast fields of wildflowers.

TORTILLA FLAT

18 mi southwest of Roosevelt Dam, 18 mi northeast of Apache Junction.

Close to the end of the Apache Trail, this old-time restaurant and country store are what is left of an authentic stagecoach stop at **Tortilla Flat**. This is a fun place to stop for a well-earned rest and refreshment—miner- and cowboy-style grub, of course—before heading back the last 18 mi to civilization. Enjoy a hearty bowl of killer chili and some prickly pear cactus ice cream while sitting at the counter on a saddle bar stool.

Grand Canyon National Park

WORD OF MOUTH

"My favorite thing to do at the South Rim is to walk along the rim from Bright Angel Trail to Hopi Point. The beauty of this is you have several places you can pick up the free shuttle. Walking from Mather Point to Bright Angel trailhead is another one to do, too. Great views and plenty of places to take photos!"

—utahtea

WELCOME TO
GRAND CANYON NATIONAL PARK

TOP REASONS
TO GO

★ **Its status:** This is one of those places where you really want to say, "Been there, done that!"

★ **Awesome vistas:** Painted Desert, sandstone canyon walls, pine and fir forests, mesas, plateaus, volcanic features, the Colorado River, streams, and waterfalls make for some jaw-dropping moments.

★ **Year-round adventure:** Outdoor junkies can bike, boat, camp, fish, hike, ride mules, white-water raft, watch birds and wildlife, cross-country ski, and snowshoe.

★ **Continuing education:** Adults and kids can have fun learning, thanks to free park-sponsored nature walks and interpretive programs.

★ **Sky-high and river-low experiences:** Experience the canyon via plane, train, and automobile, as well as helicopter, oar- or motor-boat, bike, mule, or on foot.

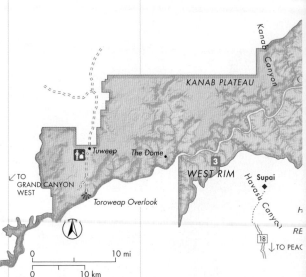

1 South Rim. The South Rim is where the action is: Grand Canyon Village's lodging, camping, eateries, stores, and museums, plus plenty of trailheads into the canyon. Visitor services and facilities are open and available daily, including holidays. Four free shuttle routes cover more than 35 stops, and visitors who'd rather relax than rough it can treat themselves to comfy hotel rooms and elegant restaurant meals (lodging and camping reservations are essential).

2 North Rim. Of the nearly 5 million people who visit the park annually, 90% enter at the South Rim, but many consider the North Rim even more gorgeous—and worth the extra effort. Open only from mid-May to about mid-October (or the first good snowfall), the North Rim has legitimate bragging rights: at more than 8,000 feet above sea level (1,000 feet higher than the South Rim), it has precious solitude and seven developed viewpoints. Rather than staring into the canyon's depths, you get a true sense of its expanse.

3 West Rim and Havasu Canyon. Though not in Grand Canyon National Park, the far-off-the-beaten-path western end of the canyon,

Beavertail cactus in bloom.

3

often called the West Rim, has some spectacular scenery. In Havasu Canyon, on the Havasupai Reservation, you can view some of the most gorgeous waterfalls in the United States. On the Hualapai Reservation, the Skywalk has become a major draw. This U-shape glass-floored deck juts out 3,600 feet above the Colorado River and is not for the faint of heart.

Desert view watchtower was designed by Mary Colter in 1932.

GETTING ORIENTED

Grand Canyon National Park is a superstar—biologically, historically, and recreationally. One of the world's best examples of arid-land erosion, the canyon provides a record of three of the four eras of geological time. Almost 2 billion years worth of Earth's history is written in the colored layers of

rock stacked from the river bottom to the top of the plateau. In addition to its diverse fossil record, the park reveals long-ago traces of human adaptation to an unforgiving environment. It's also home to several major ecosystems, five of the world's seven life zones, three of North America's four desert types, and all kinds of rare, endemic, and protected plant and animal species.

GRAND CANYON NATIONAL PARK PLANNER

When to Go

There's no bad time to visit the canyon, though the busiest times of year are summer and spring break. Visiting during these peak seasons, as well as holidays, requires patience and a tolerance for crowds. Note that weather changes on a whim in this exposed high-desert region. *The North Rim shuts down from mid-October through mid-May due to weather conditions and related road closures.*

AVG. HIGH/LOW TEMPS.

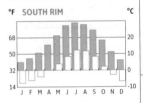

°F SOUTH RIM °C

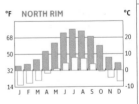

°F NORTH RIM °C

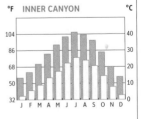

°F INNER CANYON °C

Planning Your Trip

Plan ahead: mule rides require at least a six-month advance reservation, and longer for the busy season (most can be reserved up to 13 months in advance). Multiday rafting trips should be reserved at least a year in advance. For lodgings in the park, reservations are also essential; they're taken up to 13 months in advance. **Xanterra Parks & Resorts** (☎ 888/297–2757 ⊕ www.grandcanyonlodges.com) runs the South Rim park lodging as well as Phantom Ranch, deep inside the canyon. For North Rim reservations, contact **Grand Canyon Lodge** (☎ 877/386–4383 ⊕ www.grandcanyonlodgenorth.com).

Before you go, get the complimentary *Trip Planner,* updated regularly, from the **Grand Canyon National Park** (⊕ www.nps.gov/grca). Once you arrive, pick up the free detailed map and *The Guide,* a newspaper with a schedule of free programs.

The park is most crowded near the east and, especially, the south entrances and in Grand Canyon Village, as well as on the scenic drives, particularly the 23-mi Desert View Drive. ⇨ *See Tips for Avoiding Grand Canyon Crowds.*

Admission Fees and Permits

A fee of $25 per vehicle or $12 per person for pedestrians and cyclists is good for one week's access at both rims.

The $50 Grand Canyon Pass gives unlimited access to the park for 12 months. The annual America the Beautiful **National Parks and Recreational Land Pass** (☎ 888/275–8747 ⊕ store.usgs.gov/pass ✉ $80) provides unlimited access to all national parks and federal recreation areas for 12 months.

No permits are needed for day hikers; but **backcountry permits** (☎ 928/638–7875 or 928/638–2125 ⊕ www.nps.gov/grc ✉ $10, plus $5 per person per night) are necessary for overnight hikers. Permits are limited, so make your reservation as far in advance as possible—they're taken up to four months ahead of arrival. **Camping** in the park is restricted to designated campgrounds (☎ 877/444–6777 ⊕ www.recreation.gov).

Getting Here and Around: South Rim

Air Travel: North Las Vegas Airport in Las Vegas is the primary air hub for charter flights to **Grand Canyon National Parks Airport** (GCN ☎ 928/638–2446).

Car Travel: The best route into the park from the east or south is from Flagstaff. Take U.S. 180 northwest to the park's southern entrance and Grand Canyon Village. An excellent alternative if you'd rather forgo bringing a car to the South Rim is to take the Grand Canyon Railway from Williams. From the west on Interstate 40, the most direct route to the South Rim is on U.S. 180 and Highway 64.

Park Shuttle Travel: The South Rim is open to car traffic year-round, though access to Hermits Rest is limited to shuttle buses part of the year. There are four free shuttle routes: **The Hermits Rest Route** operates March through November, between Grand Canyon Village and Hermits Rest. **The Village Route** operates year-round in the village area near the Grand Canyon Visitor Center. **The Kaibab Trail Route** goes from the visitor center to Yaki Point, including a stop at the South Kaibab Trailhead. **The Tusayan Route** operates summer only and runs from Grand Canyon Visitor Center to the town Tusayan.
■TIP➔ In summer, South Rim roads are congested, and it's easier, and sometimes required, to park your car and take the free shuttle. Running from one hour before sunrise until one hour after sunset, shuttles arrive every 15 to 30 minutes at 30 clearly marked stops.

Shuttle Travel: Xanterra (☎ 928/638–2822) offers 24-hour taxi service in Tusayan and the South Rim. **Arizona Shuttle** (☎ 928/226–8060 or 877/226–8060 ⊕ www.arizonashuttle.com) has service from Phoenix to Flagstaff and Grand Canyon Village. **Open Road Tours** (☎ 928/226–8060 or 877/226–8060 ⊕ www.openroadtours.com) will transport you from Flagstaff and Williams to Tusayan and Grand Canyon Village.

Getting Here and Around: North Rim

Park services on the more remote North Rim shut down in winter and following the first major snowfall (usually around mid-November); Highway 67 south of Jacob Lake is closed. The nearest airport to the North Rim is **St. George Municipal Airport** (☎ 435/634–5822 ⊕ www.sgcity.org/airport) in Utah, 164 mi north, with regular service provided by both Delta and United Airlines.

From mid-May to mid-October, the **Trans Canyon Shuttle** (☎ 928/638–2820 ⊕ www.trans-canyonshuttle.com) travels daily between the South and North rims—the ride takes 4½ hours each way. One-way fare is $80, round-trip $150. Reservations are required.

What Time Is It?

The park is in the mountain standard time zone year-round. Daylight savings time is not observed.

Updated
by Andrew
Collins

When it comes to the Grand Canyon, there are statistics, and there are sensations. While the former are impressive—the canyon measures in at an average width of 10 mi, length of 277 river mi, and depth of 1 mi—they don't truly prepare you for that first impression. Seeing the canyon for the first time is an astounding experience—one that's hard to wrap your head around. In fact, it's more than an experience, it's an emotion, one that is only just beginning to be captured with the superlative "Grand."

Roughly 5 million visitors come to the park each year. They can access the canyon via two main points: the South Rim and the North Rim. The width from the North Rim to the South Rim varies from 600 feet to 18 mi, but traveling between rims by road requires a 215-mi drive. Hiking arduous trails from rim to rim is a steep and strenuous trek of at least 21 mi, but it's well worth the effort. You'll travel through five of North America's seven life zones. (To do this any other way, you'd have to journey from the Mexican desert to the Canadian woods.) In total, more than 600 mi of mostly very primitive trails traverse the canyon, with about 51 of those miles maintained. West of Grand Canyon National Park, the tribal lands of the Hualapai and the Havasupai lie along the so-called West Rim of the canyon.

GRAND CANYON SOUTH RIM

Visitors to the canyon converge mostly on the South Rim, and mostly in summer. Grand Canyon Village is here, with most of the park's lodging and camping, trailheads, restaurants, stores, and museums, along with a nearby airport and railroad depot. Believe it or not, the average stay in the park is a mere half day or so; this is not advised! You need to spend several days to truly appreciate this marvelous place, but at the very least, give it a full day. Hike down into the canyon, or along the rim, to get away from the crowds and experience nature at its finest.

SCENIC DRIVES

Desert View Drive. This heavily traveled 23-mi stretch of road follows the rim from the East entrance to the Grand Canyon Village. Starting from the less-congested entry near Desert View, road warriors can get their first glimpse of the canyon from the 70-foot-tall watchtower, the top of which provides the highest viewpoint on the South Rim. Eight overlooks, the remains of an Ancestral Puebloan dwelling at the Tusayan Ruin and Museum, and the secluded and lovely Buggeln picnic area make for great stops along the South Rim. The Kaibab Trail Route shuttle bus travels a short section of Desert View Drive and takes 30 minutes to ride round-trip without getting off at any of the three stops: South Kaibab Trailhead, Yaki Point, and Pipe Creek Vista.

Hermit Road. The Santa Fe Company built Hermit Road, formerly known as West Rim Drive, in 1912 as a scenic tour route. Nine overlooks dot this 7-mi stretch, each worth a visit. The road is filled with hairpin turns, so make sure you adhere to posted speed limits. A 1.5-mi Greenway trail offers easy access to cyclists looking to enjoy the original 1912 Hermit Rim Road. From March through November, Hermit Road is closed to private auto traffic because of congestion; during this period, a free shuttle bus carries visitors to all the overlooks. Riding the bus round-trip without getting off at any of the viewpoints takes 75 minutes; the return trip stops only at Pima, Mohave, and Powell points.

EXPLORING

HISTORIC SITES

Kolb Studio. Built over several years beginning in 1904 by the Kolb brothers as a photographic workshop and residence, this building provides a view of Indian Garden, where, in the days before a pipeline was installed, Emery Kolb descended 3,000 feet each day to get the water he needed to develop his prints. Kolb was doing something right; he operated the studio until he died in 1976 at age 95. The gallery here has changing exhibitions of paintings, photography, and crafts. There's also a bookstore. During the winter months, a ranger-led tour of the studio illustrates the role the Kolb brothers had on the development of the Grand Canyon. Call ahead to sign up for the tour. ⊠ *Grand Canyon Village near Bright Angel Lodge* ☎ *928/638–2771* ☎ *Free* ☉ *Mid-May–mid-Oct., daily 8–7; mid-Oct.–mid-May, daily 8–5.*

Lookout Studio. Built in 1914 to compete with the Kolbs' photographic studio, the building was designed by architect Mary Jane Colter. The combination lookout point and gift shop has a collection of fossils and geologic samples from around the world. An upstairs loft provides another excellent overlook into the gorge below. ⊠ *About 0.25 mi west of Hermit Rd. Junction on Hermit Rd.* ☎ *Free* ☉ *Daily 9–5.*

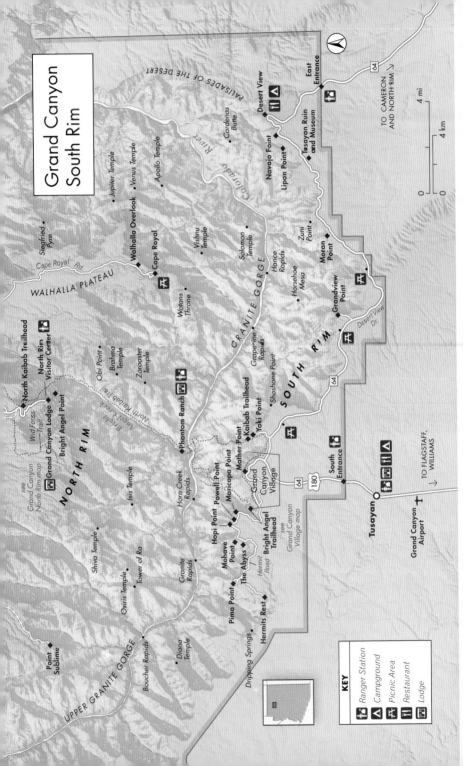

Grand Canyon South Rim

PALISADES OF THE DESERT

Colorado River

GRANITE GORGE

UPPER GRANITE GORGE

WALHALLA PLATEAU

Cape Royal Rd.

NORTH RIM

SOUTH RIM

Temples and Buttes:
Siegfried Pyre
Jupiter Temple
Venus Temple
Apollo Temple
Cardenas Butte
Vishnu Temple
Solomon Temple
Zuni Point
Obi Point
Brahma Temple
Zoroaster Temple
Isis Temple
Shiva Temple
Osiris Temple
Tower of Ra
Diana Temple
Dripping Springs
Wotans Throne

Points and Locations:
Point Sublime
Walhalla Overlook
Cape Royal
North Kaibab Trailhead
North Rim Visitor Center
Grand Canyon Lodge
Bright Angel Point
Phantom Ranch
Wid Forss
Horn Creek Rapids
Hopi Point
Powell Point
Maricopa Point
Mohave Point
The Abyss
Pima Point
Hermits Rest
Granite Rapids
Boucher Rapids
Grape Creek Rapids
Mather Point
Kaibab Trailhead
Yaki Point
Shoshone Point
Grandview Point
Grapevine Rapids
Horseshoe Mesa
Moran Point
Hance Rapids
Lipan Point
Navajo Point
Desert View
East Entrance
Tusayan Ruin and Museum
Canyon Village
Bright Angel Trailhead
South Entrance
Tusayan
Grand Canyon Airport

North Kaibab Trail
Bright Angel Trail
Hermit Road
Desert View Dr.

see Grand Canyon North Rim map

see Grand Canyon Village map

Roads: 64, 180

TO CAMERON AND NORTH RIM →

TO FLAGSTAFF, WILLIAMS →

0   4 mi
0   4 km

KEY

- Ranger Station
- Campground
- Picnic Area
- Restaurant
- Lodge

BEST GRAND CANYON VIEWS

The best time of day to see the canyon is before 10 AM and after 4 PM, when the angle of the sun brings out the colors of the rock, and clouds and shadows add dimension. Colors deepen dramatically among the contrasting layers of the canyon walls just before and during sunrise and sunset.

Hopi Point is the top spot on the South Rim to watch the sun set; Yaki and **Pima** points also offer vivid views. For a grand sunrise, try **Mather** or Yaki points.

■TIP➜ Arrive at least 30 minutes early for sunrise views and as much as 90 minutes for sunset views at these points. For another point of view, take a leisurely stroll along the Rim Trail and watch the color change along with the views. Timetables are listed in *The Guide* and are posted at park visitor centers.

Powell Memorial. A granite platform honors the memory of John Wesley Powell, who measured, charted, and named many of the canyons and creeks of the Colorado River. It was here that the dedication ceremony for Grand Canyon National Park took place on April 3, 1920. ⊠ *About 3 mi west of Hermit Rd. Junction on Hermit Rd.*

Tusayan Ruin and Museum. Completed in 1932, the museum offers a quick orientation to the lifestyles of the prehistoric and modern Indian populations associated with the Grand Canyon and the Colorado Plateau. Adjacent, an excavation of an 800-year-old dwelling gives a glimpse at the lives of some of the area's earliest residents. ⊠ *About 20 mi east of Grand Canyon Village on Desert View Dr.* ☎ 928/638–7968 ➩ *Free* ☽ *Daily 9–5.*

SCENIC STOPS

The Abyss. At an elevation of 6,720 feet, the Abyss is one of the most awesome stops on Hermit Road, revealing a sheer drop of 3,000 feet to the Tonto Platform, a wide terrace of Tapeats sandstone about two-thirds of the way down the canyon. From the Abyss you'll also see several isolated sandstone columns, the largest of which is called the Monument. ⊠ *About 5 mi west of Hermit Rd. Junction on Hermit Rd.*

★ **Desert View and Watchtower.** From the top of the 70-foot stone-and-mortar watchtower, even the muted hues of the distant Painted Desert to the east and the Vermilion Cliffs rising from a high plateau near the Utah border are visible. In the chasm below, angling to the north toward Marble Canyon, an imposing stretch of the Colorado River reveals itself. Up several flights of stairs, the watchtower houses a glass-enclosed observatory with powerful telescopes. ⊠ *About 23 mi east of Grand Canyon Village on Desert View Dr.* ☎ 928/638–2736 ☽ *Daily 8–8; hrs vary in winter.*

Grandview Point. At an elevation of 7,399 feet, the view from here is one of the finest in the canyon. To the northeast is a group of dominant buttes, including Krishna Shrine, Vishnu Temple, Rama Shrine, and Sheba Temple. A short stretch of the Colorado River is also visible. Directly below the point, and accessible by the steep and rugged Grandview Trail, is Horseshoe Mesa, where you can see remnants of Last

Chance Copper Mine. ⊠ *About 12 mi east of Grand Canyon Village on Desert View Dr.*

★ **Hermits Rest.** This westernmost viewpoint and Hermit Trail, which descends from it, were named for "hermit" Louis Boucher, a 19th-century French-Canadian prospector who had a number of mining claims and a roughly built home down in the canyon. Views from here include Hermit Rapids and the towering cliffs of the Supai and Redwall formations. In the stone building at Hermits Rest you can buy curios and snacks. ⊠ *About 8 mi west of Hermit Rd. Junction on Hermit Rd.*

★ **Hopi Point.** From this elevation of 6,800 feet, you can see a large section of the Colorado River; although it appears as a thin line, the river is nearly 350 feet wide below this overlook. The overlook extends farther into the canyon than any other point on Hermit Road. The unobstructed views make this a popular place to watch the sunset. Across the canyon to the north is Shiva Temple, which remained an unexplored section of the Kaibab Plateau until 1937. That year, Harold Anthony of the American Museum of Natural History led an expedition to the rock formation in the belief that it supported life that had been cut off from the rest of the canyon. Imagine the expedition members' surprise when they found an empty Kodak film box on top of the temple—it had been left behind by Emery Kolb, who felt slighted for not having been invited to partake of Anthony's tour. Directly below Hopi Point lies Dana Butte, named for a prominent 19th-century geologist. In 1919, an entrepreneur proposed connecting Hopi Point, Dana Butte, and the Tower of Set across the river with an aerial tramway, a technically feasible plan that fortunately has not been realized. ⊠ *About 4 mi west of Hermit Rd. Junction on Hermit Rd.*

Lipan Point. Here, at the canyon's widest point, you can get an astonishing visual profile of the gorge's geologic history, with a view of every eroded layer of the canyon—you can also observe one of the longest stretches of visible Colorado River. The spacious panorama stretches to the Vermilion Cliffs on the northeastern horizon and features a multitude of imaginatively named spires, buttes, and temples—intriguing rock formations named after their resemblance to ancient pyramids. You can also see Unkar Delta, where a creek joins the Colorado to form powerful rapids and a broad beach. Ancestral Puebloan farmers worked the Unkar Delta for hundreds of years, growing corn, beans, and melons. ⊠ *About 25 mi east of Grand Canyon Village on Desert View Dr.*

Maricopa Point. This site merits a stop not only for the arresting scenery, which includes the Colorado River below, but also for its view of a defunct mine operation. On your left, as you face the canyon, are the Orphan Mine, a mine shaft, and cable lines leading up to the rim. The

DID YOU KNOW?

From the Grand Canyon's edge, the Colorado River is up to 1 mi deep. Almost 40 exposed bands of rocks represent different geological periods—the oldest sections date back some 2 billion years.

GRAND CANYON, GREAT ITINERARIES

GRAND CANYON IN 1 DAY

Start early, pack a picnic lunch, and drive to **Grand Canyon Visitor Center** just north of the south entrance, to pick up info and see your first incredible view at **Mather Point**. Continue east along **Desert View Drive** for about 2 mi to **Yaki Point**. Next, continue driving 7 mi east to **Grandview Point** for a good view of the buttes Krishna Shrine and Vishnu Temple. Go 4 mi east and catch the view at **Moran Point**, then 3 mi to the **Tusayan Ruin and Museum**, where a small display is devoted to the history of the Ancestral Puebloans. Continue another mile east to **Lipan Point** to view the Colorado River. In less than a mile, you'll arrive at **Navajo Point**, the highest elevation on the South Rim. **Desert View and Watchtower** is the final attraction along Desert View Drive.

On your return drive, stop off at any of the picnic areas for lunch. Once back at Grand Canyon Village, walk the paved **Rim Trail** to **Maricopa Point**. Along the way, pick up souvenirs in the village and stop at historic **El Tovar Hotel** for dinner (be sure to make reservations well in advance). If you have time, take the shuttle on **Hermit Road** to **Hermits Rest**, 7 mi away. Along that route, Hopi Point and Powell Point are excellent spots to watch the sunset.

GRAND CANYON IN 3 DAYS

On Day 1, follow the one-day itinerary for the morning, but spend more time exploring Desert View Drive and enjoy a leisurely picnic lunch. Later, drive 30 mi beyond Desert View to Cameron Trading Post, which has a good restaurant and is an interesting side trip. Travel Hermit Road on your second morning, and drive to Grand Canyon Airport for a late-morning small plane or helicopter tour. Have lunch in **Tusayan** and cool off at the IMAX film *Grand Canyon: Discovery & Adventure*. Back in the village, take a free ranger-led program. On your third day, hike partway down the canyon on **Bright Angel Trail**. It takes twice as long to hike back up, so plan accordingly. Get trail maps at **Grand Canyon Visitor Center**, and bring plenty of water.

Alternatively, spend days 2 and 3 exploring the remote **West Rim**, 150 mi towards Nevada or California and far away from major highways. Fill the first day with a Hummer tour along the rim, a helicopter ride into the canyon, or a pontoon boat ride on the Colorado River. The next day, raft the Class V and VI rapids or get a tribal permit and hike 8 mi into **Havasu Canyon** to the small village of Supai and the Havasupai Lodge.

GRAND CANYON IN 5 DAYS

Between mid-May and mid-October, you can visit the North Rim as well as the South. Follow the three-day South Rim itinerary and, early on your fourth day, start the long but rewarding drive to the North Rim. The most popular short trails here are **Transept Trail**, which starts near the Grand Canyon Lodge, and **Cliff Springs Trail**, which starts near **Cape Royal**. Before leaving the area, drive Cape Royal Road 11 mi to **Point Imperial**—at 8,803 feet, it's the highest vista on either rim. A visit to the North Rim can also work well with a three-day trip, especially if you are headed north toward Zion or Bryce national parks in southern Utah.

mine, which started operations in 1893, was worked first for copper and then for uranium until the venture came to a halt in 1969—little remains of the mine infrastructure today, but some displays along the Rim Trail discuss its history. The Battleship, the red butte directly ahead of you in the canyon, was named during the Spanish-American War, when warships were in the news. ⊠ *About 2 mi west of Hermit Rd. Junction on Hermit Rd.*

★ **Mather Point.** You'll likely get your first glimpse of the canyon from this viewpoint, one of the most impressive and accessible (and most crowded) on the South Rim. Named for the National Park Service's first director, Stephen Mather, this spot yields extraordinary views of the Grand Canyon, including deep into the inner gorge and numerous buttes: Wotans Throne, Brahma Temple, and Zoroaster Temple, among others. The Grand Canyon Lodge, on the North Rim, is almost directly north from Mather Point and only 10 mi away—yet you have to drive 215 mi to get from one spot to the other. ⊠ *Near Grand Canyon Visitor Center.*

Mohave Point. Some of the canyon's most magnificent stone spires and buttes visible from this lesser-known overlook include the Tower of Set; the Tower of Ra; and Isis, Osiris, and Horus temples. From here you can view the 5,401-foot Cheops Pyramid, a grayish rock formation behind Dana Butte, plus some of the strongest rapids on the Colorado River. The Granite and Salt Creek rapids are navigable, but not without plenty of effort. ⊠ *About 5 mi west of Hermit Rd. Junction on Hermit Rd.*

Moran Point. This point was named for American landscape artist Thomas Moran, who was especially fond of the play of light and shadows from this location. He first visited the canyon with John Wesley Powell in 1873. "Thomas Moran's name, more than any other, with the possible exception of Major Powell's, is to be associated with the Grand Canyon," wrote noted canyon photographer Ellsworth Kolb. It's fitting that Moran Point is a favorite spot of photographers and painters. ⊠ *About 17 mi east of Grand Canyon Village on Desert View Dr.*

Navajo Point. A possible site of the first Spanish view into the canyon in 1540, this overlook is also at the highest natural elevation (7,461 feet) on the South Rim. ⊠ *About 21 mi east of Grand Canyon Village on Desert View Dr.*

Pima Point. Enjoy a bird's-eye view of Tonto Platform and Tonto Trail, which winds its way through the canyon for more than 70 mi. Also to the west, two dark, cone-shape mountains—Mount Trumbull and Mount Logan—are visible on the North Rim on clear days. They rise in stark contrast to the surrounding flat-top mesas and buttes. ⊠ *About 7 mi west of Hermit Rd. Junction on Hermit Rd.*

Trailview Overlook. Look down on a dramatic view of the Bright Angel and Plateau Point trails as they zigzag down the canyon. In the deep gorge to the north flows Bright Angel Creek, one of the region's few permanent tributary streams of the Colorado River. Toward the south is an unobstructed view of the distant San Francisco Peaks, as well as Bill Williams Mountain (on the horizon) and Red Butte (about 15 mi

CLOSE UP

Tips for Avoiding Grand Canyon Crowds

It's hard to commune with nature while you're searching for a parking place, dodging video cameras, and stepping away from strollers. However, this scenario is likely only during the peak summer months. One option is to bypass Grand Canyon National Park altogether and head to the West Rim of the canyon, tribal land of the Hualapai and Havasupai. If only the park itself will do, the following tips will help you to keep your distance and your cool.

TAKE ANOTHER ROUTE

Avoid road rage by choosing a different route to the South Rim, foregoing the traditional highways 64 and U.S. 180 from Flagstaff. Take U.S. 89 north from Flagstaff instead, passing near Sunset Crater and Wupatki national monuments. When you reach the junction with Highway 64, take a break at Cameron Trading Post (1 mi north of the junction)—or stay overnight. This is a good place to shop for Native American artifacts, souvenirs, and the usual postcards, dream-catchers, recordings, and T-shirts. There are also high-quality Navajo rugs, jewelry, and other authentic handicrafts, and you can sample Navajo tacos. U.S. 64 to the west takes you directly to the park's east entrance; the scenery along the Little Colorado River gorge en route is eye-popping. It's 23 mi from the east entrance to the visitor center at Grand Canyon Visitor Center.

SKIP THE SOUTH RIM

Although the North Rim is just 10 mi across from the South Rim, the trip to get there by car is a five-hour drive of 215 mi. At first it might not sound like the trip would be worth it, but the payoff is huge. Along the way, you will travel through some of the prettiest parts of the state and be granted even more stunning views than those on the more easily accessible South Rim. Those who make the North Rim trip often insist it has the canyon's most beautiful views and best hiking. To get to the North Rim from Flagstaff, take U.S. 89 north past Cameron, turning left onto U.S. 89A at Bitter Springs. En route you'll pass the area known as Vermilion Cliffs. At Jacob Lake, take Highway 67 directly to the Grand Canyon North Rim. North Rim services are closed from mid-October through mid-May because of heavy snow, but in summer months and early fall, it's a wonderful way to beat the crowds at the South Rim.

RIDE THE RAILS

There is no need to deal with all of the other drivers racing to the South Rim. Sit back and relax in the comfy train cars of the **Grand Canyon Railway**. Live music and storytelling enliven the trip as you journey past the landscape through prairie, ranch, and national park land to the log-cabin train station in Grand Canyon Village. You won't see the Grand Canyon from the train, but you can walk or catch the shuttle at the restored, historic Grand Canyon Railway Station. The vintage train departs from the Williams Depot every morning, and makes the 65-mi journey in 2¼ hours. You can do the round-trip in a single day; however, it's a more relaxing and enjoyable strategy to stay for a night or two at the South Rim before returning to Williams. ⇨ *See Grand Canyon Railway Hotel in Where to Stay.* ☏ *800/843–8724* ⊕ *www. thetrain.com* ✉ *$70–$130 round-trip.*

south of the canyon rim). ⊠ *About 2 mi west of Hermit Rd. Junction on Hermit Rd.*

Yaki Point. Stop here for an exceptional view of Wotan's Throne, a flat-top butte named by François Matthes, a U.S. Geological Survey scientist who developed the first topographical map of the Grand Canyon. The overlook juts out over the canyon, providing unobstructed views of inner-canyon rock formations, South Rim cliffs, and Clear Creek canyon. About a mile south of Yaki Point, you'll come to the trailhead for the South Kaibab Trail. The point is one of the best places on the South Rim to watch the sunset. ⊠ *2 mi east of Grand Canyon Village on Desert View Dr.*

Fodor'sChoice **Yavapai Point.** This is also one of the best locations on the South Rim
★ to watch the sunset. Dominated by the Yavapai Observation Station, this point displays panoramic views of the mighty gorge through a wall of windows. Exhibits here include videos of the canyon floor and the Colorado River, a scaled diorama of the canyon with national park boundaries, fossils and rock fragments used to re-create the complex layers of the canyon walls, and a display on the natural forces used to carve the chasm. Rangers dig even deeper into Grand Canyon geology with free ranger programs. A guided afternoon nature walk completes the options. Check ahead for special events and walk and program schedules. There's also a bookstore. ⊠ *Adjacent to Grand Canyon Village* 🚳 *Free* ⊙ *Daily 8–8; hrs vary in winter.*

VISITOR CENTERS

Grand Canyon Visitor Center. The park's main orientation center, known formerly as Canyon View Information Plaza, near Mather Point, provides pamphlets and resources to help plan your sightseeing as well as engaging interpretive exhibits on the park. Rangers are on hand to answer questions and aid in planning canyon excursions. A bookstore is stocked with books covering all topics on the Grand Canyon, and a daily schedule of ranger-led hikes and evening lectures is posted on a bulletin board inside. There's ample parking by the information center, which you can also reach by a short walk from Mather Point, by a short ride on the shuttle bus Village Route, or by a leisurely 1-mi walk on the Greenway Trail—a paved pathway that meanders through the forest. ⊠ *East side of Grand Canyon Village* 🖀 *928/638–7888* ⊙ *Daily 8–5, outdoor exhibits may be viewed anytime.*

Desert View Information Center. Near the watchtower, at Desert View Point, the Grand Canyon Association has a nice selection of books, park pamphlets, and educational materials. ⊠ *East entrance* 🖀 *800/858–2808 or 928/638–7893* ⊙ *Daily 9–5; hrs vary in winter.*

Verkamp's Visitor Center. After 102 years of selling memorabilia and knickknacks on the South Rim across from El Tovar Hotel, Verkamp's Curios moved to the park's newest visitor center in 2008. The building now serves as a bookstore, ranger station, and museum with exhibits on the pioneer history of the region. ⊠ *Desert View Dr. across from El Tovar Hotel, Grand Canyon Village* 🖀 *928/638–7146* ⊙ *Daily 8–5.*

Switchbacks on the canyon's trails make the steep grade level enough for hikers (and mules)

Yavapai Observation Station. Shop in the bookstore, catch the park shuttle bus, or pick up information for the Rim Trail here. The canyon views from inside this historic building are stupendous. ⊠ *1 mi east of Market Plaza, Grand Canyon Village* ☎ *928/638–7890* ☉ *Daily 8–8; hrs vary in winter.*

SPORTS AND THE OUTDOORS

AIR TOURS

★ Flights by plane and helicopter over the canyon are offered by a number of companies, departing for the Grand Canyon Airport at the south end of Tusayan. Though the noise and disruption of so many aircraft buzzing the canyon is controversial, flightseeing remains a popular, if expensive, option. You'll have more visibility from a helicopter but they are louder and more expensive than the fixed-wing planes. Prices and lengths of tours vary, but you can expect to pay about $100–$125 per adult for short plane trips and approximately $145–$235 for brief helicopter tours (and about $350 for tours leaving from Vegas). These companies often have significant discounts in winter—check the company Web sites to find the best deals.

OUTFITTERS AND EXPEDITIONS **Air Grand Canyon** (⊠ *Grand Canyon Airport, Tusayan* ☎ *928/638–2686 or 800/247–4726* ⊕ *www.airgrandcanyon.com*) runs 40- to 50-minute fixed-wing air tours over the North Rim, the Kaibab Plateau, and the Dragon Corridor, one of the cross canyons. Tours start at 9 AM and run every hour on the hour. **Grand Canyon Airlines** (⊠ *Grand Canyon Airport Tusayan* ☎ *928/638–2359 or 866/235–9422* ⊕ *www.grandcanyonairlines.com*)

flies a fixed-wing on a 50-minute tour of the eastern edge of the Grand Canyon, the North Rim, and the Kaibab Plateau. All-day combination tours combine flight-seeing with jeep tours and float trips on the Colorado River. The company also schedules helicopter tours that leave from Las Vegas. Get an up-close view of Grand Canyon geology and the Colorado River on 30- and 50-minute tours with **Grand Canyon Helicopters** (⌧ *Grand Canyon Airport Tusayan* ☎ *928/638–2764 or 800/541–4537* ⊕ *www.grandcanyonhelicoptersaz.com/gch*). **Maverick Helicopters** (⌧ *Grand Canyon Airport Tusayan* ☎ *928/638–2622 or 800/962–3869* ⊕ *www.maverickhelicopters.com*) offers 25- and 45-minute tours of the eastern Grand Canyon, the North Rim, and the Dragon Corridor. A landing tour option sets you down in the canyon for a short snack below the rim. **Papillon Grand Canyon Helicopters** (⌧ *Grand Canyon Airport Tusayan* ☎ *928/638–2419 or 800/528–2418* ⊕ *www.papillon.com*) offers a variety of fixed-wing and helicopter tours, leaving both from Grand Canyon Airport and Vegas, of the canyon and combination tours with off-road jeep tours and smooth-water rafting trips.

BICYCLING

The South Rim's limited opportunities for off-road biking, narrow shoulders on park roads, and heavy traffic may disappoint hard-core cyclists. Bicycles are permitted on all park roads and on the multiuse Greenway System, as well as Bridle Trail (⇨ *North Rim*). Bikes are prohibited on all other trails, including the Rim Trail. Mountain bikers visiting the South Rim may be better off meandering through the ponderosa pine forest on the Tusayan Bike Trail. Currently, no rentals are available at the South Rim, but as of this writing, plans were being considered to introduce rentals by 2011. Bicycle camping sites are available at Mather Campground for $6 per person.

HIKING

Although permits are not required for day hikes, you must have a backcountry permit for longer trips (⇨ *See Admission Fees and Permits at the start of this chapter*). Some of the more popular trails are listed in this chapter; more detailed information and maps can be obtained from the Backcountry Information Centers. Also, rangers can help design a trip to suit your abilities.

Remember that the canyon has significant elevation changes and, in summer, extreme temperature ranges, which can pose problems for people who aren't in good shape or who have heart or respiratory problems. Carry plenty of water and energy foods. The majority of each year's 400 search-and-rescue incidents result from hikers underestimating the size of the canyon, hiking beyond their abilities, or not packing sufficient food and water.

GRAND CANYON FESTIVALS AND EVENTS

May **Williams Rendezvous Days**. A black-powder shooting competition, 1800s-era crafts, and a parade fire up Memorial Day weekend in honor of Bill Williams, the town's namesake mountain man. ☎ 928/635–4061 ⊕ www.williamschamber.com.

Late August–early September **Grand Canyon Music Festival**. Three weekends when mostly chamber music fills the Shrine of Ages amphitheater at Grand Canyon Village. In the early 1980s, music aficionados Robert Bonfiglio and Clare Hoffman hiked through the Grand Canyon and decided the stunning spectacle should be accompanied by the strains of a symphony. One of the park rangers agreed, and the wandering musicians performed an impromptu concert. Encouraged by the experience, Bonfiglio and Hoffman started the festival. ☎ 928/638–9215 or 800/997–8285 ⊕ www.grandcanyonmusicfest.org.

December–early January **Mountain Village Holiday**. Williams hails the holidays with a parade of lights, ice-skating rink, and live entertainment. ☎ 928/635–4061 ⊕ www.williamschamber.com.

⚠ Under no circumstances should you attempt a day hike from the rim to the river and back. Remember that when it's 80°F on the South Rim, it's 110°F on the canyon floor. Allow two to four days if you want to hike rim to rim (it's easier to descend from the North Rim, as it is more than 1,000 feet higher than the South Rim). Hiking steep trails from rim to rim is a strenuous trek of at least 21 mi and should only be attempted by experienced canyon hikers.

EASY

Fodor's Choice
★

Rim Trail. The South Rim's most popular walking path is the 12-mi (one-way) Rim Trail, which runs along the edge of the canyon from Pipe Creek Vista (the first overlook on Desert View Drive) to Hermits Rest. This walk, which is paved to Maricopa Point and for the last 1.5 mi to Hermits Rest, visits several of the South Rim's historic landmarks. Allow anywhere from 15 minutes to a full day; the Rim Trail is an ideal day hike, as it varies only a few hundred feet in elevation from Mather Point (7,120 feet) to the trailhead at Hermits Rest (6,650 feet). The trail also can be accessed from several spots in Grand Canyon Village and from the major viewpoints along Hermit Road, which are serviced by shuttle buses during the busy summer months. ■TIP→ On the Rim Trail, water is only available in the Grand Canyon Village area and at Hermits Rest.

MODERATE
★

Bright Angel Trail. Well maintained, this is one of the most scenic hiking paths from the South Rim to the bottom of the canyon (9.6 mi each way). Rest houses are equipped with water at the 1.5- and 3-mi points from May through September and at Indian Garden (4 mi) year-round. Water is also available at Bright Angel Campground, 9.25 mi below the trailhead. Plateau Point, on a spur trail about 1.5 mi below Indian Garden, is as far as you should attempt to go on a day hike; plan on spending six to nine hours. Bright Angel Trail is the easiest of all the footpaths into

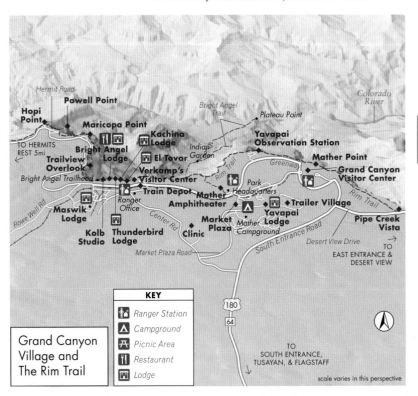

Grand Canyon Village and The Rim Trail

KEY

🧍	Ranger Station
⛺	Campground
🎋	Picnic Area
🍴	Restaurant
🏠	Lodge

the canyon, but because the climb out from the bottom is an ascent of 5,510 feet, the trip should be attempted only by those in good physical condition and should be avoided in midsummer due to extreme heat. The top of the trail can be icy in winter. Originally a bighorn sheep path and later used by the Havasupai, the trail was widened late in the 19th century for prospectors and is now used for both mule and foot traffic. ■ TIP➔ Hikers going downhill should yield to those going uphill. Also note that mule trains have the right-of-way—and sometimes leave unpleasant surprises in your path. ✉ *Trailhead: Kolb Studio, Hermits Rd.*

DIFFICULT **Grandview Trail.** Accessible from the parking area at Grandview Point, the trailhead is at 7,400 feet. The path heads steeply down into the canyon for 4.8 mi to the junction and campsite at East Horseshoe Mesa Trail. Classified as a wilderness trail, the route is aggressive and not as heavily traveled as some of the more well-known trails, such as Bright Angel and Hermit; allow six to nine hours, round-trip. There is no water available along the trail, which follows a steep descent to 4,800 feet at Horseshoe Mesa, where Hopi Indians once collected mineral paints. ✉ *Trailhead: Grandview Point, Desert View Dr.*

Hermit Trail. Beginning on the South Rim just west of Hermits Rest (and 7 mi west of Grand Canyon Village), this steep, 9.7-mi (one way) trail drops more than 5,000 feet to Hermit Creek, which usually flows year-round. It's a strenuous hike back up and is recommended for experienced long-distance hikers only; plan for six to nine hours. There's an abundance of lush growth and wildlife, including desert bighorn sheep, along this trail. The trail descends from the trailhead at 6,640 feet to the Colorado River at 2,300 feet. Day hikers should not go past Santa Maria Spring at 5,000 feet. For much of the year, no water is available along the way; ask a park ranger about the availability of water at Santa Maria Spring and Hermit Creek before you set out. All water from these sources should be treated before drinking. The route leads down to the Colorado River and has inspiring views of Hermit Gorge and the Redwall and Supai formations. Six miles from the trailhead are the ruins of Hermit Camp, which the Santa Fe Railroad ran as a tourist camp from 1911 until 1930. ⊠ *Trailhead: Hermits Rest, Hermits Rd.*

> **WORD OF MOUTH**
>
> "Taking the first step into the canyon was just amazing. We started down the series of switchbacks. We took the obligatory pictures at Ooh-Ahh Point and continued on to Cedar Ridge. The views were magnificent. This highlights the reason to hike into the canyon. You get such a different perspective with all of the rock formations right around you. I can't really find the words to express what it is like to travel down into the canyon and be surrounded by so many ancient rocks and buttes."
> —caligirl56

★ **South Kaibab Trail.** This trail starts near Yaki Point, 4 mi east of Grand Canyon Village and is accessible via the free shuttle bus. Because the route is so steep (and sometimes icy in winter)—descending from the trailhead at 7,260 feet down to 2,480 feet at the Colorado River—and has no water, many hikers return via the less-demanding Bright Angel Trail; allow four to six hours. During this 6.4-mi trek to the Colorado River, you're likely to encounter mule trains and riders (although mule rides are prohibited on the trail through at least 2011 while crews work on improving sections of the trail). At the river, the trail crosses a suspension bridge and runs on to Phantom Ranch. Along the trail there is no water and very little shade. There are no campgrounds, though there are portable toilets at Cedar Ridge (6,320 feet), 1.5 mi from the trailhead. Toilets and an emergency phone are also available at the Tipoff, 4.6 mi down the trail (3 mi past Cedar Ridge). The trail corkscrews down through some spectacular geology. Look for (but don't remove) fossils in the limestone when taking water breaks. ■TIP→ **Even though an immense network of trails winds through the Grand Canyon, the popular corridor trails (Bright Angel and South Kaibab) are recommended for hikers new to the region.** ⊠ *Trailhead: Yaki Point, Desert View Dr.*

JEEP TOURS

Jeep rides can be rough; if you have had back injuries, check with your doctor before taking a 4X4 tour. It's a good idea to book a week or two ahead, and even further if you're visiting in summer or on busy weekends.

OUTFITTERS AND EXPEDITIONS

Grand Canyon Jeep Tours & Safaris. If you'd like to get off the pavement and see parts of the park that are accessible only by dirt road, a jeep tour can be just the ticket. From March through November, this tour operator leads daily, 1½- to 4½-hour, off-road tours within the park, as well as in Kaibab National Forest. Combo tours adding helicopter and airplane rides are also available. ⌂ *Box 1772, Grand Canyon 86023* ☎ *928/638–5337 or 800/320–5337* ⊕ *www.grandcanyonjeeptours.com* ✉ *$45–$222.*

ARRANGING TOURS

Transportation-services desks are maintained at Bright Angel, Maswik Lodge, and Yavapai Lodge (closed in winter) in Grand Canyon Village. The desks provide information and handle bookings for sightseeing tours, taxi and bus services, mule rides (but don't count on last-minute availability). There's also a concierge at El Tovar that can arrange most tours, with the exception of mule rides. On the North Rim, Grand Canyon Lodge has general information about local services.

Grand Canyon Old West Jeep Tours. This tour company offers off-road jeep adventures and backcountry ATV adventures. From March through November, there are two- and three-hour, off-road and helicopter-jeep combo tours of the South Rim—optional smooth-water raft tours through the canyon are available as an add-on to any trip for $179. The all-day trip to the inner canyon on the Hualapai Indian Reservation is offered year-round. ✉ *Grand Canyon* ☎ *928/638–2000 or 800/716–9389* ⊕ *www.grandcanyonjeeps.com* ✉ *$63–$259.*

Marvelous Marv's Grand Canyon Tours. For a personalized experience, take this private tour of the Grand Canyon and surrounding sights any time of year. Tours include round-trip transportation from your hotel or campground in Williams, Tusayan, or Grand Canyon; admission to the park; scenic viewpoint stops; a short hike; and personal narration of the geology and history of the area. Note that credit cards are not accepted. ⌂ *Box 544, Williams 86046* ☎ *928/707–0291* ⊕ *www. marvelousmarv.com* ✉ *$85.*

MULE RIDES

★ Mule rides provide an intimate glimpse into the canyon for those who have the time, but not the stamina, to see the canyon on foot. ■ TIP➔ **Reservations are essential and are accepted up to 13 months in advance.**

These trips have been conducted since the early 1900s. A comforting fact as you ride the narrow trail: no one's ever been killed while riding a mule that fell off a cliff. (Nevertheless, the treks are not for the faint of heart or people in questionable health.)

OUTFITTERS **Xanterra Parks & Resorts Mule Rides.** These trips delve into the canyon from the South Rim to Phantom Ranch, or west along the canyon's

GRAND CANYON NATIONAL PARK: TOP PICKS HIKING TRAILS

	Grade	Miles (One Way)	Beginning Elevation	Hiking Level	Ending Elevation	Mules	Campground	Open Info*	Water	Shuttle Access	Ranger Station	Toilet/Restroom	Emergency Telephone	Trail Conditions
SOUTH RIM														
Bright Angel Trail South	Steep	9.6 mi	6,860 ft	Moderate-Difficult	2,480 ft (Colorado River)	Y	Y	Y/R	(Seasonal)	Y	Y	Y	Y	Maintained
Grandview Trail	Very Steep	3.2 mi	7,400 ft	Difficult	4,800 ft (Horseshoe Mesa)			Y/R	(Untreated)	Y		Y		Maintained
Hermit Trail	Steep	9.7 mi	6,640 ft	Difficult	2,300 ft (Colorado River)			Y/R	(Untreated)	Y		Y ‡	Y **	Unmaintained
New Hance Trail	Steep	8 mi	6,982 ft	Difficult	2,600 ft (Colorado River)			Y/R						Unmaintained
Rim Trail	Level	9 mi	6,640 ft	Easy-Difficult	7,120 ft (Mather Point)		Y	Y/R	Y **	Y	Y	Y	Y	Maintained
South Kaibab Trail	Steep	6.4 mi	7,260 ft	Difficult	2,400 ft (Colorado River)	Y	Y	Y/R	Y **	Y	Y	Y	Y	Unmaintained
NORTH RIM														
Cape Final Trail	Level/Incline	2.0 mi	7,840 ft	Easy-Moderate	7,916 ft (Cape Final)			mid-May–mid-Oct.						Maintained
Ken Patrick Trail	Level/Incline	10 mi	8,250 ft	Easy-Difficult	8,803 ft (Point Imperial)			mid-May–mid-Oct.						Unmaintained
North Kaibab Trail	Steep	7.1 mi	8,241 ft	Moderate	2,400 ft (Colorado River)	Y	Y	mid-May–mid-Oct.	Y	Y	Y	Y	Y	Maintained
Transept Trail	Level	1.5 mi	8,255 ft	Easy	8,200 ft (Campground)			mid-May–mid-Oct.			Y	Y		Maintained
Uncle Jim Trail	Level	2.5 mi	8,300 ft	Easy-Difficult	8,244 ft (Uncle Jim Point)	Y		mid-May–mid-Oct.						Maintained
Widforss Trail	Level/Incline	4.9 mi	8,080 ft		7,900 ft (Widforss Point)			mid-May–mid-Oct.						Unmaintained

*(South Rim trails occasionally close due to weather or trail conditions) **(Trailhead) Y/R = year-round

edge to a famed viewpoint called the Abyss (the Plateau Point rides were discontinued in 2009). Riders must be at least 55 inches tall, weigh less than 200 pounds, and understand English. Children under 15 must be accompanied by an adult. Riders must be in fairly good physical condition, and pregnant women are advised not to take these trips. The three-hour ride to the Abyss costs $117.40 (box lunch included). An overnight with a stay at Phantom Ranch at the bottom of the canyon is $477.34 ($842.60 for two riders). Two nights at Phantom Ranch, an option available from November through March, will set you back $667.69 ($1,111.22 for two). Meals are included. Reservations, especially during the busy summer months, are a must, but you can check at the Bright Angel Transportation Desk to see if there's last-minute availability. ⌂ *6312 S. Fiddlers Green Circle, Suite 600, N. Greenwood Village CO 80111* ☎ *303/297–2757 or 888/297–2757* ⊕ *www. grandcanyonlodges.com* ☽ *Phantom Ranch rides May–Sept., daily; Abyss rides mid-Mar.–Oct., twice daily; Nov.–mid-Mar., once daily.* ⌦ *Reservations essential.*

SKIING

Although you can't schuss down into the Grand Canyon, you can cross-country ski in the woods near the rim when there's enough snow, usually mid-December though early March. Trails, suitable for beginner and intermediate skiers, begin 0.3 mi north of the Grandview Lookout and travel through the Kaibab National Forest. For details, contact the **Tusayan Ranger District** (⌂ *Box 3088, Grand Canyon 86023* ☎ *928/638–2443* ⊕ *www.fs.fed.us/r3/kai*).

EDUCATIONAL OFFERINGS

Grand Canyon Field Institute. Instructors lead guided educational tours, hikes around the canyon, and weekend programs at the South Rim. With more than 100 classes a year, tour topics include everything from archaeology and backcountry medicine to photography and natural history. Contact GCFI for a schedule and price list. Discounted classes are available for members; annual dues are $35. ⌂ *Box 399, Grand Canyon 86023* ☎ *928/638–2485 or 866/471–4435* ⊕ *www.grandcanyon. org/fieldinstitute* ▨ *$125–$725 for most classes.*

Interpretive Ranger Programs. The National Park Service sponsors all sorts of orientation activities, such as daily guided hikes and talks. The focus may be on any aspect of the canyon—from geology and flora and fauna to history and early inhabitants. For schedules on the South Rim, go to Grand Canyon Visitor Center, pick up a free copy of *The Guide*, or check online. ☎ *928/638–7888* ⊕ *www.nps.gov/grca* ▨ *Free.*

☺ **Junior Ranger Program for Families.** The Junior Ranger Program provides a free, fun way to look at the cultural and natural history of this sublime destination. These hands-on educational programs for children ages 4 to 14 include guided adventure hikes, ranger-led "discovery" activities, and book readings. ☎ *928/638–7888* ⊕ *www.nps.gov/grca* ▨ *Free.*

Xanterra Motorcoach Tours. Narrated by knowledgeable guides, tours include the Hermits Rest Tour, which travels along the old wagon road

CLOSE UP

Freebies at the Grand Canyon

While you're here, be sure to take advantage of the many complementary services offered at Grand Canyon National Park.

■ The most useful is undoubtedly the system of free shuttle buses at the South Rim; it caters to the road-weary, with four routes winding through or just outside the park—Hermits Rest Route, Village Route, Kaibab Trail Route, and Tusayan Route. Of the bus routes, the Hermits Rest Route runs only from March through November and the Tusayan Route only in summer; the other two run year-round, and the Kaibab Trail Route provides the only access to Yaki Point. Hikers coming or going from the Kaibab Trailhead can catch the Hikers Express, which departs three times each morning from the Bright Angel Lodge, makes a quick stop at the Backcountry Information Center, and then heads out to the South Kaibab Trailhead.

■ Ranger-led programs are always free and offered year-round, though more are scheduled during the busy spring and summer seasons. These programs might include activities such as stargazing and topics such as geology and the cultural history of prehistoric peoples. Some of the more in-depth programs may include a fossil walk or a condor talk. Check with the visitor center for seasonal programs including wildflower walks and fire ecology.

■ Kids ages 4 to 14 can get involved with the park's Junior Ranger program, with ever-changing activities including hikes and hands-on experiments.

■ Despite all of these options, rangers will tell you that the best free activity in the canyon is watching the magnificent splashes of color on the canyon walls during sunrise and sunset.

built by the Santa Fe Railway; the Desert View Tour, which glimpses the Colorado River's rapids and stops at Lipan Point; Sunrise and Sunset Tours; and combination tours. Children 16 and younger are free when accompanied by a paying adult. ☎ *303/297–2757 or 888/297–2757* ⊕ *www.grandcanyonlodges.com* ✉ *$20–$57.*

SHOPPING

Nearly every lodging facility and retail store at the South Rim stocks Native American arts and crafts and Grand Canyon books and souvenirs. Prices are comparable to other souvenir outlets, though you may find some better deals in Williams. However, a portion of the proceeds from items purchased at Kolb Studio, Tusayan Museum, and the visitor centers go to the Grand Canyon Association.

Desert View Trading Post (⊠ *Desert View Dr. near the watchtower at Desert View* ☎ *928/638–3150*) sells a mix of traditional Southwestern souvenirs and authentic Native American arts and crafts.

★ **Hopi House** (⊠ *Desert View Dr. east of El Tovar Hotel, Grand Canyon Village* ☎ *928/638–2631*) has the widest selection of Native American handicrafts in the vicinity.

GRAND CANYON NORTH RIM

The North Rim stands 1,000 feet higher than the South Rim and has a more alpine climate, with twice as much annual precipitation. Here, in the deep forests of the Kaibab Plateau, the crowds are thinner, the facilities fewer, and the views even more spectacular. Due to snow, the North Rim is off-limits in winter. The park buildings and concessions are closed mid-October through mid-May. The road closes when the snow makes it impassable—usually by the end of November.

Lodgings are available but limited; the North Rim only offers one historic lodge and restaurant and a single campground. Dining options have opened up a little with the addition of the Grand Cookout, offered nightly with live entertainment under the stars. Your best bet may be to pack your camping gear and hiking boots and take several days to explore the lush Kaibab Forest. The canyon's highest, most dramatic rim views also can be enjoyed on two wheels (via primitive dirt access roads) and on four legs (courtesy of a trusty mule).

SCENIC DRIVE

★ **Highway 67**. Open mid-May to roughly mid-November (or the first big snowfall), the two-lane paved road climbs 1,400 feet in elevation as it passes through the Kaibab National Forest. Also called the "North Rim Parkway," this scenic route crosses the limestone-capped Kaibab Plateau—passing broad meadows, sun-dappled forests, and small lakes and springs—before abruptly falling away at the abyss of the Grand Canyon. Wildlife abounds in the thick ponderosa pine forests and lush mountain meadows. It's common to see deer, turkeys, and coyotes as you drive through this remote region. Point Imperial and Cape Royal can be reached by spurs off this scenic drive running from Jacob Lake to Bright Angel Point.

EXPLORING

HISTORIC SITE

Grand Canyon Lodge. Built in 1937 by the Union Pacific Railroad (replacing the original 1928 building, which burned in a fire), the massive stone structure is listed on the National Register of Historic Places. Its huge sunroom has hardwood floors, high-beam ceilings, and a marvelous view of the canyon through plate-glass windows. On warm days, visitors sit in the sun and drink in the surrounding beauty on an outdoor viewing deck, where National Park Service employees deliver free lectures on geology and history. ⊠ *Off Hwy. 67 near Bright Angel Point.*

SCENIC STOPS

★ **Bright Angel Point**. The trail, which leads to one of the most awe-inspiring overlooks on either rim, starts on the grounds of the Grand Canyon Lodge and runs along the crest of a point of rocks that juts into the canyon for several hundred yards. The walk is only 0.5 mi round-trip, but it's an exciting trek accented by sheer drops on each side of the trail. In a few spots where the route is extremely narrow, metal railings ensure

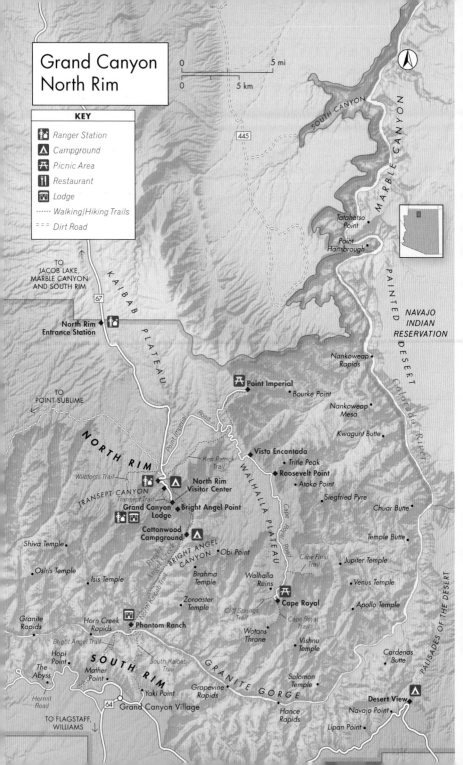

visitors' safety. The temptation to clamber out to precarious perches to have your picture taken could get you killed—every year several people die from falls at the Grand Canyon. ⊠ *North Rim Dr.*

Cape Royal. A popular sunset destination, Cape Royal showcases the canyon's jagged landscape; you'll also get a glimpse of the Colorado River, framed by a natural stone arch called Angels Window. In autumn, the aspens turn a beautiful gold, adding even more color to an already magnificent scene of the forested surroundings. At Angels Window Overlook, **Cliff Springs Trail** starts its 1-mi route (round-trip) through a forested ravine. The trail terminates at Cliff Springs, where the forest opens to another impressive view of the canyon walls. ⊠ *Cape Royal Scenic Dr., 23 mi southeast of Grand Canyon Lodge.*

Point Imperial. At 8,803 feet, Point Imperial has the highest vista point at either rim; it offers magnificent views of both the canyon and the distant country: the Vermilion Cliffs to the north, the 10,000-foot Navajo Mountain to the northeast in Utah, the Painted Desert to the east, and the Little Colorado River canyon to the southeast. Other prominent points of interest include views of Mount Hayden, Saddle Mountain, and Marble Canyon. ⊠ *2.7 mi left off Cape Royal Scenic Dr. on Point Imperial Rd., 11 mi northeast of Grand Canyon Lodge.*

Fodor's Choice
★

Point Sublime. Talk about solitude. Here you can camp within feet of the canyon's edge. Sunrises and sunsets are spectacular. The winding road, through gorgeous high country, is only 17 mi, but it will take you at least two hours, one way. The road is intended only for vehicles with high-road clearance (pickups and four-wheel-drive vehicles). It is also necessary to be properly equipped for wilderness road travel. Check with a park ranger or at the information desk at Grand Canyon Lodge before taking this journey. You may camp here only with a permit from the Backcountry Information Center. ⊠ *North Rim Dr., Grand Canyon; about 20 mi west of North Rim Visitor Center.*

Roosevelt Point. Named after the president who gave the Grand Canyon its national monument status in 1908 (it was upgraded to national park status in 1919), this is the best place to see the confluence of the Little Colorado River and the Grand Canyon. The cliffs above the Colorado River south of the junction are known as the Palisades of the Desert. A short woodland loop trail leads to this eastern viewpoint. ⊠ *Cape Royal Rd., 18 mi east of Grand Canyon Lodge.*

Vista Encantada. This point on the Walhalla Plateau offers views of the upper drainage of Nankoweap Creek, a rock pinnacle known as Brady Peak, and the Painted Desert to the east. This is an enchanting place

Flora and Fauna of the Grand Canyon

Eighty-nine mammal species inhabit Grand Canyon National Park, as well as 355 species of birds, 56 kinds of reptiles and amphibians, and 17 kinds of fish. The rare Kaibab squirrel is found only on the North Rim—you can recognize them by their all-white tails and black undersides. The pink Grand Canyon rattlesnake lives at lower elevations within the canyon. Hawks and ravens are visible year-round. The endangered California condor has been reintroduced to the canyon region. Park rangers give daily talks on the magnificent birds, whose wingspan measures 9 feet. In spring, summer, and fall, mule deer, recognizable by their large ears, are abundant at the South Rim. Don't be fooled by gentle appearances; these guys can be aggressive. It's illegal to feed them, as it will disrupt their natural habitats, and increase your risk of getting bitten or kicked.

The best times to see wildlife are early in the morning and late in the afternoon. Look for out-of-place shapes and motions, keeping in mind that animals occupy all layers in a natural habitat and not just at your eye level. Use binoculars for close-up views. While out and about try to fade into the woodwork by keeping your movements limited and noise at a minimum.

More than 1,700 species of plants color the park. The South Rim's Coconino Plateau is fairly flat, at an elevation of about 7,000 feet, and covered with stands of piñon and ponderosa pines, junipers, and Gambel's oak trees. On the Kaibab Plateau on the North Rim, Douglas fir, spruce, quaking aspen, and more ponderosas prevail. In spring you're likely to see asters, sunflowers, and lupine in bloom at both rims.

for a picnic lunch. ⊠ *Cape Royal Rd., 16 mi southeast of Grand Canyon Lodge.*

Walhalla Overlook. One of the lowest elevations on the North Rim, this overlook has views of the Unkar Delta, a fertile region used by Ancestral Puebloans as farmland. These ancient people also gathered food and hunted game on the North Rim. A flat path leads to the remains of the Walhalla Glades Pueblo, which was inhabited from 1050 to 1150. ⊠ *Cape Royal Rd., 22.5 mi southeast of Grand Canyon Lodge.*

VISITOR CENTER

North Rim Visitor Center. View exhibits, peruse the bookstore, and pick up useful maps and brochures. Interpretive programs are often scheduled in summer. If you're craving coffee, it's a short walk from here to the Roughrider Saloon at the Grand Canyon Lodge. ⊠ *Near the parking lot on Bright Angel Peninsula* ☎ *928/638–7864* ⊙ *Mid-May–mid-Oct., daily 8–6.*

SPORTS AND THE OUTDOORS

BICYCLING

Mountain bikers can test the many dirt access roads found in this remote area, including the 17-mi trek to Point Sublime. It's rare to spot other people on these primitive roads.

Bicycles and leashed pets are allowed on the well-maintained 1.2-mi (one way) **Bridle Trail,** which follows the road from Grand Canyon Lodge to the North Kaibab Trailhead. Bikes are prohibited on all other national park trails.

OUTFITTERS **The Outfitters Station** offers Schwinn bicycles on an hourly, half-day, or full-day basis. Be sure to take a cruise on the tandem bicycle or the retro surrey for a leisurely ride in a place you won't soon forget. Children's bikes are available. ⊠ *Grand Canyon Lodge* ☎ *928/638–2611* ⊕ *www. grandcanyonforever.com.*

HIKING

EASY **Cape Final Trail.** This 2-mi hike follows an old jeep trail through a ponderosa pine forest to the canyon overlook at Cape Final with panoramic views of the northern canyon, the Palisades of the Desert, and the impressive spectacle of Juno Temple. ⊠ *Trailhead: dirt parking lot 5 mi south of Roosevelt Point on Cape Royal Rd.*

☾ **Roosevelt Point Trail.** This easy 0.2-mi round-trip trail loops through the ★ forest to the scenic viewpoint. Allow 20 minutes for this short, secluded hike. ⊠ *Trailhead: Cape Royal Rd.*

☾ **Transept Trail.** This 3-mi (round-trip), 1½-hour trail begins at 8,255 feet near the Grand Canyon Lodge. Well maintained and well marked, it has little elevation change, sticking near the rim before reaching a dramatic view of a large stream through Bright Angel Canyon. The route leads to a side canyon called Transept Canyon, which geologist Clarence Dutton named in 1882, declaring it "far grander than Yosemite." Check the posted schedule to find a ranger talk along this trail; it's also a great place to view fall foliage. Flash floods can occur any time of the year, especially June through September when thunderstorms develop rapidly. ⚠ Check forecasts before heading into the canyon and use caution when hiking in narrow canyons and drainage systems. ⊠ *Trailhead: near the Grand Canyon Lodge's east patio.*

MODERATE **Ken Patrick Trail.** This primitive trail travels 10 mi one way (allow six hours) from the trailhead at 8,250 feet to Point Imperial at 8,803 feet. It crosses drainages and occasionally detours around fallen trees. The end of the road brings the highest views from either rim. Note that there is no water along this trail. ⊠ *Trailhead: east side of North Kaibab trailhead parking lot.*

Uncle Jim Trail. This 5-mi, three-hour loop trail starts at 8,300 feet and winds south through the forest, past Roaring Springs and Bright Angel canyons. The highlight of this rim hike is Uncle Jim Point, which, at 8,244 feet, overlooks the upper sections of the North Kaibab Trail. ⊠ *Trailhead: North Kaibab Trail parking lot.*

★ **Widforss Trail.** Round-trip, Widforss Trail is 9.8 mi, with an elevation change of 200 feet. Allow five to seven hours for the hike, which starts at 8,080 feet and passes through shady forests of pine, spruce, fir, and aspen on its way to Widforss Point, at 7,900 feet. Here you'll have good views of five temples: Zoroaster, Brahma, and Deva to the southeast and Buddha and Manu to the southwest. You are likely to see wildflowers in summer, and this is a good trail for viewing fall foliage. It's named in honor of artist Gunnar M. Widforss, renowned for his paintings of national park landscapes. ⊠ *Trailhead: across from the North Kaibab Trail parking lot.*

DIFFICULT **North Kaibab Trail.** At 8,241 feet, this trail, like the roads leading to the North Rim, is open only from May through late October or early November (depending on the weather). It is recommended for experienced hikers only, who should allow four days for the full hike. The long, steep path drops 5,840 feet over a distance of 14.5 mi to Phantom Ranch and the Colorado River, so the National Park Service suggests that day hikers not go farther than Roaring Springs (5,020 feet) before turning to hike back up out of the canyon. After about 7 mi, Cottonwood Campground (4,080 feet) has drinking water in summer, restrooms, shade trees, and a ranger. ∎ **TIP→ For a fee, a shuttle takes hikers to the North Kaibab trailhead twice daily from Grand Canyon Lodge.** ⊠ *Trailhead: 2 mi north of the Grand Canyon Lodge.*

MULE RIDES

OUTFITTER **Canyon Trail Rides.** This company leads mule rides on the easier trails of
⟳ the North Rim. A one-hour ride (minimum age seven) runs $40. Half-day trips on the rim or into the canyon (minimum age 10) cost $75; full-day trips (minimum age 12) go for $165. Full-day trips into the canyon follow the North Kaibab Trail to Roaring Springs where you'll have time to explore and eat a sack lunch. Weight limits vary from 200 to 220 pounds. Available daily from May 15 to October 15, these excursions are popular, so make reservations far in advance. ⌂ *Box 128, Tropic, UT 84776* ☎ *435/679–8665* ⊕ *www.canyonrides.com/grand_canyon_rides.html.*

EDUCATIONAL OFFERINGS

⟳ **Discovery Pack Junior Ranger Program.** Children ages 9 to 14 can take part in these hands-on educational programs and earn a Junior Ranger certificate and badge. ☎ *928/638–7967* ⊕ *www.nps.gov/grca* ✉ *Free.*

Interpretive Ranger Programs. Daily guided hikes and talks may focus on any aspect of the canyon—from geology and flora and fauna to history and the canyon's early inhabitants. For schedules, go to the Grand Canyon Lodge or pick up a free copy of *The Guide* to the North Rim. ☎ *928/638–7967* ⊕ *www.nps.gov/grca* ✉ *Free.*

DID YOU KNOW?

Sure-footed mules take riders along the rim for half-day trips and down into the canyon for longer excursions. Two-day trips include an overnight stay at Phantom Ranch on the canyon floor.

THE WEST RIM AND HAVASU CANYON

Known as "The People" of the Grand Canyon, the Pai Indians—the Hualapai and Havasupai—have lived along the Colorado River and the vast Colorado Plateau for more than 1,000 years. Both tribes traditionally moved seasonally between the plateau and the canyon, alternately hunting game and planting crops. Today, they rely on their tourism offerings outside the national park as an economic base.

GRAND CANYON WEST

186 mi northwest of Williams, 70 mi north of Kingman

The plateau-dwelling Hualapai ("people of the tall pines") acquired a larger chunk of traditional Pai lands with the creation of their reservation in 1883. Hualapai tribal lands include diverse habitats ranging from rolling grasslands to rugged canyons, and travel from elevations of 1,500 feet at the Colorado River to more than 7,300 feet at Aubrey Cliffs. In recent years, the Hualapai have been attempting to foster tourism on the West Rim—most notably with the spectacular Skywalk, a glass walkway suspended 70 feet over the edge of the canyon rim. Not hampered by the regulations in place at Grand Canyon National Park, Grand Canyon West offers helicopter flights down into the bottom of the canyon, horseback rides to rim viewpoints, and boat trips on the Colorado River.

The Hualapai Reservation encompasses a million acres along 108 mi of the Colorado River in the Grand Canyon. Peach Springs, on historic Route 66, is the tribal capital and the location of the Hualapai Lodge. Although increasingly popular, the West Rim is still relatively remote and visited by far fewer people than the South Rim—keep in mind that it's more than 120 mi away from the nearest interstate highways.

GETTING HERE AND AROUND

GETTING HERE   The West Rim is a 5-hour drive from the South Rim of Grand Canyon National Park or a 2½-hour drive from Las Vegas. From Kingman, drive north 30 mi on U.S. 93, and then turn right onto Pierce Ferry Road and follow for 28 mi. (A shorter, more scenic alternative is to drive 42 mi north on Stockton Hill Road, turning right onto Pierce Ferry Road for 7 mi, but this takes a bit longer because Stockton Hill Road has a lower speed limit than the wide, divided U.S. 93 highway.) Turn right (east) on to Diamond Bar Road and follow for 21 mi to Grand Canyon West entrance.

The dusty, 14-mi stretch of unpaved road leading to Grand Canyon West is not recommended for RVs and low-clearance vehicles (as of this writing, plans are underway to pave this road by early 2011). For a different approach along Diamond Bar Road, visitors can schedule shuttle services from the Grand Canyon West Welcome Center on Pierce Ferry Road for a nominal fee; reservations are required. The Hualapai Tribe requires visitors to obtain permits to travel on tribal lands, although no permit is required to drive to the West Rim if you take a tour while there.

GETTING AROUND

Visitors aren't allowed to travel in their own vehicles to the viewpoints once they reach the West Rim and must purchase a tour package from Destination Grand Canyon West.

TOURS

In addition to the exploring options by the Hualapai Tribe, more than 30 tour and transportation companies service Grand Canyon West from Las Vegas, Phoenix, and Sedona by airplane, helicopter, coach, SUV, and Hummer. Perhaps the easiest way to visit the West Rim from Vegas is with a tour. Bighorn Wild West Tours will pick you up in a Hummer at your Vegas hotel for an all-day trip that includes the shuttle-bus package and lunch, for $219.

> ### EXPLORING INDIAN COUNTRY
>
> When visiting Native American reservations, respect tribal laws and customs. Remember you are a guest in a sovereign nation. Do not wander into residential areas or take photographs of residents without first asking permission. Possessing or consuming alcohol is illegal on tribal lands. In general, the Hualapai and Havasupai are quiet, private people. Offer respect and do not pursue conversations or personal interactions unless invited to do so.

ESSENTIALS

Information Contacts Destination Grand Canyon West (☎ 877/716–9378 ⊕ www.destinationgrandcanyon.com)

Tour Operators Bighorn Wild West Tours (☎ 702/385–4676 or 888/385–4676).

Transportation Contacts Park and Ride Shuttle (☎ 702/878–9378 ✐ reservations@destinationgrandcanyon.com).

EXPLORING

Destination Grand Canyon West is run by the Hualapai Tribe, who offers the basic Hualapai Legacy tour package ($43.05 per person, including taxes and fees), which includes a Hualapai visitation permit and shuttle transportation. The shuttle will take you to Eagle Point, where the Indian Village walking tour visits authentic dwellings; Hualapai Ranch, site of Western performances, cookouts, and horseback and wagon rides; and Guano Point, where the "High Point Hike" offers panoramic views of the Colorado River. For an extra cost you can add a helicopter trip into the canyon, a boat trip on the Colorado, an off-road Hummer adventure, a horseback or wagon ride to the canyon rim, or a walk on the Skywalk. Local Hualapai guides add a Native American perspective to a canyon trip that you won't find on North and South Rim tours.

The **Skywalk,** which opened in 2007, is a cantilevered glass terrace suspended nearly 4,000 feet above the Colorado River and extending 70 feet from the edge of the Grand Canyon. Approximately 10 feet wide, the bridge's deck, made of tempered glass several inches thick, has 5-foot glass railings on each side making an unobstructed open-air platform. Visitors must store all personal effects, including cameras, cell phones, and video cameras, in lockers before entering the Skywalk. A professional photographer takes personal photographs on the walkway, which can be purchased from the gift shop. At this writing, a three-level, 6,000-square-foot visitor center was under construction at the site. The date of completion is currently uncertain, but eventually this complex is expected to include a museum, movie theater, gift shop, and at least two restaurants. A short walk takes visitors to the Indian Village, where educational displays uncover the culture of five different Native American tribes (Havasupai, Plains, Hopi, Hualapai, and Navajo). Intertribal, powwow-style dance performances entertain visitors at the nearby amphitheater. ⊠ *Grand Canyon West* ☎ *702/878–9378 or 877/716–9378* ⊕ *www.destinationgrandcanyon.com* ✍ *$43.05 entrance fee and taxes; Skywalk $29.95* ◷ *Daily.*

SPORTS AND THE OUTDOORS

ADVENTURE TOURS One-day combination river trips are offered by the Hualapai Tribe through the **Hualapai River Runners** (⊠ *887 Rte. 66, Peach Springs* ☎ *928/769–2219 or 888/255–9550* ⊕ *www.grandcanyonwest.com*) from mid-March through October. The trips, which cost $328, leave from Peach Springs and include rafting, a hike, helicopter ride, and transport. Lunch, snacks, and beverages are provided. Children must be eight or older to take the trip, which runs several rapids with the most difficult rated as Class V or VI, depending on the river flow.

HAVASU CANYON

141 mi northwest from Williams to the head of Hualapai Hilltop.

With the establishment of Grand Canyon National Park in 1919, the Havasupai ("people of the blue green water") were confined to their summer village of Supai and the surrounding 518 acres in the 5-mi-wide and 12-mi-long Havasu Canyon. In 1975, the reservation was substantially enlarged, but is still completely surrounded by national park lands on all but its southern border. Each year, about 25,000 tourists fly, hike, or ride into Havasu Canyon to visit the Havasupai. Despite their economic reliance on tourism, the Havasupai take their guardianship of the Grand Canyon seriously, and severely limit visitation in order to protect the fragile canyon habitats. Dubbed the "Shangri-la of the Grand Canyon," the waterfalls have drawn visitors to this remote Indian reservation.

Major flooding in 2008 altered Havasu Canyon's famous landscape and it was closed to visitors for almost 10 months. Supai reopened in June 2009 but water and mud damage have changed some of the beautiful waterfalls, their streams and pools, and the amount of blue-green travertine. ■TIP→ Be sure to call the Havasupai Tourist Enterprise (☎ *928/448–2121*) before visiting for reservations.

GETTING HERE AND AROUND

Hualapai Hilltop is reached via Indian Route 18, which you follow about 65 mi north from historic Route 66 (34 mi west of Seligman and 50 mi east of Kingman). The total driving distance from the South Rim of the Grand Canyon is about 200 mi.

TRAVEL INTO
THE CANYON

The Havasupai restrict the number of visitors to the canyon; you must have reservations. They ask that hikers call ahead before taking the trek into the canyon. Hualapai Trail leaves from Hualapai Hilltop. From an elevation of 5,200 feet, the trail travels down a moderate grade to Supai village at 3,200 feet. Bring plenty of water and avoid hiking during the middle of the day, when canyon temperatures can reach into the 100s. If you'd rather ride, you can rent a horse for the trip down for $187 round-trip, or $94 one way. Riders must be able to mount and dismount by themselves; be at least 4 feet, 7 inches; and weigh less than 250 pounds. Reservations must be made at least six weeks in advance with Havasupai Tourist Enterprise, which requires a 50% deposit. You'll need to spend the night if you're hiking or riding.

> **MAIL BY MULE**
>
> Arguably, the most remote mail route in the United States follows a steep 8-mi trail to the tiny town of Supai in Havasu Canyon. Havasupai tribal members living deep within the confines of the Grand Canyon rely on this route for the delivery of everything from food to furniture. During a typical week, more than a ton of mail is sent into the canyon by mule, with each animal carrying a cargo of about 130 pounds.

Another option is a helicopter ride into the canyon with Air West Helicopters. Flights leave from Hualapai Hilltop and cost $85 per person each way. Reservations are not accepted and visitors are transported on a first-come, first-served basis. Tribal members are boarded prior to tourists.

ESSENTIALS

Information Contacts Havasupai Tourist Enterprise (☎ *928/448–2121* ⊕ *www.havasupaitribe.com*).

Transportation Contacts Air West Helicopters (☎ *623/516–2790* ☽ *Mid-Mar.– mid-Oct., Thurs., Fri., Sun., and Mon. 10–1; mid-Oct.–mid-Mar., Fri. and Sun. 10–1*)

EXPLORING

Havasu Canyon, south of the middle part of Grand Canyon National Park's South Rim and away from the crowds, is the home of the Havasupai, a tribe that has lived in this isolated area for centuries. You'll discover why they are known as the "people of the blue green waters" when you see the canyon's waterfalls. Accumulated travertine formations in some of the most popular pools were washed out in massive flooding decades ago and again in 2008, destroying some of the otherworldly scenes pictured in older photos, but the place is still magical.

The 600 tribal members now live in the village of Supai, accessible only down the 8-mi-long **Hualapai Trail,** which drops 2,000 feet from the canyon rim to the tiny town. The quiet and private Havasupai mostly remain apart from the modest flow of tourists, which nevertheless plays a vital role in the tribal economy.

To reach Havasu's waterfalls, you must hike downstream from the village of Supai. Both **Havasu Falls** and **Mooney Falls** are still flowing and as beautiful as ever but flooding in 2008 washed out well-known Navajo Falls completely. Pack adequate food and supplies. Prices for food and sundries in Supai are more than double what they would be outside the reservation. The tribe does not allow alcohol, drugs, pets, or weapons. ⊠ *Havasupai Tourist Enterprise, Supai* ☏ *928/448–2141, 928/448–2121 general information, 928/448–2111, 928/448–2201 lodging reservations* ⊕ *www.havasupaitribe.com* ✉ *$35 entrance fee, $5 impact fee.*

WHAT'S NEAR THE GRAND CANYON?

The northwest section of Arizona is geographically fascinating. In addition to the Grand Canyon, it's home to national forests, national monuments, and national recreation areas. Towns, however, are small and scattered. Many of them cater to visiting adventurers, and Native American reservations dot the map.

NEARBY TOWNS AND ATTRACTIONS

NEARBY TOWNS

Towns near the canyon's South Rim include the tiny town of Tusayan, just 1 mi south of the entrance station, and Williams, the "Gateway to the Grand Canyon," 58 mi south.

Tusayan has the basic amenities and an airport that serves as a starting point for airplane and helicopter tours of the canyon. The cozy mountain town of **Williams,** founded in 1882 when the railroad passed through, was once a rough-and-tumble joint, replete with saloons and bordellos. Today it reflects a much milder side of the Wild West, with 3,300 residents and more than 25 motels and hotels. Wander along main street—part of historic Route 66, but locally named, like the town, after trapper Bill Williams—and indulge in Route 66 nostalgia inside antiques shops or souvenir and T-shirt stores.

The communities closest to the North Rim—all of them tiny and with limited services—include Fredonia, 76 mi north; Marble Canyon, 80 mi northeast; Lees Ferry, 85 mi east; and Jacob Lake, 45 mi north.

Fredonia, a small community of about 1,050, approximately an hour's drive north of the Grand Canyon, is often referred to as the gateway to the North Rim; it's also relatively close to Zion and Bryce Canyon national parks in Utah. **Marble Canyon** marks the geographical beginning of the Grand Canyon at its northeastern tip. It's a good stopping point if you are driving U.S. 89 to the North Rim. En route from the South Rim to the North Rim is **Lees Ferry,** where most of the area's river rafts start their journey. The tiny town of **Jacob Lake,** nestled high in pine country at an elevation of 7,925 feet, was named after Mormon explorer Jacob Hamblin, also known as the "Buckskin Missionary." It has a hotel, café, campground, and lush mountain countryside.

ESSENTIALS

Visitor Information Kaibab National Forest, North District (⊠ *430 S. Main St., Fredonia* ☎ *928/643–7395* ⊕ *www.fs.fed.us/r3/kai*). **Kaibab National Forest, Tusayan Ranger District** (⊠ *Hwy. 64 Grand Canyon* ☎ *928/638–2443* ⊕ *www.fs.fed.us/r3/kai*). **Kaibab National Forest, Williams Ranger District** (⊠ *742 S. Clover Rd., Williams* ☎ *928/635–5600* ⊕ *www.fs.fed.us/r3/kai*). **Kaibab Plateau Visitor Center** (⊠ *Hwy. 89A/AZ 67, HC 64, Jacob Lake* ☎ *928/643–7298* ⊕ *www.fs.fed.us/r3/kai*). **Williams Visitor Center** (⊠ *200 W. Railroad Ave., at Grand Canyon Blvd., Williams* ☎ *928/635–1418 or 800/863–0546* ⊕ *www.williamschamber.com* ⊙ *Spring, fall, and winter, daily 8–5; summer, daily 8–6:30*).

3

NEARBY ATTRACTIONS

National Geographic Visitor Center Grand Canyon. Here you can schedule and purchase tickets for air tours and daily Colorado River trips; buy a national park pass, and access the park by special entry lanes. However, the biggest draw at the visitor center is the six-story IMAX screen that features the 34-minute movie *Grand Canyon: Discovery & Adventure*. You can learn about the geologic and natural history of the canyon, soar above stunning rock formations, and ride the rapids through the rocky gorge. ⊠ *Hwy. 64/U.S. 180, 2 mi south of the Grand Canyon's south entrance, Box 3309, Tusayan* ☎ *928/638–2203 or 928/638–2468* ⊕ *www.explorethecanyon.com* ⊠ *$13.34 for IMAX movies* ⊙ *Mar.–Oct., daily 8:30–8:30; Nov.–Feb., daily 10:30–6:30*

ᗑ **Planes of Fame Museum.** A good stop 30 mi north of Williams, at the junction of U.S. 180 and State Route 64 in Valle, this satellite of the Air Museum Planes of Fame in Chino, California, chronicles the history of aviation with an array of historic and modern aircraft. One of the featured pieces is a C-121A Constellation "Bataan," the personal aircraft General MacArthur used during the Korean War. Guided tours of this historic plane are offered for $3. Visitors are not allowed inside the cockpits. ⊠ *755 Mustang Way, Valle* ☎ *928/635–1000* ⊕ *www.planesoffame.org* ⊠ *$5.95* ⊙ *Daily 9–5; extended summer hrs.*

★ **Vermilion Cliffs.** West from the town of Marble Canyon are these spectacular cliffs, more than 3,000 feet high in many places. Keep an eye out for condors; the giant endangered birds were reintroduced into the area in 1996. Reports suggest that the birds, once in captivity, are surviving well in the wilderness.

SCENIC DRIVES AND VISTAS

U.S. 89. The route north from Cameron Trading Post (Cameron, Arizona) on U.S. 89 offers a stunning view of the **Painted Desert** to the right. The desert, which covers thousands of square miles stretching to the south and east, is a vision of subtle, almost harsh beauty, with windswept plains and mesas, isolated buttes, and barren valleys in pastel patterns. About 30 mi north of Cameron Trading Post, the Painted Desert country gives way to sandstone cliffs that run for miles. Brilliantly hued and ranging in color from light pink to deep orange, the **Echo Cliffs** rise to more than 1,000 feet in many places. They are essentially devoid of

Lava Falls is the largest and most well known of the rapids in the Grand Canyon.

vegetation, but in a few high places, thick patches of tall cottonwood and poplar trees, nurtured by springs and water seepage from the rock escarpment, manage to thrive.

U.S. 89A. At Bitter Springs, 60 mi north of Cameron, U.S. 89A branches off from U.S. 89, running north and providing views of **Marble Canyon,** the geographical beginning of the Grand Canyon. Like the Grand Canyon, Marble Canyon was formed by the Colorado River. Traversing a gorge nearly 500 feet deep is **Navajo Bridge,** a narrow steel span built in 1929 and listed on the National Register of Historic Places. Formerly used for car traffic, it now functions only as a pedestrian overpass.

AREA ACTIVITIES

SPORTS AND THE OUTDOORS

BICYCLING Pedal the depths of the Kaibab National Forest on the **Arizona Bike Trail** (✉ *Tusayan Ranger District, Hwy. 64, Box 3088, Tusayan* ☎ *928/638–2443* ⊕ *www.fs.fed.us/r3/kai*). Following linked loop trails at an elevation of 6,750 feet, you can bike as few as 3 mi or as many as 38 mi round-trip along old logging roads (parts of it paved) through ponderosa pine forest. Keep an eye out for elk, mule deer, hawks, eagles, pronghorn antelope, turkeys, coyote, and porcupines. Open for biking year-round (but most feasible March through October), the trail is accessed on the west side of Highway 64, a half mile north of Tusayan.

Cyclists also can enjoy the scenery along abandoned sections of Route 66 on the **Historic Route 66 Mountain Bike Tour.** Maps of the tour, which include the 6-mi **Ash Fork Hill Trail** and the 5-mi **Devil Dog Trail,** are available at the Williams Visitor Center.

FISHING   Fish for trout, crappie, catfish, and smallmouth bass at a number of lakes surrounding Williams. To fish on public land, anglers ages 14 and older are required to obtain a fishing license from the **Arizona Game and Fish Department** (☎ *928/774–5045* ⊕ *www.gf.state.az.us*).

The stretch of ice-cold, crystal-clear water at Lees Ferry off the North Rim provides arguably the best trout fishing in the Southwest. Many rafters and anglers stay the night in a campground near the river or in nearby Marble Canyon before hitting the river at dawn. **Marble Canyon Outfitters** (✉ *0.25 mi west of Navajo Bridge on U.S. 89A, Marble Canyon 86036* ☎ *928/355–2225 or 800/726–1789* ⊕ *www.leesferryflyfishing. com*), at Marble Canyon Lodge, sells Arizona fishing licenses and offers guided fishing trips. **Lees Ferry Anglers** (✉ *Milepost 547, N. U.S. 89A, HC 67, Marble Canyon 86036* ☎ *928/355–2261 or 800/962–9755* ⊕ *www. leesferry.com*) has guides and state fishing licenses and gear for sale.

HORSEBACK   **Apache Stables.** There's nothing like a horseback ride to immerse you in
RIDING   the Western experience. From stables near Tusayan, these folks offer gentle horses and a ride that will meet most budgets. Choose from one- and two-hour trail rides or the popular campfire rides and horse-drawn wagon excursions. ✉ *Forest Service Rd. 328, 1 mi north of Tusayan* ✍ *Box 158, Grand Canyon 86023* ☎ *928/638–2891 or 928/638–3105* ⊕ *www.apachestables.com* 💲 *$25.50–$85.50* ⊙ *Mar.–Nov., daily.*

RAFTING   The National Park Service authorizes 16 concessionaires to run rafting
★   trips through the canyon—you can view a full list at the park Web site (⊕ *www.nps.gov/grca/planyourvisit/river-concessioners.htm*). You can also experience one-day trips in Grand Canyon West with the Hualapai Tribe or Page (⇨ *Northeast Arizona*); here are a few of the best operators for multiday trips:

Arizona Raft Adventures (✉ *4050 E. Huntington Rd., Flagstaff* ☎ *928/526– 8200 or 800/786–7238* ⊕ *www.azraft.com*) organizes 6- to 16-day paddle and/or motor trips for all skill levels. Trips, which run $1,920 to $3,916, depart April through October.

With a reputation for high quality and a roster of 3- to 14-day trips, **Canyoneers** (✍ *Box 2997, Flagstaff 86003* ☎ *928/526–0924 or 800/525– 0924* ⊕ *www.canyoneers.com*) is popular with those who want to do some hiking as well. The five-day "Best of the Grand" trip includes a hike down to Phantom Ranch. The motorized and oar trips, available April through September, cost between $995 and $3,250.

You can count on **Grand Canyon Expeditions** (✍ *Box 0, Kanab, UT 84741* ☎ *435/644–2691 or 800/544–2691* ⊕ *www.gcex.com*) to take you down the Colorado River safely and in style: it limits the number of people on each boat to 14, and evening meals might include filet mignon, pork chops, or shrimp. The mid-April through mid-September trips cost $2,500 to $3,600 for 8 to 16 days.

One of the canyon's larger rafting outfitters, **Wilderness River Adventures** (✍ *Box 717, Page 86040* ☎ *928/645–3296 or 800/992–8022* ⊕ *www.*

Continued on page 198

EXPLORING THE
COLORADO RIVER

By Carrie Frasure

High in Colorado's Rocky Mountains, the Colorado River begins as a catch-all for the snowmelt off the mountains west of the Continental Divide. By the time it reaches the Grand Canyon, the Colorado has been joined by multiple tributaries to become a raging river, red with silt as it sculpts spectacular landscapes. A network of dams can only partially tame this mighty river.

Snaking its way through five states, the Colorado River is an essential water source to the arid Southwest. Its natural course runs 1,450 mi from its origin in Colorado's La Poudre Pass Lake in Rocky Mountain National Park to its final destination in the Gulf of California, also called the Sea of Cortez. In northern Arizona, the Colorado River has been a powerful force in shaping the Grand Canyon, where it flows 4,000 to 6,000 feet below the rim. Beyond the canyon, the red river takes a lazy turn at the Arizona–Nevada border, where Hoover Dam creates the reservoir at Lake Mead. The Colorado continues at a relaxed pace along the Arizona–California border, providing energy and irrigation in Arizona, California, and Nevada before draining into northwestern Mexico.

A RIVER RUNS THROUGH IT

Stretching along 277 mi of the Colorado River is one of the seven natural wonders of the world, the Grand Canyon ranges in width from 4 to 18 mi, while the walls around it soar up to a mile high. Nearly 2 billion years of geologic history and majesty are revealed in exposed tiers of rock cut deep in the Colorado Plateau. What caused this incredible marvel of nature? Erosion by water coupled with driving wind are most likely the major culprits: under the sculpting power of wind and water, the shale layers eroded into slopes and the harder sandstone and limestone layers created terraced cliffs. Other forces that may have helped shape the canyon include ice, volcanic activity, continental drift, and earthquakes.

WHO LIVES HERE
Native tribes have lived in the canyon for thousands of years and continue to do so, looking to the river for subsistence. The plateau-dwelling Hualapai ("people of the tall pines") live on a million acres along 108 mi of the Colorado River in the West Rim. The Havasupai ("people of the blue green water") live deep within the walls of the 12-mi-long Havasu Canyon—a major side canyon connected to the Grand Canyon.

ENVIRONMENTAL CONCERNS
When the Grand Canyon achieved national park status in 1919, only 44,173 people made the grueling overland trip to see it—quite a contrast from today's nearly 5 million annual visitors. The tremendous increase in visitation has greatly impacted the fragile ecosystems, as has Lake Powell's Glen Canyon Dam, which was constructed in the 1950s and '60s. The dam has changed the composition of the Colorado River, replacing warm water rich in sediments (nature's way of nourishing the riverbed and banks) with mostly cool, much clearer water. This has introduced nonnative plants and animals that threaten the extinction of several native species. Air pollution has also affected visibilty and the constant buzz of aerial tours has disturbed the natural solitude.

DID YOU KNOW?

The North Rim's isolated Toroweap overlook (also called Tuweep) is perched 3,000 feet above the canyon floor: a height equal to stacking the Sears Tower and Empire State Building on top of each other.

RIVER RAFTING THROUGH THE GRAND CANYON

Viewing the Colorado River from a canyon overlook is one thing, but looking up at the canyon from the middle of the river is quite another experience. If you're ready to tackle the churning white water of the Colorado River as it rumbles and hisses its way through the Grand Canyon, take a look at this map of what you might encounter along the way.

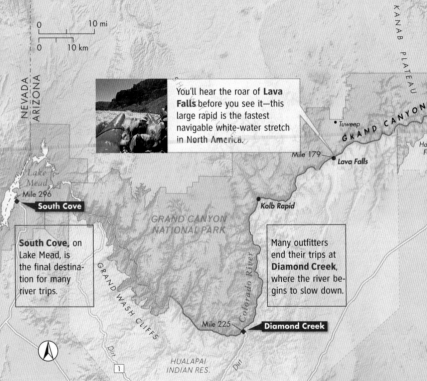

KANAB PLATEAU

NEVADA
ARIZONA

0   10 mi
0   10 km

You'll hear the roar of **Lava Falls** before you see it—this large rapid is the fastest navigable white-water stretch in North America.

Tuweep

GRAND CANYON

Havasu Falls

Mile 179   Lava Falls

Lake Mead

Mile 296

South Cove

Kolb Rapid

GRAND CANYON NATIONAL PARK

South Cove, on Lake Mead, is the final destination for many river trips.

GRAND WASH CLIFFS

Colorado River

Many outfitters end their trips at **Diamond Creek**, where the river begins to slow down.

Mile 225   **Diamond Creek**

Dirt

HUALAPAI INDIAN RES.

Dirt

Peach Springs

Valentine

COLORADO RIVER TRIPS

Time and Length	Entry and Exit points	Cost/person
1 day	Glen Canyon Dam to Lees Ferry	$75–$400
3–4 days	Lees Ferry to Phantom Ranch	*$650–$1,200
6 days, 89 mi	Phantom Ranch to Diamond Creek	$1,800–$2,100
9–10 days, 136 mi	Lees Ferry to Diamond Creek	$2,300–$3,000
14–16 days, 225 mi	Lees Ferry to South Cove	$3,250–$3,900

*Trips either begin or end at Phantom Ranch/Bright Angel Beach at the bottom of the Grand Canyon, at river mile 87

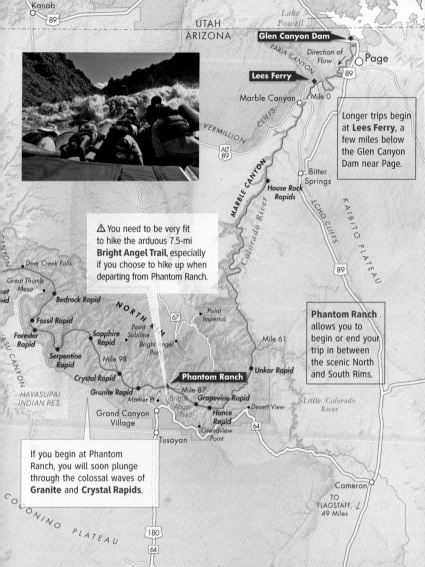

Kanab
89
UTAH
ARIZONA
Lake Powell
Glen Canyon Dam
Direction of Flow
Page
89
Lees Ferry
Marble Canyon
Mile 0
PARIA CANYON
VERMILLION CLIFFS
ALT 89
ECHO CLIFFS
KAIBITO PLATEAU
Bitter Springs
MARBLE CANYON
House Rock Rapids
Colorado River
89

Longer trips begin at **Lees Ferry**, a few miles below the Glen Canyon Dam near Page.

Deer Creek Falls
Great Thumb Mesa
Bedrock Rapid
NORTH RIM
Fossil Rapid
Forester Rapid
Sapphire Rapid
Point Sublime
Bright Angel Point
67
Point Imperial
Serpentine Rapid
Mile 98
Crystal Rapid
HAVASUPAI INDIAN RES.
Granite Rapid
Mather Pt.
Phantom Ranch
Bright Angel Trail
Mile 87
Grapevine Rapid
Hance Rapid
Unkar Rapid
Mile 61
Grand Canyon Village
Grandview Point
Desert View
64
Little Colorado River
Tusayan
COCONINO PLATEAU
180
64
Cameron
TO FLAGSTAFF, 49 Miles

⚠ You need to be very fit to hike the arduous 7.5-mi **Bright Angel Trail**, especially if you choose to hike up when departing from Phantom Ranch.

Phantom Ranch allows you to begin or end your trip in between the scenic North and South Rims.

If you begin at Phantom Ranch, you will soon plunge through the colossal waves of **Granite** and **Crystal Rapids**.

NOT JUST RAPIDS

Don't think that your experience will be non-stop white-water adrenaline. Most of the Colorado River features long, relaxing stretches of water, where you drift amid grandiose rock formations. You might even spot a mountain goat or two. Multiday trips include camping on the shore.

PLANNING YOUR RIVER RAFTING TRIP

OAR, MOTOR, OR HYBRID?

Base the type of trip you choose on the amount of effort you want to put in. Motor rafts, which are the roomiest of the choices, cover the most miles in less time and are the most comfortable. Guides do the rowing on oar boats and these smaller rafts offer a wilder ride. All-paddle trips are the most active and require the most involvement from guests. Hybrid trips are popular because they offer both the opportunity to paddle and to relax.

THE GEAR

Life jackets, beverages, tents, sheets, tarps, sleeping bags, dry bags, first aid, and food are provided—but you'll still need to plan ahead by packing clothing, hats, sunscreen, toiletries, and other sundries. Commercial outfitters allow each river runner two waterproof bags to store items during the day—just keep in mind that one of these will be filled up with the provided sleeping bag and tarp. ■TIP➔ Bring a rain suit: summer thunderstorms are frequent and chilly.

WHEN TO GO

Lots of people book trips for summer's peak period: June through August. If you're flexible, take advantage of the Arizona weather and go from May to early June or in September. ■TIP➔ Seats fill up quickly; make reservations for multiday trips a year or two in advance.

TOUR OPERATORS

Arizona Raft Adventures ☎ 928/526–8200 or 800/786–7238 ⊕ www.azraft.com

Canyoneers ☎ 928/526–0924 or 800/525–0924 ⊕ www.canyoneers.com

Grand Canyon Expeditions ☎ 435/644–2691 or 800/544–2691 ⊕ www.gcex.com

Hualapai River Runners ☎ 928/769–2219 or 888/255–9550 ⊕ www.destinationgrand-canyon.com

Wilderness River Adventures ☎ 928/645–3296 or 800/992–8022 ⊕ www.riveradventures.com

⇨ See "Rafting" in the Sports and the Outdoors section of What's Nearby for more information.

Above, Getting wet—and loving it—on an oar boat.

DID YOU KNOW?

As you're hanging on for dear life, consider this: Civil War veteran John Wesley Powell chartered these treacherous rapids in 1869—not only were conditions more dangerous then, but he had only one arm.

riveradventures.com) runs a wide variety of trips from 5 days to 16 days, oar or motorized, from April to October. Their most popular trip is the seven-day motor trip.

SKIING   **Elk Ridge Ski and Outdoor Recreation**
(✉ *2467 S. Perkinsville Rd., off I-40, Williams 86046* ☎ *928/814–5038* ⊕ *www.elkridgeski.com*) is usually open from mid-December through much of March, weather permitting. There are four groomed runs (including one for beginners), areas suitable for cross-country skiing, and a hill set aside for tubing. The lodge rents skis, snowboards, and inner tubes. From Williams, take South 4th Street/Perkinsville Road for 2.5 mi, and then turn right at Ski Run Road/Forest Road 106 and go another 1.5 mi. During heavy snows, four-wheel drive or chains may be necessary.

WHERE TO EAT AND STAY

ABOUT THE RESTAURANTS

INSIDE THE PARK   Within the park, you can find everything from cafeteria food to casual café fare to creatively prepared, Western- and Southwestern-inspired American cuisine. There's even a coffeehouse with organic joe. Reservations are accepted (and recommended) only for dinner at El Tovar Dining Room; they can be made up to six months in advance with El Tovar room reservations, 30 days in advance without. You can also make dinner reservations at the Grand Canyon Lodge Dining Room on the North Rim—they're less essential here but still a good idea in summer. The dress code is casual across the board, but El Tovar is your best option if you're looking to dress up a bit and thumb through an extensive wine list. On the North Rim there's a restaurant, a cafeteria, and a chuck-wagon-style Grand Cookout experience. Drinking water and restrooms are not available at most picnic spots.

OUTSIDE THE PARK   Options outside the park generally range from mediocre to terrible—you didn't come all the way to the Grand Canyon for the food, did you? Our selections highlight your best options. Of towns near the park, Williams definitely has the leg up on culinary variety and quality, with Tusayan and Jacob Lake to the north mostly either fast food or merely adequate sit-down restaurants. Near the park, even the priciest places welcome casual dress. On the Hualapai and Havasupai reservations in Havasu Canyon and on the West Rim, dining is limited and basic.

ABOUT THE HOTELS

INSIDE THE PARK   The park's accommodations include three "historic rustic" facilities and four motel-style lodges, all of which have undergone significant upgrades over the past decade. Of the 922 rooms, cabins, and suites, only 203, all at the Grand Canyon Lodge, are at the North Rim. Outside

El Tovar Hotel, the canyon's architectural highlight, accommodations are relatively basic but comfortable, and the most sought-after rooms have canyon views. Rates vary widely, but most rooms fall in the $150 to $190 range, though the most basic units at the South Rim go for just $90.

Reservations are a must, especially during the busy summer season. ■TIP→ **If you want to get your first choice (especially Bright Angel Lodge or El Tovar), make reservations as far in advance as possible; they're taken up to 13 months ahead.** You might find a last-minute cancellation, but you shouldn't count on it. Although lodging at the South Rim will keep you close to the action, the frenetic activity and crowded facilities are off-putting to some. With short notice, the best time to find a room on the South Rim is in winter. And though the North Rim is less crowded than the South Rim, lodging is available only from mid-May through mid-October, though remember that rooms are limited.

OUTSIDE THE PARK Just south of the park's boundary, Tusayan's hotels are in a convenient location but without bargains, while Williams can provide price breaks on food and lodging, as well as a respite from the crowds. Extra amenities (e.g., swimming pools and gyms) are also more abundant. Reservations are always a good idea. Lodging options are extremely limited and very basic at the West Rim.

ABOUT THE CAMPGROUNDS

INSIDE THE PARK Within the national park, camping is permitted only in designated campsites. Some campgrounds charge nightly camping fees in addition to entrance fees, and some accept reservations up to five months in advance through ⊕ *www.recreation.gov*. Others are first-come, first-served. The South Rim has three campgrounds, one with RV hookups. The North Rim's single in-park campground does not offer hookups. All four campgrounds are near the rims and easily accessible. In-park camping in a spot other than a developed rim campground requires a permit from the Backcountry Information Center, which also serves as your reservation. Permits can be requested by mail or fax; applying well in advance is recommended. Call ☎ 928/638–7875 between 1 and 5 Monday through Friday for information. Numerous backcountry campsites dot the canyon—be prepared for a considerable hike. The three established backcountry campgrounds require a trek of 4.6 to 16.6 mi.

OUTSIDE THE PARK Outside the park boundaries, two campgrounds, one with hookups, are within 7 mi of the South Rim, and two are within about 45 mi of the North Rim. Developed and undeveloped campsites are available, first-come, first-served, in the Kaibab National Forest. There is no camping on the West Rim, but you can pitch a tent on the beach near the Colorado River at the primitive campground on Diamond Creek Road. Hikers heading to the falls in Havasu Canyon can stay at the primitive campground in Supai.

WHAT IT COSTS					
	¢	$	$$	$$$	$$$$
Restaurant	under $8	$8–$12	$13–$20	$21–$30	over $30
Hotel	under $70	$70–$120	$121–$175	$176–$250	over $250

Restaurant prices are per person for a main course at dinner. Hotel prices are for a standard double in high season, excluding taxes and service charges.

WHERE TO EAT

IN THE PARK: SOUTH RIM

$$$
STEAK
✕**Arizona Room.** The canyon views from this casual Southwestern-style steak house are the best of any restaurant at the South Rim. The menu includes such delicacies as chile-crusted pan-seared wild salmon, chipotle barbecue baby back ribs, pulled-pork-and-avocado quesadillas, and half-pound buffalo burgers with Gorgonzola aioli. For dessert, try the cheesecake with prickly-pear syrup paired with one of the house's specialty coffee drinks. Seating is first-come, first served, so arrive early to avoid the crowds. ⊠ *Bright Angel Lodge, Desert View Dr., Grand Canyon Village* ☎ *928/638–2631* ⊕ *www.grandcanyonlodges.com* ⚲ *Reservations not accepted* ⊟ *AE, D, DC, MC, V* ☾ *Closed Jan. and Feb. No lunch Nov. and Dec.*

$
SOUTHWESTERN
✕**Bright Angel Restaurant.** The draw here is casual, affordable, if uninspired dining. No-surprises dishes will fill your belly at breakfast, lunch, or dinner. Entrées include such basics as salads, steaks, lasagna, fajitas, and fish tacos. Or you can step it up a notch and order some of the same selections straight from the Arizona Room menu including prime rib, baby back ribs, and wild salmon. For dessert try the warm apple grunt cake topped with vanilla ice cream. Be prepared to wait for a table: the dining room bustles all day long. The plain decor is broken up with large-pane windows and original artwork. ⊠ *Bright Angel Lodge, Desert View Dr., Grand Canyon Village* ☎ *928/638–2631* ⊕ *www.grandcanyonlodges.com* ⚲ *Reservations not accepted* ⊟ *AE, D, DC, MC, V.*

¢
AMERICAN
✕**Canyon Café.** Fast-food favorites here include pastries, burgers, and pizza. Open for breakfast, lunch, and dinner, this cafeteria in the Market Plaza also serves specials such as chicken potpie, fried catfish, and fried chicken. There isn't a fancy bar here, but you can order beer and wine with your meal. Resembling an old-fashioned diner, this cafeteria seats 345 guests and has easy-to-read signs that point the way to your favorite foods. Hours are limited in winter—it's best to call ahead then. ⊠ *Yavapai Lodge, Desert View Dr., Grand Canyon Village* ☎ *928/638–2631* ⊕ *www.grandcanyonlodges.com* ⚲ *Reservations not accepted* ⊟ *AE, D, DC, MC, V.*

$$$
SOUTHWESTERN
Fodor's Choice
★
✕**El Tovar Dining Room.** No doubt about it—this is the best restaurant for miles. Modeled after a European hunting lodge, this rustic 19th-century dining room built of hand-hewn logs is worth a visit. The cuisine is modern Southwestern with an exotic flair. Start with the smoked salmon–and–goat cheese crostini or the acclaimed black bean soup.

TOP PICNIC SPOTS

Bring your picnic basket and enjoy dining alfresco surrounded by some of the most beautiful backdrops in the country. Be sure to bring water, as it's unavailable at many of these spots, as are restrooms.

■ **Buggeln**, 15 mi east of Grand Canyon Village on Desert View Drive, has some secluded, shady spots.

■ **Cape Royal**, 23 mi south of the North Rim Visitor Center, is the most popular designated picnic area on the North Rim due to its panoramic views.

■ **Grandview Point** has, as the name implies, grand vistas; it is 12 mi east of the village on Desert View Drive.

■ **Point Imperial**, 11 mi northeast of the North Rim Visitor Center, has shade and some privacy.

The dinner menu includes such hearty yet creative dishes as citrus-marmalade-glazed duck with roasted poblano black bean rice, grilled New York strip steak with buttermilk-cornmeal onion rings, and a wild salmon tostada topped with organic greens and tequila vinaigrette. The dining room also has an extensive wine list. ■TIP→ **Dinner reservations can be made up to six months in advance with room reservations and 30 days in advance for all other visitors.** If you can't get a dinner table, consider lunch or breakfast—the best in the region with dishes like polenta corncakes with prickly pear–pistachio butter, and blackened breakfast trout and eggs. ⊠ *El Tovar Hotel, Desert View Dr.* ⌂ *10 Albright Ave., Grand Canyon Village 86023* ☎ *303/297–2757, 888/297–2757 reservations only, 928/638–2631 Ext. 6432* ⊕ *www.grandcanyonlodges.com* ⌂ *Reservations essential* ⊟ *AE, D, DC, MC, V.*

¢ ✕**Maswik Cafeteria.** You can get a burger, hot sandwich, pasta, or Mexi-
AMERICAN can fare at this food court, as well as pizza by the slice and wine and beer in the adjacent Maswik Pizza Pub. This casual eatery is 0.25 mi from the rim. Lines can be long during high-season lunch and dinner, but everything moves fairly quickly. ⊠ *Maswik Lodge, Desert View Dr., Grand Canyon Village* ☎ *928/638–2631* ⊕ *www.grandcanyonlodges. com* ⌂ *Reservations not accepted* ⊟ *AE, D, DC, MC, V.*

IN THE PARK: NORTH RIM

¢ ✕**Deli in the Pines.** Dining choices are very limited on the North Rim,
AMERICAN but this is your best bet for a meal on a budget. Selections include pizza, salads, deli sandwiches, hot dogs, homemade breakfast pastries, and soft-serve ice cream. Best of all, there is an outdoor seating area for dining alfresco. It's open for breakfast, lunch, and dinner. ⊠ *Grand Canyon Lodge, Bright Angel Point, North Rim* ☎ *928/638–2611 Ext. 766* ⊕ *www.grandcanyonforever.com* ⌂ *Reservations not accepted* ⊟ *AE, D, DC, MC, V* ⊙ *Closed mid-Oct.–mid-May.*

$$$ ✕**Grand Canyon Lodge Dining Room.** The historic lodge has a huge, high-
AMERICAN ceilinged dining room with spectacular views and decent food, though
★ the draw here is definitely the setting. You might find pork medallions, bison flank steak, and grilled ruby trout for dinner. The filling, simply prepared food here takes a flavorful turn with Southwestern spices

and organic selections. It's also open for breakfast and lunch. A full-service bar and an impressive wine list add to the relaxed atmosphere of the only full-service, sit-down restaurant on the North Rim. Dinner reservations aren't required, but they're a good idea in summer and on spring and fall weekends. ⊠ *Grand Canyon Lodge, Bright Angel Point, North Rim* ☎ *928/638–2611 Ext. 760* ⊕ *www.grandcanyonforever.com* ⊟ *AE, D, DC, MC, V* ⊘ *Closed mid-Oct.–mid-May.*

$$$$ ✕ **Grand Cookout.** Dine under the stars and enjoy live entertainment at
AMERICAN this chuck-wagon-style dining experience—a popular family-friendly
ⓒ choice among the North Rim's limited dining options. Fill up on Western favorites including barbecue beef brisket, roasted chicken, baked beans, and cowboy biscuits. The food is basic and tasty, but the real draw is the nightly performance of Western music and tall tales. Transportation from the Grand Canyon Lodge to the cookout is included in the price. Be sure to call before 4 PM for dinner reservations. Advance reservations are taken up to seven days ahead at the Grand Canyon Lodge registration desk. ⊠ *Grand Canyon Lodge, North Rim* ☎ *928/638–2611* ⚼ *Reservations essential* ⊟ *AE, D, DC, MC, V* ⊘ *Closed mid-Oct.–mid-May.*

OUTSIDE THE PARK: TUSAYAN

$$ ✕ **Canyon Star Restaurant and Saloon.** Relax in the rustic timber-and-stone
AMERICAN dining room at the Grand Hotel for reliable if uninspired American
ⓒ food, with an emphasis at dinner on steaks and barbecue. Other popular options include barbecue chicken and ribs, and traditional Mexican fare. Most nights there's entertainment: live music, karaoke, or Native American dance performances—all great for families. There's a kids' menu, and the Canyon Star also serves breakfast and lunch daily. In summer, be sure to reserve a table. There's also a coffee bar in the hotel lobby. ⊠ *Hwy. 64/U.S. 180, Tusayan* ☎ *928/638–3333* ⊕ *www. grandcanyongrandhotel.com* ⊟ *AE, DC, MC, V.*

$$$ ✕ **The Coronado Room.** Inside the Best Western Grand Canyon Squire
AMERICAN Inn is the most sophisticated cuisine in Tusayan in an upscale dining room with attentive service. The menu includes well-prepared, hearty American food, with an emphasis on game (elk, venison, buffalo), plus grilled seafood, escargot, and oversize desserts. There's a good-size wine list, too. Although classier than most eateries in these parts, dress is still casual and the vibe relaxed. Reservations are a good idea, particularly in the busy season. ⊠ *Hwy. 64/U.S. 180, Tusayan* ☎ *928/638–2681* ⊟ *AE, D, DC, MC, V* ⊘ *No lunch.*

OUTSIDE THE PARK: WILLIAMS

$ ✕ **Cruisers Café 66.** A festive spot for a nostalgic meal, this diner pat-
AMERICAN terned after a classic '50s-style, high-school hangout (but with cocktail
ⓒ service) pleases kids and adults with a large menu of family-priced
★ American classics—good burgers and fries, barbecue pork sandwiches, salads, and thick malts, plus a choice steak that'll set you back about $25. The Grand Canyon Brewery, accessed by a side entrance, adds to the casual fun—just saddle up to a hand-carved log bar stool and order one of five microbrews on tap. A large mural of the town's heyday along the "Mother Road" and historic cars out front make this a

Route 66 favorite. Kids enjoy the relaxed atmosphere and jukebox tunes. ☒ *233 W. Rte. 66, Williams* ☏ *928/635–2445* ▭ *AE, D, MC, V.*

$ × **Pancho McGillicuddy's.** Established
MEXICAN in 1893 as the Cabinet Saloon, this
★ restaurant is on the National Register of Historic Places. Gone are the spittoons and pipes—the colorful dining area now has Mexican-inspired decor and serves such specialties as "armadillo eggs" (deep-fried jalapeños stuffed with cheese). Other favorites include fish tacos, buzzard wings—better known as hot wings—and *pollo verde* (chicken breasts smothered in a sauce of cheese, sour cream, and green chiles). The bar has TVs tuned to sporting events and pours more than 30 tequilas, and there's live old-school rock and country many evenings. ☒ *141 Railroad Ave., Williams* ☏ *928/635–4150* ▭ *AE, D, MC, V.*

$$ × **Red Raven.** Chef-owned David Haines cultivates a devoted foodie
ECLECTIC following with this dapper storefront bistro in the heart of downtown
Fodor's Choice Williams, with warm lighting and romantic booth seating. Creatively
★ presented fare blends American, Italian, and Asian ingredients—specialties include a starter of crisp tempura shrimp salad with a ginger-sesame dressing, and mains like charbroiled salmon with basil butter over cranberry–pine nut couscous, and pork scallopine with a roasted-tomato sauce, served with angel hair pasta and sautéed local vegetables. The well-selected wine and beer list is one of the most extensive in the region. ☒ *135 W. Rte. 66, Williams* ☏ *928/635–4980* ⊕ *www. redravenrestaurant.com* ▭ *AE, D, MC, V.*

¢ × **Twisters.** Kick up some Route 66 nostalgia at this old-fashioned soda
AMERICAN fountain and kitschy gift shop. Dine on burgers and hot dogs, a famous
☺ Twisters sundae (topped with raspberry sauce, nuts, and hot fudge), Route 66 beer float, or cherry phosphate—all to the sounds of '50s tunes. The kids' menu features cartoon characters and a selection of corn dogs, hot dogs, hamburgers, chicken strips, and peanut-butter-and-jelly sandwiches. The adjoining gift shop is a blast from the past, with Route 66 tchotchkes, classic Coca-Cola memorabilia, and fanciful items celebrating the careers of Betty Boop, James Dean, Elvis, and Marilyn Monroe. ☒ *417 E. Rte. 66, Williams* ☏ *928/635–0266* ▭ *AE, D, MC, V* ☺ *Closed Sun.*

3

WHERE TO STAY

IN THE PARK: SOUTH RIM

$-$$ ⊞ **Bright Angel Lodge.** Famed architect Mary Jane Colter designed this
☺ 1935 log-and-stone structure, which sits within a few yards of the
★ canyon rim and blends superbly with the canyon walls. Its location is similar to El Tovar but for about half the price. Accommodations are in surprisingly attractive motel-style rooms or cabins. Lodge rooms

don't have TVs, and some rooms share a bath. Scattered among the pines are 50 cabins, which do have TVs and private baths; some have fireplaces, and a few have virtually unobstructed canyon views. Expect rustic, historic charm but not luxury. The Bright Angel Dining Room serves casual, affordable meals all day and the Arizona Room serves dinner only. Adding to the experience are an ice-cream parlor, gift shop, and small history museum. **Pros:** some rooms have canyon vistas; all are steps away from the rim; Internet kiosks and transportation desk for the mule ride check-in are in the lobby; good value for the amazing location. **Cons:** the popular lobby is always packed; parking is a bit of a hike; lack of elevators make accessibility an issue for lodge rooms. ✉ *Desert View Dr., Grand Canyon Village* ✆ *Box 699, Grand Canyon 86023* ☎ *888/297–2757 reservations only, 928/638–2631* ⊕ *www.grandcanyonlodges.com* ➳ *37 rooms, 18 with bath; 49 cabins* ☖ *In-room: a/c (some), safe (some), refrigerator (some), no TV (some), Wi-Fi (some). In-hotel: 2 restaurants, bar* ⊟ *AE, D, DC, MC, V.*

$$$–$$$$
Fodor's Choice
★

🏨 **El Tovar Hotel.** A registered National Historic Landmark, the "architectural crown jewel of the Grand Canyon" was built in 1905 of Oregon pine logs and native stone. The hotel's proximity to all of the canyon's facilities, European hunting-lodge atmosphere, attractively updated rooms and tile baths, and renowned dining room make it the best place to stay on the South Rim. It's usually booked well in advance (up to 13 months ahead), though it's easier to get a room during winter months. Three suites (El Tovar, Fred Harvey, and Mary Jane Colter) and several rooms have canyon views (these book *very* early), but you can enjoy the view anytime from the cocktail-lounge back porch. **Pros:** historic lodging just steps from the South Rim; fabulous lounge with outdoor seating and canyon views; best in-park dining on-site. **Cons:** books up quickly. ✉ *Desert View Dr., Grand Canyon Village* ✆ *Box 699, Grand Canyon 86023* ☎ *888/297–2757 reservations only, 928/638–2631* ⊕ *www.grandcanyonlodges.com* ➳ *66 rooms, 12 suites* ☖ *In-room: a/c, refrigerator, Wi-Fi. In-hotel: restaurant, room service, bar, Wi-Fi hotspot* ⊟ *AE, D, DC, MC, V.*

$$

🏨 **Kachina Lodge.** On the rim halfway between El Tovar and Bright Angel Lodge, this motel-style lodge has many rooms with partial canyon views ($10 extra). Although lacking the historical charm of the neighboring lodges, these well-outfitted (safes, coffeemakers, irons) rooms are a good bet for families and are within easy walking distance of dining facilities at El Tovar and Bright Angel Lodge—they're identical in look and amenities to rooms at the Thunderbird Lodge. There are also several rooms for people with physical disabilities. There's no air-conditioning, but evaporative coolers keep the heat at bay. **Pros:** partial canyon views in half the rooms; family-friendly; steps from the best restaurants in the park. **Cons:** check-in takes place at El Tovar Hotel; limited parking; pleasant but bland furnishings. ✉ *Desert View Dr., Grand Canyon Village* ✆ *Box 699, Grand Canyon 86023* ☎ *888/297–2757 reservations only, 928/638–2631* ⊕ *www.grandcanyonlodges.com* ➳ *49 rooms* ☖ *In-room: no a/c, safe, refrigerator, Wi-Fi (some)* ⊟ *AE, D, DC, MC, V.*

3

$-$$ 🛏 **Maswik Lodge.** The lodge, named for a Hopi kachina who is said to guard the canyon, is 0.25 mi from the rim. Accommodations are far from crowds and noise and nestled in a shady ponderosa pine forest, with options ranging from rustic cabins to more modern motel-style rooms. The cabins are the cheapest option but are available only spring through fall. Rooms in the South Section have the fewest frills and resemble what you'd find at a typical budget chain property (though with wall-mounted fans instead of air-conditioning). The North Section rooms cost nearly twice as much but are larger and have brighter, newer furnishings, air-conditioning, and plenty of extras—refrigerators, coffeemakers, and safes. Families appreciate the pizza pub, a casual spot with a big-screen TV. Kids under 16 stay free. **Pros:** larger rooms here than in older lodgings; good for families; affordable dining options. **Cons:** rooms lack historic charm and cabins as well as rooms in the South Section are quite plain; tucked away from the rim in the forest. ⊠ *Grand Canyon Village* 🖉 *Box 699, Grand Canyon 86023* 📷 *888/297–2757 reservations only, 928/638–2631* ⊕ *www.grandcanyonlodges.com* 🛏 *250 rooms, 28 cabins* ⚒ *In-room: a/c (some), safe (some), refrigerator (some), Wi-Fi (some). In-hotel: restaurant, bar, Internet terminal* ⊟ *AE, D, DC, MC, V.*

¢ 🛏 **Phantom Ranch.** In a grove of cottonwood trees on the canyon floor, Phantom Ranch is accessible only to hikers and mule trekkers. The wood-and-stone buildings originally made up a hunting camp built in 1922. There are 40 dormitory beds and 14 beds in cabins, all with shared baths. Seven additional cabins are reserved for mule riders, who buy their trips as a package. The mess hall–style restaurant, one of the most remote eating establishments in the United States, serves family-style meals, with breakfast, dinner, and box lunches available. Reservations, taken up to 13 months in advance, are a must for services and lodging. **Pros:** only inner-canyon lodging option; fabulous canyon views; remote access limits crowds. **Cons:** accessible only by foot or mule; few amenities or means of outside communication. ⊠ *On canyon floor, at intersection of Bright Angel and Kaibab trails* 🖉 *Box 699, Grand Canyon 86023* 📷 *303/297–2757 or 888/297–2757* ⊕ *www.grandcanyonlodges.com* 🛏 *4 dormitories and 2 cabins for hikers, 7 cabins with outside showers for mule riders* ⚒ *In-room: no a/c, no phone, no TV. In-hotel: restaurant* ⊟ *AE, D, DC, MC, V.*

$$ 🛏 **Thunderbird Lodge.** This motel with comfortable, simple rooms with the modern amenities you'd expect at a typical mid-price chain hotel is next to Bright Angel Lodge in Grand Canyon Village. For $10 more, you can get a room with a partial view of the canyon. Rooms have either two queen beds or one king. Some rooms have evaporative coolers (they're very effective) instead of air-conditioning. **Pros:** partial canyon views in some rooms; family-friendly. **Cons:** rooms lack personality; check-in takes place at Bright Angel Lodge; limited parking. ⊠ *Desert View Dr., Grand Canyon Village* 🖉 *Box 699, Grand Canyon 86023* 📷 *888/297–2757 reservations only, 928/638–2631* ⊕ *www.grandcanyonlodges.com* 🛏 *55 rooms* ⚒ *In-room: a/c (some), safe, refrigerator, Wi-Fi (some)* ⊟ *AE, D, DC, MC, V.*

Perched on the North Rim's edge—1,000 feet higher than the South Rim—is the Grand Canyon Lodge.

$–$$ 🏨 **Yavapai Lodge.** The largest motel-style lodge in the park is tucked in a piñon and juniper forest at the eastern end of Grand Canyon Village, near the RV park. The basic rooms are near the park's general store, the visitor center (0.25 mi), and the rim (0.5 mi). The cafeteria, open for breakfast, lunch, and dinner, serves standard park-service food. Rates drop, depending on availability, in winter. **Pros:** transportation-activities desk on-site in the lobby; near Market Plaza in Grand Canyon Village; forested grounds. **Cons:** farthest in-park lodging from the rim. ⊠ *Grand Canyon Village* ☎ *Box 699, Grand Canyon 86023* ✆ *888/297–2757 reservations only, 928/638–2961* ⊕ *www.grandcanyonlodges.com* ⤵ *358 rooms* ♻ *In-room: a/c (some), refrigerator, Wi-Fi (some). In-hotel: restaurant, Internet terminal* ⊟ *AE, D, DC, MC, V* ⊗ *Closed Jan. and Feb.*

CAMP-
GROUNDS
AND RV PARKS
¢

⛺ **Bright Angel Campground.** This campground is near Phantom Ranch on the South and North Kaibab trails, at the bottom of the canyon. There are toilet facilities and running water, but no showers. If you plan to eat at the Phantom Ranch Canteen, book your meals ahead of time. Reservations for all services, taken up to four months in advance, are a must. A backcountry permit, which serves as your reservation, is required to stay here. **Pros:** incredible setting in bottom of canyon; close to Phantom Ranch. **Cons:** extremely remote; long hike from either rim. ⊠ *Intersection of South and North Kaibab trails, Grand Canyon* ☎ *Backcountry Information Center, Box 129, Grand Canyon 86023* ✆ *928/638–7875* ✆ *928/638–2125* ⤵ *30 tent sites, 2 group sites* ♻ *Flush toilets, drinking water, picnic tables* ☞ *Backcountry permit required* ⊗ *Open year-round.*

¢ 🏕 **Desert View Campground.** Popular for spectacular views of the canyon from the nearby watchtower, this campground fills up fast in summer. Fifty RV (without hookups) and tent sites are available on a first-come, first-served basis. **Pros:** right off the main road, steps from wonderful canyon views; farther from crowds and RVs than other South Rim campgrounds. **Cons:** no RV hookups; fills up fast. ⊠ *Desert View Dr., 23 mi east of Grand Canyon Village off Hwy. 64* 🚲 *Backcountry Information Center, Box 129, Grand Canyon 86023* 🕾 *928/638–7875* 🖷 *928/638–2125* 🛏 *50 campsites* 🚻 *Flush toilets, drinking water, grills, picnic tables* 🚫 *Reservations not accepted* 🕐 *May–mid-Oct.*

> **DUFFEL SERVICE: LIGHTEN YOUR LOAD**
>
> Hikers staying at either Phantom Ranch or Bright Angel campground can also take advantage of the ranch's duffel service: bags or packs weighing 30 pounds or less can be transported to the ranch by mule for a fee of $64.04 each way. As is true for many desirable things at the canyon, reservations are a must.

¢ 🏕 **Indian Garden.** Halfway down the canyon is this campground, en route to Phantom Ranch on the Bright Angel Trail. Running water and toilet facilities are available, but not showers. A backcountry permit, which serves as a reservation, is required. You can book up to four months in advance by fax or mail. **Pros:** pristine setting with potential for spotting wildlife; far from Grand Canyon Village crowds. **Cons:** remote; accessed via a long hike. ⊠ *Bright Angel Trail, Grand Canyon* 🚲 *Backcountry Information Center, Box 129, Grand Canyon 86023* 🕾 *928/638–7875* 🖷 *928/638–2125* 🛏 *15 tent sites, 1 large site* 🚻 *Pit toilets, drinking water, picnic tables* 🗹 *Reservations essential* 🕐 *Open year-round.*

¢ 🏕 **Mather Campground.** Mather has RV and tent sites but no hookups.
★ No reservations are accepted from mid-November through February (when rates drop slightly), but the rest of the year, especially during the busy spring and summer seasons, they are a good idea, and can be made up to five months in advance. Ask at the campground entrance for same-day availability. **Pros:** walking distance to several South Rim restaurants and grocery store; open year-round; great for tent campers. **Cons:** no hookups for RVs; in crowded part of South Rim. ⊠ *Off Village Loop Dr., Grand Canyon Village* 🕾 *877/444–6777* ⊕ *www.recreation.gov* 🛏 *308 sites for RVs and tents* 🚻 *Flush toilets, dump station, drinking water, guest laundry, showers, fire grates, picnic tables, public telephone* 🕐 *Open year-round.*

IN THE PARK: NORTH RIM

$–$$ 🏨 **Grand Canyon Lodge.** This historic property, constructed mainly in the
Fodor'sChoice 1920s and '30s, is the premier lodging facility in the North Rim area.
★ The main building has locally quarried limestone walls and timbered ceilings. Lodging options include small, rustic cabins; larger cabins (some with a canyon view and some with two bedrooms); and slightly more modern motel rooms. The two-bedroom Pioneer cabins sleep up to six people. The hand-carved Aspen lodge furniture adds to the rustic atmosphere. However, the best of the bunch are the Rim View Western,

especially log cabins 301 and 306, which have private porches perched on the lip of the canyon. Other cabins with fabulous canyon views include 305, 309, and 310. Because of their premier location, these cabins are snapped up fast and need to be reserved a year in advance. **Pros:** steps away from gorgeous North Rim views; close to several easy hiking trails. **Cons:** as the only in-park North Rim lodging option, this lodge fills up fast; few amenities and no Internet access. ⊠ *Grand Canyon National Park, Hwy. 67, North Rim* ☎ *877/386–4383, 928/638–2611 May–Oct., 928/645–6865 Nov.–Apr.* ⊕ *www.grandcanyonforever.com* ⟿ *40 rooms, 178 cabins* ⌂ *In-room: no a/c, refrigerator (some), no TV. In-hotel: 3 restaurants, bar, bicycles, laundry facilities (at the campground)* ⊟ *AE, D, MC, V* ⊙ *Closed mid-Oct.–mid-May.*

CAMPGROUND
¢   ⚠ **North Rim Campground.** The only designated campground at the North Rim of Grand Canyon National Park sits 3 mi north of the rim, and has 83 RV and tent sites (no hookups). You can reserve a site up to five months in advance. Leashed pets are allowed at the campground. **Pros:** only camping at North Rim and mostly geared towards tents; attractive pine-shaded setting. **Cons:** no hookups for RVs; closed much of the year. ⊠ *Hwy. 67, North Rim* ☎ *877/444–6777* ⊕ *www.recreation.gov* ⟿ *83 campsites* ⌂ *Flush toilets, dump station, drinking water, guest laundry, showers, fire grates, picnic tables, general store* ⌂ *Reservations essential* ⊙ *Mid-May–mid-Oct., possibly later, weather permitting.*

OUTSIDE THE PARK: TUSAYAN

$$$
☺   ⛆ **Best Western Grand Canyon Squire Inn.** About 1 mi from the park's
★   south entrance, this motel lacks the historic charm of the older lodges at the canyon rim, but has more amenities, including a small cowboy museum in the lobby, an upscale gift shop, and one of the better restaurants in the region. Children enjoy the bowling alley, arcade, and outdoor swimming pool. Updated rooms with flat-screen TVs are spacious and furnished in Southwestern style. Those in the rear have a view of the woods. Kiosks in the lobby provide Internet access to registered guests. **Pros:** a cool pool in summer and a steamy sauna for cold winter nights; children's activities at the Family Fun Center; close to South Rim. **Cons:** hall noise can be an issue with all of the in-hotel activities. ⊠ *100 Hwy. 64, Grand Canyon* ☎ *928/638–2681 or 800/622–6966* ⊕ *www.grandcanyonsquire.com* ⟿ *250 rooms, 4 suites* ⌂ *In-room: a/c, refrigerator (some), Wi-Fi. In-hotel: restaurant, bar, pool, gym, laundry facilities, Wi-Fi hotspot* ⊟ *AE, D, DC, MC, V.*

$$$
★   ⛆ **The Grand Hotel.** At the south end of Tusayan, this popular hotel has bright, clean rooms decorated in Southwestern colors. The lobby has a stone-and-timber design, cozy seating areas, and free Wi-Fi. Live Native American dancing and cowboy singers lead the entertainment in the Canyon Star Wild West Saloon during evenings in the peak season. At the bar, you can sit on a saddle that was once used for canyon mule trips. **Pros:** coffee stand for a quick morning pick-me-up; gift shop stocked with outdoor gear and regional books. **Cons:** no in-room Internet access; restaurant and lounge hours are not reliable; facilities often closed during off-season. ⊠ *Hwy. 64/U.S. 180, Grand Canyon* ☎ *928/638–3333 or 888/634–7263* ⊕ *www.grandcanyongrandhotel.*

com ➚ *109 rooms, 12 suites* ⟲ *In-room: a/c. In-hotel: restaurant, bar, pool, gym, laundry facilities, Wi-Fi hotspot* ☰ *AE, D, DC, MC, V.*

$$ 🏨 **Red Feather Lodge.** This motel and adjacent hotel are a good value about 6 mi from the canyon. A Southwestern theme dominates the large rooms. The motel portion of the lodge is closed January through March, except to guests with pets and smokers. Rooms have cable TV with movies and video games, and there is Internet access in the rooms and lobby for a fee. An outdoor pool and hot tub are open seasonally. **Pros:** good price for being so close to park; complimentary Continental breakfast. **Cons:** this older hotel shows more wear and tear than other nearby lodging facilities. ⊠ *Hwy. 64/U.S. 180, Tusayan* ☎ *928/638–2414 or 866/561–2425* ⊕ *www.redfeatherlodge.com* ➚ *215 rooms, 1 suite* ⟲ *In-room: a/c, refrigerator (some), Wi-Fi. In-hotel: restaurant, pool, gym, some pets allowed* ☰ *AE, D, DC, MC, V* ⭤ *CP.*

OUTSIDE THE PARK: WILLIAMS

¢–$ 🏨 **Canyon Motel and RV Park.** Railcars, cabooses, and cottages make up
☉ this 13-acre property on the outskirts of Williams, about a one-hour drive to the park. The best room is the 1929 Santa Fe red caboose: It's family-friendly, with two sides separated by a bathroom, giving parents a little privacy. The original wooden floor and tool equipment add to the authenticity. Another caboose looks much like a standard hotel room inside, as do the flagstone cottage rooms built from the local sandstone known for its variegated colors. A Pullman passenger car holds three rooms (railcar suites), each with its own bathroom. The motel also has a few dry campsites (no water available) and a 47-space RV park with full hookups. **Pros:** family-friendly property with hiking, horseshoes, and playground; general store and recreation room; owners are friendly and helpful. **Cons:** a few miles from Williams dining options; RV park traffic. ⊠ *1900 E. Rodeo Rd., Williams* ☎ *928/635–9371 or 800/482–3955* ⊕ *www.thecanyonmotel.com* ➚ *18 rooms, 5 railcar suites* ⟲ *In-room: no a/c (some), no phone, refrigerator. In-hotel: pool, laundry facilities, Wi-Fi hotspot* ☰ *D, MC, V* ⭤ *CP.*

$$ 🏨 **Grand Canyon Railway Hotel.** This hotel was designed to resemble the
★ train depot's original Fray Marcos lodge. Neoclassical Greek columns flank the grand entrance, which leads to a lobby with maple-wood balustrades, an enormous flagstone fireplace, and oil paintings of the Grand Canyon by local artist Kenneth McKenna. Original bronzes by Frederic Remington also adorn the lobby. The attractive Southwestern-style accommodations have large bathrooms and comfy beds with upscale linens. Adjacent to the lobby is Spenser's, a pub with an ornate 19th-century hand-carved bar. Riding the train to the canyon in sleek '50s-era railcars can be a relaxing alternative to the long drive. The hotel also operates an adjacent RV park and a "pet resort" that provides comfy accommodations for dogs and cats. **Pros:** railway package options; game room and outdoor playground; short walk from historic downtown restaurants and bars. **Cons:** railroad noise; limited food options. ⊠ *235 N. Grand Canyon Blvd., Williams* ☎ *928/635–4010 or 800/843–8724* ⊕ *www.thetrain.com* ➚ *287 rooms, 11 suites* ⟲ *In-room: refrigerator (some). In-hotel: restaurant, bar, pool, gym, laundry facilities, Wi-Fi hotspot* ☰ *AE, D, MC, V.*

$-$$ 🏨 **Red Garter B&B.** This restored saloon and bordello from 1897 now houses a small, antiques-filled B&B. Guest rooms are on the second floor; ask for the "Best Gal's Room," which has its own sitting room overlooking the train tracks. All four rooms (two are interior, with skylights) are very quiet, as the only train traffic is the Grand Canyon Railway. Even if you don't stay here, the fresh pastries served in the first-floor coffee shop are worth a stop. **Pros:** on-site coffeehouse and bakery; decorated in antiques and period pieces; steps from several restaurants and bars. **Cons:** all rooms are only accessible by stairs; parking is across the street; over an hour drive to canyon. ⊠ *137 W. Railroad Ave., Williams* ☎ *928/635–1484 or 800/328–1484* ⊕ *www.redgarter. com* ↩ *4 rooms* ♿ *In-room: a/c, no phone, Wi-Fi. In-hotel: no kids under 8* ➡ *D, MC, V* ⊙*CP* ☾ *Closed Dec.–mid-Feb.*

$$-$$$ 🏨 **Sheridan House Inn.** Nestled among 2 acres of pine trees near Route
★   66, this upscale B&B has decks looking to the tall ponderosa pines and a flagstone patio with a hot tub. Average-size bedrooms all have king beds, CD stereos, and marble bathrooms. Hearty breakfasts—scrambled eggs, fruit plates, bacon, sausage, potatoes, eggs Benedict, and buttermilk pancakes—will ready you for the hour-long drive to the canyon. K.C. and Mary Seidner are gracious hosts who will gladly help guests plan itineraries. **Pros:** quiet location; game room has puzzles and board games; entertainment room has a pool table and piano. **Cons:** a long drive to the canyon and a short drive from downtown Williams; parking is at the bottom of the hill. ⊠ *460 E. Sheridan Ave., Williams* ☎ *928/635–9441 or 888/635–9345* ⊕ *www. grandcanyonbbinn.com* ↩ *6 rooms, 2 suites* ♿ *In-room: no a/c, DVD (some), Wi-Fi* ➡ *AE, D, MC, V* ⊙*BP.*

CAMP-   ⛺ **Kaibab National Forest.** Both developed and undeveloped campsites
GROUNDS   are available on a first-come, first-served basis at this forest that sur-
¢   rounds Williams and extends to the Grand Canyon, encompassing Cataract Lake, Kaibab Lake, Dogtown Lake, and White Horse Lake. Campgrounds are open May through September and range in rates from $14 to $18 per night. Developed campgrounds have pit toilets, fire rings, and picnic tables. There is a dump station, but no hookups at Kaibab, Dogtown, and White Horse Lake. **Pros:** pristine setting far from crowds. **Cons:** primitive camping areas only; fairly remote location. ☎ *928/699–1239 or 877/444–6777* ⊕ *www.fs.fed.us/r3/kai.*

OUTSIDE THE PARK: NORTH RIM

$-$$ 🏨 **Jacob Lake Inn.** The bustling lodge at Jacob Lake Inn is a popular stop for those heading to the North Rim, 45 mi south. This 5-acre complex in Kaibab National Forest has basic cabins and standard motel rooms that overlook the highways. Avoid the older facilities by asking for one of the new rooms. They aren't as nostalgic and private as the cabins, but they do have fresher surroundings. **Pros:** grocery store, coffee shop, and restaurant; quiet rooms. **Cons:** small bathroom in cabins; worn furnishings; old-fashioned key locks. ⊠ *Hwy. 67/U.S. 89A, Fredonia* ☎ *928/643–7232* ⊕ *www.jacoblake.com* ↩ *32 rooms, 26 cabins* ♿ *In-room: no a/c (some), no phone (some), no TV (some) Wi-Fi (some). In-hotel: restaurant, some pets allowed* ➡ *AE, D, MC, V.*

$ ⊞ **Marble Canyon Lodge.** This Arizona Strip lodge popular with anglers
★   and rafters opened in 1929 on the same day the Navajo Bridge was
dedicated. Three types of accommodations are available: rooms in the
original building, standard motel rooms in the newer building, and two-
bedroom apartments. You can play the 1920s piano or sit on the porch
swing of the native-rock lodge and look out on Vermilion Cliffs and
the desert. Zane Grey and Gary Cooper are among well-known past
guests. **Pros:** convenience store and trading post; great fishing on the
Colorado River. **Cons:** no-frills rustic lodging; more than 70 mi to the
Grand Canyon North Rim. ⊠ *0.25 mi west of Navajo Bridge on U.S. 89A*
⬩ Box 6001, Marble Canyon 86036 ☎ *928/355–2225 or 800/726–1789*
⊕ *www.leesferryflyfishing.com/thelodge* ⬐ *46 rooms, 8 apartments* ⌂ *In-
room: a/c, no phone, kitchen (some), Wi-Fi. In-hotel: restaurant, bar,
laundry facilities, some pets allowed* ⊟ *AE, D, MC, V.*

OUTSIDE THE PARK: WEST RIM

$$ ⊞ **Havasupai Lodge.** These are fairly spartan accommodations, but you
won't mind much when you see the natural beauty surrounding you.
The lodge and restaurant are at the bottom of Havasu Canyon and are
operated by the Havasupai Tribe. In addition to the room rate, there
is a $35 per-person tribal entry fee and a $5 environmental-care fee.
Reservations are essential and can be made up to a year in advance.
Pros: near the famous waterfalls; Native American perspective on the
natural and cultural history of the Grand Canyon. **Cons:** accessible
only by foot, horseback, or helicopter; rooms are plain and worn; no
phones, Internet, or TVs. ⊠ *Supai Village Trail* ☎ *928/448–2111 or
928/448–2201* ⊕ *www.havasupaitribe.com* ⬐ *24 rooms* ⌂ *In-room:
no phone, no TV* ⊟ *MC, V.*

$ ⊞ **Hualapai Lodge.** In Peach Springs on the longest stretch of the origi-
nal historic Route 66, the hotel has a comfortable lobby with a large
fireplace that is welcoming on chilly nights—it's a 19-mi scenic drive
to the West Rim. The rooms are clean but basic. **Pros:** concierge desk
arranges river trips with the Hualapai River Runners; good on-site res-
taurant with Native American dishes; Hualapai locals add a different
perspective to the canyon experience. **Cons:** basic rooms lack historic
charm; location is off the beaten path. ⊠ *900 Rte. 66, Peach Springs*
☎ *928/769–2230 or 888/255–9550* ⊕ *www.grandcanyonwest.com/
lodge.html* ⬐ *60 rooms* ⌂ *In-room: a/c. In-hotel: restaurant, pool, gym,
laundry facilities, Wi-Fi hotspot* ⊟ *AE, D, MC, V.*

$$ ⊞ **Hualapai Ranch.** Cabins are clean and neat, but also very small and
unassuming. The front porches make for a good place to sit and
unwind after a hectic day exploring the sights at the West Rim. The
cabins are adjacent to a small "Western" town, where visitors can pose
for snapshots, sign up for guided horseback tours and wagon rides,
watch gunfight re-enactments in the dusty streets, and visit a petting
zoo. Accommodations include two meals, a Hualapai visitation permit,
and motor-coach transfers to the rim overlooks at Guano Point and
Eagle Point. **Pros:** front porches have relaxed desert views; rustlers
tell tall tales and strike up a tune at campfire programs; dining room
serves meals all day long. **Cons:** no phones, Internet, or TVs. ⊠ *US
66, West Rim* ⬩ *6206 W. Desert Inn, Suite B, Las Vegas, NV 89146*

☎ *702/878–9378 or 888/868–9378* ⊕ *www.grandcanyonwest.com*
⇲ *20 cabins* ☖ *In-room: no phone, no TV, Wi-Fi. In-hotel: restaurant*
▭ *AE, MC, V.*

CAMP-
GROUNDS
¢ ⛺ **Diamond Creek**. The Hualapai permit camping on their tribal lands here, with an overnight camping permit of $25 per person per night, which can be purchased at the Hualapai Lodge. You can camp on the beach of the Colorado River, but your peace might be interrupted by the fact that this smooth beach is a launch point for river runners and the only place on the river accessed by road other than Lees Ferry. The dispersed camping area is primitive, with only a picnic table and pit toilets. No fires are allowed, but grills may be used, and rock pit barbecues are available. The campground is accessed by a 22-mi drive down the gravel Diamond Creek Road. The road can be braved by high-clearance passenger vehicles, but your best bet is one with four-wheel-drive capabilities, especially in summer when storms are commonplace. **Pros:** easy access to river-rafting; only drive-to site in Grand Canyon region where you can camp right by river; beneath beautiful cliffs. **Cons:** hard to get to; remote; primitive. ⌂ *900 Rte. 66, Peach Springs 86434* ☎ *928/769–2210 or 888/255–9550* ⇲ *Open camping* ☖ *Portable toilets, picnic tables* ⊙ *Mid-Mar.–Oct.*

¢ ⛺ **Havasu Canyon**. You can stay in the primitive campgrounds in Havasu Canyon for $17 per person per night, in addition to the $35-per-person entry fee plus a $5 environmental-care fee. The extensive campground has 100 sites and is 2 mi from Supai village. Cottonwood trees provide plenty of shade and picnic tables can be found near many of the campsites. You can pack in a stove, but no campfires are allowed. **Pros:** shaded and peaceful grounds; good base for hiking to Havasu waterfalls. **Cons:** accessible only by foot, horseback, or helicopter. ⌂ *Havasupai Tourist Enterprises, Box 160, Supai 86435* ☎ *928/448–2121, 928/448–2174, 928/448–2180, or 928/448–2141* ⊕ *www.havasupaitribe.com* ⇲ *100 campsites* ☖ *Pit toilets, drinking water, picnic tables, food service, general store* ⚠ *Reservations essential.*

North-Central Arizona

WORD OF MOUTH

"We are so glad we [visited the Chapel of the Holy Cross]. The chapel looks as though it is somehow growing out of the red rock. And the views from the chapel itself are amazing . . . It's a very peaceful and beautiful place, a lovely way to end our trip . . . our only regret was that our vacation couldn't have lasted longer!"
                                                        —caligirl56

WELCOME TO NORTH-CENTRAL ARIZONA

TOP REASONS TO GO

★ **Mother Nature:** Stunning red rocks, snowcapped mountains, and crisp country air rejuvenate the most cynical city dwellers. Nature lovers should visit either the Coconino or Prescott national forest.

★ **Father Time:** Ancient Native American sites, such as Walnut Canyon and Montezuma's Castle, show life before Columbus "discovered" America. You can learn their history in the excellent national monument visitor centers.

★ **Main Street charm:** Jerome and Prescott exude small-town hospitality with turn-of-the-20th-century architecture and charming bed-and-breakfasts.

★ **Cool escapes:** Beat the heat in the high desert; temperatures throughout north-central Arizona are typically 20°F cooler than in the Phoenix area.

★ **Free spirits:** The energy of Sedona is delightfully infectious; even skeptics might be tempted to get their aura read.

1 Flagstaff. College-town enthusiasm and high-country charm combine to make this one of Arizona's most outdoors-friendly towns. Hiking, biking, skiing, and climbing are local passions, and there are state and national parks to explore. Stop in at a local coffeehouse and get sandwiches for a picnic, then head out on a scenic trail to enjoy some solitude.

2 Sedona. Surrounded by the Coconino National Forest, Sedona's residents call their home a museum without walls. The town's red rocks lure visitors from around the world. You'll enjoy breathtaking views, fantastic cuisine, and a dash of New Age whimsy.

3 The Verde Valley, Jerome, and Prescott. Remote but still accessible, the towns of the Verde Valley embrace the life of yesteryear. You can take the Verde Canyon Railroad or visit Montezuma's Castle and see nature's untouched beauty and history. Whiskey Row in Prescott still exudes turn-of-the-20th-century charm, and Jerome, less commercial than Sedona, is emerging as a new hub for artisans and antiques dealers.

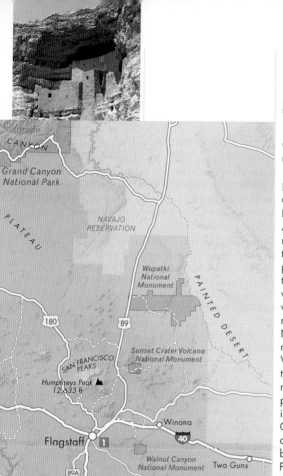

4

GETTING ORIENTED

Nestled between the Grand Canyon and Phoenix, north-central Arizona has enough natural beauty and sophisticated attractions to compete with its neighbors to the north and south. Most visitors flock to Sedona, world renowned for red rocks, pink jeeps, and New Age energy. The surrounding area of Verde Valley may not attract the same hordes, but this means some welcome peace and quiet. Flagstaff is surrounded by the Coconino National Forest and wrapped around the base of the San Francisco Peaks, the tallest mountains in the state. Phoenicians flee the summertime heat to cool off in the mountains and explore Prescott and Jerome.

Old Flagstaff sandstone courthouse from 1894.

NORTH-CENTRAL ARIZONA PLANNER

When to Go

Autumn, when the wet season ends, the stifling desert temperatures moderate (it's 20°F cooler than Phoenix), and the mountain aspens reach their full golden splendor, is a great time to visit this part of Arizona. During the summer months many Phoenix residents travel north to escape the 100°F temperatures, meaning excessive traffic along Interstate 17 just north of Phoenix on Friday and Sunday evenings. Hotels are less expensive in winter, but mountain temperatures dip below zero, and snowstorms can occur weekly, especially near Flagstaff.

Sedona has springlike temperatures even in January, when it's snowing in Flagstaff, but summer temperatures above 90°F are common.

Getting Here and Around

Getting Here: Don't plan on flying into Flagstaff, Sedona, or Prescott: commercial flights are limited, and besides, getting here is half the fun; the scenery is gorgeous. You'll definitely want a car, and north-central Arizona is only a two-hour drive from Phoenix.

Getting Around: It makes sense to rent a car in this region, since trails and monuments stretch miles past city limits and many area towns cannot be reached by the major bus companies. The major rental agencies have offices in Flagstaff, Prescott, and Sedona. Avoid interstates when possible; the back ways can be more direct and have the best views of the stunning landscape. Instead of Route 17, take AZ 89A through Verde Valley and Oak Creek canyon. Weekend traffic around Sedona can be heavy, so leave early and allow for extra time.

Making the Most of Your Time

Sedona will probably occupy most of your time, so plan to spend at least two days there, hiking or shopping. Oak Creek canyon and Chapel of the Holy Cross are must-sees. Then, depending on your preferences, spend your time looking (window-shopping or stargazing) or doing (hiking, exploring). If you can, plan to be in Sedona midweek, when the weekend crowds aren't around.

Outdoors enthusiasts should head to Flagstaff for a day to enjoy the Mount Elden Trail System or hit the slopes at Arizona Snowbowl. The evening can be spent enjoying dinner at one of downtown Flagstaff's many restaurants followed by constellation viewing at the Lowell Observatory.

Prescott and Jerome can be combined for a day or less. You can check out the pulse of downtown Prescott and famous Whiskey Row, then spend a night in a historic hotel; Jerome has several quaint B&Bs, as well as a shopping district with more-affordable treasures than Sedona.

For scenic views, nothing beats the Verde Canyon Railroad. Native American historic sites such as Montezuma Castle and Tuzigoot National Monument offer perspective on local life centuries ago.

Hiking Highlights

Ancient seas, colliding landmasses, spewing volcanoes, and other geological forces have cast and recast northern Arizona into a sprawling sculpture of contrasts. Hikes along canyon rims often look out among red-rock monoliths, and treks to the barren crests of the San Francisco Peaks overlook verdant forests stretching to the edge of the Grand Canyon to the north and Mogollon Rim to the south. You can hike through thick woods in the Verde Valley and the Prescott National Forest (and even ascend a volcano), and amid rock formations around Sedona. Check out ⊕ *www. fs.fed.us/r3/coconino* for info on the Coconino, and ⊕ *www.fs.fed.us/r3/prescott* for more info on Prescott.

Local Food and Lodging

You'll find lots of American comfort food in this part of the country: barbecue restaurants, steak houses, and burger joints predominate. If you're looking for something different, Sedona and Flagstaff have the majority of good, multiethnic restaurants in the area, and if you're craving Mexican, you're sure to find something authentic and delicious (note that burritos are often called "burros" around here). Sedona is the best place in the area for fine dining, although Flagstaff and Prescott now boast a few upscale eateries. Some area restaurants close in January and February—the slower months in the area—so call ahead. Reservations are suggested from April through October.

Flagstaff and Prescott have the more-affordable lodging options, with lots of comfortable motels and B&Bs, but no real luxury. The opposite is true in Sedona, which is filled with opulent resorts and hideaways, most offering solitude and spa services—just don't expect a bargain. Reservations are essential for Sedona and suggested for Flagstaff and Prescott. Little Jerome has a few B&Bs, but call ahead if you think you might want to spend the night. If you're in for a thrill, many of the historic hotels have haunted rooms.

Altitude Adjustment

It's wise, especially if you're an outdoors enthusiast, to start in the relatively lowland areas of Prescott and the Verde Valley, climbing gradually to Sedona and Flagstaff—it can take several days to grow accustomed to the high elevation in Flagstaff.

4

Festivals and Events

Sedona Jazz on the Rocks Festival. Top jazz musicians attract a sellout crowd that fills the town to capacity for a few days in early October. ☎ 928/282–1985 ⊕ *www.sedonajazz.com.*

Route 66 Days. Classic and muscle cars roar into Flagstaff the second weekend in September for this fun auto show with live music and a host of vendors. ☎ 928/779–0898 ⊕ *www. flagstaffroute66days.com.*

Festival of Science. This 10-day series of exhibits and guest speakers in Flagstaff is made stellar by its observatories. ☎ 800/842–7293 ⊕ *www. scifest.org.*

WHAT IT COSTS

	¢	$	$$	$$$	$$$$
Restaurant	under $8	$8–$12	$13–$20	$21–$30	over $30
Hotel	under $70	$70–$120	$121–$175	$176–$250	over $250

Restaurant prices are per person for a main course at dinner. Hotel prices are for a standard double in high season, excluding taxes and service charges.

Updated by
Mara Levin

Red-rock buttes ablaze in the slanting light of late afternoon, the San Francisco Peaks tipped white from a fresh snowfall, pine forests clad in dark green needles—north-central Arizona is rich in natural attractions, a landscape of vast plateaus punctuated by steep ridges and canyons.

To the north of Flagstaff the San Francisco Peaks, a string of tall volcanic mountains, rise over 12,000 feet, tapering to the 9,000-foot Mount Elden and a scattering of diminutive cinder cones. To the south, ponderosa pines cover the Colorado Plateau before the terrain plunges dramatically into Oak Creek canyon. The canyon then opens to reveal red buttes and mesas in the high-desert areas surrounding Sedona. The desert gradually descends to the Verde Valley, crossing the Verde River before reaching the 7,000-foot Black Range, over which lies the Prescott Valley.

Flagstaff, the hub of this part of Arizona, was historically a way station en route to Southern California via the railroads and then Route 66. Many of those who were "just passing through" stayed and built a community, revitalizing downtown with cafés, an activity-filled square, eclectic shops, and festivals. The town's large network of bike paths and parks abuts hundreds of miles of trails and forest roads, an irresistible lure for outdoors enthusiasts. Not surprisingly, the typical resident of Flagstaff is outdoorsy, young, and has a large, friendly dog in tow.

Down AZ 89A in Sedona, the average age and income rises considerably. This was once a hidden hamlet used by Western filmmakers, but New Age enthusiasts flocked to the region in the 1980s believing it was the center of spiritual powers. Well-off executives and retirees followed soon after, building clusters of McMansions. Sophisticated restaurants, upscale shops, luxe accommodations, and New Age entrepreneurs cater to both these populations, and to the thriving tourist trade. It can be difficult, though not impossible, to find a moment of serenity, even in wilderness areas.

Pioneers and miners are now part of north-central Arizona's past, but the wild and woolly days of the Old West are not forgotten. The preserved fort at Camp Verde recalls frontier life, and the decrepit facades of the funky former mining town of Jerome have an infectious charm. The many Victorian houses in temperate Prescott attest to the attempt to bring "civilization" to Arizona's territorial capital.

North-central Arizona is also rich in artifacts from its earliest inhabitants: several national and state parks—among them Walnut Canyon, Wupatki, Montezuma Castle, and Tuzigoot national monuments—hold well-preserved evidence of the architectural accomplishments of Native American Sinagua and other Ancestral Puebloans.

FLAGSTAFF

146 mi northwest of Phoenix, 27 mi north of Sedona via Oak Creek canyon.

Few travelers slow down long enough to explore Flagstaff, a town of 54,000 known locally as "Flag"; most stop only to spend the night at one of the town's many motels before making the last leg of the trip to the Grand Canyon, 80 mi north. Flag makes a good base for day trips to ancient Native American sites and the Navajo and Hopi reservations, as well as to the Petrified Forest National Park and the Painted Desert, but the city is a worthwhile destination in its own right. Set against a lovely backdrop of pine forests and the snowcapped San Francisco Peaks, downtown Flagstaff retains a frontier flavor.

In summer, Phoenix residents head here seeking relief from the desert heat, since at any time of the year temperatures in Flagstaff are about 20°F cooler than in Phoenix. They also come to Flagstaff in winter to ski at the small Arizona Snowbowl, about 15 mi northeast of town among the San Francisco Peaks.

GETTING HERE AND AROUND

GETTING HERE Flagstaff lies at the intersection of Interstate 40 (east–west) and Interstate 17 (running south from Flagstaff), 134 mi north of Phoenix via Interstate 17. If you're driving from Sedona to Flagstaff or the Grand Canyon, head north through the wooded Oak Creek canyon: it's the most scenic route.

Flagstaff Pulliam Airport is 3 mi south of town off Interstate 17 at Exit 337. US Airways Express flies from Phoenix to Flagstaff. Amtrak comes into the downtown Flagstaff station twice daily. There's no rail service into Prescott or Sedona, but Arizona Shuttle provides transportation via shuttle van or private car between Phoenix, Sedona, Flagstaff, Williams, and the Grand Canyon. Sun Taxi will take you around Flagstaff or to any place in northern Arizona.

GETTING AROUND A walking-tour map of the area is available at the visitor center in the Tudor Revival–style Santa Fe Depot, an excellent place to begin sightseeing.

PLANNING YOUR TIME

You can see most of Flagstaff's attractions in a day—especially if you visit the Lowell Observatory or the Northern Arizona University Observatory in the evening, which is also when the Museum Club is best experienced.

Consult the schedule of tour times if you want to visit the Riordan State Historic Park. Devote at least an hour to the excellent Museum of Northern Arizona. The Historic Downtown District is a good place for lunch or dinner. If you're a skier, spend part of a winter's day at the Arizona Snowbowl; in summer you can spend a couple of hours on the skyride and scenic trails at the top. Take your time enjoying the trails on Mount Elden, and remember to pace yourself in the higher elevations; allow a full day for hiking. The Lava River Cave is an easy—if dark—hike that can be done comfortably in an hour.

ESSENTIALS

Visitor Info Flagstaff Visitor Center (⊠ *Santa Fe Depot, 1 E. Rte. 66, Downtown* ☎ *928/774–9541 or 800/842–7293* ⊕ *www.flagstaffarizona.org*).

Transportation Contacts A Friendly Cab (☎ *928/774–4444*) **Arizona Shuttle** (☎ *877/226–8060* ⊕ *www.arizonashuttle.com*). **Flagstaff Pulliam Airport** (☎ *928/556–1234*). **Sun Taxi** (☎ *928/779–1111*).

EXPLORING

TOP ATTRACTIONS

❼ Arizona Snowbowl. Although still one of Flagstaff's largest attractions, droughts can make snowy slopes a luxury. Fortunately, visitors can enjoy the beauty of the area year-round. The Agassiz ski lift climbs to a height of 11,500 feet in 25 minutes, and doubles as a skyride through the Coconino National Forest in summer. From this vantage point you can see up to 70 mi; views may even include the North Rim of the Grand Canyon. There's a lodge at the base with a restaurant, bar, and ski school. To reach the ski area, take U.S. 180 north from Flagstaff; it's 7 mi from the Snowbowl exit to the skyride entrance. ⊠ *Snowbowl Rd., North Flagstaff* ☎ *928/779–1951* ⊕ *www.arizonasnowbowl.com* ⛷ *Skyride $12* ☉ *Skyride: Memorial Day–early Sept., daily 10–4; early Sept.–mid-Oct., Fri.–Sun. 10–4, weather permitting.*

❶ Historic Downtown District. Storied Route 66 runs right through the heart of downtown Flagstaff. The late-Victorian, Tudor Revival, and early–art deco architecture in this district recall the town's heyday as a logging and railroad center. The **Santa Fe Depot** (⊠ *1 E. Rte. 66, Downtown*) now houses the visitor center. Highlights include the 1927 **Hotel Monte Vista** (⊠ *100 N. San Francisco St., Downtown* ⊕ *www.hotelmontevista. com*), built after a community drive raised $200,000 in 60 days. The construction was promoted as a way to bolster the burgeoning tourism in the region, and the hotel was held publicly until the early 1960s. The 1888 **Babbitt Brothers Building** (⊠ *12 E. Aspen Ave., Downtown*) was constructed as a building-supply store and then turned into a department store by David Babbitt, the mastermind of the Babbitt empire. The Babbitts are one of Flagstaff's wealthiest founding families. Bruce Babbitt, the most recent member of the family to wield power and influence, was the governor of Arizona from 1978 through 1987 and Secretary of the Interior under President Clinton (1993–2001). Most of the area's first businesses were saloons catering to railroad construction workers, which was the case with the 1888 **Vail Building** (⊠ *5 N. San Francisco St.,*

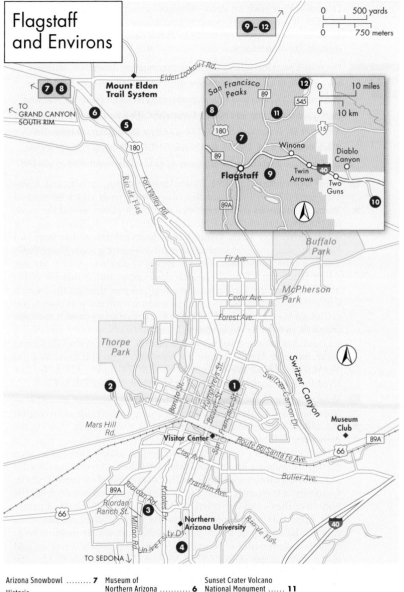

Flagstaff and Environs

Downtown), a brick art deco–influenced structure covered with stucco in 1939. It now houses Crystal Magic, a New Age shop. ⊠ *Downtown Historic District, Rte. 66 north to Birch Ave., and Beaver St. east to Agassiz St., Downtown.*

QUICK BITES

The town's most interesting shops are concentrated downtown, and there are a couple of brewpubs and some spots where you can grab a quick bite. Students, skiers, new and aging hippies, and just about everyone else who likes good coffee jam into **Macy's European Coffee House and Bakery** (⊠ *14 S. Beaver St., Downtown* ☎ *928/774–2243*) for the best cup in town. The **Black Bean** (⊠ *12 E. Rte. 66, Downtown* ☎ *928/779–9905*) is the place for do-it-yourself burritos, as healthful or as guacamole-smothered as you like.

② **Lowell Observatory.** In 1894 Boston businessman, author, and scientist Percival Lowell founded this observatory from which he studied Mars. His theories of the existence of a ninth planet sowed the seeds for the discovery of Pluto at Lowell in 1930 by Clyde Tombaugh. The 6,500-square-foot Steele Visitor Center hosts exhibits and lectures and has a gift shop. Several interactive exhibits—among them Pluto Walk, a scale model of the solar system—appeal to children. At this writing, a new Discovery Channel research telescope is anticipated for 2011, and visitors are invited, on some evenings, to peer through the 24-inch Clark telescope. Day and evening viewings are offered year-round, but call ahead for a schedule. ■ TIP➔ The Clark observatory dome is open and unheated, so dress for the outdoors. To reach the observatory, less than 2 mi from downtown, drive west on Route 66, which resumes its former name, Santa Fe Avenue, before it merges into Mars Hill Road. ⊠ *1400 W. Mars Hill Rd., West Flagstaff* ☎ *928/774–3358, 928/233–3211 recorded info* ⊕ *www.lowell.edu* ⊠ *$6* ☉ *Hrs vary; call ahead.*

⑥ **Museum of Northern Arizona.** This institution, founded in 1928, is respected worldwide for its research and its collections centering on the natural and cultural history of the Colorado Plateau. Among the permanent exhibitions are an extensive collection of Navajo rugs and a Hopi kiva (men's ceremonial chamber). A gallery devoted to area geology is usually a hit with children: it includes a life-size model dilophosaurus, a carnivorous dinosaur that once roamed northern Arizona. Outdoors, a life-zone exhibit shows the changing vegetation from the bottom of the Grand Canyon to the highest peak in Flagstaff. A nature trail, open only in summer, heads down across a small stream into a canyon and up into an aspen grove. Also in summer, the museum hosts exhibits and the works of Native American artists, whose wares are sold in the museum gift shop. ⊠ *3101 N. Fort Valley Rd., North Flagstaff* ☎ *928/774–5213* ⊕ *www.musnaz.org* ⊠ *$7* ☉ *Daily 9–5.*

WORTH NOTING

⑧ **Lava River Cave.** Subterranean lava flow formed this mile-long cave roughly 700,000 years ago. Once you descend into its boulder-strewn maw, the cave is spacious, with 40-foot ceilings, but claustrophobes take heed: about halfway through, the cave tapers to a 4-foot-high squeeze that can be a bit unnerving. A 40°F chill pervades the cave throughout the year so take warm clothing. To reach the turnoff for the cave, go approximately 9 mi north of Flagstaff on U.S. 180, then turn west onto FR 245. Turn left at the intersection of FR 171 and look for the sign to the cave. The trip is approximately 45 minutes from Flagstaff. Although the cave is on Coconino National Forest Service property, the only thing here is an interpretive sign, so it's definitely something you tackle at your own risk. ■ TIP→ Pack a flashlight (or two). ⊠ *FR 171B.*

4 **Northern Arizona University Observatory.** This observatory was built in 1952 by Dr. Arthur Adel, a scientist at Lowell Observatory whose study of infrared astronomy pioneered research into molecules that absorb light passing through Earth's atmosphere. Today's studies of Earth's shrinking ozone layer rely on some of Dr. Adel's early work. Visitors to the observatory—which houses one of the largest research-grade telescopes that the public is allowed to move and manipulate—are usually hosted by friendly students and faculty members of the university's Department of Physics and Astronomy. Dr. Adel's 24-inch telescope—the first infrared scope—is also on display. ⊠ *Bldg. 47, Northern Arizona Campus Observatory, Dept. of Physics and Astronomy, S. San Francisco St., just north of Walkup Skydome, University* ☎ *928/523–7170* ⊕ *www.physics. nau.edu* ⊠ *Free* ⊙ *Viewings Fri. 7:30–10 PM, weather permitting.*

5 **Pioneer Museum.** The Arizona Historical Society operates this museum in a volcanic-rock building constructed in 1908. The structure was Coconino County's first hospital for the poor, and the current displays include one of the depressingly small nurses' rooms, an old iron lung, and a reconstructed doctor's office. Most of the exhibits, however, touch on more-cheerful aspects of Flagstaff history—like road signs and children's toys. The museum holds a folk-crafts festival on July 4, with blacksmiths, weavers, spinners, quilters, and candle makers. Their crafts, and those of other local artisans, are sold in the museum's gift shop. In a wooded residential section at the northwest end of town, the museum is part of the Fort Valley Park complex. ⊠ *2340 N. Fort Valley Rd., North Flagstaff* ☎ *928/774–6272* ⊕ *www.arizonahistoricalsociety.org* ⊠ *$3* ⊙ *Mon.–Sat. 9–5.*

3 **Riordan State Historic Park.** This artifact of Flagstaff's logging heyday is near Northern Arizona University. The centerpiece is a mansion built in 1904 for Michael and Timothy Riordan, lumber-baron brothers who married two sisters. The 13,300-square-foot, 40-room log-and-stone structure—designed by Charles Whittlesley, who was also responsible for El Tovar Hotel at the Grand Canyon—contains furniture by Gustav Stickley, father of the American Arts and Crafts design movement. One room holds "Paul Bunyan's shoes," a 2-foot-long pair of boots made by Timothy in his workshop. Everything on display is original to the house. The mansion may be explored on a guided tour only; reservations are suggested. ⊠ *409 W. Riordan Rd., University* ☎ *928/779–4395* ⊕ *www. azstateparks.com* ⊠ *$6* ⊙ *May–Oct., daily 8:30–5, with tours on the hr 9–4; Nov.–Apr., daily 10:30–5, with tours on the hr 11–4.*

SPORTS AND THE OUTDOORS

HIKING

You can explore Arizona's alpine tundra in the San Francisco Peaks, part of the Coconino National Forest, where more than 80 species of plants grow on the upper elevations. The habitat is fragile, so hikers are asked to stay on established trails (there are lots of them). ■ TIP→ Flatlanders should give themselves a day or two to adjust to the altitude before lengthy or strenuous hiking. The altitude here will make even the hardiest hikers breathe a little harder, so anyone with cardiac or respiratory problems should be cautious about overexertion.

The rangers of the **Coconino National Forest** (✉ *1824 S. Thompson St., North Flagstaff* ☎ *928/527–3600* ⊕ *www.fs.fed.us/r3/coconino*) maintain many of the region's trails, and can provide you with details on hiking in the area; the forest's main office is open weekdays 8–4:30.

Mount Elden Trail System. Most trails in the 35-mi-long Mount Elden Trail System lead to views from the dormant volcanic field, across the vast ponderosa pine forest, all the way to Sedona. The most challenging trail in the Mount Elden system, which happens to be the route with the most rewarding views, is along the steep switchbacks of the **Elden Lookout Trail** (✉ *Trailhead: Off U.S. 89, 3 mi east of downtown Flagstaff*). If you traverse the full 3 mi to the top, keep your focus on the landscape rather than the tangle of antennae and satellite dishes that greets you at the top. The 4-mi-long **Sunset Trail** (✉ *Trailhead: Off U.S. 180, 3 mi north of downtown Flagstaff, then 6 mi east on FR 420/Schultz Pass Rd.*) proceeds with a gradual pitch through the pine forest, emerging onto a narrow ridge nicknamed the Catwalk. By all means take pictures of the stunning valley views, but make sure your feet are well placed. The access road to this trail is closed in winter.

Flagstaff is in the **Peaks District** (✉ *Peaks Ranger Station, 5075 N. U.S. 89* ☎ *928/526–0866*) of the Coconino National Forest, and there are many trails to explore. The **Humphreys Peak Trail** (✉ *Trailhead: Snowbowl Rd., 7 mi north of U.S. 180*) is 9 mi round-trip, with a vertical climb of 3,843 feet to the 12,643-foot summit of Arizona's highest mountain. Those who don't want a long hike can do just the first mile of the adjacent, 5-mi-long **Kachina Trail** (✉ *Trailhead: Snowbowl Rd., 7 mi north of U.S. 180*) ; gently rolling, this route is surrounded by huge stands of aspen and offers fantastic vistas. In fall, changing leaves paint the landscape shades of yellow, russet, and amber.

HORSEBACK RIDING

The wranglers at **Hitchin' Post Stables** (✉ *4848 Lake Mary Rd., South Flagstaff* ☎ *928/774–1719*) lead rides into Walnut Canyon and operate horseback or horse-drawn wagon rides with sunset barbecues. In winter they'll take you through Coconino National Forest on a sleigh.

MOUNTAIN BIKING

With more than 30 mi of challenging trails a short ride from town, it was inevitable that one of Flagstaff's best-kept secrets would leak out. The mountain biking on Mount Elden is on par with that of more-celebrated trails in Colorado and Utah.

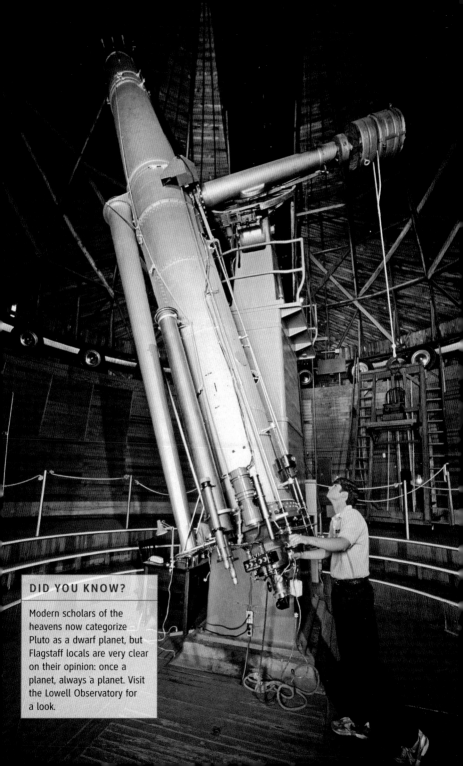

The **Coconino National Forest** has some of the best trails in the region. A good place to start is the **Lower Oldham Trail** (⊠ *Trailhead: Cedar St.*), which originates on the north end of Buffalo Park in Flagstaff; there's a large meadow with picnic areas and an exercise path. The terrain rolls, climbing about 800 feet in 3 mi, and the trail is technical in spots but easy enough to test your tolerance of the elevation. Many fun trails spur off this one. They're all hemmed in by roads and cabins so it's difficult to get too lost.

The very popular **Schultz Creek Trail** (⊠ *Trailhead: Schultz Pass Rd. near intersection with U.S. 180*) is fun and suitable for strong beginners, although seasoned experts will be thrilled as well. Most opt to start at the top of the 600-foot-high hill and swoop down the smooth, twisting path through groves of wildflowers and stands of ponderosa pines and aspens, ending at the trailhead 4 giddy mi later.**Sunset Trail** (⊠ *Trailhead: Elden Lookout Rd., 7 mi from intersection with Schultz Pass Rd.*), near the summit of Mount Elden, has amazing views off the ridge rendered barren by a 1977 fire. The trail narrows into the aptly nicknamed Catwalk, with precipitous drops a few feet on either side. Fear, either from the 9,000-foot elevation or the sheer exposure, is not an option. You need to be at least a moderately experienced mountain biker to attempt this trail. When combined with Elden Lookout Road and Schultz Creek Trail, the usual loop, the trail totals 15 mi and climbs almost 2,000 feet. You can avoid the slog up Mount Elden by parking one vehicle at the top of Elden Lookout Road, at the trailhead, and a friend's vehicle at the bottom.

You can rent mountain bikes, get good advice, and purchase trail maps at **Absolute Bikes** (⊠ *202 E. Rte. 66, Downtown* ☎ *928/779–5969*). From mid-June through mid-October, the **Flagstaff Nordic Center** (⊠ *U.S. 180, 16 mi north of Flagstaff, North Flagstaff* ☎ *928/220–0550* ⊕ *www. flagstaffnordiccenter.com*) opens its cross-country trails—good for families and beginners, because they're scenic and not technically challenging—to mountain bikers. A map of the **Urban Trails System** (⊠ *1 E. Rte. 66, Downtown* ☎ *928/774–9541 or 800/842–7293*), available at the Flagstaff Visitor Center, details low and no-traffic bike routes around town.

ROCK CLIMBING

Vertical Relief Rock Gym (⊠ *205 S. San Francisco St., Downtown* ☎ *928/556– 9909*) has the tallest indoor climbing walls in the Southwest, as well as guided climbing excursions throughout the Flagstaff area.

SKIING AND SNOWBOARDING

The ski season usually starts in mid-December and ends in mid-April. The **Arizona Snowbowl** (⊠ *Snowbowl Rd., North Flagstaff* ☎ *928/779– 1951, 928/779–4577 snow report* ⊕ *www.arizonasnowbowl.com*), 7 mi north of Flagstaff off U.S. 180, has 32 downhill runs (37% beginner, 42% intermediate, and 21% advanced), four chairlifts, and a vertical drop of 2,300 feet. There are a couple of good bump runs, but it's better for beginners or those with moderate skill; serious area skiers take a road trip to Telluride. Still, it's a fun place to ski or snowboard. The Hart Prairie Lodge has an equipment-rental shop and a SKIwee center for ages four to seven. All-day adult lift tickets are $49. Half-day discounts are available, and group-lesson packages (including two hours of instruction, an all-day lift ticket, and equipment rental) are a good buy at $74. A children's program, which includes progress card and full supervision 9–3:30, runs $70. Many Flagstaff motels have ski packages that include transportation to Snowbowl.

The **Flagstaff Nordic Center** (⊠ *U.S. 180, 16 mi north of Flagstaff, North Flagstaff* ☎ *928/220–0550* ⊕ *www.flagstaffnordiccenter.com*) is 9 mi north of Snowbowl Road. There are 25 mi of well-groomed cross-country trails here that are open 9–4 daily. Coffee, hot chocolate, and snacks are served at the lodge. A day pass for skiing costs $12 on weekdays and $18 on weekends. An instruction package costs $45, including equipment. Renting equipment by itself is $16.

4

WHERE TO EAT

$ ✕**Beaver Street Brewery and Whistle Stop Cafe.** Popular among the wood-

AMERICAN fired pizzas is the Enchanted Forest, with Brie, portobello mushrooms, roasted red peppers, spinach, and artichoke pesto. Whichever pie you order, expect serious amounts of garlic. Sandwiches, such as the Southwestern chicken with three types of cheese, come with a hefty portion of tasty fries. You won't regret ordering one of the down-home desserts, like the super-gooey chocolate bread pudding. Among the excellent microbrews usually on tap, the raspberry ale is a local favorite. ⊠ *11 S. Beaver St., Downtown* ☎ *928/779–0079* ⊕ *www.beaverstreetbrewery. com* ⊟ *AE, D, DC, MC, V.*

$$$ ✕**Black Bart's Steakhouse Saloon.** The Wild West decor at this rollicking,

AMERICAN brightly lighted barn of a restaurant is a bit cornball, but the barbecued chicken is tender and flavorful; just don't expect to see vegetables on your plate unless they're deep-fried. Northern Arizona University music students entertain while they wait on tables, so don't be surprised if your server suddenly jumps onstage to belt out a couple of show tunes. ⊠ *2760 E. Butler Ave., Downtown* ☎ *928/779–3142 or 800/574–4718* ⊕ *www. blackbartssteakhouse.com* ⊟ *AE, D, DC, MC, V* ⊗ *No lunch.*

$$$ ✕ **Brix Restaurant & Wine Bar.** A redbrick carriage house, built around 1910

AMERICAN as a garage for one the first automobiles in Flagstaff, is now home to one of Flagstaff's most sophisticated restaurants. With a seasonally updated menu, the chef pairs locally raised pork and roasted duck entrées with wines from a list of almost 200 bottles (Brix refers to the sugar content of grapes at harvest). The cheese plate, served with poached natural apricots, is a great accompaniment to a glass of wine at the counter bar. The servers are friendly, the vibe is casually upscale, and the food is outstanding. ⊠ *413 N. San Francisco St., Downtown* ☎ *928/213–1021* ⊕ *www.brixflagstaff.com* ⊟ *AE, D, MC, V* ⊗ *No lunch.*

¢ ✕**Bun Huggers.** Since 1979 the best burger in town has been flipped

AMERICAN over a mesquite-fired grill at this no-frills joint. Also try the tasty, if decadent, deep-fried zucchini served with shredded cheddar cheese and ranch dressing. There's a small salad bar here, but it seems like an afterthought, existing only to appease guilty consciences. ⊠ *901 S. Milton Rd., University* ☎ *928/779–3743* ⊟ *AE, D, MC, V.*

$$ ✕ **Buster's Restaurant.** At lunchtime, families and students from nearby
AMERICAN Northern Arizona University settle into comfy booths to enjoy fresh sea-
food, homemade soups, salads, giant burgers, and steaks. What better
environment in which to ask Mom or Dad for some extra money, or to
discuss those first-semester grades? Try the *lahvosh* appetizer—a huge
cracker heaped with toppings ranging from smoked salmon to mush-
rooms—or the Caesar salad with grilled Cajun chicken. At night single
professionals and skiers crowd the bar and work through its impres-
sive beer selection. ✉ *1800 S. Milton Rd., University* ☎ *928/774–5155*
⊕ *www.busters-restaurant.com* ▭ *AE, D, DC, MC, V.*

$$$ ✕ **Cottage Place.** Regarded by locals as one of the best special-occasion
CONTINENTAL dining venues in the area, this restaurant in a cottage built in 1909
★ has intimate dining rooms and an extensive wine list. The menu strays
slightly from Continental to include some classic American dishes, such
as charbroiled lamb chops. The grilled herb salmon and the chateau-
briand for two are recommended. Dinner includes soup and salad, but
save room for chocolate decadence. ✉ *126 W. Cottage Ave., Downtown*
☎ *928/774–8431* ⊕ *www.cottageplace.com* ▭ *AE, MC, V* ☯ *Closed
Mon. and Tues. No lunch.*

¢–$ ✕ **La Bellavia.** At this favorite bohemian breakfast and lunch nook the
CAFÉ trout and eggs platter is the standard—two eggs served with Idaho
★ trout flavored with a hint of lemon, rounded off by a buttermilk pan-
cake. Other options include Swedish oat pancakes, seven-grain French
toast, and a dozen varieties of eggs Benedict. A palette of creative sandwiches and familiar salads makes this a worthwhile lunch stop as well.
The café doubles as a gallery for local artists, whose work hangs on
the walls. ✉ *18 S. Beaver St., Downtown* ☎ *928/774–8301* ⊕ *www.
labellaviarestaurant_az.com* ▭ *MC, V* ☯ *No dinner.*

$ ✕ **Salsa Brava.** This cheerful Mexican restaurant, with light-wood
MEXICAN booths and colorful designs, eschews heavy Sonoran-style fare in favor
of the grilled dishes found in Guadalajara. It's considered the best Mexican food in town—but there's not much competition. The fish tacos
are particularly good. Or wake up your taste buds with a breakfast of
huevos rancheros. ✉ *2220 E. Rte. 66, East Flagstaff* ☎ *928/779–5293*
⊕ *www.salsabravaflagstaff.com* ▭ *AE, D, MC, V.*

WHERE TO STAY

Trains pass through the downtown area along Route 66 (also called
Santa Fe Avenue) about every 15 minutes throughout the day and night.
Light sleepers may prefer to stay in the south or east sections of town
to avoid hearing trains rumbling through; at least the whistles are no
longer blown within the downtown district.

$$ ⊡ **Abineau Lodge.** This contemporary mountain inn with a rustic feel
is on 4 acres bordering the immense Coconino National Forest. Two
separate living rooms, one on each level, and a deck for stargazing
make for a comfortable retreat. A big draw here for dog-lovers is play-
ing with the pack of retired sled dogs, the owners' well-loved Siberian
huskies. Canine visitors are welcome, but they must stay in a separate
climate-controlled kennel area. **Pros:** pleasant common areas; hot tub

and sauna. **Cons:** 7 mi south of town; huskies howl "The Siberian Serenade" in early morning. ⊠ *10155 Mountainaire Rd., South Flagstaff* ☎ *928/525–6212 or 888/715–6386* ⊕ *www.abineaulodge.com* ⮌ *8 rooms, 1 suite* ⬧ *In-room: a/c, no TV. In-hotel: Wi-Fi hotspot, no kids under 8* ▭ *AE, D, MC, V* ⧈ *BP.*

¢–$ ⊡ **Hotel Weatherford.** With a columned veranda, this hotel, built in 1897, is a dramatic presence at the hub of town. Imbued with a creaky charm, some rooms are spartan and a bit worn around the edges but comfortable. Three rooms with a shared bath are an especially good value. Forgo TV, telephones, and reliable hot water for a taste of the Old West. The two clubs downstairs have a bustling nightlife scene. **Pros:** historical charm mixes with a cool music scene. **Cons:** guests will hear noise from bars until the wee hours; dated plumbing; no elevator (all rooms require climbing one or two flights of stairs). ⊠ *23 N. Leroux St., Downtown* ☎ *928/779–1919* ⊕ *www.weatherfordhotel.com* ⮌ *10 rooms, 7 with bath* ⬧ *In-room: no a/c, no phone, no TV. In-hotel: restaurant, bars* ▭ *AE, D, DC, MC, V.*

$$–$$$ ⊡ **Inn at 410.** This downtown B&B is an inviting alternative to Flag's chain motels. All the accommodations in the beautifully restored 1907 residence are spacious suites with private baths and fireplaces; some also have two-person Jacuzzi tubs. Pancakes with blue cornmeal and piñon nuts, and curried corn-bread pudding with pumpkin sauce highlight a tantalizing breakfast menu. **Pros:** convenient downtown location; romantic; complimentary cookies and cocktails every afternoon. **Cons:** some train noise. ⊠ *410 N. Leroux St., Downtown* ☎ *928/774–0088 or 800/774–2008* ⊕ *www.inn410.com* ⮌ *9 suites* ⬧ *In-room: a/c, no phone, refrigerator, DVD* ▭ *MC, V* ⧈ *BP.*

$$ ⊡ **Little America of Flagstaff.** The biggest hotel in town is deservedly popu-
★ lar. It's a little distance from the roar of the trains, the grounds are surrounded by evergreen forests, and it's one of the few places in Flagstaff with room service. Plush rooms have comfortable sitting areas with French provincial–style furniture. Other pluses are an above-average in-house restaurant, courtesy van service to the airport and the Amtrak station, a deli, and a great Southwestern gift shop. **Pros:** large, very clean rooms; many amenities including walking trails. **Cons:** large-scale property can feel impersonal. ⊠ *2515 E. Butler Ave., Downtown* ☎ *928/779–7900 or 800/352–4386* ⊕ *www.littleamerica.com/flagstaff* ⮌ *247 rooms* ⬧ *In-room: a/c, safe, kitchen (some), refrigerator, Wi-Fi. In-hotel: restaurant, room service, bar, pool, gym, laundry facilities, laundry service* ▭ *AE, D, DC, MC, V.*

$$–$$$ ⊡ **Starlight Pines Bed and Breakfast.** If you prefer the clean lines of 1920s design to Victorian froufrou, consider staying at this stylish B&B on the city's east side. Guest rooms are lovely, with art deco pieces including Tiffany lamps and other antiques. Enjoy a soak in your claw-foot tub after a day's hike. **Pros:** pretty, immaculate rooms; very hospitable hosts. **Cons:** a short drive from downtown; train whistles can still be heard. ⊠ *3380 E. Lockett Rd., East Flagstaff* ☎ *928/527–1912 or 800/752–1912* ⊕ *www.starlightpinesbb.com* ⮌ *4 rooms* ⬧ *In-room: a/c, no TV (some), Wi-Fi* ▭ *D, MC, V* ⧈ *BP.*

A visit to Meteor Crater complements Arizona's many observatories for a different look at the impact of the heavens.

SHOPPING

For fine arts and crafts—everything from ceramics and stained glass to weaving and painting—visit the **Artists Gallery** (⊠ *17 N. San Francisco St., Downtown* ☎ *928/773–0958* ⊕ *www.theartistsgallery.net*), a local artists' cooperative. **Babbitt's Backcountry Outfitters** (⊠ *12 E. Aspen Ave., Downtown* ☎ *928/774–4775* ⊕ *www.babbittsbackcountry.com*) is the place to pick up any sporting-goods needs. The **Black Hound Gallerie** (⊠ *120 N. Leroux St., Downtown* ☎ *928/774–2323* ⊕ *www. blackhoundgallerie.com*) specializes in posters, prints, and funky kitsch of all kinds. **Bookman's** (⊠ *1520 S. Riordan Ranch Rd., University* ☎ *928/774–0005* ⊕ *www.bookmans.com*) is packed solid with used books on every topic; a cybercafe and live folk music occupy a corner of the store. **Carriage House Antique & Gift Mall** (⊠ *413 N. San Francisco St., Downtown* ☎ *928/774–1337*) has vendors selling vintage clothing and jewelry, furniture, fine china, Mexican folk art, and other collectibles. The **Museum of Northern Arizona Gift Shop** (⊠ *3101 N. Fort Valley Rd., University* ☎ *928/774–5213* ⊕ *www.musnaz.org*) carries high-quality jewelry and crafts. **Winter Sun Trading Company** (⊠ *107 N. San Francisco St., Downtown* ☎ *928/774–2884* ⊕ *www.wintersun.com*) sells medicinal herbs, unique fragrances, jewelry, and crafts. **Zani** (⊠ *107 W. Phoenix Ave., Downtown* ☎ *928/774–9409* ⊕ *www.zani-online.com*) stocks hip jewelry and gifts, handmade paper, and greeting cards.

NIGHTLIFE AND THE ARTS

NIGHTLIFE

Flagstaff's large college contingent has plenty of places to gather after dark; most are in historic downtown and most charge little or no cover. It's easy to walk from one rowdy spot to the next. For information on what's going on, pick up the free *Flagstaff Live*.

Flagstaff's Green Room (⌂ *15 N. Agassiz St., Downtown* ☎ *928/226–8669* ⊕ *flagstaffgreenroom.com*), an environmentally conscious bar, rolls out an eclectic mix of live music and hardy stout nightly until 2 AM. The **Hotel Weatherford** (⌂ *23 N. Leroux St., Downtown* ☎ *928/779–1919* ⊕ *www.weatherfordhotel.com*) has a double bill: Charly's hosts late-night jazz and blues bands; the Exchange Pub tends to attract folksy ensembles. The **Monte Vista Lounge** (⌂ *100 N. San Francisco St., Downtown* ☎ *928/774–2403* ⊕ *www.hotelmontevista.com/mvlounge.php*) packs 'em in with nightly live blues, jazz, classic rock, and punk. **San Felipe's Coastal Cantina** (⌂ *103 N. Leroux, Downtown* ☎ *928/779–6000* ⊕ *www.sanfelipescantina.com*) is the place for tequila, fish tacos, dancing, and a raucous spring-break atmosphere.

THE ARTS

There is no shortage of cultural entertainment in Flagstaff, including several summer festivals.

A Celebration of Native American Art (⌂ *3101 N. Fort Valley Rd., North Flagstaff* ☎ *928/774–5213* ⊕ *www.musnaz.org*), featuring exhibits of work by Zuni, Hopi, and Navajo artists, is held at the Museum of Northern Arizona from late May through September.

Flagstaff Cultural Partners/Coconino Center for the Arts (⌂ *2300 N. Fort Valley Rd., North Flagstaff* ☎ *928/779–2300* ⊕ *www.culturalpartners.org*) has gallery space for exhibitions, a theater, and performance space. The **Flagstaff Symphony Orchestra** (☎ *928/774–5107* ⊕ *www.flagstaffsymphony.org*) has year-round musical events. The 1917 **Orpheum Theater** (⌂ *15 W. Aspen St., Downtown* ☎ *928/556–1580* ⊕ *www.orpheumpresents.com*) features music acts, films, lectures, and plays. **Theatrikos Theatre Company** (⌂ *11 W. Cherry Ave., Downtown* ☎ *928/774–1662* ⊕ *www.theatrikos.com*) is a highly regarded performance-art group.

SIDE TRIPS NEAR FLAGSTAFF

Travelers heading straight through town bound for the Grand Canyon often neglect the area north and east of Flagstaff, but a detour has its rewards. If you don't have time to do everything, take a quick drive to Walnut Canyon—it's only about 15 minutes out of town.

EAST OF FLAGSTAFF

GETTING HERE AND AROUND

From Flagstaff, follow Interstate 40 a few miles east to Exit 204 for Walnut Canyon National Monument. Continue east along the highway for Meteor Crater off Exit 233, a 45-minute drive.

EN
ROUTE

Museum Club Roadhouse and Danceclub. For real Route 66 color, check out this local institution fondly known as the Zoo, because the building housed an extensive taxidermy collection in the 1930s. Most of the animals are gone, but some owls still perch above the dance floor of what is now a popular country-and-western club. Even if you don't like crowds or country music, it's worth stopping in for a drink and to see this gigantic log cabin constructed around five trees; the entryway is a huge wishbone-shape pine. ✉ *3404 E. Rte. 66, East Flagstaff* ☎ *928/526–9434* ⊕ *www.museumclub.com* 🖃 *Free* ☉ *Daily 11AM–2AM.*

9 **Walnut Canyon National Monument** consists of a group of cliff dwellings
★ constructed by the Sinagua people, who lived and farmed in and around the canyon starting around AD 700. The more than 300 dwellings here were built between 1080 and 1250, and abandoned, like those at so many other settlements in Arizona and New Mexico, around 1300. The Sinagua traded far and wide with other Native Americans, including people at Wupatki. Even macaw feathers, which would have come from tribes in what is now Mexico, have been excavated in the canyon. Early Flagstaff settlers looted the site for pots and "treasure"; Woodrow Wilson declared this a national monument in 1915, which began a 30-year process of stabilizing the site.

Part of the fascination of Walnut Canyon is the opportunity to enter the dwellings, stepping back in time to an ancient way of life. Some of the Sinagua homes are in near-perfect condition in spite of all the looting, because of the dry, hot climate and the protection of overhanging cliffs. You can reach them by descending 185 feet on the 1-mi, 240-stairs, stepped **Island Trail,** which starts at the visitor center. As you follow the trail, look across the canyon for other dwellings not accessible on the path. Island Trail takes about an hour to complete at a normal pace. Those with health concerns should opt for the easier 0.5-mi **Rim Trail,** which has overlooks from which dwellings, as well as an excavated, reconstructed pit house, can be viewed. Picnic areas dot the grounds and line the roads leading to the park. ✉ *Walnut Canyon Rd., 3 mi south of I–40, Exit 204, Winona* ☎ *928/526–3367* ⊕ *www.nps.gov/waca* 🖃 *$5* ☉ *Nov.–Apr., daily 9–5; May–Oct., daily 8–5.*

10 **Meteor Crater,** a natural phenomenon in a privately owned park 43 mi
☺ east of Flagstaff, is impressive if for no other reason than its sheer size. A hole in the ground 600 feet deep, nearly 1 mi across, and more than 3 mi in circumference, Meteor Crater is large enough to accommodate the Washington Monument or 20 football fields. It was created by a meteorite crash 49,000 years ago. The area looks so much like the surface of the moon that NASA made it one of the official training sites for the Project Apollo astronauts. You can't descend into the crater because of the efforts of its owners to maintain its condition—scientists consider this to be the best-preserved crater on Earth—but guided rim tours, given every hour on the hour 9–3, give useful background information. There's a small snack bar, and the Rock Shop sells specimens from the area and jewelry made from native stones. Take Interstate 40 east of Flagstaff to Exit 233, then drive 6 mi south on Meteor Crater Road. ✉ *Meteor Crater Rd. (43 mi east of Flagstaff), Winslow* ☎ *928/289–5898 or 800/289–5898* ⊕ *www.meteorcrater.com* 🖃 *$15* ☉ *June–Aug., daily 7–7; Sept.–May, daily 8–5.*

SAN FRANCISCO VOLCANIC FIELD

The San Francisco Volcanic Field north of Flagstaff encompasses 2,000 square mi of fascinating geological phenomena, including ancient volcanoes, cinder cones, valleys carved by water and ice, and the San Francisco Peaks themselves, some of which soar to almost 13,000 feet. There are also some of the most extensive Native American dwellings in the Southwest: don't miss Sunset Crater and Wupatki. These national monuments can be explored in relative solitude during much of the year. ■TIP➔ The area is short on services, so fill up on gas and consider taking a picnic.

GETTING HERE AND AROUND

To get to both Sunset Crater and Wupatki national monuments, take U.S. 89 north out of Flagstaff. After 12 mi, turn right for Sunset Crater. Wupatki National Monument is another 19 mi north on this road.

> ### THE SINAGUA PEOPLE
>
> The achievements of the Sinagua people, who lived in north-central Arizona from the 8th through the 15th century, reached their height in the 12th and 13th centuries, when related groups occupied most of the San Francisco Volcanic Field and a large portion of the upper and middle Verde Valley. The Sinagua sites around modern-day Camp Verde, Clarkdale, and Flagstaff provide a window onto this remarkable culture. Some of the best examples of surviving Sinagua architecture can be found at Walnut Canyon and Wupatki National Monument, northeast of Flagstaff.

4

⓫ ★ Sunset Crater Volcano National Monument lies 14 mi northeast of Flagstaff off U.S. 89. Sunset Crater, a cinder cone that rises 1,000 feet, was an active volcano 900 years ago. Its final eruption contained iron and sulfur, which give the rim of the crater its glow and thus its name. You can walk around the base, but you can't descend into the huge, fragile cone. The **Lava Flow Trail,** a half-hour, mile-long, self-guided walk, provides a good view of the evidence of the volcano's fiery power: lava formations and holes in the rock where volcanic gases vented to the surface.

If you're interested in hiking a volcano, head to **Lenox Crater,** about 1 mi east of the visitor center, and climb the 280 feet to the top of the cinder cone. The cinder is soft and crumbly, so wear closed, sturdy shoes. From **O'Leary Peak,** 5 mi from the visitor center on Forest Route 545A, enjoy great views of the San Francisco Peaks, the Painted Desert, and beyond. The road is unpaved and rutted, though, so it's advisable to take only high-clearance vehicles, especially in winter. In addition, there's a gate, about halfway along the route, which is usually closed, and when it is it means a steep 2.5-mi hike to the top on foot. To get to the area from Flagstaff, take Santa Fe Avenue east to U.S. 89, and head north for 12 mi; turn right onto the road marked Sunset Crater and go another 2 mi to the visitor center. ⊠ *Sunset Crater–Wupatki Loop Rd., 14 mi northeast of Flagstaff* ☎ *928/526–0502* ⊕ *www.nps. gov/sucr* ⊠ *$5, including Wupatki National Monument and Doney Mountain* ⊘ *Nov.–Apr., daily 9–5; May–Oct., daily 8–5.*

⑫ Families from the Sinagua and other Ancestral Puebloans are believed to
★ have lived together in harmony on the site that is now **Wupatki National
Monument**, farming and trading with one another and with those who
passed through. The eruption of Sunset Crater may have influenced
migration to this area a century after the event, as freshly laid volcanic
cinders held in moisture needed for crops. Although there's evidence of
earlier habitation, most of the settlers moved here around 1100 and left
the pueblo by about 1250. The 2,700 identified sites contain archaeological evidence of a Native American settlement.

The national monument was named for the Wupatki (meaning "tall
house" in Hopi) site, which was originally three stories high, built
above an unexplored system of underground fissures. The structure had
almost 100 rooms and an open ball court—evidence of Southwestern
trade with Mesoamerican tribes for whom ball games were a central
ritual. Next to the ball court is a blowhole, a geologic phenomenon in
which air is forced upward by underground pressure.

Other sites to visit are Wukoki, Lomaki, and the Citadel, a pueblo on a
knoll above a limestone sink. Although the largest remnants of Native
American settlements at Wupatki National Monument are open to the
public, other sites are off-limits. If you're interested in an in-depth tour,
consider a ranger-led overnight hike to the **Crack-in-Rock Ruin**. The
14-mi (round-trip) trek covers areas marked by ancient petroglyphs and
dotted with well-preserved sites. The trips are only conducted in April
and October; call by February or August if you'd like to take part in the
lottery for one of the 100 available places on these $50 hikes. Between
the Wupatki and Citadel ruins, **Doney Mountain** affords 360-degree
views of the Painted Desert and the San Francisco Volcanic Field. It's a
perfect spot for a sunset picnic. In summer, rangers give lectures. ⊠ *Sunset Crater–Wupatki Loop Rd., 19 mi north of Sunset Crater visitor
center* ☎ *928/679–2365* ⊕ *www.nps.gov/wupa* ✏ *$5, including Sunset
Crater National Monument and Doney Mountain* ☼ *Daily 9–5.*

SEDONA AND OAK CREEK CANYON

*27 mi south of Flagstaff on AZ 89A; 119 mi north of Phoenix, I–17 to
AZ 179 to AZ 89A; 60 mi northeast of Prescott, U.S. 89 to AZ 89A.*

It's easy to see what draws so many people to Sedona. Red-rock
buttes—Cathedral Rock, Bear Mountain, Courthouse Rock, and Bell
Rock, among others—reach up into an almost always blue sky, and
both colors are intensified by dark-green pine forests. Surrealist Max
Ernst, writer Zane Grey, and many filmmakers drew inspiration from
these vistas—more than 80 Westerns were shot in the area in the 1940s
and '50s alone.

These days, Sedona lures enterprising restaurateurs and gallery owners
from the East and West coasts. New Age followers, who believe that
the area contains some of Earth's more-important vortexes (energy centers), also come in great numbers believing that the "vibe" here confers
a sense of balance and well-being, and enhances creativity.

Sedona Vortex Tour

What is a vortex? The word "vortex" comes from the Latin *vertere*, which means "to turn or whirl." In Sedona, a vortex is a funnel created by the motion of spiraling energy. Sedona has long been believed to be a center for spiritual power because of the vortexes of subtle energy in the area. This energy isn't described as electricity or magnetism, though it's said to leave a slight residual magnetism in the places where it's strongest.

New Agers believe there are four major vortexes in Sedona: Airport, Cathedral Rock, Boynton Canyon, and Bell Rock. Each manifests a different kind of energy, and this energy interacts with the individual in its presence. People come from all over the world to experience these energy forms, hoping for guidance in spiritual matters, health, and relationships.

Juniper trees, which are all over the Sedona area, are said to respond to vortex energy in a way that reveals where this energy is strongest. The stronger the energy, the more axial twist the junipers bear in their branches.

Airport Vortex is said to strengthen one's "masculine" side, aiding in self-confidence and focus. **Cathedral Rock Vortex** nurtures one's "feminine" aspects, such as patience and kindness. You'll be directed to **Boynton Canyon Vortex** if you're seeking balance between the masculine and feminine. And finally **Bell Rock Vortex**, the most powerful of all, strengthens all three aspects: masculine, feminine, and balance.

These energy centers are easily accessed, and vortex maps are available at crystal shops all over Sedona.

4

Expansion since the early 1980s has been rapid, and lack of planning has taken its toll in unattractive developments and increased traffic.

The town itself is young, and there are few historic sites; the main downtown activity is shopping, mostly for Southwestern-style paintings, clothing, rugs, jewelry, and Native American artifacts. Just beyond the shops and restaurants, however, canyons, creeks, ancient dwellings, and the red rocks beckon. The area is easy to hike or bike, or you can take a jeep tour.

GETTING HERE AND AROUND

GETTING HERE Sedona stretches along AZ 89A, its main thoroughfare, which runs roughly east–west through town. Uptown, the section with most of the shops and restaurants, is at the east end. Free parking is plentiful throughout Sedona, but especially in Uptown: the visitor center, a half block off 89A on Forest Road, has an adjacent parking lot; parking spaces along the streets are free for three hours; or park all day in the large municipal lot a few blocks farther east, off Jordan Road.

The most scenic route into town from Phoenix is taking Interstate 17 to AZ 260 toward Cottonwood, then going northeast on AZ 89A. To reach Sedona more directly from Phoenix, take Interstate 17 north for 113 mi until you come to AZ 179; it's another winding 15 mi on that road into town. The trip should take about 2½ hours. The 27-mi drive north from

Sedona to Flagstaff on AZ 89A, which winds its way through Oak Creek canyon, is breathtaking.

Sedona Airport, in West Sedona, is a base for several air tours but has no regularly scheduled flights.

The Sedona–Phoenix Shuttle makes eight trips daily between those cities; the fare is $45 one-way, $85 round-trip. You can also get on or off at Camp Verde, Cottonwood, or the Village of Oak Creek (7 mi outside Sedona on AZ 179). Reservations are required.

FLAGSTAFF AND SEDONA

There might only be 27 mi separating Flagstaff and Sedona, but they're very different places. Flagstaff's natural terrain and earthiness lend a "granola-y" feel to the city, and the Northern Arizona University students here enhance it. Meanwhile, Sedona's beauty is no secret, and residents (full- and part-time) pay a premium to enjoy it.

Weekend traffic near Sedona, especially during the high season, can approach gridlock on the narrow highways. Leave for your destination at first light to bypass the day-trippers, late risers, and midday heat.

GETTING AROUND

Sedona is roughly divided into three neighborhoods: Uptown, which is a walkable shopping district; West Sedona, which is a 4-mi-long commercial strip; and Central Sedona, which encompasses everything south of the "Y" where AZ 179 and AZ 89A intersect. The Sedona RoadRunner provides free bus transportation daily along AZ 89A, looping over to Tlaquepaque and into Uptown, every 15 minutes 9 AM–6 PM.

Sedona Trolley offers two types of daily orientation tours, both departing from the main bus stop in Uptown and lasting less than an hour. One goes along AZ 179 to the Chapel of the Holy Cross, with stops at Tlaquepaque and some galleries; the other passes through West Sedona to Boynton Canyon (Enchantment Resort). Rates are $12 for one or $22 for both.

If you want to explore the red rocks of Sedona, you can rent a four-wheel drive from one of the local agencies such as Barlow Jeep Rentals.

PLANNING YOUR TIME

In warmer months visit air-conditioned shops at midday and do hiking and jeep tours in the early morning or late afternoon, when the light is softer and the heat less oppressive. Many of the most memorable spots in Sedona are considered energy centers; vortex maps of the area are available at most of Sedona's New Age stores.

The vistas of Sedona from Airport Mesa at sunset can't be beat. The Upper Red Rock Loop has great photo opportunities.

ESSENTIALS

Visitor Info Sedona Visitor Center (✉ 331 Forest Rd., just off AZ 89A ☎ 928/282–7722 or 800/288–7336 ⊕ www.visitsedona.com).

Transportation Contacts Barlow Jeep Rentals (☎ 928/282–8700 ⊕ www.barlowjeeprentals.com). **RoadRunner Shuttle** (⊕ www.roadrunner.az.gov). **Sedona Airport** (☎ 928/282–4487). **Sedona–Phoenix Shuttle Service** (☎ 928/282–2066, 800/448–7988 in Arizona ⊕ www.sedona-phoenix-shuttle.com). **Sedona Taxi** (☎ 928/204–9111). **Sedona Trolley** (☎ 928/282–4211 ⊕ www.sedonatrolley.com).

Sedona and Oak Creek Canyon

EXPLORING

TOP ATTRACTIONS

Bell Rock. With its distinctive shape right out of your favorite Western film and its proximity to the main drag ensuring a steady flow of admirers, you may want to arrive early to see this popular butte. The parking lot next to the Bell Rock Pathway often fills by mid-morning even midweek. The views from here are good, but an easy and fairly accessible path follows mostly gentle terrain for 1 mi to the base of the butte. Mountain bikers, parents with all-terrain baby strollers, and not-so-avid hikers should have little problem getting there. No official paths climb the rock itself, but many forge their own routes (at their own risk). ⊠ *AZ 179, several hundred yards north of Bell Rock Blvd., Village of Oak Creek.*

Cathedral Rock. It's almost impossible not to be drawn to this butte's towering, variegated spires. The approximately 1,200-foot-high Cathedral Rock looms dramatically over town. When you emerge from the narrow gorge of Oak Creek canyon, this is the first recognizable formation you'll spot. ■ **TIP→ The butte is best seen toward dusk from a distance.** Hikers may want to drive to the Airport Mesa and then hike the rugged but generally flat path that loops around the airfield. The trail is 0.5 mi up Airport Road off AZ 89A in West Sedona; the reward is a panoramic view of Cathedral Rock without the crowds. Those not hiking should drive through the Village of Oak Creek and 5 mi west on Verde Valley School Road to its end, where you can view the butte from a beautiful streamside vantage point and take a dip in Oak Creek if you wish. ⊠ *5 mi to end of Verde Valley School Rd., west off AZ 179, Village of Oak Creek.*

Cathedral Rock Trail. A vigorous but nontechnical 1.5-mi scramble up the slickrock (smooth, rather than slippery, sandstone), this path leads to a nearly 360-degree view of red-rock country. Follow the cairns (rock piles marking the trail) and look for the footholds in the rock. Carry plenty of water: though short, the trail offers little shade and the pitch is steep. You can see the Verde Valley and Mingus Mountain in the distance. Look for the barely discernible "J" etched on the hillside marking the former ghost town of Jerome 30 mi distant. ⊠ *Trailhead: About 0.5 mi down Back O' Beyond Rd. off AZ 179, 3 mi south of Sedona.*

Chapel of the Holy Cross. You needn't be religious to be inspired by the setting and the architecture here. Built in 1956 by Marguerite Brunwige Staude, a student of Frank Lloyd Wright, this modern landmark, with a huge cross on the facade, rises between two red-rock peaks. Vistas of the town and the surrounding area are spectacular. Though there is only one regular service—a beautiful Taizé service of prayer and song on Monday at 5 PM—all are welcome for quiet meditation. A small gift shop sells religious artifacts and books. A trail east of the chapel leads you—after a 20-minute walk over occasional loose-rock surfaces—to a seat surrounded by voluptuous red-limestone walls, worlds away from the bustle and commerce around the chapel. ⊠ *Chapel Rd. off AZ 179, Village of Oak Creek* ☎ *928/282–4069* ⊕ *www.chapeloftheholycross. com* ⊠ *Free* ☉ *Daily 9–5.*

★ **Oak Creek canyon.** Whether you want to swim, hike, picnic, or enjoy beautiful scenery framed through a car window, head north through the wooded Oak Creek canyon. It's the most scenic route to Flagstaff and the Grand Canyon, and worth a drive-through even if you're not heading north. The road winds through a steep-walled canyon, where you crane your neck for views of the dramatic rock formations above. Although the forest is primarily evergreen, the fall foliage is glorious. Oak Creek, which runs along the bottom, is lined with tent campgrounds, fishing camps, cabins, motels, and restaurants. ⊠ *AZ 89A, beginning 1 mi north of Sedona, Oak Creek Canyon.*

☾ **Slide Rock State Park.** A good place for a picnic, Slide Rock is 7 mi north of Sedona. On a hot day you can plunge down a natural rock slide into a swimming hole (bring an extra pair of jeans or a sturdy bathing suit and river shoes to wear on the slide). The site started as an early-20th-century apple orchard, and the natural beauty attracted Hollywood—a

DID YOU KNOW?

Between Flagstaff and Sedona, Route 89A runs through Oak Creek canyon. Over time, softer rock has eroded to carve out the canyon and create the dramatic rock formations you see today.

Red-Rock Geology

It's hard to imagine that the land-locked desert surrounding Sedona was, for much of prehistoric time, an area of dunes and swamps on the shore of an ancient sea. The ebb and flow of this sea shaped the land. When the sea rose, it planed the dunes before dropping more sediment on top. The process continued for a few hundred million years. Eventually the sediment hardened into gray layers of limestone on top of the red sandstone. When North America collided with another continental plate, the land buckled and lifted, forming the Rocky Mountains and raising northern Arizona thousands of feet. Volcanoes erupted in the area, capping some of the rock with erosion-resistant basalt.

Oak Creek started flowing at this time, eroding through the layers of sandstone and limestone. Along with other forces of erosion, the creek carved out the canyons and shaped the buttes. Sedona's buttes stayed intact because a resilient layer of lava had hardened on top and slowed the erosion process considerably. As iron minerals in the sandstone were gradually exposed to the elements, they turned red in a process similar to rusting. The iron minerals, in turn, stained the surrounding colorless quartz and grains of sand—it only takes 2% red-iron material to give the sandstone its red color.

Like the rings of a tree, the striations in the rock document the passage of time and the events, limestone marking the rise of the sea, sandstone when the region was coastline.

---

number of John Wayne and Jimmy Stewart movies were filmed here. A few easy hikes run along the rim of the gorge. Fly-fishing for trout is possible when it's too cold for swimming. One downside is the traffic, particularly on summer weekends; you might have to wait to get into the park after mid-morning. Unfortunately, the popularity of the stream has led to the occasional midsummer closing due to E. coli–bacteria infestations; the water is tested daily and there is a water-quality hotline at ☎ 602/542–0202. ⊠ 6871 N. AZ 89A, Oak Creek Canyon ☎ 928/282–3034 ⊕ www.azstateparks.com ☜ $10 per vehicle for up to 4 persons; $20 per vehicle in summer ⊗ Labor Day–Memorial Day, daily 8–5; Memorial Day–Labor Day, weekdays 8–6, Fri.–Sun. 8–7, last entrance 1 hr before closing.

☾ **Snoopy Rock.** Kids love this: when you look almost directly to the east, this butte really does look like the famed Peanuts beagle lying atop red rock instead of his doghouse. You can distinguish the formation from several places around town, including the mall in Uptown Sedona, but to get a clear view, venture up Schnebly Hill Road. Park by the trailhead on the left immediately before the paved road deteriorates to dirt. Marg's Draw, one of several trails originating here, is worthwhile, gently meandering 100 feet down-canyon, through the tortured desert flora to Morgan Road. Backtrack to the parking lot for close to a 3-mi hike. ■ TIP➔ Always carry plenty of water, no matter how easy the hike appears. ⊠ Schnebly Hill Rd. off AZ 179, Central.

WORTH NOTING

Courthouse Butte. The red sandstone seems to catch on fire toward sunset, when this monolith is free of shadow. From the highway, Courthouse Butte sits in back of Bell Rock and can be viewed without any additional hiking or driving. ⊠ *AZ 179, Village of Oak Creek.*

Rainbow Trout Farm. North-central Arizona may not be the most obvious fishing destination, but this stocked farm is a fun way to spend a few hours if you're so inclined. Anglers young and old almost always enjoy a sure catch, and you can rent a cane pole here with a hook and bait for $1. There's no charge if your catch is under 8 inches; above that it's $8 to $12, depending on the length. The real bargain is that the staff will clean and pack your fish for 50¢ each. ⊠ *3500 N. AZ 89A, 3 mi north of Sedona, Oak Creek Canyon* ☎ *928/282–5799* ☉ *Daily 9–5.*

Red Rock State Park. Two miles west of Sedona via AZ 89A is the turnoff for this 286-acre state park, a less crowded alternative to Slide Rock State Park, though without the possibility for swimming. The 5 mi of interconnected park trails are well marked, and provide beautiful vistas. There are daily ranger-guided nature walks at 10 AM and 2 PM, and bird-watching excursions on Wednesday and Saturday. ⊠ *4050 Red Rock Loop Rd., West* ☎ *928/282–6907* ⊕ *www.azstateparks.com* ✉ *$10 per car for up to 4 persons* ☉ *Daily 8–5.*

SPORTS AND THE OUTDOORS

The Brins Fire consumed 4,500 acres in Sedona in 2006. Although no people or structures were harmed, the human-ignited fire threatened the Oak Creek canyon area and serves as a reminder for fire safety. Take precautions and use common sense. Extinguish all fires with water. Never toss a cigarette butt. And don't hesitate to ask questions of local park rangers.

■ TIP→ A Red Rock Pass is required to park in the Coconino National Forest from Oak Creek canyon through Sedona and the Village of Oak Creek. Passes cost $5 for the day, $15 for the week, or $20 for an entire year, and can be purchased online and at the National Forest Service Ranger Station, Sedona Chamber of Commerce, and Circle K stores within Sedona. Passes are also available from vending machines at popular trailheads— including Boynton Canyon and Bell Rock—and at many Sedona hotels. Locals widely resent the pass, feeling that free access to national forests is a right. The **Coconino Forest Service** (⊠ *8375 AZ 179, just south of the Village of Oak Creek* ☎ *928/282–4119* ⊕ *www.redrockcountry. org*) counters that it doesn't receive enough federal funds to maintain the land surrounding Sedona, trampled by 5 million visitors each year, and that a parking fee is the best way to raise revenue.

BALLOONING

Northern Light Balloon Expeditions (☎ *928/282–2274 or 800/230–6222* ⊕ *www.northernlightballoon.com*) one of only two companies with permits to fly over Sedona, offers sunrise flights including a post-flight breakfast picnic for $195. **Red Rock Balloon Adventures** (☎ *928/284–0040 or 800/258–3754* ⊕ *www.redrockballoons.com*) flies guests over the red rocks for $195 per person for one to two hours.

GOLF

The **Oak Creek Country Club** (⊠ *690 Bell Rock Blvd., Village of Oak Creek* ☎ *928/284–1660* ⊕ *www.oakcreekcountryclub.com*) is a good semiprivate 18-hole, par-72 course designed by Robert Trent Jones. Green fees are $115 in high season and $69 during the summer months. Lessons and rental clubs are available.

Fodor's Choice **Sedona Golf Resort** (⊠ *35 Ridge Trail Dr., Village of Oak Creek* ☎ *928/*
★ *284–9355 or 877/733–6630* ⊕ *www.sedonagolfresort.com*), a gorgeous par-71 course, was designed by Gary Panks to take advantage of the many changes in elevation and scenery. Golf courses are a dime a dozen in Arizona, but this one is regarded as one of the best in the state. The restaurant—with panoramic red-rock vistas—serves breakfast and lunch daily.

HIKING AND BACKPACKING

For free detailed maps, hiking advice, and information on campgrounds, contact the rangers of the **Coconino National Forest** (⊠ *Sedona Ranger District, 250 Brewer Rd., West* ☎ *928/282–4119* ⊕ *www.fs.fed.us/r3/coconino* ⊙ *Weekdays 8–4:30*). Ask here or at your hotel for directions to trailheads for Doe's Mountain (an easy ascent, with many switchbacks), Loy Canyon, Devil's Kitchen, and Long Canyon.

Among the paths in Coconino National Forest, the popular West Fork Trail (⊠ *Trailhead: AZ 89A, 9.5 mi north of Sedona*) traverses the Oak Creek canyon for a 3-mi hike. A walk through the woods between sheer red-rock walls and a dip in the stream make a great summer combo. The trailhead is about 3 mi north of Slide Rock State Park.

HORSEBACK RIDING

Among the tour options at **Trail Horse Adventures** (⊠ *Dead Horse Ranch State Park, Cottonwood* ☎ *866/958–7245* ⊕ *www.trailhorseadventures.com*) are a midday ride with picnic, a ride along the Verde River to Native American cliff dwellings, and a full-moon ride with a campfire cookout. Rides range from about $60 for an hour to about $125 for an entire day.

JEEP TOURS

Several jeep-tour operators headquartered along Sedona's main Uptown drag conduct excursions, some focusing on geology, some on astronomy, some on vortexes, some on all three. You can even find a combination jeep tour and horseback ride. Prices start at about $55 per person for two hours and go upward of $100 per person for four hours. Although all the excursions are safe, many are not for those who dislike heights or bumps.

A Day in the West (☎ *928/282–4320 or 800/973–3662* ⊕ *www.adayinthewest.com*) can take you to all the prime spots and combine a jeep tour with a horseback ride or local wine tasting. The ubiquitous **Pink Jeep Tours** (⊠ *204 N. AZ 89A,* ☎ *928/282–5000 or 800/873–3662* ⊕ *www.pinkjeep.com*) are a popular choice. **Sedona Red Rock Jeep Tours** (⊠ *270 N. AZ 89A,* ☎ *928/282–6826 or 800/848–7728* ⊕ *www.redrockjeep.com*) is a reliable operator that spins some good cowboy tales on its jeep tours.

MOUNTAIN BIKING

Given the red-rock splendor, challenging terrain, miles of single track, and mild weather, you might think Sedona would be a mountain-biking destination on the order of Moab or Durango. Inexplicably, you won't find the Lycra-clad throngs patronizing pasta bars or throwing back microbrews on the Uptown mall, but all the better for you: the mountain-biking culture remains fervent but low-key. A few strategically located, excellent bike shops can outfit you and give advice.

BOYNTON CANYON

You might want to drive out to Boynton Canyon, sacred to the Yavapai Apache, who believe it was their ancient birthplace. This is also the site of the Enchantment Resort, where all are welcome to hike the canyon and stop in for lunch or a late-afternoon drink on the terrace.

As a general rule, mountain bikes are allowed on all trails and jeep paths unless designated as wilderness or private property. The rolling terrain, which switches between serpentine trails of buff red clay and mounds of slickrock, has few sustained climbs but be careful of blind drop-offs that often step down several feet in unexpected places. The thorny trailside flora makes carrying extra inner tubes a must, and an inner-tube sealant is a good idea, too. If you plan to ride for several hours, pack a gallon of water and start early in the morning on hot days. Shade is rare, and with the exception of (nonpotable) Oak Creek, water is nonexistent.

For the casual rider, **Bell Rock Pathway** ($\boxtimes$ *Trailhead: 5 mi south of Sedona on AZ 179*) is a scenic and easy ride traveling 3 mi through some of the most breathtaking scenery in red-rock country. Several single-track trails spur off this one making it a good starting point for many other rides in Sedona. **Submarine Rock Loop** is perhaps the most popular single-track loop in the area, and for good reason. The 10-mi trail is a heady mixture of prime terrain and scenery following slickrock and twisty trails up to Chicken Point, a sandstone terrace overlooking colorful buttes. The trail continues as a bumpy romp through washes almost all downhill. Be wary of blind drop-offs in this section. It wouldn't be overly cautious to scout any parts of the trail that look sketchy.

RENTALS A few hundred yards south of Bell Rock Pathway, **Bike and Bean** ($\boxtimes$ *6020 AZ 179, Village of Oak Creek* ☎ *928/284–0210* ⊕ *www.bike-bean. com*) offers rentals, tours, trail maps, their own blend of coffee, and advice on trails and conditions.

WHERE TO EAT

Some Sedona restaurants close in January and February, so call before you go; if you're planning a visit in high season (April to October), make reservations.

¢ ✕ **Coffee Pot Restaurant.** Locals and tourists alike swarm to this spacious
AMERICAN diner for scrumptious breakfast and brunch food served by a friendly waitstaff. One hundred and one omelet options are the stars of the show, and include such concoctions as the quirky peanut butter and jelly or the basic ham and cheese. Warm homemade biscuits always hit the spot.

Jeep tours get you close to Sedona's red rocks while someone else does the driving.

An extensive lunch menu that includes everything from Mexican dishes to a Greek salad rounds out the offerings. ✉ *2050 W. AZ 89A, West* ☏ *928/282–6626* ⊕ *coffeepotsedona.com* ▭ *D, MC, V* ✪ *No dinner.*

$$–$$$
STEAK

✕ **Cowboy Club.** At this upscale restaurant you can hang out in the casual Cowboy Club or dine in the more-formal Silver Saddle Room, where suede booths are surrounded by cowboy art and a pair of large cattle horns. High-quality cuts of beef are the specialty, but the burgers and the fried chicken served with cumin mashed potatoes are delicious, too. ✉ *241 AZ 89A, Uptown* ☏ *928/282–4200* ⊕ *www.cowboyclub.com* ▭ *AE, D, DC, MC, V.*

$$$
ITALIAN
★

✕ **Dahl & DiLuca.** Andrea DiLuca and Lisa Dahl have created one of the most popular Italian restaurants in town: Andrea runs the kitchen, and Lisa meets and greets diners when she's not making delicious homemade soups like white bean with ham and hearty minestrone. Specialties here include tortellini with a portobello mushroom sauce and *pollo piccata* (chicken in a lemon, capers, and chardonnay sauce). Renaissance reproductions and café seating give the impression of a Roman piazza. Make reservations or you may be seated at the bar—good food but far less romantic. ✉ *2321 W. AZ 89A, West* ☏ *928/282–5219* ⊕ *www. dahlanddiluca.com* ▭ *AE, D, MC, V* ✪ *No lunch.*

$$
MEXICAN

✕ **Elote Café.** Traditional Mexican recipes get a creative and tasty update at this deservedly popular restaurant. Start with the namesake *elote*, roasted corn on a stick, for an appetizer: this favorite street food in Mexico is transformed into an addictive dip of grilled corn kernels, cojita cheese, lime, and chiles. Small plates like chicken tacos with mole sauce are delicious and affordable, and larger dishes like braised lamb shank in ancho chile sauce or chiles rellenos are equally satisfying.

Enjoy the colorful interior or sit on the open-air deck for fabulous Sedona views. Just come prepared for a wait on weekends. ⊠ *771 AZ 179, Kings Ransom Sedona Hotel, Central* ☎ *928/203–0105* ⊕ *www. elotecafe.com* ⌘ *Reservations not accepted* ⊟ *AE, D, MC, V* ⊘ *Closed Sun. and Mon. No lunch.*

\$\$–\$\$\$ ✕ **Heartline Café and Fireside Room.** Fresh flowers and innovative cuisine that
CONTINENTAL   even the staff struggles to characterize are this attractive café's hallmarks.
★   Local ingredients pepper the menu, giving a Sedona twist to Continental fare, and favorites include pecan-crusted, Sedona-raised trout with Dijon sauce and seafood cioppino stew. Appealing vegetarian plates are also available, and small and large portion options help keep the prices down. Desserts include a phenomenal crème brûlée, as well as homemade truffles at the chef's whim. ■ TIP➔ Breakfast and lunch are served daily in the more-casual Fireside Room next door, where you can also get gourmet takeout—perfect prep for picnics under the red rocks. ⊠ *1610 W. AZ 89A, West* ☎ *928/282–0785* ⊕ *www.heartlinecafe.com* ⊟ *AE, D, MC, V.*

\$\$\$–\$\$\$\$ ✕ **L'Auberge.** The most formal dining room in Sedona, on the L'Auberge
FRENCH   de Sedona resort property, promises a quiet, civilized evening of indul-
★   gence. Chef David Schmidt offers a fusion of American cuisine with French influences, and among the house favorites is the filet mignon with mushroom risotto. You can make the most of L'Auberge's 1,200-bottle wine cellar by enjoying the four-course wine-paired tasing menu for \$110. The lavish Sunday brunch is well worth the splurge. ⊠ *L'Auberge de Sedona, 241 AZ 89A, Uptown* ☎ *928/282–1667* ⊕ *www.lauberge. com* ⊟ *AE, D, DC, MC, V.*

¢–\$ ✕ **New Frontiers Natural Marketplace.** Healthful fare at this mostly organic
CAFÉ   grocery and deli runs the gamut from grab-and-go sandwiches to the well-stocked salad bar to hot items like honey-glazed salmon, cheese or chicken enchiladas, and turkey meat loaf. Get supplies for your red-rock picnic or relax at the indoor-outdoor dining area. ⊠ *1420 W. AZ 89A, West* ☎ *928/282–6311* ⊟ *AE, D, MC, V.*

\$–\$\$ ✕ **Oaxaca Restaurant.** Tasty standards complement some of the best
MEXICAN   Uptown canyon vistas at this modern Mexican restaurant with a lovely balcony. The smoky kick of the salsa, along with the sun-kissed scenery, may transport you south of the border, but dishes are prepared under the auspices of owner Carla Butler, a dietitian who shuns the traditional use of lard and cholesterol-containing oils in favor of healthier options—with delicious results. A south-of-the-border breakfast is served on weekends. ⊠ *321 N. AZ 89A, Uptown* ☎ *928/282–4179* ⊕ *www.oaxacarestaurant.com* ⊟ *AE, D, MC, V.*

\$\$\$–\$\$\$\$ ✕ **René at Tlaquepaque.** Ease into the plush banquettes at this lace-curtained
CONTINENTAL   restaurant for classic French and Continental dishes. Recommended starters include French onion soup and the spinach-and-wild-mushroom salad in a hazelnut vinaigrette. Rack of lamb is the house specialty, and the Dover sole is a real find, far from the white cliffs. Crêpes suzette for two, prepared table-side, is an impressive dessert. There's a well-selected wine list, too. Service is formal, but resort-casual attire is acceptable. ⊠ *Tlaquepaque Arts & Crafts Village, Unit B–117, AZ 179, Central* ☎ *928/282–9225* ⊕ *www.rene-sedona.com* ⊟ *AE, MC, V.*

¢ ✕ **Sally's Mesquite Grill and BBQ.** Although it offers limited indoor seat-
SOUTHERN ing, this Uptown hideaway behind a long row of tourist shops is worth
★ a visit. It's supercasual, with just an ordering window where you can
select pulled-pork sandwiches and homemade comfort food such as
beans or coleslaw. The barbecue sauce has a bit of a kick, and the french
fries (also made from scratch) are fabulous. Hours vary with the season, so call ahead. ⊠ *250 Jordan Rd., No. 9, Uptown* ☎ *928/282–6533*
⊕ *www.sallyshbq.com* ▭ *MC, V.*

$$–$$$ ✕ **Shugrue's Hillside.** Almost everything is good here—including the red-
AMERICAN rock views from every seat—which has made this one of the most popular
restaurants in Sedona, but the salads and meats are particularly noteworthy. The Caesar salad is refreshingly traditional, and the inventive
ginger-walnut chicken salad is large enough to share. Rack of lamb and
filet mignon are prepared and presented simply, and there's a small, well-
priced wine list. Full entrées include soup or salad; smaller à la carte
selections are lower priced. Service is friendly rather than formal, and
dining views don't get much better than the upstairs deck. ⊠ *671 AZ 179,
Central* ☎ *928/282–5300* ⊕ *www.shugrues.com* ▭ *AE, DC, MC, V.*

$$$ ✕ **Takashi.** Anyone seeking serenity and a respite from heavy meals will
JAPANESE enjoy this Japanese restaurant, which provides aesthetic pleasure in
everything from tea (with little bits of floating popcorn and brown
rice) to dessert (sweet ginger or red-bean ice cream). Salads include
spicy sushi-quality tuna with Japanese mayonnaise on a bed of cab-
bage and fresh vegetables. Combination dinners such as sashimi with
tempura or teriyaki let you sample a bit of everything. ⊠ *465 Jordan
Rd., Uptown* ☎ *928/282–2334* ⊕ *www.takashisedona.com* ▭ *AE, DC,
MC, V* ☾ *Closed Mon. No lunch weekends.*

WHERE TO STAY

$$$–$$$$ ⛨ **Adobe Village and Graham Inn.** Some of the rooms and suites at this
★ inn south of Sedona have Jacuzzi tubs and balconies that look out onto
the red rocks. Each of the four individually decorated casitas on the
lot next door has a gas fireplace that opens into both the sitting area
and the bathroom area, which is outfitted with a two-person Jacuzzi
tub. What makes this place really special, though, is the impeccable yet
casual service. **Pros:** way-above-average hospitality; extras like compli-
mentary trail mix to go and hearty afternoon snacks; walk to hiking
trails. **Cons:** some road noise; drive to town. ⊠ *150 Canyon Circle
Dr., Village of Oak Creek* ☎ *928/284–1425 or 800/228–1425* ⊕ *www.
adobevillagegrahaminn.com* ➶ *6 rooms, 5 suites, 4 private villas* ⚘ *In-
room: a/c, kitchen (some), refrigerator (some), DVD, Wi-Fi. In-hotel:
pool* ▭ *AE, D, MC, V* ⊠⊠ *BP.*

$$$–$$$$ ⛨ **Alma de Sedona.** The Alma de Sedona continues to be an enchanting
bed-and-breakfast, with spectacular views and ultracomfortable beds.
The inn was built well off the main drag and in the shadow of the
buttes for views and privacy. Understated, elegant, and inviting rooms
all have private entrances and patios. Bath salts and candles await in
the bathrooms, most of which have two-person Jacuzzi tubs. **Pros:**
central location; excellent views. **Cons:** overpriced for a B&B; decor
could use updating; no elevator (some rooms require climbing stairs).

⊠ *50 Hozoni Dr., West* ☎ *928/282–2737 or 800/923–2282* ⊕ *www. almadesedona.com* ⇗ *12 rooms* ♨ *In-room: a/c, refrigerator, Wi-Fi. In-hotel: pool* ⊟ *MC, V* ⊺⊙⊺ *BP.*

$$$ ⊡ **Amara Resort.** You might not expect to find a boutique hotel in small, outdoorsy Sedona, but here at the Amara, next to gurgling Oak Creek, sleek rooms deviate from the usual Sedona look, with low-slung beds and work desks with ergonomic seating. Other cushy extras include in-room DVD players and Aveda bath products. Step out onto your room's private balcony or terrace to take in expansive red-rock views. **Pros:** good spa and restaurant; walk to Uptown. **Cons:** city-chic feels somewhat incongruous with natural setting. ⊠ *310 N. AZ 89, Uptown* ☎ *928/282–4828 or 866/455–6610* ⊕ *www.amararesort.com* ⇗ *92 rooms, 8 suites* ♨ *In-room: a/c, DVD, Wi-Fi. In-hotel: restaurant, bar, gym, Internet terminal* ⊟ *AE, D, DC, MC, V.*

$$$–$$$$ ⊡ **Boots & Saddles.** Irith and Sam are the worldly and consummate hosts at this quiet inn tucked behind the main street in West Sedona. The romantic rooms are decorated in an upscale Western motif, complete with genuine cowboy artifacts, and most have decks with hot tubs and telescopes for stargazing. **Pros:** hosts go the extra mile to pamper and advise; private decks. **Cons:** first-floor rooms can get noise from upstairs guests. ⊠ *2900 Hopi Dr., West* ☎ *928/282–1944 or 800/201–1944* ⊕ *www.oldwestbb.com* ⇗ *6 rooms* ♨ *In-room: a/c, refrigerator, DVD, Wi-Fi. In-hotel: no kids under 12* ⊟ *AE, D, MC, V* ⊺⊙⊺ *BP.*

$$$–$$$$ ⊡ **Briar Patch Inn.** This B&B in verdant Oak Creek canyon has Southwestern-themed rooms in wooden cabins, many with decks overlooking the creek. On summer mornings you can sit outside and enjoy home-baked breads and fresh egg dishes while listening to live classical music. Yoga classes are also held on the premises. **Pros:** tranquil creek-side setting with beautiful gardens. **Cons:** somewhat rustic; cabins can be dark. ⊠ *3190 N. AZ 89A, Oak Creek Canyon* ☎ *928/282–2342 or 888/809–3030* ⊕ *www. briarpatchinn.com* ⇗ *19 cottages* ♨ *In-room: a/c, kitchen (some), refrigerator, no TV (some). In-hotel: Wi-Fi hotspot* ⊟ *AE, MC, V* ⊺⊙⊺ *BP.*

$$
★ ⊡ **The Canyon Wren.** The best value in the Oak Creek canyon area, this small B&B across the road from the creek has freestanding cabins with views of the canyon walls, and hosts Milena and Mike regard guests' privacy first and foremost. It's likely that their two lovable dogs, Zoey and Wookiee, will greet you on arrival. Cabins have private decks and fireplaces. **Pros:** romantic yet homey; wonderful hosts and breakfast. **Cons:** may be too rustic for some; 6 mi to town. ⊠ *6425 N. AZ 89A, Oak Creek Canyon* ☎ *928/282–6900 or 800/437–9736* ⊕ *www. canyonwrencabins.com* ⇗ *4 cabins* ♨ *In-room: a/c, no phone, kitchen, no TV* ⊟ *AE, D, MC, V* ⊺⊙⊺ *CP.*

$–$$ ⊡ **Desert Quail Inn.** Close to a lion's share of the trailheads, this is a good base for outdoor adventures, and the front desk has plenty of maps and advice on offer. Rooms, though dated (circa 1980), are spacious and bright, and the in-room refrigerators are stocked with fresh fruit—a nice touch. **Pros:** large, clean rooms. **Cons:** two-story roadside motel. ⊠ *6626 AZ 179, Village of Oak Creek* ☎ *928/284–1433 or 800/385–0927* ⊕ *www. desertquailinn.com* ⇗ *41 rooms* ♨ *In-room: a/c, refrigerator. In-hotel: pool, laundry facilities, some pets allowed (fee)* ⊟ *AE, D, DC, MC, V.*

Local arts and crafts often represent the Native American heritage in Arizona.

$$$$ **El Portal Sedona.** This stunning hacienda is one of the most beautifully designed boutique hotels in the Southwest. Decor accents include authentic Tiffany and Roycroft pieces, French doors leading to balconies or a grassy central courtyard, stained-glass windows and ceiling panels, river-rock or tile fireplaces, and huge custom-designed beds. Wine and hors d'oeuvres like cheese and lavosh crackers are served in the afternoon. Breakfast is delicious, but not included in the room rates. **Pros:** very attractive building; central location next to Tlaquepaque shops and restaurants. **Cons:** even breakfast is expensive. ⊠ *95 Portal La., Central* ☎ *928/203–9405 or 800/313–0017* ⊕ *www.elportalsedona.com* ⬎ *11 rooms, 1 suite* ♿ *In-room: a/c, refrigerator, DVD, Wi-Fi. In-hotel: some pets allowed* ▭ *AE, D, MC, V* ⑩ *BP.*

$$$$ **Enchantment Resort.** The rooms and suites at this resort are tucked
★ into small, pueblo-style buildings in serene Boynton Canyon. Accommodations come in many configurations, and multiple bedrooms can be joined to create large, elaborate suites. All have beehive gas fireplaces, private decks, and superb views. The resort's world-class spa, Mii Amo, offers all-inclusive packages with separate rooms and suites in the spa complex, as well as myriad treatments and innovative spa cuisine. **Pros:** gorgeous setting; state-of-the-art spa; numerous on-site activities. **Cons:** 20-minute drive into town. ⊠ *525 Boynton Canyon Rd., West* ☎ *928/282–2900 or 800/826–4180* ⊕ *www.enchantmentresort.com* ⬎ *107 rooms, 115 suites* ♿ *In-room: a/c, safe, kitchen (some), Wi-Fi. In-hotel: 3 restaurants, bar, tennis courts, pools, gym, spa, bicycles, children's programs (ages 4–12)* ▭ *AE, D, MC, V.*

$$$–$$$$ **Junipine Resort.** These one- and two-bedroom cabins nestled in a juniper and pine forest (hence the name) are spacious and airy, with vaulted ceilings, wood-burning fireplaces, and large decks overlooking either the creek or the canyon. An excellent value for groups of four or more, some of the cabins are more than 1,400 square feet and sleep up to eight people. Junipine's most enchanting feature might be the sound of Oak Creek roaring below, lulling you to sleep by the fire. **Pros:** huge, well-equipped cabins; trailheads on-site. **Cons:** individually owned condo units have been individually decorated in styles that may not appeal to everyone; the group appeal can mean some partying neighbors. ⊠ *8351 N. AZ 89A, Oak Creek Canyon* ☎ *928/282–3375 or 800/742–7463* ⊕ *www.junipine.com* ⤴ *50 suites* ⚉ *In-room: a/c, kitchen, DVD (some), Wi-Fi. In-hotel: restaurant* ☰ *AE, D, MC, V.*

$$$–$$$$
★ ⌂ **L'Auberge de Sedona.** This hillside resort consists of a central lodge building with elegant rooms and—the major attraction—private cottages in the woods along Oak Creek. Rooms in the lodge are decorated in lush country-European style, and the cottages—some with Jacuzzi tubs—all have wood-burning fireplaces. Phoenix couples flock to this hideaway and dine in the hotel's French restaurant, one of the most romantic eateries in Arizona. **Pros:** luxurious rooms and cabins; secluded setting yet close to town. **Cons:** exclusive feel; in-house restaurant very pricey. ⊠ *301 L'Auberge La., Uptown* ⌆ *Box B, Sedona 86336* ☎ *928/282–1661 or 800/905–5745* ⊕ *www.lauberge.com* ⤴ *21 rooms, 31 cottages* ⚉ *In-room: a/c, safe, refrigerator, Wi-Fi. In-hotel: 2 restaurants, pool, spa* ☰ *AE, D, DC, MC, V.*

$$$–$$$$ ⌂ **Lodge at Sedona.** Rooms in this rambling wood-and-stone Craftsman house have a refined rustic style; some have fireplaces, redwood decks, or hot tubs. For solitude, walk the seven-path classic labyrinth (made of local rock) and through the gardens. A chef prepares a five-course breakfast each morning. **Pros:** tranquil setting yet short walk from West Sedona; friendly staff. **Cons:** limited views. ⊠ *125 Kallof Pl., West* ☎ *928/204–1942 or 800/619–4467* ⊕ *www.lodgeatsedona.com* ⤴ *5 rooms, 9 suites* ⚉ *In-room: a/c, no phone, DVD (some), no TV (some), Wi-Fi. In-hotel: pool, gym, some pets allowed* ☰ *D, MC, V* ⍾❘ *BP.*

$ ⌂ **Sedona Motel.** Built on a terrace removed from the highway in order to afford it the same expansive views as the pricier resorts, this motel is pretty typical in all other respects. It's within easy reach of most of Sedona's attractions, and the rooms are well kept. **Pros:** good value; convenient walk to shops and restaurants; red-rock views. **Cons:** some road noise. ⊠ *218 AZ 179, Central* ☎ *928/282–7187 or 877/828–7187* ⊕ *www.thesedonamotel.com* ⤴ *16 rooms* ⚉ *In-room: a/c, refrigerator, Wi-Fi* ☰ *D, MC, V.*

$–$$ ⌂ **Sky Ranch Lodge.** There may be no better vantage point in town from which to view Sedona's red-rock canyons than the private patios and balconies at Sky Ranch Lodge, near the top of Airport Mesa. Some rooms have stone fireplaces and some have kitchenettes. Paths on the grounds wind around fountains and, in summer, through colorful flower gardens. **Pros:** good value; great views. **Cons:** less-expensive rooms have few amenities. ⊠ *Top of Airport Rd., West* ☎ *928/282–6400 or 800/708–6400* ⊕ *www.skyranchlodge.com* ⤴ *92 rooms, 2 cottages* ⚉ *In-room: a/c, kitchen (some), refrigerator (some), Wi-Fi. In-hotel: pool, some pets allowed* ☰ *AE, MC, V.*

¢–$ 🛏 **Sugar Loaf Lodge**. Though it may be hard to believe, there are still bargains in Sedona, and this one-story, family-run motel delivers. All rooms have refrigerators and microwaves, and the pool and hot-tub area serves as a gathering spot for swapping tales with fellow travelers—many from Europe—at the end of the day. **Pros:** it's cheap; it's clean. **Cons:** older furnishings; part of the driveway is unpaved. ⊠ *1870 W. AZ 89A, West* ☎ *928/282–9451 or 877/282–0632* ⊕ *www.sedonasugarloaf.com* ⤵ *16 rooms* △ *In-room: a/c, refrigerator, Wi-Fi. In-hotel: pool, some pets allowed* ⊟ *AE, MC, V* ❄ *CP.*

SHOPPING

With a few exceptions, most of the stores in Uptown Sedona (north of the "Y," running along AZ 89A to the east of its intersection with AZ 179) cater to the tour-bus trade with Native American jewelry and New Age souvenirs. If this isn't your style, the largest concentration of stores and galleries is in Central Sedona, along AZ 179, south of the "Y," with plenty of offerings for serious shoppers.

There are three main art-gallery complexes in Sedona—Hozho and Tlaquepaque are the best of the three, though Hillside is very close to Hozho. Each has smaller galleries within the larger complex; *several are listed below.* The **Hillside Courtyard & Marketplace** (⊠ *671 AZ 179, Central* ☎ *928/282–4500*) has several galleries. The **Hozho Center** (⊠ *431 AZ 179, Central* ☎ *928/204–2257*), a minute or two north of Hillside on AZ 179, is a small, upscale complex in a beige Santa Fe–style building, with galleries and fine-art souvenirs. **Tlaquepaque Arts & Crafts Village** (⊠ *AZ 179 just south of "Y," Central* ☎ *928/282–4838* ⊕ *www. tlaq.com*) is home to more than 100 shops and galleries and several restaurants, and remains one of the best places for travelers to find mementos from their trip to Sedona. The complex of clay-tile-roofed buildings arranged around a series of courtyards shares its name and architectural style with a crafts village just outside Guadalajara. It's a lovely place to browse, but beware: prices tend to be high, and locals joke that it's pronounced "to-lock-your-pocket."

STORES AND GALLERIES

Souvenirs in Sedona run the gamut, from authentic Southwestern art to jewelry, and more than enough crystals to bring you inner harmony.

Crystal Magic (⊠ *2978 W. AZ 89A, West* ☎ *928/282–1622*) dabbles in the metaphysical, with crystals, jewelry, and books for the New Age.

ARTS AND CRAFTS

El Prado Galleries (⊠ *Tlaquepaque, 336 AZ 179, No. 101, Bldg. E, Central* ☎ *928/282–7390* ⊕ *www.elpradogalleries.com*) is a good bet for Southwestern art. **Esteban's** (⊠ *Tlaquepaque, 336 AZ 179, No. 103, Bldg. B, Central* ☎ *928/282–4686*) focuses on ceramics and Native American crafts.

Garland's Navajo Rugs (⊠ *411 AZ 179, Central* ☎ *928/282–4070* ⊕ *www.garlandsrugs.com*) has a collection of new and antique rugs, as well as Native American kachina dolls, pottery, and baskets. **James Ratliff Gallery** (⊠ *Hozho Center, 431 AZ 179, Central* ☎ *928/282–1404* ⊕ *www.jamesratliffgallery.com*) has fun and functional pieces by not-

SPAS IN SEDONA

While some prefer to harness Sedona's rejuvenating energy at a vortex site, others seek renewal at one of the many spas in town. From all-inclusive spa retreats nestled in red-rock canyons to inexpensive bodywork performed by healing arts students, Sedona has relaxing options for every budget and preference.

With its history of Native American traditions, Sedona is thought of as one of the most sacred healing spots on Earth. Spas incorporate indigenous materials, like red-rock clay, into their spa services—and choosing your treatments is part of the pleasure. Some of Sedona's spas are destinations in themselves, offering all-inclusive experiences tailored to individual needs and desires.

If you're staying at the Enchantment Resort, you can enjoy the revered **Mii Amo Spa** (☎ *928/203-8500* ⊕ *www.miiamo.com*). Set in spectacular Boynton Canyon, Mii Amo is a state-of-the-art facility with indoor and outdoor pools and treatment rooms. Meditate in the sand-floor crystal grotto before your Watsu water therapy or deep-tissue massage. Afterward, dine in the spa's healthful and tasty café (no egg yolks in these omelets), wearing only your spa robe if you like.

The **Sedona Rouge Hotel and Spa** (☎ *866/312-4111* ⊕ *www.*sedonarouge.com*) is a more-understated healing environment, open to the public as well as to its boutique hotel guests. Deepak Chopra chooses this simple and tranquil setting for his weeklong "SynchroDestiny" workshops each year. Skilled therapists meet with clients first to discuss individual goals before embarking on treatments like the Seven Sacred Pools Massage which brings balance to the body's seven energy centers or chakras.

Sedona's upscale resorts also offer an array of spa amenities for their guests. At the luxurious **L'Auberge** (☎ *800/905-5745* ⊕ *www.lauberge. com*) you can indulge in an outdoor massage on the bank of gurgling Oak Creek, or restore balance to your skin with a grape-seed antioxidant scrub. Better yet, select four treatments and lunch for a custom spa package here.

Students at the Northern Arizona Massage Therapy Institute, **NAMTI** (☎ *928/282-7737* ⊕ *www.namti. com*), offer quality one-hour massage, craniosacral, and reflexology treatments for the bargain price of $30.

The popular **Sedona New Day Spa** (☎ *928/282-7502* ⊕ *www. sedonanewdayspa.com*) uses local ingredients for clay masks, body wraps, and crystal therapy. They also have a separate spa for men.

---

yet-established artists. **Kuivato Glass Gallery** (⊠ *Tlaquepaque, 336 AZ 179, No. 125, Bldg. B, Central* ☎ *928/282-1212* ⊕ *www.kuivato. com*) carries gorgeous glassware. **Lanning Gallery** (⊠ *Hozho Center, 431 AZ 179, Central* ☎ *928/282-6865* ⊕ *www.lanninggallery.com*) sells Southwestern art and jewelry. **Sedona Pottery** (⊠ *411 AZ 179, Central* ☎ *928/282-1192* ⊕ *www.sedonapottery.net*) sells unusual pieces, including flower-arranging bowls, egg separators, and life-size ceramic statues by shop owner Mary Margaret Sather.

CLOTHING

Isadora (✉ *Tlaquepaque, 336 AZ 179, No. 120, Bldg. A, Central* ☎ *928/ 282–6232* ⊕ *www.isadoragallery.com*) has beautiful handwoven jackets and shawls.**Looking West** (✉ *242 N. AZ 89A, Uptown* ☎ *928/282–4877*) sells the spiffiest cowgirl-style getups in town.

SPORTS

Canyon Outfitters (✉ *2701 W. AZ 89A, West* ☎ *928/282–5293*) is good for gearing up with maps, clothing, and camping equipment before your outdoor adventures.

NIGHTLIFE AND THE ARTS

Nightlife in Sedona tends to be sedate, although on high-season weekends there's usually live music at the Enchantment Resort. Shugrue's Hillside also regularly presents local musicians. Options vary from jazz to rock and pop; in all cases, call ahead.The two-day Sedona **Jazz on the Rocks Festival** (☎ *928/282–1985* ⊕ *www.sedonajazz.com*), held every October, attracts a sellout crowd at their outdoor concerts.**Chamber Music Sedona** (☎ *928/204–2415* ⊕ *www.chambermusicsedona.org*) hosts a concert series from October through May.

The **Sedona Arts Center** (✉ *N. AZ 89A and Art Barn Rd., Uptown* ☎ *928/282 3809* ⊕ *www.sedonaartscenter.com*) offers classes in all mediums and hosts the Plein Air Art Festival in October. The innovative Sedona International Film Festival (☎ *928/282–1177* ⊕ *www. sedonafilm.org*) takes place in late February.

The closest thing to a rollicking cowboy bar in Sedona is **Relics Restaurant & Nightclub at Rainbow's End** (✉ *3235 W. AZ 89A, West* ☎ *928/282–1593* ⊕ *www.relicsrestaurant.com*), a steak house with a dance floor and live rock or country-and-Western music most nights.

THE VERDE VALLEY, JEROME, AND PRESCOTT

About 90 mi north of Phoenix, as you round a curve approaching Exit 285 off Interstate 17, the valley of the Verde River suddenly unfolds in a panorama of grayish-white cliffs, tinted red in the distance and dotted with desert scrub, cottonwood, and pine. For hundreds of years many Native American communities, especially those of the southern Sinagua people, lined the Verde River. Rumors of great mineral deposits brought Europeans to the Verde Valley as early as 1583, when Hopi Indians guided Antonio de Espejo here, but it wasn't until the second half of the 19th century that this wealth was commercially exploited. The discovery of silver and gold in the Black Hills, which border the valley on the southwest, gave rise to boomtowns like Jerome—and to military installations such as Fort Verde, set up to protect the white settlers and wealth seekers from the Native American tribes they displaced. Mineral wealth was also the impetus behind the establishment of Prescott as a territorial capital by President Lincoln and other Unionists who wanted to keep the riches out of Confederate hands.

VERDE VALLEY

18 mi southwest of Sedona on U.S. 89A; 94 mi north of Phoenix on I-17.

Often overlooked by travelers on trips to Sedona or Flagstaff, the Verde Valley offers several enjoyable diversions, including wine-tasting in Cornville and the historical wonders at Montezuma Castle and Tuzigoot. And if you're tired of the car, the Verde Canyon Railroad in Clarkdale is a great way to get off road without doing the driving.

GETTING HERE AND AROUND

From Phoenix, it's a leisurely and picturesque route through Verde Valley. Follow Interstate 17 north 25 mi past Cordes Junction until you see the turnoff for AZ 260, which will take you to Cottonwood in 12 mi. Here you can pick up AZ 89A, which leads southwest to Prescott (41 mi) or northeast to Sedona (19 mi).

EXPLORING

TOP ATTRACTIONS

The five-story, 20-room cliff dwelling at **Montezuma Castle National Monument** was named by explorers who believed it had been erected by the Aztecs. Southern Sinagua Native Americans actually built the roughly 600-year-old structure, which is one of the best-preserved prehistoric dwellings in North America—and one of the most accessible. An easy paved trail (0.3 mi round-trip) leads to the dwelling and to adjacent Castle A, a badly deteriorated six-story living space with about 45 rooms. No one is permitted to enter the site, but the viewing area is close by. From Camp Verde, take Main Street to Montezuma Castle Road.

Somewhat less accessible than Montezuma Castle—but equally striking—is the **Montezuma Well** (☎ *928/567–4521 ✉ Free*), a unit of the national monument. Although there are some Sinagua and Hohokam sites here, the limestone sinkhole with a limpid blue-green pool lying in the middle of the desert is the park's main attraction. This cavity—55 feet deep and 365 feet across—is all that's left of an ancient subterranean cavern; the water remains at a constant 76°F year-round. It's a short hike, but the peace, quiet, and views of the Verde Valley reward the effort. To reach Montezuma Well from Montezuma Castle, return to Interstate 17 and go north to Exit 293; signs direct you to the well, which is 4 mi east of the freeway. The drive includes a short section of dirt road. ⊠ *Montezuma Castle Rd., 7 mi northeast of Camp Verde, Camp Verde* ☎ *928/567–3322* ⊕ *www.nps.gov/moca* ✉ *$5 for Montezuma Castle* ⊙ *Labor Day–Memorial Day, daily 8–5; Memorial Day–Labor Day, daily 8–6.*

★ Train buffs come to the Verde Valley to catch the 22-mi **Verde Canyon Railroad**, which follows a dramatic route through the Verde Canyon, the remains of a copper smelter, and much unspoiled desert that is inaccessible by car. The destination—the city of Clarkdale—might not be that impressive, but the ride is undeniably scenic. Knowledgeable announcers regale riders with the area's colorful history and point out natural attractions along the way—in winter you're likely to see bald

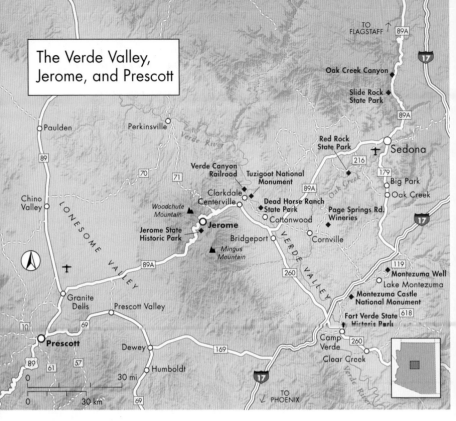

The Verde Valley,
Jerome, and Prescott

TO
FLAGSTAFF 89A

17

Oak Creek Canyon

Slide Rock
State Park

89A

Paulden

Perkinsville

Verde River

Red Rock
State Park

216

Sedona

179

89

70

71

Verde Canyon
Railroad

Tuzigoot National
Monument

Big Park

Oak Creek

Chino
Valley

Woodchute
Mountain

Clarkdale

Centerville

89A

Dead Horse Ranch
State Park

Cottonwood

Page Springs Rd.
Wineries

LONESOME VALLEY

Jerome State
Historic Park

Jerome

Bridgeport

Cornville

VERDE VALLEY

Mingus
Mountain

89A

260

119

Montezuma Well

Lake Montezuma

Granite
Dells

Prescott Valley

Montezuma Castle
National Monument

Fort Verde State
Historic Park

618

10

69

Prescott

Dewey

Camp
Verde

260

89

61

57

Humboldt

169

Clear Creek

17

Verde River

0   30 mi

0   30 km

TO
PHOENIX

eagles. This four-hour trip is especially popular in fall-foliage season and
in spring, when the desert wildflowers bloom; book well in advance.
Round-trip rides cost $54.95. For $79.95 you can ride the much more
comfortable living-room-like first-class cars, where hors d'oeuvres, coffee, and a cocktail are included in the price. ■ TIP→ Reservations are
required. ⊠ *Arizona Central Railroad, 300 N. Broadway, Clarkdale*
☎ *800/320–0718* ⊕ *www.verdecanyonrr.com.*

WORTH NOTING

The military post for which **Fort Verde State Historic Park** is named was
built between 1871 and 1873 as the third of three fortifications in this
part of the Arizona Territory. To protect the Verde Valley's farmers and
miners from Tonto Apache and Yavapai raids, the fort's administrators
oversaw the movement of nearly 1,500 Native Americans to the San
Carlos and Fort Apache reservations. A museum details the history of
the area's military installations, and three furnished officers' quarters
show the day-to-day living conditions of the top brass—it's a good
break from the interstate if you've been driving for too long. Signs
from any of Interstate 17's three Camp Verde exits will direct you to
the 10-acre park. ⊠ *125 E. Hollomon St. Camp Verde* ☎ *928/567–3275*
⊕ *www.azstateparks.com/Parks/fove* 🎫 *$4* ⏱ *Thurs.–Mon. 9–5.*

The 423-acre spread of **Dead Horse Ranch State Park**, which combines high-desert and wetlands habitats, is a pleasant place to while away the day. You can fish in the Verde River or the well-stocked Park Lagoon, or hike on some 6 mi of trails that begin in a shaded picnic area and wind along the river; adjoining forest service pathways are available for those who enjoy longer treks. Birders can check off more than 100 species from the Arizona Audubon Society lists provided by the rangers. Bald eagles perch along the Verde River in winter, and the common black hawks—a misno-

mer for these threatened birds—nest here in summer. It's 1 mi north of Cottonwood, off Main Street. ☒ *675 Dead Horse Ranch Rd., Cottonwood* ☏ *928/634–5283* ⊕ *www.azstateparks.com/Parks/deho* ☒ *$7 per car for up to 4 persons* ☉ *Daily 8–5.*

Tuzigoot National Monument isn't as well preserved as Montezuma Castle, but it's more impressive in scope. Tuzigoot is another complex of the Sinagua people, who lived on this land overlooking the Verde Valley from about AD 1000 to 1400. The pueblo, constructed of limestone and sandstone blocks, once rose three stories and incorporated 110 rooms. Inhabitants were skilled dry farmers and traded with peoples hundreds of miles away. Implements used for food preparation, as well as jewelry, weapons, and farming tools excavated from the site, are displayed in the visitor center. Within the site, you can step into a reconstructed room. ☒ *3 mi north of Cottonwood on Broadway Rd., between Cottonwood's Old Town and Clarkdale, Clarkdale* ☏ *928/634–5564* ⊕ *www.nps.gov/tuzi* ☒ *$5* ☉ *Sept.–May, daily 8–5; June–Aug., daily 8–6.*

WINERIES

The high-desert soil of the Verde Valley seems to be working for growing grapes, and several vineyards have sprouted on the hillsides above Lower Oak Creek. Three notable vineyards are nestled together along Page Springs Road in Cornville, recently dubbed Winery Row, and offer daily wine-tasting.

The award-winning wines at **Page Springs Cellars** (☒ *1500 N. Page Springs Rd., Cornville* ☏ *928/639–3004* ⊕ *www.pagespringscellars.com* ☉ *Daily 11–6*), produced by grape guru Eric Glomski, focus on grapes popular in the Rhône wine region of France.

At **Oak Creek Vineyards** (☒ *1555 Page Springs Rd., Cornville* ☏ *928/649–0290* ⊕ *www.oakcreekvineyards.net* ☉ *Daily 11–5*), winemaker Deb Wahl offers Syrah, merlot, chardonnay, and dessert wines. You can also pick up fixings for a picnic here—salami, cheeses, crackers, and chocolates.

Javelina Leap Vineyard (✉ *1565 Page Springs Rd., Cornville* ☎ *928/649–2681* ⊕ *www.javelinaleapwinery.com* ☉ *Daily 11–5*) produces predominantly red wines with bold, dry flavors. Taste a few here and you'll be welcomed by owners Rod and Cynthia as if you were family.

SPORTS AND THE OUTDOORS

The **Verde Ranger District** office of the **Prescott National Forest** (✉ *300 E. AZ 260, Camp Verde* ☎ *928/567–4121* ⊕ *www.fs.fed.us/r3/prescott*) is a good resource for places to hike, fish, and boat along the Verde River.

The **Black Canyon Trail** (✉ *Trailhead: AZ 260, 4 mi south of Cottonwood, west on FR 359 4.5 mi*) is a bit of a slog, rising more than 2,200 feet in 6 mi, but the reward is grand views from the gray cliffs of Verde Valley to the red buttes of Sedona to the blue range of the San Francisco Peaks.

WHERE TO EAT

¢   **✗ Casa Antigua.** Conveniently tucked into the Basha's shopping cen-
MEXICAN   ter just off Interstate 17 at the exit for Camp Verde, this tiny eatery serves consistently good traditional Mexican food. Try the *carne asada* (marinated, grilled beef) tacos and the chicken *burros* (as burritos are often called in this part of Arizona). For a larger appetite, the Steak Ranchero Plate—steak strips grilled with onions and peppers, served with guacamole, sour cream, and flour tortillas—is a house favorite. ✉ *522 W. Finnie Flat Rd., Camp Verde* ☎ *928/567 6300* ▭ *AE, D, MC, V* ☉ *Closed Sun.*

$$ **✗ Manzanita Restaurant.** You might not expect to find sophisticated cook-
CONTINENTAL   ing in Cornville, 6 mi east of Cottonwood, but a European-born chef prepares Continental fare here, using organic produce and locally raised meat whenever possible. Roast duckling à l'orange and rack of lamb are beautifully presented; try the mushroom soup if it's available. ✉ *11425 E. Cornville Rd., Cornville* ☎ *928/634–8851* ⊕ *www.themanzanitarestaurant. com* ▭ *AE, D, MC, V* ☉ *No lunch Mon. and Tues.*

JEROME

★   *20 mi northwest of Camp Verde, 3.5 mi southwest of Clarkdale, 33 mi northeast of Prescott, 25 mi southwest of Sedona on AZ 89A.*

Jerome was once known as the Billion Dollar Copper Camp, but after the last mines closed in 1953 the booming population of 15,000 dwindled to 50 determined souls. Although its population has risen back to almost 500, Jerome still holds on to its "ghost town" designation, and several B&Bs and eateries regularly report spirit sightings. It's hard to imagine that this town was once the location of Arizona's largest JCPenney store and one of the state's first Safeway supermarkets. Jerome saw its first revival during the mid-1960s, when hippies arrived and turned it into an arts colony of sorts, and it has since become a tourist attraction. In addition to its shops and historic sites, Jerome is worth visiting for its scenery: it's built into the side of Cleopatra Hill, and from here you can see Sedona's red rocks, Flagstaff's San Francisco Peaks, and even eastern Arizona's Mogollon Rim country.

Jerome is about a mile above sea level, but structures within town sit at elevations that vary by as much as 1,500 feet, depending on whether

Getting there is the fun with a classic train ride on the Verde Canyon Railroad.

they're on Cleopatra Hill or at its foot. Blasting at the United Verde (later Phelps Dodge) mine regularly shook buildings off their foundations—the town's jail slid across a road and down a hillside, where it sits today. And that's not all that was unsteady about Jerome. In 1903 a reporter from a New York newspaper called Jerome "the wickedest town in America," due to its abundance of drinking and gambling establishments; town records from 1880 list 24 saloons. Whether by divine retribution or drunken accidents, the town burned down several times.

GETTING HERE AND AROUND

You can get a map of the town's shops and its attractions at the visitor-information trailer on AZ 89A. The three streets in the main shopping area—Hull, Main, and Hill—run parallel to each other on the hillside. Street parking is easy to come but be prepared for some steep climbing up and down Cleopatra Hill when you're exploring by foot.

PLANNING YOUR TIME

The town can easily be explored in an afternoon with a stop for lunch, but the historic charm and shopping opportunities entice some visitors to stay overnight. Jerome currently has around 50 retail establishments (that's more than one for every 10 residents). Attractions and businesses don't always stay open as long as their stated hours if things are slow.

ESSENTIALS

Visitor Info Jerome Chamber of Commerce (☎ 928/634-2900 ⊕ www.jeromechamber.com).

Cliff dwellings of the Sinagua people have been preserved for about 600 years at Montezuma Castle.

EXPLORING

The **Mine Museum** in downtown Jerome is staffed by the Jerome Historical Society. The museum's collection of mining stock certificates alone is worth the (small) price of admission—the amount of money that changed hands in this town 100 years ago boggles the mind. ⊠ *200 Main St.* ☎ *928/634–5477* 🎫 *$2* ⊙ *Daily 9–4:30.*

WHERE TO EAT

$$–$$$
AMERICAN
✕ **The Asylum.** Don't be put off by the name, a tribute to its past identity—this charming restaurant inside the Jerome Grand Hotel is the standout choice in town for fine dining, good wines, and wonderful vistas. Interior burgundy walls hung with local artists' work create a warm and romantic setting. Signature dishes include achiote-rubbed pork tenderloin and sea bass with a poblano chile–chardonnay lemon sauce. Don't miss the roasted butternut squash soup, with just the right blend of sweetness and spice. ⊠ *200 Hill St.* ☎ *928/639–3197* ⊕ *www. asylum.biz* ▭ *AE, D, MC, V.*

¢
AMERICAN
✕ **Flatiron Cafe.** Ask where to have lunch or a late-afternoon snack, and nearly every Main Street shop owner will direct you to a tiny eatery at the fork in the road. The menu includes healthful sandwiches, such as black-bean hummus with feta cheese, and many coffee drinks. Breakfast is also served. ⊠ *416 Main St.* ☎ *928/634–2733* ⊕ *www. flatironcafejerome.com* ▭ *MC, V* ⊙ *Closed Tues. No dinner.*

$
AMERICAN
✕ **Haunted Hamburger/Jerome Palace.** After the climb up the stairs from Main Street to this former boardinghouse, you'll be ready for the hearty burgers, chili, cheese steaks, and ribs that dominate the menu. Lighter fare, including such meatless selections as the guacamole quesadilla, is

also available. Eat on the outside deck overlooking Verde Valley or in the upstairs dining room, where "Claire," the resident ghost, purportedly hangs out. ✉ *410 Clark St.* ☎ *928/634–0554* ▭ *MC, V.*

WHERE TO STAY

$–$$ 🏨 **Ghost City Inn.** The outdoor veranda at this 1898 B&B affords sweeping views of the Verde Valley and Sedona. Most rooms are decorated in Victorian style and all have private entrances and baths. Afternoon tea with cookies is an unexpected luxury for this formerly rough-and-ready town. **Pros:** authentic historic charm; fabulous views. **Cons:** some smaller rooms; many stairs. ✉ *541 N. Main St.* 📠 *928/634–4678 or 888/634–4678* ⊕ *www.ghostcityinn.com* ⇪ *6 rooms* ⚙ *In-room: a/c, Wi-Fi. In-hotel: some pets allowed, no kids under 10* ▭ *AE, D, MC, V* ⋈*BP.*

$–$$ 🏨 **Jerome Grand Hotel.** This full-service hotel at the highest point in town is housed in the Jerome's former hospital, built in 1927. Rooms are comfy, with homey furnishings that part with the institutional past, and many have splendid views. The hotel's restaurant, the Asylum, is superb. **Pros:** great restaurant; historic property; great ghost-hunting. **Cons:** creaky; sharing your room with ghosts. ✉ *200 Hill St.* ☎ *928/634–8200 or 888/817–6788* ⊕ *www.jeromegrandhotel.com* ⇪ *25 rooms* ⚙ *In-room: a/c, Wi-Fi. In-hotel: restaurant, bar* ▭ *D, MC, V* ⋈*CP.*

$–$$ 🏨 **Surgeon's House.** Plants, knickknacks, bright colors, and plenty of
★ sunlight make this Mediterranean-style home a welcoming place to stay. Multicourse breakfasts might include overstuffed burritos or a marinated fruit compote. There are two suites and two rooms, including a former chauffeur's quarters that has a skylight and private patio. **Pros:** friendly host; knockout vistas; unique gardens. **Cons:** rigid breakfast time; some rooms have tiny bathrooms; climbing some stairs is required. ✉ *101 Hill St.* ☎ *928/639–1452 or 800/639–1452* ⊕ *www.surgeonshouse.com* ⇪ *2 rooms, 2 suites* ⚙ *In-room: a/c, kitchen (some), no TV, Wi-Fi. In-hotel: some pets allowed* ▭ *MC, V* ⋈*BP.*

SHOPPING

Jerome has its share of art galleries (some perched precariously on Cleopatra Hill), along with boutiques, and they're funkier than those in Sedona. Main Street and, just around the bend, Hull Avenue are Jerome's two primary shopping streets. Your eyes may begin to glaze over after browsing through one boutique after another, most offering tasteful Southwestern paraphernalia.

Aurum (✉ *369 Main St.* ☎ *928/634–3330* ⊕ *www.aurumjewelry.com*) focuses on contemporary art jewelry in silver and gold; about 30 artists are represented. **Designs on You** (✉ *233 Main St.* ☎ *928/634–7879* ⊕ *designsonyoujeromeaz.com*) carries attractively styled women's clothing. **Jerome Artists Cooperative Gallery** (✉ *502 Main St.* ☎ *928/639–4276*

4

⊕ *jeromecoop.com*) specializes in jewelry, sculpture, painting, and pottery by local artists. **Nellie Bly** (⊠ *136 Main St.* ☏ *928/634–0255* ⊕ *nellieblyscopes.com*), specializing in art glass, stocks perfume bottles and outstanding kaleidoscopes. **Raku Gallery** (⊠ *250 Hull Ave.* ☏ *928/639–0239* ⊕ *www.rakugallery.com*) stocks the work of 300 artists; you'll find wrought-iron furniture, free-blown glass, and fountains. **Sky Fire** (⊠ *140 Main St.* ☏ *928/634–8081*) has two floors of items to adorn your person and your house, from Southwestern-pattern dishes to hand-crafted Mission-style hutches.

NIGHTLIFE

Jerome's a ghost town, so don't expect a hopping nightlife, although there are some places to have fun. **Paul & Jerry's Saloon** (⊠ *Main St.* ☏ *928/634–2603*) attracts a (relative) crowd to its two pool tables and old wooden bar. On weekends there's live music and a lively scene at the **Spirit Room** (⊠ *Main St. and AZ 89A* ☏ *928/634–8809* ⊕ *www.spiritroombar.com*); the mural over the bar harks back to the days when it was a dining spot for the prostitutes of the red-light district.

EN ROUTE

The drive down a mountainous section of AZ 89A from Jerome to Prescott is gorgeous (if somewhat harrowing in bad weather), filled with twists and turns through **Prescott National Forest** (⊕ *www.fs.fed.us/r3/prescott*). A scenic turnoff near Jerome provides one last vista and a place to apply chains during surprise snowstorms. There's camping, picnicking, and hiking at the crest of Mingus Mountain. If you're coming to Prescott from Phoenix, the route that crosses the Mogollon Rim, overlooking the Verde Valley, has nice views of rolling hills and is less precipitous.

PRESCOTT

33 mi southwest of Jerome on AZ 89A to U.S. 89, 100 mi northwest of Phoenix via I–17 to AZ 69.

In a forested bowl 5,300 feet above sea level, Prescott is a prime summer refuge for Phoenix-area dwellers. It was proclaimed the first capital of the Arizona Territory in 1864 and settled by Yankees to ensure that gold-rich northern Arizona would remain a Union resource. (Tucson and southern Arizona were strongly pro-Confederacy.) Although early territorial settlers thought that the area's original inhabitants were of Aztec origin, today it's believed that they were ancestors of the Yavapai, whose reservation is on the outskirts of town. The Aztec theory—inspired by *The History and Conquest of Mexico*, a popular book by historian William Hickling Prescott, for whom the town was named—has left its mark on such street names as Montezuma, Cortez, and Alarcon.

Despite a devastating downtown fire in 1900, Prescott remains the "West's most Eastern town" with a rich trove of late-19th-century New England–style architecture. With two institutions of higher education, Yavapai College and Prescott College, Prescott could be called a college town, but it doesn't really feel like one, perhaps because so many retirees also reside here, drawn by the temperate climate and low cost of living.

The 1916 Yavapai County Courthouse stands in the heart of Prescott, bounded by Gurley, Goodwin, Cortez, and Montezuma streets, and guarded by an equestrian bronze of turn-of-the-20th-century journalist and lawmaker Bucky O'Neill, who died while charging San Juan Hill in Cuba with Teddy Roosevelt during the Spanish-American War. Those interested in architecture will enjoy the Victorian neighborhoods. Many Queen Annes have been beautifully restored, and a number are now B&Bs.

GETTING HERE AND AROUND

The most direct route to Prescott from Phoenix is to take Interstate 17 north for 60 mi to Cordes Junction and then drive northwest on AZ 69 for 36 mi into town. Interstate 17, a four-lane divided highway, has several steep inclines and descents (complete with a number of runaway-truck ramps), but it's generally an easy and scenic thoroughfare.

Prescott Municipal Airport is 8 mi north of town on U.S. 89. United Airlines and Frontier Airlines offer connecting service to Prescott Municipal Airport from Phoenix.

The city's main drag is Gurley Street, which AZ 69 turns into from the east. You can usually find street parking along Gurley or on the side streets as you approach town; or use the large (free) public lot on the corner of Gurley and Marina, across the street from the Hassayampa Inn. Most of the town's Victorian neighborhoods, shops, and restaurants, best explored on foot, are within walking distance of the Courthouse Plaza, sitting just off Gurley Street on Montezuma. Art galleries and saloons line Cortez and Montezuma streets to the north and west of the courthouse.

PLANNING YOUR TIME

Tourism in Prescott can be bustling on weekends but is rarely overwhelming. Any day will do to tour the Victorian homes and antiques shops, but if you enjoy museums, note that museum hours are stunted on Sunday, and you won't want to rush through the extensive grounds of the Sharlot Hall Museum. Devoting a full day to tour Prescott is ample, and an overnight allows for hearing plenty of live music on Whiskey Row.

ESSENTIALS

Visitor Info Prescott Area Coalition for Tourism (☎ 928/708–9336 ⊕ www.visit-prescott.com).

Transportation Contact Prescott Municipal Airport (☎ 928/445–7860).

EXPLORING

❶ **Phippen Museum of Western Art.** The paintings and bronze sculptures of George Phippen, along with works by other artists of the West, form the permanent collection of this museum about 5 mi north of downtown. Phippen met with a group of prominent cowboy artists in 1965 to form the Cowboy Artists of America, a group dedicated to preserving the Old West as they saw it. He became the president but died the next year. A memorial foundation set up in his name opened the doors of this museum in 1984. ⊠ 4701 U.S. 89N Downtown ☎ 928/778–1385 ⊕ www.phippenartmuseum.org ⛄ $5 ☉ Tues.–Sat. 10–4, Sun. 1–4.

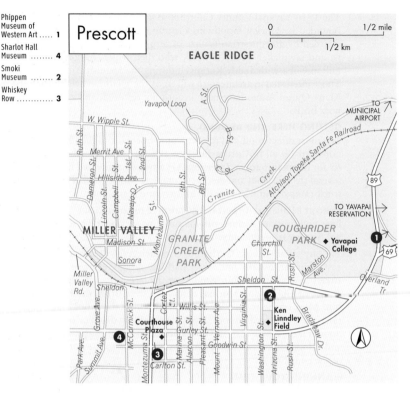

Sharlot Hall Museum. Local history is documented at this remarkable museum. Along with the original ponderosa pine log cabin, which housed the territorial governor, and the museum, named for historian and poet Sharlot Hall, the parklike setting contains three fully restored period homes and a transportation museum. Territorial times are the focus, but natural history and artifacts of the area's prehistoric peoples are also on display. Kids under 18 get in free. ⊠ *415 W. Gurley St., 2 blocks west of Courthouse Plaza, Downtown* ☎ *928/445–3122* ⊕ *www.sharlot.org* ☒ *$5* ⊘ *Mon.–Sat. 10–4, Sun. noon–4.*

Smoki Museum. The 1935 stone-and-log building, which resembles an Indian pueblo, is almost as interesting as the Native American artifacts inside. Baskets, kachinas, pottery, rugs, and beadwork make up the collection, which represents Native American culture from the pre-Columbian period to the present. ⊠ *147 N. Arizona St., Downtown* ☎ *928/445–1230* ⊕ *www.smokimuseum.org* ☒ *$5* ⊘ *Tues.–Sat. 10–4, Sun. 1–4.*

Whiskey Row. Twenty saloons and houses of pleasure once lined this stretch of Montezuma Street, along the west side of Courthouse Plaza. Social activity is more subdued these days, and the historic bars provide an escape from the street's many boutiques. ⊠ *Downtown.*

Bistro St. Michael is a great place to relax over a coffee or grab a bowl of black-bean chili and watch the people on Whiskey Row. The café/bar has been restored to its original 1901 style. The service at the counter is brisk, and will leave you plenty of time for antiquing or museum browsing for the remainder of the day. ⌧ *205 W. Gurley St., Downtown* ☎ *928/778–2500.*

SPORTS AND THE OUTDOORS

HIKING AND
CAMPING

More than a million acres of national forest land surround Prescott. Thumb Butte is a popular hiking spot, but there are lots of other trekking and overnighting options. Contact the **Bradshaw Ranger District** (⌧ *2230 E. AZ 69, Hwy. 69* ☎ *928/443–8000* ⊕ *www.fs.fed.us/r3/prescott*) for information about hiking trails and campgrounds in the Prescott National Forest south of town down to Horse Thief Basin. Campgrounds near Prescott are generally not crowded.

The **Thumb Butte Loop Trail** (⌧ *Trailhead: Thumb Butte Rd., 3 mi west of Prescott following Gurley St., which turns into Thumb Butte*), a 2-mi trek on a paved yet steep loop, takes you 600 feet up near the crest of its namesake. The vistas are large, but you won't be alone on this popular trail.

HORSEBACK
RIDING

Granite Mountain Stables (⌧ *2400 W. Shane Dr., 7 mi northeast of Prescott* ☎ *928/771–9551* ⊕ *www.granitemountainstables.com*) has daily guided trail rides and lessons costing about $35.

WHERE TO EAT

$
ITALIAN

✕ **Genovese's**. Reasonably priced, classic southern Italian fare makes this restaurant near Courthouse Plaza a local favorite. The decor is right out of 1975, but the family recipes, like chicken marsala, make up for the lack of ambience. Try the cannelloni stuffed with shrimp, crab, ricotta cheese, and spinach. Save room for spumoni ice cream or a cannoli. ⌧ *217 W. Gurley St., Downtown* ☎ *928/541–9089* ⊕ *www.genovesesrestaurant.net* ▬ *AE, MC, V.*

¢
AMERICAN

✕ **Kendall's Famous Burgers and Ice Cream**. A classic diner, replete with booths and a 1950s-style soda fountain, Kendall's serves hamburgers cooked to order with your choice of 14 condiments. If you've seen the movie *Billy Jack*, you'll probably recognize this place from the scene where the Native Americans and the townies get into a big fight in an ice-cream shop. Make sure to try the homemade french fries. ⌧ *113 S. Cortez St., Downtown* ☎ *928/778–3658* ▬ *D, MC, V.*

$$–$$$
AMERICAN

✕ **Murphy's**. Mesquite-grilled meats and beer brewed exclusively for the restaurant are the specialties at this classy bar and grill, a sort of local institution set in a restored, polished-up 1890 mercantile building. The baby back ribs, fresh steamed clams, and fresh fried catfish are standouts. Businessfolk do their moving and shaking at lunchtime here, and the spirited bar stays open until 1 AM. ⌧ *201 N. Cortez St., Downtown* ☎ *928/445–4044* ▬ *AE, D, MC, V.*

$$
AMERICAN

✕ **The Palace**. Legend has it that the patrons who saved the Palace's ornately carved 1880s Brunswick bar from a Whiskey Row fire in 1900 continued drinking at it while the row burned across the street. Whatever the case, the bar remains the centerpiece of the beautifully restored turn-of-the-20th-century structure, with a high, pressed-tin ceiling. Steaks and chops are the stars here, but the grilled fish and hearty corn chowder are fine, too. ⊠ *120 S. Montezuma St., Downtown* 🕾 *928/541–1996* ⊕ *www.historicpalace.com* ▭ *AE, MC, V.*

$ ✕**Prescott Brewing Company.** Good beer, good food, good service, and
AMERICAN good prices—for a casual meal, it's hard to beat this cheerful restaurant on the town square. In addition to chili, fish-and-chips, and British-style bangers and mash, vegetarian enchiladas made with tofu and pasta salad are on the menu. Ponderosa IPA and Lodgepole Light are two popular microbrews; fresh-baked beer bread comes with many entrées. ⊠ *130 W. Gurley St., Downtown* 🕾 *928/771–2795* ⊕ *www. prescottbrewingcompany.com* ▭ *AE, D, DC, MC, V.*

$$$ ✕**The Rose Restaurant.** In a well-maintained Victorian home, the Rose
AMERICAN serves inspired dishes that straddle nouvelle and Continental fare. Choose from entrées like braised lamb shank, duck breast with sweet-potato cake and raspberry sauce, or almond-crusted halibut as Sinatra music plays softly in the background. Desserts, especially the apple-cara-mel tart, are equally stellar. ⊠ *234 S. Cortez St., Downtown* 🕾 *928/777–8308* ⊕ *www.theroserestaurant.com* ▭ *AE, MC, V* ☺ *Closed Mon. and Tues. No lunch.*

WHERE TO STAY

$$–$$$ ☷ **Hassayampa Inn.** Built in 1927 for early automobile travelers, the Hassayampa Inn oozes character. The ceiling in the lobby is hand-painted, and some rooms still have the original furnishings. Don't get a room by the old-fashioned elevator or you'll be jarred by the clanging metal gate every time it opens and closes. The Peacock Room, the hotel's pretty—if overly formal—dining room, has tapestried booths and better-than-average Continental food. In the cocktail lounge, listen to live jazz while you sip a martini. **Pros:** cental location; historic charm. **Cons:** thin walls; small bathrooms. ⊠ *122 E. Gurley St., Downtown* 🕾 *928/778–9434 or 800/322–1927* ⊕ *www.hassayampainn.com* 🛏 *58 rooms, 10 suites* ♿ *In-room: a/c, Wi-Fi. In-hotel: restaurant, bar* ▭ *AE, D, DC, MC, V* ⦿❘ *BP.*

¢–$ ☷ **Hotel St. Michael.** Don't expect serenity on the busiest corner of Court-house Plaza, but for low rates and historic charm it's hard to beat this hotel in operation since 1900. Rooms have 1920s–'40s-era antiques; some face the plaza and others look out on Thumb Butte. The first-floor Bistro St. Michael, where a full breakfast is included with your stay, serves great coffee and croissants. **Pros:** excellent breakfast; has character. **Cons:** noise from bars until the wee hours; some rooms are very worn. ⊠ *205 W. Gurley St., Downtown* 🕾 *928/776–1999 or 800/678–3757* ⊕ *www.stmichaelhotel.com* 🛏 *71 rooms* ♿ *In-room: a/c. In-hotel: restaurant* ▭ *AE, D, DC, MC, V* ⦿❘ *BP.*

$–$$ ☷ **Hotel Vendome.** This World War I–era hostelry has seen miners, health seekers, and such celebrities as cowboy star Tom Mix walk through its doors. Old-fashioned touches, including the original claw-foot tubs, remain, and like many other historic hotels the Vendome has its obligatory resident ghost (her room costs slightly more). **Pros:** central location; good value. **Cons:** creaky floors raise noise factor. ⊠ *230 Cortez St., Downtown* 🕾 *928/776–0900 or 888/468–3583* ⊕ *www.vendomehotel.com* 🛏 *16 rooms, 4 suites* ♿ *In-room: a/c, Wi-Fi* ▭ *AE, D, DC, MC, V* ⦿❘ *CP.*

$$ ☷ **Prescott Resort Conference Center and Casino.** On a hill on the outskirts of town, this upscale property run by the Yavapai tribe has views of the mountain ranges surrounding Prescott and the valley, although many guests hardly notice, so riveted are they by the poker machines and slots in Arizona's only hotel casino. There are plenty of recreational facilities to occupy those able to resist the one-armed bandits. **Pros:** nicely updated; comfortable rooms. **Cons:** large-scale property feels impersonal; drive to town center. ⊠ *1500 AZ 69* ☎ *928/776–1666 or 800/967–4637* ⊕ *www.prescottresort.com* ⤴ *161 rooms* ⚐ *In-room: a/c, refrigerator, safe, Wi-Fi. In-hotel: restaurant, bar, tennis courts, pool, gym* ⊟ *AE, D, DC, MC, V.*

SHOPPING

Shops selling antiques and collectibles line Cortez Street, just north of Courthouse Plaza. You'll find fun stuff—especially Western kitsch—as well as some good buys on valuable pieces. Courthouse Plaza, especially along Montezuma Street, is lined with specialty and gift shops. Many match those in Sedona for quality. Be sure to check out **Arts Prescott** (⊠ *134 S. Montezuma St., Downtown* ☎ *928/776–7717* ⊕ *www. artsprescott.com*), a cooperative gallery of talented local artisans. **Bella Home Furnishings** (⊠ *115 W. Willis St., Downtown* ☎ *928/445–0208* ⊕ *www.bellahomefurnishings.com*) has vintage home furnishings and artwork. At 14,000 square feet, the **Merchandise Mart Antique Mall** (⊠ *205 N. Cortez St., Downtown* ☎ *928/776–1728* ⊕ *prescottantiquestores. com*) is the largest of the town's collections of collectors. **Sun West Gallery** (⊠ *152 S. Montezuma St., Downtown* ☎ *928/778–1204*) has artwork, furnishings, and Native American Zapotec rugs. Don't miss the back room's selection of beads from around the world. Exquisite work of local and national artists is beautifully displayed at **Van Gogh's Ear** (⊠ *156 S. Montezuma St., Downtown* ☎ *928/776–1080* ⊕ *vgegallery.com*).

NIGHTLIFE AND THE ARTS

THE ARTS

Prescott's popular **Bluegrass Festival on the Square** (⊕ *www. prescottbluegrassfestival.com*) takes place in June. The town had its first organized cowboy competition in 1888, and lays claim to having the world's oldest rodeo: the annual **Frontier Days** (⊕ *www.worldsoldestrodeo. com*) roundup, held on July 4 weekend at the Yavapai County Fairgrounds. In August the **Cowboy Poets Gathering** (⊕ *www.azcowboypoets. org*) brings together campfire bards from around the country.

The **Prescott Fine Arts Association** (⊠ *208 N. Marina St., Downtown* ☎ *928/445–3286* ⊕ *www.pfaa.net*) sponsors musicals and dramas, plays for children, and a concert series. The association's gallery also presents rotating exhibits by local, regional, and national artists. The **Prescott Jazz Society** (☎ *928/237–7908* ⊕ *www.pjazz.org*) organizes jazz music events in and around town. The **Yavapai Symphony Association** (⊠ *228 N. Alarcon St., Suite B, Downtown* ☎ *928/776–4255* ⊕ *www. yavapaisymphony.org*) hosts performances by the Phoenix and Flagstaff symphonies; call ahead for schedules and venues.

NIGHTLIFE

Montezuma Street's Whiskey Row, off Courthouse Plaza, is nowhere near as wild as it was in its historic heyday, but most bars have live music—with no cover charge—on weekends. The **Hassayampa Inn** (✉ *122 E. Gurley St., Downtown* ☎ *928/778–9434* ⊕ *www.hassayampainn. com*) is an upscale, art nouveau piano bar. **Jersey Lilly Saloon** (✉ *116 Montezuma St., Downtown* ☎ *928/771–0997* ⊕ *www.jerseylillysaloon. com*), above the Palace, is a former brothel with live entertainment, a great patio, and a large dance floor. The classic Brunswick bar at **Lyzzard's Lounge** (✉ *120 N. Cortez St., Downtown* ☎ *928/778–2244*) was shipped from England via the Colorado River. **Raven Cafe** (✉ *142 N. Cortez St., Downtown* ☎ *928/717–0009*) is a contemporary, attractive coffeehouse and bar that doubles as a live-music venue in the evening. **129 1/2** (✉ *129 Cortez St., Downtown* ☎ *928/443—9292*) has live jazz music Thursday–Sunday evenings.

Northeast Arizona

WORD OF MOUTH

"Canyon de Chelly is spectacular in a completely different way
from the Grand Canyon, but really impressive just the same. The
cliffs are a deep, deep red, without the horizontal variations in
color of the Grand Canyon."

—Toucan2

WELCOME TO NORTHEAST ARIZONA

TOP REASONS TO GO

★ **Drive the rim roads at Canyon de Chelly:** Visit one of the most spectacular natural wonders in the Southwest—it rivals the Grand Canyon for beauty. It's a must for photography buffs.

★ **Go boating at Glen Canyon:** Get to know this stunning, mammoth reservoir by taking a boat out on Lake Powell amid the towering cliffs.

★ **Explore Hubbell Trading Post:** Take the self-guided tour to experience the relationship between the traders and the Navajo.

★ **Shop for handmade crafts on the Hopi Mesas:** Pick up crafts by some of Arizona's leading Hopi artisans, who sustain their culture through continuous occupation of the ancient villages on these mesas.

★ **Take a jeep tour through Monument Valley:** On an excursion through this 92,000-acre area, see firsthand the landscape depicted in such iconic Western films as *Stagecoach* and *The Searchers*.

Antelope Canyon

1 Navajo Nation East. Vastly underrated Canyon de Chelly National Monument offers some of the most spectacular panoramas in the world, and Window Rock is the governmental and cultural hub of the Navajo people.

2 The Hopi Mesas. An artistically rich and dramatically situated tribal land entirely surrounded by the Navajo Nation, the Hopi Mesas rise above the high-desert floor, rife with trading posts and art galleries selling fine weavings, jewelry, and crafts.

3 Navajo Nation West. Just 80 mi east of the Grand Canyon's South Rim, the bustling community of Tuba City anchors the western portion of the Navajo Nation—it's an excellent base for checking out the region's painted-desert landscapes and Navajo trading posts.

4 Monument Valley. You've probably seen images of this Ancestral Puebloan stomping ground in everything from classic Western movies to Ansel Adams photos; you can explore this sweeping valley on a variety of Navajo-led tours.

Rainbow Bridge
National Monument

UTAH

Four Corners
Monument

CO

Monument Valley
Navajo Tribal
Park

Teec Nos
Pos

Mexican
Water

Navajo
National
Monument

Kayenta

BLACK MESA

Chilchinbito

Round
Rock

Red
Rock

CHUSKA MOUNTAINS

NEW MEXICO

Cow Springs

Rough Rock

Many
Farms

HOPI
RESERVATION

Canyon de Chelly
National
Monument

Pinon

Chinle

Cottonwood

Hotevilla

Kykotsmovi

Shungopavi

Hopi
Cultural
Center

Polacca

Keams Canyon
Trading Post

Second
Mesa

Fort
Defiance

Ganado

Window
Rock

Hubbell Trading Post
National Historic Site

White Cone

Dilkon

Bidahochi

Greasewood

Klagetoh

NAVAJO
RESERVATION

Petrified Forest
National Park

Sanders

Winslow

Holbrook

0   40 miles

0   60 km

GETTING ORIENTED

Relatively few visitors experience the vast, sweeping northeast quadrant of Arizona, which comprises the Navajo and Hopi reservations, but efforts to spend a few days here are rewarded with stunning scenery and the chance to learn about some of the world's most vibrant indigenous communities. This is part of the West's great Four Corners Region, home to the underrated and spectacular Canyon de Chelly National Monument as well as the dramatic buttes and canyons of Monument Valley. The one portion of the area outside tribal lands is Page, the base for exploration of crystalline Lake Powell's 2,000 mi of shoreline.

Lake Powell Resort

5 **Glen Canyon Dam and Lake Powell.** The one section of northeastern Arizona not set on tribal lands is dominated by the nation's second-largest man-made body of water, Lake Powell, and 710-foot-tall Glen Canyon Dam; it's a boating paradise, and the town of Page has the greatest number of hotels and restaurants in the region.

NORTHEAST ARIZONA PLANNER

Making the Most of Your Time

Northeastern Arizona encompasses an enormous area but relatively few key attractions, so it's best to use one or two primary communities (Page or Tuba City on the west side, Kayenta on the north, and Chinle or Window Rock on the east) as bases for day trips to outlying attractions.

If your time is limited, put Canyon de Chelly and Monument Valley at the top of your list—if you're ambitious, you could explore these two sites on consecutive days, spending the night in either Chinle, Kayenta, or in Monument Valley itself. Focus on the South Rim Drive at Canyon de Chelly, and in Monument Valley book a jeep tour with the highly respected Sacred Monument Tours. On travel days from one base community to another, plan a scenic drive, such as AZ 264 from Tuba City to Window Rock (don't miss the great crafts shopping at Second Mesa) or AZ 98 to U.S. 160 to U.S. 191 from Page to Chinle. Give yourself at least two days to get to know any one part of the region, and as much as a week to fully explore all of it.

Getting Here and Around

Car Travel: It's virtually impossible to see much of northeastern Arizona without a car—this is your best bet not only for getting here, but also for visiting attractions and communities throughout the region.

Many visitors see northeastern Arizona as part of a road-tripping adventure through the Four Corners Region, perhaps combining their visit with trips to the national parks of southern Utah and southwestern Colorado. This "en route" road-tripping strategy makes the most sense, especially given the region's stunningly scenic drives—the Navajo Nation has a terrific Web site (⊕ *NavajoScenicRoads.com*) geared toward road-tripping.

Road Conditions and Services: Most of the 27,000 square mil of the Navajo Reservation and other areas of northeastern Arizona are off the beaten track. It's prudent to stay on the well-maintained paved thoroughfares. If you don't have the equipment for wilderness travel—including a four-wheel-drive vehicle and provisions—and lack backcountry experience, stay off dirt roads unless they are signed and graded and the skies are clear. Be on the lookout for ominous rain clouds in summer or signs of snow in winter. Never drive into dips or low-lying areas during a heavy rainstorm, and be vigilant for both wildlife and livestock (the Navajo Nation is open range, meaning cattle roam freely). If you heed these simple precautions, car travel through the region is as safe as anywhere else in the Southwest.

■TIP→ While driving around the Navajo Nation, tune in to 660 AM (KTNN) for local news and weather.

A tour of Navajo-Hopi country can involve driving significant distances between widely scattered communities, so a detailed, up-to-date road map is essential. Road service, auto repairs, and other automotive services are few and far between, so service your vehicle before venturing into the Navajo and Hopi reservations (or do so in the larger communities, such as Tuba City, Kayenta, and Window Rock), and carry emergency equipment and supplies.

If You Like Hiking

Some of the best hikes in this region are in Canyon de Chelly, up the streambed between the soaring vermilion, orange, and white sandstone cliffs, with the remains of the ancient Ancestral Puebloan communities frequently in view. The Navajo National Monument offers impressive hikes to Betatakin, a settlement dating back to AD 1250, and Keet Seel, which dates back as far as AD 950. Both are in alcoves at the base of gigantic overhanging cliffs. Remember, you cannot hike or camp on private property or tribal land without a backcountry permit.

Local Food and Lodging

Northeastern Arizona is a vast area with small hamlets and towns scattered miles apart, and there are few stores or restaurants. With the exception of Page, which has slightly more culinary variety, the region's towns mostly offer restaurants serving basic but tasty Native American and Southwestern cuisine. Navajo and Hopi favorites include mutton stew, Hopi *piki* (paper-thin, blue-corn bread), and Navajo fry bread.

Page also has the area's greatest concentration of lodgings, most of them fairly standard chain motels and hotels, but this base camp for exploring Lake Powell also has a few B&Bs as well as houseboat rentals, and the area is also home to the ultraluxurious Amangiri resort. You'll find a handful of well-maintained chains in the Navajo Nation, mostly in Kayenta, Chinle, Tuba City, and Window Rock. Additionally, Navajo's View Hotel in Monument Valley, and the Hopi's Moenkopi Legacy Inn in Tuba City are beautifully designed, contemporary hotels. This is a popular area for both tent and RV camping—you can obtain a list of campgrounds from the Page/Lake Powell Chamber of Commerce and the Navajo Nation Tourism Office.

WHAT IT COSTS					
	¢	$	$$	$$$	$$$$
Restaurant	under $8	$8–$12	$13–$20	$21–$30	over $30
Hotel	under $70	$70–$120	$121–$175	$176–$250	over $250

Restaurant prices are per person for a main course at dinner. Hotel prices are for a standard double in high season, excluding taxes and service charges.

Festivals and Events

A number of festivals and events take place among the Navajo and Hopi communities.

Aug. Central Navajo Fair. Several horse races, an arts-and-crafts market, the Miss Central Navajo Pageant, and several live-music performances are part of this celebration in Chinle. ☎ 928/674–9448.

Aug. and Sept. Hopi Harvest Festival. A celebration featuring Harvest and Butterfly social dances. ☎ 928/737–2754.

Sept. Navajo Nation Annual Tribal Fair. The world's largest Native American fair includes a rodeo, traditional Navajo music and dances, food booths, and an intertribal powwow over the first weekend of September after Labor Day, at Window Rock. ☎ 928/871–6647 ⊕ www. navajonationfair.com.

What Time Is It?

Unlike the rest of Arizona (including the Hopi Reservation), the Navajo Reservation observes daylight saving time. Thus for half the year—late March to early November—it's an hour later on the Navajo Reservation than everywhere else in the state.

5

NATIVE AMERICAN EXPERIENCE

With roots tracing back more than 12,000 years, Native Americans have lived in Arizona for hundreds of generations. Today more than 250,000 people reside in sovereign nations within Arizona's state borders. Alongside ancient cliff dwellings and stunning natural monuments, the reality of the 21 tribes' cultures is best experienced on the reservations.

Above: Colorful beadwork is a popular adornment for clothing. Top right: Apache warrior Geronimo. Bottom right: Each Navajo community is known for specific rug colors and designs.

Arizona's tribes live on reservations that comprise more than a quarter of the state's lands. Though some tribes are similar to one another in certain aspects, most are culturally and spiritually distinct. Many tribes live on lands that enable them to derive income from natural resources, such as coal, but most rely upon tourism to some extent for revenue. Some tribes, such as the Navajo, open up much of their culture to visitors. Native American artisans are famed for handmade items popular with tourists, but casinos are increasingly vital to tribal economies. These often include dining, lodging, and entertainment as well.

RESERVATION REALITIES

For all the richness in culture, reservations are places where poverty is often prevalent. Some liken the tourist experience to that of visiting a developing country. Some panhandlers cluster at shopping centers and view sites. Visitors should respond to panhandlers with a polite but firm "no." If you wish to help, make a donation to a legitimate organization.

NAVAJO NATION AND HOPI RESERVATION RULES

Each reservation has its own government that dictates and enforces visitation rules.

Alcohol and Drugs: The possession and consumption of alcoholic beverages or illicit drugs is illegal on Hopi and Navajo land.

Camping: No open fires are allowed in reservation campgrounds; you must use grills or fireplaces. You may not gather firewood on the reservation—bring your own. Camping areas have quiet hours from 11 PM to 6 AM. Pets must be kept on a leash or confined.

Hopi Shrines: Hopi spirituality is intertwined with daily life, and objects that seem ordinary to you may have deeper significance. If you see a collection of objects at or near the Hopi Mesas do not disturb them.

Permits and Permissions: No off-trail hiking, rock climbing, or other off-road travel is allowed unless you are accompanied by a local guide. A tribal permit is required for fishing. Violations of fish and game laws are punishable by heavy fines, imprisonment, or both.

Photography: Always ask permission before taking photos of locals. Even if no money is requested, consider offering a dollar or two to the person whose photo you have taken. The Navajo are very open about photographs; the Hopi do not allow photographs at all, including videos, and tape recordings.

Religious Ceremonies: Should you see a ceremony in progress, look for posted signs indicating who is welcome or check with local shops or the village community. Unless you're specifically invited, stay out of kivas (ceremonial rooms) and stay on the periphery of dances or processions.

Respect for the Land: Do not wander through residential areas or disturb property. Do not disturb or remove animals, plants, rocks, petrified wood, or artifacts.

TRIBAL TIMELINE

1120–1210 Ancestral Puebloans occupy Wupatki Pueblo.

1150 The Hopi build the (still-occupied) village of Old Orabi.

1250 Ancestral Puebloans are living at Keet Seel.

1276–1300 Tribes abandon northern Arizona during the "big drought."

1540–1542 Francisco Vásquez de Coronado leads an expedition in search of gold.

1863 Congress creates the Arizona Territory.

1864 Navajos forced to march 300 mi to Fort Sumner during the "Long Walk."

1868 The Navajo and the United States sign a treaty.

1886 Geronimo surrenders after evading U.S. troops for over a year.

1907 Arizona outlaws gambling.

1912 Arizona becomes 48th state.

1993 16 Arizona tribes sign gambling compacts with state

SHOPPING TIPS	CULTURE
For big-ticket items, buy directly from the craftsmen themselves or a reputable dealer. Most products sold on the Hopi and Navajo reservations are authentic, but fakes are not unheard of.	**Heritage flavors:** Native American food staples are well adapted to living in Arizona's arid lands. Corn is a universal ingredient—ground into flour to make tortillas, included in stew, or simply steamed and left on the cob. The fruits of the saguaro, prickly pear, and other cacti are commonly harvested by tribes as well as tepary beans grown from seeds handed down over generations. Fry bread—a flat piece of fried dough—is the basis of the popular Navajo taco, usually topped with beans, ground beef, and shredded cheese.

If you're traveling in Navajoland, the Cameron Trading Post north of Flagstaff or the Hubbell Trading Post at Ganado are two spots where you can find exemplary items.

In Phoenix, the Heard Museum offers some of the finest Native American handicrafts at reasonable prices.

Trading posts are reliable, as are most roadside stands, which can offer some outstanding values, but be wary of solo vendors around parking lots.

If you're planning on shopping on the Hopi Reservation or elsewhere outside the Navajo trading posts, it's a good idea to carry cash, as not all vendors accept credit cards.

The famous squash-blossom necklaces can run more than $1,000, especially if the silver beads are handmade as two separate hemispheres. A medium-size handwoven rug (5 by 7 feet) may require more than half a year to create, so don't be shocked if it costs over $30,000.

Song and dance: Ceremonies involving music and dance are central to Native American culture. Not every ceremony is accessible to visitors. Cultural centers and museums, such as the Heard in Phoenix, frequently hold powwows and other festivals that often celebrate more than one tribe.

Sacred spaces: The Hopi kiva are square- or circular-walled, mostly underground structures that are used exclusively for religious ceremonies, and often are accessed by a ladder from above. Most kivas, including ruins, are off-limits to tourists. The hogan is the traditional dwelling of the Navajo and the door always faces east to welcome the rising sun. Though used as homes, hogans play an important part in Navajo spirituality and represent the universe and all things in it.

Arts and crafts: Many of the craftspeople on the reservations sell their wares, with specialties that include pottery, turquoise and sterling-silver jewelry, handwoven baskets, and Navajo wool rugs. As the Spanish ventured northward from Mexico in the late 1500s and early 1600s, they taught the Native Americans their silver-crafting skills, while tribes specializing in pottery and weaving carry on a tradition that began hundreds of years ago. Native beadwork traces its origins to trade beads from early explorers.

(Below: Not every ceremony is accessible to visitors—tribes vary on their policies.)

THE NAVAJO AND THE HOPI PEOPLE

Both the Navajo and Hopi base their culture on the land around them, but they are very different from one another. The Navajo refer to themselves as the Diné (pronounced din-eh)—"the people"—and live on 17 million acres in Arizona, New Mexico, Utah, and Colorado, the largest Native American reservation in the country. The Hopi trace their roots back to the original settlers of the area, whom they call the Hisatsinom, or "people of long ago"—they are also known as Anasazi, meaning both "ancient ones" and "ancient enemies." Hopi culture is more formal and structured than that of the Navajo, and their religion has remained stronger and purer. For both tribes unemployment is high on the reservation, and poverty a constant presence.

The **Navajo** use few words and have a subtle sense of humor that can pass you by quickly if you're not a good listener. From childhood they are taught not to talk too much, be loud, or show off. Eye contact is considered impolite. If you're conversing with Navajos, some may look down or away even though they are paying attention to you. Likewise, touching is seen differently; handshaking may be the only physical contact that you see. When shaking hands, a light touch is preferred to a firm grip, which is considered overbearing.

Although most Navajos speak English with varying degrees of mastery, listen closely to the language of the Diné. Stemming from the Athabascan family of languages, it is difficult for outsiders to learn because of subtle accentuation. The famous Marine Corps Navajo "code talkers" of World War II saved thousands of lives in the South Pacific by creating a code within their native Navajo language. Many "code talkers" still alive today reside in the area around Tuba City.

The **Hopi** Reservation is surrounded by the far larger Navajo Reservation. Over the years the proximity of the two tribes has been the cause of contention, often involving the assistance of the United States Government in settling land claims, yet the spirituality of the Hopi—"the peaceful ones"—is decidedly anti-war. In fact, Hopi mythology holds that a white-skinned people will save the tribe from its difficult life. Long ago, however, in the face of brutal treatment by whites, most Hopi became convinced that salvation would originate elsewhere. (Some Hopi now look to the Dalai Lama for redemption.)

ON THE GROUND

Visiting the Navajo: The Navajo are generally more relaxed than the Hopi when it comes to recording, but always ask for permission before taking someone's picture. If you aren't asked for a gratuity consider giving one anyway ($1 is recommended). **Canyon De Chelly, Chaco Canyon, Monument Valley Navajo Tribal Park**, and **Navajo National Monument** each offers a glimpse into both the past and present of Native American life and culture, including ruins of ancient dwellings and visitor centers with informative dioramas.

Visiting the Hopi: Recordings of any kind, including photographs, are prohibited throughout the Hopi Reservation. Central to the reservation are a handful of **Hopi Mesas** that contain two of the oldest continually inhabited villages in North America. Though all **Hopi villages** offer visitors restricted or no access, visitors can buy handicrafts directly from Hopi artisans at a number of shops and galleries.

(Above: A traditional Navajo Hogan dwelling)

5

Updated
by Andrew
Collins

Northeast Arizona is a vast and magnificent land of lofty buttes, towering cliffs, and turquoise skies. Most of the land in the area belongs to the Navajo and Hopi, who adhere to ancient traditions based on spiritual values, kinship, and an affinity for nature. Life here has changed little during the last two centuries, and visiting this land can feel like traveling to a foreign country or going back in time.

In such towns as Tuba City and Window Rock it's not uncommon to hear the gliding vowels and soft consonants of the Navajo language, a tongue as different from Hopi as English is from Chinese. As you drive in the vicinity, tune your radio to 660 AM KTNN (⊕ *www.ktnnonline. com*), the Voice of the Navajo Nation since 1985. You'll quickly understand why the U.S. Marine Navajo "code talkers" communicating in their native tongue were able to devise a code within their language that was never broken by the Japanese.

In the Navajo Nation's approximate center sits the nearly 2,600-square-mi Hopi Reservation, a series of adobe villages built on high mesas overlooking the cultivated land. On Arizona's borders, where the Navajo Nation continues into Utah and New Mexico, the Navajo and Canyon de Chelly national monuments contain haunting cliff dwellings of ancient people who lived in the area some 1,500 years ago. Glen Canyon Dam, which abuts the northwestern corner of the reservation, holds back 185 mi of emerald waters known as Lake Powell.

Most of northeast Arizona is desert country, but it's far from boring: eerie and spectacular rock formations as colorful as desert sunsets highlight immense mesas, canyons, and cliffs; towering stands of ponderosa pine cover the Chuska Mountains to the north and east of Canyon de Chelly. Navajo Mountain to the north and west in Utah soars more than 10,000 feet, and the San Francisco Peaks climb to similar heights to the south and west by Flagstaff. According to the Navajo creation myth, these are two of the four mountainous boundaries of the sacred land where the Navajo first emerged from Earth's interior.

NAVAJO NATION EAST

Land has always been central to the history of the Navajo people: it's embedded in their very name. The Tewa were the first to call them *Navahu*, which means "large area of cultivated land." But according to the Navajo creation myth, they were given the name *ni'hookaa diyan diné*—"holy earth people"—by their creators. Today tribal members call themselves the Diné (pronounced din-*eh*)—"the people". The eastern portion of the Arizona Navajo Nation (in Navajo, *diné bikéyah*) is a dry but often surprisingly green land, especially in the vicinity of the aptly named Beautiful Valley, south of Canyon de Chelly along U.S. 191. A landscape of rolling hills, wide arroyos, and small canyons, the area is dotted with traditional Navajo hogans, sheepfolds, cattle tanks, and wood racks. The region's easternmost portion is marked by tall mountains and towering sandstone cliffs cut by primitive roads that are generally accessible only on horseback or with four-wheel-drive vehicles.

ESSENTIALS

Visitor Info Navajo Nation Tourism Office (☎ 928/810–8501 ⊕ www.discovernavajo.com)

WINDOW ROCK

192 mi from Flagstaff; 26 mi from Gallup, New Mexico.

Named for the immense arch-shape "window" in a massive sandstone ridge above the city, Window Rock is the capital of the Navajo Nation and the center of its tribal government. With a population of around 3,000, this community serves as the business and social center for Navajo families throughout the reservation. Window Rock is a good place to stop for food, supplies, and gas.

GETTING HERE AND AROUND

From Flagstaff follow Interstate 40 east for 160 mi, then Highway 12 north. From Gallup, New Mexico follow U.S. 491 north and then NM 264 west (which becomes AZ 264).

EXPLORING

The **Navajo Nation Council Chambers** is a handsome structure that resembles a large ceremonial hogan. The murals on the walls depict scenes from the history of the tribe, and the bell beside the entrance was a gift to the tribe by the Santa Fe Railroad to commemorate the thousands of Navajos who worked to build the railroad. Visitors can observe sessions of the council, where 88 delegates representing 110 reservation chapters meet on the third Monday of January, April, July, and October. Turn east off Indian Highway 12, about 0.5 mi north of AZ 264, to reach the Council Chambers. **Window Rock Navajo Tribal Park & Veteran's Memorial,** near the Council Chambers, is a memorial park honoring Navajo veterans, including the famous World War II code talkers. ⊠ *AZ 264* ☎ *928/871–6417* ⊕ *www.navajo.org* ☉ *Daily 8–5.*

The **Navajo Nation Museum,** on the grounds of the former Tse Bonito Park off AZ 264, is devoted to the art, culture, and history of the Navajo people and has an excellent library on the Navajo Nation. The

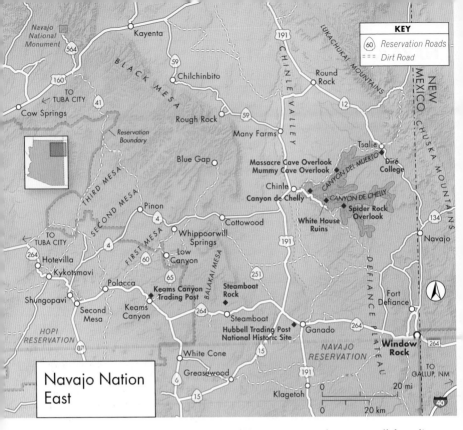

Navajo
National
Monument
564

Kayenta

191

LUKACHUKAI MOUNTAINS

59

Chilchinbito

Round
Rock

CHINLE VALLEY

12

NEW MEXICO

CHUSKA MOUNTAINS

160

TO
TUBA CITY 41

Cow Springs

BLACK MESA

Rough Rock

59

Many Farms

Tsalie

Diné
College

Reservation
Boundary

Blue Gap

Massacre Cave Overlook
Mummy Cave Overlook

CANYON DEL MUERTO

THIRD MESA

SECOND MESA

Pinon

Chinle

Canyon de Chelly

CANYON DE CHELLY

Spider Rock
Overlook

134

Cottonwood

White House
Ruins

Navajo

TO
TUBA CITY 4

Hotevilla

4

Whippoorwill
Springs

191

264

Kykotsmovi

FIRST MESA

60

Low
Canyon

BALAKAI MESA

251

DEFIANCE PLATEAU

Polacca

65

Keams Canyon
Trading Post

Steamboat
Rock

Fort
Defiance

Shungopavi

Second
Mesa

Keams
Canyon

264

Steamboat

264

Window
Rock

HOPI
RESERVATION

07

White Cone

15

Hubbell Trading Post
National Historic Site

Ganado

NAVAJO
RESERVATION

264

TO
GALLUP, NM

Greasewood

6

191

15

Klagetoh

0   20 mi
0   20 km

40

**Navajo Nation
East**

museum hosts exhibitions of Native artists each season; call for a list of shows. In the same building as the Navajo Nation Museum is the Navajo Nation Visitor Center, a great resource for all sorts of information on reservation activities. ✉ *AZ 264 next to Quality Inn Navajo Nation* ☎ *928/871–7941* ⊕ *www.navajonationmuseum.org* 🎫 *Free* ☉ *Mon. and Sat. 8–5, Tues.–Fri. 8–8.*

Within walking distance of the Navajo Museum, the **Navajo Arts and Crafts Enterprises** (☎ *866/871–4090* ⊕ *www.gonavajo.com/navajoart*) has been selling local artwork, including pottery, jewelry, and blankets, since 1941.

Amid the sandstone monoliths on the border between Arizona and New Mexico, the **Navajo Nation Botanical and Zoological Park** displays about 30 species of domestic and wild animals, birds, and amphibians that figure in Navajo legends, as well as examples of plants used by traditional people. Most of the animals here were brought in as orphans or after sustaining injuries—they include black bears, mountain lions, Mexican gray wolves, bobcats, golden eagles, Gila monsters, and western rattlesnakes. It's the only Native American–owned-and-operated zoo in the United States. ✉ *AZ 264 northeast of Navajo Nation Museum* ☎ *928/871–6644* ⊕ *www.navajozoo.org* 🎫 *Free* ☉ *Mon.–Sat. 10–5.*

🕐 Many all-Indian rodeos are held near the center of downtown at the **Navajo Tribal Fairgrounds.** The community hosts the annual multiday Fourth of July celebration with a major rodeo, ceremonial dances, and a parade. The Navajo Nation Tribal Fair, much like a traditional state fair, is held in early September. It offers standard county-fair rides, midway booths, contests, powwow competitions, and an all-Indian rodeo. ✉ *AZ 264* ☎ *928/871–6647, 928/871–6478 Navajo Nation Fair Office* ⊕ *www.navajonationfair.com.*

WHERE TO STAY

¢–$ 🛏 **Navajoland Inn and Suites.** This well-kept, affordable property in St. Michaels, formerly a Days Inn, is 3 mi west of Window Rock, and has standard rooms decorated in contemporary Southwestern style with 25-inch TVs, irons and boards, and free local phone calls. Guests appreciate the indoor pool and hot tub. **Pros:** friendly staff; closest reliable accommodation to Hubbell Trading Post; very well maintained. **Cons:** basic rooms; not much curb appeal. ✉ *392 W. AZ 264, St. Michaels* ☎ *928/871–5690* ⊕ *www.navajoland-innsuites.com* 🛏 *65 rooms, 8 suites* ⚇ *In-room: a/c, refrigerator, Wi-Fi. In-hotel: restaurant, pool, gym, some pets allowed* ⊟ *AE, D, MC, V.*

$ 🛏 **Quality Inn Navajo Nation Capital.** Rooms in this two-story beam-and-stucco hotel are decorated with an earthy Navajo-inspired palette that complements the rustic pine furniture. The decor, bedding, and amenities exceed typical Quality Inn standards and are nicer than you might guess given the hotel's drab exterior. The Diné Restaurant serves tasty Navajo and Southwestern fare (roasted corn chowder, Indian tacos, veggie burritos) plus a handful of American standards, and the gift shop sells authentic Navajo jewelry. **Pros:** within walking distance of Navajo Museum; decent restaurant; rooms are bright and attractively furnished. **Cons:** on busy road with dull setting. ✉ *48 W. AZ 264 at Hwy. 12* ☎ *928/871–4108 or 800/662–6189* ⊕ *www.qualityinn.com* 🛏 *56 rooms* ⚇ *In-room: a/c, refrigerator, Wi-Fi. In-hotel: restaurant, Internet terminal, some pets allowed* ⊟ *AE, D, MC, V* ⎟◎⎟ *CP.*

SHOPPING

★ An outlet of the **Navajo Arts and Crafts Enterprises** (✉ *AZ 264 at Hwy. 12, next to Quality Inn Navajo Nation Capital* ☎ *928/871–4090* ⊕ *www. gonavajo.com/navajoart*) stocks tribal art purchased from craftspeople across the reservation, including stunning silverwork, traditional Navajo dolls, pottery, and rugs. Local artisans are occasionally at work here. Major credit cards are accepted.

CANYON DE CHELLY

30 mi west of Window Rock on AZ 264, then north 25 mi on U.S. 191.

GETTING HERE AND AROUND

U.S. 191 runs north–south through the town of Chinle, the closest town to the Canyon de Chelly entrance.

Guided tours allow visits directly into the canyons, not just the park drives high above them; jeep tours even have the option of camping overnight. Each kind of tour has its pros and cons: you'll cover the most ground in a jeep; horseback trips get you close to one of the park's most notable geological formations, Spider Rock; and guided walks provide the most leisurely pace and an excellent opportunity to interact with your guide and ask questions. You can also plan custom treks lasting up to a week.

PLANNING YOUR TIME

To get even a basic sense of the park's scope and history, plan to spend at least a full day here. If time is short, the best strategy is to spend some time at the visitor center, where you can watch an informative 23-minute video about the canyons, and then drive the most magnificent of the two park roads, South Rim Drive. You could, theoretically, drive both park roads in one day, but it's better to set aside a second day for North Rim Drive, or take the North Rim Drive as an alternative route to Kayenta, by way of Tsaile. From the different overlooks along the park roads you'll be treated to amazing photo ops of the valley floors below, and you can also access certain dwellings. For a more in-depth look at Canyon de Chelly, consider one of the guided hiking, jeep, or horseback tours into the canyon.

Both Canyon de Chelly and Canyon del Muerto have a paved rim drive with turnoffs and parking areas. Each drive takes a minimum of two hours—allow more if you plan to hike to White House Rim, picnic, or spend time photographing the sites. Overlooks along the rim drives provide incredible views of the canyon; be sure to stay on trails and away from the canyon edge, and to control children and pets at all times.

The visitor center has exhibits on the history of the cliff dwellers and provides information on scheduled hikes, tours, and National Park Service programs offered throughout the summer months.

ESSENTIALS

Visitor Info Canyon de Chelly Visitor Center *Indian Hwy. 7, 3 mi east of U.S. 191 Chinle* ☎ *928/674–5500* ⊕ *www.nps.gov/cach*

EXPLORING

Fodor'sChoice
★

Home to Ancestral Puebloans from AD 350 to 1300, the nearly 84,000-acre **Canyon de Chelly** (pronounced d'*shay*) is one of the most spectacular natural wonders in the Southwest. On a smaller scale, it rivals the Grand Canyon for beauty. Its main gorges—the 26-mi-long Canyon de Chelly ("canyon in the rock") and the adjoining 35-mi Canyon del Muerto ("canyon of the dead")—comprise sheer, heavily eroded sandstone walls that rise to 1,100 feet over dramatic valleys. Ancient pictographs and petroglyphs decorate some of the cliffs, and within the canyon complex there are more than 7,000 archaeological sites. Stone walls rise hundreds of feet above streams, hogans, tilled fields, and sheep-grazing lands.

You can view prehistoric sites near the base of cliffs and perched on high, sheltering ledges, some of which you can access from the park's two main drives along the canyon rims. The dwellings and cultivated fields of the present-day Navajo lie in the flatlands between the cliffs, and those who inhabit the canyon today farm much the way their ancestors did. Most residents leave the canyon in winter but return in early spring to farm.

★ Canyon de Chelly's **South Rim Drive** (36 mi round-trip with seven over-looks) starts at the visitor center and ends at **Spider Rock Overlook,** where cliffs plunge nearly 1,000 feet to the canyon floor. The view here is of two pinnacles, Speaking Rock and Spider Rock. Other highlights on the South Rim Drive are Junction Overlook, where Canyon del Muerto joins Canyon de Chelly; White House Overlook, from which a 2.5-mi round-trip trail leads to the **White House Ruin,** with remains of nearly 60 rooms and several kivas; and Sliding House Overlook, where you can see dwellings on a narrow, sloped ledge across the canyon. The carved and sometimes narrow trail down the canyon side to White House Ruin is the only access into Canyon de Chelly without a guide—but if you have a fear of heights, this may not be the hike for you.

The only slightly less breathtaking **North Rim Drive** (34 mi round-trip with four overlooks) of Canyon del Muerto also begins at the visitor center and continues northeast on Indian Highway 64 toward the town of Tsaile. Major stops include Antelope House Overlook, a large site named for the animals painted on an adjacent cliff; **Mummy Cave Overlook,** where two mummies were found inside a remarkably unspoiled pueblo dwelling; and **Massacre Cave Overlook,** which marks the spot where an estimated 115 Navajo were killed by the Spanish in 1805. (The rock walls of the cave are still pockmarked by the Spaniards' ricocheting bullets.) ⊠ *Indian Hwy. 7, 3 mi east of U.S. 191, Chinle* ☎ *928/674–5500 visitor center* ⊕ *www.nps.gov/cach* ⊠ *Free* ☉ *Daily 9–5.*

In Tsaile, Navajo medicine men worked with architects to design the town's six-story **Diné College,** the first Native American–owned community college in the country. Because all important Navajo activities traditionally take place in a circle (a hogan is essentially circular), the campus was laid out in the round, with the buildings inside its perimeter covered in reflective glass to mirror the piñon-covered landscape surrounding the campus. Diné College's **Hatathli Museum and Art Gallery** contains art and exhibits on Navajo culture as well as intertribal exhibits from across the United States. ⊠ *Indian Hwy. 12 south of Indian Hwy. 64, Tsaile* ☎ *928/724–3311 college, 928/724–6654 museum* ⊕ *www.dinecollege. edu* ⊠ *Donations accepted* ☉ *Museum weekdays 8:30–4.*

To the north of Tsaile are the impressive **Chuska Mountains,** covered with sprawling stands of ponderosa pine. There are no established hiking trails in the Chuska Mountains, but up-to-date hiking information and backcountry-use permits (rarely granted if a Navajo guide does not accompany the trip) can be obtained through the Navajo Nation. ⊠ *Navajo Nation Parks and Recreation Department, Bldg. 36A, E. AZ 264, Window Rock* ☎ *928/871–6647* ⊕ *www.navajonationparks.org.*

SPORTS AND THE OUTDOORS

HIKING From late May through early September, free three-hour ranger-led hikes depart daily at 9 AM from the visitor center. Also at this time, two four-hour hikes (about $10 per person) leave from the visitor center and again in afternoon. Some trails are strenuous and steep; others are easy or moderate. Those with health concerns or a fear of heights should proceed with caution. Call ahead: hikes are occasionally canceled in deference to local customs or events.

CLOSE UP

Who Were the Cliff Dwellers?

The first inhabitants of the canyons arrived more than 2,000 years ago—anthropologists call them the basket makers, because baskets were the predominant artifacts they left behind. By AD 750, however, the basket makers had disappeared—their reason for leaving the region is unknown, but some speculate they were forced to leave because of encroaching cultures or climatic changes—and they were replaced by Pueblo tribes who constructed stone cliff dwellings. The departure of the Pueblo people around AD 1300 is widely believed to have resulted from changing climatic conditions, soil erosion, dwindling local resources, disease, and internal conflict. Present-day Hopi see these people as their ancestors. Beginning around AD 780, Hopi farmers settled here, followed by the Navajo around 1300. The Navajo migrated from far northern Canada; no one is sure when they first arrived in the Southwest. Despite evidence to the contrary, most Navajos hold that their people have always lived here and that the Diné passed through three previous underworlds before emerging into this, the fourth or Glittering World.

Only one hike within Canyon de Chelly National Monument—the **White House Ruin Trail** on the South Rim Drive—can be undertaken without an authorized guide. The trail starts near White House Overlook and runs along sheer walls that drop about 550 feet. If you have concerns about height, be aware that the path gets narrow and requires careful footing. The hike is 2.5 mi round-trip, and hikers should carry their own drinking water.

Private guided hikes to the interior of the canyons cost about $15 per hour, with a three-hour minimum for groups of up to four people. (Don't venture into the canyon without a guide or you'll face a stiff fine.) For overnights you'll need a guide as well as permission to stay on private land. If you have a four-wheel-drive vehicle and want to drive yourself, guides will accompany you for a charge of about $15 an hour, with a three-hour minimum for up to three vehicles. All Navajo guides are members of the **Tsegi Guide Association** (⊠ *Canyon de Chelly Visitor Center, Indian Hwy. 7, Chinle* ☎ *928/674–5500*). You can hire a guide on the spot at the visitor center, or you can call ahead and make a reservation.

HORSEBACK
RIDING
★

Totsonii Ranch (⊠ *South Rim Dr., Chinle* ☎ *928/755–2037* ⊕ *www. totsoniiranch.com*), 13 mi from the visitor center at the end of the paved portion of South Rim Drive, offers several types of horseback tours into different parts of Canyon de Chelly: Canyon Rim (two hours), Three Turkey Ruins (four hours), Spider Rock (four hours), White House Ruins (six to seven hours), Canyon de Chelly overview (eight to nine hours), and one- and two-night treks. Some of these trips are geared only toward skilled adult riders, such as the Canyon Rim trips, which encounter steep terrain and offer amazing views. Spider Rock is a great choice for virtually any skill level, and can be done in a half day—the ride leads right to the base of this 800-foot iconic pillar. Rates are $15 per hour per person plus $15 per hour per guide.

JEEP TOURS **Canyon de Chelly Tours** (📞 928/674–5433 ⊕ *www.canyondechellytours.com*) offers private jeep tours into Canyon de Chelly and arranges group tours and overnight camping in the canyon as well as late-afternoon and evening tours. Entertainment such as storytellers, music, and Navajo legends can be arranged with advance reservation. Rates begin at $66 per person for three-hour tours, or $44 per hour per vehicle if you use your own SUV (about a 10% discount if you pay in cash). Treks with **Thunderbird Lodge Canyon Tours** (✉ *Thunderbird Lodge Gift Shop, Indian Hwy. 7, Chinle* 📞 *928/674–5841 or 800/679–2473* ⊕ *www.tbirdlodge.com*), in six-wheel-drive vehicles, are available from late spring to late fall. Half-day tours are $49 and start at 9 AM and 1 or 2 PM daily; all-day tours cost $79 and include lunch.

WALKING TOURS **Footpath Journey Tours** (📞 928/724–3366 ⊕ *www.footpathjourneys.com*) offers custom four- to seven-day treks into the canyon starting at $800 per person, not including food.

WHERE TO EAT

Chinle is the closest town to Canyon de Chelly. There are good lodgings with restaurants, as well as a supermarket and a campground. Be aware that you may be approached by panhandlers in the grocery store parking lot. In late August each year, Chinle is host to the Central Navajo Fair, a public celebration complete with a rodeo, carnival, and traditional dances.

$$ ✕ **Garcia's Restaurant.** The lobby restaurant at Chinle's Holiday Inn is
AMERICAN low-key, a bit lacking in natural light, and rather ordinary by most standards, but it is one of the area's more reliable dining options, especially for dinner. You can count on well-prepared specialties such as mutton stew with fry bread and honey. They also sell a box picnic for guests. ✉ *Indian Hwy. 7 Chinle* 📞 *928/674–5000* ⊕ *www.holidayinn.com* ▭ *AE, D, DC, MC, V* ☉ *No lunch mid-Nov.–Mar.*

$ ✕ **The Junction.** Across the parking lot from the Best Western Canyon
AMERICAN de Chelly Inn, this sun-filled, airy dining room with cream-color walls, large windows, a long granite counter, and a mix of attractive booths and tables has a cheerier feel than any other restaurant in town, and the kitchen turns out pretty tasty American, Southwestern, and Chinese food, too. Specialties include posole stew, chicken-fried steak, and sheepherder's sandwiches (their vision consists of a tortilla or fry bread stuffed with steak, Swiss cheese, grilled onions, chiles, and tomatoes). A small kiosk by the front door sells gifts and jewelry. ✉ *100 Main St.* ⌂ *Box 295, Chinle 86503* 📞 *928/674–5875 or 800/327–0354* ⊕ *www.canyondechelly.com* ▭ *AE, D, DC, MC, V.*

WHERE TO STAY

$–$$ **Best Western Canyon de Chelly Inn.** This two-story motel about 3 mi from Canyon de Chelly but close to the junction with U.S. 191 has cheerful rooms with modern, no-frills oak furnishings. All rooms have coffeemakers. The on-site Junction restaurant is one of the few spots in town to serve three meals a day, year-round, and there's a very good gift shop off the lobby. **Pros:** usually slightly less expensive than the Holiday Inn; fun retro-motel exterior; indoor pool with hot tub and sauna is open 24 hours. **Cons:** not within walking distance of the park. ⊠ *100 Main St.* ⌂ *Box 295, Chinle 86503* ☏ *928/674–5875 or 800/327–0354* ⊕ *www.canyondechelly.com* ⌨ *102 rooms* ⌂ *In-room: a/c, Wi-Fi. In-hotel: restaurant, room service, pool* ▤ *AE, D, DC, MC, V.*

$–$$ **Holiday Inn Canyon de Chelly.** Once Garcia's Trading Post, this hotel near Canyon de Chelly is less generic than you might expect: the exterior is territorial fort in style, although the rooms are predictably pastel and contemporary. Off the lobby there's a gift shop stocked with local Native American arts and crafts, plus a decent restaurant. **Pros:** attractive adobe-style building; nice pool and gym; a short drive from park entrance. **Cons:** not especially memorable decor; dull roadside setting. ⊠ *Indian Hwy. 7* ⌂ *Box 1889, Chinle 86503* ☏ *928/674–5000 or 888/465–4329* ⊕ *www.holidayinn.com* ⌨ *108 rooms* ⌂ *In-room: a/c, refrigerator, Wi-Fi. In-hotel: restaurant, pool, gym* ▤ *AE, D, DC, MC, V.*

$ **Thunderbird Lodge.** In an ideal location within the national monument's
★   borders, this pleasant establishment has stone-and-adobe units that match the site's original 1896 trading post. The cafeteria is in the original trading post and serves reasonably priced soups, salads, sandwiches, and entrées, including charbroiled steaks. The lodge also offers jeep tours of Canyon de Chelly and Canyon del Muerto. **Pros:** inside the actual park borders; steeped in history; tours offered right from hotel. **Cons:** rustic decor; no high-speed Internet. ⊠ *Indian Hwy. 7* ⌂ *Box 548, Chinle 86503* ☏ *928/674–5841 or 800/679–2473* ⊕ *www.tbirdlodge.com* ⌨ *73 rooms* ⌂ *In-room: a/c. In-hotel: restaurant* ▤ *AE, D, DC, V.*

CAMPGROUND   **Spider Rock Campground.** Cordial Navajo owner Howard Smith
¢   makes everyone feel comfortable at this informal campground nestled in low piñons within a few hundred yards of the canyon. The camp is just a short drive from the famous Spider Rock site and overlook and has tent sites as well as authentically designed Navajo hogans. There's a 3-mi self-guided hike to the rim overlooking Ancestral Puebloan ruins in Wild Cherry Canyon, and Howard will also customize guided hikes into the canyon on such routes as Grandmother's Trail, which has Ancestral Puebloan footholds and handholds worn into the sandstone. Wi-Fi was added in 2009. **Pros:** friendly and knowledgeable staff; hiking on-site; the chance to stay in an authentic hogan. **Cons:** far from restaurants and town. ⊠ *Indian Hwy. 7, 10 mi east of Canyon de Chelly Visitor Center* ⌂ *Box 2509, Chinle 86503* ☏ *928/674–8261 or 877/910–2267* ⊕ *www.spiderrockcampground.com* ⌨ *30 campsites, 2 hogans* ⌂ *Pit toilets, partial hookups (electricity), dump station, drinking water, showers, fire pits, picnic tables* ⊙ *Open year-round.*

SHOPPING

★ Chinle's branch of **Navajo Arts and Crafts Enterprises** (✉ *AZ 64 at U.S. 191,Chinle* ☎ *928/674–5338* ⊕ *www.gonavajo.com/navajoart*) carries an excellent selection of locally made art and crafts.

HUBBELL TRADING POST NATIONAL HISTORIC SITE

40 mi south of Canyon de Chelly, off AZ 264; 30 mi west of Window Rock.

GETTING HERE AND AROUND

The National Park Service visitor center exhibits illustrate the post's history, and you can take a self-guided tour of the grounds and Hubbell home and visit the Hubbell Trading Post, which contains a fine display of Native American artistry. The visitor center has a fairly comprehensive bookstore specializing in Navajo history, art, and culture; local weavers often demonstrate their craft on-site.

EXPLORING

Hubbell Trading Post National Historic Site. John Lorenzo Hubbell, a merchant and friend of the Navajo, established this trading post in 1876. Hubbell taught, translated letters, settled family quarrels, and explained government policy to the Navajo, and during an 1886 smallpox epidemic he turned his home into a hospital and ministered to the sick and dying. He died in 1930, and is buried near the trading post.

The Hubbell Trading Post National Historic Site is famous for "Ganado red" Navajo rugs, which are sold at the store here. The quality is outstanding, and prices are high but fair—rugs can cost anywhere from $100 to more than $30,000. Considering the time that goes into weaving each one, the prices are quite reasonable. It's hard to resist the beautiful designs and colors, and it's a pleasure just to browse around this rustic spot, where Navajo artists frequently show their work. Documents of authenticity are provided for all works. Note: when photographing weavers, ask permission first. They expect a few dollars in return. ✉ *AZ 264, 1 mi west of town, Ganado* ☎ *928/755–3475 park office, 928/755–3254 store* ⊕ *www.nps.gov/hutr* 🎟 *Free, $2 to tour Hubbell home* ☉ *May–mid Sept., daily 8–6; mid-Sept.–Apr., daily 8–5.*

EN ROUTE
About 20 mi west of Hubbell Trading Post on AZ 264 is **Steamboat Rock**, an immense, jutting peninsula of stone that resembles an early steamboat, complete with a geologically formed waterline. At Steamboat Rock you are only 5 mi from the eastern boundary of the Hopi Reservation.

THE HOPI MESAS

The Hopi occupy 12 villages in regions referred to as First Mesa, Second Mesa, and Third Mesa. Although these areas have similar languages and traditions, each has its own individual features. Generations of Hopitu, "the peaceful people," much like their Puebloan ancestors, have lived in these largely agrarian settlements of stone-and-adobe houses, which blend in with the earth so well that they

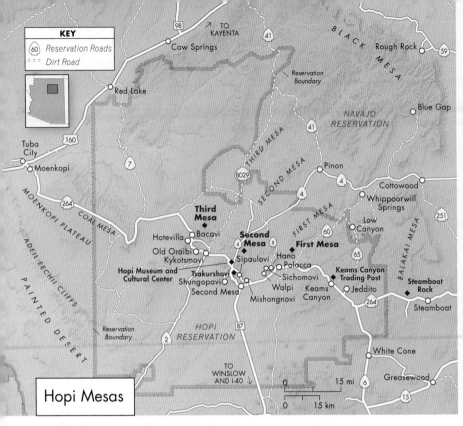

Hopi Mesas

appear to be natural formations. Television antennae, satellite dishes, and automobiles notwithstanding, these Hopi villages still exude the air of another time.

Descendants of the ancient Hisatsinom, the Hopi number about 12,000 people today. Their culture can be traced back more than 2,000 years, making them one of the oldest known tribes in North America. They successfully developed "dry farming," and grow many kinds of vegetables and corn (called maize) as their basic food—in fact the Hopi are often called the "corn people." They incorporate nature's cycles into most of their religious rituals. In the celebrated Snake Dance ceremony, dancers carry venomous snakes in their mouths to appease the gods and to bring rain. In addition to farming the land, the Hopi create fine pottery and basketwork and excel in wood carving of kachina dolls.

ESSENTIALS
Vistor Info Inter Tribal Council of Arizona: Hopi Tribe (☎ 928/734–2441 ⊕ www.itcaonline.com/tribes_hopi.html).

KEAMS CANYON TRADING POST

43 mi west of Hubbell Trading Post on AZ 264.

The trading post established by Thomas Keam in 1875 to do business with local tribes is now the area's main tourist attraction, offering a primitive campground, restaurant, service station, and shopping center, all set in a dramatic rocky canyon. An administrative center for the Bureau of Indian Affairs, Keams Canyon also has a number of government buildings. A road, accessible by passenger car, winds northeast 3 mi into the 8-mi wooded canyon. At **Inscription Rock,** about 2 mi down the road, frontiersman Kit Carson engraved his name in stone. There are several picnic spots in the canyon.

GETTING HERE AND AROUND

Keams Canyon is along AZ 264, the main route between Window Rock and Tuba City.

WHERE TO EAT

5

$ ✗ **Keams Canyon Restaurant.** A typical no-frills roadside diner with For-
AMERICAN mica tabletops, Keams offers both American and Native American dishes, including Navajo tacos heaped with ground beef, chili, beans, lettuce, and grated cheese. Daily specials, offered at $1 to $2 off the regular price, may include anything from barbecued ribs to lamb chops to crab legs. There's also an ice-cream stand in the same building. ⊠ *Keams Canyon Shopping Center, AZ 264, Keams Canyon* ☎ *928/738–2296* ⊟ *D, MC, V* ⊗ *No dinner weekends.*

SHOPPING

Keams Canyon Arts and Crafts and McGee's Art Gallery (⊠ *AZ 264, Keams Canyon* ☎ *928/738–2295* ⊕ *www.hopiart.com*), upstairs from the Keams Canyon Restaurant, sells first-rate, high-quality Hopi crafts such as handcrafted jewelry, pottery, beautiful carvings, basketry, and artwork.

FIRST MESA

★ *11 mi west of Keams Canyon, on AZ 264.*

GETTING HERE AND AROUND

The first village that you approach is Polacca; the older and more impressive villages of Hano, Sichomovi, and Walpi are at the top of the sweeping mesa. From Polacca a paved road (off AZ 264) angles up to a parking lot near the village of Sichomovi, and to the Punsi Hall Visitor Center. ■ TIP➜ **You must get permission at Punsi Hall to take the guided walking tour of Hano, Sichomovi, and Walpi. Admission is by tour only, so call ahead to find out when they're offered.**

EXPLORING

First Mesa villages are renowned for their polychrome pottery and kachina-doll carvings. The older Hopi villages have structures built of rock and adobe mortar in simple architectural style. **Hano** actually belongs to the Tewa, a New Mexico Pueblo tribe. In 1696 the Tewa Indians sought refuge with the Hopi on First Mesa after an unsuccessful rebellion against the Spanish in the Rio Grande Valley. Today the Tewa live close to the Hopi but maintain their own language and ceremonies.

Sichomovi is built so close to Hano that only the residents can tell where one ends and the other begins. Constructed in the mid-1600s, this village is believed to have been built to ease overcrowding at Walpi, the highest point on the mesa. **Walpi,** built on solid rock and surrounded by steep cliffs, frequently hosts ceremonial dances. It's the most pristine of the Hopi villages, with cliff-edge houses and vast scenic vistas. Inhabited for more than 1,100 years (dating back to 900 AD, Walpi's cliff-edge houses seem to grow out of the nearby terrain. Today only about 10 residents occupy this settlement, which has neither electricity nor running water; one-hour guided tours of the village are available. Note that Walpi's steep terrain makes it a less than ideal destination for acrophobes. ⊠ *Punsi Hall Visitor Center, First Mesa* ☎ 928/737–2670 ⊕ *www.experiencehopi.com/walpi.html* ✉ *Guided tours $13* ⊙ *Tours daily 9–3, except when ceremonies are being held.*

SECOND MESA

8 mi southwest of First Mesa, on AZ 264.

GETTING HERE AND AROUND

The Second Mesa communities are reached via the main highway (AZ 264) through the Hopi Reservation.

EXPLORING

The Mesas are the Hopi universe, and Second Mesa is the "Center of the Universe." **Shungopavi,** the largest and oldest village on Second Mesa, which was founded by the Bear Clan, is reached by a paved road angling south off AZ 264, between the junction of AZ 87 and the Hopi Cultural Center. The villagers here make silver overlay jewelry and coil plaques. Coil plaques are woven from galleta grass and yucca and are adorned with designs of kachinas, animals, and corn. The art of making the plaques has been passed from mother to daughter for generations, and fine coil plaques have become highly sought-after collector's items. The famous Hopi snake dances (closed to the public) are held here in August during even-numbered years.

Two smaller villages are off a paved road that runs north from AZ 264, about 2 mi east of the Hopi Cultural Center. **Mishongnovi,** the easternmost settlement, was established in the late 1600s. Set on a high mesa with views for more than 100 mi in every direction, **Sipaulovi** (☎ 928/737–5426 ⊕ *www.sipaulovihopiinformationcenter.org* ✉ *Guided tours $15* ⊙ *Tours weekdays 9–4*) was originally at the base of the mesa before moving to its present site in 1680. You can learn more about the community and its centuries-old traditions by watching a video at the small visitor center and taking one of the guided walking tours through the community. On these tours you have the chance to stop by local studios and talk with artists.

At the **Hopi Museum and Cultural Center,** you can stop for the night, learn about the people and their communities, and eat authentic Hopi cuisine. The museum here is dedicated to preserving Hopi traditions and to presenting those traditions to non-Hopi visitors. A gift shop sells works by local Hopi artisans at reasonable prices, and a modest picnic area on the west side of the building is a pleasant spot for lunch with a view of the San Francisco Peaks. ⊠ *AZ 264, Second Mesa* ☎ *928/734–2401* ⊕ *www.hopiculturalcenter.com* ☜ *Museum $4* ⊙ *Mid-Mar.–Oct., weekdays 8–4:30, weekends 9–3; Nov.–mid-Mar., weekdays 8–4:30.*

WHERE TO EAT AND STAY

$ ✕ **Hopi Cultural Center Restaurant.** The restaurant at the Hopi Cultural Cen-
SOUTHWESTERN ter is an attractive, light-filled room where you can sample traditional
★ tribal fare. Authentic dishes include Indian tacos, Hopi blue-corn pancakes, piki (paper-thin, blue-corn bread), fry bread (delicious with honey
or salsa), and *nok qui vi* (a tasty stew made with tender bits of lamb,
hominy, and mild green chiles). Breakfast is served starting at 6 in summer, an hour later in winter. ⊠ *5 mi west of AZ 87 on AZ 264, Second
Mesa* ☎ *928/734–2402* ⊕ *www.hopiculturalcenter.com* ☰ *DC, MC, V.*

$ ▦ **Hopi Cultural Center Motel.** This Hopi-run establishment is the only
place to eat or sleep in the immediate area, but because of its remote
location it usually has some vacancies. The attractive adobe building
with a tan-and-reddish-brown exterior contains clean, quiet, moderately priced rooms with coffeemakers. **Pros:** adjacent to cultural center;
only place to stay for miles in either direction; peaceful setting. **Cons:**
remote unless you are here to explore Hopi culture; fairly basic rooms;
no high-speed Internet. ⊠ *5 mi west of AZ 87 on AZ 264, Second Mesa*
☎ *928/734–2401* ⊕ *www.hopiculturalcenter.com* ☜ *30 rooms* ⌂ *In-
room: a/c. In-hotel: restaurant* ☰ *DC, MC, V.*

SHOPPING

The venerable **Hopi Arts and Crafts/Silvercrafts Cooperative Guild** (⊠ *383 AZ
264, Second Mesa* ☎ *928/734–2463*), just west of the Hopi Cultural Center and in existence since the 1940s, hosts craftspeople selling their wares;
you might even see silversmiths at work here. Shops at the **Hopi Cultural
Center** (⊠ *AZ 264, Second Mesa* ☎ *928/734–2401*) carry the works of
local artists and artisans. At **Hopi Fine Arts** (⊠ *AZ 264 at AZ 87, Second
Mesa* ☎ *928/737–2222*), proprietor and musician Alph Secakuku is a
native of the Hopi Pueblo and an authority on all arts and crafts of the
Hopi people. He represents about 75 active artisans in his user-friendly
gallery. **Tsa-Kursh-Ovi** (⊠ *AZ 264, Second Mesa* ☎ *928/734–2478*), 1.5 mi
east of the Hopi Cultural Center, is a small shop where Hopi come to buy
bundles of sweetgrass and sage, deer hooves with which to make rattles,
and ceremonial belts adorned with seashells. The proprietor's wife, Janice
Day, is a renowned Hopi basket maker. The shop has one of the largest
collections of Hopi baskets in the Southwest.

THIRD MESA

12 mi northwest of Second Mesa, on AZ 264.

GETTING HERE AND AROUND

The Third Mesa communities are the closest to Tuba City, about 50 mi
away along AZ 264.

EXPLORING

Third Mesa villages are known for their agricultural accomplishments,
textile weaving, wicker baskets, silver overlay, and plaques. You'll find
crafts shops and art galleries, as well as occasional roadside vendors,

along AZ 264. ■TIP→ The Hopi Tribal Headquarters and Office of Public Relations in Kykotsmovi should be visited first for necessary permissions to visit the villages of Third Mesa.

Kykotsmovi, at the eastern base of Third Mesa, is literally translated as "ruins on the hills" for the many sites on the valley floor and in the surrounding hills. Present-day Kykotsmovi was established by Hopi people from Oraibi—a few miles west—who either converted to Christianity or who wished to attend school and be educated. Kykotsmovi is the seat of the Hopi Tribal Government.

Old Oraibi, a few miles west and on top of Third Mesa at about 7,200 feet in elevation, is believed to be the oldest continuously inhabited community in the United States, dating from around AD 1150. It was also the site of a rare, bloodless conflict between two groups of the Hopi people; in 1906, a dispute, settled uniquely by a "push of war" (a pushing contest), sent the losers off to establish the town of Hotevilla. Oraibi is a dusty spot and, as a courtesy, tourists are asked to park their cars outside and approach the village on foot.

Hotevilla and **Bacavi** are about 4 mi west of Oraibi, and their inhabitants are descended from the former residents of that village. The men of Hotevilla continue to plant crops and beautiful gardens along the mesa slopes. ⊠ *Cultural Preservation Office, AZ 264* ⊕ *Box 123, Kykotsmovi 86039* ☎ *928/734–3000 or 928/734–3612* ⊕ *www.nau. edu/~hcpo-p* ☉ *Weekdays 8:30–5.*

EN ROUTE Beyond Hotevilla, AZ 264 descends from Third Mesa, exits the Hopi Reservation, and crosses into Navajo territory, past **Coal Canyon**, where Native Americans have long mined coal from the dark seam just below the rim. The colorful mudstone, dark lines of coal, and bleached white rock have an eerie appearance, especially by the light of the moon. Twenty miles west of Coal Canyon, at the junction of AZ 264 and U.S. 160, is the town of Moenkopi, the last Hopi outpost. Established as a farming community, it was settled by the descendants of former Oraibi residents.

NAVAJO NATION WEST

The Hopi Reservation is like a doughnut hole surrounded by the Navajo Nation. If you approach the Grand Canyon from U.S. 89, via Flagstaff, north of the Wupatki National Monument, you'll find two significant sites in the western portions of the Navajo Reservation, the Cameron Trading Post and Tuba City. Situated 45 mi west of the Hopi town of Hotevilla, Tuba City is a good stopover if you're traveling east to the Hopi Mesas or northeast to Page.

At Cameron, the turnoff point for the South Rim of the Grand Canyon, the Cameron Trading Post was built in 1916 and commemorates Ralph Cameron, a pre-statehood territorial-legislative delegate. The sheer walls of the Little Colorado River canyon about 10 mi west of U.S. 89 along AZ 64 are quite impressive, and also worth a stop.

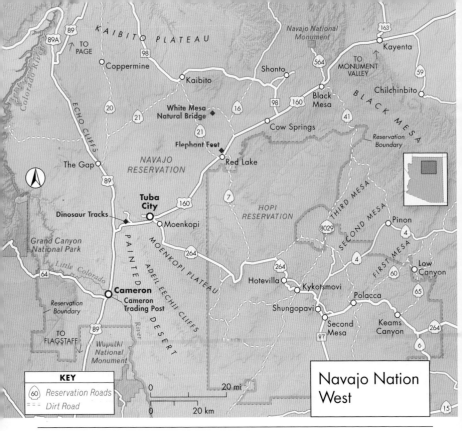

TUBA CITY

52 mi northwest of Third Mesa on AZ 264.

Tuba City, believed to be named after a Hopi chief "Tsuve," has about 8,200 permanent residents and is the administrative center for the western portion of the Navajo Nation. In addition to a hotel, hostel, and a few restaurants, this small town has a hospital, a bank, a trading post, and a movie theater. In late October Tuba City hosts the Western Navajo Fair, a celebration combining traditional Navajo song and dance with a parade, pageant, and countless arts-and-crafts exhibits.

GETTING HERE AND AROUND

Tuba City is one of the main base communities in the Navajo and Hopi region as well as a potential base for exploring either rim of the Grand Canyon from the east. The town lies about midway between Flagstaff and Page (80 mi from each) via U.S. 89 and U.S. 160, and 60 mi from the eastern entrance to the South Rim of the Grand Canyon via AZ 64, U.S. 89, and U.S. 160.

EXPLORING

The octagonal **Tuba City Trading Post** (⊠ *Main St. at Moenave Rd.* ☎ *928/283–5441*), founded in the early 1870s, sells groceries and authentic, reasonably priced Navajo rugs, pottery, baskets, and jewelry—it's adjacent to the Quality Inn Navajo Nation.

★ The tribe operates the dramatic 7,000-square-foot **Explore Navajo Interactive Museum**, which is set inside a geodesic dome–shape structure, meant to recall a traditional Navajo hogan, and contains a vast trove of artifacts, photos, artwork, and memorabilia. One of the more poignant exhibits tells of the infamous "Long Walk" of 1864, when the U.S. military forced the Navajo to leave their native lands and march to an encampment at Fort Sumner, New Mexico, where they were confined for more than four years. The museum also operates the small **Navajo Code Talkers Memorial Museum** in the back of the Tuba City Trading Post next door. Both facilities are adjacent to the Quality Inn Navajo Nation. ⊠ *Main St.* ☎ *800/644–8383* ⊕ *www.explorenavajo.com* 🖃 *$9* ☉ *Mon.–Sat. 8–6, Sun. noon–6.*

☼ About 5.5 mi west of Tuba City, between mileposts 316 and 317 on U.S. 160, is a small sign for the **Dinosaur Tracks**. More than 200 million years ago a dilophosaurus—a carnivorous bipedal reptile over 10 feet tall—left tracks in mud that turned to sandstone. There's no charge for a look. Ask the locals about guiding you to the nearby petroglyphs and freshwater springs.

Four miles west of the dinosaur tracks on U.S. 160 is the junction with U.S. 89. This is one of the most colorful regions of the **Painted Desert**, with amphitheaters of maroon, orange, and red rocks facing west; it's especially glorious at sunset.

WHERE TO EAT

$$
SOUTHWESTERN
✕**Hogan Restaurant**. The fare at this spot adjacent to the Quality Inn Navajo Nation is mostly Southwestern and Mexican, but the kitchen also serves basic American and Navajo dishes, including tasty barbecue ribs, honey-glazed ham, and herb-roasted chicken. The chicken enchiladas and beef tamales are also quite good. Breakfast is served, too. ⊠ *Main St. (AZ 264)* ☎ *928/283–5260* ⊕ *www.qualityinntubacity.com* 🖃 *AE, D, DC, MC, V.*

$
AMERICAN
✕**Kate's Cafe**. A favorite of locals, this all-American café in a simple adobe house serves breakfast—try the vegetarian omelet—lunch, and dinner. At lunch choose from hearty charbroiled Baja burgers (topped with tomato, avocado, bacon, and Monterey Jack), Kate's club sandwich, grilled chicken, or salads. Dinner selections include several pasta specials and charbroiled New York strip steak. For local color and fine food at reasonable prices, this is the place to go. Espresso and designer-coffee drinks are also served. ⊠ *Edgewater Dr. at Main St. (AZ 264)* ☎ *928/283–6773* 🖃 *No credit cards.*

¢
SOUTHWESTERN
✕**Tuuvi Cafe**. This casual spot inside the largest truck stop and travel center in the region serves simple but well-prepared Southwestern and American food, from native fry bread tacos to charbroiled burgers. There's always a stew of the day—perhaps corn-squash-and-mutton, or green-chile-and-chicken—and homemade peach pie is a dessert specialty. Noteworthy,

too, are the hearty breakfasts, such as chicken-fried steak with eggs, and the Hopi Special of eggs, bacon or Spam, and homemade biscuits and gravy. ⊠ *U.S. 160 at AZ 264* ☎ *928/283–4374* ▭ *AE, D, MC, V.*

WHERE TO STAY

$–$$ 🖬 **Moenkopi Legacy Inn & Suites**. Opened by the Hopi tribe in early 2010 across the street from the Tuuvi Travel Center, this striking, contemporary hotel contains light-filled, boldly colored rooms, flat-screen TVs, work desks, and coffeemakers—those on the third floor have impressive views of the San Francisco Peaks in the distance (as does a large common lounge). Suites have granite counters and more legroom. Off the lobby are an attractively landscaped saltwater pool, hot tub, and garden. Complimentary Continental breakfast is prepared each morning by the Tuuvi Cafe, across the street, and served in the art-filled, high-ceilinged lobby. **Pros:** high-quality furnishings and linens; several public areas for lounging; pool is perfect spot to end a day of hiking. **Cons:** no restaurant on-site (although Hopi run a café across the street and there's a Denny's next door); at a busy intersection. ⊠ *AZ 264 at U.S. 160* ✉ *Box 2260, Moenkopi 86045* ☎ *928/283–4500* ⊕ *www.experiencehopi.com* ⇥ *84 rooms, 16 suites* ⚷ *In-room: a/c, refrigerator (some), Wi-Fi. In-hotel: pool, gym, laundry facilities, some pets allowed* ▭ *AE, D, DC, MC, V.*

$ 🖬 **Quality Inn Navajo Nation**. This hotel has a trading post and shops for essentials, gifts, and souvenirs. Standard rooms are spacious and well maintained, fine for an overnight stop before or after a visit to the Hopi Mesas. To better compete with Tuba City's new Moenkopi Legacy Inn, the somewhat aged property has made a number of improvements, including upgraded room furnishings. **Pros:** rooms have attractive Navajo-style prints and furnishings; Navajo museum and trading post are within walking distance; decent restaurant on-site. **Cons:** rates are a little high for what you get; an older property. ⊠ *Main St. at Moenave Rd.* ✉ *Box 247, Tuba City 86045* ☎ *928/283–4545 or 800/644–8383* ⊕ *www.qualityinntubacity.com* ⇥ *78 rooms, 2 suites* ⚷ *In-room: a/c, refrigerator (some), Wi-Fi. In-hotel: restaurant, laundry facilities, some pets allowed* ▭ *AE, D, DC, MC, V.*

SHOPPING

The **Native American swap meet** (⊠ *Main St.*), behind the community center and next to the baseball field, held every Friday from 8 AM on, has great deals on jewelry, jewelry-making supplies, semiprecious stones, rugs, pottery, and other arts and crafts; there are also food concessions and booths selling herbs.

CAMERON TRADING POST

25 mi southwest of Tuba City on U.S. 89.

Cameron Trading Post and Motel, established in 1916 overlooking a spectacular gorge and vintage suspension bridge, is one of the few remaining authentic trading posts in the Southwest. A convenient stop if you're driving from the Hopi Mesas to the Grand Canyon, it has reasonably priced dining, lodging, camping, and shopping.

GETTING HERE AND AROUND

The trading post is along the main highway (U.S. 89) between Flagstaff and Page and just 30 mi from the eastern entrance to the South Rim of the Grand Canyon.

WHERE TO STAY

$ ⛄ **Cameron Trading Post.** At the turnoff for the western entrance to the Grand Canyon's South Rim, this trading post dates back to 1916. Southwestern-style rooms have carved-oak furniture, tile baths, and balconies overlooking the Colorado River. Native-stone landscaping—including fossilized dinosaur tracks—and a small, well-kept garden are pleasant. Make your reservations far in advance for high season. **Pros:** impressive collection of Southwestern art in the trading post gallery and gift shop; restaurant serves up Native American specialties and American favorites; historic lodging with campground next door.**Cons:** high traffic volume; highway noise; basic rooms. ⊠ *U.S. 89, milepost 466* ⌖ *Box 339, Cameron 86020* ☎ *928/679–2231, 800/338–7385 Ext. 414 (for hotel)* ⊕ *www.camerontradingpost.com* ⮑ *62 rooms, 4 suites* ⚷ *In-room: a/c, Wi-Fi. In-hotel: restaurant, some pets allowed* ⊟ *AE, D, DC, MC, V.*

SHOPPING

Fine authentic Navajo products are sold at an outlet of the **Navajo Arts and Crafts Enterprises** (⊠ *U.S. 89 at AZ 64, Cameron* ☎ *928/679–2244* ⊕ *www.gonavajo.com/navajoart*), open since 1941.

EN ROUTE As you proceed toward Kayenta, 22 mi northeast of Tuba City on U.S. 160, you'll come to the tiny community of Red Lake. Off to the left of the highway is a geologic phenomenon known as **Elephant Feet.** These massive eroded-sandstone buttes offer a great family photo opportunity: pose under the enormous columns. Northwest of here at the end of a graded dirt road in Navajo backcountry is **White Mesa Natural Bridge,** a massive arch of white sandstone that extends from the edge of White Mesa. The long **Black Mesa** plateau runs for about 15 mi along U.S. 160. Above the prominent escarpments of this land formation, mining operations—a major source of revenue for the Navajo Nation—delve into the more than 20 billion tons of coal deposited there.

MONUMENT VALLEY

The magnificent Monument Valley stretches to the northeast of Kayenta into Utah. At a base altitude of about 5,500 feet, the sprawling, arid expanse was once populated by Ancestral Puebloan people (more popularly known by the Navajo word *Anasazi,* which means both "ancient ones" and "ancient enemies") and in the last few centuries has been home to generations of Navajo farmers. The soaring red buttes, eroded mesas, deep canyons, and naturally sculpted rock formations of Monument Valley are easy to enjoy on a leisurely drive.

At U.S. 163 and the Monument Valley entrance is a street of disheveled buildings called Vendor Village. Here you can purchase trinkets and souvenirs; bartering is perfectly acceptable and expected.

KAYENTA

75 mi northeast of Tuba City, on U.S. 160, 22 mi south of Monument Valley.

Kayenta, a small and rather dusty town with a couple of convenience stores, three chain motels, and a hospital, is a good base for exploring nearby Monument Valley Navajo Tribal Park and the Navajo National Monument. The Burger King in town has an excellent "Navajo Code Talker" exhibit, with lots of memorabilia relating to this heroic World War II marine group.

GETTING HERE AND AROUND

Kayenta is the first sizable community you reach if driving to the Navajo Nation via the Four Corners on U.S. 160 or U.S. 163.

EXPLORING

Take a self-guided walking tour through the small outdoor cultural park, the **Navajo Cultural Center of Kayenta,** which describes the beliefs and traditions that have shaped North America's largest Native American tribe. ⊠ *U.S. 160 between Hampton Inn and Burger King* ☎ *928/697–3170* ⊕ *www.kayenta.nndes.org* 🖼 *Free* ☉ *Daily 7AM–sunset.*

WHERE TO EAT

¢
SOUTHWESTERN

✕ **Amigo Cafe.** The tables are packed with locals who frequent this small establishment, where everything is made from scratch. The delicious fry bread is the real draw. If you've never had a Navajo taco or Navajo hamburger, this is a good place to be initiated. The café also serves excellent Mexican fare and traditional American dishes. Dine on the adobe-walled patio in warm weather. ⊠ *U.S. 163 just north of U.S. 160* ☎ *928/697–8448* 🖃 *MC, V* ☉ *Closed Sun.*

$$
AMERICAN
★

✕ **Reuben Heflin Restaurant.** Hampton Inn hotels aren't known for their restaurants, but this attractive spot just off the lobby serves the best food in town. Upholstered Navajo-print chairs with rustic lodgepole frames, hammered-tin sconces, a wood-beam ceiling, and a mammoth adobe fireplace set an inviting mood for the American fare with a regional bent. The sheepherder's sandwich (roast beef, provolone, and green chile in a Navajo taco) is a local favorite, but also consider chicken-fried steak, fajitas, and sautéed Idaho trout. ⊠ *Hampton Inn, U.S. 160* ☎ *928/697–3170* 🖃 *AE, D, DC, MC, V* ☉ *No lunch mid-Oct.–mid-Mar.*

WHERE TO STAY

$–$$

🏨 **Best Western Wetherill Inn.** This clean two-story motel with a red-tile roof has Southwestern decor and a well-stocked gift shop. Rooms have basic furnishings and open to a parking lot, but attractive shrubbery and trees provide a bit of greenery, and there's a very basic but simple diner called Golden Sands a short stroll away. **Pros:** a little closer to Monument Valley than other properties in town; clean rooms; slightly cheaper than competitors. **Cons:** bland setting; ordinary room furnishings. ⊠ *U.S. 163* 🖂 *Box 175, Kayenta 86033* ☎ *928/697–3231 or 800/528–1234* ⊕ *www.bestwesternarizona.com* 🛏 *54 rooms* 🖔 *In-room: a/c, Wi-Fi. In-hotel: pool, Wi-Fi hotspot* 🖃 *AE, D, DC, MC, V.*

$–$$

🏨 **Hampton Inn of Kayenta.** This warm and inviting hotel is the best accommodation in the area, and it's little different from any other in the chain,

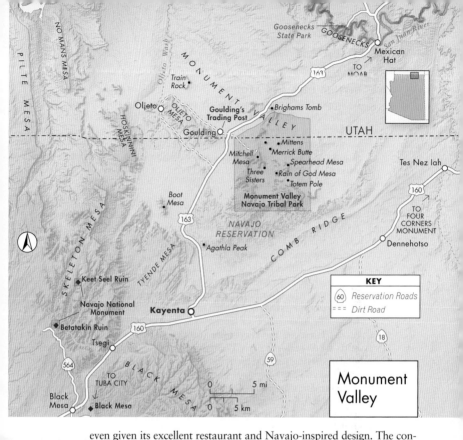

Monument Valley

KEY
(60) Reservation Roads
= = = Dirt Road

even given its excellent restaurant and Navajo-inspired design. The contemporary, comfortable rooms and lobby are tastefully decorated with Southwest textures, and the restaurant is staffed by Native Americans wearing traditional Navajo garb. There's a free Continental-breakfast bar, a patio with a beehive fireplace, and a notably impressive gift shop with top-quality Native American art and unique gifts. Packages are available that include discounted guided tours of Monument Valley. **Pros:** clean and updated rooms; welcoming staff; excellent restaurant. **Cons:** on busy and unattractive road. ⊠ *U.S. 160* 🖃 *Box 1219, Kayenta 86033* ☎ *928/697–3170* ⊕ *www.hamptoninn.com* ⟿ *73 rooms* ⚏ *In-room: a/c, Wi-Fi. In-hotel: restaurant, pool, some pets allowed* ⊟ *AE, D, DC, MC, V* ⏐⏐CP.

$–$$　⛺ **Holiday Inn Monument Valley**. This '70s-style, bland-looking cluster of buildings overlooking a bland highway lined with gas stations doesn't offer much curb appeal. But a welcoming staff, prosaic but clean rooms, and a commendable on-site restaurant make it a worthwhile option, especially if the nearby Hampton Inn is already booked. The gift shop offers traditional local arts and crafts. **Pros:** nice restaurant; friendly staff. **Cons:** on an unappealing stretch of road; a bit dated. ⊠ *U.S. 160 just south of junction with U.S. 163* 🖃 *Box 307, Kayenta 86033* ☎ *928/697–3221 or 888/465–4329* ⊕ *www.holidayinn.com* ⟿ *162 rooms* ⚏ *In-room: a/c, Wi-Fi. In-hotel: restaurant, pool, gym, laundry facilities* ⊟ *AE, D, DC, MC, V*.

MONUMENT VALLEY NAVAJO TRIBAL PARK

24 mi northeast of Kayenta, off U.S. 163.

GETTING HERE AND AROUND

It's impossible not to drive slowly on this park's bumpy roads, which are best conquered with an SUV or all-wheel-drive vehicle (especially during rainy times of year), but if you take your time and exercise caution, you can make the entire drive in a conventional car. If in doubt, inquire at the drive's entrance gate. Call ahead for road conditions in winter. The park is just off U.S. 163 north of the Arizona/Utah border and very well marked.

EXPLORING

© **Monument Valley Navajo Tribal Park.** For generations, the Navajo have

Fodor's Choice grown crops and herded sheep in Monument Valley, considered to be

★ one of the most scenic and mesmerizing destinations in the Navajo Nation. Within Monument Valley lies the 30,000-acre Monument Valley Navajo Tribal Park, where eons of wind and rain have carved the mammoth red-sandstone monoliths into memorable formations. The monoliths, which jut hundreds of feet above the desert floor, stand on the horizon like sentinels, frozen in time and unencumbered by electric wires, telephone poles, or fences—a scene virtually unchanged for centuries. These are the very same nostalgic images so familiar to movie buffs who recall the early Western films of John Wayne. A 17-mi self-guided driving tour on an extremely rough dirt road (there's only one road, so you can't get lost) passes the memorable **Mittens** and **Totem Pole** formations, among others. Also be sure to walk (15 minutes round-trip) from North Window around the end of Cly Butte for the views.

The **Monument Valley Visitor Center** was handsomely redesigned and expanded in 2009 and has an extensive crafts shop and exhibits devoted to ancient and modern Native American history. Most of the independent guided tours here use enclosed vans and charge about $20 to $25 for 2½ hours. You can generally find Navajo guides—who will escort you to places that you are not allowed to visit on your own—in the center or through the booths in the parking lot. It adjoins the stunning View Hotel, which sits on a gradual rise overlooking the valley, with big-sky views in every direction. The park also has a 99-site campground, which closes from early October through April. ⊠ *Visitor center, off U.S. 163, 24 mi north of Kayenta, Monument Valley* ✆ *Box 2520, Window Rock 86515* ☎ *435/727–5874* ⊕ *www.navajonationparks.org* ⬧ *$5* ☉ *Visitor center: May–Sept., daily 6 AM–8:30 PM; Oct.–Apr., daily 7–7.*

SPORTS AND THE OUTDOORS

HIKING, **Monument Valley Tours** (☎ *435/727–3313 or 866/422–8687* ⊕ *www.*
HORSEBACK *moab-utah.com/totempole*) offers jeep tours, some including entertain-
RIDING, AND ment and outdoor barbecues. Jeep tours of the valley, from hour-long
JEEP TOURS to overnight, can be arranged through Roland Cody Dixon at **Roland's Navajoland Tours** (☎ *520/697–3524*); he offers cultural tours with crafts demonstrations, camping, and photography. **Sacred Monument Tours** (☎ *435/727–3218 or 928/380–4527* ⊕ *www.monumentvalley. net*) has hiking, jeep, photography, and horseback-riding tours into Monument Valley. **Simpson's Trailhandler Tours** (☎ *435/727–3362* ⊕ *www.*

DID YOU KNOW?

If Monument Valley looks familiar, it probably should. Scenes from many movies, including *How the West Was Won, Forrest Gump, Stagecoach, 2001: A Space Odyssey,* and *Wind Talkers* have been filmed here.

trailhandlertours.com) offers four-wheel-drive jeep trips, photography and hiking tours, and the chance to stay overnight in a traditional Navajo hogan.

WHERE TO EAT

SOUTHWESTERN

★

✕ **View Restaurant.** Connected to the View Hotel through a second-floor breezeway, this airy space comprises a few high-ceilinged rooms with massive plate-glass windows framing mesmerizing views of the valley—in warm weather you can dine outside on a terrace, awed by the same panorama. Navajo rugs and local art hang on the walls above the light-wood tables and chairs, and the tribal visitor center's extensive curio shop is attached. The food is well prepared if fairly typical of the region: green chile stew, Navajo tacos, steaks, and the like. There's also a smaller self-serve section where you can grab sandwiches and light snacks. ⊠ *Off U.S. 163, 24 mi north of Kayenta* ☎ *435/727–5555* ⊕ *www.monumentvalleyview.com* ⊟ *AE, MC, V.*

WHERE TO STAY

$$$
Fodor'sChoice
★

⊡ **View Hotel.** The Navajo tribe opened this sleek, three-story, red-stucco hotel on a bluff beside the visitor center in fall 2008. It's the first lodging ever to open inside the Monument Valley Navajo Tribal Park, and the astounding vistas from every room in the hotel—even the elevators, which have windows—live up to the name. Nearly all the rooms face east toward the iconic Mittens and Totem Pole formations (a few look west and still enjoy terrific views). All have private balconies, flat-screen TVs, tile floors, and brightly hued Navajo bedspreads. You can read or relax in a cavernous lobby with tall windows, leather chairs, and hand-carved furnishings, or work out in a small gym looking out toward Mitchell Butte. More rooms and a full-service spa are planned with a further expansion in the next year or two. **Pros:** unbelievable panoramas from every room; stylish furnishings; eco-conscious bath products, appliances, and buildings standards. **Cons:** priciest lodging in the region; very remote. ⊠ *Off U.S. 163, 24 mi north of Kayenta* ⊡ *Box 360289, Monument Valley, UT 84536* ☎ *435/727–5555* ⊕ *www.monumentvalleyview. com* ⇶ *96 rooms* ⅄ *In-room: a/c, refrigerator, Wi-Fi (some). In-hotel: restaurant, gym, Wi-Fi hotspot* ⊟ *AE, D, DC, MC, V.*

OFF THE
BEATEN
PATH

Four Corners Monument. An inlaid brass plaque marks the only point in the United States where four states meet: Arizona, New Mexico, Colorado, and Utah. Despite the Indian wares and booths selling greasy food, there's not much else to do here but pay a fee and stay long enough to snap a photo; you'll see many a twisted tourist trying to get an arm or a leg in each state. The monument is a 75-mi drive from Kayenta and is administered by the Navajo Nation Parks and Recreation Department. ⊠ *7 mi northwest of the U.S. 160 and U.S. 64 junction, Teec Nos Pos* ☎ *928/871–6647 Navajo Parks & Recreation Dept.* ⊕ *www. navajonationparks.org* ⊠ *$3* ⊘ *Oct.–May, daily 8–5; June–Sept., daily 7AM–8 PM.*

> **WORD OF MOUTH**
>
> "I have been to the View Hotel in the Monument Valley twice now since it opened in December 08. It's absolutely the most spiritual and miraculous place you can go."
> —Jengle09

GOOSENECKS REGION, UTAH

Fodor'sChoice
★

33 mi north of Monument Valley Navajo Tribal Park, on U.S. 163.

Monument Valley's scenic route, U.S. 163, continues from Arizona into Utah, where the land is crossed, east to west, by a stretch of the San Juan River known as the Goosenecks—named for the myriad twists and curves it takes. This barren, erosion-blasted gorge has a stark beauty. This spot is a well-known take-out point for white-water runners on the San Juan, a river that vacationing sleuths will recognize as the setting of many of Tony Hillerman's Jim Chee mystery novels.

GETTING HERE AND AROUND

The scenic overlook for the Goosenecks is reached by turning west from U.S. 163 onto UT 261, 4 mi north of the small community of **Mexican Hat,** then proceeding on UT 261 for 1 mi to a directional sign at the road's junction with UT 316. Turn left onto UT 316 and proceed 4 mi to the vista-point parking lot.

WHERE TO STAY

$
★

San Juan Inn & Trading Post. The inn's Southwestern-style, rustic rooms overlooking the river at Mexican Hat are clean and well maintained, and the setting against the red rocks is quite inspiring. Diners can watch the river at the Old Bridge Grille, which serves great grilled steak and juicy hamburgers, fresh trout, and inexpensive Navajo dishes—it's also the only place for 100 mi in any direction with a liquor license. **Pros:** magnificent setting; affordable rooms; parking is right outside your room. **Cons:** very basic room decor; no high-speed Internet. ⊠ *U.S. 163* ✆ *Box 310276, Mexican Hat, UT 84531* ☎ *435/683–2220 or 800/447–2022* ⊕ *www.sanjuaninn.net* ⊐ *36 rooms* ⌂ *In-room: a/c, Internet. In-hotel: restaurant, gym, laundry facilities, some pets allowed* ▭ *AE, D, DC, MC, V.*

GOULDING'S TRADING POST

2 mi west of entrance road to Monument Valley Navajo Tribal Park, off U.S. 163 on Indian Hwy. 42.

Established in 1924 by Harry Goulding and his wife "Mike," this trading post provided a place where Navajos could exchange livestock and handmade goods for necessities. Goulding's is probably best known, though, for being used as a headquarters by director John Ford when he filmed the Western classic *Stagecoach*. Today the compound has a lodge, restaurant, museum, gift shop, grocery store, and campground. The Goulding Museum displays Native American artifacts and Goulding family memorabilia, as well as an excellent multimedia show about Monument Valley.

WHERE TO STAY

$$–$$$

Goulding's Lodge. Nestled beneath a massive red-rock monolith, this two-level property affords spectacular views of Monument Valley from each room's private balcony. Before the View Hotel opened nearby with even more impressive views, this was the only lodging in the region offering truly knockout views. It has more history than its new competitor, but it's not nearly as plush. The on-premises Stagecoach restaurant, serving American fare, is decorated with Western movie memorabilia. Goulding's also conducts custom guided tours and provides Navajo guides into the backcountry. **Pros:** right in heart of Monument Valley; incredibly peaceful; indoor pool open all year. **Cons:** remote location; simple rooms; not cheap. ⊠ *Off U.S. 163, 24 mi north of Kayenta Goulding* ⌂ *Box 360001, Monument Valley, UT 84536* ☎ *435/727–3231* ⊕ *www.gouldings.com* ⇝ *62*

rooms ⚂ *In-room: a/c, refrigerator, DVD, Wi-Fi. In-hotel: restaurant, pool, laundry facilities* ▤ *AE, D, DC, MC, V.*

CAMPGROUND   ⚠ **Goulding's Good Sam Campground.** Views of Monument Valley are the
⚲   draw at this clean, modern campground. Check in at Goulding's grocery store (in Goulding's Trading Post). Campers have access—at no additional charge—to the 17-mi-loop drive around Monument Valley. Shuttle vans provide free transportation to Goulding's restaurant and museum. **Pros:** wonderful views; price includes admission to tribal park. **Cons:** somewhat pricey for tent sites. ⊠ *Off U.S. 163, 24 mi north of Kayenta* ⌂ *Box 360001, Monument Valley, UT 84536* ☎ *435/727–3235* ⇝ *66 RV sites, 50 tent sites* ⚂ *Flush toilets, full hookups, guest laundry, showers, grills, general store, play area, swimming (indoor pool)* ▤ *AE, D, DC, MC, V* ☉ *Open year-round; limited service Nov.–Mar. 15.*

NAVAJO NATIONAL MONUMENT

53 mi southwest of Goulding's Trading Post, 21 mi west of Kayenta.

GETTING HERE AND AROUND

From Kayenta, take U.S. 160 southwest to AZ 564 and follow signs 9 mi north to monument.

AZ 564 turns north off U.S. 160 at the Black Mesa gas station and convenience store, and leads to the visitor center. No food, gasoline, or hotel lodging is available at the monument.

The visitor center houses a small museum, exhibits of prehistoric pottery, and a good crafts shop. Free campground and picnic areas are nearby, and rangers sometimes present campfire programs in summer.

EXPLORING

Fodor'sChoice   At the **Navajo National Monument** two unoccupied 13th-century cliff
★   pueblos, Betatakin and Keet Seel, stand under the overhanging cliffs of Tsegi Canyon. The largest ancient dwellings in Arizona, these stone-and-mortar complexes were built by Ancestral Puebloans, obviously for permanent occupancy, but abandoned after less than half a century.

The well-preserved, 135-room **Betatakin** (Navajo for "ledge house") is a cluster of cliff dwellings from AS 1250 that seem to hang in midair before a sheer sandstone wall. When discovered in 1907 by a passing American rancher, the apartments were full of baskets, pottery, and preserved grains and ears of corn—as if the occupants had been chased away in the middle of a meal. For an impressive view of Betatakin, walk to the rim overlook about 0.5 mi from the visitor center. Ranger-led tours (a 5-mi, four-hour, strenuous round-trip hike including a 700-foot descent into the canyon) leave once a day from late May to early September at 8 AM and return between noon and 1 PM. No reservations are accepted; groups of no more than 25 form on a first-come, first-served basis.

Keet Seel (Navajo for "broken pottery") is also in good condition in a serene location, with 160 rooms and five kivas dating from AD 950. Explorations of Keet Seel, which lies at an elevation of 7,000 feet and is 8.5 mi from the visitor center on foot, are restricted: only 20 people are allowed to visit per day, and only between late May and early September, when a ranger is present at the site. A permit—which also allows campers to stay overnight nearby—is required. ■TIP→ Trips to Keet Seel are very popular, so reservations are taken up to two months in advance. Anyone who suffers from vertigo might want to avoid this trip: the trail leads down a 1,100-foot, near-vertical rock face. ⊠ *AZ 564, Black Mesa* ☎ *HC 71, Box 3, Tonalea 86044* ☏ *928/672–2700* ⊕ *www.nps.gov/nava* ✉ *Free* ☉ *Mid-May.–mid-Sept., weekdays 8–5, weekends 8–7; mid-Sept.–mid-May., daily 9–5; tours late May–early Sept.*

SPORTS AND THE OUTDOORS

HIKING Hiking is the best way for adventurous souls to see the Navajo National Monument. It's a fairly strenuous hike to the sites, but if you're fit and leave early enough, it's well worth it to visit some of the best-preserved ancient dwellings in the Southwest. It's free, but the trail is open only from late May through early September, and you need to call ahead to make a reservation, usually at least two months in advance. ☎ *Navajo National Monument, HC 71, Box 3, Tonalea 86044* ☏ *928/672–2366* ✉ *Free* ☉ *weekdays 8–5, weekends 8–7; tours late May–early Sept.*

WHERE TO STAY

$ ⓨ **Anasazi Inn–Tsegi Canyon.** On U.S. 160, 10 mi east of Black Mesa and

AMERICAN 9 mi west of Kayenta, this is the closest lodging to Navajo National Monument. The one-story property with a bright turquoise roof offers basic, clean accommodations with exterior entrances and commanding views of Tsegi Canyon. There's also a well-stocked gift shop and a restaurant that serves sandwiches, burgers, and basic Navajo fare—it's decent if nothing special, but it's also the only dining option for miles around. **Pros:** close to Navajo National Monument; affordable. **Cons:** dated furnishings; remote location; no high-speed Internet. ⊠ *Off U.S. 160, 9 mi west of Kayenta* ☎ *Box 1543, Kayenta 86033* ☏ *928/697–3793* ⊕ *www.anasaziinn.com/tsegicanyon* ⌑ *57 rooms* ⌂ *In-room: a/c. In-hotel: restaurant* ⊟ *AE, D, MC, V.*

GLEN CANYON DAM AND LAKE POWELL

Lake Powell is the heart of the huge 1.25-million-acre Glen Canyon National Recreation Area. Created by the barrier of Glen Canyon Dam in the Colorado River, Lake Powell is ringed by red cliffs that twist off into 96 major canyons and countless inlets (most accessible only by boat) with huge, red-sandstone buttes randomly jutting from the sapphire waters. It extends through terrain so rugged it was the last major area of the United States to be mapped. You could spend 30 years exploring the lake and still not experience everything there is to see. The Sierra Club has started a movement to drain the lake to restore water-filled Glen Canyon, which some believe was more spectacular than the Grand Canyon, but the lake is likely to be around for years to come.

South of Lake Powell the landscape gives way to **Echo Cliffs,** orange-sandstone formations rising 1,000 feet and more above the highway in places. At **Bitter Springs** the road ascends the cliffs and provides a spectacular view of the 9,000-square-mi Arizona Strip to the west and the 3,000-foot Vermilion Cliffs to the northwest.

PAGE

90 mi west of the Navajo National Monument, 136 mi north of Flagstaff on U.S. 89.

Built in 1957 as a Glen Canyon Dam construction camp, Page is now a tourist spot and a popular base for day trips to Lake Powell; it has also become a major point of entry to the Navajo Nation. The nearby Vermilion Cliffs are where the California condor, an endangered species, has been successfully reintroduced into the wild. The town's human population of nearly 7,100 makes it the largest community in far-northern Arizona, and each year more than 3 million people come to play at Lake Powell.

GETTING HERE AND AROUND

Most of the motels, restaurants, and shopping centers are concentrated along **Lake Powell Boulevard,** the name given to U.S. 89 as it loops through the business district.

The only airline that offers service directly to northeastern Arizona is Great Lakes Aviation, which flies into Page Municipal Airport from Phoenix as well as from Denver (with a stop in Farmington, New Mexico).

ESSENTIALS

Visitor Info Page/Lake Powell Chamber of Commerce (☎ 928/645–2741 or 888/261–7243 ⊕ www.pagelakepowelltourism.com)

Transportation Contacts Great Lakes Aviation (☎ 800/554–5111 ⊕ www.greatlakesav.com). **Page Municipal Airport** (☎ 928/645–4337 ⊕ www.cityofpage.org/airport.htm).

EXPLORING

At the corner of North Navajo Drive and Lake Powell Boulevard is the **John Wesley Powell Memorial Museum,** whose namesake led the first known expeditions down the Green River and the rapids-choked Colorado

Ancestral Puebloans' construction methods and their mysterious fate are worth pondering during a visit to Navajo National Monument.

through the Grand Canyon between 1869 and 1872. Powell mapped and kept detailed records of his trips, naming the Grand Canyon and many other geographic points of interest in northern Arizona. Artifacts from his expeditions are displayed in the museum. The museum also doubles as the town's visitor information center. A travel desk dispenses information and allows you to book boating tours, raft trips, scenic flights, accommodations in Page, or Antelope Canyon tours. When you sign up for tours here, concessionaires give a donation to the nonprofit museum with no extra charge to you. ⊠ *6 N. Lake Powell Blvd.* ☎ *928/645-9496 or 888/597-6873* ⊕ *www.powellmuseum.org* ▨ *$5* ☼ *Weekdays 9–5; Memorial Day–Labor Day also open Sat., call for hrs.*

The **Navajo Village Heritage Center** imparts an understanding of life on the reservation. You can take a guided tour of a traditional Navajo hogan and bread oven. For $50 per person (or $130 per family) the village hosts a 2½-hour "Evening with the Navajo–Grand Tour," which includes an hour of cultural entertainment and a Navajo taco dinner around a campfire. Less-extensive (and less-expensive) versions of the tour are also available. ⊠ *531 Haul Rd.* ☎ *928/660-0304* ⊕ *www. navajo-village.com* ▨ *$5* ☼ *Apr.–Oct., daily 10–3.*

SPORTS AND THE OUTDOORS
For water sports on Lake Powell, see Wahweap below.

Glen Canyon Recreation Area (☎ *928/608-6200* ⊕ *www.nps.gov/glca*) has a helpful Web site.

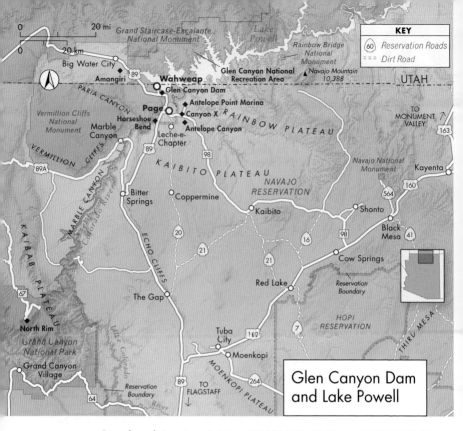

Glen Canyon Dam and Lake Powell

AIR TOURS Page-based **American Aviation** (☎ 928/608–1060 or 866/525–3247 ⊕ *www.americanaviationwest.com*) offers flightseeing tours of Monument Valley, Lake Powell and Rainbow Bridge, and Bryce.

FLOAT TRIPS **Colorado River Discovery** (☎ *888/522–6644 ⊕ www.raftthecanyon.com*) offers waterborne tours, including a 5½-hour guided rafting excursion down a calm portion of the Colorado River on comfortable, motorized pontoon boats ($78). The scenery—multicolor-sandstone cliffs adorned with Native American petroglyphs—is spectacular. The trips are offered twice daily from May through September, and once a day in March, April, October, and November (no tours in winter). The company also offers full-day rowing trips along the river, using smaller boats maneuvered by well-trained guides ($155). These trips—offered Sunday, Monday, and Wednesday—are quieter and more low-key, and provide a more intimate brush with this magnificent body of water.

GOLF **Lake Powell National Golf Course** (✉ *400 Clubhouse Dr., off U.S. 89* ☎ *928/645–2023 ⊕ www.golflakepowell.com ⌘ 18 holes. Par 72. 7064 yards. 139 slope. Green Fee: $69 ☞ Facilities: Golf carts*) has wide fairways, tiered greens with some of the steepest holes in the Southwest, and a generous lack of hazards. From the fairways you can enjoy spectacular vistas of Glen Canyon Dam and Lake Powell.

HIKING   The **Glen Canyon Hike** (⌧ *Off U.S. 89*), a short walk from the parking lot down a flight of uneven rock steps, takes you to a viewpoint on the canyon rim high above the Colorado River, and provides fantastic views of the Colorado as it flows through Glen Canyon. To reach the parking lot, turn west on Scenic View Drive, 1.5 mi south of Carl Hayden Visitor Center.

The **Horse Shoe Bend Trail** (⌧ *Off U.S. 89*) has some steep up-and-down paths and a bit of deep sand to maneuver; however, the views are well worth the hike. The trail leads up to a bird's-eye view of Glen Canyon and the Colorado River downstream from Glen Canyon Dam. There are some sheer drop-offs here, so watch children. To reach the trail, drive 4 mi south of Page on U.S. 89 and turn west onto a blacktop road 0.20 mi south of mile marker 545. It's a 0.75-mi hike from the parking area to the top of the canyon.

WHERE TO EAT

$$ ✗**Dam Bar and Grille.** The Dam's vaguely industrial-looking decor is
AMERICAN   quite urbane for this part of the world, and the kitchen turns out filling,
★   well-prepared food. Consider the 8-ounce cowboy steak topped with sautéed mushrooms and Swiss cheese, the smoked baby back ribs, the Southwest Cobb salad, or the burger topped with bacon, cheddar, and barbecue sauce. The Dam comprises a whole complex of establishments that also includes a sushi bar, coffeehouse, and saloon. ⌧ *644 N. Navajo Dr.* ☏ *928/645–2161* ⊕ *www.damplaza.com* ▤ *AE, MC, V.*

$ ✗**Fiesta Mexicana.** From the faux village-plaza decor, carved-wood
MEXICAN   booths, and piped-in mariachi music, this festive downtown eatery feels entirely predictable but quite pleasant. Part of a regional chain of Four Corners Mexican restaurants, Fiesta Mexicana prepares a nice range of traditional favorites, including particularly good chicken fajitas and massive margaritas. Dine on the covered patio for the best people-watching. ⌧ *125 S. Lake Powell Blvd.* ☏ *928/645–4082* ▤ *AE, D, MC, V.*

WHERE TO STAY

$–$$ ☷ **Best Western Arizonainn.** On a bluff at the northern end of Page, this modern, well-run motel has large rooms with queen-size beds and Southwestern-print bedspreads, and has fantastic views of Lake Powell, just 2 mi away. Butterfield Steakhouse serves Southwestern and standard American fare. **Pros:** panoramic views; close to downtown shopping and dining; nice gym and pool. **Cons:** run-of-the-mill decor. ⌧ *716 Rim View Dr.* ✑ *Box 250, Page 86040* ☏ *928/645–2466 or 800/826–2718* ⊕ *www.bestwestern.com/arizonainn* ➪ *103 rooms* ♿ *In-room: a/c, Internet. In-hotel: restaurant, bar, pool, gym, laundry facilities, some pets allowed* ▤ *AE, D, DC, MC, V* ¹⊙¹ *CP.*

$$–$$$ ☷ **Best Western at Lake Powell.** The newer of the two Best Westerns in town is a modern, three-story motel on a high bluff overlooking Glen Canyon Dam with dazzling views of the Vermilion Cliffs. The large rooms are functional but with tasteful, Southwest-inspired color schemes and designs, and the beds are quite plush. **Pros:** attractive room interiors; excellent views; close to downtown shopping and dining. **Cons:** pricier than the other Best Western. ⌧ *208 N. Lake Powell Blvd.* ☏ *928/645–5988 or 888/794–2888* ⊕ *www.bestwestern.com/atlakepowell* ➪ *132*

rooms ⚐ *In-room: a/c, Wi-Fi. In-hotel: pool, gym, laundry facilities* ▤ *AE, D, DC, MC, V* ⍐ *CP.*

$$
★ 🔲 **Canyon Colors B&B.** Run by personable New England transplants Bev and Rich Jones, this desert-country B&B occupies a simple, modern house in a quiet residential neighborhood near downtown. The

Sunflower and Paisley rooms, which can accommodate three and two, respectively, have queen beds and wood-burning stoves. The B&B also has an extensive video library, including many videos of Lake Powell and the Navajo Nation. **Pros:** personal attention; peaceful setting; central location. **Cons:** very small; need to book well ahead in summer. ⊠ *225 S. Navajo Dr.* ⬡ *Box 3657, Page 86040* ☎ *928/645–5979 or 800/536–2530* ⊕ *www.canyoncolors. com* ⬎ *2 rooms* ⚐ *In-room: a/c, refrigerator, Wi-Fi. In-hotel: pool, Internet terminal* ▤ *AE, MC, V* ⍐ *BP.*

$$–$$$ 🔲 **Courtyard by Marriott.** Page's top hotel lies just below the stunning grounds of Lake Powell National Golf Course, and has airy rooms decorated in a Southwestern motif with plush bedding and large TVs, health and fitness facilities, and dining at Peppers (closed late October through April), which serves predictable but consistent American and Mexican standards. **Pros:** lovely setting by golf course; good restaurant; the best and most modern room amenities in town. **Cons:** uphill walk to downtown restaurants and shopping. ⊠ *600 Clubhouse Dr.* ⬡ *Box 4150, Page 86040* ☎ *928/645–5000 or 888/236–2427* ⊕ *www. courtyard.com* ⬎ *153 rooms* ⚐ *In-room: a/c, Wi-Fi. In-hotel: restaurant, bar, pool, gym, laundry facilities* ▤ *AE, D, DC, MC, V.*

$ 🔲 **Days Inn & Suites.** Although part of an uneven chain of low-frills ★ motels, the Page Days Inn is first-rate among budget-friendly properties in the region. The attractive Southwest-style building sits atop a plateau with expansive views of the region, although it doesn't directly view Lake Powell. Rooms are plainly furnished, but have large windows or doors opening to small balconies. **Pros:** many rooms have balconies; super-friendly staff; panoramic views. **Cons:** need a car to get to downtown shopping and restaurants; rooms look rather ordinary; on a busy road at edge of town. ⊠ *961 N. U.S. 89* ☎ *928/645–2800 or 877/525–3769* ⊕ *www.daysinn.net* ⬎ *82 rooms* ⚐ *In-room: a/c, refrigerator, Wi-Fi. In-hotel: pool, laundry facilities, some pets allowed* ▤ *AE, D, MC, V* ⍐ *CP.*

CAMPGROUND ⚠ **Page–Lake Powell Campground.** Lake Powell is a popular destination ¢ and very busy in summer months, so make reservations if you're planning to stay at this in-town campground. The Antelope Point launch ramp on Lake Powell is 7 mi away. **Pros:** close to local restaurants. **Cons:** prosaic setting; can get crowded in summer. ⊠ *849 S. Coppermine Rd.* ☎ *928/645–3374* ⊕ *www.pagecampground.com* ⬎ *85 RV sites, 20 tent sites* ⚐ *Flush toilets, full hookups, partial hookups (electric and water), dump station, guest laundry, showers, picnic tables, general store, swimming (indoor pool)* ▤ *MC, V* ☺ *Open year-round.*

SHOPPING

★ There are numerous gift shops and clothing stores in the downtown area along Lake Powell Boulevard. There's lots of junk, but you can find authentic Native American arts and crafts, too. **Big Lake Trading Post** (✉ *1501 AZ 98* ☎ *928/645–2404* ⊕ *www.biglaketradingpost. com*) has a gas station, convenience store, car wash, and coin laundry. **Blair's Dinnebito Trading Post** (✉ *626 Navajo Dr.* ☎ *928/645–3008* ⊕ *www.blairstradingpost.com*) has been around for more than half a century. Authentic Native American arts and crafts are only a small part of what this store sells. Need tack equipment, rodeo ropes, rugs, saddlery, pottery? It's all here and reasonably priced. Wander upstairs and visit the Elijah Blair collection and memorabilia rooms.

LAKE POWELL FAST FACTS

■ Lake Powell is 185 mi long with 2,000 mi of shoreline—longer than America's Pacific Coast.

■ This is the second-largest man-made lake in the nation and it took 17 years to fill.

■ The Glen Canyon Dam is a 710-foot-tall wall of concrete.

ANTELOPE CANYON

4 mi east of Page on the Navajo Reservation, on AZ 98.

GETTING HERE AND AROUND

Access to Antelope Canyon is restricted by the Navajo tribe to licensed tour operators. The tribe charges a $6 per-person fee, included in the price of tours offered by the licensed concessionaires in Page. The easiest way to book a tour is in town at the John Wesley Powell Memorial Museum Visitor Center; you pay nothing extra for the museum's service. If you'd like to go directly to the tour operators, you can do that, too; visit ⊕ *www.navajonationparks.org/htm/antelopecanyon.htm* for a list of approved companies. Most companies offer 1- to 1½-hour sightseeing tours for about $25 to $32, or longer photography tours for $40 to $50. ■ TIP➔ The best time to see the canyon is between 8 AM and 2 PM.

EXPLORING

★ **Antelope Canyon.** You've probably seen dozens of photographs of Antelope Canyon, a narrow, red-sandstone slot canyon with convoluted corkscrew formations, dramatically illuminated by light streaming down from above. And you're likely to see assorted shutterbugs waiting patiently for just the right shot of these colorful, photogenic rocks, which are actually petrified sand dunes of a prehistoric ocean that once filled this portion of North America. The best photos are taken at high noon, when light filters through the slot in the canyon surface. This is one place where you'll need to protect your camera equipment against blowing dust. ✉ *AZ 98, Page* ☍ *Box 2520, Window Rock 86515* ☎ *928/871–6647 Navajo Parks & Recreation Dept.* ⊕ *www.navajonationparks.org* ☎ *$6 (included in tour cost).*

Houseboats are a unique lodging option; they're also great for exploring Lake Powell's almost 2,000 miles of shoreline.

ANTELOPE CANYON TOURS

Antelope Canyon Navajo Tours (☎ 928/698–3384 ⊕ *www.navajotours.com*) offers one-hour sightseeing tours and two-hour photography tours.

Antelope Canyon Tours (☎ 928/645–9102 or 866/645–9102 ⊕ *www. antelopecanyon.com*) offers several tours daily 8 AM–3 PM for sightseers and photographers. The photo tour gives serious and amateur photographers the opportunity to wait for the right light to photograph the canyon and get basic information on equipment setup.

John Wesley Powell Memorial Museum Visitor Center (☎ 928/645–9496 ⊕ *www.powellmuseum.org*) arranges and books 1½-hour tours and 2-hour photography tours, which leave at different times throughout the morning and early afternoon.

Overland Canyon Tours (☎ 928/608–4072 ⊕ *www.overlandcanyontours. com*) is one of only a few Native American–operated tour companies in Page. Tours include a narrative explaining the canyon's history and geology. On private property, the isolated slot canyon known as **Canyon X** can be toured only by Navajo guide Harley Klemm and his company, Overland Canyon Tours, which also operates popular tours to Antelope Canyon as well as guide service to the famed but hard-to-reach Wave sandstone formations in North Coyote Buttes, about 20 mi west of Page. Only one tour is given per day—departure times vary—and tours are offered by advance reservation only, with a limit of six participants. Because the area is rugged, children are not allowed, and participants should have good physical mobility to climb crevasses and some rough terrain.

SPORTS AND THE OUTDOORS

BOATING About 5 mi north of AZ 98, opposite the turnoff for Antelope Canyon, the Navajo Nation built **Antelope Point Marina** ✉ *End of Indian Rte. N22B, off AZ 98, 9 mi northeast of Page* ☎ *602/645–4500 Navajo Parks & Recreation Dept.* ⊕ *www.antelopepointlakepowell. com*) in 2003 on a scenic canyon of Lake Powell. This impressive 27,000-square-foot floating village has 300 wet slips for houseboats and watercraft, the very good Ja'di' Tooh restaurant and lounge, a seasonal ice-cream stand, a fishing dock, and a market. From here, boaters can access the other points along the lake, including the development at Wahweap. Eventually, the Navajo plan to add luxury casitas and a Navajo Cultural Center to this dramatic compound.

SLOT CANYONS

Slot canyons are unique to the Southwest. Carved through sandstone by wind and water, they are narrow at the top—some are only a foot wide on the surface—and wider at the bottom, which can be more than 100 feet below ground level. The play of light as it filters down through the slot onto the sandstone walls makes them remarkable subjects for photographs, but they are dangerous, particularly during the summer rainy season when flash floods can rush through them and sweep away an unwary hiker. Before hiking into a slot canyon, consult with locals and pay attention to weather forecasts.

5

WHERE TO EAT

AMERICAN ✗ **Ja'di' Tooh at Antelope Point Marina.** The floating, sandstone restaurant and lounge at the Navajo-operated Antelope Point Marina serves reliably well-prepared American food with contemporary accents— wood-fire pizzas, roast duck breast with cherry sauce, and a decadent white-chocolate truffle cake. You'll also find one of the better wine lists in the region. As good as the food is, the dramatic dining room with soaring windows overlooking a red-rock-wall section of Lake Powell is what really makes this place special. It's a long walk from the parking area to the front door, but staff whisk visitors to and fro in golf carts. ✉ *End of Indian Rte. N22B, off AZ 98, 9 mi northeast of Page* ☎ *928/645–5900* ⊕ *www.antelopepointlakepowell.com* ▭ *AE, D, MC, V* ☯ *Closed Mon.–Wed. in winter.*

GLEN CANYON NATIONAL RECREATION AREA

1 mi north of Page on U.S. 89.

GETTING HERE AND AROUND

Just off the highway at the north end of the bridge is the **Carl Hayden Visitor Center,** where you can learn about the controversial creation of Glen Canyon Dam and Lake Powell and enjoy panoramic views of both. To enter the visitor center you must go through a metal detector. Absolutely no bags are allowed inside.

EXPLORING

Glen Canyon Dam National Recreation Area. Once you leave the Page business district heading northwest, the Glen Canyon Dam National Recreation Area and Lake Powell behind it immediately become visible. This concrete-arch dam—all 5 million cubic feet of it—was completed in September 1963, its power plant an engineering feat that rivaled the Hoover Dam. The dam's crest is 1,560 feet across and rises 710 feet from bedrock and 583 feet above the waters of the Colorado River. When Lake Powell is full, it's 560 feet deep at the dam. The plant generates some 1.3 million kilowatts of electricity when each generator's 40-ton shaft is producing nearly 200,000 horsepower. Power from the dam serves a five-state grid consisting of Colorado, Arizona, Utah, California, and New Mexico, and provides energy for some 1.5 million users.

With only 8 inches of annual rainfall, the Lake Powell area enjoys blue skies nearly year-round. Summer temperatures range from the 60s to the 90s. Fall and spring are usually balmy, with daytime temperatures often in the 70s and 80s, but chilly weather can set in. Nights are cool even in summer, and in winter the risk of a cold spell increases, but all-weather houseboats and tour boats make for year-round cruising.

Boaters and campers should note that regulations require the use of portable toilets on the lake and lakeshore to prevent water pollution.

✉ *U.S. 89, 2 mi west of town, Page* ☎ *928/608–6404* 💲 *$15 per vehicle or $7 per person (entering on foot or by bicycle), good for up to 7 days; $16 per wk boating fee* ☼ *Visitor center: June–Aug., daily 8–6; Sept.–Nov. and Mar.–May, daily 8–5; Dec.–Feb., daily 8–4.*

WAHWEAP

5 mi north of Glen Canyon Dam on U.S. 89.

Most waterborne-recreational activity on the Arizona side of the lake is centered on this vacation village, where everything needed for a lakeside holiday is available: tour boats, fishing, boat rentals, dinner cruises, and more. The Lake Powell Resort has excellent views of the lake area, and you can take a boat tour from the Wahweap Marina.

GETTING HERE AND AROUND

Wahweap has two well-marked entrance roads off U.S. 89, one just north of Glen Canyon Dam, and the other about 3.5 mi north and more direct if arriving from Utah. Keep in mind that you must pay the Glen Canyon National Recreation Area entry fee upon entering Wahweap—this is true even if you're just passing through or having a meal at Lake Powell Resort (although the fee collection stations are often closed in winter, meaning you can pass through freely).

EXPLORING

★ A boat tour to **Rainbow Bridge National Monument** is a great way to see the enormity of the lake and its incredible, rugged beauty. This 290-foot red-sandstone arch is the world's largest natural bridge, and can be reached by boat or strenuous hike *(⇨ See Hiking)*. The lake level is down due to the prolonged drought throughout the region, so expect a 1.5-mi hike from the boat dock to the monument. The bridge can also

Midday light on Antelope Canyon's sandstone walls is a favorite shot for many photographers.

be viewed by air. To the Navajos this is a sacred area with deep religious and spiritual significance, so outsiders are asked not to hike underneath the arch itself. ☎ *928/608–6200* ⊕ *www.nps.gov/rabr*.

SPORTS AND THE OUTDOORS

BOAT TOURS Excursions on double-decker scenic cruisers piloted by experienced guides leave from the dock of **Lake Powell Resort** (⊠ *100 Lake Shore Dr.,* ☎ *928/645–2433 or 800/528–6154* ⊕ *www.lakepowell.com*). The most popular tour is the full-day trip to Rainbow Bridge National Monument for $100 (a box lunch is included); a half-day version is available, too. There's also a two-hour sunset dinner cruise ($75) featuring a prime-rib dinner—vegetarian lasagna meals are available if ordered in advance. It's served on the fully enclosed decks of the 95-foot *Canyon King* paddle wheeler, a reproduction of a 19th-century bay boat. Two-hour Antelope Canyon cruises are another favorite, costing about $32.

BOATING One of the most scenic lakes of the American West, Lake Powell has 185 mi of clear sapphire waters edged with vast canyons of red and orange rock. Ninety-six major side canyons intricately twist and turn into the main channel of Lake Powell, into what was once the main artery of the Colorado River through Glen Canyon. In some places the lake is 500 feet deep, and by June the lake's waters begin to warm and stay that way well into October.

At **Aramark's Lake Powell Resorts & Marinas** (☎ *928/645–1004 or 800/528–6154* ⊕ *www.visitlakepowell.com*) houseboat rentals range widely in size, amenities, and price, depending upon season. ⇨ *For more information on houseboats, see Houseboating in Where to Stay, below.* You may want to rent a powerboat or personal watercraft along with a houseboat to explore the many narrow canyons and waterways on the lake. A 19-foot powerboat for seven passengers runs approximately $400 and up per day. **Wahweap Marina** (⊠ *100 Lake Shore Dr.* ☎ *928/645–2433*) is the largest of the five full-service Lake Powell marinas run by Aramark's Lake Powell Resorts & Marinas. There are 850 slips and the most facilities, including a decent diner, public launch ramp, fishing dock, and marina store where you can buy fishing licenses and other necessities. It's the only full-service marina on the Arizona side of the lake (the other four—Dangling Rope, Hite, Bullfrog, and Halls Crossing—are in Utah).

FISHING Anglers delight in the world-class bass fishing on Lake Powell. You'll hear over and over how the big fish are "biting in the canyons," so you'll need a small vessel if you plan on fishing for the big one. Landing a 20-pound striper isn't unusual (the locals' secret is to use anchovies for bait). Fishing licenses for both Arizona and Utah are available at the **Marina Store at Wahweap Marina** (⊠ *100 Lake Shore Dr.* ☎ *928/645–1136*). **Stix Bait & Tackle** (⊠ *5 S. Lake Powell Blvd., Page* ☎ *928/645–2891* ⊕ *www.stixbaitandtackle.com*) can recommend local fishing guides.

HIKING Bring plenty of water when hiking and drink often. It's important to remember when hiking at Lake Powell to watch the sky for storms: it may not be raining where you are, but flooding can occur in downstream canyons—particularly slot canyons—from a storm miles away.

Only seasoned hikers in good physical condition will want to try either of the trails leading to **Rainbow Bridge**; both are about 26 to 28 mi round-trip through challenging and rugged terrain. This site is considered sacred by the Navajo, and it's requested that visitors show respect by not walking under the bridge. Take Indian Highway 16 north toward the Utah state border. At the fork in the road, take either direction for about 5 mi to the trailhead leading to Rainbow Bridge. Excursion boats pull in at the dock at the arch, but no supplies are sold there. **Navajo Nation Parks and Recreation Department** (⊠ *Bldg. 36A, E. AZ 264* ✉ *Box 2520, Window Rock 86515* ☎ *928/871–6647* ⊕ *www.navajonationparks.org*) provides backcountry permits (a small fee is charged), which must be obtained before hiking to Rainbow Bridge. Write to the office, and allow about a month to process the paperwork.

WHERE TO EAT AND STAY

$$$ ✕ **Rainbow Room.** The bi-level signature restaurant at the Lake Pow-
AMERICAN ell Resort occupies a cavernous round room affording 270-degree
Fodor's Choice views of the lake, surrounding vermilion cliffs, and massive Navajo
★ Mountain in the distance. Serving the best food in the region, the kitchen focuses on organic, healthful ingredients in producing such toothsome dishes as a Southwestern Cobb salad with crispy chicken, fire-roasted chiles, and smoked jalapeño-buttermilk dressing; and wild-mushroom-stuffed quail with roast-shallot-mashed potatoes, roasted organic veggies, and a bourbon-molasses glaze. ⊠ *100 Lake Shore Dr., 7 mi north of Page off U.S. 89* ☎ *928/645–2433* ⊕ *www.lakepowell.com* ⊟ *AE, D, DC, MC, V.*

Amangiri. Self-described "Amanjunkies" rejoiced with the 2009

Fodor'sChoice opening of the beloved Aman resort company's second American
★ property, just a few miles north of Lake Powell on a 600-acre plot of rugged high desert, soaring red-rock cliffs, and jagged mesas. This ultracushy, all-suites spa comprises 34 artfully designed units, each with an extensive private terrace and outdoor fireplace; top units have private pools. High-ceilinged rooms with stone floors, concrete walls, and timber and steel finishes adjoin massive bathrooms, each with a deep sunken tub and tall window that's perfect for stargazing. The eager-to-help staff can tailor guided day hikes or private dinners on your private terrace, and a dramatically situated spa offers treatments in both indoor and outdoor areas. Guests dine on first-rate Mediterranean and American cuisine in a softly lighted dining room, warmed by a crackling fireplace—the clientele is mostly hotel guests, but the public is welcome by reservation. **Pros: stunning accommodations inside and out; exceedingly gracious and professional staff; world-class restaurant and spa. Cons:** it's about 10 times more expensive than most accommodations in the area; extremely secluded. ✉ *1 Kayenta Point Rd., 15 mi north of Page off U.S. 89, Canyon Point, UT* ☎ *435/675–3999 or 877/695–3999* ⊕ *www.amanresorts.com* ➴ *34 suites* ⚐ *In-room: a/c, safe, refrigerator, DVD, Wi-Fi. In-hotel: restaurant, bar, room service, pool, gym, spa* ▭ *AE, D, DC, MC, V.*

$–$$ **Lake Powell Resort.** This sprawling property consisting of several one-
★ and two-story buildings, run by Aramark, sits on a promontory above Lake Powell and serves as the center for recreational activities in the area. The brightly colored Southwest-style suites in the newest building are particularly attractive, and most have wonderful lake views. Restaurants include the airy Rainbow Room, a coffeehouse, and a seasonal pizza parlor. **Pros: stunning lake setting; couldn't be closer to the water; nice range of restaurants. Cons:** rooms aren't especially fancy; it can be a long way from your room to the restaurant and lobby. ✉ *100 Lake Shore Dr., 7 mi north of Page off U.S. 89, Wahweap* ✉ *Box 1597, Page 86040* ☎ *928/645–2433 or 800/528–6154* ⊕ *www.lakepowell.com* ➴ *350 rooms* ⚐ *In-room: a/c, refrigerator, Wi-Fi. In-hotel: 3 restaurants, bar, pools, Wi-Fi hotspot, some pets allowed* ▭ *AE, D, DC, MC, V.*

CAMP- Beautiful campsites are abundant on Lake Powell, from large beaches
GROUNDS to secluded coves, with the most desirable areas accessible only by boat. You're allowed to camp anywhere along the shores of the lake unless it's restricted by the National Park Service; however, camping within 0.25 mi of the shoreline requires a portable toilet or bathroom facilities on your boat. Campfires are allowed on the shoreline, but since there's little firewood available around the lake you'll need to bring your own.

¢ **Wahweap Campground.** This campground in the Wahweap Marina complex, which is run by the National Park Service concessionaire, has views of the lake and serves both RVers and tent campers. There are showers and coin-laundry services at the nearby grocery store. **Pros:** convenient to restaurants and marina; nice lake views; some sites pick up campground Wi-Fi. **Cons:** Can get noisy and crowded during busy times; not much shade during hot summer months. ✉ *U.S. 89, 5 mi north of Page near shore of Lake Powell, Wahweap* ☎ *928/645–1059*

5

⚲ *112 tent sites, 94 full hookups* ⚐ *Flush toilets, full hookups, dump station, drinking water, fire pits, grills, picnic tables* ⊟ *AE, D, DC, MC, V* ⊙ *Open year-round.*

HOUSEBOATS Without a doubt, the most popular and fun way to vacation on Lake Powell is to rent a houseboat. Houseboats, ranging in size from 46 to 59 feet and sleeping 6 to 12 people, come complete with marine radios, fully equipped kitchens, and bathrooms with hot showers; you need only bring sheets and towels. The larger, deluxe boats are a good choice in hot summer months, since they have air-conditioning. **Aramark's Lake Powell Resorts & Marinas** (☎ *800/528–6154* ⊕ *www.lakepowell.com*) is the only concessionaire that rents boats on Lake Powell. There are many vacation packages available. One houseboat that sleeps 10 runs from $2,000 for a week in winter to about $3,400 for a week during the summer peak. At the other end of the spectrum, 75-foot luxury houseboats, which sleep 12, cost as much as $12,485 for seven nights. You receive hands-on instruction before you leave the marina.

SHOPPING

The gift shop at **Lake Powell Resort** (✉ *100 Lake Shore Dr., Wahweap* ☎ *928/645–2433* ⊕ *www.lakepowell.com*) carries authentic Native American rugs, pottery, jewelry, and baskets, as well as tourist T-shirts and postcards.

Eastern Arizona

WORD OF MOUTH

"At last we hit I-40 and the delight that is roadside attraction sign-age in America. Dinosaurs! Real pieces of the Petrified Forest! Cow-boys! Indians! Arrowheads! . . . We had us some driving to do. And drive we did. We could see the famous Route 66 Wigwams as we drove by . . . love 75 MPH on many Arizona highways."

—Toucan2

WELCOME TO EASTERN ARIZONA

TOP REASONS TO GO

★ **Get outside:** No place for couch potatoes, eastern Arizona is home to some of the state's best recreation areas for skiing, fishing, golfing, camping, and exploring. If you love the outdoor life, you might fall in love with this place.

★ **Be petrified:** Marvel at huge fossilized logs and the dazzling colors of nature at Petrified Forest National Park.

★ **View nature's handiwork at Salt River canyon:** Watch the desert cacti disappear as the country's pine delights your senses. U.S. 60 dramatically switchbacks down—and back up—2,000 feet of eroded canyon.

★ **Hit the road:** Whether you're traveling the Colorado Trail National Scenic Byway or getting your kicks on Route 66, these roads were made for travelers.

★ **Discover native traditions:** The rich culture and heritage of Native American tribes permeates this area.

Salt River Canyon

1 The White Mountains. In a state known for its extreme temperatures, residents of the White Mountains are proud of their home's relatively staid climate. The comfortable conditions and panoramic mountain views draw thousands here in summer, making the region a playground for golfers, hikers, and fishermen. But there's plenty to do if you don't want to get your hands dirty.

2 The Petrified Forest and the Painted Desert. Forget about indoor natural history exhibits—the Petrified Forest actually takes you back in time. One of Arizona's most unusual sites, the park has yielded fossils dating back 225 million years. A visit to the forest is like exploring an outdoor museum. It's worth the trip to the park's beautiful Painted Desert setting—especially if you catch the brilliant colors of the landscape at midday.

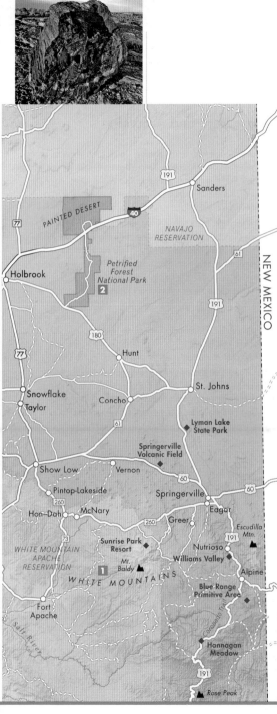

GETTING ORIENTED

Eastern Arizona is a large, somewhat loosely defined series of small towns and historic sites along the Mogollon Rim. Pronounced "*muh*-gee-on," the rim is is a 200-mi-long area of volcanic and sedimentary rock that marks a distinct change in topography of the state. Say goodbye to cacti and desert, and hello to forests of towering trees. Visitors searching for an escape from the desert heat head for the White Mountains and their majestic vistas of ponderosa pines. Others seek history and head northeast to the 186,000-acre Petrified Forest National Park and the Painted Desert. No matter the destination, don't forget to stop and experience the area's local flavor, whether it's a museum of Native American crafts or a drive through a town whose name was derived from a losing hand of cards.

Petroglyph

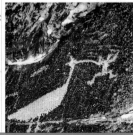

6

EASTERN ARIZONA PLANNER

When to Go

If you're not a winter-sports enthusiast, it's probably best to plan your trip to eastern Arizona for the high season (May through October). Residents of Phoenix and Tucson flock here to escape unbearably hot temperatures, but you can still find some solitude if you rent a cabin or choose a smaller, more remote resort or bed-and-breakfast.

If you're a skier, winter is the time to tour the White Mountains. Sunrise Park Resort has 10 lifts and 65 trails, and a private snowboarders' park. ■ TIP → Eastern Arizona is enjoyable year-round, but many lodging facilities, restaurants, and tourist attractions are closed in autumn and winter. It's wise to call ahead from November through April, as the opening and closing dates of many seasonal properties are dependent on when the snow starts (and when it melts). Snowstorms can close the highways that lead into the area, so if you plan on making the trip from Phoenix or even Flagstaff, make sure you have an alternate option.

Getting Here and Around

Car Travel: There isn't much choice: you'll be driving to and around eastern Arizona. Amtrak runs limited service, but it isn't that helpful for travelers. Part of the experience in eastern Arizona is the drive. Rent a car in Phoenix or Tucson, or even Flagstaff, and enjoy the open road.

If you're arriving from points west via Flagstaff, Interstate 40 leads directly to Holbrook, where drivers can take AZ 77 south into Show Low or U.S. 180 southeast to Springerville-Eagar. From the Phoenix, take the scenic drive northeast on U.S. 60, or the only slightly faster AZ 87 north to AZ 260 east, both of which lead to Show Low. From Tucson, AZ 77 north connects with U.S. 60 at Globe, and continues through Show Low up to Holbrook. For those who want to drive the Coronado Trail south-to-north, U.S. 70 and AZ 78 link up with U.S. 191 from Globe to the west and New Mexico to the east, respectively.

Winter Road Conditions: Weather conditions change rapidly in eastern Arizona. Before heading out on a daylong excursion—particularly in winter—be sure to call the Arizona Department of Transportation's Traveler Information Service (☎ 511).

Making the Most of Your Time

The Petrified Forest is the main attraction for most of eastern Arizona's visitors; it's easy to see the fossils in just a few hours. Plan to reserve a day for the park and the surrounding Painted Desert, with one or two additional days for exploring the surrounding towns and areas. Depending on your preferences, you can add day trips and excursions. Fans of the great outdoors have their choice of activities in the White Mountains. Those who like a little less sweat in their vacations can hit the open road and explore historic Route 66 or the Colorado Trail.

Pinetop-Lakeside may be the best base for your trip, with a wide range of lodging facilities and amenities. Neighboring area towns, such as Snowflake-Taylor or Holbrook, have storied motels and B&Bs. If solitude is your goal, consider staying at a lodge surrounded by private forest.

Native American Sites

North of Springerville-Eagar, Casa Malpais Archaeological Park is a prehistoric pueblo site with construction characteristics of both the Ancient Puebloan and Mogollon peoples. Petroglyphs and pueblos dating back more than 600 years can be found at stops along the 28-mi park road in Petrified Forest National Park. Closed at this writing, Lyman Lake and Homolovi Ruins state parks are known for petroglyphs and ancient pueblo sites, respectively.

Local Food and Lodging

Luxury travel this is not. Some local lodges, such as the Greer Lodge Resort, are expanding and providing more luxury services such as massages. Most places, however, have clean rooms without many frills. Fine dining is difficult to find; home-style cooking, steak houses, and the occasional authentic Mexican joint pepper most towns. Reservations are suggested during the busy summer months, and remember that some places are closed from November to April.

Like camping? Apache-Sitgreaves National Forest (☎ 928/333–4301 ⊕ www.fs.fed.us/r3/asnf) has a listing of all public camping facilities in the region, most of which operate from April to November. To reserve a site at a fee campground, use the **National Recreation Reservation Service** (☎ 877/444–6777 ⊕ www.recreation.gov), which charges a reservation fee of $10 per transaction. Book your campground site well in advance with the Game and Fish Division of the **White Mountain Apache Tribe** (☎ 928/338–4385 ⊕ www.wmat.nsn.us).

WHAT IT COSTS

	¢	$	$$	$$$	$$$$
Restaurant	under $8	$8–$12	$13–$20	$21–$30	over $30
Hotel	under $70	$70–$120	$121–$175	$176–$250	over $250

Restaurant prices are per person for a main course at dinner. Hotel prices are for a standard double in high season, excluding taxes and service charges.

Outdoor Activities

Hiking: Hikers and mountain bikers of all abilities enjoy the White Mountains' 225 mi of interconnecting loop trails, open to visitors on foot or on nonmotorized wheels. Ranger stations have maps. Allow an hour for each 2 mi of trail, plus an additional hour for every 1,000 feet gained in altitude. Carry water and watch out for poison ivy.

Fishing: Anglers flock to the more than 65 lakes, streams, and reservoirs in the White Mountains. In winter only artificial lures and flies are permitted. An Arizona fishing license is required; on tribal land you'll also need a White Mountain Apache fishing license. Want an easier catch? Some lodges have private lakes stocked with trout.

Golfing: The high country's links draw golfers from all over, and these mountain fairways angle through lush forests and past lakes and springs.

Skiing: The 11,000-foot White Mountains have hilly, wooded landscapes that invite downhill and cross-country skiing adventurers. Greer's nearby Pole Knoll Trail System and surrounding Forest Service roads make for 33 mi of cross-country trails. No matter where you stay in the White Mountains, Sunrise Park Resort is never more than an hour's drive away.

6

Updated by
Cara LaBrie

In a state of dramatic natural wonders, eastern Arizona is often overlooked—truly a tragedy, as it's one of Arizona's great outdoor playgrounds. In the White Mountains, northeast of Phoenix, you can hike, fish, swim, and, at night, gaze upward at millions of twinkling stars. The region's winter sports are just as varied: you can ski downhill or cross-country, snowboard, snowshoe, and snowmobile.

The White Mountains are unspoiled high country at its best. In vast tracts preserved primitive wilderness, the air is rent with piercing cries of hawks and eagles, and majestic herds of elk graze in verdant, wildflower-laden meadows. Past volcanic activity has left the land strewn with cinder cones, and the whole region is bounded by the Mogollon Rim (pronounced *muh*-gee-on)—a 200-mi geologic upthrust that splits the state—made famous as the "Tonto Rim" in Zane Grey's books. Much of the plant life is unique to this region; this is one of the few places in the country where such desert plants as juniper and manzanita grow intermixed with mountain pines and aspen.

The human aspects of the landscape are equally appealing. Historic Western towns are outposts of down-home hospitality, and the prehistoric sites are reminders of the native cultures that once flourished here and are still a vital presence. The Fort Apache Reservation, home to the White Mountain Apache Tribe, is north of the Salt River, and the San Carlos Apache Tribal Reservation is south of the river. Visitors are welcome to explore most reservation lands with a permit, easily obtained from tribal offices.

Historic sites and natural wonders also attract visitors to eastern Arizona. To the north, along historic Route 66, are the Painted Desert and Petrified Forest National Park. The austere mesas of the Painted Desert are famous for their multihued sedimentary layers. In Triassic times the Petrified Forest was a great, steamy swampland; some 225 million years ago, seismic activity forced the swamp's decaying plant matter deep underground, where it eventually turned to stone.

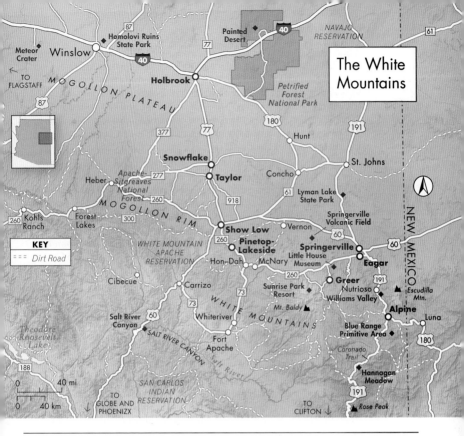

THE WHITE MOUNTAINS

With elevations climbing to more than 11,000 feet, the White Mountains area of east-central Arizona is a winter wonderland and a summer haven from the desert heat. In the 1870s, U.S. soldier and diarist John Gregory Bourke labeled the White Mountains region "a strange upheaval, a freak of nature, a mountain canted up on one side; one rides along the edge and looks down two or three thousand feet into a weird scene of grandeur and rugged beauty." The area, although much less remote than in Bourke's time, is still grand and rugged, carved by deep river canyons and tall cliffs covered with ponderosa pine.

SALT RIVER CANYON

40 mi north of Globe on U.S. 60.

Exposing a time lapse of 500 million years, the multicolor spires, buttes, mesas, and walls of the **Salt River canyon** have inspired its nickname, the mini–Grand Canyon. Approaching the Salt River canyon from Phoenix, U.S. 60 climbs through rolling hills, and the terrain changes from high desert with cactus and mesquite trees to forests of ponderosa pine. After entering the San Carlos Indian Reservation, the highway drops

2,000 feet and makes a series of hairpin turns to the Salt River. **Hiero-glyphic Point** is just one of the viewpoints along the scenic drive. Stop at the viewing and interpretive display area before crossing the bridge to stretch your legs. Wander along the banks below and enjoy the rock-strewn rapids. On hot days slip your shoes off and dip your feet into the chilly water. ■TIP➔ The river and canyon are open to hiking, fishing, and white-water rafting, but you need a permit, as this is tribal land. For information and recreational permits, contact the individual tribes.

The Apache people migrated to the Southwest around the 10th century. Divided into individual bands instead of functioning as a unified tribe, they were a hunting and gathering culture, moving with the seasons to gather food, and their crafts—baskets, beadwork, and cradleboards—were compatible with their mobile lifestyle. The U.S. government didn't understand that different Apache bands might be hostile to each other, and tried to gather separate tribes on one reservation, compounding relocation problems. Eventually, the government established San Carlos Apache Indian Reservation in 1871 and Fort Apache Indian Reservation in 1897. Both tribes hold fiercely to their cultures. The native language is still spoken and taught in schools, and tribal ceremonies continue to be held. Both tribes have highly acclaimed "hot-shot" crews that immediately respond to forest fires throughout the West. The Salt River forms the boundary between these two large Apache reservations of eastern Arizona.

GETTING HERE AND AROUND
From the Phoenix area, take U.S. 60 east through Globe, and then continue north for 40 mi. From rim to rim, the road into the canyon itself is 9 mi but allow extra time to slow down for the hairpin turns—and to enjoy the views. It's a three-hour drive from Phoenix through Globe.

WHEN TO GO
Just like most of eastern Arizona, it's best to visit Salt River canyon in the summer, when there are no worries about winter storms.

ESSENTIALS
Recreational Permits and Information San Carlos Apache Tribe (☎ 928/475–2343 or 888/475–2344 ⊕ www.sancarlosapache.com). **White Mountain Apache Tribe** (☎ 928/338–4385 ⊕ www.wmat.nsn.us).

EXPLORING
Apache Cultural Museum. The entrance price buys access to three great places to visit on the Fort Apache Indian Reservation. The museum explains the history, culture, and artistic traditions of the Apaches, and sells local crafts and books. The **Fort Apache Historical Park** harks back to cavalry days with horse barns, parade grounds, log cabins, and officers' homes. **Kinishba Ruins,** 5 mi west of Fort Apache (get directions and a map at the Cultural Center), is a partly restored sandstone pueblo, and the only Native American ruin on the reservation open to visitors. ⊠ 0.5 mi east of junction of AZ 73 and Indian Rte. 46, 5 mi south of Whiteriver ☎ 928/338–4625 ⊡ $5 ☉ Sept.–May, weekdays 8–5; June–Aug., Mon.–Sat. 8–5.

The **Cultural Center** houses displays of Apache history and culture, along with explanations of cultural traditions like Changing Women

U.S. 60 descends 2,000 feet into the Salt River Canyon on a series of tight switchbacks with great views.

Ceremony, a girls' puberty rite. Crafts are sold here. ⊠ *Hwy. 70, Mile-post 272, Peridot* ☎ *928/475–2894* ☎ *$4* ⊙ *Weekdays 9–5.*

The 1.6-million-acre **Fort Apache Indian Reservation** (☎ *928/338–4346* ⊕ *www.wmat.nsn.us*) is the ancestral home of the White Mountain Apache Tribe. The elevation of the tribal lands ranges from 3,000 feet at the bottom of Salt River to 11,000 feet in the White Mountains, and the area provides some of the best outdoor recreation in the state. Most of the more than 15,000 tribal members live in nine towns, the largest, Whiteriver (population 5,200), serving as tribal headquarters. Tribal enterprises include Sunrise Ski Resort, Hon-Dah Resort Casino, cattle ranching, and lumber.

The **San Carlos Apache Indian Reservation** (☎ *928/475–2361 for tribal offices* ⊕ *www.sancarlosapache.com*), established in 1871 for various Apache tribes, covers 1.8 million acres southeast of Salt River canyon. One-third of the reservation is covered with forest, and the rest is desert. The San Carlos Apaches number about 12,500 and are noted for their beadwork and basketry. Peridot, a beautiful yellow-green stone resembling the emerald, is mined near the town of the same name and made into jewelry.

EN ROUTE The road out of the Salt River canyon climbs along the canyon's northern cliffs, providing views of this truly spectacular chasm, unfairly overlooked in a state full of world-famous gorges. The highway continues some 50 mi northward to the **Mogollon Rim**—a huge geologic ledge that bisects much of Arizona—and its cool upland pine woods.

SHOW LOW

60 mi north of the Salt River canyon on U.S. 60.

Show Low has little of the charm of its neighboring White Mountains communities, but it's the main commercial center for the high country. Additionally, the city is a crossing point for east–west traffic along the Mogollon Rim and traffic headed for Holbrook and points north. If you're heading up to the Painted Desert and Petrified Forest from Phoenix, you might want to spend the night here.

GETTING HERE AND AROUND

Show Low is a fairly good central location from which to explore eastern Arizona by car. You can take AZ 260 south to reach Pinetop-Lakeside, or travel north on AZ 77 to Springerville and, eventually, Holbrook and the Petrified Forest National Park.

WHEN TO GO

You'll have to pass through the Salt River canyon to reach Show Low (or take Interstate 40 east of Flagstaff, and then head south). Either way, it means you'll be driving through mountains; be prepared in winter for storms and cold weather.

SPORTS AND THE OUTDOORS

FISHING **Fool Hollow Lake Recreational Area** (✉ *1500 N. Fool Hollow Lake Rd., 2 mi north of U.S. 60 off AZ 260* ☎ *928/537-3680*) is open year-round for camping, fishing, and boating. Set amid a piney 800 acres, the lake is stocked with rainbow trout, walleye, and bass, and the surrounding area provides wonderful opportunities for wildlife-viewing.

♻ **Show Low Lake** (✉ *Show Low Lake Rd.* ☎ *928/537-4126*), south of town and 1 mi off AZ 260, holds the state record for the largest walleye catch and is well stocked with largemouth bass, bluegill, and catfish. Lucky anglers have pulled out 9-pound rainbow trout. Facilities include a bait shop, a marina with boat rentals, and campsites with bathrooms and showers.

OUTFITTERS **Troutback Flyfishing** (✉ *450 S. Clark Rd., 85901* ☎ *928/242-3931* ⊕ *www. troutback.com*) has access to some of the most scenic lakes and private waters in the region. From April through October this company specializes in fly-fishing instruction, guided walk-wades, and float-tube and boating trips.

GOLF **Bison Golf & Country Club** (✉ *860 N. 36th Dr., at AZ 260* ☎ *928/537-4564* ⊕ *www.bisongolf.net* ⚐ *18 holes. 5916 yds. Par 71. Slope 114. Green Fee: $30–$42* ☞ *Facilities: Driving range, putting green, golf carts, rental clubs, pro shop*) has a back nine in the pines and a front nine in a more open meadow. Need to practice driving or putting? You can do it here and this Billy Mayfair–designed course also has a fitness center. The course is open year-round.

Silver Creek Golf Club (✉ *2051 Silver Lake Blvd.* ☎ *928/537-2744* ⊕ *www.silvercreekgolfclub.com* ⚐ *18 holes. 6813 yds. Par 71. Slope 135. Green Fee: $45–$55* ☞ *Facilities: Driving range, putting green, golf carts, rental clubs, lessons, restaurant, bar*) is 5 mi east of town on U.S. 60, then 7.5 mi north on Bourdon Ranch Road. This championship course opened to rave reviews in the 1980s, and was voted by the PGA as one of the top 10 golf courses in Arizona—no small feat in a state that lives and breathes golf. It's also one of the more affordable courses in the area. Given its lower elevation, this course is usually a few degrees warmer than Show Low and stays open year-round. Sandbaggers Bar & Grill has breakfast and lunch (dinner on weekends).

WHERE TO EAT

$$ ✕ **Licano's Mexican Food and Steak-**
MEXICAN **house.** Licano's serves what locals
★ claim are the best enchiladas on the mountain, along with shrimp tacos, prime rib, and lobster tail, making for a fairly broad menu. The spacious lounge, with a weekday happy hour from 4:30 to 6:30, stays open to 9 nightly. Its convenient downtown location places it within walking distance from most Show Low hotels. ☒ *573 W. Deuce of Clubs* ☎ *928/537–8220* ⊕ *www.licanos.com* ▭ *AE, D, MC, V.*

$ ✕ **Native New Yorker.** If you want to catch your favorite sporting event,
AMERICAN this regional chain restaurant has 30 TVs in the dining room and the adjacent sports bar. Like any sports bar, they're famous for their wings and bar food, but the soup in the sourdough bread bowl is good, too. If you're looking for a late-night scene, this is your best bets for the area: the bar stays open on weekends until 2 AM. ☒ *391 W. Deuce of Clubs* ☎ *928/532–5100* ⊕ *www.nativenewyorker.com* ▭ *AE, D, MC, V.*

WHERE TO STAY

$ ▣ **Best Western Paint Pony Lodge.** Spacious rooms have wood accents and picture windows overlooking Arizona's pine-studded high country. Suites and some rooms include fireplaces, and use of an off-property gym is free for you. **Pros:** affordable, clean and large rooms; complimentary hot breakfast; modern conveniences. **Cons:** no-frills environment not ideal for leisure travelers. ☒ *581 W. Deuce of Clubs* ☎ *928/537–5773* ⊕ *www.bestwestern.com* ⤹ *48 rooms, 2 suites* ⌂ *In-room: refrigerator, Wi-Fi. In-hotel: some pets allowed* ▭ *AE, D, DC, MC, V* ☉ *Closed Oct.–May* ⦿| *CP.*

$ ▣ **Holiday Inn Express.** Larger rooms and more conveniences than its Show Low neighbors make for a comfortable night's rest. All rooms include microwaves and refrigerators. Feel like working out? Check out the cardio equipment, and cool off with a complimentary bottle of water and a dip in the indoor pool. **Pros:** closest thing to a "big-city" hotel in Show Low; everything you expect from a brand-name property. **Cons:** limited sightseeing opportunities nearby make this a site for a pit stop and not a vacation. ☒ *151 W. Deuce of Clubs* ☎ *928/537–5115* ⊕ *www.hiexpress.com* ⤹ *71 rooms* ⌂ *In-room: refrigerator, Wi-Fi. In-hotel: pool, gym, laundry facilities* ▭ *AE, D, DC, MC, V* ⦿| *CP.*

6

$ ⊡ **KC Motel.** Victorian decorating and large rooms make this a not-so-typical two-story motel. Well-stocked rooms with microwaves and coffeemakers include four-poster beds. Chances are good the owner will check you in. **Pros:** nice for the price; Continental breakfast included. **Cons:** as expected for a motel, there are few frills; style not for everyone. ⊠ *60 W. Deuce of Clubs* ☎ *928/537–4433 or 800/531–7152* ⊕ *www.kcmotelinshowlow.com* ⤳ *35 rooms* ♿ *In-room: refrigerator, Wi-Fi* ▭ *AE, D, DC, MC, V* ⓘ *CP.*

PINETOP-LAKESIDE

15 mi southeast of Show Low on AZ 260.

At 7,200 feet, the community of Pinetop-Lakeside borders the world's largest stand of ponderosa pine. Two towns, Pinetop and Lakeside, were incorporated in 1984 to form this municipality—although they still retain separate post offices. The modest year-round population is 4,200, but in summer months it can jump to as high as 30,000. Once popular only with the retirement and summer-home set, the city now lures thousands of "flatlanders" up from the Valley of the Sun with its gorgeous scenery, excellent multiuse trails, premier golf courses, and temperatures rarely exceeding 85°F.

GETTING HERE AND AROUND

Just a 15 minute drive from Show Low, Pinetop-Lakeside is also ideal for exploring by car. The main drag is known as both AZ 260 and White Mountain Boulevard.

WHEN TO GO

Desert dwellers flock to Pinetop-Lakeside in summer to escape the heat. In winter, it's a wonderland of snow and mountains, but be prepared, as U.S. 60 and Interstate 40 are routinely closed and impassable during snowstorms.

SPORTS AND THE OUTDOORS

BICYCLING AND HIKING

Listed in the country's "Trail Town Hall of Fame" by the American Hiking Society, Pinetop-Lakeside is the primary trailhead for the White Mountains Trails System, which includes roughly 200 mi of interconnecting multiuse loop trails that span the White Mountains. All these trails are open to mountain bikers, horseback riders, and hikers.

Half a mile off AZ 260 on Woodland Road, **Big Springs Environmental Study Area** is a 0.5–mi loop trail that wanders by riparian meadows, two streams, and a spring-fed pond. A series of educational signs is devoted to the surrounding flora and fauna. The trailhead for **Country Club Trail** is at the junction of Forest Service roads 182 and 185; these 3.5 mi of moderately difficult mountain-biking and hiking trails can be spiced up by following the spur-trail to the top of Pat Mullen Mountain and back. The well-traveled and easy **Mogollon Rim Interpretive Trail** follows a small part of the 19th-century **Crook Trail** along the Mogollon Rim; the 0.25-mi path, with a trailhead just west of the Pinetop-Lakeside city limits, is well marked with placards describing local wildlife and geography. The 8-mi **Panorama Trail**, rated moderate, affords astonishing views from the top of extinct double volcanoes known as the Twin Knolls, and passes though a designated wildlife habitat area; the trailhead is 6 mi east on Porter Mountain Road, off AZ 260.

You can get trail brochures or other information from the **Apache-Sitgreaves National Forests** (✉ *Lakeside Ranger Station, 2022 W. White Mountain Blvd., Lakeside* ☎ *928/368–2100* ⊕ *www.fs.fed.us/r3/asnf*), including a $2 booklet on the White Mountains Trail System.

FISHING East of Pinetop-Lakeside and 9 mi south of AZ 260, 260-acre **Hawley Lake** (✉ *AZ 473, Hawley Lake* ☎ *928/338–4385*) sits on Apache territory and yields mostly rainbow trout; rental boats are available in the marina. Tribal permits are required for all recreational activities: contact **White Mountain Apache Fish & Game Department** (☎ *928/338–4385*) for details.

OUTFITTERS **Paradise Creek Anglers** (✉ *560 W. White Mountain Blvd., Lakeside* ☎ *928/367–6200 or 800/231–3831* ⊕ *www.paradisecreekanglers.com*) offers fishing advice, lessons, and equipment rentals.

GOLF **Pinetop Lakes Golf & Country Club** (✉ *4643 Buck Springs Rd., Pinetop* ☎ *928/369–4531* ⊕ *www.pinetoplakesgolf.com* ⚑ *18 holes. 4558 yds. Par 63. Slope 94. Green Fee: $30–$47* ☞ *Facilities: Driving range, putting green, golf carts, rental clubs, lessons, restaurant, bar*) has fewer trees than other area courses, but it includes several water hazards to compensate. The shorter course is wonderful for public play. The club also has tennis courts; it's open April to October.

HORSEBACK RIDING **Porter Mountain Stables** (✉ *4048 Porter Mountain Rd., Lakeside* ☎ *928/368–5306*) runs one-hour to all-day horseback trips in summer; they are open from Memorial Day to Labor Day.

SKIING AND SNOW SPORTS The **Skier's Edge** (✉ *560 W. White Mountain Blvd., Pinetop* ☎ *928/367–6200 or 800/231–3831* ⊕ *www.skiersedgepinetop.com*) has cross-country and downhill skis as well as snowboards and boots. **Snowriders** (✉ *857 E. White Mountain Blvd., Pinetop* ☎ *928/367–5638 or 800/762–0256* ⊕ *www.azsnowriders.com*) sells and rents skis and snowboards and gear from December through mid-March, weather permitting.

WHERE TO EAT

$$$$ ✕ **Charlie Clark's Steak House.** From golfers relishing a successful day on
AMERICAN the links to locals in search of good food, Charlie Clark's has been the meeting place of the White Mountains since it opened in 1938. Prime rib is the house specialty—a delicate "ladies cut" is available for those with smaller appetites. Minnesota walleye pike adds a Midwestern spin to the menu. ✉ *1701 E. White Mountain Blvd., Pinetop* ☎ *928/367–4900* ⊕ *www.charlieclarks.com* ▭ *AE, D, MC, V.*

$$ ✕ **Los Corrales.** Bright yellows and oranges make for a cheerful family-
MEXICAN style eatery, which attracts locals with Mexican seafood dishes such as *camarones a la crema* (shrimp and mushrooms in cream sauce) and luncheon specials. Dessert specialties include fried ice cream and apple chimichanga. A small bar serves drinks. ✉ *845 E. White Mountain Blvd., Lakeside* ☎ *928/367–5585* ▭ *AE, D, DC, MC, V.*

6

WHERE TO STAY

$ 🏨 **Hon-Dah Resort Casino and Conference Center.** Stuffed high-country animals atop a mountain of boulders welcome you to Apache Tribe–operated Hon-Dah. The main draw is the casino, with hundreds of slot machines, live poker and blackjack, and weekend entertainment. Large guest rooms all have coffeemakers and wet bars. A high-roof atrium holds the pool and hot tub. The Indian Pine Restaurant serves three daily meals, and a small gift shop sells local Apache crafts. **Pros:** best destination for travelers who aren't interested in roughing it; big draw for the casino crowd. **Cons:** the resort can get noisy in the evening. ⊠ *777 AZ 260, Pinetop* ☎ *928/369–0299 or 800/929–8744* ⊕ *www. hon-dah.com* ⤴ *126 rooms, 2 suites* ⟳ *In-room: refrigerator, Wi-Fi. In-hotel: restaurant, bars, pool* ⊟ *AE, D, DC, MC, V.*

$$ 🏨 **Lake of the Woods Resort.** Janet Pierson was so taken with Lakeside after her first visit that she and two friends decided to buy Lake of the Woods Resort. Housed next to the resort's private lake, you can fish for trout, hike, rent a boat, and enjoy the natural surroundings of the area. Novice fishermen take note: Pierson and crew stock the lake a half dozen times a year with trout. It's almost as easy as shooting fish in a barrel. **Pros:** on Lakeside's main street, with a rural, but not removed, atmosphere; stocked private lake. **Cons:** only phone on-site for you is a pay phone in the main building; no Internet. ⊠ *2244 W. White Mountain Blvd., Lakeside* ☎ *928/368–5353* ⊕ *www.lakeofthewoodsaz.com* ⤴ *26 cabins, / houses* ⟳ *In-room: no phone, kitchen. In-hotel: some pets allowed* ⊟ *MC, V.*

$ 🏨 **Northwoods Resort.** Each of the 14 fully furnished cottages at this moun-
♻ tain retreat has its own covered porch and barbecue. Inside, natural wood paneling, brick fireplaces, and wall-to-wall carpeting add to the homey feeling. Full electric kitchens have refrigerators, ovens, microwaves, and adjacent dinette sets. Proprietors here keep their promise to provide "meticulously maintained" accommodations, including daily replenishment of firewood. Master bedrooms have king-size beds, and the two-story chalets can accommodate up to 18 people. **Pros:** no highway noise; well removed for a family vacation of solitude; extremely friendly for families traveling with children. **Cons:** no on-site restaurant; you'll have to hike up to the main road if you want to visit any local attractions on foot. ⊠ *AZ 260, Milepost 352* ⊡ *Box 397N, Pinetop 85935* ☎ *928/367–2966 or 800/813–2966* ⊕ *www.northwoodsaz.com* ⤴ *14 cabins* ⟳ *In-room: no a/c, kitchen. In-hotel: laundry facilities* ⊟ *D, MC, V.*

$ 🏨 **Whispering Pines Resort.** These well-maintained cabins have fireplaces (wood or natural gas), grills, and double sofa beds. One-, two-, and three-bedroom units—some with second bathrooms—have either handsome knotty-pine or more modern wood-panel interiors. The four log cabins, three of them studio units, have that hideaway cabin vibe. Couples may want to request one of the alpine suites, with whirlpool tubs. On 12 acres bordering the Apache-Sitgreaves National Forest, cabins are in walking distance of Woodland Lake and Walnut Creek. It'll feel like home after a while: the resort doesn't offer daily housekeeping. **Pros:** great accommodations for large parties; extremely private. **Cons:** older furnishings in rooms; icy roads in the resort can be difficult to navigate in winter. ⊠ *AZ 260, just beyond Milepost 352* ⌕ *Box 1043, Pinetop 85935* ☎ *928/367–4386 or 800/840–3867* ⊕ *www.whisperingpinesaz. com* ⌐ *38 cabins* ⚭ *In-room: no a/c, kitchen (some), In-hotel: laundry facilities, Wi-Fi hotspot, some pets allowed* ⊟ AE, D, MC, V.

SHOPPING

Many of Pinetop-Lakeside's shops are open only in summer.

ANTIQUES **Antique Mercantile Company** (⊠ *2106 W. White Mountain Blvd., Lakeside* ☎ *928/368–9090*) has century-old collectibles ranging from first-edition law encyclopedias to working Victrolas. Upscale-quality glass, china, furniture, military items, and vintage sports and camera equipment are all for sale. In winter it's open by appointment only. The log-cabin **Harvest Moon Antiques** (⊠ *392 W. White Mountain Blvd., Pinetop* ☎ *928/367–6973*), open Memorial Day through Thanksgiving weekend, specializes in Old West relics, ranging from buckskins and Apache wares to old guns and U.S. Cavalry items. This is an excellent place to find affordable Native American jewelry and Navajo rugs. **Orchard Antiques** (⊠ *1664 W. White Mountain Blvd., Lakeside* ☎ *928/368–6563*), open from April to October, is a reliable purveyor of high-quality furniture, glass, china, and sterling, and deals in some quilts and vintage clothing.

NIGHTLIFE

There isn't much nightlife in the White Mountains area, but **Charlie Clark's Steak House** (⊠ *1701 E. White Mountain Blvd., Pinetop* ☎ *928/367–4900*) has a lounge with a full bar, pool tables, and a bouncing jukebox that stays open until midnight at the latest on weekends. **Hon-Dah Resort Casino** (⊠ *777 AZ 260, Pinetop* ☎ *928/369–0299 or 800/929–8744* ⊕ *www. hon-dah.com*) is the spot where you can always find live music, concerts, and comedy. Check online to find out about upcoming performances.

SNOWFLAKE-TAYLOR

30 mi north of Pinetop-Lakeside on Route 260 and AZ 77.

Snowflake-Taylor is a good jumping-off point for exploring eastern Arizona. The towns are also a less-crowded alternative for summer excursions into the nearby White Mountains. Most Phoenix weekenders head for the higher towns, so Snowflake and Taylor avoid the crush of summer visitors that results in higher prices at hotels and restaurants. Sandwiched between the White Mountains and the Colorado Plateau, the communities enjoy year-round pleasant weather, with summer highs in the 90s. Yes, it snows in Snowflake, but it seldom lasts more than a day. It's also an easy day trip to the Petrified Forest.

Snowflake and Taylor were settled by Mormons in the 1870s and named for Mormon church leaders. Snowflake's unusual name is a combination of Erastus Snow, an apostle in the early Mormon church of Salt Lake City, Utah, and William Flake, one of the town founders. One of Arizona's two Mormon temples sits on Temple Hill west of Snowflake, and the towns still have a large Mormon contingent in their combined population of 9,000. You can take a walking tour of Snowflake's historical district, with pioneer homes and antiques stores.

GETTING HERE AND AROUND

From Show Low off AZ 77, Snowflake-Taylor is about one-third of the way to Holbrook and Interstate 40.

WHEN TO GO

As Snowflake-Taylor isn't as far into the White Mountains as other communities it is somewhat easier to reach in winter. Still, most visitors explore this area in summer.

EXPLORING

The **Stinson Museum** once served as a schoolhouse. James Stinson, the first rancher in the valley, was the original resident of the small adobe home. William J. Flake bought out Stinson's holdings and founded the town of Snowflake. Flake added on to the structure, which today is a museum containing pioneer memorabilia, quilts, Native American artifacts, and a small gift shop. ⊠ *102 N. 1st East, Snowflake* ☎ *928/536–4881* 🖃 *Donations accepted* ☉ *Mon., Tues., and Thurs–Sat. 10–2.*

The **Taylor Museum**, a small local museum with pioneer and Native American exhibits, celebrates July 4 by "firing the anvil" at sunrise. At 4 AM revelers place an anvil on the ground, a newspaper and gunpowder on top, then another anvil. When the gunpowder is lighted, the anvil flies 3 feet into the air with a deafening bang. The rest of the year, the anvil resides at the museum along with the Jennings drum, which was brought to town by early Mormon settlers. ⊠ *2 N. Main St., Taylor* ☎ *928/536–6649* 🖃 *Donations accepted* ☉ *Mon., Tues., and Thurs.–Sat. 10–2.*

SPORTS AND THE OUTDOORS

GOLF One of the least expensive golf courses in the White Mountains, the **Snowflake Municipal Golf Course** (⊠ *90 N. Country Club Dr., Snowflake* ☎ *928/536–7233* 🏌 *18 holes. 6172 yds. Par 72. Slope 116. Green Fee: $20–$40* ⚷ *Facilities: Driving range, putting green, golf carts, rental clubs, restaurant*) is open year-round. Especially scenic with red rocks and waterfalls, the course includes a water hazard. The restaurant is open May through October. Green fees are lower October through April.

HIKING At the junction of Silver Creek Canyon and Five-Mile Canyon, 5 mi north of Snowflake, ancient peoples left petroglyphs carved through the dark desert varnish revealing the light sandstone of the canyon walls. **Petroglyph Hike** (⊠ *Silver Creek Canyon Snowflake*), the trail from the canyon top down to the petroglyphs, is short but steep. Trail access is regulated by the city of Snowflake. To check in and get directions, contact the **Snowflake-Taylor Chamber of Commerce** (☎ *928/536–4331* ⊕ *www.snowflaketaylorchamber.org*).

WHERE TO EAT

$$ ✕ **Enzo's Ristorante Italiano.** The only Italian restaurant in town is in
ITALIAN Snowflake's historic district. Sauces and breads are made from scratch by Enzo himself, and although they may take a while, the minestrone soup, baked pastas, and shrimp Alfredo are worth the wait. A delicious calzone is sure to warm you on a cold winter night. ⊠ *423 W. 3rd St. N, Snowflake* ☎ *928/243–0450* ⚭ *Reservations not accepted* ▭ *No credit cards* ☉ *Closed Sun.–Tues. No lunch.*

$ ✕ **La Cocina de Eva.** Any trip to Arizona should become a tour of different MEXICAN styles of Mexican food, and if you like trying different interpretations of ★ Sonoran cuisine, stop here. The green-corn tamales and enchiladas are delicious, and locals go for the bean burrito smothered in green chile sauce. Portions are large and service is friendly. A combination of South-of-the-border knickknacks and Western paintings gives this popular spot a homey vibe. ✉ *201 N. Main St., Snowflake* ☎ *928/536–7683* ▤ *D, MC, V* ☉ *Closed Sun.*

$ ✕ **Trapper's Cafe.** Opened in 1973 by "Trapper" Hatch, and still family-AMERICAN owned, this hometown diner is decorated with Hatch's old trapping equipment and animal paintings by local artists. Chicken-fried steak and homemade barbecue sauce draw a loyal crowd, as do the steaks. People drive out of their way just for a piece of Trapper's pies, especially banana cream. Have a slice at the counter with a cup of coffee. ✉ *9 S. Main St., Taylor* ☎ *928/536–7758* ▤ *MC, V* ☉ *Closed Sun.*

WHERE TO STAY

$ ▥ **Comfort Inn.** Large rooms and the complimentary Continental break-fast make the reliable hotel a great deal for families. A large river-rock fireplace and rustic furniture adorn the comfortable lobby. **Pros:** the only lodging in either Snowflake or Taylor with a pool (indoor); good value. **Cons:** not enough amenities to encourage a multinight vacation stay; lacks the charm of nearby historic properties. ✉ *2055 S. Main St., Snowflake* ☎ *928/536–3888 or 877/505–3888* ⊕ *www.comfortinn.com* ⮑ *64 rooms* ♿ *In-room: refrigerator (some), Wi-Fi. In-hotel: pool, gym, laundry facilities, some pets allowed* ▤ *AE, D, MC, V* ✽⃝ *CP.*

$–$$ ▥ **Osmer D. Heritage Inn.** Elegantly furnished with period antiques, this popular redbrick bed-and-breakfast with a white-picket fence was built in 1890 by Mormon pioneer Osmer D. Flake. Filled with pioneer style, Osmer D.'s is next door to Heritage Antiques and between two restaurants—making it the best place to start Snowflake's historic walk-ing tour. **Pros:** quiet B&B setting with modern conveniences, includ-ing Internet access and DVD players. **Cons:** only 10 rooms, so book early—up to six months—for summer travel. ✉ *161 N. Main St., Snow-flake* ☎ *928/536–3322 or 866/486–5947* ⊕ *www.heritage-inn.net* ⮑ *10 rooms* ♿ *In-room: DVD (some), Wi-Fi* ▤ *AE, D, MC, V* ✽⃝ *BP.*

¢–$ ▥ **Silver Creek Rodeway Inn.** Simply furnished, clean, and near fast-food restaurants, Silver Creek sees many regulars who travel through the area often. There's ample parking for RVs and trailers. It's close to Taylor's only grocery store, and rooms have refrigerators and micro-waves. A complimentary daily "hot breakfast" has biscuits, gravy, and sausage. **Pros:** convenient town location; inexpensive. **Cons:** best for travelers just passing through; no on-site restaurant. ✉ *825 N. Main St., Taylor* ☎ *928/536–2600* ⊕ *www.choicehotels.com* ⮑ *42 rooms* ♿ *In-room: refrigerator. In-hotel: Wi-Fi hotspot* ▤ *AE, D, DC, MC, V* ✽⃝ *CP.*

6

SUNRISE PARK RESORT

27 mi southeast of Pinetop-Lakeside on AZ 260 and 273.

GETTING HERE AND AROUND

The resort is 7 mi south of the intersection of AZ 260 on AZ 273.

WHEN TO GO

Sunrise is one of Arizona's top two destinations for skiing and winter recreation. You can visit in summer, however, and enjoy horseback riding, mountain biking, and chairlift rides—all with great views of the White Mountains.

WORD OF MOUTH

"I would head up over the White Mountains. It will (literally!) be like a breath of fresh air after Phoenix and Tucson, a very different Arizona. Reminded me of the Black Forest! From there you could go to the Petrified Forest."
—wildblueyonder

EXPLORING

Sunrise Park Resort. In winter and early spring, skiers and other snow lovers flock to Sunrise Park Resort. There's plenty more than downhill and cross-country skiing here, including snowboarding, snowmobiling, snowshoeing, ice fishing, and sleigh rides. The resort has 10 lifts and 65 trails on three mountains rising to 11,000 feet. Eighty percent of the downhill runs are for beginning or intermediate skiers, and many less-intense trails begin at the top, so skiers of varying skill levels can ride the chairlifts together. There's a "ski-wee" hill for youngsters. The Sunrise Express high-speed chairlift anchors the 10 lifts. One-day lift tickets are $49. Sunrise's Snowboard Park has jumps of all difficulty levels and its own sound system, and is exclusively for snowboarders—so there's no tension on the hill between boarders and skiers. Cross-country skiers enjoy 13.5 mi of interconnecting trails. You can rent equipment at the ski shop. In summer a marina is open for boat rentals on Sunrise Lake. ✉ *AZ 273, 7 mi south of AZ 260* ⓓ *Box 117, Greer 85927* ☎ *928/735–7669, 800/772–7669 hotel reservations and snow reports* 🌐 *www.sunriseskipark.com* ▭ *AE, D, MC, V.*

WHERE TO STAY

$$ **Sunrise Park Lodge.** Catering to those who want to be as close as possible to the lifts, this hotel has comfortable rooms with ski racks and runs a shuttle to the slopes every half hour. Save with a lodging-and-lift-ticket package. The VIP Suite, with its wet bar, refrigerator, microwave oven, and hot tub, comes with two lift tickets that grant the holders line-cutting privileges on the slopes. In summer you can enjoy boating on Sunrise Lake, "3-D" archery, scenic chairlift rides, horseback riding, and mountain biking on designated trails. ■ **TIP→ Call ahead, because the lodge closes twice a year:** from the end of ski season until Memorial Day weekend in spring and then again in fall from mid-October until the first heavy snowfall. **Pros:** comfortable accommodations; best access to ski amenities. **Cons:** not the best winter destination for those who don't want to hit the slopes; closed between seasons. ✉ *AZ 273, 7 mi south of AZ 260* ⓓ *Box 117, Greer 85927* ☎ *928/735–7669 or 800/772–7669* 🌐 *www.sunriseskipark.com* *100 rooms, 1 suite* *In-room: no a/c, refrigerator (some). In-hotel: 2 restaurants, bar, pool, Wi-Fi hotspot* ▭ *AE, D, DC, MC, V.*

Eastern Arizona attracts outdoor lovers for horseback riding, hiking, fishing, golfing, and skiing.

GREER

★ *12 mi east of Sunrise Park resort, 35 mi southeast of Pinetop-Lakeside, 15 mi southwest of Eagar on AZ 260.*

The charming community of Greer sits just south of AZ 260 among pine, spruce, willow, and aspen on the banks of the Little Colorado River. At an elevation of 8,500 feet, this portion of gently sloping National Forest land is covered with meadows and reservoirs and is dominated by 11,590-foot Baldy Peak. Much of the surrounding area remains under the control of the White Mountain Apache tribe, so visitors must take care to respect Apache law and land.

GETTING HERE AND AROUND

Take AZ 373 south from AZ 260. AZ 373 is also Greer's main street and after it crosses the Little Colorado River it eventually comes to a dead end. It's affectionately called the Road to Nowhere.

WHEN TO GO

When compared to other areas of eastern Arizona, Greer is relatively temperate. Like most towns in the area, summers are great here for getting away from the heat; winters are snowy but not frigid.

EXPLORING

Listed on the National Register of Historic Places, the **Butterfly Lodge Museum** was built as a hunting lodge in 1914 by John Butler, the husband of "Aunt Molly" (of Molly Butler Lodge fame), for author James Willard Schultz and his artist son, Lone Wolf, a prolific painter of Indian and Western scenes. There's a small gift shop. Take time to watch the surrounding meadow come to life with fluttering butterflies, from which the lodge got its name. ⊠ *AZ 373 at CR 1126* ☎ *928/735–7514* ⊕ *www.wmonline.com/butterflylodge.htm* ⊿ *$2* ⊙ *June–Aug., Thurs.–Sun. 10–5.*

SPORTS AND THE OUTDOORS

The **Tin Star Trading Post** (⊠ *38940 AZ 373* ☎ *928/735–7540*) sells sleds in winter and tackle the rest of the year. Fishing licenses, groceries, and camping supplies are also for sale. You can grab a cup of joe at the Post's coffee shop. Buy supplies for an afternoon picnic and feel free to use their wireless Internet service for a quick e-mail check.

FISHING The three **Greer Lakes** are actually the Bunch, River, and Tunnel reservoirs. Bait and fly-fishing options are scenic and plentiful, and there are several places to launch a boat. Winding through Greer, the Little Colorado River's West Fork is well stocked with brookies and rainbows, and has 23 mi of fishable waters.

HIKING The difficult but accessible **Mount Baldy Trail** begins at **Sheeps Crossing**, southwest of Greer on AZ 273. In just under 8 mi (one way) the trail climbs the northern flank of 11,590-foot Mount Baldy, the second-highest peak in Arizona. Note that the summit of Baldy is on the White Mountain Apache Reservation. Considered sacred land, this final 0.25 mi is off-limits to non-Apaches. The boundary is clearly marked; please respect it, no matter how much you wish to continue to the peak.

SKIING Cross-country skiers find Greer an ideally situated hub for some of the mountain's best trails. About 2.5 mi west of AZ 373 on AZ 260, a trailhead marks the starting point for the **Pole Knoll Trail System,** nearly 30 mi of well-marked, groomed cross-country trails interlacing through the Apache-Sitgreaves National Forest and color-coded by experience level. Trail maps are available from the **Apache-Sitgreaves National Forest** (⊠ *Springerville Ranger District, 165 S. Mountain Ave., Springerville* ☎ *928/333–6200* ⊕ *www.fs.fed.us/r3/asnf*).

WHERE TO EAT

$ ✕ **Greer Mountain Resort Country Cafe.** This plant-hung diner-café is open
AMERICAN 7 AM–3 PM. Grab a seat by the fireplace and sample the homemade ranch beans, a signature grilled-cheese sandwich with green chiles and tomato—because every dish in Arizona tastes better with green chiles—or fresh-baked cobbler. On those cooler days, the homemade soups will warm any belly. ⊠ *38742 AZ 373, 1.5 mi south of AZ 260* ☎ *928/735–7560* ⊕ *www.greermountainresort.com* ▬ *MC, V* ⊙ *Closed Wed. No dinner.*

¢ ✕ **Rendezvous Diner.** The popular local diner has earned a reputation
AMERICAN for serving up some of Greer's tastiest dishes, not to mention the area's best hot spiced cider, a perfect choice during the chilly winter months. Of particular note are the pineapple teriyaki, green-chile burgers, and generous portions of homemade cobblers. The rhubarb is a specialty. The place is open year-round for breakfast and lunch. ⊠ *117 Main St.* ☎ *928/735–7483* ▬ *MC, V* ⊙ *Closed Tues. No dinner.*

WHERE TO STAY

$$–$$$ ⬛ **Greer Lodge Resort.** Designed for travelers on all budgets, the lodge's
★ accommodations range from basic rooms to four-bedroom luxury cabins. Situated on a mile-long property, the resort continues to expand as the years go on. You can enjoy fly-fishing in three private trout ponds or fish along the Little Colorado River (provided you have a public fishing license); and hiking, cross-country skiing, and opportunities for viewing wildlife are close by. Two on-site restaurant-bars have casual and finer dining, making it unnecessary to leave the property. Feel pampered with luxury beds and high thread-count sheets that make the country a bit more comfortable. **Pros:** great place for city slickers to escape to the country but still feel spoiled; range of accommodations. **Cons:** luxury cabins are expensive. ✉ *44 Main St.* ⬥ *Box 244, Greer 85927* ☎ *928/735–7216* ⊕ *www.greerlodgeaz.com* ⬦ *140 rooms* ⬧ *In-room: Wi-Fi, no a/c (some). In-hotel: 2 restaurants, bar, spa, some pets allowed* ⬒ *AE, D, DC, MC, V.*

$–$$ ⬛ **Greer Mountain Resort.** Budget travelers and families appreciate these cabin-style accommodations. Each of the nine units are different, but most can sleep up to six people and contain either a fireplace or a gas- or wood-burning stove. The smallest, one-bedroom, knotty-pine units have no fireplaces, but they're reasonably priced and good for couples. You may want to enjoy breakfast or lunch at the resort's roadside restaurant, or you can whip up your own feast in the fully equipped kitchens. **Pros:** on-site restaurant and in-room kitchens; good value. **Cons:** small resort has few other amenities. ✉ *AZ 373, 1.5 mi south of AZ 260* ⬥ *Box 145, Greer 85927* ☎ *928/735–7560* ⊕ *www. greermountainresort.com* ⬦ *9 units* ⬧ *In-room: no a/c, kitchen, no TV. In-hotel: Wi-Fi hotspot* ⬒ *MC, V.*

$–$$ ⬛ **Molly Butler Lodge.** Colorful quilts and wood furnishings fill the history-themed rooms at Arizona's oldest lodge, which also includes cabins for larger parties and extended stays. The lodge includes four suites, each themed to honor a historic figure with ties to the area—Herbert Hoover, Zane Grey, John Wayne, and local pioneer Molly Butler. These luxury suites have updated, comfortable furnishings in what the general manager calls an "opulent rustic" vibe. The 49 cabins at Molly's "Cabin Capers" can sleep up to 16 and include complete kitchens, linens, and living areas. You can bring food to stock the pantries at the cabins, but Molly's famous on-site restaurant could lure you from the rooms with its prime rib, steaks, and famous chili. **Pros:** historic charm; range of accommodations. **Cons:** two-night minimum for weekend stays, three nights for holidays. ✉ *109 Main St.* ☎ *928/735–7226* ⊕ *www.mollybutlerlodge.com* ⬦ *49 cabins, 6 rooms, 4 suites* ⬧ *In-room: no a/c, no phone (some), Wi-Fi (some). In-hotel: restaurant, bar, some pets allowed* ⬒ *AE, D, MC, V.*

NIGHTLIFE

Tiny Greer's nightlife is limited to the bar and lounge of the **Molly Butler Lodge** (✉ *109 Main St.* ☎ *928/735–7226*), where you can listen to vintage tunes on the jukebox, sink into a cozy seat near the fireplace, play an arcade game, or challenge a local to a game of pool or darts. Don't expect to be out too late: the bar usually closes by 11 in winter and just past midnight during the busier summer months.

SPRINGERVILLE-EAGAR

17 mi northeast of Greer, 45 mi east of Pinetop-Lakeside on AZ 260, 67 mi southeast of Petrified Forest National Park on U.S. 180.

Sister cities Springerville and Eagar are tucked into a circular, high-mountain basin christened "Valle Redondo," or Round Valley, by Basque settlers in the late 1800s. Nestled on the back side of massive 10,912-foot Escudilla Mountain, this self-proclaimed "Gateway to the White Mountains" sits in a different climate belt from nearby Greer and Sunrise Resort; insulated by its unique geography, Springerville-Eagar has markedly less-severe winter temperatures and lighter snowfall than neighboring mountain towns. Geographically, the Round Valley also served as a unique Old West haven for the lawless—a great place to conceal stolen cattle and hide out for a while. Butch Cassidy, the Clantons, and the Smith gang all spent time here. So did the late John Wayne, whose former 26-Bar Ranch lies just west of Eagar off AZ 260.

GETTING HERE AND AROUND

It's about an hour drive from Pinetop-Lakeside to this isolated area. ■TIP→ **The Round Valley is the favorite of skiers in the know,** who appreciate the location as they commute to the lifts at Sunrise with the sun always at their back—important when you consider the glare off those blanketed snowscapes between the resort and Pinetop-Lakeside—and the dramatically lighter traffic on this less-icy stretch of AZ 260.

WHEN TO GO

While Springerville-Eagar might not get as much snow as other parts of the region, this is also a very remote area. And that means it can be hard to reach—and leave—in winter.

EN ROUTE The junction of U.S. 180/191 and U.S. 60, just north of Springerville, is the perfect jumping-off spot for a driving tour of the **Springerville Volcanic Field.** On the southern edge of the Colorado Plateau, it covers a total area larger than the state of Rhode Island, and is spread across a high-elevation plain similar to the Tibetan Plateau. Six miles north of Springerville on U.S. 180/191 are sweeping westward views of the **Twin Knolls**—double volcanoes that erupted twice here about 700,000 years ago. As you travel west on U.S. 60, Green's Peak Road and various south-winding Forest Service roads make for a leisurely, hour-long drive past **St. Peter's Dome** and a stop for impressive views from **Green's Peak,** the topographic high point of the Springerville Field. A free, detailed driving-tour brochure of the Springerville Volcanic Field is available from the **Springerville-Eagar Regional Chamber of Commerce** (✉ *318 Main St.* 🗐 *Box 31, Springerville 85938* ☎ *928/333–2123* ⊕ *www.springerville-eagarchamber.com*).

EXPLORING

The 14.5-acre **Casa Malpais Archaeological Park** pueblo complex is piquing the interest of a growing number of anthropologists and astronomers. The "House of the Badlands" (a sobriquet for the rough-textured ground's effect on bare feet) has a series of narrow terraces lining eroded edges of basalt (hardened lava flow) cliff, as well as an extensive system of subterranean rooms nestled within Earth's fissures underneath.

Strategically designed gateways in the walls of the complex allow streams of sunlight to precisely illuminate significant petroglyphs prior to the setting equinox or solstice sun. Casa Malpais's **Great Kiva** (any kiva over 30 feet is considered great) is square-cornered instead of round, consistent with Ancestral Puebloan heritage. Some archaeologists believe the pueblo served as a regional ceremonial center for the Mogollon people. Both Hopi and Zuni tribes trace their history to Casa Malpais. The site has a small museum in town, with artifacts from the Casa Malpais site, a butterfly collection, and items from early-days Springerville; a small gift shop sells Native American jewelry and local history books. The site itself may only be visited on a two-hour tour; these leave from the museum at 9, 11, and 2. ⊠ *318 E. Main St., Springerville* ☏ *928/333–5375* ⊡ *$8* ☉ *Museum Tues.–Sat. 8–4, weather permitting; call ahead to confirm.*

The **Little House Museum** has a collection of local pioneer and ranching memorabilia, but it's the mesmerizing tones from a rare collection of automatic musical instruments that you remember—as well as the museum's colorful curator, Wink Crigler, with her tales of this region's lively past. Tours to archaeological digs and petroglyphs are available by appointment. To reach the ranch, go 10 mi southwest of Eagar on AZ 260, turn south onto South Fork Road, and go 3 mi. ⊠ *X Diamond Ranch, S. Fork Rd., 10 mi southwest of Eagar* ☏ *928/333–2286* ⊕ *www.xdiamondranch.com* ⊡ *$12* ☉ *By reservation only.*

The **Renée Cushman Art Collection Museum** is open to the public only by appointment, but a visit is worth the effort. Renée Cushman's extensive collection of objets d'art—some acquired on her travels, some collected with the accumulated resources of three wealthy husbands, and some willed to her by her artistic father—is administered by the Church of Latter-day Saints. Her treasure includes a Rembrandt engraving, Tiepolo pen-and-inks, and an impressive collection of European antiques, some dating back to the 15th century. Call the Springerville-Eagar Chamber of Commerce (☏ *928/333–2123*) to arrange your visit.

SPORTS AND THE OUTDOORS

For your mountain-sports needs the **Sweat Shop** (⊠ *42 N. Main St., Eagar* ☏ *928/333–2950*) rents skis, snowboards, and mountain bikes.

FISHING **Becker Lake** (⊠ *U.S. 60, 2 mi northwest of Springerville* ☏ *928/367–4281*) is a specialty lake for trout fishing; call for seasonal bait requirements. **Big Lake** (⊠ *AZ 273, 24 mi south of AZ 260* ☏ *928/521–1387*), known to many as the "queen of all trout lakes," is stocked each spring and fall with rainbow, brook, and cutthroat trout. **Nelson Reservoir** (⊠ *U.S. 191, Nutrioso*), between Springerville-Eagar and Alpine, is well stocked with rainbow, brown, and brook trout.

Troutback (⊠ *450 S. Clark Rd., Show Low* ☏ *928/532–3474 or 800/403–4092* ⊕ *www.troutback.com*) is a fly-fishing guide service that will create half- or full-day fishing trips for novices and seasoned anglers alike throughout the White Mountains. Equipment, including boats, waders, fly rods and reels, and float tubes, is available for rent. **Western United Drug** (⊠ *105 E. Main St., Springerville* ☏ *928/333–4321*) stays open 365 days a year, and has a well-stocked sporting-goods and outdoor-equipment section.

The White Mountains' elevation makes the area a great place to stay cool in summer.

WHERE TO EAT

$ ✗ **Booga Reds**. The delicious home-style cooking, such as fish-and-chips
AMERICAN and roast-beef dinner, is worth a stop. Should your palate demand
something spicier, try one of the many Mexican dishes—the enchiladas
are wonderful. Save room for the daily fruit or cream pie. Booga Reds
opens at 6 AM for an early breakfast but closes relatively early—at 9
PM—so make your dinner an early one, too. ⊠ *521 E. Main St., Spring-*
erville 🖾 *928/333–2640* ⊟ *MC, V.*

$$ ✗ **Java Blues**. Not your typical mountain eatery, Java Blues oozes a cof-
AMERICAN feehouse vibe with its overstuffed couches and stained-glass windows.
Salads, soups, sandwiches, and a Greek Board—a variety of Greek
meats and cheeses served with toasted baguette—are on the lunch menu.
A separate dinner menu and a full bar make it a favorite evening spot,
too, featuring the only fettuccine Alfredo in town and chicken-fried
steak. The restaurant opens early and serves dinner six nights a week.
⊠ *341 E. Main St., Springerville* 🖾 *928/333–5282* ⊟ *MC, V.*

WHERE TO STAY

¢–$ 🛏 **Reed's Lodge**. It's an older motel, but a town favorite. The rooms of
this mostly single-story lodge have Western accents such as knotty-pine
paneling and Navajo-print bedspreads. Perks include a recreation room
with pool table, video games, and a pinball machine; a gift shop; and
complimentary bicycles. Enjoy coffee, tea, cocoa, or cider every morning.
Proprietor Roxanne Knight will arrange visits for guests on a working
(not dude) ranch, cattle drives, horseback adventures, four-wheel-drive
tours, wildlife- and petroglyph-viewing trips, or fossil-hunting expedi-
tions. **Pros:** well priced. **Cons:** modest accommodations; few frills. ⊠ *514*

E. Main St., Springerville ☎ *928/333–4323 or 800/814–6451* ⊕ *www. k5reeds.com* ⤴ *45 rooms, 5 suites* ⟁ *In-room: refrigerator (some), Wi-Fi. In-hotel: some pets allowed* ☰ *AE, D, DC, MC, V.*

$–$$ 🏨 **Rode Inn.** Don't let the John Wayne motif scare you away—two cardboard figures of "The Duke" in full cowboy regalia are perched on a walkway above the lobby, and his photos decorate the walls; the rooms and service here are excellent. John Wayne did in fact stay here (when it was a Ramada Inn), and the room in which he slept has been converted into a plush suite. **Pros:** kitschy, but comfortable. **Cons:** take away the accessories and it's just an old Ramada Inn. ⊠ *242 E. Main St., Springerville* ☎ *928/333–4365* ⊕ *www.rodeinnmotels.com* ⤴ *60 rooms, 3 suites* ⟁ *In-room: refrigerator, Wi-Fi. In-hotel: laundry facilities, some pets allowed* ☰ *AE, D, DC, MC, V* ⦿ *CP.*

$–$$ 🏨 **X Diamond Ranch.** This magnificent ranch has log cabins complete
★ with porches, fireplaces, and full kitchens. Most sleep two to six, but the Butler House and the Beaver Lodge sleep eight. Most cabins include hot tubs or Jacuzzis, and all have high-definition TVs. Activities include fly-fishing, horseback riding, and tours of Little Bear archaeological site on the ranch land—in June you can even take part in the excavation yourself. Nonguests are welcome to participate in activities. **Pros:** one of the best known and most picturesque spots in the area. **Cons:** no on-site restaurant, so plan on making your own meals. ⊠ *S. Fork Rd., 10 mi southwest of Eagar off AZ 260* ⊕ *Box 791, Springerville 85938* ☎ *928/333–2286* ⊕ *www.xdiamondranch.com* ⤴ *7 cabins* ⟁ *In-room: no a/c, kitchen* ☰ *AE, D, MC, V.*

SHOPPING

K-5 Western Gallery (⊠ *Reed's Lodge, 514 E. Main St., Springerville* ☎ *928/333–4323*) sells wares created by White Mountains artists and local craftspeople, including those from nearby reservations. The gallery teems with Western-themed paintings, books on local history, wildlife, and cowboy poetry, and even John Wayne paper dolls.

NIGHTLIFE

Springerville and Eagar aren't known for their nightlife, but **Tequila Reds** (⊠ *521 E. Main St., Springerville* ☎ *928/333–5036*) is the best place around to catch a televised sporting event. It's behind Booga Reds restaurant and stays open until at least 11 most nights.

CORONADO TRAIL

The 127-mi stretch of U.S. 191 from Springerville to Clifton.

GETTING HERE AND AROUND

Take U.S. 191 for 127 mi from Springerville to Clifton, and be prepared for an eye-opening ride. Allow a good four hours to make the steep, winding drive, more if you plan to stop and leisurely explore.

WHEN TO GO

It's best to drive in summer. The road is curvy—the name Devil's Highway exists for a reason—and is not to be driven in snow or ice.

EXPLORING

Surely one of the world's curviest roads, the twisting **Coronado Trail** portion of U.S. 191 was referred to as the Devil's Highway in its prior incarnation as U.S. 666. More significantly, the route parallels the one allegedly followed more than 450 years ago by Spanish explorer Francisco Vásquez de Coronado on his search for the legendary Seven Cities of Cibola, where the streets were reputedly paved with gold and jewels.

This 127-mi stretch of highway is renowned for the transitions of its spectacular scenery over a dramatic 5,000-foot elevation change—from rolling meadows to spruce- and ponderosa pine–covered mountains, down into the Sonoran Desert's piñon pine, grassland savannas, juniper stands, and cacti. A trip down the Coronado Trail crosses through Apache-Sitgreaves National Forest, as well as the White Mountain Apache and San Carlos Apache Indian reservations.

Pause at **Blue Vista,** perched on the edge of the Mogollon Rim, about 30 mi outside Alpine, to take in views of the Blue Range Mountains to the east and the succession of tiered valleys dropping some 4,000 feet back down into the Sonoran Desert. Still above the rim, this is one of your last opportunities to enjoy the blue spruce, ponderosa pine, and high-country mountain meadows.

About 17 mi south of Blue Vista, the Coronado Trail continues to twist and turn, eventually crossing under 8,786-foot **Rose Peak.** Named for the wild roses growing on its mountainside, Rose Peak is also home to a fire lookout tower from which peaks more than 100 mi away can be seen on a clear day. This is a great picnic-lunch stop.

After Rose Peak, enjoy the remaining scenery some 70 more mi until you reach the less-scenic towns of Clifton and Morenci, homes to a massive copper mine. U.S. 191 then swings back west, links up with U.S. 70, and provides a fairly straight shot to Globe.

ALPINE

27 mi south of Springerville-Eagar on U.S. 191.

Known as the Alps of Arizona, the tiny, scenic village of Alpine promotes its winter recreation opportunities, but outdoors enthusiasts will find that the town, sitting on the lush plains of the San Francisco River, is an ideal base for hiking, fishing, and mountain-biking excursions during the warmer months. With summer cabins tucked in the pines, campgrounds, 11 lakes, and 200 mi of trout streams within a 30-mi radius, outdoor recreation drives this mountain burg.

GETTING HERE AND AROUND

Take U.S. 191 south from Springerville 27 mi. This is a good stop along the Coronado Trail.

WHEN TO GO

This area of the Apache National Forest is remote as it gets, and the name Alpine should indicate the climate. If you're there in winter, expect road closures or delays if there's a storm. In summer, this is a great place to transition from green forests to, eventually, brown desert and cacti.

SPORTS AND THE OUTDOORS

BICYCLING The 8-mi **Luna Lake Trail** (✉ *U.S. 180, Alpine 85925*), 5 mi east of U.S. 191, is a good two-hour cruise for beginner and intermediate cyclists. The trailhead is on the north side of the lake, before the campground entrance.

FISHING A divergence of the San Francisco River's headwaters, 80-acre **Luna Lake** (✉ *U.S. 180, Alpine 85925*), 5 mi east of U.S. 191, is well stocked with rainbow trout. **Tackle Shop** (☎ *928/339–4338*), at the junction of U.S. 180 and 191, carries trout and fly-fishing supplies. **Arizona Mountain Flyfishing** (☎ *928/339–4829* ⊕ *www.azmtflyfishing.com*) guides anglers to top fishing streams and teaches novices.

GOLF **Alpine Country Club** (✉ *58 County Rd. 2122, Alpine 85920* ☎ *928/339–4944* ✵. *18 holes. 5595 yds. Par 70. Slope 107. Green Fee: $20* ⌕ *Facilities: restaurant*) is off U.S. 180, 3 mi east of U.S. 191. At 8,500 feet above sea level, it's one of the highest golf courses in the Southwest. Even if you don't play golf, stop in for New Mexican–style food—enchiladas here are stacked, not rolled—and breathtaking scenery at the club's Aspen Room Restaurant. It's 1 mi south of Alpine on Blue River Road. The course is closed from November to April, and the restaurant is closed Monday.

HIKING The **Escudilla National Recreation Trail** (✉ *U.S. 191, Hulsey Lake*) is more idyllic than arduous; the 3-mi trail wends through the Escudilla Wilderness to the summit of towering, 10,912-foot **Escudilla Mountain**, Arizona's third-tallest peak. The trail climbs 1,300 feet to a fire tower 0.25 mi from the summit. From Alpine, take U.S. 191 north and follow the signs to Hulsey Lake (about 5 mi).

SNOW SPORTS **Williams Valley Winter Sports Area** (✉ *FSR 249, Alpine 85929* ☎ *928/339–5000 for Alpine Ranger District information*), 2.5 mi west of town, has 12.5 mi of cross-country and snowshoe trails of varying difficulty maintained by the Alpine Ranger District. Toboggan Hill is a favorite for families, with sleds, toboggans, and tubes. Shelters, picnic facilities, and toilets are available. Pick up an Apache-Sitgreaves National Forest map and "Winter Sports" brochure from the Alpine Ranger District, and call for conditions prior to heading out.

WHERE TO STAY

$ ⛺ **Downs' Ranch Hide-Away.** Looking for a vacation that is really back-of-beyond? For stress relief, do as the locals do and go "down on the Blue." Blue, Arizona, on the Blue River in the Blue Range Primitive Area, along the Arizona–New Mexico border, is one of the most remote sections of the state and a sure cure for the city-life blues. Try hiking or horseback riding to explore Blue River, pine forests, canyons, Native American dwellings, wildlife—or just sit on the porch and enjoy a hefty helping of serenity. Cabins have complete kitchens, and owners Bill and Mona Bunnell suggest you bring food. Let them know in advance if you need meals arranged. The ranch accepts only cash, checks, traveler's checks, or money orders. **Pros:** a truly one-of-a-kind way to commune with Mother Nature; open year-round. **Cons:** zero amenities; limited payment options. ⌂ *Box 77, Blue 85922* ☎ *928/339–4952* ⊕ *www.dcoutfitters.com/downsRanch.php* ⇦ *4 cabins* ⌂ *In-room: Kitchen, no phone, no tv.* ▭ *No credit cards.*

$ ⊞ **Tal-Wi-Wi Lodge.** This lodge draws many repeat visitors—particularly
★   car and motorcycle enthusiasts—to its lush meadows, a favorite for
bird-watchers. Motel-style rooms are simple and clean, with three of
the most popular rooms having wood-burning fireplace-stoves, indoor
hot tubs, or both. In the evening stroll the grounds and gaze at the
Milky Way in the brilliant night sky. With satellite TV and live country music on weekends, the lodge saloon draws a loyal local following. The cozy, casual restaurant is open May through November and
serves breakfast on weekends and dinner Thursday through Saturday.
Prime rib is the house specialty, but they also serve pizza and homemade pies. **Pros:** best place to stay in Alpine, with absolutely majestic
views of the area. **Cons:** bare-bones and rustic. ⊠ *U.S. 191* ⊕ *Box 169,
Alpine 85920* ☎ *928/339–4319* ⊕ *www.talwiwilodge.com* ☞ *20 rooms*
⚘ *In-room: no a/c, no TV. In-hotel: restaurant, bar, Wi-Fi, some pets
allowed* ⊟ *MC, V.*

▮ **OFF THE
BEATEN
PATH**   **Blue Range Primitive Area.** Directly east of Hannagan Meadow, these
unspoiled 170,000 acres, lovingly referred to by locals as "the Blue,"
comprise the last designated primitive area in the United States. The
diverse terrain surrounds the Blue River and is crossed by the Mogollon Rim from east to west. No motorized or mechanized equipment
is allowed—including mountain bikes; passage is restricted to foot
or horseback. Many trails interlace the Blue: prehistoric paths of the
ancient native peoples, cowboy trails to move livestock between pas-
tures and water sources, access routes to lookout towers and fire trails.
Avid backpackers and campers may want to spend a few days exploring the dozens of hiking trails. Even though trail access is fairly good,
hikers need to remember that this is primitive, rough country, and it's
essential to carry adequate water supplies.

HANNAGAN MEADOW

23 mi south of Alpine, 50 mi south of Springerville-Eagar.

GETTING HERE AND AROUND

The Coronado Trail stretch of U.S. 191 passes through this remote
part of the state.

WHEN TO GO

Just like other towns of eastern Arizona, Hannagan Meadow is warm
(not hot!) in summer and cold and snowy in winter. You'll have
to drive a while to get here, so stay at least a day to make the trip
worthwhile.

EXPLORING

★   **Hannagan Meadow** is a pastorally mesmerizing location. Lush and isolated at a 9,500-foot-plus elevation, the meadow is home to elk, deer,
and range cattle, as well as blue grouse, wild turkeys, and the occasional
eagle. Adjacent to the meadow, the Blue Range Primitive Area provides
access to miles of untouched wilderness and some stunning rugged terrain, and it's a designated recovery area for the endangered Mexican
gray wolf. It's believed that Francisco Vásquez de Coronado and his
party came through the meadow on their famed expedition in 1540 to
find the Seven Cities of Cibola.

SPORTS AND THE OUTDOORS

Want to get away from it all? The **Apache Ranger District** of the Apache-Sitgreaves National Forest has secluded spaces for outdoors adventures year-round. Hikers and anglers can check out the 11,000-acre **Bear Wallow Wilderness Area** (west of U.S. 191 and bordered by FSR 25 and 54), which has cool, flowing streams stocked with native Apache trout. The **Rose Spring Trail** is a pleasant 5.5-mi hike with a moderate gradient and magnificent views from the Mogollon Rim's edge; the trailhead is at the end of Forest Service Road 54. **Reno Trail** and **Gobbler Trail** both drop into the main canyon from well-marked trailheads off Forest Service Road 25. Reno Trail meanders 2 mi through conifer forest and aspen, while Gobbler Trail is 2.5-mi long with views overlooking the Black River and Fort Apache Indian Reservation. This designated wilderness (and some of its trails) borders the San Carlos Apache Indian Reservation, where an advance permit is required for entry.

In winter, try the 8.5 mi of groomed cross-country trails of the **Hannagan Meadow Winter Recreation Area** (⊠ *U.S. 191, Hannagan Meadow*), which also is part of the Apache-Sitgreaves National Forest. The 4.5-mi **Clell Lee Loop** is an easy route; the advanced-level, ungroomed **KP Rim Loop** traverses upper elevations of the Blue Range Primitive Area and provides some of the most varied (and tranquil) remote skiing in the state. The area just northeast of U.S. 191 is a snowmobiling playground. Trailheads are at U.S. 191 and Forest Service Road 576. There are no rental shops nearby, so bring your own equipment.

Contact **Apache-Sitgreaves National Forest** (⊠ *Alpine Ranger District, U.S. 191* ✆ *Box 469, Alpine 85920* ☎ *928/339–5000* ⊕ *www.fs.fed. us/r3/asnf*) for trail maps and information.

WHERE TO STAY

$–$$ ★ 🏨 **Hannagan Meadow Lodge.** Antiques and floral prints impart a genteel, Victorian quality to this lodge. The dining room has hewn-log beams and a glass wall that overlooks a pristine meadow. Log cabins are more rustic; some have full kitchens and fireplaces, whereas others are equipped with microwaves, stove tops, and wood-burning stoves. The solitude of the area is enhanced by the absence of phones and TVs in rooms and cabins. The general store sells sundries as well as fishing supplies, and rents snowshoes, cross-country skis, and mountain bikes. Continental breakfast is provided in summer. **Pros:** gorgeous surroundings. **Cons:** you should not rely on daily room cleaning; much more lodge than hotel. ⊠ *U.S. 191, 22 mi south of Alpine, Hannagan Meadow* ✆ *HC 61, Box 335, Alpine 85920* ☎ *928/339–4370* ⊕ *www. hannaganmeadow.com* ⇌ *7 rooms, 10 cabins* ⚑ *In-room: no a/c, no phone, kitchen (some), no TV. In-hotel: restaurant, bicycles, Wi-Fi hotspot, some pets allowed* ═ *MC, V.*

CLOSE UP

Petroglyphs: The Writing on the Wall

The rock art of early Native Americans is carved or painted on basalt boulders, on canyon walls, and on the underside of overhangs throughout the area. No one knows the exact meaning of these signs, and interpretations vary; they have been seen as elements in shamanistic or hunting rituals, as clan signs, maps, or even indications of visits by extraterrestrials.

WHERE TO FIND IT
Damaged by vandalism, many rock-art sites are not open to the public. Two good petroglyphs to check out at **Petrified Forest National Park** are Newspaper Rock, an overlook near mile marker 12, and the Puerco Pueblo Trail near mile marker 11. Other sites in Arizona include **Hieroglyphic Point** in Salt River canyon, and **Five-Mile Canyon** in Snowflake.

DETERMINING ITS AGE
It's just as difficult to date a "glyph" as it is to understand it. Archaeologists try to determine a general time frame by judging the style, the date of the ruins and pottery in the vicinity, the amount of patination (formation of minerals) on the design, or the superimposition of newer images on top of older ones. Most of eastern Arizona's rock art is estimated to be at least 1,000 years old, and many of the glyphs were created even earlier.

VARIETY OF IMAGES
Some glyphs depict animals like bighorn sheep, deer, bear, and mountain lions; others are geometric patterns. The most unusual are the anthropomorphs, strange humanlike figures with elaborate headdresses. Concentric circles are a common design. A few of these circles served as solstice signs, indicating the summer and winter solstice and other important dates. At the solstice, when the angle of the sun is just right, a shaft of light shines through a crack in a nearby rock, illuminating the center of the circle. Archaeologists believe that these solar calendars helped determine the time for ceremonies and planting.

Many solstice signs are in remote regions, but you can visit the Petrified Forest National Park around June 20 to see a concentric circle illuminated during the summer solstice. The glyph, reached by paved trail just a few hundred yards from the parking area, is visible year-round, but a finger of light shines directly in the center during the week of the solstice. The phenomenon occurs at 9 AM, a reasonable hour for looking at the calendar.

■TIP➜ Do not touch petroglyphs or pictographs—the oils from your hands can cause damage to the image.

THE PETRIFIED FOREST AND THE PAINTED DESERT

Only about 1½ hours from Show Low and the lush, verdant forests of the White Mountains, Arizona's diverse and dramatic landscape changes from pine-crested mountains to the sunbaked terrain. Inside the lunarlike landscape of the Painted Desert is the fossil-filled Petrified Forest.

PETRIFIED FOREST NATIONAL PARK

Northern Entrance: 160 mi north of Hannagan Meadow on AZ 191 and I-40, 27 mi east of Holbrook on I-40; Southern Entrance: 18 mi east of Holbrook on U.S. 180.

Though named for its famous fossilized trees, Petrified Forest National Park has something to see for history buffs of all stripes, from a segment of Route 66 to ancient dwellings to even more ancient fossils. And the good thing is that most of Petrified Forest's treasures can easily be viewed without a great amount of athletic conditioning. Much can be seen by driving along the main road, from which historic sites are readily accessible. By combining a drive along the park road with a short hike here and there and a visit to one of the park's landmarks, you can see most of the sights in as little as half a day.

GETTING HERE AND AROUND

Holbrook, the nearest larger town, is roughly 20 mi from either of the park's two entrances on U.S. 40.

Parking is free, and there's ample space at all trailheads, as well as at the visitor center and the museum. The main park road extends 28 mi from the Painted Desert Visitor Center (north entrance) to the Rainbow Forest Museum (south entrance). For park road conditions, call ☎ 928/524–6228.

TIMING

The park is rarely crowded. Weather-wise, the best time to visit is autumn, when nights are chilly but daytime temperatures hover near 70°F. Half of all yearly rain falls between June and August, so it's a good time to spot blooming wildflowers. The park is least crowded in winter, because of cold winds and occasional snow, though daytime temperatures are in the 50s and 60s.

ESSENTIALS

Accessibility The visitor center, museum, and overlooks on the scenic drive are wheelchair accessible. All trails are paved, and all are accessible except Blue Mesa, which is very steep.

Admission Fees Entrance fees are $10 per car for seven consecutive days or $5 per person on foot, bicycle, motorcycle, or bus.

Admission Hours The park is open daily 8 AM–5 PM from Labor Day through Memorial Day, and daily 7 AM–7 PM Memorial Day through Labor Day.

Permits Backcountry hiking and camping permits are free (limit of 15 days) at Painted Desert Visitor Center or the Rainbow Forest Museum before 4 PM.

Visitor Information Petrified Forest National Park (✉ *1 Park Rd., Petrified Forest 86028* ☎ *928/524–6228* ⊕ *www.nps.gov/pefo*).

EXPLORING

There are few places where the span of geologic and human history is as wide or apparent as it is at **Petrified Forest National Park**. Fossilized trees and countless other fossils date back to the Triassic Period, while a stretch of the famed Route 66 of more modern lore is protected within park boundaries. Ancestors of the Hopi, Zuni, and Navajo left petroglyphs, pottery, and even structures built of petrified wood. Nine park sites are on the National Register of Historic Places; one, the Painted Desert Inn, is one of only 3% of such sites that are further listed as National Historic Landmarks.

LOOK AND TOUCH— BUT DONT TAKE

One of the most commonly asked questions about the Petrified Forest is, "Can I touch the wood?" Yes! Feel comfortable to touch anything, pick it up, inspect it...just make sure you put it back exactly where you found it. It is illegal to remove even a small sliver of fossilized wood from the park.

SCENIC DRIVE

Painted Desert Scenic Drive. A 28-mi scenic drive takes you through the park from one entrance to the other. If you begin from the north, the first 5 mi of the drive takes you along the edge of a high mesa, with spectacular views of Painted Desert. Beyond lies the desolate Painted Desert Wilderness Area. After the 5-mi point, the road crosses Interstate 40, then swings south toward the Puerco River across a landscape covered with sagebrush, saltbrush, sunflowers, and Apache plume. Past the river, the road climbs onto a narrow mesa leading to Newspaper Rock, a panel of Pueblo Indian rock art. Then the road bends southeast, enters a barren stretch, and passes tepee-shape buttes in the distance. Next you come to Blue Mesa, roughly the park's midpoint and a good place to stop for views of petrified logs. The next stop on the drive is Agate Bridge, really a 100-foot log over a wide wash. The remaining overlooks are Jasper Forest and Crystal Forest, where you can get a further glimpse of the accumulated petrified wood. On your way out of the park, stop at the Rainbow Forest Museum for a rest and to shop for a memento. ⊠ *Begins at Painted Desert Visitor Center.*

HISTORIC SITES

Agate House. This eight-room pueblo is thought to have been built entirely of petrified wood 700 years ago. Researchers believe it might have been used as a temporary dwelling by seasonal farmers or traders from one of the area tribes. ⊠ *Rainbow Forest Museum parking area.*

Newspaper Rock. See huge boulders covered with petroglyphs believed to have been carved by the Pueblo Indians more than 500 years ago. ⊠ *6 mi south of Painted Desert Visitor Center.*

Painted Desert Inn National Historic Site. You'll find cultural-history exhibits, as well as the murals of Fred Kabotie, a popular 1940s artist whose work was commissioned by Mary Jane Colter. Native American crafts are displayed in this museum and mini visitor center. Check the schedule for daily events. ⊠ *2 mi north of Painted Desert Visitor Center* ☎ *928/524–6228* ⊕ *www.nps.gov/pefo* ⊠ *Free* ☉ *Labor Day–Memorial Day, daily 8–5; Memorial Day–Labor Day, daily 7–6.*

Puerco Pueblo. This is a 100-room pueblo, built before 1400 and said to have housed Ancestral Puebloan people. Many visitors come to see petroglyphs, as well as a solar calendar. ⊠ *10 mi south of the Painted Desert Visitor Center on the main park road.*

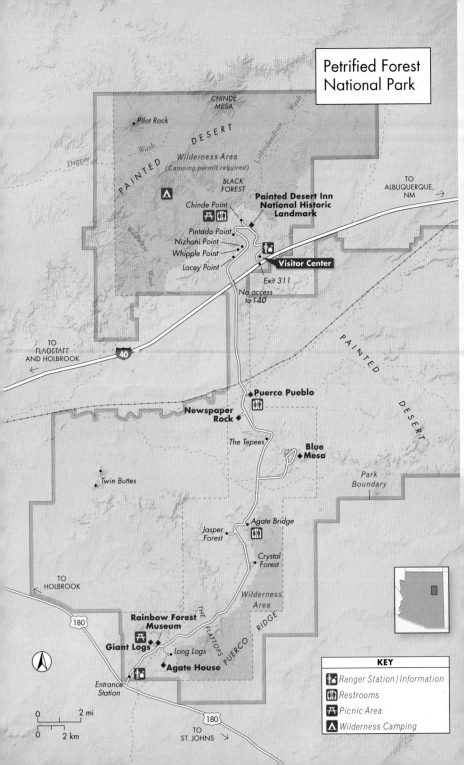

Petrified Forest National Park

CHINDE MESA

PAINTED DESERT

Pilot Rock

Wash

Digger

Wash

Wilderness Area
(Camping permit required)

Libhodendron Wash

BLACK FOREST

Chinde Point

Painted Desert Inn National Historic Landmark

Pintado Point

Nizhoni Point

Whipple Point

Lacey Point

Wilderness

Wash

Visitor Center

Exit 311

No access to I-40

TO ALBUQUERQUE, NM

TO FLAGSTAFF AND HOLBROOK

40

Puerco Pueblo

Newspaper Rock

The Tepees

Blue Mesa

PAINTED DESERT

Twin Buttes

Park Boundary

Agate Bridge

Jasper Forest

Crystal Forest

Wilderness Area

THE FLATTOPS   PUERCO RIDGE

TO HOLBROOK

180

Rainbow Forest Museum

Giant Logs

Long Logs

Agate House

Entrance Station

TO ST. JOHNS

180

0   2 mi

0   2 km

KEY

🛈	Ranger Station / Information
🚻	Restrooms
⛱	Picnic Area
⛺	Wilderness Camping

PETRIFIED FOREST IN ONE DAY

A nonstop drive through the park (28 mi) takes only 45 minutes, but you can spend a half day or more exploring if you stop along the way. From almost any vantage point you can see the multicolor rocks and hills that were home to prehistoric humans and ancient dinosaurs.

Entering from the north, stop at **Painted Desert Visitor Center** and see a 20-minute introductory film. **Painted Desert Inn Visitor Center**, 2 mi south of the north entrance, provides guided ranger tours. Drive south 8 mi to reach **Puerco Pueblo**, a 100-room pueblo built before 1400. Continuing south, you'll find Puebloan petroglyphs at **Newspaper Rock** and, just beyond, **the Tepees**, cone-shape rock formations.

Blue Mesa is roughly the midpoint of the drive, and the start of a 1-mi, moderately steep loop hike that leads you around badland hills made of bentonite clay. Drive on for 5 mi until you come to **Jasper Forest**, just past **Agate Bridge**, with views of the landscape strewn with petrified logs. **Crystal Forest**, 18 mi south of the north entrance, is named for the smoky quartz, amethyst, and citrine along the 0.8-mi loop trail. **Rainbow Forest Museum**, at the park's south entrance, has restrooms, a bookstore, and exhibits. Just behind Rainbow Forest Museum is **Giant Logs**, a 0.4-mi loop that takes you to "Old Faithful," the largest log in the park, estimated to weigh 44 tons.

6

SCENIC STOPS

★ **Agate Bridge.** Here you'll see a 100-foot log spanning a 40-foot-wide wash. ⊠ *19 mi south of Painted Desert Visitor Center.*

Crystal Forest. The fragments of petrified wood strewn here once held clear quartz and amethyst crystals. ⊠ *20 mi south of Painted Desert Visitor Center.*

★ **Giant Logs.** A short walk leads you past the park's largest log, known as "Old Faithful." It's considered the largest because of its diameter (9 feet, 9 inches), weight (44 tons), and as well as how tall it once was. ⊠ *28 mi south of Painted Desert Visitor Center.*

Jasper Forest. More of an overlook than a forest, this spot has a large concentration of petrified trees in jasper or red. ⊠ *17 mi south of Painted Desert Visitor Center.*

The Tepees. Witness the effects of time on these cone-shape rock formations colored by iron, manganese, and other minerals. ⊠ *8 mi south of Painted Desert Visitor Center.*

VISITOR CENTERS

Painted Desert Visitor Center. This is the place to go for general park information and an informative 20-minute film on the park. Proceeds from books purchased here will fund continued research and interpretive activities for the park. ⊠ *North entrance, off I–40, 27 mi east of Holbrook* ☎ *928/524–6228* ☽ *Labor Day–Memorial Day, daily 8–5; Memorial Day–Labor Day, daily 7–6. Post office weekdays 11–1.*

Walking Petrified Forest's short trails can be a nice break from driving along Interstate 40, which crosses the park.

Rainbow Forest Museum and Visitor Center. The museum houses artifacts of early reptiles, dinosaurs, and petrified wood. Be sure to see Gurtie, a skeleton of a phytosaur, a crocodile-like carnivore. ⊠ *South entrance, off U.S. 180, 18 mi southeast of Holbrook* ☏ *928/524–6228* ☉ *Labor Day–Memorial Day, daily 8–5; Memorial Day–Labor Day, daily 7–6.*

Painted Desert Inn National Historic Site. This third visitor center at the park isn't as large, but here you can get information as well as view cultural history exhibits. ⊠ *2 mi north of Painted Desert Visitor Center* ☏ *928/524–6228* ☉ *Labor Day–Memorial Day, daily 8–5; Memorial Day–Labor Day, daily 7–6.*

SPORTS AND THE OUTDOORS

Because the park goes to great pains to maintain the integrity of the fossil- and artifact-strewn landscape, sports and outdoor options in the park are limited to on-trail hiking.

HIKING

All trails begin off the main road, with restrooms at or near the trailheads. Most maintained trails are relatively short, paved, clearly marked, and, with a few exceptions, easy to moderate in difficulty. Hikers with greater stamina can make their own trails in the wilderness area, located just north of the Painted Desert Visitor Center. Watch your step for rattlesnakes, which are common in the park—if left alone and given a wide berth, they are passed easily enough.

EASY **Crystal Forest.** The easy 0.8-mi loop leads you past petrified wood that once held quartz crystals and amethyst chips. ⊠ *20 mi south of the Painted Desert Visitor Center.*

CLOSE UP

Petrified Forest Flora and Fauna

Engelmann's asters and sunflowers are among the blooms in the park each summer. Juniper trees, cottonwoods, and willows grow along Puerco River wash, providing shelter for all manner of wildlife. You might spot mule deer, coyotes, prairie dogs, and foxes, while other inhabitants, like porcupines and bobcats, tend to hide. Bird-watchers should keep an eye out for mockingbirds, red-tailed and Swainson's hawks, roadrunners, swallows, and hummingbirds. Look for all three kinds of lizards—collared, side-blotched, and southern prairie—in rocks.

Beware of rattlesnakes. They are common but can generally be easily avoided: Watch where you step, and don't step anywhere you can't see. If you do come across a rattler, give it plenty of space, and let it go its way before you continue yours. Other reptiles are just as common but not as worrisome. The gopher snake looks similar to a rattlesnake, but is nonpoisonous. The collared lizard, with its yellow head, can be seen scurrying out of your way in bursts measured at up to 15 MPH. They are not poisonous, but will bite in the rare instance of being caught.

6

Giant Logs. At 0.4 mi, Giant Logs is the park's shortest trail. The loop leads you to "Old Faithful," the park's largest log—it's 9 feet, 9 inches at its base, weighing 44 tons. ⊠ *Directly behind Rainbow Forest Museum, 28 mi south of Painted Desert Visitor Center.*

Long Logs. While barren, the easy 0.6-mi loop passes the largest concentration of wood in the park. ⊠ *26 mi south of Painted Desert Visitor Center.*

♿ **Puerco Pueblo.** A relatively flat and interesting 0.3-mi trail takes you past remains of a home of the Ancestral Puebloan people, built before 1400. The trail is paved and handicapped accessible. ⊠ *10 mi south of Painted Desert Visitor Center.*

MODERATE **Agate House.** A fairly flat 1-mi trip takes you to an eight-room pueblo
Fodor's Choice sitting high on a knoll. ⇨ *See Historic Sites in Exploring.* ⊠ *26 mi south*
★ *of Painted Desert Visitor Center.*

Blue Mesa. Although it's only 1 mi long and it's significantly steeper than the rest, this trail at the park's midway point is one of the most popular. ⊠ *14 mi south of Painted Desert Visitor Center.*

Painted Desert Rim. The 1-mi trail is at its best in early morning or late afternoon, when the sun accentuates the brilliant red, blue, purple, and other hues of the desert and Petrified Forest landscape. ⊠ *Tawa Point and Kachina Point, 1 mi north of Painted Desert Visitor Center.*

DIFFICULT **Kachina Point.** This is the trailhead for wilderness hiking. A 1-mi trail leads to the wilderness area, but from there you're on your own. With no developed trails, hiking here is cross-country style, but expect to see strange formations, beautifully colored landscape, and maybe, just maybe, a pronghorn antelope. ⊠ *On the northwest side of the Painted Desert Inn Museum.*

Different minerals in different concentrations cause the rich colors in petrified wood and in the Painted Desert.

EDUCATIONAL OFFERINGS

Children 12 and younger can learn more about the park's extensive human, animal, and geologic history in the Junior Ranger program.

Park Rangers lead regular programs along the Great Logs Trail, inside the Painted Desert Inn Museum, and to the Puerco Pueblo. Check online at ⊕ *www.nps.gov/pefo* and ask at either visitor center for the availability of **special tours,** such as the after-hours lantern tour of the Painted Desert Inn Museum.

WHERE TO EAT AND STAY

There is no lodging or campgrounds within the Petrified Forest. Backcountry camping is allowed if you obtain a free permit at the visitor center or museum; the only camping allowed is minimal-impact camping in a designated zone in the wilderness area. Group size is limited to eight. RVs are not allowed. There are no fire pits, nor is any shade available. Also note that if it rains, that pretty Painted Desert rock formation turns to sticky clay.

Dining in the park is limited to a cafeteria in the Painted Desert Visitor Center and snacks in the Rainbow Forest Museum. You may want to pack a lunch and eat at one of the park's picnic areas.

HOLBROOK

27 mi west of Petrified Forest National Park via I–40.

Downtown Holbrook is a monument to Route 66 kitsch. The famous "Mother Road" traveled through the center of Holbrook before Interstate 40 replaced it as the area's major east–west artery, and remnants of the "good ole days" can be found all over town. Route 66 itself still runs through Holbrook, following Navajo Boulevard and Hopi Drive. It makes a sharp corner at the intersection of these two roads, and used to cause traffic jams. The Downtowner, a popular coffee shop on this corner, served simple meals and coffee to sleepy truck drivers. Crowds from the movie theater at what is today East Hopi Drive brought Route 66 to a standstill. Moviegoers, who filled the streets after shows, considered it their right to block traffic; after all, many had traveled over 100 mi to see the movie.

Before Route 66 rolled into Holbrook, the town was a notorious hangout for cowboys from the vast Aztec Land and Cattle Company, better known as the Hashknife Outfit for the shape of their brand. For a walking-tour map, call the Chamber of Commerice and see the sites, including the infamous Bucket of Blood Saloon.

GETTING HERE AND AROUND
Holbrook is on Interstate 40, approximately 90 mi east of Flagstaff, and just 20 mi west of Petrified Forest National Park. You can access AZ 77, en route to Snowflake, Taylor, and other eastern Arizona recreation towns, directly from Interstate 40 in Holbrook.

ESSENTIALS
Information Holbrook Chamber of Commerce (⌂ *100 E. Arizona St., Holbrook 86025* ☎ *928/524–6558 or 800/524–2459* ⊕ *www.ci.holbrook.az.us*).

EXPLORING
★ The **Old Courthouse Museum**, at the corner of Arizona Street and Navajo Boulevard, holds memorabilia from the Route 66 heyday along with Old West and railroad records. ⌂ *100 E. Arizona St.* ☎ *800/524–2459* ⊕ *www.ci.holbrook.az.us* ⌂ *Free* ☉ *Daily 8–5.*

WHERE TO EAT AND STAY

$ ✕ **Mesa Italiana Restaurant.** While you're cruising on Route 66, stop by
ITALIAN to enjoy a hearty meal at one of Holbrook's most popular restaurants, where the chef prepares authentic-tasting traditional red-sauce dishes. Locals recommend the fresh pasta, including the spaghetti with Italian mushrooms. Don't forget the spumoni for dessert. For a more low-key environment, check out its adjoining grill that serves burgers and steak. ⌂ *2318 E. Navajo Blvd., Holbrook 86025* ☎ *928/524–6696* ▭ *AE, D, MC, V* ☉ *No lunch.*

$ ▦ **Holbrook Days Inn.** This clean, simple hotel has free Continental breakfast and local phone calls; it's a pleasant, convenient choice for a good price. Rooms have coffeemakers, hair dryers, and cable TV. **Pros:** heated indoor pool and hot tub; close to local restaurants. **Cons:** lacks the historic charm of most of its lodging neighbors. ⌂ *2601 Navajo Blvd.* ☎ *928/524–6949* ⊕ *www.daysinn.com* ⊸ *52 rooms, 3 suites* ⌂ *In-room: refrigerator (some), Wi-Fi. In-hotel: pool, laundry facilities* ▭ *AE, D, MC, V* ❍ *CP.*

¢ ▦ **Wigwam Motel.** One of the iconic images of Route 66 and listed on
★ the National Register of Historic Places, the Wigwam consists of 15 bright-white concrete tepees where you can sleep inexpensively in a quirky environment. As you might expect, wigwams are phoneless, but—here's to Mother Progress—these have cable TV. A small lobby museum exhibits Mexican, Native American, and military relics collected by the owner's family. The 180-pound, polished, petrified-wood

6

sphere is one of the largest in the Southwest. All the classic cars parked by the tepees also belong to the owners. **Pros:** impeccably kitschy; one of the signature spots along Route 66. **Cons:** very sparse accommodations. ✉ *711 W. Hopi Dr.* ☎ *928/524–3048* ⊕ *www.galerie-kokopelli. com/wigwam* ⟿ *15 rooms* ⧖ *In-room: no phone* ⊟ *MC, V.*

SHOPPING

McGees Beyond Native Tradition (✉ *2114 E. Navajo Blvd.* ☎ *928/524– 1977 or 800/524–9183* ⊕ *www.hopiart.com*) is the area's premier source of high-quality Native American jewelry, rugs, Hopi baskets, and kachina dolls. The owners have longstanding relationships with reservation artisans and a knowledgeable staff that adroitly assists first-time buyers and seasoned collectors.

WINSLOW

34 mi west of Holbrook on I-40, 58 mi east of Flagstaff.

Frequent flooding on the Little Colorado River frustrated the attempts of Mormon pioneers to settle here, but with the coming of the railroad the town roared into life. Later, Route 66 sustained the community until Interstate 40 passed north of town. New motels and restaurants sprouted near the interstate exits, and downtown was all but abandoned. Downtown Winslow is now revitalizing, with La Posada Winslow Hotel as its showpiece, but dining options are still scarce. Homolovi Ruins State Park, 5 mi north of Winslow, is closed at this writing. Sacred to the Hopi people, the park includes 40 ceremonial kivas and two pueblos containing more than 1,000 rooms each from between 1200 and 1425 AD.

GETTING HERE AND AROUND

Amtrak trains depart daily from Flagstaff to Winslow. From Albuquerque, Winslow is only a four-hour ride, with trains leaving daily.

WHERE TO STAY

$–$$ 🏨 **La Posada Winslow.** One of the great railroad hotels, La Posada ("resting place") exudes the charm of an 18th-century Spanish hacienda. Architect Mary Jane Colter, famous for her work at the Grand Canyon, designed and decorated the 68,000-square-foot hotel. Spanish and Native American furniture, antiques, and art permeate her designs. The lobby is a gallery for paintings by Tina Mion, one of the owners. Individually finished rooms are restored to 1930s style, and the lush gardens are a swath of green in the red-rock Colorado Plateau. At this writing, renovations are ongoing to open La Posada's East Wing for the first time, and add 14 rooms to the property. If you can't stay for the night, take a self-guided tour of the hotel ($3 donation). **Pros:** historic charm; unique architecture. **Cons:** dated rooms; ongoing renovations. ✉ *303 E. 2nd St., Winslow 86047* ☎ *928/289–4366* ⊕ *www.laposada.org* ⟿ *37 rooms* ⧖ *In-room: no phone. In-hotel: restaurant, bar* ⊟ *AE, D, MC, V.*

Tucson

WORD OF MOUTH

"If you enjoy being out in the desert among the cacti then Tucson is the place. Tucson is considerably smaller than Phoenix and . . . surrounded on the east and west by Saguaro National Park . . . there's the Sonoran Desert Museum which is an amazing natural history museum plus a zoo of native critters!"

—peterboy

WELCOME TO TUCSON

TOP REASONS TO GO

★ **Get close to the cacti:**
Unique to this region, the saguaro is the quintessential symbol of the Southwest. See them at Sabino Canyon and Saguaro National Park.

★ **Enjoy Mexican food:**
Tucson boasts that it's the "Mexican Food Capital," and you won't be disappointed at any of the authentic restaurants listed in this section.

★ **Explore the Arizona–Sonora Desert Museum:**
Anyone who thinks that museums are boring hasn't been here, where you can learn about the region in a gorgeous, mostly outdoor, setting.

★ **Tour Mission San Xavier del Bac:** The "White Dove of the Desert" is the oldest building in Tucson. Ornate carvings and frescoes inside add to the mystical quality of this active parish on the Tohono O'odham reservation.

★ **Stroll the U of A campus:** Stop in at one of the five museums, then walk University Boulevard and 4th Avenue for a taste of Tucson's hipper element.

1 **Downtown.** Three historic districts here—Barrio Historico, El Presidio, and Armory Park—encompass the Downtown area.

2 **The University of Arizona.** The 353-acre campus, classified as an arboretum, has several top-rated museums. At the west entrance, University Boulevard is lined with boutiques, cafés, and bookstores.

3 **Central and Eastside.** This mostly residential area is home to Tucson's zoo, its largest indoor shopping mall (Park Place), and its best municipal golf course (Randolph Park).

4 **Catalina Foothills.** North of River Road the land

GETTING ORIENTED

The metropolitan Tucson area covers more than 500 square mi in a valley ringed by mountains—the Santa Catalinas to the north, the Santa Ritas to the south, the Rincons to the east, and the Tucson Mountains to the west. Saguaro National Park bookends Tucson, with one section on the far east side and the other out west near the world-class Arizona–Sonora Desert Museum. The central portion of the city has most of the shops, restaurants, and businesses, but not many tourist sights. Downtown's historic district and the neighboring University area are much smaller and easily navigated on foot. Up north in the Catalina Foothills, you'll find first-class resorts, restaurants, and hiking trails, most with spectacular views of the entire valley.

becomes hilly and streets wind up to beautiful homes and resorts. At the east end, Sabino Canyon is a must for hikers.

5 Northwest. Suburban sprawl at it finest, this part of town just keeps growing. A dude ranch and a few riding stables are holdouts from a quieter era.

6 Westside. The untamed Tucson Mountain region embraces miles of saguaro forests, the Arizona–Sonora Desert Museum, and Mission San Xavier del Bac on the Tohono O'odham reservation.

Agave plant

TUCSON PLANNER

When to Go

Summer lodging rates (late May–September) are hugely discounted, even at many of the resorts, but there's a good reason: summer in Tucson is hot! Swimming and indoor activities like visiting museums (and spa treatments) are doable; but only the hardiest hikers and golfers stay out past noon in summer.

Tucson averages only 12 inches of rain a year. Winter temperatures hover around 65°F during the day and 38°F at night. Summers are unquestionably hot—July averages 104°F during the day and 75°F at night—but, as Tucsonans are fond of saying, "it's a dry heat."

The International Gem and Mineral Show descends on Tucson in February; book your hotel in advance or you'll be hard-pressed to find a room.

Visitor Information

Metropolitan Tucson Convention and Visitors Bureau. La Placita Village visitor center is open 9–5 weekdays and 9–4 weekends. ✉ 100 S. Church Ave., Suite 7199, Downtown ☎ 520/624–1817 or 800/638–8350 ⊕ www. visittucson.org

Getting Here and Around

You can fly to Tucson International Airport, but cheaper, nonstop flights into Phoenix—a two-hour drive away down Interstate 10—are often easier to find. Once in town, a car is essential to get to the outlying tourist sights.

Air Travel: Tucson International Airport (TUS) (☎ 520/573–8000 ⊕ www.tucsonairport.org) is 8.5 mi south of Downtown, off the Valencia exit of Interstate 10. Many hotels have a courtesy airport shuttle; inquire when making reservations. **Arizona Stagecoach** (☎ 520/889–1000 ⊕ www.azstagecoach.com) will carry you between the airport and all parts of Tucson and Green Valley for $9 to $41, depending on the location.

Bus Travel: Within the city limits, public transportation, which is geared primarily to commuters, is available through Sun Tran (☎ 520/792–9222 ⊕ www.suntran. com), Tucson's bus system.

Car Travel: You'll need a car to get around Tucson and the surrounding area, and it makes sense to rent at the airport; all the major car-rental agencies are represented. To save a little on cost, **Carefree Rent-a-Car** (☎ 520/790–2655), a local company, rents reliable used cars at good rates. Driving time from the airport to the center of town varies, but it's usually less than a half hour; add 15 minutes to any destination during rush hours (7:30 AM–9 AM and 4:30 PM–6 PM). Parking is not a problem in most parts of town, except near the university, where there are several pay lots.

Taxi Travel: Taxi rates vary widely since they're unregulated, but the taxi companies listed below charge $2 per mile plus an initial pickup fee ($4.50 from the airport, $2 from elsewhere in town). It's always wise to inquire about the cost before getting into a cab. It should be about $20 from the airport to central Tucson. One of the more reliable cab companies is **Allstate Taxi** (☎ 520/798–1111). **Yellow Cab** (☎ 520/624–6611 ⊕ www.yellowcabtucson.com) also operates **Fiesta Taxi** (☎ 520/622–7777), whose drivers speak English and Spanish.

Train Travel: Amtrak (✉ 400 E. Toole Ave., Downtown ☎ 520/623–4442 or 800/872–7245 ⊕ www.amtrak. com) serves the city with westbound and eastbound trains six times a week.

Outdoor Activities

Fall, winter, and spring in Tucson are mild with little rainfall, making the Tucson area wonderful for outdoor sports. The city has miles of bike paths (shared by joggers and walkers) and plenty of open spaces with memorable desert views, and some of the best golf courses in the country. Hikers enjoy the desert trails in Saguaro National Park, Sabino Canyon, and Catalina State Park—all within 20 minutes of central Tucson; in summer there are cooler treks in nearby mountain ranges—Mount Lemmon to the north and Madera Canyon to the south. Equestrians can find scenic trails at one of the many area stables or dude ranches.

Making the Most of Your Time

Even if you have only one day, you can experience both the wild and developed parts of Tucson. You can visit the Arizona–Sonora Desert Museum in the morning and combine it with a stop at Mission San Xavier del Bac or Old Tucson Studios. On the way back to town, stop in Downtown's Barrio Historico and El Presidio neighborhoods to meander the adobe-lined streets, then have dinner at one of the outstanding Mexican restaurants in Downtown or South Tucson.

Another option is spending a half day in Saguaro National Park. ■TIP→ Set out for a desert visit in the early morning when it's cooler and the liveliest time for wildlife. If you're based in the Foothills, you can choose Sabino Canyon instead; the saguaros are almost as plentiful and the vistas are equally rewarding. Nature in the morning can be combined with an afternoon in the University area: visit any of the five campus museums, then stroll University Boulevard and 4th Avenue for ethnic eats and vintage boutiques.

If you have another day for exploring and like to shop, head south towards the Mexican border. If you haven't seen Mission San Xavier yet, it's directly en route to Tubac, an artists' colony with historic sights as well as galleries. You can then head back toward Tucson, stopping at the Titan Missile Museum or at one of the casinos.

Native Cultures

Mexican-Americans make up about 30% of Tucson's population, and play a major role in all aspects of daily life. The city's south-of-the-border soul is visible in its tile-roof architecture, mariachi festivals, and abundance of Mexican restaurants. Native Americans have a strong presence as well, especially the Tohono O'odham and the Pascua Yaqui. Mission San Xavier del Bac, a thriving reservation parish, is a good spot to experience religious festivals around Christmas and Easter, and to sample fry bread, a favorite Indian snack.

Festivals and Events

Feb. Tucson Gem and Mineral Show. This huge trade show is the largest of its kind in the world. ☎ 800/638-8350 ⊕ www.tgms.org.

Feb. La Fiesta de los Vaqueros. America's largest outdoor midwinter rodeo is at the Tucson Rodeo Grounds. ☎ 520/741-2233 ⊕ www.tucsonrodeo.com.

Apr. Fiesta de Saguaro. Hispanic culture and heritage are celebrated at Saguaro National Park. ☎ 520/733-5153 ⊕ www.nps.gov/sagu.

July Saguaro Harvest. The majestic saguaro's fruit is harvested at Colossal Cave Mountain Park. ☎ 520/647-7121 ⊕ www.colossalcave.com.

7

TUCSON FOOD: NORTH OF THE BORDER

While Tucson ensures that authentic south-of-the-border culinary and cultural influences are not lost in translation, it also cooks up plenty of cross-border sway. The growing University metropolis boasts eats from around the world and mixes these tastes with more-local flavors.

Above: Peppers are the star ingredient in many Southwestern dishes. Top right: Tamales use corn flour and corn husks. Lower right: Chocolate, chiles, and spices make a savory mole sauce.

Emerging from an era of meat and potatoes and carne and frijoles—all of which it still does exceptionally well, Tucson has become a foodie tour de force. You can indulge in authentic chicken mole (rich sauce including chiles and chocolate) and *carne seca* (dried beef); fill up on some local/world food fusion; or get good and greasy with a Mexican corn dog.

Start with some classic Mexican dishes such as tamales (filled masa dough wrapped in a corn husk) or enchiladas (corn tortillas filled with meat or cheese). But today even Mexican-American foods are evolving into a new generation of creations. Do you prefer the chimichangas (deep-fried burritos) that purportedly originated at El Charro Café or the mango-filled ones at Mi Nidito for dessert? Taste and decide for yourself.

FOODIE FESTIVALS

In October visit the upscale Loew's Ventana Canyon Resort for the **Tucson Culinary Festival** (⊕ *www.tucsonculinaryfestival.com*), where more than 40 local indie restaurateurs and chefs showcase their talents. Feeling casual and eclectic? Hit Tucson's **4th Avenue Street Fair,** usually held in spring and late fall, where you can munch on every kind of festival food imaginable (⊕ *www.fourthavenue.org*).

SAY CHEESE

Many identify Mexican food by bright, glistening layers of cheddar that render the entrée below it unrecognizable. Not that there's anything wrong with that, but true Mexico-style meals are untouched by orange cheese. Authentic dishes are served with much smaller rations of white cheese, usually *queso blanco* or *panela*—mild cheeses that become soft and creamy when heated, but do not melt—and *cotija*, a Mexican-style Parmesan. These cheeses now appear in non-Hispanic menus, too.

as a garnish for everything from salads to nachos.

PICK A PEPPER

Another key to authentic Mexican food is its heat source: fresh peppers. Once a south-of-the-border specialty, increased demand moved production of the heat-tolerant plants into the southern United States where they have had a growing impact on regional cuisine. There are endless varieties of the spicy fruit, but here are some more commonly seen on local menus.

GREEN AND RED: Often roasted and peeled for stews and broths, sauces, rubs, marinades, confectionery, chili, and chiles rellenos. Green chiles are unripe with mild to medium-high heat. Red chiles are ripe with maximum heat.

JALAPEÑO: These flavorful green peppers can range from mild to hot and are served pickled, canned, deep-fried for "poppers," or

CHIPOTLE: When select jalapeños mature from green to a deep red, they're prime for the wood-smoking process that creates chipotle (chee-pote-lay) peppers. Their distinct flavor is popular in sauces, marinades, and salsas.

HABAÑERO: This thumblike pepper is one of the hottest. A little goes a long way in cooking. It's most often found in chili recipes and hot sauces.

POBLANO: This green pepper, aka *pasilla*, is usually mild, but can sometimes pack a punch. Dried, it's an ancho chile. The poblano is used for moles (mo-lays).

TAKE A STAND

Talk about fusion. Take the American tradition of ballpark franks, give it a Sonoran spin, and you'll have a Mexican hot dog, created by and sold in **El Guero Canelo** (*201 S. 12th Ave., Downtown 520/295–9005* ⊕ *elguero-canelo.com*)restaurant and their strategically placed taco stands. The dogs are made with *bolillos* (oval-shape baguettes) and topped with beans, cheese, and *crema*—a thin sour cream. Be on the lookout for the variety of other food stands around Tucson specializing in *tortas* (sandwiches) and burritos.

TUCSON AND SOUTHERN ARIZONA SHOPPING

Despite the waves of modernity that continue to wash over it, southern Arizona always emerges with reverence for its cultural influences and attention to detail, making it one of the best places to shop in the Southwest—even if you're just browsing.

Above: Papier mache skulls celebrate *El Dia de los Muertes* (The Day of the Dead). Right: Ceramics are popular crafts in Tucson and nearby Tubac.

With its proximity to Mexico, its numerous artisan and Indian communities, a prominent wine region, and a storied past, this booming area is bursting with rare culinary and curio items, home and garden decor, fine art, folklore, and clothing. Tucson is a wealth of wares, but a great way to find some firsthand bargains and fun is to go straight to the source—like Amado, Tubac, and Bisbee for resident fine art and serious souvenir shopping; Tombstone, where Old West kitsch and curios are alive and well; Sonoita, Elgin, and Willcox for some of the state's award-winning wines. The shopping list goes on, but your bucks can stop right here. There are many southern Arizona specialties to leave room for in your suitcase, or for which to bring an extra bag altogether.

EVENTS TO SHOP

A rural artisan extravaganza, **Tubac Festival of the Arts** (☎ 520/398–2704 ⊕ *www.tubacaz.com/festival.asp*) brings artists from around the country to exhibit their eclectic, fine, and tourist-oriented art. Shop like a rock star at the annual February **Tucson Gem and Mineral Show** (☎ 520/322–5773 ⊕ *www.tgms.org*), the world's largest, exhibiting precious stones, fossils, and jewels from around the globe.

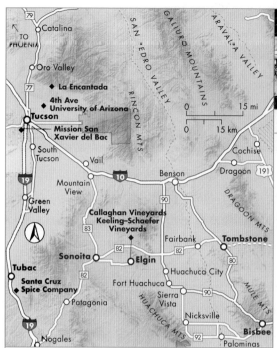

TOP SHOPS

Native and Mexican influence: Given the influences of the area, "ethnic" art is always in, especially pottery, baskets, rugs, furniture, and Mexican crafts including signature folk art depicting skeletons of the dearly departed honoring *El Dia de los Muertos* (The Day of the Dead). Check out **Del Sol** in Tucson or visit **San Xavier Plaza** on the Tohono O'odham Indian Reservation.

Consumables: For flavorful finds, wines from regional vineyards such as **Callaghan Vineyards** and **Keeling Schaefer Vineyards** are a winning gift, as are local seasonings from **Santa Cruz Spice Factory.**

Fashionable Finds: Not so much into local flare or things that don't relate to fashion? Make your way to outdoor mall **La Encantada** for upscale, limited-location clothing boutiques like J. Jill and Lucy.

QUICK BITES

Tucson's St. Philip's Plaza is near La Encantada and Tucson Mall and features upscale shops, great atmosphere, and acclaimed eats including **Acacia** (⊠ *4340 N. Campbell Ave. Foothills* ☎ *520/232–0101* ⊕ *www.acaciatucson.com*), which serves fresh, organic, and sustainable salads and sandwiches and more.

If you're in the Downtown, University, and 4th Avenue area, pop into **Delectables** (⊠ *533 N. 4th Ave, University* ☎ *520/884–9289* ⊕ *www.delectables.com*) for fresh gourmet salads, soups, sandwiches, and desserts.

7

Updated by
Mara Levin

The Old Pueblo, as Tucson is affectionately known, is built upon a deep Native American, Spanish, Mexican, and Old West foundation. Arizona's second-largest city is both a bustling center of business and a relaxed university and resort town. Metropolitan Tucson has more than 850,000 residents, including thousands of snowbirds, who flee colder climes to enjoy the sun that shines on the city more than 340 days out of 365.

The city has a tri-cultural (Hispanic, Anglo, Native American) population, and the chance to see how these cultures interact—and to sample their cuisines—is one of the pleasures of a visit. The city is particularly popular among golfers, but the area's many hiking trails will keep nonduffers busy, too. If the weather is too hot to stay outdoors comfortably, consider a cooler alternative at a museum like the Arizona State Museum or the Center for Creative Photography.

This college town has Mexican and Native American cultural influences, a striking landscape, and all the amenities of a resort town, as well as its fair share of ubiquitous strip malls and tract-home developments. High-tech industries have moved into the area, but the economy still relies heavily on tourism and the university—although, come summer, you'd never guess; when the snowbirds and students depart, Tucson can be a sleepy place.

EXPLORING TUCSON

Central Tucson—which has most of the shops, restaurants, and businesses—is roughly bounded by Craycroft Road to the east, Oracle Road to the west, River Road to the north, and 22nd Street to the south. The older Downtown section, east of Interstate 10 off the Broadway-Congress exit, is smaller and easy to navigate on foot. Downtown streets don't run on any sort of grid, however, and many are one-way, so it's best to get a good, detailed map. The city's Westside area is the vast region west of Interstate 10 and Interstate 19, which includes the western section of Saguaro National Park and the San Xavier Indian Reservation.

DOWNTOWN

The area bordered by Franklin Street on the north, Cushing Street on the south, Church Avenue on the east, and Main Avenue on the west contains more than two centuries of Tucson's history, dating from the original walled fortress, El Presidio de Tucson, built by the Spanish in 1776, when Arizona was still part of New Spain. A good deal of the city's history was destroyed in the 1960s, when large sections of Downtown's barrio were bulldozed to make way for the Tucson Convention Center, high-rises, and parking lots. However, within the area's three small historic districts it's still possible to explore Tucson's architectural and cultural past.

GETTING HERE AND AROUND Downtown only approaches bustling during the weekdays, at lunchtime and 5-6 PM for the evening rush hour. Otherwise, it's pretty quiet and easy to find metered street parking.

Numbers in the text correspond to numbers in the margin and on the Downtown Tucson map.

TOP ATTRACTIONS

1 **"A" Mountain.** The original name of this mountain, Sentinel Peak, west of Downtown, came from its function as a lookout point for the Spanish, though the Pima village and cultivated fields that once lay at the base of the peak are long gone. In 1915 fans of the University of Arizona football team whitewashed a large "A" on its side to celebrate a victory, and the tradition has been kept up ever since—the permanent "A" is now red, white, and blue. During the day the peak's a great place to get an overview of the town's layout; at night the city lights below form a dazzling carpet, but the teenage hangout–make-out scene may make some uncomfortable. ⊠ *Congress St. on Sentinel Peak Rd., Downtown.*

Downtown Historic Districts. El Presidio Historic District, north of the Convention Center and the government buildings that dominate Downtown, is an architectural thumbnail of the city's former self. The north–south streets Court, Meyer, and Main are sprinkled with traditional Mexican adobe houses sitting cheek by jowl with territorial-style houses, with wide attics and porches. Paseo Redondo, once called Snob Hollow, is the wide road along which wealthy merchants built their homes. The area most closely resembling 19th-century Tucson is the **Barrio Historico,** also known as Barrio Viejo. The narrow streets of this neighborhood, including Convent Avenue, have a good sampling of thick-wall adobe houses. The colorfully painted houses are close to the street, hiding the yards and gardens within. To the east of the Barrio Historico, across Stone Avenue, is the **Armory Park** neighborhood, mostly constructed by and for the railroad workers who settled here after the 1880s. The brick or wood territorial-style homes here were the Victorian era's adaptation to the desert climate. ⊠ *Downtown.*

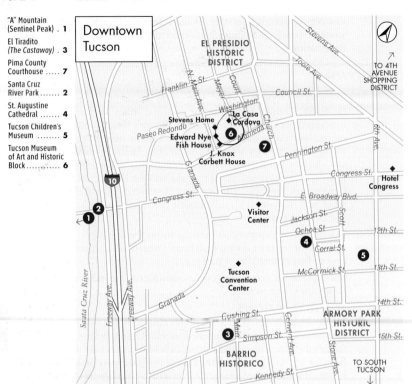

3 **El Tiradito (*The Castaway*).** No one seems to know the details of the story behind this little shrine, but everyone agrees a tragic love triangle was involved. A bronze plaque indicates only that it's dedicated to a sinner who is buried here on unconsecrated ground. The candles that line the cactus-shrouded spot attest to its continuing importance in local Catholic lore. People light candles and leave *milagros* (miracles; little icons used in prayers for healing) for loved ones. A modern-day miracle: the shrine's inclusion on the National Register of Historic Places helped prevent a freeway from plowing through this section of the Barrio Historico. ⊠ *Main Ave. south of Cushing St., Downtown.*

7 **Pima County Courthouse.** This pink Spanish colonial–style building with a
★ mosaic-tile dome is among Tucson's most beautiful historic structures. Still in use, it was built in 1927 on the site of the original single-story adobe court of 1869; a portion of the old presidio wall can be seen in the south wing of the courthouse's second floor. At the side of the building, the county assessor's office has a diorama depicting the area's early days. ⊠ *115 N. Church Ave., between Alameda and Pennington Sts., Downtown* ⊕ *www.jp.co.pima.az.us* ✉ *Free* ☉ *Weekdays 8–4:30, Sat. 8–noon.*

5 **Tucson Children's Museum.** Youngsters are encouraged to touch and
☺ explore the science, language, and history exhibits here. They can

examine a patient in the Medical Center or shop for healthy food in the Wellness Town Grocery Store. Dinosaur Canyon has mechanical prehistoric creatures, and there's an Enchanted Forest where toddlers can climb, build, and burn off steam. ✉ *200 S. 6th Ave., Downtown* ☎ *520/792–9985* ⊕ *www. tucsonchildrensmuseum.org* ✐ *$8* ⊙ *Tues.–Fri. 9–5, weekends 10–5.*

❻ ★ Tucson Museum of Art and Historic Block. The five historic buildings on this block are listed in the National Register of Historic Places. You can enter La Casa Cordova, the Stevens Home, the J. Knox Corbett House, and the Edward Nye Fish House,

LONG LIVE ADOBE!

Adobe—brick made of mud and straw, cured in the hot sun—was used widely as a building material in early Tucson because it provides natural insulation from the heat and cold and because it's durable in Tucson's dry climate. When these buildings are properly made and maintained, they can last for centuries. Driving around Downtown Tucson, you'll see adobe houses painted in vibrant hues such as bright pink and canary yellow.

but the Romero House, believed to incorporate a section of the presidio wall, is not open to the public. In the center of the museum complex, connecting the modern buildings to the surrounding historic houses, is the Plaza of the Pioneers, honoring Tucson's early citizens. The museum building, the only modern structure of the complex, houses a permanent collection of modern, contemporary, and Asian art and hosts traveling shows.

Permanent and changing exhibitions of Western art fill the **Edward Nye Fish House,** an 1868 adobe that belonged to an early merchant, entrepreneur, and politician, and his wife. The building is notable for its 15-foot beamed ceilings and saguaro cactus–rib supports. There are free docent tours of the museum, and you can pick up a self-guided tour map of El Presidio district. **La Casa Cordova,** one of the oldest buildings in Tucson, is also one of the best local examples of a Sonoran row house. This simple but elegant design is a Spanish style adapted to adobe construction. The oldest section of La Casa Cordova, constructed around 1848, has been restored to its original appearance, and is the Mexican Heritage Museum. El Nacimiento, a permanent installation of nativity scenes and depictions of Mexican family life, is on display here from November through March. The **J. Knox Corbett House** was built in 1906–07, and occupied by members of the Corbett family until 1963. The original occupants were J. Knox Corbett, successful businessman, postmaster, and mayor of Tucson, and his wife Elizabeth Hughes Corbett, an accomplished musician and daughter of Tucson pioneer Sam Hughes. Tucson's Hi Corbett field (the spring training field for the Colorado Rockies) is named for their grandnephew, Hiram. The two-story, Mission Revival–style residence has been furnished with Arts and Crafts pieces: Stickley, Roycroft, Tiffany, and Morris are among the more famous manufacturers represented. The **Stevens Home** was where the wealthy politician and cattle rancher Hiram Stevens and his Mexican wife, Petra Santa Cruz, entertained many of Tucson's leaders during the 1800s. A drought brought the Stevens's cattle ranching to a halt in 1893, and Stevens killed himself in despair after unsuccessfully attempting to shoot his wife (the bullet was deflected by the comb she wore in her hair). The 1865 house was restored in 1980, and now houses the Tucson Museum of Art's permanent collections of pre-Columbian, Spanish-colonial, and Latin American folk art. Admission to the museum and all four homes is free on the first Sunday of every month. ■TIP→ There's free parking in a lot behind the museum at Washington and Meyer streets. ⊠ *140 N. Main Ave., Downtown* ☎ *520/624–2333* ⊕ *www.tucsonmuseumofart.org* ☑ *$8* ☉ *Tues.–Sat. 10–5, Sun. noon–5. Free guided tours Oct.–Apr., Tues.–Sun.*

QUICK BITES

On the patio of the Stevens Home, part of the Tucson Museum of Art and Historic Block, Cafe A La C'Arte (⊠ *150 N. Main Ave., Downtown* ☎ *520/628–8533*) serves fanciful salads, soups, and sandwiches weekdays 11–3.

WORTH NOTING

❷ **Santa Cruz River & River Park.** When Europeans arrived in what is now Arizona, the Santa Cruz River had wide banks suitable for irrigation; over time its banks have been narrowed and contained and are now lined by River Park. These days it's a dry wash, or arroyo, most of the year, but sudden summer thunderstorms and rainwater from upper elevations can turn it into a raging river in a matter of hours. It's a favorite spot for walkers, joggers, bicyclists, and horseback riders. The park has a bike path, restrooms, drinking fountains, and sculptures created by local artists. ⊠ *W. Congress St. at Bonita Ave., Downtown* ⊕ *www.pima.gov/nrpr/parks.*

❹ **St. Augustine Cathedral.** Although the imposing white-and-beige, late-19th-century, Spanish-style building was modeled after the Cathedral of Queretaro in Mexico, a number of its details reflect the desert setting: above the entryway, next to a bronze statue of St. Augustine, are carvings of local desert scenes with saguaro cacti, yucca, and prickly pears—look closely and you'll find the horned toad. Compared with the magnificent facade, the modernized interior is a bit disappointing. ■TIP→ For a distinctly Southwestern experience, attend the mariachi mass celebrated Sunday at 8 AM. ⊠ *192 S. Stone Ave., Downtown* ☎ *520/623–6351* ⊕ *www.staugustinecathedral.com* ☑ *Free* ☉ *Daily 7–6.*

THE UNIVERSITY OF ARIZONA

The U of A (as opposed to rival ASU, in Tempe) is a major economic influence in Tucson, with a student population of more than 34,000. The land for the university was "donated" by a couple of gamblers and a saloon owner in 1891—their benevolence reputedly inspired by a bad hand of cards—and $25,000 of territorial (Arizona was still a territory back then) money was used to build Old Main, the original building, and hire six faculty members. Money ran out before Old Main's roof was placed, but a few enlightened citizens pitched in funds to finish it. Most of the city's populace was less than enthusiastic about the institution: they were disgruntled when the 13th Territorial Legislature

Colorful adobe buildings come in many shades beyond the natural clay color.

granted the University of Arizona to Tucson and awarded Phoenix what was considered the real prize—an insane asylum and a prison.

The university's flora is impressive—it represents a collection of plants from arid and semiarid regions around the world. An extremely rare mutated, or "crested," saguaro grows at the northeast corner of the Old Main building. The long, grassy mall in the heart of campus—itself once a vast cactus garden—sits atop a huge underground student activity center, and makes for a pleasant stroll on a balmy evening.

GETTING HERE AND AROUND
If you drive, leave your car in a university garage or lot; those on 2nd Street at Mountain Avenue, on Speedway Boulevard at Park Avenue, on Tyndall Avenue south of University Boulevard, and on 2nd Street at Euclid Avenue are the most convenient. Parking is free in these garages on weekends and holidays.

TIMING
Call ahead to verify hours for the university's museums, as yearly budget revisions often cause schedule changes. Visit the University of Arizona Web site (⊕ *www.arizona.edu*) for parking maps and the latest visitor information.

Numbers in the text correspond to numbers in the margin and on the University of Arizona map.

TOP ATTRACTIONS

❷ Arizona History Museum. Flanking the entrance to the museum are statues of two men: Father Kino, the Jesuit who established San Xavier del Bac and a string of other missions, and John Greenaway, indelibly linked to Phelps Dodge, the copper-mining company that helped Arizona earn statehood in 1912. The museum houses the headquarters of the state

U of A Campus Walking Tour

This tour takes in the highlights of the university area: Start at the northwest corner of campus, at Euclid and 2nd streets, at the public parking garage, then walk a half block east on 2nd Street to the **Arizona History Museum** to see how far the Old Pueblo has come in 100 years. A block south on Park Avenue, just inside the main gate of the university, is the **Arizona State Museum**, the place to explore Native American culture. Heading east on University Boulevard and deeper into the campus, you'll pass Old Main and the crested saguaro. As the road curves to the left, University Boulevard turns into the campus mall. The Student Union and University Bookstore are on your left; the sculpture in front of the complex depicts Arizona–Mexico border struggles. Cross over to the south side of the mall (watch out for Frisbees) and take a peek inside the old gymnasium, then continue east, passing the steps leading down to the underground activity center, and you'll come to the **Flandrau Science Center and Observatory**. Check telescope-viewing schedules, see a light show, or stock up on science-oriented gifts here.

Walk north on Cherry, then turn left onto 2nd Street, passing several fraternity and sorority houses. Turn right on Olive Road to find the **Center for Creative Photography**, home to most of photographer Ansel Adams's negatives and a slew of other exhibits in this medium. Across from the center is the **University of Arizona Museum of Art**. From here it's a short walk west on Speedway Boulevard to Park Avenue, where you can go south to 2nd Street and return to the Arizona Historical Society's Museum and the parking lot.

For more college culture, continue down Park to University Boulevard and turn right. This area is the hub of off-campus activity, with restaurants, cafés, and trendy boutiques. You can walk—or on weekends ride the **Old Pueblo Trolley** along University to **4th Avenue**, Tucson's last bastion of bohemia, for shopping and people-watching.

If you drive, leave your car in a university garage or lot; those on 2nd Street at Mountain Avenue, on Speedway Boulevard at Park Avenue, on Tyndall Avenue south of University Boulevard, and on 2nd Street at Euclid Avenue are the most convenient. Parking is free in these garages on weekends and holidays.

Historical Society and has exhibits exploring the history of southern Arizona, the Southwest United States, and northern Mexico, starting with the Hohokam Indians and Spanish explorers. The harrowing "Life on the Edge: A History of Medicine in Arizona" exhibit promotes a new appreciation of modern drugstores in present-day Tucson. Children enjoy the exhibit on copper mining (complete with an atmospheric replica of a mine shaft and camp) and the stagecoaches in the transportation area. The library has an extensive collection of historic Arizona photographs and sells inexpensive reprints. Admission is free on the first Saturday of every month. Park in the garage at the corner of 2nd and Euclid streets and get a free parking pass in the museum. ⊠ *949 E.*

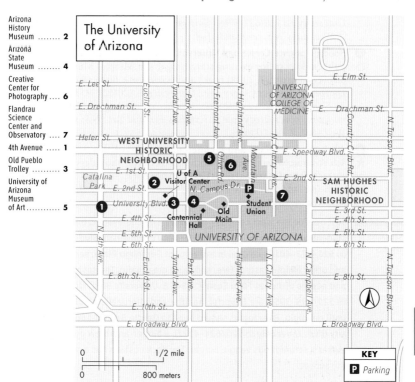

The University of Arizona

7

KEY

P Parking

0 _____ 1/2 mile

0 _____ 800 meters

2nd St., University ☎ *520/628–5774* ⊕ *www.arizonahistoricalsociety. org* 🖃 *$5* ⊙ *Mon.–Sat. 10–4; library weekdays 10–2, Sat. 10–1.*

❹ Arizona State Museum. Inside the main gate of the university is Arizona's oldest museum, dating from territorial days (1893) and recognized as one of the world's most important resources for the study of Southwestern cultures. Exhibits in the original (south) building focus on the state's ancient history, including fossils and a fascinating sample of tree-ring dating. "Paths of Life: American Indians of the Southwest" is a permanent exhibit that explores the cultural traditions, origins, and contemporary lives of 10 native tribes of Arizona and Sonora, Mexico. ✉ *1013 E. University Blvd., at Park Ave. University* ☎ *520/621–6302* ⊕ *www.statemuseum.arizona.edu* 🖃 *$5* ⊙ *Mon.–Sat. 10–5.*

❻ Center for Creative Photography. Ansel Adams conceived the idea of a ★ photographer's archive and donated the majority of his negatives to this museum. In addition to its superb collection of his work, the center has works by other major photographers, including Paul Strand, W. Eugene Smith, Edward Weston, and Louise Dahl-Wolfe. Changing exhibits in the main gallery display selected pieces from the collection, but if you'd like to see the work of a particular photographer in the archives, call to arrange an appointment. ✉ *1030 N. Olive Rd., north of 2nd St.,*

University ☎ *520/621–7968* ⊕ *www.creativephotography.org* ✉ *Free* ☉ *Weekdays 9–5, weekends 1–4.*

❼ Flandrau Science Center and Observatory. Attractions include a 16-inch public telescope for evening stargazing and a Mineral Museum, which displays more than 2,000 rocks and gems, some quite rare. ⊠ *1601 E. University Blvd., at Cherry Ave., University* ☎ *520/621–4515, 520/621–7827 recorded message* ⊕ *www.uasciencecenter.org* ✉ *$4 for mineral museum, observatory free* ☉ *Exhibits Fri. and Sat. 9–5; Observatory Wed.–Sat. 7 PM–10 PM.*

❶ 4th Avenue. Students and counterculturists favor this 0.5-mi strip of ★ 4th Avenue, where vintage-clothing stores rub shoulders with ethnic eateries from Guatemalan to Greek. After dark, 4th Avenue bars pulse with live and recorded music. ⊠ *Between University Blvd. and 9th Ave. University.*

QUICK BITES

Just outside the west campus gate, University Boulevard is lined with student-oriented eateries. Sinbad's (⊠ *810 E. University Blvd., University* ☎ *520/623–4010*), nestled in the verdant Geronimo Plaza, serves falafel and other Middle Eastern fare, and has a great patio. The sushi, rice bowls, and noodle dishes at **Fuku Sushi** (⊠ *940 E. University Blvd., University* ☎ *520/798–3858*) are flavorful, healthy, and affordable. It's also open until midnight. Beer lovers should head to Gentle Ben's (⊠ *865 E. University Blvd., University* ☎ *520/624–4177*), a burger-and-brew pub that also makes a scrumptious veggie burger. The deck upstairs has a good view of the sunset.

WORTH NOTING

❸ Old Pueblo Trolley. You can ride historic electric trolleys through the streets of Tucson along University Boulevard and 4th Avenue past shops and restaurants Friday through Sunday. The route passes restored historic buildings on part of the original 1898 streetcar track and terminates near the west gate of the university campus. ⊠ *360 E. 8th St., University* ☎ *520/792–1802* ⊕ *www.oldpueblotrolley.org* ✉ *Fri. and Sat. $1, Sun. 25¢* ☉ *Fri. 6 PM–10 PM, Sat. noon–midnight, Sun. noon–6.*

❺ University of Arizona Museum of Art. This small museum houses a collection of European paintings from the Renaissance through the 17th century, along with modern works by Georgia O'Keeffe and Jackson Pollock. A highlight is the Kress Collection's *retablo* from Ciudad Rodrigo: 26 panels of an altarpiece made in 1488 by Fernando Gallego. ⊠ *Fine Arts Complex, Bldg. 2, southeast corner of Speedway Blvd. and Park Ave., University* ☎ *520/621–7567* ⊕ *www.artmuseum.arizona.edu* ✉ *$5* ☉ *Tues.–Fri. 9–5, weekends noon–4.*

CENTRAL AND EASTSIDE

Tucson expanded north and east from the university during the 1950s and '60s, and currently continues to spread southeast. The sights worth seeing in this mostly residential area include the Tucson

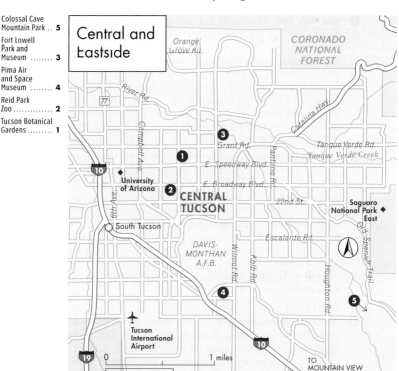

Botanical Gardens, the small Reid Park Zoo, and the Fort Lowell Park and Museum. Colossal Cave Mountain Park and Pima Air and Space Museum are on the southeast outskirts. Saguaro National Park East is also on the far east side of town.

TIMING   If it's warm, visit outdoor attractions such as the zoo or Tucson Botanical Gardens in the morning; note that Colossal Cave stays at a constant, cool temperature, so it's a good option on a hot day.

Numbers in the text correspond to numbers in the margin and on the Central and Eastside and Catalina Foothills maps.

CENTRAL TUCSON

③ **Fort Lowell Park and Museum.** Fertile soil and proximity to the Rillito River once enticed the Hohokam to construct a village on this site. Centuries later, a fort (in operation from 1873 to 1891) was built here to protect the fledgling city of Tucson against the Apaches. The former commanding officer's quarters at this tiny museum has artifacts from military life in territorial days. Admission to the museum is free on the first Saturday of every month. The park has a playground, ball fields, tennis courts, and a duck pond. ✉ *2900 N. Craycroft Rd., Central* ☎ *520/885–3832* ⊕ *www.arizonahistoricalsociety.org* ☞ *Museum $3* ⊙ *Fri. and Sat. 10–4.*

② **Reid Park Zoo**. This small but well-designed zoo won't tax the children's—or your—patience. There are plenty of shady places to sit, a wonderful gift shop, and a snack bar to rev you up when your energy flags. The zoo's friendly giraffes—who come quite close to visitors—and the South American section with its rain forest and exotic birds are popular. If you're visiting in summer, go early in the day when the animals are active. The park surrounding the zoo has multiple and imaginative playground structures and a lake where you can feed ducks and rent paddleboats. ⊠ *Reid Park, 1100 S. Randolph Way, off 22nd St., Central* ☎ *520/791–3204* ⊕ *www.tucsonzoo.org* 🖾 *$7* ☉ *Daily 9–4.*

① **Tucson Botanical Gardens**. The 5 acres are home to a variety of experiences: a tropical greenhouse; a sensory garden, where you can touch and smell the plants and listen to the abundant birdlife; historical gardens that display the Mediterranean landscaping the property's original owners planted in the 1930s; a garden designed to attract birds; and a cactus garden. Other special gardens showcase wildflowers, Australian plants, and Native American crops and herbs. Call ahead to find out what's blooming. A delightful café is open daily October–early May. All paths are wheelchair accessible. ⊠ *2150 N. Alvernon Way, Central* ☎ *520/326–9686* ⊕ *www.tucsonbotanical.org* 🖾 *$7* ☉ *Daily 8:30–4:30.*

EASTSIDE

⑤ **Colossal Cave Mountain Park**. This limestone grotto 20 mi east of Tucson is the largest dry cavern in the world. Guides discuss the fascinating crystal formations and relate the many romantic tales surrounding the cave, including the legend that an enormous sum of money stolen in a stagecoach robbery is hidden here. Forty-five-minute cave tours begin every 30 minutes and require a 0.5-mi walk and climbing 363 steps. The park includes a ranch area with trail rides ($27 per hour), a gemstone-sluicing area, a small museum, nature trails, a butterfly garden, a snack bar, and a gift shop. Parking is $5 per vehicle. Take Broadway Boulevard or 22nd Street East to Colossal Cave Road. ⊠ *16721 E. Old Spanish Trail, Eastside* ☎ *520/647–7275* ⊕ *www.colossalcave.com* 🖾 *$11* ☉ *Oct.–mid-Mar., daily 9–5; mid-Mar.–Sept., daily 8–5.*

④ **Pima Air and Space Museum**. This huge facility ranks among the largest private collections of aircraft in the world. More than 200 airplanes are on display in hangars and outside, including a presidential plane used by both John F. Kennedy and Lyndon B. Johnson, a full-scale replica of the Wright brothers' 1903 Wright Flyer; the SR-71 reconnaissance jet; and a mock-up of the X-15, the world's fastest aircraft. World War II planes are particularly well represented. Meander on your own or take a free walking tour of the hangars led by volunteer docents every day at 10:15. The open-air tram tour (an additional $6 fee) narrates all outside aircraft. Hour-long van tours of Aerospace Maintenance and Regeneration Center (AMARC)—affectionately called "The Boneyard"—at Davis-Monthan Air Force Base provide an eerie glimpse of hundreds of mothballed aircraft lined up in rows on a vast tract of desert. This $7 AMARC tour, which is available only on weekdays on a first-come, first-served basis, is a photographer's delight. A combination ticket is also available with the Titan Missile Museum *(⇨ see Side Trips Near*

Tucson History: City in the Foothills

Native Americans have lived along the waterways in this valley for thousands of years. During the 1500s Spanish explorers arrived to find Pima Indians growing crops in the area. Father Eusebio Francisco Kino, a Jesuit missionary whose influence is still strongly felt throughout the region, first visited the area in 1687, and returned a few years later to build missions.

NATIVE AMERICANS AND THE PRESIDIO

The name "Tucson" came from the Native American word *stjukshon* (pronounced *stook*-shahn), meaning "spring at the foot of a black mountain." The springs at the foot of Sentinel Peak, made of black volcanic rock, are now dry. The name was pronounced *tuk*-son by the Spanish explorers who built a wall around the city in 1776 to keep Native Americans from reclaiming it. At the time, this *presidio* (fortified city), called San Augustin del Tuguison, was the northernmost Spanish settlement in the area, and present-day Main Avenue is a quiet reminder of the former Camino Real ("royal road") that

stretched from this tiny walled fort all the way to Mexico City.

CHANGING ALLEGIANCES

Four flags have flown over Tucson— Spanish, Mexican, Confederate, and, finally, the Stars and Stripes. Tucson's allegiance changed in 1820 when Mexico declared independence from Spain, and again in 1853 when the Gadsden purchase made it part of the United States, though Arizona didn't become a state until 1912. In the 1850s the Butterfield stage line was extended to Tucson, bringing adventurers, a few settlers, and more than a handful of outlaws. The arrival of the railroad in 1880 marked another spurt of growth, as did the opening of the University of Arizona in 1891.

MODERN TIMES

Tucson's 20th-century growth occurred after World War I, when veterans with damaged lungs sought the dry air and healing power of the sun, and again during World War II with the opening of Davis-Monthan Air Force Base and the rise of local aeronautical industries. It was also around this time that air-conditioning made the desert climate hospitable year-round.

Tucson). ✉ 6000 E. Valencia Rd., I–10, Exit 267, Eastside ☎ 520/574–0462 ⊕ www.pimaair.org ✉ $15.50; combination with the Titan Missile Museum $18 ☉ Daily 9–5, last admission at 4.

CATALINA FOOTHILLS

Considered by some to be the "Beverly Hills of Tucson," the Catalina Foothills area is home to posh resorts and upscale shopping. Because the neighborhood backs on the beautiful Santa Catalina Mountains, it also has an abundance of hiking trails.

TIMING If you want to venture farther into the mountains, head northeast up to Mount Lemmon: it's time-consuming (a one-hour drive each way), but the higher elevation and cooler temperatures make it an excellent midday destination in summer.

Catalina
Foothills

TOP ATTRACTION

❶ Sabino Canyon. Year-round, but especially in summer, locals flock to
★ Coronado National Forest to hike, picnic, and enjoy the waterfalls,
streams, swimming holes, and shade trees. No cars are allowed, but a
narrated tram ride (about 45 minutes round-trip) takes you up a WPA-
built road to the top of the canyon; you can hop off and on at any of
the nine stops or hike any of the numerous trails. There's also a shorter
tram ride to adjacent Bear Canyon, where a much more rigorous but
rewarding hike leads to the popular Seven Falls (it'll take about 1½–2
hours each way from the drop-off point, so carry plenty of water). If
you're in Tucson near a full moon between April and November, take
the special night tram and watch the desert come alive with nocturnal
critters. ⊠ *Sabino Canyon Rd. at Sunrise Dr., Foothills* ☎ *520/749–
2861 recorded tram information, 520/749–8700 visitor center* ⊕ *www.
fs.fed.us/r3/coronado* ⊠ *$5 per vehicle, tram $3–$8* ☉ *Visitor center:
weekdays 8–4:30, weekends 8:30–4:30; call for tram schedules.*

WORTH NOTING

❷ De Grazia's Gallery in the Sun. Arizonan artist Ted De Grazia, who depicted
Southwest Native American and Mexican life in a manner some find
kitschy and others adore, built this sprawling, spacious, single-story
museum with the assistance of Native American friends, using only

natural material from the surrounding desert. You can visit De Grazia's workshop, former home, and grave. Although the original works are not for sale, the museum's gift shop has a wide selection of prints, ceramics, and books by and about the colorful artist. ⊠ *6300 N. Swan Rd., Foothills* ☎ *520/299–9191* ⊕ *www.degrazia.org* ✆ *Free* ☉ *Daily 10–4.*

❸ **Mount Lemmon.** Part of the Santa Catalina range, Mount Lemmon—named for Sara Lemmon, the first woman to reach the peak of this mountain, in 1881—is the southernmost ski slope in the continental United States, but you don't have to be a skier to enjoy the area: in summer, it's a popular place for picnicking, and there are 150 mi of marked and well-maintained trails for hiking. The mountain's 9,157-foot elevation brings relief from summer heat.

Mount Lemmon Highway twists its way for 28 mi up the mountainside. Every 1,000-foot climb in elevation is equivalent, in terms of climate, to traveling 300 mi north: you'll move from typical Sonoran Desert plants in the Foothills to vegetation similar to that found in southern Canada at the top. Rock formations along the way look as though they were carefully balanced against each other by sculptors from another planet.

At milepost 18 of your ascent, on the left-hand side of the road, is the Palisades Ranger Station of **Coronado National Forest** (☎ *520/749–8700* ⊕ *www.fs.fed.us/r3/coronado* ☉ *8–4:30 Daily*). Rangers have information on the mountain's campgrounds, hiking trails, and picnic spots.< Even if you don't make it to the top of the mountain, you'll find stunning views of Tucson at Windy Point, about halfway up. Look for a road on your left between the Windy Point and San Pedro lookouts; it leads to Rose Canyon lake, a lovely reservoir.

Just before you reach the ski area, you'll pass through the tiny alpine-style village of **Summerhaven,** which has some casual restaurants, gift shops, and pleasant lodges.

Mount Lemmon Highway ends at **Mount Lemmon Ski Valley** (☎ *520/576–1321* ⊕ *www.skithelemmon.com*). Skiing depends on natural conditions—there's no artificial snow, so call ahead. There are 21 runs, open daily in winter, ranging from beginner to advanced. Lift tickets cost $37 for an all-day pass and $22 for a half-day pass starting at 1 PM. Equipment rentals and instruction are available. Off-season you can take a ride on the chairlift ($9), which whisks you to the top of the slope—some 9,100 feet above sea level. Many ride the lift, then hike on one of several trails that crisscross the summit. There are some concessions right at the ski lift; the Iron Door Restaurant, across the road, serves sandwiches, soups, and homemade pies alongside gorgeous views.

7

■TIP→ There are no gas stations on Mount Lemmon Highway, so gas up before you leave town and check the road conditions in winter. To reach the highway, take Tanque Verde Road to Catalina Highway, which becomes Mount Lemmon Highway as you head north. ⊠ *Mount Lemmon Hwy., Northeast* ☎ *520/576–1400 recorded snow report, 520/547–7510 winter road conditions* ⬚ *$5 per vehicle* ☉ *Daily, depending on snow in ski season.*

NORTHWEST TUCSON AND THE WESTSIDE

Once a vast, open space dotted with horse ranches, Northwest Tucson is now a rapidly growing residential area encompassing the townships of Oro Valley and Marana. Families and retirees are moving here in droves, and the traffic congestion proves the point, but you'll also find first-rate golf resorts and restaurants here, as well as the oases of Tohono Chul Park and Catalina State Park, which calm the senses.

The Westside is far less developed, and beautiful vistas of saguaro-studded hills are around every bend. Saguaro National Park West, the Desert Museum, Old Tucson Studios, and the San Xavier mission are all in this section of town. If you're interested in the flora and fauna of the Sonoran Desert—as well as some of its appearances in the cinema—heed the same advice given the pioneers: go west.

TIMING　A good idea is to start the morning at Saguaro National Park and then head over to the Arizona–Sonora Desert Museum, where you can lunch at the Ironwood Terrace or the more upscale Ocotillo Café. How long you spend at Saguaro National Park depends on whether you choose a short walk to see petroglyphs at Signal Hill on the Loop Drive (an hour should suffice) or hike a longer mountain trail, but leave yourself at least two hours for your visit at the Desert Museum. The hottest part of an afternoon can be spent ducking in and out of attractions at Old Tucson Studios or enjoying the indoor sanctuary of San Xavier mission, although the mission is also a good stop if you're heading out of town to Tubac or Tumacácori.

TOP ATTRACTIONS

❶ **Arizona–Sonora Desert Museum.** The name "museum" is a bit misleading, since this delightful site is actually a beautifully planned zoo and botanical garden featuring the animals and plants of the Sonoran Desert. Hummingbirds, cactus wrens, rattlesnakes, scorpions, bighorn sheep, and prairie dogs all busy themselves in ingeniously designed habitats. An Earth Sciences Center has an artificial limestone cave to climb through and a hands-on meteor and mineral display. The coyote and javelina (wild, piglike mammals with oddly oversize heads) exhibits have "invisible" fencing that separates humans from animals, and the Riparian Corridor section has great underwater views of otters and beavers. The restaurants are above average, and the gift shop, which

Fodor's Choice
★

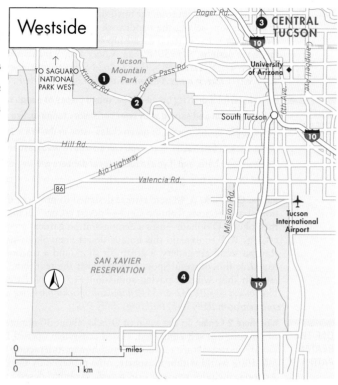

carries books, jewelry and crafts, is outstanding. ✉ *2021 N. Kinney Rd.,
Westside* ☎ *520/883–2702* ⊕ *www.desertmuseum.org* ✉ *$13* ☯ *Mar.–
Sept., daily 7:30–5; Oct.–Feb., daily 8:30–5.*

❹ **Mission San Xavier del Bac.** The oldest Catholic church in the United
Fodor's Choice States still serving the community for which it was built, San Xavier
★ was founded in 1692 by Father Eusebio Francisco Kino, who established
22 missions in northern Mexico and southern Arizona. The current
structure was made out of native materials by Franciscan missionaries
between 1777 and 1797, and is owned by the Tohono O'odham tribe.

The beauty of the mission, with elements of Spanish, baroque, and
Moorish architectural styles, is highlighted by the stark landscape
against which it is set, inspiring an early-20th-century poet to dub it
the White Dove of the Desert. Inside, there's a wealth of painted statues,
carvings, and frescoes. Paul Schwartzbaum, who helped restore Michel-
angelo's masterwork in Rome, supervised Tohono O'odham artisans in
the restoration of the mission's artwork, completed in 1997; Schwartzbaum has called the mission the Sistine Chapel of the United States.
Mass is celebrated at 8:30 AM Tuesday through Friday in the church,
Saturday afternoon at 5:30, and three times on Sunday morning. Call
ahead for information about special celebrations.

Across the parking lot from the mission, San Xavier Plaza has a number of crafts shops selling the handiwork of the Tohono O'odham tribe, including jewelry, pottery, friendship bowls, and baskets with man-in-the-maze designs. ⊠ *1950 W. San Xavier Rd., 9 mi southwest of Tucson on I–19, Westside* ☎ *520/294–2624* ⊕ *www.sanxaviermission.org* ☞ *Free* ☉ *Church daily 8–5, museum and gift shop daily 8–5.*

For wonderful Indian fry bread—large, round pieces of dough taken fresh from the hot oil and served with sweet or savory toppings like honey, powdered sugar, beans, meats, or green chiles—stop in the **Wa:k Snack Shop** at the back of San Xavier Plaza. You can also have breakfast or a lunch of Mexican food here, and if you're lucky, local dancers will be performing for one of the many tour groups that stop here.

❸ **Tohono Chul Park.** A 48-acre retreat designed to promote the conservation of arid regions, Tohono Chul—"desert corner" in the language of the Tohono O'odham—uses a demonstration garden, greenhouse, and geology wall to explain this unique desert area. Shady nooks, nature trails, a small art gallery, a great gift shop, and a tearoom can all be found at this peaceful spot. You can visit the tearoom, greenhouse, and gift shop without paying admission. ⊠ *7366 N. Paseo del Norte, Northwest* ☎ *520/742–6455* ⊕ *www.tohonochulpark.org* ☞ *$7* ☉ *Park and tearoom daily 8–5, buildings daily 9–5.*

Biosphere 2 Center. In the town of Oracle, about 30 minutes northwest of Tucson, this self-contained, closed ecosystem opened in 1991 as a facility to test nature technology and human interaction with it. The miniature world within Biosphere, now managed by the University of Arizona, includes tropical rain forest, savanna, desert, thorn scrub, marsh, ocean, and agricultural areas, including almost 3,000 plant and animal species. A film and a large, rotating cutaway model in the visitor center explain the project, which included two "human missions" wherein scientists entered the ecosystem for extended periods of time—once for six months, once for two years. Guided walking tours, which last about two hours, take you inside some of the biomes, and observation areas let you peer in at the rest. A snack bar overlooks the Santa Catalina Mountains. ⊠ *AZ 77, Milepost 96.5, Oracle* ☎ *520/838–6200* ⊕ *www.b2science.org* ☞ *$20* ☉ *Daily 9–4.*

WORTH NOTING

❷ **Old Tucson Studios.** This film studio–theme park, originally built for the 1940 motion picture *Arizona,* has been used to shoot countless movies, such as *Rio Bravo* (1959) and *The Quick and the Dead* (1994), and the TV shows *Gunsmoke, Bonanza,* and *Highway to Heaven.* Actors in Western garb perform and roam the streets talking to visitors. Youngsters enjoy the simulated gunfights, rides, stunt shows, and petting farm, while adults might appreciate the screenings of old Westerns and the little-bit-bawdy Grand Palace Hotel's Dance Hall Revue. There are plenty of places to eat and to buy souvenirs. Horseback riding is available for an additional charge. ⊠ *Tucson Mountain Park, 201 S. Kinney Rd., Westside* ☎ *520/883–0100* ⊕ *www.oldtucson.com* ☞ *$16.95* ☉ *Daily 10–4.*

SPORTS AND THE OUTDOORS

Tucson's urban status doesn't prevent visitors from enjoying outdoor activites within the city and in the nearby area. Though summer heat can limit your options, golf and hiking are popular year-round.

ADVENTURE TOURS

Baja's Frontier Tours (☎ *520/887–2340 or 800/726–7231* ⊕ *www.bajasfrontiertours.com*) explores the natural and cultural history of Tucson and the greater Southwest by van and motorcoach. **Southwest Trekking** (✉ *Box 57714, Tucson* ☎ *520/296–9661* ⊕ *www.swtrekking.com*) arranges top-notch guided mountain biking, hiking, and camping outings. **Trail Dust Adventures** (☎ *520/747–0323* ⊕ *www.traildustadventures.com*) runs open-air jeep tours that explore the Sonoran Desert and mountains outside the city. Cookouts and cattle drives are added options.

BALLOONING

Balloon America (✉ *Box 31255, Tucson 85751* ☎ *520/299–7744* ⊕ *www.balloonrideusa.com*) flies passengers above the Santa Catalinas on hot-air balloon tours departing from the east side of Tucson from October through May. **Fleur de Tucson Balloon Tours** (✉ *4635 N. Caida Pl., Tucson 85718* ☎ *520/529–1025* ⊕ *www.fleurdetucson.net*), operates out of Northwest from October through April and flies over the Tucson Mountains and Saguaro National Park West.

BASEBALL

It doesn't have as many teams as Phoenix, but Tucson does have its share of baseball spring training action: the Arizona Diamondbacks and the Colorado Rockies are in the Tucson area from mid-February until the end of March. The Diamondbacks play at Tucson Electric Park, south of town near the airport. The Rockies play at Hi Corbett Field, which is adjacent to Reid Park. Not surprisingly, some people plan vacations around scheduled training dates; there are plenty of local fans, too.

Arizona Diamondbacks (✉ *Tucson Electric Park, 2400 E. Ajo Way, Central* ☎ *520/434–1367 or 866/672–1343* ⊕ *www.dbacks.com*) **Colorado Rockies** (✉ *Hi Corbett Field, 3400 E. Camino Campestre, Central* ☎ *520/327–9467 or 800/388–7625* ⊕ *www.coloradorockies.com*)

BICYCLING

Tucson, ranked among America's top five bicycling cities by *Bicycling* magazine, has well-maintained bikeways, routes, lanes, and paths all over the city. Scenic-loop roads in both sections of Saguaro National Park are rewarding rides for all levels of cyclists.

Most bike stores in Tucson carry the monthly newsletter of the Tucson chapter of **GABA** (*Greater Arizona Bicycling Association* ✉ *Box 43273, Tucson 85733* ⊕ *www.bikegaba.org*), which lists rated group rides, local bike rentals, and more. You can pick up a map of Tucson-area bike routes at the **Pima Association of Governments** (✉ *177 N. Church Ave., Suite 405, Downtown 85701* ☎ *520/792–1093* ⊕ *www. pagnet.org*).

7

RENTALS   Mountain bikes, comfort bikes, and road bikes can be rented by the day or week at **Fair Wheel Bikes** (⊠ *1110 E. 6th St., University* ☎ *520/884–9018*). They also organize group rides of varying difficulty. **Tucson Bicycles** (⊠ *4743 E. Sunrise Dr., Foothills* ☎ *520/577–7374*) rents a selection of road and mountain bikes in the Catalina Foothills.

BIRD-WATCHING

The naturalist and illustrator Roger Tory Peterson (1908–96) considered Tucson one of the country's top birding spots, and avid "life listers"—birders who keep a list of all the birds they've sighted and identified—soon see why. In the early morning and early evening Sabino Canyon is alive with cactus and canyon wrens, hawks, and quail. Spring and summer, when species of migrants come in from Mexico, are great hummingbird seasons. In the nearby Santa Rita Mountains and Madera Canyon you can see elegant trogons nesting in early spring. The area also supports species usually found only in higher elevations. You can get the latest word on the bird on the 24-hour line at the **Tucson Audubon Society** (☎ *520/798–1005* ⊕ *www.tucsonaudubon.org*) ; sightings of rare or interesting birds in the area are recorded regularly.

RESOURCES   The society's **Audubon Nature Shop** (⊠ *300 E. University Blvd., Suite 120, University* ☎ *520/629–0510*) organizes local outings and carries field guides, bird feeders, binoculars, and natural-history books. The **Wild Bird Store** (⊠ *3526 E. Grant Rd., Central* ☎ *520/322–9466*) is an excellent resource for bird-watching information, books, and trail guides.

TOURS   Several companies operate birding tours in the Tucson area. **Borderland Tours** (⊠ *2550 W. Calle Padilla, Northwest* ☎ *520/882–7650 or 800/525–7753* ⊕ *www.borderland-tours.com*) leads bird-watching tours in Arizona. **Wings** (⊠ *1643 N. Alvernon Way, Suite 105, Central, Tucson* ☎ *520/320–9868* ⊕ *www.wingsbirds.com*), a Tucson-based company, leads ornithological expeditions worldwide and locally.

GOLF

Tee off after 1 PM at many of Tucson's courses, and you can shave off nearly half the green fee. Some courses also have lower fees Monday through Thursday. All Tucson area courses dramatically reduce green fees in summer.

RESOURCES   For a detailed listing of the state's courses, contact the **Arizona Golf Association** (☎ *602/944–3035 or 800/458–8484* ⊕ *www.azgolf.org*). The **Golf Stop Inc.** (⊠ *6155 E. Broadway, Eastside* ☎ *520/790–0941*), a shop owned and run by two LPGA pros, can fit you with pro shop brands and custom clubs, repair your old irons, or give you lessons.

MUNICIPAL COURSES   One of Tucson's best-kept secrets is that the city's five low-price municipal courses are maintained to standards usually found only at the best country clubs. All five have pro shops, driving ranges and putting greens, snack bars, and rental clubs. To reserve a tee time at one of the city's courses, call the **Tucson Parks and Recreation Department** (☎ *520/791–4653 general golf information, 520/791–4336 automated tee-time reservations* ⊕ *www.tucsoncitygolf.com*) at least a week in advance.

Dell Urich Golf Course (⊠ *600 S. Alvernon Way, Central* ☎ *520/791–4161* ⊕ *www.tucsoncitygolf.com*), adjacent to Randolph and formerly known

These slabs contain fossil replicas from three different eras in Arizona's past. Fossils provide clues that help us visualize how ancient landscapes may have looked.

Hills and Forests

Don't let the name fool you, the Arizona–Sonora Desert Museum is also a zoo and botanical garden.

as Randolph South, is a par-70, 18-hole course with tall trees and dramatic elevation changes ($54 to walk, $64 with a cart).

El Rio Golf Course (⊠ *1400 W. Speedway Blvd., Westside* ☎ *520/791–4229* ⊕ *www.tucsoncitygolf.com*) is a par-70 course with 18 holes of tight fairways, small greens, and two lakes on fairly flat terrain ($30 to walk, $35 with a cart).

Fred Enke Golf Course (⊠ *8251 E. Irvington, Eastside* ☎ *520/791–2539* ⊕ *www.tucsoncitygolf.com*) is a hilly, semi-arid (less grass and more native vegetation), par-72, 18-hole course ($36 to walk, $48 with a cart). It's southeast of town.

Fodor's Choice
★ **Randolph Park Golf Course–North Course** (⊠ *600 S. Alvernon Way, Central* ☎ *520/791–4161* ⊕ *www.tucsoncitygolf.com*), a long, scenic 18-hole, par-72 course that has hosted the LPGA Tour for many years, is the flagship of Tucson's municipal courses ($56 to walk, $64 with a cart).

Silverbell Golf Course (⊠ *3600 N. Silverbell Rd., Northwest* ☎ *520/791–5235* ⊕ *www.tucsoncitygolf.com*), with spacious fairways and ample greens, has an 18-hole, par-70 layout along the Santa Cruz River ($38 to walk, $48 with a cart).

PUBLIC COURSES **Arizona National Golf Club** (⊠ *9777 E. Sabino Greens Dr., Eastside* ☎ *520/749–3636* ⊕ *www.arizonanationalgolfclub.com*) is a gorgeous 18-hole, par-71 course with a restaurant and snack bar ($175).

Dorado Golf Course (⊠ *6601 E. Speedway Blvd., Eastside* ☎ *520/885–6751*) has an 18-hole, par-62 executive course, good for those who want to play just a few short rounds ($23 to walk, $32 with a cart). There is a putting green but no driving range, club rentals, or lessons.

Esplendor Resort & Country Club (✉ *1069 Camino Carampi, Rio Rico* ☎ *800/288–4746* ⊕ *www.esplendor-resort.com*), south of Tucson, was designed by Robert Trent Jones Sr. This 18-hole, par-72 course, with pro shop, driving range, and on-site restaurant and county club facilities, is one of Arizona's lesser-known gems ($59).

San Ignacio Golf Club (✉ *4201 S. Camino del Sol, Green Valley* ☎ *520/648–3468* ⊕ *www.sanignaciogolfclub.com*), designed by Arthur Hills, is a challenging 18-hole, par-71 desert course. Facilities include a driving range, practice area, and restaurant, and rental clubs are available ($77).

Tubac Golf Resort (✉ *1 Otero Rd., Tubac* ☎ *520/398–2021* ⊕ *www. tubacgolfresort.com*), a par-72 course 45 minutes south of Tucson, will look familiar to you if you've seen the movie *Tin Cup*. The rolling hills and pastoral land surrounding these 27 holes are a change from desert golf environs. A pro shop, practice areas, and restaurant are on-site ($109).

RESORT COURSES   Avid golfers check into one of Tucson's many tony resorts and head straight for the links. The resort courses listed below are open to the public, but resort guests pay slightly lower green fees. All have complete country-club facilities. Those who don't mind getting up early to beat the heat will find some excellent golf packages at these places in summer.

Hilton Tucson El Conquistador (✉ *10555 N. La Canada Dr., Northwest* ☎ *520/544–1800* ⊕ *www.hiltonelconquistador.com*) has 45 holes of golf tucked into the Santa Catalina Foothills. The three courses—one par-71, one par-72, and one 9-hole, par 35—have panoramic views of the city ($89).

Fodor's Choice ★   **Lodge at Ventana Canyon** (✉ *6200 N. Clubhouse La., Foothills* ☎ *520/577– 4015 or 800/828–5701*) has two beautiful 18-hole, par-72 Tom Fazio– designed courses ($175). Their signature hole, No. 3 on the mountain course, is a favorite of golf photographers. Guests staying up the road at Loews Ventana Canyon Resort also have privileges here.

★   **Omni Tucson National Golf Resort** (✉ *2727 W. Club Dr., Northwest* ☎ *520/575–7540* ⊕ *www.tucsonnational.com*), cohost of an annual PGA winter open, offers 36 holes: one traditional par-73 course with gorgeous, long par 4s; and one par-70 desert course. The resort's orange and gold courses were designed by Robert Van Hagge and Bruce Devlin ($188).

Starr Pass Golf Resort (✉ *3645 W. Starr Pass Blvd., Westside* ☎ *520/670– 0406* ⊕ *www.jwmarriottstarrpass.com*), with 27 magnificent holes in the Tucson Mountains, was developed as a Tournament Player's Course. Managed by Arnold Palmer, Starr Pass has become a favorite of visiting pros; playing its No. 15 signature hole has been likened to threading a moving needle ($215). Guests at the JW Marriott Starr Pass Resort have privileges here.

HIKING

For hiking inside Tucson city limits, you can test your skills climbing trails up "A" Mountain (Sentinel Peak), but there are also hundreds of other trails in the immediate Tucson area. The Santa Catalina Mountains, Sabino Canyon, and Saguaro National Park East and West beckon hikers with waterfalls, birds, critters, and huge saguaro cacti. *For hiking trails in Saguaro, ⇨ see Saguaro National Park in this chapter.*

Catalina State Park (✉ *11570 N. Oracle Rd., Northwest* ☎ *520/628–5798* ⊕ *www.azstateparks.gov*) is crisscrossed by hiking trails. One of them, the relatively easy, two-hour, 5.5-mi round-trip **Romero Canyon Trail**, leads to Romero Pools, a series of natural *tinajas,* or stone "jars," filled with water much of the year. The trailhead is on the park's entrance road, past the restrooms on the right side.

★ The **Bear Canyon Trail** in **Sabino Canyon** (✉ *Sabino Canyon Rd. at Sunrise Dr., Foothills* ☎ *520/749–8700* ⊕ *www.fs.fed.us/r3/coronado*), also known as **Seven Falls Trail**, is a three- to four-hour, 7.8-mi round-trip that is moderately easy and fun, crossing the stream several times on the way up the canyon. Be sure to bring plenty of water. Kids enjoy the boulder-hopping, and all are rewarded with pools and waterfalls as well as views at the top. The trailhead can be reached from the parking area by either taking a five-minute Bear Canyon Tram ride or walking the 1.8-mi tram route.

RESOURCES   The local chapter of the **Sierra Club** (✉ *738 N. 5th Ave., University* ☎ *520/620–6401*) welcomes out-of-towners on weekend hikes. The **Southern Arizona Hiking Club** (☎ *520/751–4513* ⊕ *www.sahcinfo.org*) leads weekend hikes of varying difficulty. For hiking on your own, a good source is **Summit Hut** (✉ *5045 E. Speedway Blvd., Central* ☎ *520/325–1554*), which has a collection of hiking reference materials and a friendly staff who will help you plan your trip. Packs, tents, bags, and climbing shoes can be rented and purchased here.

HORSEBACK RIDING

Wranglers at **Cocoraque Ranch** (✉ *6255 N. Diamond Hills La., Westside* ☎ *520/682–8594*) lead riders on real cattle drives through their working cattle ranch and along trails into Saguaro National Park West. **Colossal Cave Stables** (✉ *16600 Colossal Cave Rd., Eastside* ☎ *520/647–3450*) takes riders into Saguaro National Park East on one-hour, two-hour, all-day, or sunset rides. **Pantano Riding Stables** (✉ *4450 S. Houghton Rd., Eastside* ☎ *520/298–8980* ⊕ *www.horsingaroundarizona.com*) is a reliable operator of one-hour to all-day rides. **Pusch Ridge Stables** (✉ *13700 N. Oracle Rd., Northwest* ☎ *520/825–1664*), adjacent to Catalina State

Park, can serve up a cowboy-style breakfast on your trail ride; one-hour, sunset, and overnight rides are available.

RODEO

In the last week of February, Tucson hosts **Fiesta de Los Vaqueros,** the largest annual winter rodeo in the United States, a five-day extravaganza with more than 600 events and a crowd of more than 44,000 spectators a day at the **Tucson Rodeo Grounds** (✉ *4823 S. 6th Ave., South* ☎ *520/294–8896* ⊕ *www.tucsonrodeo.com*). The rodeo kicks off with a 2-mi parade of horseback riders (Western and fancy-dress Mexican *charro*, wagons, stagecoaches, and horse-drawn floats; it's touted as the largest nonmotorized parade in the world. Local schoolkids especially love the celebration—they get a two-day holiday from school. Daily seats at the rodeo vary from $12 to $25.

WHERE TO EAT

Tucson boldly proclaims itself to be the "Mexican Food Capital of the United States" and most of the Mexican food in town is Sonoran style. This means prolific use of cheese, mild peppers, corn tortillas, pinto beans, and beef or chicken. The majority of the best Mexican restaurants are concentrated in South Tucson and Downtown, though some favorites have additional locations around town. If Mexican's not your thing, there are plenty of other options: you won't have any trouble finding excellent sushi, Thai, Italian, and Ethiopian food at reasonable prices.

For sampling local cuisine, there are several Southwestern restaurants in town. Up in the Foothills, upscale Southwestern cuisine flourishes at such restaurants as Janos at the Westin La Paloma and the Grill at Hacienda del Sol Resort. A recent trend in Tucson dining is combining hip restaurants with chic shopping locations. Choose from sushi, steak, Italian, or Mexican at La Encantada in the Foothills. Casas Adobes Plaza, in the Northwest, is home to upscale shops alongside Wildflower Grill, Bluefin Seafood, and trendy, thin-crust pizza at Sauce—and the gelato shop here is handy for dessert. At St. Philip's Plaza, in the lower Foothills, art galleries and boutiques surround Acacia and Vivace, both with lovely patio dining.

Cheaper but no less tasty fare as varied as Japanese, Guatemalan, and Middle-Eastern can be enjoyed on the west side of U of A's campus, along University Boulevard and 4th Avenue, a great area for people-watching and barhopping as well as quelling hunger pangs.

PLANNING INFORMATION

On Friday and Saturday nights and during the Gem Show (first two weeks of February), reservations are usually a good idea at upscale and popular restaurants, which we've noted with Reservations Essential. Dress ranges from casual to casual dressy here—jackets for men are not required at any restaurant, even at resorts. Although the city's selection of restaurants is impressive, Tucson doesn't have much in the way of late-night dining. Most restaurants in town are shuttered by 9 PM; some spots that keep later hours are noted below.

WHAT IT COSTS				
¢	$	$$	$$$	$$$$
AT DINNER	under $8	$8–$12	$13–$20	$21–$30	over $30

Prices are per person for a main course.

Use the coordinate (✛ B2) at the end of each listing to locate a site on the corresponding map.

DOWNTOWN TUCSON

$$
SOUTHWESTERN

✕**Barrio.** Lively at lunchtime, this trendy grill serves innovative Southwestern cuisine. Try a "little plate" of black tiger shrimp rubbed with tamarind paste, or stuffed Anaheim chile in red bell-pepper cream. Entrées are as varied as the simple but delicious fish tacos and the linguine with chicken, dried papaya, and mango in a chipotle-chardonnay cream sauce. Save room for an elegant dessert of fresh berries drenched in crème anglaise or a chilled chocolate custard topped with caramel. ⊠ *135 S. 6th Ave., Downtown* ☎ *520/629–0191* ⊕ *barriofoodanddrink.com* ▭ *AE, DC, MC, V* ⊗ *No lunch weekends* ✛ *B5.*

$$
MEXICAN
Fodor's Choice
★

✕**Café Poca Cosa.** In what is arguably Tucson's most creative Mexican restaurant, the chef prepares recipes inspired by different regions of her native country. The menu, which changes daily, might include chicken mole or pork *pibil* (made with a tangy Yucatecan barbecue seasoning). Servings are plentiful, and each table gets a stack of warm corn tortillas and a bowl of beans to share. Order the daily Plato Poca Cosa, and the chef will select one beef, one chicken, and one vegetarian entrée for you to sample. The bold-color walls are hung with Latin American art. ⊠ *110 E. Pennington St., Downtown* ☎ *520/622–6400* ⊕ *cafepocacosainc.com* ▭ *MC, V* ⊗ *Closed Sun. and Mon.* ✛ *B5.*

$
AMERICAN

✕**Cup Café.** This charming spot off the lobby of Hotel Congress is at the epicenter of Tucson's hippest Downtown scene, but it's also a down-home, friendly place. Try the eggs, potatoes, chorizo, and cheese for breakfast or a veggie burger for lunch. The Brie melted over artichoke hearts and apple slices on a baguette appetizer complements such entrées as chicken satay or "Tornados" of beef. Open until 10 PM weeknights and 1 AM weekends, it becomes interestingly crowded in the evening with patrons from Club Congress, the hotel nightclub. ⊠ *Hotel Congress, 311 E. Congress St., Downtown* ☎ *520/798–1618* ⊕ *hotelcongress.com* ▭ *AE, D, MC, V* ✛ *B5.*

$
MEXICAN

✕**El Charro Café.** Started by Monica Flin in 1922, the oldest Mexican restaurant in town still serves splendid versions of the Mexican-American staples Flin claims to have originated, most notably chimichangas and cheese crisps. The tortilla soup and *carne seca* chimichanga, made with beef that is air-dried on the premises—on the roof, actually—are delicious. Located in an old stone house in El Presidio Historic District, the colorful restaurant and bar exude festive—if slightly touristy—vibes. ⊠ *311 N. Court Ave., Downtown* ☎ *520/622–1922* ⊕ *elcharrocafe.com* ▭ *AE, D, DC, MC, V* ✛ *B5.*

7

BEST BETS FOR TUCSON DINING

Fodor's offers a listing of quality dining experiences at every price range, from the city's best cheap eateries to its most upscale restaurants. Here, we've compiled our top picks by price and experience. The best properties—in other words, those that provide a remarkable experience in their price range—are designated in the listings with the Fodor's Choice logo.

Fodor'sChoice ★

Beyond Bread, p. 398
Café Poca Cosa, p. 393
El Minuto Café, p. 395
Grill at Hacienda del Sol, p. 401
Janos, p. 401

Best by Price

¢

Beyond Bread, p. 398
Tucson Tamale Company, p. 399

$

Bangkok Cafe, p. 395
El Minuto Café, p. 395
Micha's, p. 403
Sauce, Central, p. 403
Zemam's, p. 399
Zinburger, p. 401

$$

Café Poca Cosa, p. 393
Feast, p. 398
North, p. 401

$$$

Acacia, p. 400
Grill at Hacienda del Sol, p. 401
Wildflower Grill, p. 403

$$$$

Janos, p. 401

Best by Cuisine

AMERICAN

JaxKitchen, p. 402
Kingfisher, p. 398
Wildflower, p. 403

BEST MEXICAN

Café Poca Cosa, p. 393
El Minuto, p. 395
Mi Nidito, p. 403

SOUTHWESTERN

Acacia, p. 400
Grill at Hacienda del Sol, p. 401
Janos, p. 401
Harvest, p. 402

Best by Experience

BEST BREAKFAST

Arizona Inn, p. 407
Hungry Fox, p. 398
Tohono Chul Tea Room, p. 403

BEST PATIO DINING

Acacia, p. 400
Tohono Chul Tea Room, p. 403

CHILD-FRIENDLY

Beyond Bread, p. 398
Pinnacle Peak Steakhouse, p. 399
Sauce, p. 403

GOOD FOR GROUPS

Bluefin Seafood Bistro, p. 402
Montana Avenue, p. 399
North, p. 401

HOT SPOTS

Café Poca Cosa, p. 393
Cup Café, p. 393
Zinburger, p. 401

LATE-NIGHT DINING

Bluefin Seafood Bistro, p. 402
Cup Café, p. 393
El Minuto Cafe, p. 395
Kingfisher, p. 398
Zinburger, p. 401

SPECIAL OCCASION

Acacia, p. 400
Grill at Hacienda del Sol, p. 401
Janos, p. 401

$ ✕ **El Minuto Café**. Popular with local families and the business crowd at
MEXICAN lunch, this bustling restaurant is in Tucson's Barrio Historico neighbor-
Fodor's Choice hood and open until midnight Friday and Saturday and until 10 PM the
★ rest of the week. For more than 50 years El Minuto has served *topopo*
salads (a crispy tortilla shell heaped with beans, guacamole, and many
other ingredients), huge burritos, and green-corn tamales (in season)
made just right. The spicy *menudo* (tripe soup) is reputed to be a great
hangover remedy. ⊠ *354 S. Main Ave., Downtown* ☎ *520/882–4145*
⊕ *elminutocafe.com* ▭ *AE, D, DC, MC, V* ✛ *B5.*

UNIVERSITY OF ARIZONA

$$$–$$$$ ✕ **Arizona Inn Restaurant**. At the Arizona Inn, one of Tucson's oldest and
CONTINENTAL most elegant restaurants, dine on the patio overlooking the lush grounds
or enjoy the view from the dining room, which has Southwestern details
from the 1930s. The culinary range is broad, from bouillabaisse to a
vegetarian corn and butternut squash cannelloni. Locals mostly come
for weekday power breakfasts and business lunches, Sunday brunch,
or afternoon high tea in the library. ⊠ *Arizona Inn, 2200 E. Elm St.,
University* ☎ *520/325–1541* ⊕ *arizonainn.com* ▭ *AE, MC, V* ✛ *C4.*

$$ ✕ **Athens**. The tranquil dining room in this Greek spot off 4th Avenue
GREEK is furnished with lace curtains, white stucco walls, and potted plants.
Enjoy classics like *kotopoulo stin pita* (grilled chicken breast with
a yogurt-cucumber sauce on fresh pita), moussaka, or the *pastitsio* (a
casserole made with pasta, meat, and béchamel). The house favorite is
braised lamb shoulder in a light tomato sauce over pasta or potatoes—
call to reserve your order of the lamb ahead of time. ⊠ *500 N. 4th Ave.,
at 6th St., University* ☎ *520/624–6886* ⊕ *athenson4th.com* ⬥ *Reservations not accepted* ▭ *AE, D, DC, MC, V* ⊙ *Closed Sun.* ✛ *B5.*

$ ✕ **B Line**. In the heart of 4th Avenue's amalgam of antique clothing
AMERICAN stores, pubs, and natural-food grocers, this casual café in a converted
1920s bungalow attracts a mix of students, professors, Downtown
professionals, and artists with its simple but refined meals and desserts. Homemade biscuit sandwiches and excellent coffee start the day;
the lunch–dinner menu features soups, salads, pastas, burritos, and 13
brews on tap. People-watching as a secondary pleasure doesn't get any
better than sitting against the wraparound window looking out on 4th
Avenue. ⊠ *621 N. 4th Ave., University* ☎ *520/882–7575* ⊕ *blinerestau-
rant.com* ▭ *MC, V* ✛ *B4.*

CENTRAL TUCSON

$ ✕ **Bangkok Cafe**. This is not only the best Thai food in town, it is top-
THAI notch for Thai-food fans. You'll find all your favorite dishes in this
bright, spacious café, along with exceptionally pleasant service and
reasonable prices. Thoong-Tong appetizers, fried veggie-filled pouches,
are blissfully good. The spice-heat level of any dish can be adjusted at
your request, from 1 through 5 (just keep in mind that a 5 might cause
steam to blow out the top of your head). There are plenty of options
for vegetarians, and tofu is available to add to any dish. Try to avoid
the dinner rush (6:30–8:30) on weekends, or you'll wait a while to be

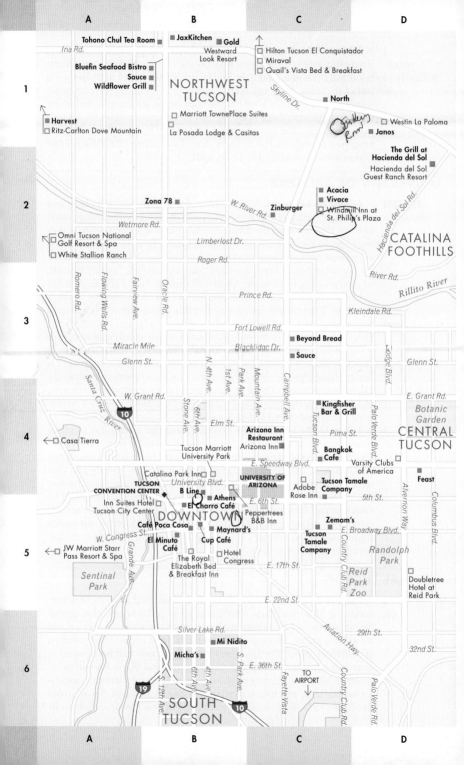

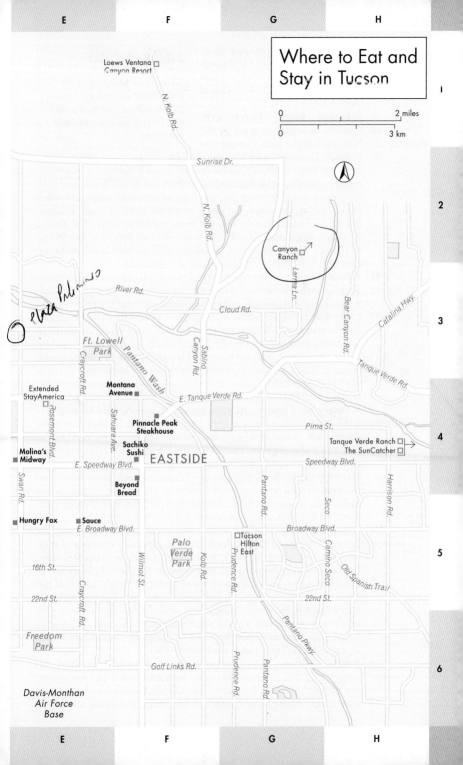

seated. ✉ *2511 E. Speedway Blvd., Central* ☎ *520/323–6555* 🌐 *bangkokcafe.net* *Reservations not accepted* 💳 *AE, MC, V* ⏱ *Closed Sun.* ✥ *C4.*

DID YOU KNOW?

Tucson is the birthplace of the *chimichanga* (Spanish for "whatchamacallit"), a flour tortilla filled with meat or cheese, rolled, and deep-fried.

¢ CAFÉ Fodor's Choice ★ **Beyond Bread.** Twenty-seven varieties of bread are made at this bustling bakery with Central and Eastside locations, and highlights from the huge sandwich menu include Annie's Addiction (hummus, tomato, sprouts, red onion, and cucumber) and Brad's Beef (roast beef, provolone, onion, green chiles, and Russian dressing); soups and salads are equally scrumptious. Eat inside or on the patio, or order takeout, but be sure to splurge on one of the incredible desserts. The second location—larger and just as busy—is at 6260 East Speedway Boulevard. ✉ *3026 N. Campbell Ave., Central* ☎ *520/322–9965* 🌐 *beyondbread.com* 💳 *AE, D, MC, V* ⏱ *Sun. closes at 6* ✥ *C3, F4.*

$$ ECLECTIC **Feast.** At this unassuming, informal bistro you order at the counter—after marveling at the display case filled with choices like potato gnocchi with sausage and spinach, sautéed sea bass with fingerling potatoes, and a beet with tarragon-cultured-mascarpone salad—then choose a table; and the friendly staff will bring you each dish as it's ready. Locals might just call in their order (after checking the daily specials online) and zip in to pick up tasty, gourmet takeout. Though the eclectic cuisine is hard to categorize, it is always yummy—including the homemade desserts. ✉ *4122 E. Speedway, Central* ☎ *520/326–9363* 🌐 *eatatfeast.com* 💳 *AE, D, MC, V* ⏱ *Closed Mon.* ✥ *D4.*

¢ AMERICAN **Hungry Fox.** Hungry customers have been coming here for good ol'-fashioned breakfasts, served until 2 PM, since 1962. It's the home of the double yolk, meaning when you order one egg, you'll get two (and so on). You'll also get a real slice of Tucson life at this cheerful, unpretentious place decorated with cow and farm photos, and a spoon collection that lines the walls. Hearty country "dinners," such as meat loaf and lasagna, are also served through lunchtime at the same bargain prices. ✉ *4637 E. Broadway Blvd., Central* ☎ *520/326–2835* 🌐 *hungryfox.com* 💳 *AE, D, MC, V* ⏱ *No dinner* ✥ *E5.*

$$$ AMERICAN **Kingfisher Bar and Grill.** Kingfisher is a standout for classic American cuisine. The emphasis is on fresh seafood, especially oysters and mussels, but the kitchen does baby back ribs and steak with equal success. Try the delicately battered fish-and-chips or the clam chowder on the late-night menu, served from 10 PM to midnight. Bright panels of turquoise and terra-cotta, black banquettes, and neon lighting make for a chic space in the main dining room, or sit in the cozy bar area with locals who appreciate a good meal with their cocktails. ✉ *2564 E. Grant Rd., Central* ☎ *520/323–7739* 🌐 *kingfishertucson.com* 💳 *AE, D, DC, MC, V* ⏱ *No lunch weekends* ✥ *C4.*

$ MEXICAN **Molina's Midway.** Tucked into a side street just north of Speedway, this unassuming and charming Mexican restaurant holds its own against any in South Tucson. Specialties include Sinchiladas (chicken or beef with chiles, cheese, and a cream sauce) and *carne asada* (chunks of mildly spiced steak) wrapped in soft corn or flour tortillas. Seating is plentiful and the service is friendly; several smaller rooms keep the noise level down. ✉ *1138 N. Belvedere, Central* ☎ *520/325–9957* ▭ *AE, D, MC, V* ☉ *Closed Mon.* ✛ *E4.*

¢ ✕ **Tucson Tamale Company.** A good homemade tamale is special and a res-
MEXICAN   taurant that prepares and serves them up fresh every day with all sorts of creative fillings is a find indeed. Carnivores can indulge in beef, pork, or chicken tamales. Traditional, cheese-filled green corn tamales are vegetarian; selections with fillings like spinach, mushrooms, and sesame seeds or sweet potatoes and sun-dried tomatoes, are vegan. Salad, rice, and black beans are side options; everything is gluten-free and made without animal fat. Eat here at one of seven tables in the no-frills dining area, or take your tamales to go. If you're inspired to try making tamales yourself, they even sell packages of corn husks to wrap them in. ✉ *2545 E. Broadway, Central* ☎ *520/305–4760* ⊕ *tucsontamalecompany.com* ▭ *D, MC, V* ☉ *Closed Sun. No dinner Sat. or Mon.* ✛ *C5.*

$ ✕ **Zemam's.** It can be hard to get a table in this small eatery—except in
ETHIOPIAN   summer, when the lack of air-conditioning presents a challenge. The sampler plate of any three items allows you to try dishes like *yesimir wat* (a spicy lentil dish) and *lega tibs* (a milder beef dish with a tomato sauce). Most of the food has a stewlike consistency, so don't come if you feel the need to crunch. Everything is served on a communal platter with *injera*, a spongy bread, and eaten with the hands. ✉ *2731 E. Broadway Blvd., Central* ☎ *520/323–9928* ⊕ *zemams.com* ⌲ *Reservations not accepted* ▭ *MC, V* ⌁ *BYOB* ☉ *Closed Mon.* ✛ *C5.*

$ ✕ **Zona 78.** Fresh food takes on a whole new meaning at this contempo-
ITALIAN   rary bistro emphasizing inventive pizzas, pastas, and salads. The casual interior's focal point is a huge stone oven, where the pies are fired with toppings like Australian blue cheese, kalamata olives, sausage, and even chicken with peanut sauce. Whole-wheat crust is an option, and there are also baked salmon and chicken entrées. The house-made mozzarella is delectable, either on top of a pizza or in a salad with organic tomatoes. The newer eastside location at 7301 East Tanque Verde Road has the same low-key, neighborhood feel. ✉ *78 W. River Rd., Central* ☎ *520/888–7878* ⊕ *zona78.com* ▭ *AE, D, MC, V* ✛ *B2.*

EASTSIDE

$$ ✕ **Montana Avenue.** The more sedate but equally charming sister restau-
AMERICAN   rant to Zinburger, North, and Wildflower, Montana Avenue satisfies with upscale comfort food in a sophisticated setting, this one named for the chic dining district in L.A.'s Santa Monica. There's no view here, but floor-to-ceiling windows create a bright backdrop for nouvelle dishes like shrimp risotto with shiitake mushrooms and buttermilk chicken with chayote squash. Just for fun, indulge in their sumptuous macaroni and cheese, grown-up style. ✉ *6390 E. Grant Rd., Eastside* ☎ *520/298–2020* ⊕ *foxrestaurantconcepts.com* ▭ *AE, D, MC, V* ✛ *F4.*

$ ✕ **Pinnacle Peak Steakhouse.** Anybody caught eating newfangled foods
STEAK   like fish tacos here would probably be hanged from the rafters—along
☺   with the ties snipped from city slickers who overdressed. This cowboy steak house serves basic, not stellar, cowboy fare: mesquite-broiled

Work up your appetite hiking through the desert before enjoying some of the best Mexican food north of the border.

steak, chicken, and grilled fish with salad and pinto beans. The restaurant is part of the somewhat kitschy Trail Dust Town, a re-creation of a turn-of-the-20th-century town, complete with a working antique carousel and a narrow-gauge train. Gunfights are staged outside nightly at 7, 8, and 9. Expect a long wait on weekends. ⊠ *6541 E. Tanque Verde Rd., Eastside* ☎ *520/296–0911* ⊕ *pinnaclepeaktucson.com* ⌧ *Reservations not accepted* ☐ *AE, D, DC, MC, V* ⊘ *No lunch* ✣ *F4.*

\$\$
JAPANESE

✕ **Sachiko Sushi.** Don't let the bland interior or the strip-mall setting dissuade you; many locals consider this the best Japanese restaurant in Tucson. Inside, you'll find perfectly prepared sushi and sashimi, generous combinations of tempura and teriyaki, and friendly service. The owner's wife is Korean, so you'll also find quite a few Korean classics, like beef and pork *bulgogi* (barbecued with vegetables) and tofu kimchi, on the menu. Try a bowl of udon noodles, served in broth with assorted meat, seafood, or vegetables; it's a satisfying meal in itself. ⊠ *1101 Wilmot Rd., Eastside* ☎ *520/886–7000* ⊕ *www.sachikorestaurant.com* ☐ *AE, DC, MC, V* ⊘ *No lunch Sun.* ✣ *F4.*

CATALINA FOOTHILLS

\$\$\$
SOUTHWESTERN

✕ **Acacia.** One of Tucson's premier chefs, Albert Hall, chose one of the area's most artistic settings to open his own beautiful restaurant in 2006. A glass waterfall sculpture by local artist Tom Philabaum graces one wall, and bold red-and-blue glass plates and stemware seem to float atop the tables. Roasted plum tomato–and–basil soup, a recipe from Hall's mom, is a favorite starter. Creative dishes like wild salmon with a pecan honey-mustard glaze and wood-roasted quail filled with pancetta, mozzarella, roasted tomatoes, and Oaxacan risotto are among the many tempting entrées. Weekend evenings bring live jazz to the patio, which overlooks pretty, flower-filled St. Philip's Plaza. ⊠ *4340 N. Campbell Ave., St. Philip's Plaza, Foothills* ☎ *520/232–0101* ⊕ *acaciatucson.com* ▭ *AE, D, MC, V* ✛ *C2.*

$$$
SOUTHWESTERN
Fodor's Choice
★

✕ **The Grill at Hacienda del Sol.** Tucked into the Foothills and surrounded by flowering gardens, this special-occasion restaurant, a favorite among locals hosting out-of-town visitors, provides an alternative to the chile-laden dishes of most Southwestern nouvelle cuisine. Wild-mushroom bisque, pecan-grilled buffalo, and pan-seared sea bass are among the menu choices at this luxurious guest ranch resort. Tapas (and most items on the full menu) can be enjoyed on the more casual outdoor patio, accented by live flamenco guitar music. The lavish Sunday brunch buffet is worth a splurge. ⊠ *Hacienda del Sol Guest Ranch Resort, 5601 N. Hacienda del Sol Rd., Foothills* ☎ *520/529–3500* ⊕ *haciendadelsol. com* ▭ *AE, DC, MC, V* ✛ *2D.*

$$$$
SOUTHWESTERN
Fodor's Choice
★

✕ **Janos.** Chef Janos Wilder was one of the first to reinvent Southwestern cuisine, and the menu, wine list, and service place this restaurant among the finest in the West. The hillside location on the grounds of the Westin La Paloma is a stunning backdrop for such dishes as sweet and spicy glazed quail with butternut-squash cannelloni, salmon with a scallop mousse served on polenta, and venison loin with chile-lime paste and pecans. Have a drink or a more casual meal of Latin-inspired fare next door at J Bar, a lively and lower-priced venue for sampling Janos's outstanding cuisine. Twinkling city lights make patio seating a romantic choice here. ⊠ *Westin La Paloma, 3770 E. Sunrise Dr., Foothills* ☎ *520/615–6100* ⊕ *janos.com* ▭ *AE, DC, MC, V* ☽ *Closed Sun. No lunch* ✛ *D1.*

$$
ITALIAN

✕ **North.** This trendy eatery in upscale La Encantada Shopping Center boasts an urban-loft look with exposed-pipe ceiling, white leather booths, dark concrete floors, and an open kitchen—and it draws crowds for its excellent thin-crust pizzas, pasta, fish, and steak. Alfresco dining on plush lounge furniture affords views of the city and quieter conversation; on most evenings the expansive bar area inside buzzes with Tucson's young professionals. ⊠ *2995 E. Skyline Dr., La Encantada, Foothills* ☎ *520/299–1600* ⊕ *foxrestaurantconcepts.com* ▭ *AE, D, MC, V* ✛ *C1.*

$$
ITALIAN

✕ **Vivace.** A nouvelle Italian bistro in the lovely St. Philip's Plaza, Vivace has long been a favorite with Tucsonans. Wild mushrooms and goat cheese in puff pastry is hard to resist as a starter. The fettuccine with grilled salmon is a nice lighter alternative to such entrées as a rich osso buco. For dessert, the molten chocolate cake with spumoni is worth the 20 minutes it takes to create. Patio seating is especially inviting on warm evenings. ⊠ *4310 N. Campbell Ave., Foothills* ☎ *520/795–7221* ▭ *AE, D, MC, V* ☽ *Closed Sun.* ✛ *C2.*

$
AMERICAN

✕ **Zinburger.** Have a glass of wine or a cocktail with your gourmet burger and fries at this high-energy, somewhat noisy, and unquestionably hip burger joint. Open until 11 PM on Friday and Saturday, late by Tucson standards, Zinburger delivers tempting burgers—try the Kobe beef with cheddar and wild mushrooms—and decadent milk shakes

7

made of exotic combinations like dates and honey or melted chocolate with praline flakes. A few creative salads, including one with ahi tuna, round out the menu. ⊠ *1865 E. River Rd., Foothills* ☎ *520/299–7799* ⊕ *foxrestaurantconcepts.com* ▤ *AE, D, DC, MC, V* ✛ *C2.*

NORTHWEST TUCSON

$$$ ✕**Bluefin Seafood Bistro.** What's a nice little fish restaurant doing in the
SEAFOOD   middle of the desert? Consistently turning out well-prepared, fresh seafood like cashew-crusted mahimahi; Scottish salmon; and a mixed grill of lobster, shrimp, and scallops in a classy setting. Tucked into the courtyard of Casas Adobes Plaza, the two-story bistro has three comfortable seating areas—in the brick-walled bar listening to live jazz, upstairs in the mellow dining room, or outside on the patio. The late-night menu, which includes New England and Manhattan clam chowder, is served until midnight on Friday and Saturday, providing a less expensive, lighter option in this part of town. ⊠ *7053 N. Oracle Rd., Northwest* ☎ *520/531–8500* ⊕ *bluefintucson.com* ▤ *AE, D, MC, V* ✛ *B1.*

$$$ ✕**Gold.** Every seat in this casually elegant and quiet dining room at the
SOUTHWESTERN   Westward Look Resort, high in the Catalina Foothills, has a spectacular view of the city below. The fare includes classics like sautéed halibut and roasted rack of lamb in truffle port sauce, as well as regional specialties such as mesquite-grilled buffalo sirloin and pine-nut-crusted chicken. All are served with organically grown vegetables picked from the chef's on-site garden. ⊠ *Westward Look Resort, 245 E. Ina Rd., Northwest* ☎ *520/297–1151* ⊕ *westwardlook.com* ▤ *AE, DC, MC, V* ✛ *B1.*

$$ ✕**Harvest.** The farm-to-table approach is the signature of this North-
SOUTHWESTERN   west bistro featuring fresh local ingredients and a solid wine list. The warm, orange-accented interior may be simple, but the food is decidedly complex and flavorful. Try the homemade gnocchi with wild mushrooms, sausage and sunchokes for a fabulous starter—it's large enough to share. The menu changes seasonally but enticing entrées in winter may include scallops with marscapone grits and Kobe beef sweetbreads in puff pastry. A sunset menu, served daily 4–5:30, has many of the same delicious dishes for only $12. ⊠ *10355 N. La Canada Dr., Northwest* ☎ *520/731–1100* ⊕ *harvest.marketrg.com* ▤ *AE, D, MC, V* ✛ *A2.*

$$ ✕**JaxKitchen.** A 2008 entry to the Tucson dining scene, Jax serves up
AMERICAN   modern comfort food in a cozy, sophisticated setting more reminiscent of Chicago or Boston than the Sonoran Desert. Their unique versions of "shrimp and grits" (sautéed shrimp atop creamy polenta) and tomato soup with grilled Brie and Gruyère cheeses are heavenly, and the daily fish entrée is served with Meyer lemon–infused risotto. The dining room is cleverly divided by a half wall, so conversation still feels intimate even when the place is bustling. Save room for milk and cookies like your mother never served—a plate of assorted warm cookies surrounding a cup of bourbon-spiked milk to dip them in. You'll want to make a reservation here, even on weeknights. ⊠ *7286 N. Oracle Rd., Northwest* ☎ *520/219–1235* ⊕ *jaxkitchen.com* ▤ *AE, MC, V* ☉ *Closed Mon. No lunch Sun.* ✛ *B1.*

$ ✕ **Sauce.** Modern Italian fuses with fast food here at North Restaurant's
ITALIAN casual little sister in Casas Adobes Plaza. Delicious thin-crust pizzas, chopped salads, pastas, and panini are ordered at the counter in this lively, family-friendly spot decorated in a contemporary twist on the colors of Italy's flag—green, white, and tomato-red. The food is fast, fresh, and affordable, without sacrificing sophisticated taste. Two additional locations, on East Broadway in Eastside and North Campbell in Central, are identical in both decor and menu. ✉ *7117 N. Oracle Rd., Northwest* ☎ *520/297–8575* ⊕ *foxrestaurantconcepts.com* ▤ *AE, D, MC, V* ✛ *B1, C3, E5.*

$ ✕ **Tohono Chul Tea Room.** The food is excellent—especially now that Chef
SOUTHWESTERN Hall of Acacia Restaurant presides over it—but what many come for is the location—inside a wildlife sanctuary, surrounded by flowering desert gardens. The Southwestern interior has Mexican tile, light wood, and a cobblestone courtyard. Dine outside on the back patio to watch hummingbirds and butterflies. House favorites include tortilla soup, grilled portabella mushroom sandwich, and southwest chopped salad. Open daily 8–5, the Tea Room is popular for Saturday and Sunday brunch. ✉ *Tohono Chul Park, 7366 N. Paseo del Norte, Northwest* ☎ *520/797–1222* ⊕ *tohonochulpark.org* ▤ *AE, MC, V* ☾ *No dinner* ✛ *B1.*

$$$ ✕ **Wildflower Grill.** A glass wall separates the bar from the dining area,
AMERICAN where an open kitchen, high ceiling with painted flowers, and blue-green banquettes complete the light and airy effect. Wildflower Grill is well known for its creative American fare and stunning presentation, and the menu has compelling choices like warm Maine lobster salad; bow-tie pasta with grilled chicken, tomatoes, spinach, and pine nuts; and rack of lamb with a Dijon crust. The decadently huge desserts are equally top-notch. Request a banquette or seating on the patio in the evening if you want quiet conversation, as the room can be noisy. ✉ *7037 N. Oracle Rd., Northwest* ☎ *520/219–4230* ⊕ *foxrestaurantconcepts.com* ▤ *AE, D, DC, MC, V* ✛ *B1.*

SOUTH TUCSON

$ ✕ **Micha's.** Family-owned for 24 years, this local institution is a non-
MEXICAN descript Mexican diner serving some of the best Sonoran classics this side of the border. House specialties include *machaca* (shredded beef) enchiladas and chimichangas, and *cocido*, a hearty vegetable-beef soup. Homemade chorizo spices up breakfast, which is served daily. ✉ *2908 S. 4th Ave., South* ☎ *520/623–5307* ⊕ *michascatering.com* ▤ *AE, DC, MC, V* ☾ *No dinner Mon.* ✛ *B6.*

$ ✕ **Mi Nidito.** A perennial favorite among locals (the wait is worth-
MEXICAN while), Mi Nidito—"my little nest"—has also hosted its share of visiting celebrities. Following President Clinton's lunch here, the rather hefty Presidential Plate (bean tostada, taco with barbecued meat, chiles rellenos, chicken enchilada, and beef tamale with rice and beans) was added to the menu. Top that off with the mango chimichangas for dessert, and you're talkin' executive privilege. ✉ *1813 S. 4th Ave., South* ☎ *520/622–5081* ⊕ *minidito.net* ▤ *AE, DC, MC, V* ☾ *Closed Mon. and Tues.* ✛ *B6.*

WHERE TO STAY

When it comes to places to spend the night, the options in Tucson run the gamut: there are luxurious desert resorts, bed-and-breakfasts ranging from bedrooms in modest homes to private cottages nestled on wildlife preserves, as well as small to medium-size hotels and motels.

If you like being able to walk to sights, shops, and restaurants, plan on staying in the Downtown or University neighborhoods. You won't find a hotter scene than Downtown's Hotel Congress, with nightly music pulsing at Club Congress or the Rialto Theatre across the street. For a quieter but equally convenient base, opt for one of the charming B&Bs near the U of A campus.

The posh resorts, primarily situated in the Catalina Foothills and Northwest areas, although farther away from town, have many activities onsite, as well as some of Tucson's top-rated restaurants, golf courses and spas, and can arrange transportation to shopping and sights. Tucson's JW Marriott Starr Pass is the only one southwest of town; seemingly isolated, it is actually closer to Downtown and the Westside sights.

For a unique experience, you can check into a Southwestern-style dude ranch—one of them a former cattle ranch from the 1800s—on the outskirts of town (unless otherwise indicated, price categories for guest ranches include all meals and most activities).

If you are seeking accommodations that can change your life, book a stay at one of Tucson's world-class health spas, Canyon Ranch or Miraval. Both provide pampering, serenity, and guidance for attaining an improved sense of well-being.

PLANNING INFORMATION

Summer rates (late May through September) are up to 60% lower than those in winter. Note that unless you book months in advance, you'll be hard-pressed to find a Tucson hotel room at any price the week before and during the huge gem and mineral show, which is held the first two weeks in February. Also, resorts typically charge an additional daily fee for "use of facilities," such as pools, tennis courts, and exercise classes and equipment, so be sure to ask what is included when you book a room.

WHAT IT COSTS				
¢	$	$$	$$$	$$$$
FOR TWO PEOPLE	under $100	$100–$150	$151–$225	$226–$350	over $350

Prices are for a standard double in high season.

Use the coordinate (✠ B2) at the end of each listing to locate a site on the corresponding map.

BEST BETS FOR TUCSON LODGING

Fodor's offers a selective listing of quality lodging experiences at every price range, from the city's best budget motel to its most sophisticated luxury hotel. Here, we've compiled our top recommendations by price and experience. The very best properties—in other words, those that provide a particularly remarkable experience in their price range—are designated in the listings with the Fodor's Choice logo.

Fodor's Choice ★

Arizona Inn, p. 407

Casa Tierra, p. 415

Hacienda del Sol Guest Ranch Resort, p. 411

Hotel Congress, p. 406

Loews Ventana Canyon Resort, p. 411

White Stallion Ranch, p. 414

Best by Price

¢

Hotel Congress, p. 406

Quail's Vista Bed & Breakfast, p. 414

$

Adobe Rose Inn, p. 406

La Posada Lodge and Casitas, p. 412

$$

Casa Tierra, p. 415

Peppertrees B&B Inn, p. 407

Westward Look Resort, p. 414

Windmill Inn, p. 412

$$$

Arizona Inn, p. 407

Hacienda del Sol Guest Ranch Resort, p. 411

Loews Ventana Canyon Resort, p. 411

Westin La Paloma, p. 412

$$$$

JW Marriott Starr Pass, p. 415

Ritz-Carlton Dove Mountain, p. 414

White Stallion Ranch, p. 414

Best By Experience

BEST B&BS

Casa Tierra, p. 415

Peppertrees B&B Inn, p. 407

Royal Elizabeth B&B Inn, p. 406

BEST RESORTS

JW Marriott Starr Pass, p. 415

Loews Ventana Canyon Resort, p. 411

Ritz-Carlton Dove Mountain, p. 414

Westin La Paloma, p. 412

BEST SPAS

Canyon Ranch, p. 410

Miraval, p. 413

Ritz-Carlton Dove Mountain, p. 414

GREAT VIEWS

Casa Tierra, p. 415

JW Marriott Starr Pass, p. 415

Westward Look Resort, p. 414

MOST KID-FRIENDLY

Hilton Tucson El Conquistador, p. 412

Tanque Verde Ranch, p. 410

Westin La Paloma, p. 412

White Stallion Ranch, p. 414

MOST ROMANTIC

Arizona Inn, p. 407

Hacienda del Sol, p. 411

JW Marriott Starr Pass, p. 415

7

DOWNTOWN TUCSON

¢ 🖼 **Hotel Congress.** This hotel built in 1919 has been artfully restored to
Fodor's Choice its original Western version of art deco. The gangster John Dillinger
★ was almost caught here in 1934—apparently his luggage, filled with
guns and ammo, was suspiciously heavy. Each room has a black-and-
white tile bath and the original iron bed frames. The convenient location Downtown means it can be noisy, so make sure you don't get a
room over the popular Club Congress unless you plan to be up until
the wee hours. A great place to stay for younger or more adventurous
visitors, it's the center of Tucson's hippest scene. **Pros:** convenient location; good restaurant; funky and fun. **Cons:** no air-conditioning (just
evaporative cooling, which isn't very effective in July and August); no
elevator to guest rooms; noise from nightclub. ⊠ *311 E. Congress St.,
Downtown* ☎ *520/622–8848 or 800/722–8848* ⊕ *www.hotelcongress.
com* ⇆ *40 rooms* ⚭ *In-room: no a/c, no TV, Wi-Fi. In-hotel: restaurant,
bar* ▭ *AE, D, MC, V* ✥ *B5.*

¢–$ 🖼 **Inn Suites Hotel Tucson City Center.** Just north of El Presidio district of
Downtown, this hotel is next to Interstate 10 but quiet nevertheless.
The large, peach-and-green Southwestern-themed rooms, circa 1980,
face an interior grassy courtyard with a sparkling pool and *palapas*
(thatched open gazebos). Free daily extras such as a breakfast buffet,
newspaper, and happy-hour cocktails make this a haven in the city
center. **Pros:** free breakfast and cocktails; affordable. **Cons:** little character; long walk to Downtown restaurants. ⊠ *475 N. Granada Ave.,
Downtown* ☎ *520/622–3000 or 877/446–6589* ⊕ *www.innsuites.com*
⇆ *265 rooms, 35 suites* ⚭ *In-room: a/c, refrigerator, Wi-Fi. In-hotel:
restaurant, bar, pool, gym, some pets allowed (paid)* ▭ *AE, D, DC,
MC, V* ⊠⊙ *BP* ✥ *B5.*

$$ 🖼 **The Royal Elizabeth Bed and Breakfast Inn.** Fans of Victoriana will
adore this B&B in the Armory Park historic district. The inn, built in
1878, is beautifully furnished with period antiques, and its six rooms
are quite spacious. Gracious hosts Jeff and Chuck take turns in the
kitchen, preparing two-course breakfasts that might include chiles rel-
lenos, a wild-mushroom frittata, or a fresh-fruit soufflé. **Pros:** large and
well-appointed rooms; perks for business travelers (Internet confer-
ence calling in-room); a sense of privacy as well as B&B camaraderie.
Cons: pricey for Downtown; neighbors aren't very lively (next door
to a funeral home). ⊠ *204 S. Scott Ave., Downtown* ☎ *520/670–9022*
⊕ *www.royalelizabeth.com* ⇆ *6 rooms* ⚭ *In-room: a/c, DVD, Wi-Fi.
In-hotel: pool* ▭ *AE, D, MC, V* ⊠⊙ *BP* ✥ *B5.*

UNIVERSITY OF ARIZONA

$–$$ 🖼 **Adobe Rose Inn.** This 1933 adobe home's six rooms vary in size and
amenities. Two have beehive fireplaces and stained-glass windows, two
have kitchenettes, and one is an upstairs suite with its own balcony.
In the historic Sam Hughes neighborhood just east of the university,
the well-maintained inn is within easy walking distance of shops and
restaurants. Breakfast dishes like Southwestern soufflés or blueberry
pancakes, always served with fruit and muffins, are enjoyed in a dining

room overlooking the bougainvillea-draped pool area. **Pros:** sumptuous breakfasts which can be prepared gluten-free; homelike yet private. **Cons:** some rooms are small; about a mile walk to the University Boulevard and 4th Avenue sights. ⊠ *940 N. Olsen Ave., University* ☎ *520/318–4644 or 800/328–4122* ⊕ *www.aroseinn.com* ⟿ *6 rooms* ⊘ *In-room: a/c, kitchen (some), Wi-Fi. In-hotel: pool; no kids under 10* ⊟ *AE, D, MC, V* ⊠*BP* ⊹ *C4.*

$$$
Fodor's Choice
★

Arizona Inn. Although near the university and many sights, the beautifully landscaped lawns and gardens of this 1930 inn seem far from the hustle and bustle. The spacious rooms are spread over 14 acres in pink adobe-style casitas—most have private patios and some have fireplaces. The resort also has two luxurious two-story houses with their own heated pools and full-hotel service. The main building has a library, a fine-dining restaurant, and a cocktail lounge where a jazz pianist plays. **Pros:** unique historical property; emphasis on service. **Cons:** rooms may not be modern enough for some; close to U of A Medical Center but long walk (1.5 mi) from the main campus. ⊠ *2200 E. Elm St., University* ☎ *520/325–1541 or 800/933–1093* ⊕ *www.arizonainn. com* ⟿ *70 rooms, 16 suites, 3 casitas* ⊘ *In-room: a/c, Internet. In-hotel: 2 restaurants, room service, bar, tennis courts, pool, gym, laundry service* ⊟ *AE, DC, MC, V* ⊹ *C3.*

$–$$
Catalina Park Inn. Classical music plays softly in the living room of this beautifully restored 1927 neoclassical house. The original art nouveau tile work and a butler's pantry are among many charming architectural details, and all rooms are spacious, quite private, and well equipped. You might be tempted to fill your suitcase with the papaya and lime scones that are part of breakfast. **Pros:** rooms are large and quiet; up-to-date technology for a small property, with DVDs, flat-screen TVs, and iPod docks; comfortable beds. **Cons:** West University location is not as bucolic as east of campus; closed late summer. ⊠ *309 E. 1st St., University* ☎ *520/792–4541 or 800/792–4885* ⊕ *www.catalinaparkinn.com* ⟿ *6 rooms* ⊘ *In-room: a/c, DVD, Wi-Fi. In-hotel: some pets allowed (paid), no kids under 10* ⊟ *AE, D, MC, V* ⊙ *Closed July and Sept.* ⏀*BP* ⊹ *B4.*

$$
Peppertrees B&B Inn. This restored 1905 Victorian is just west of the U of A campus. Two contemporary-style guesthouses at the rear of the tree-shaded main house have full kitchens, separate phone lines, private patios, and washers and dryers. The antiques-filled main house has several guest rooms and a separate one-bedroom apartment, all furnished with pieces from innkeeper Jill Light's family in England. Elaborate breakfasts are served in rooms or in the lovely garden, and dinner is available on request. **Pros:** comfortably furnished and meticulously clean; very convenient. **Cons:** often booked far in advance. ⊠ *724 E. University Blvd., University* ☎ *520/622–7167 or 800/348–5763* ⊕ *www.peppertreesinn.com* ⟿ *3 rooms, 1 suite, 2 guesthouses* ⊘ *In-room: a/c, kitchen (some), Wi-Fi* ⊟ *D, MC, V* ⏀*BP* ⊹ *B4.*

$$
Tucson Marriott University Park. With the University of Arizona less than a block from the front door, the Marriott is an ideal place to stay when visiting the campus. This clean, contemporary hotel has a lush atrium lobby area that can be enjoyed from the restaurant and bar, and

7

Loews Ventana Canyon Resort

Arizona Inn

White Stallion Ranch

the university shopping district's cafés, pubs, and stores are all within a short stroll. **Pros:** excellent location; clean. **Cons:** generic rooms; uninspired restaurant. ✉ *880 E. 2nd St., University* ☎ *520/792–4100 or 888/236–2427* ⊕ *www.marriotttucson.com* ↳ *234 rooms, 16 suites* ⌂ *In-room: a/c, refrigerator (some), Wi-Fi. In-hotel: restaurant, room service, bar, pool, gym, laundry service* ▭ *AE, D, DC, MC, V* ✛ *B4.*

CENTRAL TUCSON

$$ ⊞ **Doubletree Hotel at Reid Park.** A sprawling, 1970s-era hotel and conference center, the Doubletree sits directly across the street from Randolph Park, Tucson's best municipal golf course, and Reid Park, which houses the city zoo, a lake with paddleboats, and numerous play areas. A pleasant jogging-walking trail encircles both parks. The hotel property is well tended though generic-looking. **Pros:** attractive gardens; close to recreation and restaurants. **Cons:** large, older property; small rooms. ✉ *445 S. Alvernon Way, Central* ☎ *520/881–4200 or 800/222–8733* ⊕ *www. doubletree.com* ↳ *295 rooms* ⌂ *In-room: a/c, refrigerator, Wi-Fi. In-hotel: 2 restaurants, room service, bar, tennis courts, pool, gym, laundry service, some pets allowed (paid)* ▭ *AE, D, DC, MC, V* ❑*BP* ✛ *D5.*

¢ ⊞ **Extended Stay America.** If you're seeking convenience and value (and don't mind a certain blandness), this modern chain property will suffice. All rooms have full kitchens, queen or king-size beds, and recliner chairs, but don't expect a view or coffee in the lobby. Crossroads Shopping Center, where there are restaurants, a Starbucks, a grocery store, shops, and a cinema, is only two blocks away. **Pros:** central location; cheap. **Cons:** no pool; some road noise in front rooms. ✉ *5050 E. Grant Rd., Central* ☎ *520/795–9510 or 800/398–7829* ⊕ *www.extendedstayhotels. com* ↳ *120 rooms* ⌂ *In-room: a/c, kitchen, refrigerator, Wi-Fi. In-hotel: laundry facilities, some pets allowed (paid)* ▭ *AE, D, MC, V* ✛ *E4.*

$$ ⊞ **Varsity Clubs of America.** This sports-themed time-share facility also doubles as a hotel, so it may have some or all of its suites available for rental at any given time. Home to the Diamondbacks and the Rockies teams during spring training, it enjoys a handy and surprisingly quiet location. One- and two-bedroom suites have whirlpool tubs and full kitchens, but alternatives to cooking include the Stadium Sports Grill downstairs or any of the several restaurants within walking distance. **Pros:** apartment style; pleasant common areas include a billiards room, cozy library with fireplace, and a putting green. **Cons:** little curb appeal; bland decor in suites; availability varies by season. ✉ *3855 E. Speedway Blvd., Central* ☎ *520/318–3777 or 888/594–2287* ⊕ *www.ilxresorts. com* ↳ *59 suites* ⌂ *In-room: a/c, kitchen, Wi-Fi. In-hotel: restaurant, pool, gym, some pets allowed (paid)* ▭ *AE, D, MC, V* ✛ *D3.*

EASTSIDE

$$ ⊞ **The SunCatcher.** The three rooms in this B&B are decorated in honor of three groups who settled the Old West: Cowboys, Native Americans, and Spanish. Some have fireplaces and Jacuzzi tubs, and can be reconfigured as suites for families. The spacious common room has a sunken seating area, a huge DVD library, and a mesquite-wood bar where happy-hour snacks are served. It's a comfortable retreat after a day of sightseeing or hiking—trailheads into Saguaro National Park East are just down the road. **Pros:** quiet escape from civilization; all rooms have separate entrances; scrumptious European breakfasts. **Cons:** on the far east side of town. ⊠ *105 N. Avenida Javelina, Eastside* ☎ *520/885–0883 or 877/775–8355* ⊕ *www.suncatchertucson.com* ⤳ *3 rooms* ⌂ *In-room: a/c, DVD, Wi-Fi. In-hotel: pool, some pets allowed (free)* ⊟ *AE, MC, V* ⫟⨀⫠ *BP* ✢ *H4.*

$$$$ 🏠 **Tanque Verde Ranch.** The most upscale of Tucson's guest ranches and
☾ one of the oldest in the country, the Tanque Verde sits on 640 beautiful acres in the Rincon Mountains next to Saguaro National Park East. Rooms in one-story casitas have tasteful Western-style furnishings, fireplaces, and picture-window views of the desert. Breakfast, lunch, and dinner buffets are huge, and the spa will help remedy sore muscles. Horseback excursions are available for every skill level (lessons are included in rates), and children can participate in daylong activity programs, leaving parents to their leisure. **Pros:** authentic Western experience; loads of all-inclusive activities. **Cons:** expensive; at the eastern edge of town. ⊠ *14301 E. Speedway Blvd., Eastside* ☎ *520/296–6275 or 800/234–3833* ⊕ *www.tanqueverderanch.com* ⤳ *49 rooms, 23 suites, 2 casitas* ⌂ *In-room: a/c, no TV. In-hotel: tennis courts, pools, gym, spa, bicycles, children's programs (ages 4–11)* ⊟ *AE, D, MC, V* ⫟⨀⫠ *FAP* ✢ *H4.*

$ 🏠 **Tucson Hilton East.** This high-rise, corporate-type hotel and conference center is set back from a main road on the suburban east side of town. An airy atrium lobby takes advantage of the view of the Santa Catalina Mountains; better yet, push "6" in the glass elevator and ascend for spectacular vistas. Rooms are spacious and well maintained, but not particularly distinctive. **Pros:** comfortable and unpretentious; quiet. **Cons:** in a sleepy part of town; very generic-looking. ⊠ *7600 E. Broadway Blvd., Eastside* ☎ *520/721–5600 or 800/774–1500* ⊕ *www.tucsoneast.hilton.com* ⤳ *225 rooms, 8 suites* ⌂ *In-room: a/c, Wi-Fi. In-hotel: restaurant, bar, pool, gym, some pets allowed (paid)* ⊟ *AE, D, DC, MC, V* ✢ *G5.*

CATALINA FOOTHILLS

$$$$ 🏠 **Canyon Ranch.** The Canyon Ranch draws an international crowd of well-to-do health seekers to its superb spa facilities on 70 acres in the desert Foothills. Two activity centers include an enormous spa complex and a Health and Healing Center, where dietitians, exercise physiologists, behavioral-health professionals, and medical staff attend to body and soul. Just about every type of physical activity is possible, from Pilates to guided hiking, and the food is plentiful and healthful. Rates include all meals, activities, taxes, and gratuities. There's a four-night minimum. **Pros:** a stay here can be a life-changing experience; gorgeous setting. **Cons:** very pricey; not family-friendly. ⊠ *8600 E. Rockcliff Rd., Foothills* ☎ *520/749–9000 or 800/742–9000* ⊕ *www.canyonranch.com* ⤳ *240 rooms* ⌂ *In-room: a/c, refrigerator, Wi-Fi. In-hotel: restaurant, tennis courts, pools, gym, spa, laundry facilities, no kids under 12* ⊟ *AE, D, MC, V* ⫟⨀⫠ *AI* ✢ *G2.*

Downtown Tucson is close to the Catalina Foothills, which fill with blooms in springtime.

$$–$$$
Fodor's Choice
★

🏨 Hacienda del Sol Guest Ranch Resort. This 32-acre hideaway in the Santa Catalina Foothills is part guest ranch, part resort, and entirely gracious. It's a charming and lower-price alternative to the larger resorts. Designed in classic Mexican hacienda style, this former finishing school for girls was converted to a guest ranch during World War II and attracted stars like Clark Gable, Katharine Hepburn, and Spencer Tracy. The best rooms are the west-facing casitas with fireplaces and private porches, where you can watch the sun set over the Tucson Mountains. **Pros:** outstanding restaurant and bar; buildings and landscaping are stunningly beautiful. **Cons:** not as kid-friendly as other resorts. ⌧ *5601 N. Hacienda del Sol Rd., Foothills* ☎ *520/299–1501 or 800/728–6514* ⊕ *www.haciendadelsol.com* ↪ *22 rooms, 8 suites* ⚗ *In-room: a/c, refrigerator, Wi-Fi. In-hotel: restaurant, pool* ☰ *AE, D, MC, V* ✛ *E1.*

$$$–$$$$
🄫
Fodor's Choice
★

🏨 Loews Ventana Canyon Resort. This is one of the most luxurious and prettiest of the big resorts, with dramatic stone architecture and an 80-foot waterfall cascading down the mountains. Rooms, facing either the Catalinas or the golf course and city, are modern and elegantly furnished in muted earth tones and light woods; each bathroom has a miniature, flat-screen TV and a double-wide tub. Dining options include poolside snacks at Bill's Grill and Southwestern cuisine at the Flying V Grill (try the fresh guacamole made table-side here). The scenic Ventana Canyon trailhead is steps away, and there's a free shuttle to nearby Sabino Canyon. **Pros:** this place has everything: great golf, full spa, hiking, and even a kids' playground. **Cons:** some rooms overlook the parking lot. ⌧ *7000 N. Resort Dr., Foothills* ☎ *520/299–2020 or 800/234–5117* ⊕ *www.loewshotels.com* ↪ *384 rooms, 14 suites* ⚗ *In-room: a/c, refrigerator, Wi-Fi. In-hotel: 4 restaurants, room service, bar, golf courses,* *tennis courts, pools, gym, spa, bicycles, children's programs (ages 4–12)* ▤ *AE, D, DC, MC, V* ⚓ *E1.*

$$$–$$$$ 🏨 **Westin La Paloma.** Popular with business travelers and families, this
☾ sprawling resort has grand views of the Santa Catalina Mountains
above and the city below. It specializes in relaxation with an emphasis
on fun: the huge pool complex has an impressively long waterslide, as
well as a swim-up bar and grill for those who can't bear to leave the
water. Kids' programs, including weekly "dive-in movies," make for
a vacation the whole family can enjoy. The highly acclaimed Janos
restaurant is on-site. **Pros:** top-notch golf, tennis, and spa; great dining
at Janos and J Bar. **Cons:** so big it can feel crowded at pool areas and
mazelike going to and from guest rooms. ✉ *3800 E. Sunrise Dr., Foot-
hills* ☎ *520/742–6000 or 888/625–5144* ⊕ *www.starwood.com* ⌨ *455
rooms, 32 suites* ☾ *In-room: a/c, refrigerator, Wi-Fi. In-hotel: 4 restau-
rants, room service, bars, golf courses, tennis courts, pools, gym, spa,
children's programs (ages 6 months–12)* ▤ *AE, D, DC, MC, V* ⚓ *D1.*

$$ 🏨 **Windmill Inn at St. Philip's Plaza.** This all-suites hotel is in a chic shopping plaza filled with glitzy boutiques, galleries, and good restaurants.
Each 500-square-foot suite has a small sitting area, wet bar, two TVs,
and three telephones (local calls are free). A few dollars extra will buy
you a view of the pool and fountain rather than the parking lot. Complimentary coffee, muffins, juice, and a newspaper are delivered to your
door; additional breakfast goodies are set up in the lobby. **Pros:** so many
shops and restaurants to walk to, so little time; bicycles are available for
treks along the adjacent Rillito River Path. **Cons:** sure, it's a suite, but
both rooms are small. ✉ *4250 N. Campbell Ave., Foothills* ☎ *520/577–
0007 or 800/547–4747* ⊕ *www.windmillinns.com* ⌨ *122 suites* ☾ *In-
room: a/c, refrigerator, Wi-Fi. In-hotel: pool, bicycles, laundry facilities,
some pets allowed (free)* ▤ *AE, D, DC, MC, V* ⛉*BP* ⚓ *C2.*

NORTHWEST TUCSON

$$$ 🏨 **Hilton Tucson El Conquistador.** A huge copper mural of cowboys and
☾ cacti, and a wide view of the Santa Catalina Mountains grace the lobby
of this golf and tennis resort. A friendly upscale property, it draws fami-
lies and conventioneers, some taking advantage of low summer rates
for the excellent sports facilities, the spa, and the pool complex with a
140-foot waterslide. Rooms are either in private one-bedroom casitas
or in the main hotel building, and more than half of them have kiva-
style fireplaces. **Pros:** great variety of on-site activities, even horseback
riding; low-key. **Cons:** huge place; location is farther northwest than
most resorts, adding on driving time to restaurants and in-town sights.
✉ *10000 N. Oracle Rd., Northwest* ☎ *520/544–5000 or 800/325–3525*
⊕ *www.hiltonelconquistador.com* ⌨ *328 rooms, 57 suites, 43 casitas*
☾ *In-room: a/c, refrigerator, Wi-Fi. In-hotel: 5 restaurants, bar, golf
courses, tennis courts, pools, gym, spa, bicycles, children's programs
(ages 4–12)* ▤ *AE, D, DC, MC, V* ⚓ *C1.*

$ 🏨 **La Posada Lodge and Casitas.** This 1960s motor lodge has been reborn
as a Santa Fe–style boutique hotel with a Latin theme. Though most
rooms in the three-story building have Saltillo-tile floors and hand-
painted Mexican headboards, a few are whimsically decorated with

blue-and-lime-green–checkered bedspreads and curtains, along with kitschy furniture and lava lamps, as a tribute to the hotel's past life. Upper-floor rooms have balconies with mountain and city views. A full breakfast is included. **Pros:** good location; good restaurant; attractive grounds. **Cons:** service is inconsistent; rooms are not large. ⊠ *5900 N. Oracle Rd., Northwest* ☎ *520/887–4800 or 800/810–2808* ⊕ *www. laposadalodge.com* ⤺ *72 rooms* ⚲ *In-room: a/c, kitchen (some), refrigerator, Wi-Fi. In-hotel: restaurant, room service, bar, pool, gym* ▭ *AE, MC, V* �⑩ *BP* ⊕ *B1.*

$ ▦ **Marriott TownePlace Suites.** With full kitchens in all of its studio, one-bedroom, and two-bedroom suites, this property is suitable for short or extended stays. In fact, the longer you stay, the lower your nightly rate. Its location is handy, yet the interior hallways and the way the buildings are set back from the road make for a quiet retreat. Some suites have a view of the neighboring par-3, executive golf course. **Pros:** convenient location; well-equipped units. **Cons:** no restaurant; kind of sterile-looking. ⊠ *405 W. Rudasill Rd., Northwest* ☎ *520/292–9697 or 800/257–3000* ⊕ *www.towneplacesuites.com* ⤺ *77 suites* ⚲ *In-room: a/c, kitchen, Wi-Fi. In-hotel: pool, laundry facilities, some pets allowed (paid)* ▭ *AE, MC, V* ⑩ *CP* ⊕ *B1.*

$$$$ ▦ **Miraval.** Giving Canyon Ranch a run for its money, this New Age health spa 30 mi north of Tucson has a secluded desert setting and beautiful Southwestern rooms. Most of the spa services and wellness programs, based primarily on Eastern philosophies, help you get in touch with your inner self. Whether you prefer to be pampered with a hot stone massage or seaweed body mask, participate in fitness and nature activities, or walk a labyrinth, it's all here. All gratuities and meals, including tasty buffets (with calories and fat content noted), are included. **Pros:** very posh getaway in the middle of nowhere; tranquil. **Cons:** very posh attitude makes some uncomfortable; expensive. ⊠ *5000 E. Via Estancia Miraval, Catalina* ☎ *520/825–4000 or 800/825–4000* ⊕ *www.miravalresort.com* ⤺ *102 rooms* ⚲ *In-room: a/c, safe, refrigerator, Wi-Fi. In-hotel: 2 restaurants, bar, tennis courts, pools, gym, spa, bicycles, laundry facilities, laundry service* ▭ *AE, D, DC, MC, V* ⑩ *FAP* ⊕ *C1.*

$$$ ▦ **Omni Tucson National Golf Resort & Spa.** Perfect for couples with differing ideas on how to spend a vacation, Tucson National is both a premier golf resort (it hosts the Tucson Open) and a full-service European-style spa, where you can be coiffed, waxed, and wrapped to your heart's content. Most of the rooms, although not technically suites, are spacious with separate sitting areas. Some casitas have full kitchens and dining rooms. Although this resort is a little farther from central Tucson than others, it's still convenient to shopping and restaurants in the thriving Northwest area. **Pros:** outstanding golf; friendly, relaxed environment. **Cons:** tucked away in Northwest Tucson; too sedate for some. ⊠ *2727 W. Club Dr., Northwest* ☎ *520/297–2271 or 800/528–4856* ⊕ *www. OmniTucsonNational.com* ⤺ *143 rooms, 24 suites* ⚲ *In-room: a/c, refrigerator, Internet (some), Wi-Fi (some). In-hotel: 3 restaurants, bars, golf courses, tennis courts, pools, gym, spa* ▭ *AE, D, DC, MC, V* ⊕ *A2.*

7

¢ ☐ **Quail's Vista Bed and Breakfast.** Innkeeper and former concierge Barbara Bauer and her husband Richard can direct you to all the best things to see and do in Tucson; some activities, like bird-watching or soaking in a hot tub that faces the dramatic Santa Catalina Mountains, can be done right in the inn's backyard. Inside, peeled-spruce columns support the beamed ceiling and rounded walls of this adobe home. Fiesta dinnerware, Native American pottery, and bright Mexican blankets decorate the common area, which has cozy nooks for reading or watching the wildlife outside the windows. **Pros:** unique and comfortable rammed-earth house; friendly hosts; cheap. **Cons:** open only four months of the year. ⊠ *826 E. Palisades Rd., Northwest* ☎ *520/297–5980* ⊕ *www. quails-vista-bb.com* ⇄ *3 rooms, 1 with bath* ⊘ *In-room: a/c, no TV (some), Wi-Fi. In-hotel: laundry facilities* ⊟ *No credit cards* ⊘ *Closed May–Dec.* ⦿ *BP* ✛ *C1.*

$$$$ ☐ **The Ritz-Carlton Dove Mountain.** This 2009 addition to the golf and tennis resort scene is the ever-posh Ritz-Carlton, set in the rolling hills of Marana, about 20 mi northwest of central Tucson. Having spared no expense, the hotel has modern Southwestern-style rooms and casitas with featherbeds and Jacuzzi tubs, a top-notch spa with its own pool and luxurious lounge areas, two Jack Nicklaus–designed golf courses—site of the WGC-Accenture Match Play Tournament in February—and an indoor-outdoor restaurant with spectacular desert views. The resort accentuates the indigenous people of this region, with Native American art, a library filled with books on the area's cultural and natural history, and a sunset celebration each evening outdoors, when notes played by a Native American flutist float into the petroglyph-studded hillsides. **Pros:** great golf; top-notch service. **Cons:** somewhat isolated location in the far Northwest. ⊠ *15000 N. Secret Springs Dr., Northwest* ☎ *520/572–3000* ⊕ *ritzcarlton.com/dovemountain* ⇄ *250 rooms* ⊘ *In-room: a/c, safe, refrigerator (some), Wi-Fi. In-hotel: 3 restaurants, room service, bars, golf courses, tennis courts, pools, gym, spa, bicycles, children's programs (ages 5–12), laundry service, Wi-Fi hotspot, some pets allowed (paid), parking (paid; valet)* ⊟ *AE, D, MC, V* ✛ *A2.*

$$–$$$ ☐ **Westward Look Resort.** Originally the 1912 homestead of William and Mary Watson, this laid-back lodging has Southwestern character and all the amenities you expect at a major resort. The Watsons' original living room, with beautiful, dried ocotillo branches draped along the ceiling and antique furnishings, is now a comfortable library-lounge. The couple probably never envisioned anything like the Sonoran Spa, with hot desert-stone massages and three-mud body masks. Spacious rooms have wrought-iron beds and Mission-style furniture. **Pros:** excellent fine-dining restaurant at Gold; pleasant nature trails; you can actually park near your room. **Cons:** no golf; pool areas are rather plain. ⊠ *245 E. Ina Rd., Northwest* ☎ *520/297–1151 or 800/722–2500* ⊕ *www. westwardlook.com* ⇄ *244 rooms* ⊘ *In-room: a/c, refrigerator, Wi-Fi. In-hotel: 2 restaurants, tennis courts, pools, gym, spa, bicycles, some pets allowed (paid)* ⊟ *AE, D, DC, MC, V* ✛ *B1.*

$$$–$$$$ ☐ **White Stallion Ranch.** A 3,000-acre working cattle ranch run by the
Fodor'sChoice hospitable True family since 1965, this place is the real deal. You can
★ ride up to four times daily, hike in the mountains, enjoy a hayride

cookout, and compete in team cattle penning. Most rooms retain their original Western furniture, and newer deluxe rooms have whirlpool baths or fireplaces. A spa and fitness center bring even more comforts to this highly civilized but authentic setting. Rates include all meals, riding, and entertainment such as weekend rodeos, country line dancing, telescopic stargazing, and campfire sing-alongs. **Pros:** solid dude-ranch experience; very charming hosts; satisfying for families as well as singles or couple; airport shuttle. **Cons:** riding is somewhat structured; no room TVs. ⊠ *9251 W. Twin Peaks Rd., Northwest* ☎ *520/297–0252 or 888/977–2624* ⊕ *www.wsranch.com* ⟿ *24 rooms, 17 suites* ⚲ *In-room: a/c, no phone, no TV. In-hotel: bar, tennis courts, pool, gym* ⊟ *AE, MC, V* ⟊*FAP* ♣ *A2.*

WESTSIDE

$$ ☒ **Casa Tierra.** For a real desert experience, head to this B&B on 5 acres
Fodor's Choice near the Desert Museum and Saguaro National Park West. The last
★ 1.5 mi are on a dirt road. All rooms have private patio entrances and look out onto a lovely central courtyard. The Southwestern-style furnishings include Mexican *equipales* (chairs with pigskin seats) and tile floors. A full vegetarian breakfast served on fine china is included, and there's a media room in case you need a break from the quiet. There's a minimum stay of two nights. **Pros:** peaceful; great Southwest character. **Cons:** far from town (30-minute drive); closed in summer. ⊠ *11155 W. Calle Pima, Westside* ☎ *520/578–3058 or 866/254–0006* ⊕ *www. casatierratucson.com* ⟿ *3 rooms, 1 suite* ⚲ *In-room: a/c, refrigerator, no TV, Wi-Fi. In-hotel: gym* ⊟ *AE, D, MC, V* ⊗ *Closed mid-June–mid-Aug.* ⟊*BP* ♣ *A4.*

$$$–$$$$ ☒ **JW Marriott Starr Pass Resort & Spa.** Set amid saguaro forests and mesquite groves in the Tucson Mountains (yet only 15 minutes from Downtown), the city's largest resort opened in 2005. Massive sun-bleached stone walls blend rather than compete with the natural surroundings, and there are stunning views from the interior dining areas and lounges. Outside terraces, with chairs and sofas clustered around kiva fireplaces, overlook the pools, golf course, and desert valley. Complimentary tequila shots, along with a dramatic recitation of the story of Pancho Villa, liven up the bar during happy hour. **Pros:** posh and beautiful; excellent spa; great walking-hiking paths. **Cons:** expensive; parking structure is quite far from lobby areas and guest rooms. ⊠ *3800 W. Starr Pass Blvd., Westside* ☎ *520/792–3500* ⊕ *www.starrpassmarriott.com* ⟿ *538 rooms, 37 suites* ⚲ *In-room: a/c, refrigerator, Wi-Fi. In-hotel: 4 restaurants, room service, bar, golf courses, pools, gym, spa* ⊟ *AE, D, MC, V* ♣ *A5.*

SHOPPING

Much of Tucson's retail activity is focused around malls, but shops with more character and some unique wares can be found in the city's open plazas: St. Philip's Plaza (River Road and Campbell Avenue), Plaza Palomino (Swan and Fort Lowell roads), Casas Adobes Plaza (Oracle and Ina roads), and La Encantada (Skyline Drive and Campbell Avenue).

The 4th Avenue neighborhood near the University of Arizona—especially between 2nd and 9th streets—is fertile ground for unusual items in the artsy boutiques, galleries, and secondhand-clothing stores. For in-town deals, the outlet stores at the Foothills Mall in Northwest Tucson score high marks.

MALLS AND SHOPPING CENTERS

Broadway Village (⊠ *2926 E. Broadway Blvd., at Country Club Rd., Central* ⊕ *www.broadwayvillagetucson.com*), Tucson's first shopping center, was built in 1939. Although small by today's standards, this outdoor complex and neighboring strip of shops houses a few interesting stores such as Zocalo for colonial Mexican furniture, Yikes! for fabulous off-the-wall toys, Picante for Mexican clothing and crafts, and Bohemia for affordable local art.

★ **Casas Adobes Plaza** (⊠ *Oracle and Ina Rds., southwest corner, Northwest* ⊕ *www.casasadobesplaza.com*) originally served the ranchers and orange-grove owners in this once remote part of town, now the city's fastest-growing area. It's an outdoor, Mediterranean-style shopping center with a Whole Foods grocery store, the superb Wildflower and Blue Fin restaurants, a gelato shop, upscale pizzas at Sauce, Starbucks, and diverse boutiques and gift shops.

Foothills Mall (⊠ *7401 N. La Cholla Blvd. at Ina Rd., Northwest* ☎ *520/742–7191* ⊕ *www.shopfoothillsmall.com*) has a Barnes & Noble Superstore, a Saks Fifth Avenue outlet store, and many other outlets including Samsonite, Nike, and Adidas. A 16-screen cineplex, video arcade, and several restaurants round out the place.

La Encantada (⊠ *Skyline Dr. and Campbell Ave., Foothills* ☎ *520/299– 3566* ⊕ *www.laencantadashoppingcenter.com*), the newest outdoor mall, has close to 50 stores (and six restaurants) decidedly aimed at affluent consumers. North, a nouvelle Italian bistro, and Ra Sushi are the standout eateries. Trendy tenants include Crate & Barrel, Pottery Barn, Coach, Apple, and Tiffany & Co., plus a huge gourmet grocery that also serves casual meals.

The Lost Barrio (⊠ *Park Ave. and 12th St., south of Broadway, Central*) is a cluster of 10 shops in an old warehouse district; Southwestern and ethnic art, furniture, and funky gifts (both antique and modern) are specialties.

Old Town Artisans Complex (⊠ *186 N. Meyer Ave., Downtown* ☎ *520/623– 6024* ⊕ *www.oldtownartisans.com*), across from the Tucson Museum of Art, has a large selection of Southwestern wares, including Native American jewelry, baskets, Mexican handicrafts, pottery, and textiles.

Park Place (⊠ *5870 E. Broadway Blvd., Eastside* ☎ *520/747–7575* ⊕ *www.parkplacemall.com*) is a busy enclosed mall with an extensive food court, a 20-screen cineplex, and more than 120 stores, including Macy's and Borders.

Plaza Palomino (⊠ *2980 N. Swan Rd., at Fort Lowell Rd., Central* ☎ *520/795–1177* ⊕ *www.plazapalominotucson.com*), an outdoor mall, has unique shops, galleries, and clothing boutiques. On Saturday you can sample locally grown produce, baked goods, salsas, and tamales at the farmers' market.

St. Philip's Plaza (⊠ *4280 N. Campbell Ave., at River Rd., Foothills* ☎ *520/886–7485* ⊕ *www.stphilipsplaza.com*) has more than a dozen chic boutiques and galleries arranged around a series of Spanish-style outdoor patios. The restaurants Vivace and Acacia are located here, too.

Tucson Mall (⊠ *4500 N. Oracle Rd., at Wetmore Rd., Central* ☎ *520/293– 7330* ⊕ *www.tucsonmall.com*), an indoor mall on the Westside, has Dillard's, Macy's, JCPenney, and more than 200 specialty shops. For tasteful Southwestern-style T-shirts, belts, jewelry, and prickly pear candies, check out the shops on "Arizona Avenue," a section on the first floor that's devoted to regional items.

SPECIALTY SHOPS

ART GALLERIES
If you're seeking work by regional artists, you might want to drive down to Tubac, a community 45 mi south of Tucson (⇨ *see Side Trips Near Tucson).* **Art Life in Southern Arizona** (⊕ *artlifearizona.com*), published annually, lists galleries and artists statewide.

Dinnerware Contemporary Arts (⊠ *44 W. 6th St. Downtown* ⊕ *dinnerwarearts.com*), a nonprofit, membership gallery, focuses on artists of southern Arizona in various media, including painting, sculpture, digital art, and furniture.

Etherton Gallery (⊠ *135 S. 6th Ave., Downtown* ☎ *520/624–7370* ⊕ *www.ethertongallery.com*) specializes in vintage, classic, and contemporary photography but also represents artists in other mediums.

Gallery Row at El Cortijo (⊠ *3001 E. Skyline Dr., at Campbell Ave., Foothills*) is a complex of galleries that collectively represent regional and national artists working in all mediums, including Native American, Western, and contemporary painting, crafts, and jewelry.

Madaras Gallery (⊠ *3001 E. Skyline Dr., at Campbell Ave., Foothills* ☎ *520/615–3001* ⊕ *www.madaras.com*), at El Cortijo, has the bright watercolor prints of cacti and animals by the popular local artist Diana Madaras.

Obsidian Gallery (⊠ *St. Philip's Plaza, 4340 N. Campbell Ave., Suite 90, Central* ☎ *520/577–3598* ⊕ *www.obsidian-gallery.com*) has exquisite glass, ceramic, and jewelry pieces.

BOOKS
Book Stop (⊠ *214 N. 4th Ave., University* ☎ *520/326–6661* ⊕ *www. bookstoptucson.com*) is a wonderful browsing place for used and out-of-print books.

Bookman's (⊠ *1930 E. Grant Rd., Central* ☎ *520/325–5767* ⊕ *www. bookmans.com*), a Tucson institution, carries an eclectic selection of used and new books, music, magazines, and software in three spacious locations.

CACTI
B&B Cactus Farm (⊠ *11550 E. Speedway Blvd., Eastside* ☎ *520/721– 4687* ⊕ *www.bandbcactus.com*), which you'll pass en route to Saguaro National Park East, has a huge selection of cacti and succulents. They ship anywhere in the country.

Local ceramics and other arts and crafts are popular in Tucson and the nearby town Tubac.

★ **Native Seeds/Search** (✉ *3061 N. Campbell Ave., University* ☎ *520/622–5561* ⊕ *www.nativeseeds.org*), dedicated to preserving native crops and traditional farming methods, sells 350 kinds of seeds as well as Native American crafts.

JEWELRY **Abbott Taylor** (✉ *6383 E. Grant Rd., Eastside* ☎ *520/745–5080* ⊕ *www.atdiamonds.com*) creates custom designs in diamonds and other precious stones.

Beth Friedman (✉ *Joesler Village, 1865 E. River Rd., Suite 121, Foothills* ☎ *520/577–6858* ⊕ *www.bethfriedman.com*) sells unsurpassed designs in silver and semiprecious stones. The store also carries an eclectic selection of ladies' apparel, fine art, and home furnishings.

MEXICAN AND SOUTHWEST CRAFTS **Antigua de Mexico** (✉ *3235 W. Orange Grove Rd., Northwest* ☎ *520/742–7114* ⊕ *www.antiguademexico.us/*) sells well-made furniture and crafts that you are not likely to find elsewhere in town.

Del Sol (✉ *435 N. 4th Ave., University* ☎ *520/628–8765* ⊕ *www.delsolstores.com*) specializes in Mexican folk art, jewelry, and Southwest-style clothing.

NATIVE AMERI-CAN ARTS AND CRAFTS San Xavier Plaza, across from San Xavier mission and also part of the Tohono O'odham Reservation, is a good place to find vendors and stores selling the work of this and other area tribes. Other shops are listed below.

Bahti Indian Arts (✉ *St. Philip's Plaza, 4330 N. Campbell Ave., Foothills* ☎ *520/577–0290* ⊕ *www.bahti.com*) is owned and run by Mark Bahti, whose father, Tom, literally wrote the book on Native American art, including an early definitive work on kachinas. The store sells high-quality jewelry, pottery, rugs, art, and more.

Grey Dog Trading Company (✉ *Plaza Palomino, 2970 N. Swan Rd., Central* ☎ *520/881–6888* ⊕ *www.greydogtrading.com*) has an ample selection of jewelry, kachinas, weaving, pottery, and Zuni fetishes.

Silverbell Trading (✉ *Casas Adobes Plaza, 7119 N. Oracle Rd., Northwest* ☎ *520/797–6852*) carries the work of local and regional artists.

WESTERN WEAR
Tucsonans who wear Western gear keep it simple for the most part—jeans, a Western shirt, maybe boots. This isn't Santa Fe.

Arizona Hatters (✉ *2790 N. Campbell Ave., Central* ☎ *520/292–1320* ⊕ *www.azhatters.com*) can fit you for that Stetson you've always wanted.

Stewart Boot Manufacturing (✉ *30 W. 28th St., South* ☎ *520/622–2706*) has been making handmade leather boots since the 1940s.

NIGHTLIFE AND THE ARTS

Tuscon's college and resort aspects contribute to its lively cultural and nightlife scene.

THE ARTS

For a city of its size, Tucson is abuzz with cultural activity. It's one of only 14 cities in the United States with a symphony as well as opera, theater, and ballet companies. Wintertime, when Tucson's population swells with vacationers, is the high season, but the arts are alive and well year-round. The low cost of Tucson's cultural events comes as a pleasant surprise to those accustomed to paying East or West Coast prices: symphony tickets are as little as $10 for some performances, and touring Broadway musicals can often be seen for $24. Parking is plentiful and frequently free.

The free *Tucson Weekly* (⊕ *www.tucsonweekly.com*) and the "Caliente" section of the *Arizona Daily Star* (⊕ *www.azstarnet.com*) both hit the stands on Thursday, and have listings of what's going on in town.

Much of the city's cultural activity takes place at or near the **Tucson Convention Center** (✉ *260 S. Church St., Downtown* ☎ *520/791–4101, 520/791–4266 box office* ⊕ *www.tucsonconventioncenter.org*), which includes the **Music Hall** and the **Leo Rich Theater**. Dance, music, and other performances take place at the University of Arizona's **Centennial Hall** (✉ *1020 E. University Blvd., University* ☎ *520/621–3341* ⊕ *www. uapresents.org*).

One of Tucson's hottest rock-music venues, the **Rialto Theatre** (✉ *318 E. Congress St., Downtown* ☎ *520/798–3333* ⊕ *www.rialtotheatre.com*) was once a silent-movie theater but now reverberates with the sounds of jazz, folk, and world-music concerts, although the emphasis is on hard rock. A recently refurbished old movie palace, the art deco **Fox Theatre** (✉ *17 W. Congress St., Downtown* ☎ *520/547–3040* ⊕ *www. foxtucsontheatre.org*), hosts film festivals and folk-rock concerts.

Each season brings visiting opera, theater, and dance companies to Tucson. Tickets to many events can be purchased through **Ticketmaster** (☎ 800/745–3000 ⊕ www.ticketmaster.com), which has outlets at most Fry's Marketplace stores around town.

DANCE

The city's most established modern dance company, **Orts Theatre of Dance** (⊕ www.otodance.org), incorporates trapeze flying into their dances. Outdoor and indoor performances are staged throughout the year.

MUSIC

A Wednesday-night chamber-music series is hosted by the **Arizona Friends of Chamber Music** (☎ 520/577–3769 ⊕ arizonachambermusic.org) at the Leo Rich Theater in the Tucson Convention Center from October through April. They also have a music festival the first week of March. The **Arizona Opera Company** (☎ 520/293–4336 ⊕ www.azopera.com), based in Tucson, puts on five major productions each year at the Tucson Convention Center's Music Hall. The **Arizona Symphonic Winds** (⊕ www.azsymwinds.org) has a spring–summer schedule of performances, many of which are held outdoors at Udall Park in Northeast Tucson. Performances are usually at 7 PM, but you need to arrive at least an hour early for a good spot on the grass. From May through September the **Tucson Pops Orchestra** (☎ 520/722–5853 ⊕ www.tucsonpops.org) gives free concerts each Saturday evening at the De Meester Outdoor Performance Center in Reid Park. Arrive about an hour before the music starts (usually at 7 PM) to stake your claim on a viewing spot.

The **Tucson Symphony Orchestra** (✉ 443 S. Stone Ave., Downtown ☎ 520/882–8585 box office, 520/792–9155 main office ⊕ www.tucsonsymphony.org), part of Tucson's cultural scene since 1929, holds concerts in the Music Hall in the Tucson Convention Center and at sites in the Foothills and the Northwest as well.

Tucson's small but vibrant jazz scene encompasses everything from afternoon jam sessions in the park to Sunday jazz brunches at resorts in the Foothills. Call the **Tucson Jazz Society** (☎ 520/903–1265) for information.

POETRY

The first weekend in April brings the **Tucson Poetry Festival** (☎ 520/256–4206 ⊕ www.tucsonpoetryfestival.org) and its four days of readings and related events, including workshops, panel discussions, and a poetry slam. Such internationally acclaimed poets as Jorie Graham and Sherman Alexie have participated.

The **University of Arizona Poetry Center** (✉ 1508 E. Helen St., University ☎ 520/626–3765 ⊕ www.poetrycenter.arizona.edu) runs a free series open to the public. Check during fall and spring semesters for info on scheduled readings.

THEATER

Arizona's state theater, the **Arizona Theatre Company** (✉ Temple of Music and Art, 330 S. Scott Ave., Downtown ☎ 520/622–2823 box office, 520/884–8210 company office ⊕ www.aztheatreco.org), performs classical pieces, contemporary drama, and musical comedy at the historic

Temple of Music and Art from September through May. It's worth coming just to see the beautifully restored historic Spanish colonial–Moorish-style theater; dinner at the adjoining Temple Café is a tasty prelude.

The University of Arizona's **Arizona Repertory Theatre** (⊠ *1025 N. Olive St., University* ☎ *520/621–1162* ⊕ *www.uatheatre.org*) has performances during the academic year. **Borderlands Theater** (⊠ *40 W. Broadway, Downtown* ☎ *520/882–7406* ⊕ *www.borderlandstheater.org*) presents new plays about Southwest border issues—often multicultural and bilingual—at venues throughout Tucson, usually from late June through April.

☺ Children of all ages love the clever melodramas at the **Gaslight Theatre** (⊠ *7010 E. Broadway Blvd., Eastside* ☎ *520/886–9428* ⊕ *www. thegaslighttheatre.com*), where hissing at the villain and cheering the hero are part of the audience's duty.

Invisible Theatre (⊠ *1400 N. 1st Ave., Central* ☎ *520/882–9721* ⊕ *www. invisibletheatre.com*) presents contemporary plays and musicals.

NIGHTLIFE

BARS AND CLUBS

In addition to the places listed below, most of the major resorts have late spots for drinks or dancing. The Westward Look Resort's Lookout Bar, with its expansive view and classic rock band on Friday and Saturday nights, is a popular spot for dancing. The bars at Westin La Paloma, Hacienda del Sol, and Loews Ventana have live acoustic music on weekends.

BLUES AND JAZZ A jazz combo plays Thursday–Saturday nights and during Sunday brunch on the lovely patio of **Acacia** (⊠ *4340 N. Campbell Ave., St. Philip's Plaza, Foothills* ☎ *520/232–0101* ⊕ *acaciatucson.com*). **Boondocks** (⊠ *3306 N. 1st Ave., Central* ☎ *520/690–0991* ⊕ *boondockslounge. com*) is the unofficial home of the Blues Heritage Foundation, hosting local and touring singer-songwriters. **Old Pueblo Grille** (⊠ *60 N. Alvernon Way, Central* ☎ *520/326–6000* ⊕ *www.metrorestaurants.com*) has live jazz on Saturday and Sunday nights. **Ric's Café** (⊠ *5605 E. River Rd., Northeast* ☎ *520/577–7272*) features jazz musicians in the courtyard on Friday and Saturday nights.

COUNTRY AND WESTERN An excellent house band gets the crowd two-stepping Tuesday through Saturday nights at the **Maverick** (⊠ *6622 E. Tanque Verde Rd., Eastside* ☎ *520/298–0430* ⊕ *tucsonmaverick.com*).

GAY AND LESBIAN BARS **Ain't Nobody's Bizness** (⊠ *2900 E. Broadway Blvd., Central* ☎ *520/318–4838* ⊕ *www.thebiztuc.com*) is the most popular lesbian bar in town. **IBT's (It's 'Bout Time)** (⊠ *616 N. 4th Ave., University* ☎ *520/882–3053*) is Tucson's most popular gay men's bar, with rock and disco DJ music and drag shows Wednesday and Saturday nights. Expect long lines on weekends.

ROCK AND MORE The **Cactus Moon Café** (⊠ *5470 E. Broadway Blvd., Central* ☎ *520/748–0049* ⊕ *cactusmoon.net*), catering to a mostly yuppie crowd, plays a standard mix of Top 40, hip-hop, and modern country, often with free appetizer buffets during happy hour.

★ **Club Congress** (✉ *Hotel Congress, 311 E. Congress St., Downtown* ☎ *520/622–8848* ⊕ *www.hotelcongress.com*) is the main Friday venue for cutting-edge rock bands, with a mixed-bag crowd of alternative rockers, international travelers, and college kids. Saturday brings a more outrageous crowd dancing to an electronic beat.

El Parador (✉ *2744 E. Broadway, Central* ☎ *520/881–2744* ⊕ *elparadortucson.com*) has a live salsa band Friday and Saturday night, with dance lessons Friday at 10 PM.

★ The **Nimbus Brewing Company** (✉ *3850 E. 44th St., Southeast* ☎ *520/745–9175* ⊕ *www.nimbusbeer.com*) is the place for acoustic blues, folk, and bluegrass, not to mention good, cheap food and microbrew beer.

Plush (✉ *340 E. 6th St., at 4th Ave., University* ☎ *520/798–1298* ⊕ *plushtucson.com*) hosts alternative-rock bands like Camp Courageous and Greyhound Soul, as well as local performers with a loyal following. You can go totally retro at the **Shelter** (✉ *4155 E. Grant Rd., Central* ☎ *520/326–1345*), a former bomb shelter decked out in plastic 1960s kitsch, lava lamps, and JFK memorabilia, which plays Elvis videos and music by the likes of Burt Bacharach and Martin Denny.

CASINOS

After a long struggle with the state of Arizona, two Native American tribes operate casinos on their Tucson-area reservations west of the airport. They are quite unlike their distant and much grander cousins in Las Vegas and Atlantic City. Don't expect much glamour, ersatz or otherwise: these casinos are more like glorified video arcades, though you can lose money much faster. You'll be greeted by a wall of cigarette smoke (the reservation is exempt from antismoking laws) and the wail of slot machines, video poker, blackjack, roulette, and craps machines. The only "live" gaming is keno, bingo, blackjack, and certain types of poker. No one under age 21 is permitted.

The Pascua Yaqui tribe's **Casino of the Sun** (✉ *7406 S. Camino de Oeste, off W. Valencia Rd. about 5 mi west of I–19, Southwest* ☎ *520/883–1700 or 800/344–9435* ⊕ *www.casinosun.com*) has slot and video-gambling machines, high-stakes bingo, and live poker. A few miles west of the Casino of the Sun is their newer, larger facility, **Casino del Sol** (✉ *5655 W. Valencia, Southwest* ☎ *520/883–1700 or 800/344–9435* ⊕ *www.casinodelsol.com*), with live poker and blackjack, bingo, slots, and an above-average Italian restaurant. An adjacent 4,600-seat outdoor amphitheater books entertainers like Bob Dylan and James Taylor. Free shuttle buses operate from points all over Tucson; call for a schedule. The Tohono O'odham tribe operates the **Desert Diamond Casinos** (✉ *7350 S. Old Nogales Hwy., 1 mi south of Valencia, just west of the airport, South* ✉ *I–19 at Pima Mine Rd., South* ☎ *520/294–7777 or 866/332–9467* ⊕ *www.desertdiamondcasino.com*), which has an indoor concert venue, one-armed bandits, and video poker in addition to live keno, bingo, and Stud High, Texas Hold'em, Omaha, and Stud Lo poker.

SAGUARO NATIONAL PARK

Saguaro National Park West: 14 mi west of Central Tucson; Saguaro National Park East: 12 mi east of Central Tucson.

Updated by
Mara Levin

Saguaro National Park's two distinct sections flank the city of Tucson. Perhaps the most familiar emblem of the Southwest, the towering saguaros are found only in the Sonoran Desert. Saguaro National Park preserves some of the densest stands of these massive cacti.

ORIENTATION

Saguaro West. Also called the Tucson Mountain District, this is the park's smaller, more-visited section. Here you'll find a Native American video orientation to saguaros at the visitor center, hiking trails, an ancient Hohokam petroglyph site at Signal Hill, and a scenic drive through the park's densest desert growth. This section is near the Arizona–Sonora Desert Museum in Tucson's Westside, and many opt for combining these sights.

Saguaro East. Also called the Rincon Mountain District, this area encompasses 57,930 acres of designated wilderness area, an easily accessible scenic loop drive, several easy and intermediate trails through the cactus forest, and opportunities for adventure and backcountry camping at six rustic campgrounds.

GETTING HERE AND AROUND

Both districts are about a half-hour drive from central Tucson. To reach Rincon Mountain District (east section) from Interstate 10, take Exit 275, then go north on Houghton Road for 10 mi. Turn right on Escalante and left onto Old Spanish Trail, and the park will be on the right side. If you're coming from town, go east on Speedway Boulevard to Houghton Road. Turn right on Houghton and left onto Old Spanish Trail.

To reach the Tucson Mountain District (west section) from Interstate 10, take Exit 242 or Exit 257, then go west on Speedway Boulevard (the name will change to Gates Pass Road), follow it to Kinney Road, and turn right.

As there is no public transportation to or within Saguaro, a car is a necessity. In the western section, Bajada Loop Drive takes you through the park and to various trailheads; Cactus Forest Drive does the same for the eastern section.

TIMING

Saguaro never gets crowded; however, most people visit in milder weather, October through April. December through February can be cool, and is prone to gentle rain showers. The spring days from March through May are bright and sunny days with wildflowers in bloom. Because of high temperatures, it's best to visit the park in the early morning or late afternoon from June through September. The intense summer heat puts off most hikers, at least at lower elevations, but lodging prices are much cheaper—rates at top resorts in Tucson drop by as much as 70%. Cooler temperatures return in October and November, providing perfect weather for hiking and camping throughout the park.

ESSENTIALS

Accessibility In the western section the Red Hills Visitor Center and two nearby nature trails are wheelchair accessible. The eastern district's visitor center is accessible, as is the paved Desert Ecology Trail.

Admission Fees Admission to Saguaro is $10 per vehicle and $5 for individuals on foot or bicycle; it is good for seven days from purchase at both park districts. Annual passes cost $25.

Admission Hours The park opens at 7 AM and closes at sunset. It is in the mountain time zone.

Permits Obtain a required backcountry permit for $6 nightly per campsite from the Saguaro East Visitor Center up to two months in advance.

Visitor Information Saguaro National Park (⊠ *3693 S. Old Spanish Trail, Tucson* ☎ *520/733–5158 Saguaro West, 520/733–5153 Saguaro East* ⊕ *nps. gov/sagu*).

EXPLORING

Saguaro National Park is filled with its namesake cacti standing sentinel in the desert. Known for their height (often 50 feet) and arms reaching out in weird configurations, these slow-growing giants can take 15 years to grow a foot high and up to 75 years to grow their first arm. The cacti can live up to 200 years and weigh up to 2 tons. In late spring (usually May), the succulent's top is covered with tiny white blooms—the Arizona state flower. The cacti are protected by state and federal laws, so don't disturb them.

SCENIC DRIVES

Unless you're ready to lace up your hiking boots for a long desert hike, the best way to see Saguaro National Park is from the comfort of your car.

Bajada Loop Drive. This 6-mi drive winds through thick stands of saguaros and past two picnic areas and trailheads to a few short hikes, including one to a rock-art site. Although the road is unpaved and moderately bumpy, it's a worthwhile trade-off for access to some of the park's densest desert growth. It's one way between Hugh Norris Trail and Golden Gate Road, so if you want to make the complete circuit, travel counterclockwise. The road is susceptible to flash floods during the monsoon season (July and August), so check road conditions at the visitor center before proceeding. ⊠ *Saguaro West.*

★ **Cactus Forest Drive.** This paved 8-mi drive provides a great overview of all Saguaro East has to offer. The one-way road, which circles clockwise, has several turnouts with roadside displays that make it easy to pull over and admire the scenery; you can also stop at two picnic areas and three easy nature trails. This road is open from 7 AM to sunset daily. ⊠ *Saguaro East.*

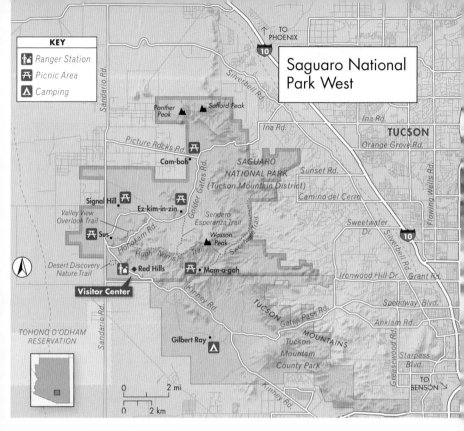

KEY

- 👥 *Ranger Station*
- 🏕 *Picnic Area*
- ⛺ *Camping*

TO
PHOENIX

10

Silverbell Rd.

Saguaro National Park West

Panther Peak

Safford Peak

Ina Rd.

Picture Rocks Rd.

Cam-boh

SAGUARO NATIONAL PARK
(Tucson Mountain District)

Sunset Rd.

Ina Rd.

TUCSON

Orange Grove Rd.

Golden Gates Rd.

Signal Hill

Ez-kim-in-zin

Valley View Overlook Trail

Sus.

Sendero Esperanza Trail

Wasson Peak

Camino del Cerro

Sweetwater Dr.

Silverbell Rd.

10

Desert Discovery Nature Trail

Red Hills

Mam-a-gah

Hugh Norris Trail

Hohokam Rd.

Sweetwater Trail

Ironwood Hill Dr.

Grant Rd.

Visitor Center

Speedway Blvd.

TOHONO O'ODHAM RESERVATION

Sandario Rd.

Kinney Rd.

Gilbert Ray

Gates Pass Rd.

Anklam Rd.

TUCSON MOUNTAINS

Tucson Mountain County Park

Greasewood Rd.

Starpass Blvd.

TO BENSON

Kinney Rd.

0 —— 2 mi

0 —— 2 km

HISTORIC SITE

Manning Camp. The summer home of Levi Manning, onetime Tucson mayor, was a popular gathering spot for the city's elite in the early 1900s. The cabin can be reached via one of several challenging high-country trails: Douglas Spring Trail to Cow Head Saddle Trail (12 mi), Turkey Creek Trail (7.5 mi), and Tanque Verde Ridge Trail (15.4 mi). The cabin itself is not open for viewing. ⊠ *Douglas Spring Trail (6 mi) to Cow Head Saddle Trail (6 mi), Saguaro East.*

SCENIC STOP

☺ **Signal Hill**. The most impressive petroglyphs, and the only ones with explanatory signs, are on the Bajada Loop Drive in Saguaro West. An easy five-minute stroll from the signposted parking area takes you to one of the largest concentrations of rock carvings in the Southwest. You'll have a close-up view of the designs left by the Hohokam people between AD 900 and 1200, including large spirals some believe are astronomical markers. ⊠ *4.5 mi north of visitor center on Bajada Loop Dr., Saguaro West.*

VISITOR CENTERS

Red Hills Visitor Center. Take in gorgeous views of nearby mountains and the surrounding desert from the center's large windows and shaded outdoor terrace. A spacious gallery is filled with educational exhibits,

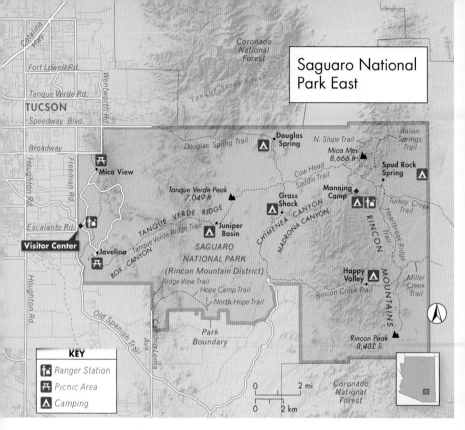

Saguaro National Park East

KEY

👤	Ranger Station
🏕	Picnic Area
▲	Camping

and a lifelike display simulates the flora and fauna of the region. A 15-minute slide show, "Voices of a Desert," provides a poetic, Native American perspective of the saguaro. Park rangers and volunteers provide maps and suggest hikes to suit your interests. A nice gift shop and bookstore add to the experience. ✉ *2700 N. Kinney Rd., Saguaro West* ☎ *520/733–5158* ⊙ *Daily 9–5.*

Saguaro East Visitor Center. Stop here to pick up free maps and printed materials on various aspects of the park, including maps of hiking trails and backcountry camping permits (Red Hills Visitor Center, in Saguaro West, does not offer permits). Exhibits at the center are comprehensive, and a relief map of the park lays out the complexities of this protected landscape. A 15-minute "Home in the Desert" slide-show program gives the history of the region, and there is a short self-guided nature hike along the Cactus Garden Trail. A small, select variety of books and other gift items are sold here, too. ✉ *3693 S. Old Spanish Trail, Saguaro East* ☎ *520/733–5153* ⊙ *Daily 9–5.*

SAGUARO IN ONE DAY

Before setting off, choose which section of the park to visit and pack a lunch. Also bring plenty of water—you are likely to get dehydrated in the dry climate, and you can't depend on finding water in the park.

In the western section, start out by watching the 15-minute slide show at the **Red Hills Visitor Center,** then stroll along the 0.5-mi-long **Desert Discovery Trail.**

In the car, head north along Kinney Road, then turn right onto the graded dirt **Bajada Loop Drive.** Before long you'll soon see a turnoff for the **Hugh Norris Trail** on your right. Hike up, and after about 45 minutes you'll reach a perfect spot for a picnic. Hike back down and drive along the Bajada Loop Drive until you reach the turnoff for **Signal Hill.** From here it's a short walk to the **Hohokam petroglyphs.**

Alternatively, in the eastern section, pick up a free map of the hiking trails at the **Saguaro East Visitor Center.** Drive south along the paved **Cactus Forest Drive** to the Javelina picnic area, where you'll see signs for the **Freeman Homestead Trail,** an easy 1-mi loop that winds through a stand of mesquite as interpretive signs describe early inhabitants in the Tucson basin. If you're up for more difficult hiking, you might want to tackle part of the **Tanque Verde Ridge Trail,** which affords excellent views of saguaro-studded hillsides.

Along the northern loop of Cactus Forest Drive is **Cactus Forest Trail,** which branches off into several fairly level paths. You can easily spend the rest of the afternoon strolling among the saguaro.

SPORTS AND THE OUTDOORS

BICYCLING

Bajada Loop Drive. This 6-mi dirt road, starting north of the Red Hills Visitor Center in Saguaro West, has "washboards" worn into the ground by seasonal drainage, which make biking a challenge. You'll share the bumpy route with cars, but most of it is one way, and the views of saguaros set against the mountains are stunning. ⊠ *Trailhead: off Kinney Rd., 1.5-mi from the Red Hills Visitor Center, Saguaro West.*

Cactus Forest Drive. Expansive vistas of saguaro-covered hills in Saguaro East highlight this paved 8-mi loop road. Go slowly during the first few hundred yards, because of an unexpectedly sharp curve. Beware of snakes and javelinas traversing the roads. ⊠ *Trailhead: Loop road begins immediately past visitor center parking area, Saguaro East.*

Cactus Forest Trail. Accessed from Cactus Forest Drive, the 2.5-mi trail near Saguaro East Visitor Center is a single sand track with varied terrain. It's good for both beginning and experienced mountain bikers who don't mind sharing the path with hikers and the occasional horse, to whom bikers must yield. You'll see plenty of wildlife and older, larger saguaro alongside paloverde and mesquite trees. ⊠ *Trailhead: 2 mi south of Saguaro East Visitor Center off Cactus Forest Dr.*

OUTFITTERS

Southwest Trekking (✉ *Box 57714, Tucson* ☎ *520/296–9661* ⊕ *www. swtrekking.com*) arranges top-notch guided mountain biking, hiking, and camping outings.

BIRD-WATCHING

To check out the more than 200 species of birds living in or migrating through the park, begin by focusing your binoculars on the limbs of the saguaros, where many birds make their home. In general, early morning and early evening are the best times for sightings. In winter and spring, volunteer-led birding hikes begin at the visitor centers.

The finest areas to flock to in Saguaro East (the Rincon Mountain District) are the Desert Ecology Trail, where you may find rufous-winged sparrows, verdins, and Cooper's hawks along the washes, and the Javelina picnic area, where you will most likely spot canyon wrens and black-chinned sparrows. At Saguaro West (the Tucson Mountain District), sit down on one of the visitor center benches and look for ash-throated flycatchers, Say's phoebes, curve-billed thrashers, and Gila woodpeckers. During the cooler months, keep a lookout for the wintering neotropical migrants such as hummingbirds, swallows, orioles, and warblers.

HIKING

The park has more than 100 mi of trails. The shorter hikes, such as the Desert Discovery and Desert Ecology trails, are perfect for those looking to learn about the desert ecosystem without expending too much energy.

■**TIP**→ Rattlesnakes are commonly seen on trails; so are coyotes, javelinas, roadrunners, Gambel's quail, and desert spiny lizards. Hikers should keep their distance from all wildlife.

EASY

Cactus Forest Trail. This 2.5-mi one-way loop drive in the east district is open to pedestrians, bicyclists, and equestrians. It is an easy walk along a dirt path that passes historic lime kilns and a wide variety of Sonoran Desert vegetation. While walking this trail, keep in mind that it is the only off-road trail for bicyclists. ✉ *Trailhead: 2 mi south of Saguaro East Visitor Center, off Cactus Forest Dr., Saguaro East.*

Cactus Garden Trail. This 100-yard paved trail in front of the Red Hills Visitor Center is wheelchair accessible, and has resting benches and interpretive signs about common desert plants. ✉ *Trailhead: across from Red Hills Visitor Center, Saguaro West.*

Desert Discovery Trail. Learn about plants and animals native to the region on this paved path in Saguaro West. The 0.5-mi loop is wheelchair accessible, and has resting benches and ramadas (wooden shelters that supply shade for your table). ✉ *Trailhead: 1 mi north of Red Hills Visitor Center, Saguaro West.*

Desert Ecology Trail. Exhibits on this 0.25-mi loop near the Mica View picnic area explain how local plants and animals subsist on limited water. ✉ *Trailhead: 2 mi north of Saguaro East Visitor Center.*

CLOSE UP

Saguaro National Park Flora and Fauna

The saguaro may be the centerpiece of Saguaro National Park, but more than 1,200 plant species, including 50 types of cactus, thrive in the park. Among the most common cacti here are the prickly pear, barrel cactus, and teddy bear cholla—so named because it appears cuddly, but rangers advise packing a comb to pull its barbed hooks from unwary fingers.

For many of the desert fauna, the saguaro functions as a high-rise hotel. Each spring the Gila woodpecker and gilded flicker create holes in the cactus and then nest there. When they give up their temporary digs, elf owls, cactus wrens, sparrow hawks, and other avians move in, as do dangerous Africanized honeybees.

You may not encounter any of the park's six species of rattlesnake or the Gila monster, a venomous lizard, but avoid sticking your hands or feet under rocks or into crevices. Look where you are walking; if you do get bitten, get to a clinic or hospital as soon as possible. Not all snakes pass on venom; 50% of the time the bite is "dry" (nonpoisonous).

Wildlife, from bobcats to jackrabbits, is most active in early morning and at dusk. In spring and summer, lizards and snakes are out and about but tend to keep a low profile during the midday heat.

7

Freeman Homestead Trail. Learn a bit about the history of homesteading in the region on this 1-mi loop. Look for owls living in the cliffs above as you make your way through the lowland vegetation. ⊠ *Trailhead: Javelina picnic area, 2 mi south of Saguaro East Visitor Center.*

Signal Hill Trail. This 0.25-mi trail in Saguaro West is an easy, rewarding ascent to ancient petroglyphs carved a millennium ago by the Hohokam people. ⊠ *Trailhead: 4.5 mi north of Red Hills Visitor Center on Bajada Loop Dr., Saguaro West.*

MODERATE

Douglas Spring Trail. This challenging 6-mi trail leads almost due east into the Rincon Mountains. After a half mile through a dense concentration of saguaros you reach the open desert. About 3 mi in is Bridal Wreath Falls, worth a slight detour in spring when melting snow creates a larger cascade. Blackened tree trunks at the Douglas Spring Campground are one of the few traces of a huge fire that swept through the area in 1989. ⊠ *Trailhead: eastern end of Speedway Blvd., Saguaro East.*

Fodor'sChoice ★ **Hope Camp Trail.** Well worth the 5.6-mi round-trip trek, this Rincon Valley Area route rewards hikers with gorgeous views of the Tanque Verde Ridge and Rincon Peak. ⊠ *Trailhead: from Camino Loma Alta trailhead to Hope Camp, Saguaro East.*

Sendero Esperanza Trail. You'll follow a sandy mine road for the first section of this 6-mi trail in Saguaro West, then ascend via a series of switchbacks to the top of a ridge where you'll cross the Hugh Norris Trail. Descending on the other side, you'll meet up with the King Canyon Trail. The Esperanza ("Hope") Trail is often rocky and sometimes steep, but rewards include ruins of the Gould Mine, dating back to

1907. ⊠ *Trailhead: 1.5 mi east of the intersection of Bajada Loop Dr. and Golden Gate Rd., Saguaro West.*

Sweetwater Trail. In Saguaro West, this one-way trail is the only footpath with access to Wasson Peak from the eastern side of the Tucson Mountains. After climbing 3.4 mi it ends at King Canyon Trail. Long and meandering, this little-used trail allows more privacy to enjoy the natural surroundings than some of the more frequently used trails. ⊠ *Trailhead: western end of El Camino del Cerro Rd., Saguaro West.*

Valley View Overlook Trail. On clear days you can spot the distinctive slope of Picacho Peak from this 1.5-mi trail in Saguaro West. Even on an overcast day you'll be treated to splendid vistas of Avra Valley. ⊠ *Trailhead: 3 mi north of Red Hills Visitor Center on Bajada Loop Dr., Saguaro West.*

DIFFICULT

Fodor's Choice **Hugh Norris Trail.** This 10-mi trail through the Tucson Mountains is
★ one of the most impressive in the Southwest. It's full of switchbacks, and some sections are moderately steep, but at the top of 4,687-foot Wasson Peak you'll enjoy views of the saguaro forest spread across the *bajada* (the gently rolling hills at the base of taller mountains). ⊠ *Trailhead: 2.5 mi north of Red Hills Visitor Center on Bajada Loop Dr., Saguaro West.*

King Canyon Trail. This 3.5 mi trail is the shortest, but steepest, route to the top of Wasson Peak in Saguaro West. It meets the Hugh Norris Trail less than half a mile from the summit. The trail, which begins across from the Arizona–Sonora Desert Museum, is named after the Copper King Mine. It leads past many scars from the search for mineral wealth. Look for petroglyphs in this area. ⊠ *Trailhead: 2 mi south of Red Hills Visitor Center, Saguaro West.*

★ **Tanque Verde Ridge Trail.** Be rewarded with spectacular scenery on this 15.4-mi trail through desert scrub, oak, alligator juniper, and piñon pine at the 6,000-foot peak, where views of the surrounding mountain ranges from both sides of the ridge delight. ⊠ *Trailhead: Javelina picnic area, 2 mi south of Saguaro East Visitor Center.*

HORSEBACK RIDING

More than 100 mi of trails in the park are open to use by livestock (mules, donkeys, and horses); however, animals are prohibited from off-trail travel and require a special permit, which can be obtained in person at one of the visitor centers or by mail. No grazing allowed in the park.

OUTFITTERS AND EXPEDITIONS

Cocoraque Ranch (⊠ 6255 N. Diamond Hills La., Tucson ☎ 520/682–8594) is a working cattle ranch; their wranglers lead riders into Saguaro West.

Pantano Riding Stables (⊠ 4450 South Houghton Rd., Tucson ☎ 520/298–8980) is a reliable operator running one-hour, two-hour and all-day rides near Saguaro East.

EDUCATIONAL OFFERINGS

Junior Ranger Program. Available several times in June, for two to three days at a time, a **camp** for kids 5–12 includes daily hikes and workshops on pottery and petroglyphs. In the **Junior Ranger Discovery program** young visitors can pick up an activity pack any time of the year and complete it within an hour or two. ⊠ *Saguaro East Visitor Center* ☎ *520/733–5153* ⊠ *Red Hills Visitor Center* ☎ *520/733–5158.*

Orientation Programs. Daily programs introduce visitors to the desert. You might find slide shows on bats, birds, or desert blooms, naturalist-led hikes (including moonlight hikes), and, in summer only, films. Check online or call for the current week's activities. ⊠ *Saguaro East Visitor Center* ☎ *520/733–5153* ⊠ *Red Hills Visitor Center* ☎ *520/733–5158* 🎫 *Free* ☉ *Daily.*

Ranger Talks. Hear about wildlife, geology, and archaeology. ⊠ *Saguaro East Visitor Center* ☎ *520/733–5153* ⊠ *Red Hills Visitor Center* ☎ *520/733–5158* 🎫 *Free* ☉ *Nov.–mid-Apr.*

WHERE TO EAT

At Saguaro you won't find more than a Southwest sampling of jams, hot sauces, and candy bars at the two visitor centers' gift shops. However, five picnic areas in the west district, and two in the east, have scenery and shade. Restaurants in the city of Tucson, sandwiched neatly between the two park districts, include some of the best Mexican and Southwestern cuisine in the country.

Each picnic area has a wheelchair-accessible pit toilet.

WHERE TO STAY

While there are no hotels within the park, its immediate proximity to Tucson makes finding a place to stay easy. A couple of B&Bs are just a short drive from the park. Some ranches and smaller accommodations close during the hottest months of summer, but many inexpensive B&Bs and hotels are open year-round.

There's no drive-up camping in the park. All six primitive campgrounds, in Saguaro East, require a hike—the shortest hikes are to Douglas Spring Campground (6 mi) and to Happy Valley (5 mi). All are open year-round. Pick up your backcountry camping permit ($6 per night) at the Saguaro East Visitor Center. Before choosing a camping destination, look over the relief map of hiking trails and the book of wilderness campground photos taken by park rangers. You can camp in the backcountry for a maximum of 14 days. Each site can accommodate up to six people. Reservations can be made via mail or in person up to two months in advance. Hikers are encouraged to set out before noon. There are several more relaxed camping opportunities, with both tent sites and RV hookups, within just a few miles of the park's west district.

SHOPPING

The visitor centers in both districts sell books, gifts, film, and single-use cameras, as well as a few necessities such as sunscreen, bug repellent, and water bottles. For other items, you'll have to drive a few miles back towards town.

SIDE TRIPS NEAR TUCSON

Interstate 19 heads south from Tucson to Tubac, carrying with it history buffs, bird-watchers, hikers, art enthusiasts, duffers, and shoppers. The road roughly follows the Camino Real (King's Road), which the conquistadors and missionaries traveled from Mexico up to what was once the northernmost portion of New Spain.

THE ASARCO MINERAL DISCOVERY CENTER

15 mi south of Tucson off I–9.

GETTING HERE AND AROUND
From Interstate 19 south take Exit 80. Turn right (west) onto Pima Mine Road and the entrance will be almost immediately on your left.

EXPLORING
The **ASARCO Mineral Discovery Center** (American Smelting and Refining Co. is abbreviated) is designed to elucidate the importance of mining to everyday life. Exhibits include a walk-through model of an ore crusher, video stations that explain refining processes, and a film on extraction of minerals from the earth. The big draw, though, is the yawning open pit of the Mission Mine, some 2 mi long and 1.75 mi wide because so much earth has to be torn up to extract the 1% that is copper. It's impressive, but doesn't bolster the case the center tries to make about how environmentally conscious mining has become. Tours of the pit take about one hour; the last one starts at 3:30. In summer, tours are only on Saturday. ✉ *1421 W. Pima Mine Rd.* ☎ *520/625–0879* ⊕ *www. mineraldiscovery.com* 💲 *$8* ☉ *Tues.–Sat. 9–5.*

TITAN MISSILE MUSEUM

25 mi south of Tucson.

GETTING HERE AND AROUND
From Interstate 19, take Exit 69, Duval Mine Road, approximately 1 mi west to museum.

EXPLORING
Now a National Historic Landmark, the **Titan Missile Museum** makes for a sobering visit. During the cold war Tucson was ringed by 18 of the 54 Titan II missiles maintained in the United States. After the SALT II treaty with the Soviet Union was signed in 1979, this was the only missile-launch site left intact. Guided tours, running every half hour, last about an hour and take you down 55 steps into the command post, where a ground crew of four lived and waited. Among the sights is the 103-foot, 165-ton, two-stage liquid-fuel rocket. Now empty, it originally held

Saguaro cacti are easy to anthropomorphize because of their giant "arms."

a nuclear warhead with 214 times the explosive power of the bomb that destroyed Hiroshima. This museum is operated by the Pima Air and Space Museum and combination tickets are available. ⊠ *1580 W. Duval Mine Rd., I–19, Exit 69, Green Valley* ☎ *520/625–7736* ⊕ *www. pimaair.org* ✉ *$9.50; combination with PASM $18* ⊗ *Daily 9–5; last tour departs at 4.*

MADERA CANYON

61.5 mi southeast of Tucson.

GETTING HERE AND AROUND
From Interstate 19, take Exit 63 (Continental Road) east for about a mile, then turn right (southeast) on White House Canyon Road for 12.5 mi (it turns into Madera Canyon Road).

EXPLORING
Madera Canyon is where the Coronado National Forest meets the Santa Rita Mountains—among them Mount Wrightson, the highest peak in southern Arizona, at 9,453 feet. With approximately 200 mi of scenic trails, the recreation area is a favorite destination for hikers. Higher elevations and thick pine cover make it especially popular with Tucsonans looking to escape the summer heat. Trails vary from a steep trek up Mount Baldy to a paved, wheelchair-accessible path. Birders flock here year-round; about 400 avian species have been spotted in the area. The small, volunteer-run visitor center is open only on weekends. ⊠ *Madera Canyon Rd., Madera Canyon* ☎ *520/281–2296 Nogales Ranger District office* ⊕ *www.fs.fed.us/r3/coronado* ✉ *$5* ⊗ *Daily.*

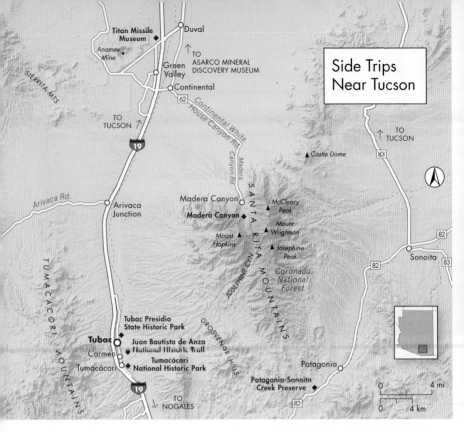

TUBAC

★ *45 mi south of Tucson at Exit 40 off I–19.*

Established in 1726, Tubac is the site of the first European settlement in Arizona. A year after the Pima Indian uprising in 1751, a military garrison was established here to protect Spanish settlers, missionaries, and peaceful Native American converts of the nearby Tumacácori Mission. It was from here that Juan Bautista de Anza led 240 colonists across the desert—the expedition resulted in the founding of San Francisco in 1776. In 1860 Tubac was the largest town in Arizona. Today, the quiet little town is a popular art colony. More than 80 shops sell such crafts as carved wooden furniture, hand-thrown pottery, delicately painted tiles, and silk-screen fabrics (many shops are closed Monday). You can also find Mexican pottery and trinkets without having to cross the border. The annual **Tubac Festival of the Arts** has been held in February for more than 30 years.

GETTING HERE AND AROUND

When you exit Interstate 19 at Tubac Road, signs will point you east into Tubac village. There is plenty of free parking.

ESSENTIALS

Vistitor Information **Tubac Chamber of Commerce** (☎ *520/398–2704* ⊕ *www.tubacaz.com*).

EXPLORING

There's an archaeological display of portions of the original 1752 fort at the **Tubac Presidio State Historic Park and Museum** in the center of town. In addition to the visitor center and the adjoining museum, which has detailed exhibits on the history of the early colony, the park includes Tubac's 1885 schoolhouse. ⊠ *1 Burruel St.* ☎ *520/398–2252* ⊕ *www.azstateparks.com* 🖾 *$3* ☉ *Thurs.–Mon. 9–5.*

WORD OF MOUTH

"Titan Missile [Museum] on Duval Mine Road in Green Valley is often highly praised for being a worthwhile stop. It is especially good if you like (or remember) history from the 60's." —CollegeMom

WHERE TO EAT AND STAY

¢ ✕ **Tubac Deli & Coffee Co.** Smack in the middle of Tubac village, this pleasant little eatery is a very convenient and friendly place to "set awhile" with the locals. Full breakfasts, 6:30–10:30 AM, include Western omelets (of course) and French toast made with homemade cinnamon raisin bread. Generous sandwiches, pizza, salads, and soups—as well as cappuccinos and homemade pastries—are served every day until 5 PM. ⊠ *6 Plaza Rd.* ☎ *520/398–3330* ⊕ *tubacdeli.com* ▭ *MC, V.*

AMERICAN

$$ 🏨 **Amado Territory Inn.** Although this quiet, friendly B&B is directly off the highway frontage road, it feels worlds away. The inn resembles a late-19th-century ranch house, but its soaring ceiling and contemporary Southwestern art make the interior distinctly modern. Western-themed rooms have a view of the gardens and the Santa Rita Mountains. Breakfast is included (try the huevos rancheros); next door, the Amado Territory Steakhouse serves burgers, steaks, and sandwiches. **Pros:** good breakfast; pleasant garden areas include two labyrinths for strolling. **Cons:** rooms are a bit spartan; only the suites have TVs; not walking distance to Tubac village. ⊠ *3001 E. Frontage Rd., off Exit 48 of I–19* ⊕ *Box 81, Amado 85645* ☎ *520/398–8684 or 888/398–8684* ⊕ *www.amado-territory-inn.com* 🛏 *9 rooms, 6 suites* ♿ *In-room: a/c, no phone, no TV (some), Wi-Fi. In-hotel: restaurant, some pets allowed (paid), no kids under 12* ▭ *MC, V* ¶ *BP.*

$–$$ 🏨 **Tubac Country Inn.** Down the lane from the shops and eateries of Tubac village is this charming two-story inn. Tastefully decorated in contemporary Southwest style, all rooms and suites have kitchenettes, and the common outdoor space is a tranquil desert flower garden with willow chairs and a Mexican fireplace. Each morning a breakfast basket of muffins, cheeses, fruits, and juice is brought to your door. **Pros:** rooms are spacious, comfortably furnished, and have separate entrances; in Tubac village. **Cons:** no B&B camaraderie here; it feels more like you're staying in someone's guest cottage. ⊠ *13 Burruel St.* ☎ *520/398–3178* ⊕ *www.tubaccountryinn.com* 🛏 *3 rooms, 2 suites* ♿ *In-room: a/c, no phone, kitchen, refrigerator, Wi-Fi* ▭ *AE, D, MC, V* ¶ *BP.*

EN ROUTE

You can tread the same road as the conquistadors: the first 4.5 mi of the **Juan Bautista de Anza National Historic Trail** (⊕ *www.nps.gov/juba*) from Tumacácori to Tubac were dedicated in 1992. You'll have to cross the Santa Cruz River—which is usually low— three times to complete the hike, and the path is rather sandy, but it's a pleasant journey along the tree-shaded banks of the river.

TUMACÁCORI NATIONAL HISTORIC PARK

3 mi south of Tubac.

GETTING HERE AND AROUND

Take Exit 29 off Interstate 19 and follow signs 0.5 mi to park (from Tucson, go under the highway to East Frontage Road and turn left).

EXPLORING

The site where **Tumacácori National Historic Park** now stands was visited by missionary Father Eusebio Francisco Kino in 1691, but the Jesuits didn't build a church here until 1751. You can still see some remnants of this simple structure, but the main attraction is the mission of San José de Tumacácori, built by the Franciscans around 1799–1803. A combination of circumstances—Apache attacks, a bad winter, and Mexico's withdrawal of funds and priests—caused the remaining inhabitants to flee in 1848. Persistent rumors of wealth left behind by both the Franciscans and the Jesuits led treasure seekers to pillage the site; it still bears those scars. The site was finally protected in 1908, when it became a national monument.

Information about the mission and the Anza trail is available at the visitor center, and guided tours are available daily October through May. A small museum displays some of the mission's artifacts, and sometimes fresh tortillas are made on a wood-fire stove in the courtyard. In addition to a Christmas Eve celebration, costumed historical high masses are held at Tumacácori in spring and fall. An annual fiesta the first weekend of December has arts and crafts and food booths. ⊠ *1891 E. Frontage Rd., I–19, Exit 29, Tumacácori* ☎ *520/398–2341* ⊕ *www.nps. gov/tuma* ☒ *$3* ☻ *Daily 9–5.*

EN ROUTE Across the street from the Tumacácori National Historic Park, the **Santa Cruz Spice Factory** (⊠ *1868 E. Frontage Rd., Tumacácori* ☎ *520/398–2591*) packs and sells various spices if you'd like to take a taste of the Southwest home. A little museum, tasting area, and store are open Monday through Saturday.

WHERE TO STAY

$$ ⚏ **Esplendor Resort.** This isolated hotel and conference center has a historic, rather than hokey, Western feel, with a working blacksmith on-site and an elongated bar reminiscent of a Tombstone saloon. Some rooms continue the theme with cowhide headboards, tepee bed canopies, or whimsical bordello furnishings. Most guests come for excellent golf, splendid views, and seclusion. **Pros:** a sense of leaving the world behind. **Cons:** mediocre restaurant; golf and tennis are across the highway (shuttle bus provided). ⊠ *1069 Camino Caralampi, off I–19 at Rio Rico Rd., Rio Rico* ☎ *520/281–1901 or 800/288–4746* ⊕ *www. esplendor-resort.com* ⚌ *166 rooms, 14 suites* ☖ *In-room: a/c, refrigerator, Wi-Fi. In-hotel: restaurant, bar, golf course, tennis courts, pool, gym, laundry service, some pets allowed (paid)* ☰ *AE, D, MC, V.*

Southern Arizona

WORD OF MOUTH

"There are some nice wineries in the area of Sonoita and Patagonia and we stopped at a couple of them. The steers came to greet
our car as we drove up one of the winery's dirt road . . . Driving
through these vast open areas which aren't desert but grasslands
was just gorgeous. So much better than staying on the Interstate."
—paula1470

WELCOME TO SOUTHERN ARIZONA

TOP REASONS TO GO

★ **Tour Kartchner Caverns:** The underground world of a living "wet" cave system is a rare and wonderful sensory experience. You'll see a multicolor limestone kingdom and probably feel "cave kiss" droplets grace your head; just *don't touch anything.*

★ **Hike in the Chiricahuas:** Stunning "upside-down" rock formations, flourishing wildlife, and relatively easy trails make for great hiking in this unspoiled region. The 3.4-mi Echo Canyon Loop Trail is a winner.

★ **Explore Bisbee:** Board the Queen Mine Train and venture into the life of a copper miner at the turn of the last century. Afterward, check out the narrow, hilly town's Victorian houses and thriving shops.

★ **Stargaze at Kitt Peak:** Clear skies and dry air provide ideal conditions for stargazing; the evening observation program, with top-notch telescopes and enthusiastic guides, is an excellent introduction to astronomy.

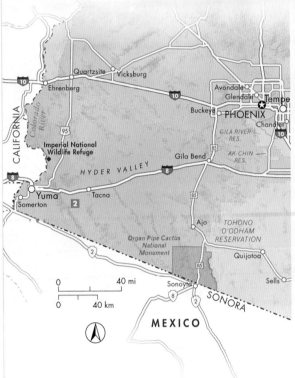

The Nature Conservancy's Patagonia-Sonoita Creek Preserve

1 Southeast Arizona. Old West history, colorful limestone caverns, bizarre hoodoo formations, sweeping "Sky Islands," Arizona's wine country, rolling grasslands, a world-renowned birding paradise, and rustic ranch retreats create a perfect mix of historical adventure and outdoor recreation.

GETTING ORIENTED

Southern Arizona ranges from the searing deserts surrounding Organ Pipe Cactus National Monument and the town of Yuma in the southwest to the soaring "Sky Islands"—steep hills that rise from the desert floor into the clouds—and rolling grasslands in the southeast. Towns are few and far between in the southwestern corner of the state, where the desert and dry climate rule. In stark contrast, the varied terrain in the southeastern region ranges from pine-forested mountains and cool canyons to desert grasslands and winding river valleys. A complex network of highways links the many communities situated in this part of the state, where the next town or attraction is just over the hill, making the decision on which way you want to go next the hardest part of traveling.

2 **Southwest Arizona.** The historical Yuma Territorial Prison, national wildlife refuges, Colorado River recreation, and Organ Pipe Cactus National Monument keep visitors busy in this remote desert region.

Kitt Peak Telescope

SOUTHERN ARIZONA PLANNER

What to Do and Where to Do It

Recreation in Cochise County centers on historic and natural treasures. History buffs can walk the streets of the Old West in Tombstone and revisit the infamous shootout at the O.K. Corral. For a look at the mineral wealth that built Bisbee, take a tour of the Copper Queen Mine and visit the historic sights in this two-canyon town. Natural beauty and some of the best birding in the world draw flocks of visitors to southeastern Arizona's "Sky Islands," Coronado National Forest, and Chiricahua National Monument. Military might takes center stage at the remote ruins found at the Fort Bowie National Historic Site and at the active outpost of Fort Huachuca. Wine-tasting in the Sonoita-Elgin area is a popular day's outing. Check out remote desert vistas in Organ Pipe Cactus National Monument; if you're out this way, you can also loop north through the old mining town of Ajo and to visit the revitalized downtown district and historic highlights in Yuma.

Getting Here and Around

Tucson is the major starting point for exploring both the southwest region and the southeast corner of the state. Yuma's remote location on the California–Arizona border makes it a destination in itself, and while it can be reached on a lengthy three-hour drive from Tucson or Phoenix, it is most easily accessed through Yuma International Airport.

The best way to explore southeastern Arizona is on a leisurely road trip. The intricate network of highways in the San Pedro Valley provides looping access to the many scenic vistas and Old West communities, which makes the drive an integral part of the adventure. In stark contrast, a drive through the southwestern portion of the state is filled with long stretches of desert broken infrequently with tiny towns and intermittent gas stations. If you're heading west, pack a lunch, a few games, and plenty of music for entertainment along the way.

A car is essential in southern Arizona. The best plan is to fly into Tucson, which is the hub of the area, or Phoenix, which has the most flights. You can rent a car from several national companies at Yuma International Airport.

Amtrak trains run three times a week from Tucson to Benson and Yuma.

Making the Most of Your Time

The diverse geography of the region and the driving distances between sights require that you strategize when planning your trip. With Tucson as a starting point, the rolling hills and grasslands of Sonoita and Patagonia are little more than an hour away, as are the underground marvels in Kartchner Caverns (to the southeast) and the starry skies above Kitt Peak Observatory (to the southwest). You can explore the Old West of Tombstone, Bisbee, and the surrounding ghost towns in one day, or more leisurely in two. If you're heading to the cactus-studded hillsides at Organ Pipe Cactus National Monument, leave yourself at least a full day to explore the monument and the nearby town of Ajo. A trek through the stunning Chiricahua rock formations calls for an overnight stay, since the area is a 2½-hour drive southeast of Tucson.

When to Go

As you might expect, the desert areas are popular in winter, and the cooler mountain areas are more heavily visited in summer. If you're seeking outdoor adventure, spring and fall are the best times to visit this part of the state. The region is in full bloom by late March and early April, and spring and fall are the peaks of birding season.

Local Food and Lodging

There are plenty of chain hotels found throughout the southern region of Arizona, especially along the interstate highways, but why settle for boring basics in this beautiful and historic corner of the state? For the best experiences, seek out an old-fashioned room in a historic hotel, a rustic casita at a working cattle ranch, or a spacious suite in a homey bed-and-breakfast. There are a few scattered dude ranches in the sweeping grasslands to the south. It's usually not hard to find a room any time of the year, but keep in mind that prices tend to go up in high season (winter and spring) and down in low season (summer through early fall).

In southern Arizona cowboy fare is more common than haute cuisine. There are exceptions, though, especially in the wine-growing area of Sonoita and in the trendy town of Bisbee, both popular for weekend outings from Tucson. And, as one would expect, Mexican food dominates menus.

WHAT IT COSTS

	¢	$	$$	$$$	$$$$
RESTAURANTS	under $8	$8–$12	$13–$20	$21–$30	over $30
HOTELS	under $70	$70–$120	$121–$175	$176–$250	over $250

Restaurant prices are per person for a main course at dinner. Hotel prices are for a standard double in high season, excluding taxes and service charges.

Festivals and Events

Jan.Wings Over Willcox. This birding extravaganza is highlighted by the morning flights of thousands of wintering sandhill cranes lifting off from the Willcox Playa. ☎ *520/384–2272* ⊕ *www.wingsoverwillcox.com.*

Feb.Cochise Cowboy Poetry and Music Gathering. In Sierra Vista, this festival showcases Western culture, history, and folklore. ☎ *520/417–6960* ⊕ *www.cowboypoets.com.*

Oct.The Rex Allen Days. A rodeo and Western music and dance fill the first weekend in October, in Willcox. ☎ *520/384–2272* ⊕ *www.rexallendays.com.*

Helldorado Days. The third weekend of October, history comes alive in Tombstone with gunfights in the streets, a parade, and an 1880s fashion show. ☎ *888/457–3929* ⊕ *www.tombstone.org.*

8

EXPERIENCE THE WILD WEST

Arizona's identity was forged like horseshoes by cattle, copper, and the men who chased both. The "Old West" stretches as long as a cowboy's yarn and as broad as a 19th-century cattle drive. Follow the echoes of gunslingers like Wyatt Earp, or drink in majestic landscapes popularized on the silver screen.

Above: You can still ride a stagecoach in Tombstone. Top right: Western watchers will find Canyon de Chelly familiar. Lower right: Tours go deep into the Cooper Queen Mine.

In 1862, when Arizona became a U.S. territory, it began to fill immediately with fortune-seekers. In towns like Bisbee (copper) and Tombstone (silver), the discovery of a single ore begot legendary boom-and-bust mining cycles. Precious metal brought miners, then speculators, real wealth, and services including saloons and brothels. Just as quickly, the ore ran out, and envy, shoot-outs, and desolation followed. With the arrival of railroads in 1880, Arizona's stock grew from a few thousand to a million plus in less than 20 years—but ranchers were also short-sighted and the "boom" subsided just as fast. Still, cowboy life is one of the most enduring icons of Americana.

TOURISM BONANZA

Movies like Gunfight at the O.K. Corral started a renaissance in many ghost towns, and the modern "boom" is tourism. Main Street's drinking and gambling establishments have given way to B&B's (try **School House Inn Bed & Breakfast**), historic bars (visit **Whiskey Row** in Prescott), and boutiques (**55 Main Gallery** in Bisbee).

SOUTHERN ARIZONA WILD WEST ROAD TRIP

Start your Old West explorations in Tucson with a half day at the **Old Tucson Studios** and **Mission San Xavier del Bac.** Kids will love the simulated gunfights, rides, and stunt shows at the studios where *Gunsmoke* and *Bonanza* were filmed. Mom and Dad can channel the West in a more contemplative way inside the 18th-century mission where the bad guys no doubt went for sanctuary or forgiveness.

Southeast Arizona may be the most dense and interesting corner in which to explore various aspects of the Old West. The Apache tribe, led by Cochise and later Geronimo, held out for decades against U.S. troops and settlers amid the 12 ranges of the Coronado National Forest, before surrendering in 1886. Imagine warrior-tribes in the canyons and rock formations of the **Chiricahua National Monument**, where spotting jaguar, rare deer, and flora are treasures in their own right.

Also in the southeast, Tombstone and Bisbee were centers of mining (silver and copper, respectively) and the wealth, larger-than-life characters, and movie depictions that came with them. **Tombstone** is more touristy, but the re-creation of the Gunfight at the O.K. Corral is so steeped in Old West history (Wyatt Earp and Doc Holliday walked away but three of the notorious Clanton gang weren't so lucky) that it's worth a visit. More-authentic experiences await in **Bisbee**. Don a light jacket when you take the 75-minute underground tour of the **Copper Queen Mine**, or if you're prone to claustrophobia, stick to the **Bisbee Mining and Historical Museum**, which served as the company's offices.

ELSEWHERE IN ARIZONA

In north-central Arizona, **Jerome** and **Prescott** are two other boom-towns worth a half-day's exploration. Jerome was once known as the Billion Dollar Copper Camp, but its 15,000-person population dwindled to 50 before rebounding to today's 500 or so. Stop for a hearty burger in the **Haunted Hamburger/Jerome Palace**, where the resident ghost purportedly hangs out upstairs. Thirty miles away, Prescott is home to the world's oldest rodeo during July's **Frontier Days** and has regular live music at the historic bars on **Whiskey Row.**

Thanks to Hollywood, the wide-open vistas of the West are some of the most recurring images of a bygone era. Fortunately for you, **Monument Valley** and **Canyon de Chelly** in northeast Arizona remain virtually unchanged from the way that cowboys and Native Americans experienced them in the 19th century.

8

RODEO LESSON

In the late 19th century, cowboys vied for recognition as best roper and rider. Skills contests have evolved into weeklong county fairs in some communities, with cowboy poetry, beauty queens, and country music accompanying the 1-ton bulls, the busting broncs, and the popular and lifesaving clowns.

The five standard events today are calf roping, bull riding, steer wrestling, saddle bronc-riding, and bareback bronc-riding. ("Bronc" is short for bronco, an unbroken range horse with a tendency to buck, or throw, a rider.) Cowboys pay entry fees, and the prize money won is usually their only compensation. The Professional Rodeo Cowboys Association (PRCA) dates to 1929 and its rules are the most commonly accepted.

Prescott has the "the World's Oldest Rodeo"—an annual affair since 1888 that concludes on July 4. Late February is the time to catch two other popular events: Tucson's rodeo has traditionally offered the most prize money in the state, more than $300,000 in recent years. Scottsdale's "Parada del Sol" includes the "World's Longest Horse Drawn Parade."

GIDDY'UP

Horseback Riding: The most iconic pictures of the American West include men on horseback. Geronimo, John Wayne, and Wyatt Earp all rode in these parts, so why not spend a day in their stirrups. You can spend as little as $15/hour at **Totsonii Ranch** in Canyon de Chelly or thousands for fully outfitted, multi-night excursions. If saddles conjure up images of painful bowlegs, **Apache Stables** near the Grand Canyon will take you on a horse-drawn wagon ride, where you'll end up at a campfire where you can grill your own dinner.

Dude Ranches: More than a dozen dude ranches (city slickers call them guest ranches) have modern charms like gourmet meals, spas, and pools accompanying the unmistakable scents and sounds of working stock. Slow, fast, mountain, and all-day rides are offered, and some allow you to help groom and feed the horses.

After a day of riding or hiking, guests find a warm welcome at happy hour, dinner, and around the campfire. Lodges are outfitted with comfortable couches, crackling fireplaces, board games, and Western saloon–type bars. As long as you expect polished ponderosa, not polished silver and marble, you may find a dude ranch more comfortable than a resort hotel. In most cases, hearty meals are included, but there's no tv in your room.

Two ranches are in the Tucson area and one is just a bit farther southeast. The large and luxurious **Tanque Verde Ranch,** on the eastern edge of town, has two swimming pools (one indoor), a tennis pro, and lavish buffet meals. The 3,000-acre **White Stallion Ranch,** adjacent to Saguaro National Park West and the setting for the *High Chaparral* TV series, has challenging riding as well as massages and a fitness center. The smaller and more rustic **Circle Z Ranch,** in Patagonia, takes riders through the picturesque Patagonia-Sonoita Creek Reserve.

(Below: Nowhere is this 19th-century American West more alive than on horseback.)

Updated by
Mara Levin

Southern Arizona can do little to escape its cliché-ridden image as a landscape of cow skulls, tumbleweed, dried-up riverbeds, and mother lodes—but it doesn't need to. Abandoned mining towns and sleepy Western hamlets dot a lonely landscape of rugged rock formations, deep pine forests, dense mountain ranges, and scrubby grasslands.

South of Sierra Vista, just above the Mexican border, a stone marker commemorates the spot where the first Europeans set foot in what is now the United States. In 1540, 80 years before the pilgrims landed at Plymouth Rock, Spanish conquistador Don Francisco Vásquez de Coronado led one of Spain's largest expeditions from Mexico along the fertile San Pedro River valley, where the little towns of Benson and St. David are found today. They had come north to seek the legendary Seven Cities of Cibola, where Native American pueblos were rumored to have doors of polished turquoise and streets of solid gold. The wealth of the region, however, lay in its rich veins of copper and silver, not tapped until more than 300 years after the Spanish marched on in disappointment. Once word of this cache spread, these parts of the West quickly became much wilder: fortune seekers who rushed to the region came face-to-face with the Chiricahua Apaches, led by Cochise and Geronimo, while Indian warriors battled encroaching settlers and the U.S. Cavalry sent to protect them.

Although the search for mineral booty in southeastern Arizona is more notorious, the western side of the state wasn't untouched by the rage to plunder. Interest in going for the gold in California gave rise to the town of Yuma: the Colorado River had to be crossed to get to the West Coast, and Fort Yuma was established in part to protect the Anglo ferry business at a good fording point from Indian competitors. The Yuma Tribe lost that battle, but another group of Native Americans, the Tohono O'odham, fared better in this part of the state. Known for a long time as the Papago—or "bean eaters"—they were deeded a large portion of their ancestral homeland by the U.S. Bureau of Indian Affairs.

SOUTHEAST ARIZONA

From the rugged mountain forests to the desert grasslands of Sierra Vista, the southeast corner of Arizona is one of the state's most scenic regions. Much of this area is part of Cochise County, named in 1881 in honor of the chief of the Chiricahua Apache. Cochise waged war against troops and settlers for 11 years, and was respected by Indian and non-Indian alike for his integrity and leadership. Today Cochise County is dotted with small towns, many of them smaller—and tamer—than they were in their heyday. Cochise County encompasses 6, and part of the 7th, of the 12 mountain ranges that compose the 1.7-million-acre Coronado National Forest.

In the valleys between southeastern Arizona's jagged mountain ranges you'll discover the 19th-century charm of Bisbee—Queen of the Copper Camps. You can explore the eerie hoodoos and spires of Chiricahua National Monument and walk in the footsteps of the legendary Apaches, who valiantly stood against the U.S. Army until Geronimo's final surrender in 1886. This is also where you can travel through the grassy plains surrounding Sonoita and Elgin—the heart of Arizona's wine country.

A trip to this historically and ecologically important corner of the state will also take you to Fort Huachuca, the oldest continuously operating military installation in the Southwest; to southeastern Arizona's "Sky islands," the lush microclimates in the Huachuca and Chiricahua mountains where jaguars roam and migratory tropical birds flit through the canopy; and to historic mining and military towns, the tenacious survivors of the Old West—including Bisbee, Sierra Vista, and Tombstone.

8

TOMBSTONE

28 mi northeast of Sierra Vista via AZ 90, 24 mi south of Benson via AZ 80.

When prospector Ed Schieffelin headed out in 1877 to seek his fortune along the arid washes of San Pedro Valley, a patrolling soldier warned that all he'd find was his tombstone. Against all odds, his luck held out: he evaded bands of hostile Apaches, braved the harsh desert terrain, and eventually stumbled across a ledge of silver ore. The town of Tombstone was named after the soldier's offhand comment.

The rich silver lodes from the area's mines attracted a wide mix of fortune seekers ranging from prospectors to prostitutes and gamblers to gunmen. But as the riches continued to pour in, wealthy citizens began importing the best entertainment and culture that silver could purchase. Even though saloons and gambling halls made up two out of every three businesses on Allen Street, the town also claimed the Cochise County seat, a cultural center, and fancy French restaurants. By the early 1880s the notorious boomtown was touted as the most cultivated city west of the Mississippi.

In 1881 a shootout between the Earp brothers and the Clanton gang ended with three of the "cowboys" (Billy Clanton and Tom and Frank McLaury) dead and two of the Earps (Virgil and Morgan) and Doc

Holliday wounded. The infamous "Gunfight at the O.K. Corral" and the ensuing feud between the Earp brothers and the Clanton gang firmly cemented Tombstone's place in the Wild West—even though the actual course of events is still debated by historians.

All in all, Tombstone's heyday lasted only a decade, but the colorful characters attached to the town's history live on—immortalized on the silver screen in such famous flicks as *Gunfight at the O.K. Corral, Tombstone,* and *Wyatt Earp.* The town's tourist industry parallels Hollywood hype. As a result, the main drag on Allen Street looks and feels like a movie set, complete with gunning desperados, satin-bedecked saloon girls, and leather-clad cowboys. Today, the "Town Too Tough to Die" attracts a kitschy mix of rough-and-tumble bikers, European tourists, and pulp-fiction thrill seekers looking to walk the boardwalks of Tombstone's infamous past.

GETTING HERE AND AROUND

Start your tour of this tiny town and pick up a free map at the visitor center. As you drive into Tombstone on U.S. 80, historic Allen Street parallels the highway one block west. The visitor center sits in the middle, on the corner of Allen and 4th Street. Park along any side street or at one of the free lots on 6th Street. There's a self-guided walking tour, but the best way to get the lay of the land is to take the 15-minute **stagecoach ride** ($10, $5 for kids) around downtown. Drivers, dressed in cowboy attire, relate a condensed version of Tombstone's notorious past. You'll also pass the Tombstone Courthouse and travel down Toughnut Street, once called Rotten Row—because of the lawyers who lived there.

ESSENTIALS

Visitor Info Tombstone Visitor Center (✉ *104 S. 4th St., at Allen St.* ☎ *520/457–3929* ⊕ *www.cityoftombstone.com* ⊗ *Daily 9–4).*

EXPLORING
TOP ATTRACTIONS

Vincent Price narrates the dramatic version of the town's past in the **Historama**—a 26-minute multimedia presentation. At the adjoining **O.K. Corral,** a recorded voice-over details the town's famous shoot-out, while life-size figures of the gunfight's participants stand poised to shoot. A reenactment of the gunfight at the O.K. Corral is held daily at 2 PM. Photographer C.S. Fly, whose studio was next door to the corral, didn't record this bit of history, but Geronimo and his pursuers were among the historic figures he did capture with his camera. Many of his fascinating Old West images may be viewed at the **Fly Exhibition Gallery.** ✉ *326 Allen St. between 3rd and 4th Sts.* ☎ *520/457–3456* ⊕ *www. ok-corral.com* ✉ *Historama, O.K. Corral, and Fly Exhibition Gallery $6; gunfight reenactment $4* ⊗ *Daily 9–5; Historama shows every half hr 9:30–4:30.*

You can see the original printing presses for the town's newspaper at the **Tombstone Epitaph Museum.** The newspaper was founded in 1880 by John P. Clum, and is still publishing today. You can purchase one of the newspaper's special editions—*The Life and Times of Wyatt Earp, The Life and Times of Doc Holliday,* or *Tombstone's Pioneering Prostitutes.* ✉ *9*

S. 5th St. ☎ *520/457–2211* 📧 *Free*
🕓 *Daily 9:30–5.*

WORTH NOTING

A Tombstone institution, known
as the wildest, wickedest night spot
between Basin Street and the Bar-
bary Coast, the **Bird Cage Theater** is
a former music hall where Enrico
Caruso, Sarah Bernhardt, and Lil-

lian Russell—among others—performed. It was also the site of the longest continuous poker game recorded: the game started when the Bird
Cage opened in 1881 and lasted eight years, five months, and three
days. Some of the better-known players included Diamond Jim Brady,
Adolphus Busch (of brewery fame), and William Randolph Hearst's
father. The cards were dealt round the clock; players had to give a
20-minute notice when they were planning to vacate their seats, because
there was always a waiting list of at least 10 people ready to shell out
$1,000 (the equivalent of about $30,000 today) to get in. In all, some
$10 million changed hands.

When the mines closed in 1889, the Bird Cage was abandoned but the
building has remained in the hands of the same family, who threw nothing out. You can walk on the stage visited by some of the top traveling
performers of the time, see the faro table once touched by the legendary
gambler Doc Holliday, and pass by the hearse that carried Tombstone's
deceased to Boot Hill. The basement, which served as an upscale bor-
dello and gambling hall, still has all the original furnishings and fixtures
intact, and you can see the personal belongings left behind by the ladies
of the night when the mines closed and they, and their clients, headed
for California. ✉ *308 E. Allen St., at 6th St.* ☎ *520/457–3421* 🌐 *www.
tombstonebirdcage.com* 📧 *$10* 🕓 *Daily 8–6.*

Boot Hill Graveyard, where the victims of the O.K. Corral shoot-out are
buried, is on the northwest corner of town, facing U.S. 80. Chinese
names in one section of the "bone orchard" bear testament to the laundry and restaurant workers who came from San Francisco during the
height of Tombstone's mining fever. One of the more amusing epitaphs
at the cemetery, however, is engraved on the headstone of Wells Fargo
agent Lester Moore; it poetically lists the cause of his untimely demise:
"Here lies Lester Moore, four slugs from a .44, no less, no more." If
you're put off by the commercialism of the place—you enter through a
gift shop that sells novelty items in the shape of tombstones—remember that Tombstone itself is the result of crass acquisition. ✉ *U.S. 80*
☎ *520/457–3300* 📧 *Free* 🕓 *Daily 8–6.*

For an introduction to the town's—and the area's—past, visit the **Tombstone Courthouse State Historic Park**. This redbrick 1882 county courthouse offers exhibits on the area's mining and ranching history and
pioneer lifestyles; you can also see the restored 1904 courtroom and
district attorney's office. The two-story building housed the Cochise
County jail, a courtroom, and public offices until the county seat was
moved to Bisbee in 1929. The stately building became the cornerstone

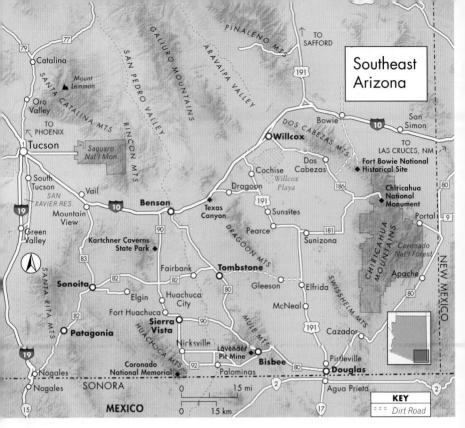

of Tombstone's historic-preservation efforts in the 1950s, and was Arizona's first operational state park. Today you can relax with an outdoor lunch at the park's tree-shaded picnic tables. ⊠ *219 E. Toughnut St., at 3rd St.* ☎ *520/457–3311* ⊕ *www.azstateparks.gov* ⊠ *$5* ☉ *Mon.– Sun. 9–5.*

Aficionados of the Old West have most likely seen the photograph of Billy Clanton in his coffin, which was taken after his demise at the infamous gunfight at the O.K. Corral. But Steve Elliott, owner of the **Tombstone Western Heritage Museum**, offers another glimpse of this cowboy—one with his eyes wide open. The 5-inch-x-7-inch black-and-white photograph, taken by C.S. Fly in the 1880s, shows the Clantons, the McLaury brothers, and Billy Claiborne all saddled up and ready to ride. According to Elliott, it is the only known photograph of Billy Clanton taken while he was still among the living. Other relics of the Old West at the museum include 1880s dentist's tools, clay poker chips, historic photographs, vintage firearms, and a stagecoach strongbox. ⊠ *515 Fremont St., at 6th St.* ☎ *520/457–3800* ⊠ *$5* ☉ *Mon.–Sat. 10–5, Sun. 1–5.*

Originally a boardinghouse for the Vizina Mining Company and later a popular hotel, the **Rose Tree Inn Museum** has 1880s period rooms. Covering more than 8,600 square feet, the Lady Banksia rose tree, planted by a homesick bride in 1885, is reported to be the largest of its kind in

The Legend of Wyatt Earp and the OK Corral

Popularized in dime novels and on the silver screen, the legend of Wyatt Earp follows the American tradition of the tall tale. This larger-than-life hero of the Wild West is cloaked with romance and derring-do. Stripped of the glamour, though, Earp emerges as a man with a checkered past who switched from fugitive to lawman several times during his long life.

Born in 1848, Wyatt Berry Stapp Earp earned renown as the assistant city marshal of Dodge City. Wyatt and his brothers James, Virgil, and Morgan moved to Tombstone in 1879, and it was here that they, along with Wyatt's friend Doc Holliday, made their mark in history. Wyatt ran a gambling concession at the Oriental Saloon, and Virgil became Tombstone's city marshal. When trouble began to brew with the Clanton gang, Virgil recruited Wyatt and Morgan as deputy policemen. The escalating animosity

between the "cowboys" and the Earps peaked on October 26, 1881, at the O.K. Corral—a 30-second gunfight that left three of the Clanton gang dead and Morgan and Virgil wounded. Doc Holliday was grazed, but Wyatt walked away from the fight uninjured. And then the real trouble for the Earps began.

In December, Virgil was shot and crippled by unknown assailants, and on March 18, 1882, Morgan was shot to death in a pool hall. In retribution, Wyatt went on a bloody vendetta. After the smoke had settled, the remaining "cowboys" were dead and Wyatt had left Tombstone for good. He made the rounds of mining camps in the West and up into Alaska, then settled in California. He died on January 13, 1929. His legend lives on in movies such as *Tombstone* and *Wyatt Earp.*

the world. The best time to see the tree is in April, when its tiny white roses bloom. Romantics can purchase a healthy clipping from the tree ($10.95 plus tax) to plant in their own yards. The museum might not look like much from the outside, but the collectibles and tree make this one of the best places to visit in town. ⊠ *116 S. 4th St., at Toughnut St.* ☎ *520/457–3326* ⊠ *$5* ⊘ *Daily 9–5.*

WHERE TO EAT AND STAY

$

AMERICAN

⟳

✕ **Longhorn Restaurant.** You won't find anything fancy at this noisy eatery across the street from Big Nose Kate's Saloon, but you will find generous helpings of basic American food at decent prices. The menu covers everything from breakfast to dinner with such entrées as omelets, burgers, steaks, tacos, and enchiladas. The food is a little bland, but the rustic environment and easy accessibility keep this longtime establishment in the running. ⊠ *501 E. Allen St.* ☎ *520/457–3405* ⊕ *www. bignosekates.com* ⊟ *AE, MC, V.*

$

🛏 **Holiday Inn Express.** Nestled into a hill just outside town, this newer two-story property offsets basic rooms with spectacular views of the mountains and desert valley. The rooms are Western-theme, of course, and every night an old Western movie is screened in the dining room. **Pros:** clean; modern; nightly movie with free popcorn. **Cons:** longer walk (or three-minute drive) into town; no elevator (request a ground-

SOUTHERN ARIZONA BIRD-WATCHING

Southern Arizona is one of the best areas for bird-watching in the United States; nearly 500 species have been spotted here. To the east, birders flock to the Patagonia–Sonoita Creek and Ramsey Canyon preserves, the San Pedro Riparian National Conservation Area, the ponds and dry lake beds south of Willcox, and the Portal–Cave Creek area in the Chiricahua Mountains near the New Mexico border. To the west, the Buenos Aires and Imperial national wildlife refuges are among the many places famed for their abundance of avian visitors. All in all, more than a quarter of the birds found in North America nest in the rich habitats provided by the secluded canyons and diverse microclimates of southern Arizona's "Sky Islands." Some of the most coveted avian species spotted in this birder's paradise include painted redstarts, elegant trogons, violet-crowned hummingbirds, northern goshawk, and sulphur-bellied flycatchers.

Nearby, Sierra Vista holds the birding claim to fame as the "Hummingbird Capital of the United States." The proliferation of the colorful, winged wonders (14 species in all) is the focus of the Southwest Wings Birding and Nature Festival, held in August. It's even possible to get up close and personal with these tiny birds by participating with Nature Conservancy researchers in weighing and banding the colorful critters. For more information on birding sites and educational programs in the area, contact the Southeastern Arizona Birding Observatory (☎ 520/432–1388 ⊕ www. sabo.org); pick up the Southeastern Arizona Birding Trail Guide for $3 at the Tucson Audubon Nature Shop (✉ 300 E. University Blvd., #120, Tucson ☎ 520/629–0510 ⊕ www. tucsonaudubon.org).

floor room if you don't want to climb stairs). ✉ *580 W. Randolph Way* ☎ *520/457–9507 or 888/465–4329* ⊕ *www.hitombstone.com* ⇆ *60 rooms, 7 suites* ⌂ *In-room: refrigerator (some). In-hotel: pool, laundry facilities, Wi-Fi hotspot* ⊟ *AE, D, MC, V* ⏐◉⏐ *BP.*

$ ⊡ **Marie's Bed & Breakfast.** Filled with Western kitsch, curios, and family portraits, Marie's has the feel of a stay at Grandma's house without the obligation. A hearty country breakfast (eggs, sausage, home-fried potatoes, and fruit) is served on fine china and crystal in the kitchen. When you've heard enough stories from effusive hosts Terry and Mike, mosey on down the street into town. **Pros:** friendly hosts; convenient location. **Cons:** two rooms in the main house share a bathroom. ✉ *101 N. 4th St* ☎ *520/457–3831 or 877/457–3831* ⊕ *www.mariesbandb. com* ⇆ *3 rooms, 1 with bath* ⌂ *In-room: a/c, no phone (some), no TV (some), Internet (some). In-hotel: Wi-Fi hotspot, parking (free)* ⊟ *AE, D, MC, V* ⏐◉⏐ *BP.*

SHOPPING

Several souvenir shops and old-time photo emporiums await in the kitschy collection of stores lining Allen Street.

★ Given the town's bloody history, it's not surprising that guns aren't permitted in most of the establishments, but it's worth visiting **Lefty's** (✉ *17 S. 4th St., at Allen St.* ☎ *520/457–3227*), on the site of G. F. Spangenberg Gun Shop, where Wyatt Earp, Virgil Earp, Doc Holliday, the Clantons, and the McLowrys all purchased weapons. The shop still sells a few period firearms.

Get into the spirit of the Old West by renting or purchasing 1880s-style costumes at **Madame Mustache** (✉ *419 E. Allen St., at 5th St.* ☎ *520/457–3815*).**Silver Hills Trading Co** (✉ *504 E. Allen St.* ☎ *520/457–3335*) offers everything from Native American jewelry to Southwestern souvenirs. Well-stocked **Tombstone Old West Books** (✉ *401 E. Allen St.* ☎ *520/457–2252*) has a wide selection of books about Cochise County and the Old West.

NIGHTLIFE

★ Another hopping bar is **Big Nose Kate's Saloon** (✉ *Allen St., between 4th and 5th Sts.* ☎ *520/457–3107* ⊕ *www.bignosekate.com*). Occasionally an acoustic concert livens things up even more at this popular pub, once part of the original Grand Hotel, built in 1881. Saloon girls encourage visitors to get into the 1880s spirit by dressing up in red-feather boas and dusters.

If you're looking to wet your whistle, stop by the **Crystal Palace** (✉ *436 E. Allen St., at 5th St.* ☎ *520/457–3611*), where a beautiful mirrored mahogany bar, wrought-iron chandeliers, and tinwork ceilings date back to Tombstone's heyday. Locals come here on weekends to dance to live country-and-western music.

BISBEE

8

★ *24 mi south of Tombstone on AZ 80.*

Like Tombstone, Bisbee was a mining boomtown, but its wealth was in copper, not silver, and its success continued much longer. The gnarled Mule Mountains aren't as impressive as some of the other mountain ranges in southern Arizona, but their rocky canyons concealed one of the richest mineral sites in the world.

Jack Dunn, a scout with Company C from Fort Huachuca chasing hostile Apaches in the area, first discovered an outcropping of rich ore here in 1877. By 1900 more than 20,000 people lived in the crowded canyons around the Bisbee mines. Phelps Dodge purchased all the major mines by the Great Depression, and mining continued until 1975, when the mines were closed for good. In less than 100 years of mining, the area surrounding Bisbee yielded more than $6.1 billion of mineral wealth.

Once known as the Queen of the Copper Camps, Bisbee is no longer one of the biggest cities between New Orleans and San Francisco. It was rediscovered in the early 1980s by burned-out city dwellers and revived as a kind of Woodstock West. The population is a mix of retired miners and their families, aging hippie jewelry makers, and enterprising restaurateurs and boutique owners from all over the country.

GETTING HERE AND AROUND

If you want to head straight into town from U.S. 80, get off at the Brewery Gulch interchange. You can cross under the highway, taking Main, Commerce, or Brewery Gulch streets, all of which intersect at the large public parking lot. Next door, the visitor center is a good place to start your visit of this historic mining town. It offers up-to-date information on attractions, dining, lodging, tours, and special events.

ESSENTIALS

Visitor InfoBisbee Visitors Center (⊠ *2 Copper Queen Plaza* ☎ *520/432–3554 or 866/224–7233* ⊕ *www.discoverbisbee.com* ⏱ *Weekdays 9–5, weekends 10–4*).

EXPLORING

TOP ATTRACTIONS

★ The **Bisbee Mining and Historical Museum** is in a redbrick structure built in 1897 to serve as the Copper Queen Consolidated Mining Offices. The rooms today are filled with colorful exhibits, photographs, and artifacts that offer a glimpse into the everyday life of Bisbee's early mining community. The exhibit "Bisbee: Urban Outpost on the Frontier" paints a fascinating portrait of how this "Shady Lady" of a mining town transformed into a true mini–urban center. Upstairs, the "Digging In" exhibit shows you everything you ever wanted to know about copper mining, including what it felt and sounded like in a mining car. This was the first rural museum in the United States to become a member of the Smithsonian Institution Affiliations Program, and it tells a story you can take with you as you wander through Bisbee's funky streets. ⊠ *5 Copper Queen Plaza* ☎ *520/432–7071* ⊕ *www.bisbeemuseum.org* 🎟 *$7.50* ⏱ *Daily 10–4*.

☾ For a lesson in mining history, take the **Copper Queen Mine Underground Tour**. The mine is less than 0.5 mi to the east of the Lavender Pit, across AZ 80 from downtown at the Brewery Gulch interchange. Tours are led by Bisbee's retired copper miners, who are wont to embellish their spiel with tales from their mining days. The 75-minute tours (you can't enter the mine at any other time) go into the shaft via a small open train, like those the miners rode when the mine was active. Before you climb aboard, you're outfitted in miner's garb—a yellow slicker and a hard hat with a light that runs off a battery pack. You may want to wear a sweater or light coat under your slicker, because temperatures inside are cool. You'll travel thousands of feet into the mine, up a grade of 30 feet (not down, as many visitors expect). Reservations are suggested. ⊠ *478 N. Dart Rd.* ☎ *520/432–2071 or 866/432–2071* ⊕ *www.queenminetour.com* 🎟 *Mine tour $13* ⏱ *Tours daily at 9, 10:30, noon, 2, and 3:30*.

Bisbee's **Main Street** is alive and retailing. This hilly commercial thoroughfare is lined with appealing art galleries, antiques stores, crafts shops, boutiques, and restaurants—many in well-preserved turn-of-the-20th-century brick buildings.

A visit to Tombstone is not complete without witnessing the re-created gunfight at the O.K. Corral.

WORTH NOTING

Brewery Gulch, a short street running north–south, is adjacent to the Copper Queen Hotel. In the old days the brewery housed here allowed the dregs of the beer that was being brewed to flow down the street and into the gutter. Nowadays, this narrow road is home to Bisbee's nightlife.

The **Copper Queen Hotel** (⊠ *11 Howell Ave.* ☎ *520/432–2216*), built a century ago and still in operation, is behind the Mining and Historical Museum. It has housed the famous as well as the infamous: General John "Black Jack" Pershing, John Wayne, Theodore Roosevelt, and mining executives from all over the world made this their home away from home. Though the restaurant has seen better days, the outdoor bar area is a great spot for enjoying a margarita and people-watching. The hotel also hosts three resident ghosts. Take a minute to look through the journal at the front desk, where guests have described their haunted encounters.

About 0.25 mi after AZ 80 intersects with AZ 92, you can pull off the highway into a gravel parking lot, where a short, typewritten history of the **Lavender Pit Mine** (⊠ *AZ 80*) is attached to the hurricane fence (Bisbee isn't big on formal exhibits). The hole left by the copper miners is huge, with piles of lavender-hue "tailings," or waste, creating mountains around it. Arizona's largest pit mine yielded some 94 million tons of copper ore before mining activity came to a halt.

WHERE TO EAT

$$ ✕**The Bisbee Grille.** You might not
AMERICAN   expect diversity at a place with
a reputation for having the best
burger in town, but this restaurant
delivers with salads, sandwiches,
fajitas, pasta, salmon, steaks, and
ribs. The dining room, built to
resemble an old train depot, fills up
fast on weekends. Its location next
to the bustling visitor center makes
for a convenient meal. ✉*2 Cop-
per Queen Plaza* ☎*520/432–6788*
▤*AE, D, MC, V.*

$$ ✕**Café Roka.** This is the deserved
ITALIAN   darling of the hip Bisbee crowd. The
★   constantly changing northern Italian–style evening menu is not extensive, but whatever you order—gulf
shrimp tossed with lobster ravioli,
roasted quail, New Zealand rack of
lamb—will be wonderful. Portions
are generous, and entrées come with soup, salad, and sorbet. Exposed-
brick walls and soft lighting form the backdrop for original artwork,
and the 1875 bar harks back to Bisbee's glory days. There's live jazz on
Friday nights. ✉*35 Main St.* ☎*520/432–5153* ⊕*www.caferoka.com*
▤*AE, MC, V* ⊗ *Closed Sun.–Wed. No lunch.*

<aside>
BISBEE TOURS

Tom Mosier, a native of Bisbee,
gives the **Lavender Jeep Tours**
(✉ *45 Gila Dr.* ☎ *520/432–5369*
⊕ *www.lavenderjeeptours.com*) for
$25 to $49. He regales locals and
visitors with tales of the town and
tours of the surrounding region.

The **Southeastern Arizona Bird
Observatory** (✉ *Box 5521,
Bisbee 85603* ☎ *520/432–1388*
⊕ *www.sabo.org*) is a nonprofit
organization that offers guided
birding tours, educational programs, and information. During
spring and summer, sign up for
a hummingbird banding session,
where you can assist researchers.
</aside>

WHERE TO STAY

$–$$ ▦**Canyon Rose Suites.** Steps from the heart of downtown, this all-suites
★   inn is in the 1905 Allen Block Building, formerly a furniture store and
miners' rooming house. Upstairs are seven pretty and spacious units
of varying size, all with hardwood floors, 10-foot ceilings, and fully
equipped kitchens. Local art (for sale) adorns the walls. **Pros:** quiet, yet
just off Main Street; easy parking behind building. **Cons:** no breakfast
or common area; no elevator (guest rooms are on second floor). ✉*27
Subway St.* ✉ *Box 1915, Bisbee85603* ☎*520/432–5098 or 866/296–
7673* ⊕*www.canyonrose.com* ⇩*7 suites* ♿*In-room: a/c, kitchen,
Wi-Fi. In-hotel: laundry facilities, parking (free)* ▤*AE, D, MC, V.*

$$ ▦**Letson Loft Hotel.** This beautifully restored boutique hotel is perched
above the galleries and shops of Main Street and well appointed with
upscale comforts. Eleven-foot ceilings and bay windows accent elegant
furnishings that blend British and Chinese influences. Don the plush
robe provided as you await an in-room massage (for an additional fee)
or indulge in a glass of champagne. **Pros:** luxurious amenities; comfy,
pillow-top mattresses. **Cons:** some noise from Main Street below; no
elevator (all guest rooms are upstairs). ✉*26 Main St.* ☎*520/432–3210
or 877/432–3210* ⊕*www.letsonlofthotel.com* ⇩*8 rooms* ♿ *In-room:
kitchen (some), DVD, Wi-Fi. In-hotel: no kids under 12* ▤*AE, D,
MC, V* ⍑⍿*CP.*

$-$$ ⊞ **School House Inn Bed & Breakfast.** You might flash back to your class-
Fodor's Choice room days at this B&B, a schoolhouse built in 1918 at the height of
★ Bisbee's mining days. Perched on the side of a hill, the two-story brick
building has a pleasant outdoor patio shaded by an oak tree. The inn's
rooms all have a theme—history, music, library, reading, arithmetic,
art, geography, and the principal's office—reflected in the decor. **Pros:**
well-preserved property; exceedingly friendly hosts; hearty vegetarian
breakfast. **Cons:** a mile walk or short drive into town. ⊠ *818 Tombstone
Canyon Rd.* ✆ *Box 32, Bisbee 85603* ☎ *520/432–2996 or 800/537–
4333* ⊕ *www.schoolhouseinnbb.com* ⊅ *7 rooms, 3 suites* ♨ *In-room:
no a/c, no phone, no TV, Wi-Fi.* ⊟ *AE, D, MC, V* ⊚◯ *BP.*

$-$$ ⊞ **Shady Dell Vintage Trailer Court.** For a blast to the past, stay in one
Fodor's Choice of the funky vintage aluminum trailers at this trailer park just south
★ of town. Choices include a 1952 10-foot homemade unit and a 1951
33-foot Royal Mansion. The entire collection is decked out 1950s style,
including vintage magazines, books, and vinyl records. Some have private bathrooms, but only a few have private showers; the park restrooms are clean, with hot showers. Dot's Diner, on-site, serves burgers,
fries, and milk shakes, as well as breakfast, Friday through Tuesday.
Pros: unique (how many vintage trailer-park hotels with a hip vibe are
out there?); fun; cheap. **Cons:** walking to the public restrooms in the
middle of the night. ⊠ *1 Old Douglas Rd.* ☎ *520/432–3567* ⊕ *www.
theshadydell.com* ⊅ *11 trailers* ♨ *In-room: no a/c, no phone, kitchen,
no TV (some). In-hotel: restaurant, laundry facilities, no kids under
10* ⊟ *D, MC, V.*

SHOPPING
★ Artist studios, galleries, and boutiques in historic buildings line Main
Street, which runs though Tombstone Canyon. **55 Main Gallery** (⊠ *55
Main St.* ☎ *520/432–4694*) is just one of many art galleries selling con-
temporary work along the main drag.

Belleza Fine Arts Gallery (⊠ *27 Main St.* ☎ *520/432–5877* ⊕ *www.
bellezagallery.org*) is owned and operated by Bisbee's Women's Transition Project, which aids homeless women and their children. This
unusual gallery features the artwork of local and national artists, as well
as Adirondack chairs and birdhouses made by women receiving assistance from the program. The gallery's 50% commission goes directly
into funding the Transition Project. A trip to Bisbee wouldn't be complete without a stop at the **Killer Bee Guy** (⊠ *15 Main St.* ☎ *520/432–2938
or 877/227–9338* ⊕ *www.killerbeeguy.com*). Beekeeper Reed Booth has
appeared on cable TV; you can sample his honey butters and mustards
and pick up some killer honey recipes. In Peddlers Alley, grab a free
cup of freshly brewed espresso from **Old Bisbee Roasters** (⊠ *7 Naco Rd.*
☎ *866/432–5063* ⊕ *www.oldbisbeeroasters.com*). Nationally renowned
Optimo Custom Panama Hatworks (⊠ *47 Main St.* ☎ *520/432–4544 or
888/346–3428* ⊕ *www.optimohatworks.com*) is popular for its custom,
handwoven Panama hats. It also sells works of beaver, cashmere, hare,
and rabbit felt.

8

NIGHTLIFE

Once known for shady ladies and saloons, Brewery Gulch retains a few shadows of its rowdy past. Established in 1902, **St. Elmo Bar** (✉ *36 Brewery Gulch* ☎ *520/432–5578*) is decorated with an assortment of the past and present—a 1922 official map of Cochise County hangs next to a neon beer sign. The jukebox plays during the week, but on weekends Buzz and the Soul Senders rock the house with rhythm and blues. The **Stock Exchange Saloon** (✉ *15 Brewery Gulch* ☎ *520/432–5240*), in the historic Muheim building, has shuffleboard, a pool table, and off-track betting. The 1914 stock board still hangs on the wall.

SONOITA

55 mi west of Bisbee on AZ 90 to AZ 82; 34 mi southeast of Tucson on I–10 to AZ 83; 57 mi west of Tombstone on AZ 82.

The grasslands surrounding modern-day Sonoita captured the attention of early Spanish explorers, including Father Eusebio Francisco Kino, who mapped and claimed the area in 1701. The Tuscan-like beauty of the rolling, often green hills framed by jutting mountain ranges has been noticed by Hollywood filmmakers. As you drive along AZ 83 and AZ 82 you might recognize the scenery from movies filmed here, including *Oklahoma* and *Tin Cup*.

Today this region is known for its family-run vineyards and wineries, as well as for its ranching history. Sonoita's "town," at the junction of AZ 83 and AZ 82 (known by locals as "the crossroads"), consists of a few restaurants and B&Bs, but it's the nearby wineries that draw the crowds. There are several events at the wineries, including the Blessing of the Vines in spring and the Harvest Festivals in fall. Summer is also a good time to visit, when you can escape the heat of Tucson, sample some of Arizona's vintages, and chat with local vintners.

GETTING HERE AND AROUND

To explore the wineries of southern Arizona, head south on AZ 83 from Sonoita and then east on Elgin Road. Most of the growers are in and around the tiny village of Elgin, 9 mi southeast of Sonoita. The best times to visit the vineyards are Friday through Sunday, when most are open for tastings. To plot your course through Arizona's wine country, check out the Arizona Wines Adventure Trail Map from Arizona Wine Growers Association.

ESSENTIALS

Winery Info Arizona Wine Growers Association (⊕ *www.arizonawine.org*).

TOP EXPERIENCE: WINERIES

Fodor's Choice ★ **Callaghan Vineyards** (✉ *336 Elgin Rd., Elgin* ☎ *520/455–5322* ⊕ *www. callaghanvineyards.com*), open Friday through Sunday 11–3, produces some of the best wine in Arizona. Its Buena Suerte ("good luck" in Spanish) Cuvée is a favorite, and its 1996 fumé blanc is considered one of the top wines in the United States.

Neighboring **Canelo Hills Winery** (✉ *342 Elgin Rd., Elgin* ☎ *520/455–5499* ⊕ *www.canelohillswinery.com*), open Friday through Sunday

ARIZONA WINERIES: A GRAPE ESCAPE

The soil and climate in the Santa Cruz Valley southeast of Tucson are ideal for growing grapes, even if "Arizona wine country" may sound odd. Wine grapes first took root in the region 400 years ago, when the Spanish missionaries planted the first vines of "mission" grapes for the production of sacramental wine. But it wasn't until the 1970s that the first commercial vinifera grapes were planted here as part of an agricultural experiment. The hardier vines, such as Syrahs, Grenaches, and Malvasias, seem to tolerate the summer heat and retain good acidity.

Connoisseurs have debated the merits of the wines produced in this area since 1974, but if you want to decide for yourself, tour some of the region's wineries. Callaghan Vineyards, Canelo Hills Winery, Rancho Rossa Vineyards, Dos Cabezas Wineworks, Village of Elgin Winery, Sonoita Vineyards, Kief-Joshua Vineyards, and Wilhelm Family Vineyards all have something to tantalize the taste buds. You can purchase a wine glass at the first tasting room you choose, then take it with you to any of the other wineries for a reduced tasting fee.

Farther east, vineyards are springing up around Willcox, and elsewhere in the state, vineyards south of Sedona along lower Oak Creek are garnering attention as well. ⇨ See the listings in this chapter and the North-Central chapter for contact info.

11–4, specializes in full-bodied red wines and chardonnays. The grapes for their wines are all grown on-site and their wine is produced here.

Award-winning reds and whites can be sampled Friday through Sunday 10:30–4:30 at **Dos Cabezas Wineworks** (✉ 3248 Hwy. 82, Elgin ☎ 520/455–5141 ⊕ www.doscabezaswinery.com), near the intersection of Highways 82 and 83.

Winemaker Kief Manning of **Kief-Joshua Vineyards** (✉ 370 Elgin Rd., Elgin ☎ 520/455–5582 ⊕ www.kiefjoshuavineyards.com), open daily 11–5, uses the traditional methods of open fermentation and barrel aging he learned in Australia. If you're here on a Sunday, Manning might just dish up an omelet to complement the wines produced from organically grown grapes.

Rancho Rossa Vineyards (✉ 32 Cattle Ranch La., Elgin ☎ 520/455–0700 ⊕ www.ranchorossa.com), known for its dry and fruity varietals, offers tastings Friday through Sunday 10:30–3:30.

Sonoita Vineyards (✉ 290 Elgin-Canelo Rd., Elgin ☎ 520/455–5893 ⊕ www.sonoitavineyards.com), known for its high-quality reds, offers tours and tastings daily 10–4. Originally planted in the early 1970s as an experiment by Dr. Gordon Dutt, former agriculture professor at the University of Arizona, this was the first commercial vineyard in Arizona.

Stop for tastings daily 10–4 at **Village of Elgin Winery** (✉ 471 Elgin Rd., Elgin ☎ 520/455–9309 ⊕ www.elginwines.com), one of the largest producers of wines in the state and the home to Tombstone Red, which the winemaker claims is "great with scorpion, tarantula, and rattlesnake meat."

You can tour as well as taste at **Wilhelm Family Vineyards** (✉ *21 Mountain Ranch Dr., Elgin* ☎ *520/455–9291* ⊕ *www.wilhelmfamilyvineyards. com*), open Friday through Sunday 11–5, which produces seven red varietals, including a homegrown Syrah and tempranillo.

WHERE TO EAT

$$ ✕ **Canela Bistro.** A cozy brick house in the center of Sonoita's tiny busi-
AMERICAN ness district is the setting for this deceptively sophisticated restaurant with small-town charm. The dinner menu, which changes with the seasons, creatively incorporates locally grown produce and—of course—showcases local wines. Sunday brunch tends towards Southwestern and Mexican egg dishes, such as *chilequiles* (a tortilla-cheese casserole), huevos rancheros, and roasted-red-pepper–and-leek quiche. ✉ *3252 AZ 82* ☎ *520/455–5783* ⊕ *canelabistro.com* ▭ *MC, V* ⊘ *Closed Mon.– Wed. No dinner Sun.*

$$ ✕ **Steak Out Restaurant & Saloon.** A frontier-style design and a weathered-
AMERICAN wood exterior help to create the mood at this Western restaurant and bar known for its tasty margaritas and live country music played on weekend evenings. Built and owned by the family that operates the Sonoita Inn next door, the restaurant serves cowboy fare: mesquite-grilled steaks, ribs, chicken, and fish. ✉ *3235 AZ 82* ☎ *520/455–5205* ⊕ *www.azsteakout.com* ▭ *AE, D, DC, MC, V* ⊘ *No lunch weekdays.*

WHERE TO STAY

$$ ⊡ **Rainbow's End.** An old ranch manager's house on a horse farm overlook-ing the Sonoita countryside is now a B&B furnished in period antiques. Four bedrooms, each with a modern bathroom, share a great room with fireplace and a big kitchen, where guests can assemble their own breakfast and organic snacks (supplied by the hosts, who live just down the hill). A comfortable two-room suite, with a kitchenette and a private dog yard, is perfect for those seeking even closer proximity to the horses—it's in the barn. **Pros:** serene setting complete with covered porches. **Cons:** minimal contact with hosts makes it feel more like a rental cottage than a B&B. ✉ *3088 AZ 83* ⊡ *Box 717, Sonoita 85637* ☎ *520/455–0202* ⊕ *www. rainbowsendbandb.com* ➮ *5 rooms* ⚷ *In-room: a/c, no TV. In-hotel: some pets allowed* ▭ *AE, D, MC, V* ⟊ *BP.*

$–$$ ⊡ **Sonoita Inn.** The owner of this small hotel also owned the Triple Crown–winning racehorse Secretariat, and the walls of the inn celebrate the horse's career with photos, racing programs, and press clippings. Hardwood floors, colorful woven rugs, and retro-cowboy bedspreads distinguish the spacious rooms, some of which have window seats with views of the Santa Rita Mountains. The inn is near the intersection of AZ 82 and AZ 83, and is adjacent to the Steak Out Restaurant & Saloon. **Pros:** cheery decor; walk to restaurants. **Cons:** some road noise. ✉ *3243 AZ 82* ⊡ *Box 99, Sonoita 85637* ☎ *520/455–5935 or 800/696–1006* ⊕ *www.sonoitainn.com* ➮ *18 rooms* ⚷ *In-room: a/c, DVD (some), Wi-Fi. In-hotel: some pets allowed* ▭ *AE, D, MC, V* ⟊ *CP.*

$–$$ ⊡ **The Walker Ranch.** If you've ever fantasized about living on a horse ranch, this B&B will be an easy place to settle into and a hard place to leave. Large and well-equipped units in separate casita areas afford privacy, and shared amenities include a pool, hot tub, pond with paddleboats, and gym with a racquetball court. There are horses and farm animals for the kids to pet; and trail rides with a local wrangler can be arranged. **Pros:** attractive rooms and suites; tranquil setting. **Cons:** breakfast costs extra. ⊠ *99 Curly Horse Rd.* ☎ *520/455–4631* ⊕ *www.thewalkerranch.com* ⤵ *8 rooms* ⚬ *In-room: no phone (some), kitchen (some), DVD (some), Wi-Fi. In-hotel: pool, gym, laundry facilities, some pets allowed* ▭ *MC, V* ⍩ *BP.*

PATAGONIA

12 mi southwest of Sonoita via AZ 82, 18 mi northeast of Nogales via AZ 82.

Served by a spur of the Atchison, Topeka & Santa Fe Railroad, Patagonia was a shipping center for cattle and ore. The town declined after the railroad departed in 1962, and the old depot is now the town hall. Today, with the migration of artists here in recent years, art galleries and boutiques coexist with real Western saloons in this tiny, tree-lined village in the Patagonia Mountains. The surrounding region is a prime birding destination, with more than 275 species of birds found around Sonoita Creek.

GETTING HERE AND AROUND

As you approach Patagonia on AZ 82 from either direction, the galleries and restaurants are either along the highway (called Naugle Avenue through town) or one block south on McKeown Avenue. There is plenty of street parking.

EXPLORING

Eleven miles south of town, **Patagonia Lake State Park** is the spot for water sports, picnicking, and camping. Formed by the damming of Sonoita Creek, the 265-acre reservoir lures anglers with its largemouth bass, crappie, bluegill, and catfish; it's stocked with rainbow trout in the wintertime. You can rent rowboats, paddleboats, canoes, and camping and fishing gear at the marina. Most swimmers head for Boulder Beach. The entrance fee is good for both Patagonia Lake State Park and the Sonoita Creek State Natural Area. ⊠ *400 Lake Patagonia Rd.* ☎ *520/287–6965* ⊕ *www.azstateparks.com* ⊡ *$8 per vehicle* ☉ *Visitor center daily 9–4:30, gates closed 10* PM*–4* AM.

At the Nature Conservancy's **Patagonia–Sonoita Creek Preserve**, 1,350 acres of cottonwood-willow riparian habitat are protected along the Patagonia–Sonoita Creek watershed. More than 275 bird species have been sighted here, along with white-tailed deer, javelina, coatimundi (raccoonlike animals native to the region), desert tortoise, and snakes. There's a self-guided nature trail; guided walks are given every Saturday at 9 AM along 2 mi of loop trails. Three concrete structures near an elevated berm of the Railroad Trail serve as reminders of the land's former use as a truck farm. To reach the preserve from Patagonia, make a right on 4th Avenue; at the stop sign, turn left onto Blue Haven Road. This paved road soon becomes dirt, and leads to the preserve in about 1.25 mi. The admission fee is good for seven days. ⊠ *150 Blue Haven Rd.* ☎ *520/394–2400* ⊕ *www.nature.org* ⊡ *$5* ☉ *Apr.–Sept., Wed.– Sun. 6:30–4; Oct.–Mar., Wed.–Sun. 7:30–4.*

Bird-watchers flock to Ramsey Canyon Preserve for rare ecosystems where deserts meet mountains.

Arizona State Parks has designated almost 5,000 acres surrounding Patagonia Lake as **Sonoita Creek State Natural Area**. This project, funded by the Arizona State Parks Heritage Fund (lottery monies) and the State Lake Improvement Fund, offers environmental educational programs and university-level research opportunities, as well as camping facilities. The riparian area is home to giant cottonwoods, willows, sycamores, and mesquites; nesting black hawks; and endangered species. Rangers offer guided birding tours, by boat and on foot, for an additional small fee every Tuesday, Saturday, and Sunday at 9, 10:15, and 11:30 AM (call to confirm schedule). The entrance fee is good for both Patagonia Lake State Park and the Sonoita Creek State Natural Area. ⊠ *AZ 82, 5 mi south of town* ☎ *520/287–2791 or 800/285–3703* ⊕ *www.azstateparks. gov* ⊠ *$8 per vehicle.*

WHERE TO EAT

¢

CAFÉ

✕ **Gathering Grounds.** This colorful café and espresso bar, which also doubles as an art gallery featuring local artists, serves healthful breakfasts and imaginative soups, salads, and sandwiches through the late afternoon. Beverage choices include organic fair-trade coffees; ice cream, cakes, and cookies draw the local younger set. ⊠ *319 McKeown Ave.* ☎ *520/394–2097* ⊕ *www.mygatheringgrounds.com* ▭ *MC, V* ☾ *No dinner.*

$

PIZZA

✕ **Velvet Elvis Pizza Co.** There aren't too many places where you can enjoy a pizza heaped with organic veggies, a crisp salad of organic greens tossed with homemade dressing, freshly pressed juice (try the beet-, apple-, and lime-juice concoction), organic wine, and microbrewed or imported beer while surrounded by images of Elvis *and* the Virgin Mary.

Owner Cecilia San Miguel uses a 1930s dough recipe for the restaurant's delightful crust, and you can pick up some pizza sauce in the gift shop if you want to try your hand at pizza making at home. They also have fabulous fruit pies. ✉ *292 Naugle Ave.* ☎ *520/394–2102* ⊕ *www. velvetelvispizza.com* ⊟ *MC, V* ⊘ *Closed Mon.–Wed.*

$ ✕ **Wagon Wheel Saloon.** The Wagon Wheel's restaurant, serving ribs,
AMERICAN steaks, and burgers, is a more recent development, but the cowboy bar, with its neon beer signs and mounted moose head, has been around since the early 1900s. This is where every Stetson-wearing ranch hand in the area comes to listen to the country jukebox and down a longneck, maybe accompanied by some jalapeño poppers. ✉ *400 W. Naugle Ave.* ☎ *520/394–2433* ⊟ *MC, V.*

WHERE TO STAY

$$$$ 🏨 **Circle Z Ranch.** Rimmed by giant sycamore, ash, and cottonwood trees
☺ and surrounded by the Patagonia–Sonoita Creek Preserve, this seasonal guest ranch served as a setting in the movie *Red River* and in several episodes of *Gunsmoke*. Rooms in the adobe-style buildings have hardwood floors and area rugs, and antique Monterey pine chests. Riders from beginner through advanced can be accommodated on adventurous, scenic trails. All meals, riding, and amenities are included. **Pros:** excellent dude ranch experience in a lush, rather than desert, setting; laid-back and friendly staff and guests. **Cons:** all-inclusive is pricey; three-night minimum stay. ✉ *AZ 82, 4 mi southwest of town* ✉ *Box 194, Sonoita 85624* ☎ *520/394–2525 or 888/854–2525* ⊕ *www.circlez.com* ⊳ *24 rooms* ☺ *In-room: no a/c, no phone, no TV. In-hotel: restaurant, tennis court, pool* ⊟ *MC, V* ⊘ *Closed mid-May–Oct.* ⎆ *AI.*

★ 🏨 **Duquesne House Bed & Breakfast/Gallery.** Built as a miners' boardinghouse at the turn of the 20th century, this adobe home has rooms painted in pastel Southwest colors, lovingly and whimsically detailed by a local artist, and decorated with hand-stitched quilts and Mexican folk art. All the rooms are suites, with sofa beds in the sitting rooms, and have private entrances. Breakfast is served in your room or in the Santa Fe–style great room. A tiered backyard garden with hammocks adds to the tranquillity. **Pros:** quiet location only a couple of blocks from town; cheerful, contemporary interior. **Cons:** few amenities. ✉ *357 Duquesne Ave.* ✉ *Box 772, Sonoita 85624* ☎ *520/394–2732* ⊳ *4 suites* ☺ *In-room: a/c, no TV, Wi-Fi* ⊟ *No credit cards* ⎆ *BP.*

SHOPPING

Patagonia is quickly turning into a shopping destination in its own right. Unlike the trendy shops in nearby Tubac, the stores here have reasonable prices in addition to small-town charm. Some of the artist spaces are open only by appointment. **Creative Spirit Gallery** (✉ *317 McKeown Ave.* ☎ *520/394–9186*) features jewelry, paintings, photography, quilts, and pottery by more than 60 local artists. **Global Arts Gallery** (✉ *315 McKeown Ave.* ☎ *520/394–0077*) showcases everything from local art and antiques to Native American jewelry, Middle Eastern rugs, and exotic musical instruments. At **High Spirits Flutes** (✉ *714 Red Rock Ave.* ☎ *520/394–2900 or 800/394–1523* ⊕ *www.highspirits.com*) you can pick up Odell Borg Native American flutes. **Mariposa Books &**

8

More (✉ *317 McKeown Ave.* ☎ *520/394–9186*) shares quarters with the visitor center, and has a nice selection of new and used books on topics ranging from cooking to regional history. The **Shooting Star Pottery** (✉ *370 Smelter Ave.* ☎ *520/394–2752*) displays clay pieces created by the village potter Martha Kelly by appointment only—or you can check out the mosaics Kelly and her students completed at the Patagonia Community Arts Center just off AZ 82.

SIERRA VISTA

42 mi southeast of Patagonia, 30 mi southeast of Sonoita, via AZ 82 to AZ 90.

A characterless military town on the outskirts of Fort Huachuca, Sierra Vista is nonetheless a good base from which to explore the more scenic areas that surround it—and at 4,620 feet above sea level the whole area has a year-round temperate climate. There are quite a few fast-food and chain restaurants for your basic dining needs, and more than 1,100 rooms in area hotels, motels, and B&Bs offer shelter for the night.

Fort Huachuca, headquarters of the army's Global Information Systems Command, is the last of the great Western forts still in operation. It dates back to 1877, when the Buffalo Soldiers (yes, Bob Marley fans—*those* Buffalo Soldiers), the first all black regiment in the U.S. forces, came to aid settlers battling invaders from Mexico, Indian tribes reluctant to give up their homelands, and assorted American desperadoes on the lam from the law back East.

GETTING HERE AND AROUND

The most direct route to Sierra Vista from Interstate 10 is a straight shot south on AZ 90 (about 30 mi). If you're not going to Fort Huachuca, take a left on the Route 90 bypass to reach the shopping centers, most of the chain motels, and the intersection of AZ 92, which takes you to Ramsey Canyon and Coronado National Memorial. If you're going to the fort, stay on AZ 90 and the fort will be on your right. From here, Fry Boulevard will lead you through town to the AZ 92.

EXPLORING

Those driving to **Coronado National Memorial**, dedicated to Francisco Vásquez de Coronado, will see many of the same stunning vistas of Arizona and Mexico the conquistador saw when he trod this route in 1540 seeking the mythical Seven Cities of Cibola. It's a little more than 3 mi via a dirt road from the visitor center to Montezuma Pass, and another 0.5 mi on foot to the top of the nearly 7,000-foot Coronado Peak, where the views are best. Other trails include Joe's Canyon Trail, a steep 3-mi route (one way) down to the visitor center, and Miller Peak Trail, 12 mi round-trip to the highest point in the Huachuca Mountains (Miller Peak is 9,466 feet). Kids ages 5 to 12 can participate in the memorial's Junior Ranger program, explore Coronado Cave, and dress up in replica Spanish armor. The turnoff for the monument is 16 mi south of Sierra Vista on AZ 92; the visitor center is 5 mi farther. ✉ *4101 E. Montezuma Canyon Rd., Hereford* ☎ *520/366–5515* ⊕ *www.nps. gov/coro* 🎫 *Free* ☾ *Visitor center daily 8–4.*

Three miles from the fort's main gate are the **Fort Huachuca museums.** The late-19th-century bachelor officers' quarters and the annex across the street provide a record of military life on the frontier. More often than not, you'll be sharing space with new cadets learning about the history of this far-flung outpost. Motion sensors activate odd little sound bites in the multimedia experience. Another half block south, the **U.S. Army Intelligence Museum** focuses on American intelligence operations from the Apache Scouts through Desert Storm. Code machines, codebooks, decoding devices, and other intelligence-gathering equipment are on display. Enter the main gate of Fort Huachuca on AZ 90, west of Sierra Vista. You need a driver's license, vehicle registration, and proof of insurance to get on base. ⊠ *Grierson St., off AZ 90, west of Sierra Vista, Fort Huachuca* ☎ *520/533–5736* ⊕ *huachuca-www.army.mil* ⊠ *Free* ⊙ *Weekdays 9–4, weekends 1–4.*

Fodor's Choice ★   **Ramsey Canyon Preserve**, managed by the Nature Conservancy, marks the convergence of two mountain and desert systems: this spot is the northernmost limit of the Sierra Madre and the southernmost limit of the Rockies, and it's at the edge of the Chihuahuan and Sonoran deserts. Visitors to this world-famous bird-watching hot spot train their binoculars skyward hoping to catch a glimpse of some of the preserve's most notable inhabitants. Painted redstarts nest, and 14 magnificent species of hummingbirds congregate here from spring through autumn—the jewels of this pristine habitat. Even for nonbirders, the beauty of the canyon makes this a destination in its own right. The rare stream-fed, sycamore-maple riparian corridor provides a lush contrast to the desert highlands at the base of the mountains. Guided hikes begin at 9 AM Tuesday, Thursday, and Saturday from March through October. Stop at the visitor center for maps and books on the area's natural history, flora, and fauna. To get here, take AZ 92 south from Sierra Vista for 6 mi, turn right on Ramsey Canyon Road, and then go 4 mi to the preserve entrance. Admission is good for seven days. ⊠ *27 Ramsey Canyon Rd., Hereford* ☎ *520/378–2785* ⊕ *www.nature.org* ⊠ *$5, free 1st Sat. of the month* ⊙ *Feb.–Oct., daily 8–5; Nov.–Jan., Thurs.–Mon. 9–4.*

OFF THE BEATEN PATH   **San Pedro Riparian National Conservation Area.** The San Pedro River, partially rerouted underground by an 1887 earthquake, may not look like much, but it sustains an impressive array of flora and fauna. To maintain this fragile creek-side ecosystem, 56,000 acres along the river were designated a protected riparian area in 1988. More than 350 species of birds come here, as well as 82 mammal species and 45 reptiles and amphibians. Forty thousand years ago this was the domain of woolly mammoths and mastodons: many of the huge skeletons in Washington's Smithsonian Institute and New York's Museum of Natural History came from the massive fossil pits in the area. As evidenced by a number of small, unexcavated ruins, the migratory Indian tribes who passed through thousands of years later also found this valley hospitable, in part because of its many useful plants. Information, guided tours, books, and gifts are available from the volunteer staff at San Pedro House, a visitor center operated by Friends of the San Pedro River (⊕ *www.sanpedroriver.org*). ⊠ *San Pedro House, 9800 AZ 90* ☎ *520/508–4445, 520/439–6400 Sierra Vista BLM Office* ⊕ *www.*

8

az.blm.gov ✉ *Free* ☺ *Visitor center daily 9:30–4:30, conservation area daily sunrise–sunset.*

BIRDING
TOURS

High Lonesome Ecotours (✉ *570 S. Little Bear Trail* ☎ *520/458–9446 or 800/743–2668* ⊕ *www.hilonesometours.com*) offers birding tours with lodging.

WHERE TO EAT

$$
AMERICAN

✕ **The Outside Inn.** Crisp white tablecloths, lace curtains, and glimmering candlelight all add to the romance of the Outside Inn, a favorite special-occasion dining destination of birders and locals alike. The prices may seem high, until you sample the delicious dinners. Delicacies include crumb-crusted lamb, prime rib, and blackened mahimahi. ✉ *4907 S. AZ 92* ☎ *520/378–4645* ▭ *AE, MC, V* ☺ *Closed Sun. No lunch Sat.*

WHERE TO STAY

$$
★

Casa de San Pedro. Bird-watchers are drawn to this contemporary hacienda-style B&B abutting the San Pedro Riparian National Conservation Area. Hiking trails pass behind the property, and guided birding tours can be arranged. Each of the bright and modern rooms has handcrafted wooden furnishings from northern Mexico. A labyrinth for meditation and butterfly gardens surround the house. **Pros:** gracious hosts; tranquil setting; midway between Bisbee and Sierra Vista. **Cons:** some may feel too isolated. ✉ *8933 S Yell La., Hereford* ☎ *520/366–1300 or 888/257–2050* ⊕ *www.bedandbirds.com* ⌯ *10 rooms* ⚇ *In-room: no phone, no TV, Wi-Fi. In-hotel: pool, laundry facilities, no kids under 12* ▭ *AE, D, MC, V* ⓘⓞⓘ *BP.*

$$–$$$
★

Ramsey Canyon Inn Bed & Breakfast. The Ramsey Canyon Preserve is an internationally renowned bird haven, and the nearby Ramsey Canyon Inn is a bird-watcher's delight. Antique furnishings and original watercolors of hummingbirds adorn the inn's rooms and apartment suites. The innkeepers serve a rotating menu of breakfast treats, such as French toast stuffed with cream cheese and nuts, as well as homemade pie in the afternoon. Reserve rooms in advance during the busy spring season. **Pros:** perfect base for birding and hiking; comfortable rooms. **Cons:** a little dull for nonbirders. ✉ *29 Ramsey Canyon Rd., Hereford* ☎ *520/378–3010* ⊕ *www.ramseycanyoninn.com* ⌯ *6 rooms, 3 suites* ⚇ *In-room: no a/c (some), no phone (some), kitchen (some), no TV. In-hotel: no kids under 12* ▭ *D, MC, V* ⓘⓞⓘ *BP.*

$

Windemere Hotel & Conference Center. This updated hotel complex, across from the area's shopping mall, is on AZ 92 in what used to be the eastern outskirts of Sierra Vista but is now a rapidly growing commercial corridor. Despite the development, it's not uncommon to see roadrunners dashing about the hotel grounds. The three-story hotel has large, comfortable rooms, most with sweeping views of the Huachuca Mountains. **Pros:** pleasant common areas and pool complex; free evening cocktails. **Cons:** generic feel compared to other lodging options. ✉ *2047 S. AZ 92* ☎ *520/459–5900 or 800/825–4656* ⊕ *www. windemerehotel.com* ⌯ *149 rooms, 3 suites* ⚇ *In-room: a/c, refrigerator, Wi-Fi. In-hotel: restaurant, bar, pool, laundry facilities, laundry service* ▭ *AE, D, DC, MC, V* ⓘⓞⓘ *BP.*

CHIRICAHUA NATIONAL MONUMENT

65 mi northeast of Sierra Vista on AZ 90 to I-10 to AZ 186; 58 mi northeast of Douglas on U.S. 191 to AZ 181, 36 mi southeast of Willcox.

GETTING HERE AND AROUND

Though more remote than other sights in southeastern Arizona, Chiricahua National Monument is well worth the two-hour drive from Tucson. You'll be rewarded with stunning scenery and unspoiled wilderness for birding and hiking. The nearest gas stations are in Willcox or Sunizona, so be sure to fill your tank first.

EXPLORING

Vast fields of desert grass are suddenly transformed into a landscape of forest, mountains, and striking rock formations as you enter the 12,000-acre **Chiricahua National Monument**. The Chiricahua Apache—who lived in the mountains for centuries and, led by Cochise and Geronimo, tried for 25 years to prevent white pioneers from settling here—dubbed it the Land of the Standing-Up Rocks. Enormous outcroppings of volcanic rock have been worn by erosion and fractured by uplift into strange pinnacles and spires. Because of the particular balance of sunshine and rain in the area, in April and May visitors will see brown, yellow, and red leaves coexisting with new green foliage. Summer in Chiricahua National Monument is exceptionally wet: from July through September there are thunderstorms nearly every afternoon. Few other areas in the United States have such varied plant, bird, and animal life. Deer, coatimundi, peccaries, and lizards live among the aspen, ponderosa pine, Douglas fir, oak, and cypress trees—to name just a few.

Chiricahua National Monument is an excellent area for bird-watchers, and hikers have more than 17 mi of scenic trails. The admission fee is good for seven days. Hiking trail maps are available at the visitor center. The most popular and rewarding hike is the moderately easy **Echo Canyon Loop Trail**. This 3.4-mi path winds through cavelike grottos, brilliant rock formations, and a wooded canyon. Birds and other wildlife are abundant here. ⊠ *AZ 181, 36 mi southeast of Willcox* ☏ *520/824–3560* ⊕ *www.nps.gov/chir* ✉ *$5* ☺ *Visitor center daily 8–4:30.*

Keeling Schaefer Vineyards (⊠ *10277 E. Rock Creek La., Pearce* ☏ *520/824–2500* ⊕ *www.keelingschaefervineyards.com*), 12 mi south of Chiricahua National Monument, is a newcomer whose fruity Grenaches and Three Sisters Syrah are garnering attention from wine mavens. Vines from the Napa Valley region of California were planted on this beautiful

Geronimo: No Bullet Shall Pass

The fearless Apache war shaman Geronimo, known among his people as "one who yawns," fought to the very last in the Apache Wars. His surrender to General Nelson Miles on September 5, 1886, marked the end of the Indian Wars in the West. Geronimo's fleetness in evading the massed troops of the U.S. Army and his legendary immunity to bullets made him the darling of sensationalistic journalists, and he became the most famous outlaw in America.

When the combined forces of the U.S. Army and Mexican troops failed to rout the powerful shaman from his territory straddling Arizona and Mexico, General Miles sent his officer Lieutenant Gatewood and relatives of Geronimo's renegade band of warriors to persuade Geronimo to parley with Miles near the mouth of Skeleton Canyon, at the edge of the Peloncillo Mountains. After several days of talks, Geronimo and his warriors agreed to the presented treaty and surrendered their arms.

Geronimo related the scene years later: "We stood between his troopers and my warriors. We placed a large stone on the blanket before us. Our treaty was made by this stone, as it was to last until the stone should crumble to dust; so we made the treaty, and bound each other with an oath." However, the political promises quickly unraveled, and the most feared of Apache medicine men spent the next 23 years in exile as a prisoner of war. He died on February 17, 1909, never having returned to his beloved homeland, and was buried in the Apache cemetery in Fort Sill, Oklahoma.

In 1934 a stone monument was built on State Route 80 in Apache, Arizona, as a reminder of Geronimo's surrender in 1886. The 16-foot-tall monument lies 10 mi northwest of the actual surrender site in Skeleton Canyon, where an unobtrusive sign and a pile of rocks mark the place where the last stone was cast.

property set among sycamores and rolling hills. Tours and tastings are available by appointment only; at this writing, the owners were preparing to open a tasting room in downtown Willcox.

WHERE TO STAY

Lodging is a bit of a challenge in this remote area. For those preferring to sleep indoors, the closest accommodations are about a half-hour drive, either north to one of several modern chain hotels in Willcox or to a B&B south of the monument. Within the monument there are 22 first-come, first-served campsites at Bonita Canyon Campground ($12). Some of the most beautiful and untouched camping areas in Arizona are nearby, in the Chiricahua Mountains. Backcountry campsites in the Cave Creek area, part of the Coronado National Forest (☎ 520/364–3468 ⊕ www.fs.fed.us/r3/coronado), have toilets but no water.

$ ☷ **Dreamcatcher Bed and Breakfast.** All five rooms of this U-shape hacienda have Jacuzzi tubs, large walk-in showers, ceiling fans, and private entrances that open onto a flower-filled courtyard. A cooked-to-order breakfast is included, and a lavish, five-course dinner with wine is

Remote Chiricahua National Monument is filled with dramatic "upside-down" or "standing-up" volcanic rock formations.

prepared upon request for an extra $35. Affable hosts John and Julia, fluent in French and German, advise guests on hiking and birding activities at the Monument, 12 mi north; you'll see plenty of wildlife—from deer to Mexican blue jays—roaming their lush 27-acre property. **Pros:** excellent value; tranquil; convenient to Chiricahuas. **Cons:** hosts take vacation in late spring—be sure to call ahead. ✉ *13097 S. Hwy 181, Pearce* ☎ *520/824–3127* 🌐 *www.dreamcatcherbnb.com* *5 rooms* *In-room: refrigerator (some), no TV (some), Wi-Fi. In-hotel: some pets allowed* *No credit cards* *BP.*

8

$ **Portal Peak Lodge.** This barracks-style structure just east of Chiricahua National Monument near the New Mexico border is notable less for its rooms (clean and pleasant but nondescript) than for its winged visitors: the elegant trogon, 14 types of hummingbird, and 10 species of owl are among the 330 varieties of birds that flock to nearby Cave Creek canyon. The café serves breakfast, lunch, and dinner, and will make sack lunches on request. **Pros:** cheap; decks outside each room; on-site restaurant and store. **Cons:** basic lodging; isolated setting on east side of Chiricahuas. ✉ *1215 Main St.* *Box 364, Portal 85632* ☎ *520/558–2223* 🌐 *www.portalpeaklodge.com* *16 rooms* *In-room: a/c, no phone, Wi-Fi. In-hotel: restaurant* *AE, D, MC, V.*

$$$–$$$$ **Sunglow Guest Ranch.** Named after the ghost town of Sunglow, this lodge consists of nine casitas decked out in Southwestern style with fireplaces. Breakfast and dinner are served in a cozy dining room with a wraparound porch, and lunches can be packed for you (for an extra fee). You can borrow mountain bikes or take a horseback ride (extra fee) to explore the trails in Coronado National Forest, which borders the property on three sides. Birding and hiking are popular, and "star

parties" attract astronomers, as this remote region offers some of the blackest skies around and perfect conditions for stargazing. **Pros:** very isolated; good for retreats. **Cons:** very isolated; it's a 30-minute drive to hike in the Chiricahuas. ⊠ *14066 S. Sunglow Rd., Pearce* ☎ *520/824–3334 or 866/786–4569* ⊕ *www.sunglowranch.com* ⇆ *4 1-room casitas, 4 2-room casitas, 1 2-bedroom casita* ♿ *In-room: no phone, refrigerator, a/c (some), no TV. In-hotel: restaurant, bicycles, Wi-Fi hotspot, some pets allowed* ⊟ *AE, D, MC, V* ⊠ *MAP*

FORT BOWIE NATIONAL HISTORICAL SITE

8 mi northwest of Chiricahua National Monument.

GETTING HERE AND AROUND

Take AZ 186 west from Chiricahua National Monument; 5 mi north of junction with AZ 181, signs direct you to an unpaved road leading to the fort. Upon entering the site, you'll drive down a winding gravel road to a parking lot, where a challenging trail leads 1.5 mi to the historic site.

EXPLORING

It's a bit of an outing to **Fort Bowie National Historical Site**, the site of Arizona's last battle between Native Americans and U.S. troops in the Dos Cabezas (Two-Headed) Mountains, but history buffs will find it an interesting diversion with the added benefit of high-desert scenic beauty. Once a focal point for military operations—the fort was built here because Apache Pass was an important travel route for Native Americans and wagon trains—it now serves as a reminder of the brutal clashes between the two cultures. The fort itself is virtually in ruins, but there's a small ranger-staffed visitor center with historical displays, restrooms, and books for sale.

Points of interest along the trail, indicated by historic markers, include the remnants of an Apache wickiup (hut), the fort cemetery, Apache Springs (their water source), and the **Butterfield stage stop,** a crucial link in the journey from east to west in the mid-19th century that happened to be in the heart of Chiricahua Apache land. Chief Cochise and the stagecoach operators ignored one another until sometime in 1861, when hostilities broke out between U.S. Cavalry troops and the Apache. After an ambush by the chief's warriors at Apache Pass in 1862, U.S. troops decided a fort was needed in the area, and Fort Bowie was built within weeks. There were skirmishes for the next 10 years, followed by a peaceful decade. Renewed fighting broke out in 1881. Geronimo, the new leader of the Indian warriors, finally surrendered in 1886. ⊠ *3203 S. Old Fort Bowie Rd., Apache Pass Rd., 26 mi southeast of Willcox* ☎ *520/847–2500* ⊕ *www.nps.gov/fobo* ⊠ *Free* ☉ *Daily 8–4:30.*

WILLCOX

26 mi northwest of Fort Bowie National Historical Site on AZ 186.

The small town of Willcox, in the heart of Arizona ranching country, began in the late 1870s as a railroad construction camp called Maley. When the Southern Pacific Railroad line arrived in 1880, the town was renamed in honor of the highly regarded Fort Bowie commander, General Orlando B. Willcox. Once a major shipping center for cattle ranchers and mining companies, the town has preserved its rustic charm; the downtown area looks like an Old West movie set. An elevation of 4,167 feet means moderate summers and chilly winters, ideal for growing apples, and apple pie fans from as far away as Phoenix make pilgrimages to sample the harvest. The climate also seems favorable for growing grapes, and Willcox has sprouted a few vineyards and tasting rooms in the last couple of years.

GETTING HERE AND AROUND

The small, historic downtown area of Willcox is just a few blocks north of Interstate 10 from Exit 336. Turn right on Maley Street and then left onto Railroad Avenue for an authentic glimpse of southern Arizona circa 1912, including mercantile stores, banks, and the railroad depot.

EXPLORING

Pick your own apples just outside town at **Apple Annie's Orchards** (✉ *2081 W. Hardy Rd.* ☎ *520/384–2084* ⊕ *www.appleannies.com*) from August to October. Peaches are ready July through September; veggies ripen in late summer and fall.

Learn about the fierce Chiricahua Apaches and the fearless leaders Cochise and Geronimo at the **Chiricahua Regional Museum and Research Center**, located in downtown Willcox. Other interesting tidbits about the area can be found in displays featuring the U.S. Cavalry, a nice collection of rocks and minerals, and relics of the famed Butterfield Overland Stage Route. One oddity the museum points out is that the memoirs of Civil War general Orlando Willcox, for whom the town was named, don't even mention a visit to Arizona. ✉ *127 E. Maley St.* ☎ *520/384–3971* 🏷 *$2* ☽ *Mon.–Sat. 10–4.*

Outside Willcox is the headquarters for the **Muleshoe Ranch Cooperative Management Area,** nearly 50,000 acres of riparian desert land in the foothills of the Galiuro Mountains that are jointly owned and managed by the Nature Conservancy, the U.S. Forest Service, and the U.S. Bureau of Land Management. It's a 30-mi drive on a dirt road to the ranch—it takes about an hour—but the scenery, wildlife, and hiking are worth the bumps. The varied terrain of mesquite bosks, desert grasslands, and rocky canyons is home to a diverse array of wildlife, including desert tortoise, javelina, mule deer, hognose skunk, Montezuma quail, and great horned owl. You might also catch a glimpse of roaming bands of coatimundi—unusual looking omnivores resembling land-bound monkeys. Backcountry hiking and mountain-biking trips can be arranged by the ranch, and overnight accommodations are available *(see below).* Guided 1-mi nature hikes are held on Saturday at 8 AM from February through April. To reach the ranch, take Exit 340 off Interstate 10, turn right on Bisbee Avenue, and continue to Airport Road, turn right again, and after 15 mi take the right fork at a junction just past a group of mailboxes and continue to the end of the road. ✉ *6502 N. Muleshoe Ranch Rd.* ☎ *520/212–4295* ⊕ *www.nature.org* ☽ *June–Aug., weekends 8–5; Sept.–May, Thurs.–Mon. 8–5.*

8

The **Rex Allen Arizona Cowboy Museum**, in Willcox's historic district, is a tribute to Willcox's most famous native son, cowboy singer Rex Allen. He starred in several rather average cowboy movies during the 1940s and '50s for Republic Pictures, but he's probably most famous as the friendly voice that narrated Walt Disney nature films of the 1960s. Check out the glittery suits the star wore on tour—they'd do Liberace proud. A special family rate is $5. ⊠ *150 N. Railroad Ave.* ☎ *520/384–4583 or 877/234–4111* ⊕ *www.rexallenmuseum.org* ☜ *$2* ⊙ *Daily 10–4.*

Don't miss the mile-high apple pies and hand-pressed cider at **Stout's Cider Mill** (⊠ *1510 N. Circle I Rd.* ☎ *520/384–3696*).

The **Willcox Commercial Store** (⊠ *180 N. Railroad Ave.* ☎ *520/384–2448*), near the Rex Allen Cowboy Museum, was established in 1881 and is the oldest retail establishment in Arizona. Locals like to say that Geronimo used to shop here. Today it's a clothing and general store, with a large selection of Western wear.

If you visit in winter, you can see some of the more than 10,000 sandhill cranes that roost at the **Willcox Playa**, a 37,000-acre area resembling a dry lake bed 12 mi south of Willcox. They migrate in late fall and head north to nesting sites in February, and bird-watchers migrate to Willcox the third week in January for the annual Wings over Willcox bird-watching event held in their honor.

WHERE TO EAT AND STAY

✗ **Salsa Fiesta Mexican Restaurant.** You can't miss the bright neon lights of

MEXICAN   this little restaurant, just south of Interstate 10 at Exit 340 in Willcox. The interior is cheerful and clean, with tables, chairs, and walls painted in a spicy medley of hot pink, purple, turquoise, green, and orange. The menu consists of Mexican standards, and the salsa bar runs the gamut from mild to superhot. There is a modest selection of domestic and Mexican beers, and takeout is available. ⊠ *1201 W. Rex Allen Dr.* ☎ *520/384–4233* ▭ *AE, D, MC, V* ⊙ *Closed Tues.*

$–$$ ⬚ **Muleshoe Ranch.** This turn-of-the-20th-century ranch is run by the Arizona chapter of the Nature Conservancy. Five casitas with kitchens sit in the pristine grassland foothills of the Galiuro Mountains, four around a courtyard hacienda-style. The fifth, a stone cabin set off by itself for more privacy, is the only unit open to families with children. The ranch has a visitor center, 22 mi of hiking trails, a guided, 0.75-mi nature walk on Saturday at 9 AM, and private natural hot springs. There's a two-night minimum stay. **Pros:** good hiking; good value for groups; hot springs. **Cons:** no services nearby; closest town is Willcox (30 mi away). ⊠ *6502 N. Muleshoe Ranch Rd.* ☎ *520/212–4295* ⊕ *www.nature.org* ⬚ *5 units* ⬚ *In-room: no a/c (some), no phone, kitchen, no TV* ▭ *AE, D, MC, V* ⊙ *Closed June–Aug.*

TEXAS CANYON

Fodor's Choice ★ *16 mi southwest of Willcox off I–10.*

A dramatic change of scenery along Interstate 10 will signal that you're entering Texas Canyon. The rock formations here are exceptional—huge boulders appear to be delicately balanced against each other.

GETTING HERE AND AROUND

Get off Interstate 10 at Exit 318, and then turn right onto Dragoon Road. The Amerind Foundation is a mile down on the left, and Triangle T Guest Ranch, with lodging and a restaurant, is next door.

EXPLORING

Texas Canyon is the home of the **Amerind Foundation** (a contraction of "American" and "Indian"), founded by amateur archaeologist William Fulton in 1937 to foster understanding about Native American cultures. The research facility and museum are housed in a Spanish colonial–style structure designed by noted Tucson architect H.M. Starkweather. The museum's rotating displays of archaeological materials, crafts, and photographs give an overview of Native American cultures of the Southwest and Mexico. The adjacent Fulton–Hayden Memorial Art Gallery displays an assortment of art collected by William Fulton. Permanent exhibits include the work of Tohono O'odham women potters, an exquisite collection of Hopi kachina dolls, prized paintings by acclaimed Hopi artists, Pueblo pottery ranging from prehistoric pieces to modern ceramics, and archaeological exhibits on the Indian cultures of the prehistoric Southwest. The museum's gift shop has a superlative selection of Native American art, crafts, and jewelry. ✉ *2100 N. Amerind Rd., 1 mi southeast of I–10, Exit 318, Dragoon* ☎ *520/586–3666* ⊕ *www.amerind.org* ⊒ *$5* ⊙ *Tues.–Sun. 10–4.*

WHERE TO STAY

$$$ ★ ⊞ **Grapevine Canyon Ranch.** Nestled deep in the Dragoon Mountains' Grapevine Canyon, this historic cattle ranch spurs the imagination with hair-raising tales of marauding Apache Indians and pioneering homesteaders. This natural stronghold once used by Chiricahua Indians led by Geronimo and Cochise is tamer these days, but the striking high-desert terrain and scattered *cienegas* (marshes) still provide enticing opportunities for adventurous exploration. Grapevine is a working cattle ranch, where visitors get the chance to watch—and, in many cases, participate in—day-to-day cowboy activities. Rooms are decorated in a mix of country and Southwestern-style furnishings—and all have spacious decks and porches. Rates include riding, meals, and all activities. **Pros:** authentic dude ranch with outstanding riding. **Cons:** expensive; way out yonder; three-night minimum. ✉ *Highland Rd.* ✉ *Box 302, Pearce 85625* ☎ *520/826–3185 or 800/245–9202* ⊕ *www.gcranch.com* ➵ *12 rooms* ⟐ *In-room: no phone, refrigerator, no TV, Wi-Fi. In-hotel: pool, no kids under 12* ⊟ *D, MC, V* ⟐⟐ *FAP.*

$$–$$$ ⊞ **Triangle T Guest Ranch.** Enjoy the romance of the Old West at this historic ranch situated on 160 acres of prime real estate in Texas Canyon. Although the cozy casitas offer Western charm, the big draw to this rustic ranch is the immediate access to the startling and stunning rock formations found in the canyon. Campsites with full hookups are

8

available for $30. **Pros:** horseback riding (extra fee) and hiking trails; good base for exploring the region. **Cons:** expensive for this area; isolated. ☒ *Dragoon Rd. at Exit 318 off I–10* ☏ *Box 218, Dragoon 85609* ☎ *520/586–7533* ⊕ *www.triangletguestranch.com* ⌁ *11 casitas* ♿ *In-room: no phone, kitchen (some), no TV, Wi-Fi. In-hotel: restaurant, bar, pool, some pets allowed* ▭ MC, V.

BENSON

12 mi west of Texas Canyon, 50 mi southeast of Tucson via I–10.

Back in its historic heyday as a Butterfield stagecoach station, and later as the hub of the Southern Pacific Railroad, Benson was just a place to stop on the way to somewhere else. Not much has changed, except that a few more visitors come through, with the 1974 discovery of a pristine cave beneath the Whetstone Mountains west of Benson, culminating 25 years later with the opening of Kartchner Caverns State Park, one of the most remarkable living cave systems in the world.

GETTING HERE AND AROUND

Amtrak runs trains from Tucson east to the Benson depot three times a week. The Benson Visitor Center is inside the train depot on 4th Street, the main drag through this sleepy town. Benson Taxi offers transport services in the Benson area, as well as to Tombstone, Bisbee, and Kartchner Caverns.

ESSENTIALS

Transportation Contacts Benson Taxi (☒ *Benson* ☎ *520/586–1294*). **Benson train station** (☒ *4th St. at San Pedro Ave., Benson*).

EXPLORING

Though the city is undergoing some modern development, you can see the story of Benson's past at the little **San Pedro Valley Arts and Historical Society Museum** (☒ *180 S. San Pedro Ave. at E. 5th St.* ☎ *520/586–3070*), a free museum open Tuesday through Saturday (but closed in August). Exhibits include a re-creation of an old-fashioned grocery store and railroad paraphernalia.

As you pass Benson on Interstate 10, watch for Ocotillo Avenue, Exit 304. Take a left and drive about 2.25 mi, where a mailbox with a backward SW signals that you've come to the turnoff for **Singing Wind Bookshop**. Make a right at the mailbox and drive 0.25 mi until you see a green gate. Let yourself in, close the gate, and go another 0.25 mi to the shop. If you don't see Winifred Bundy, who also runs the ranch, ring the gong out front. She knows just about every regional author around, so this unique bookshop-on-a-ranch has signed copies of books on almost any Southwestern topic. This chatty bibliophile also frequently shares her love of the area with visitors, throwing in choice tidbits about obscure sights and her literary friends' favorite haunts. She doesn't take credit cards, though. ☒ *700 W. Singing Wind Rd.* ☎ *520/586–2425* ☉ *Daily 9–5.*

WHERE TO EAT AND STAY

$ ✕ **Palatiano's.** The kitchen at this family-friendly roadhouse, a local
AMERICAN   favorite, turns out traditional diner fare—including great burgers and
fries—as well as pasta, Italian-style entrées, and Greek specialties like
moussaka and spanikopita. In the center of the no-frills dining room
there's a big salad bar, too—unusual in these parts. ✉ *601 W. 4th St.*
☎ *520/586–3523* ▤ *AE, MC, V* ✆ *No dinner Sun.*

–$ ✕ **Reb's Café.** For a more traditional take on Southwestern food—none
AMERICAN   of that newfangled nouvelle stuff—this unpretentious diner is of the
cowboy variety. It serves Mexican food and a little Italian, but it really
prides itself on steaks and hamburgers, and a darned good breakfast
(served all day). ✉ *1020 W. 4th St.* ☎ *520/586–3856* ▤ *MC, V.*

$–$$ 🏨 **Desert Rose Inn.** The closest lodging to Kartchner Caverns State Park,
this modern motel sits just off Interstate 10 at the "Kartchner Corridor," a few miles west of Benson. It has the comfort and amenities
you'd expect, but with a Southwestern elegance rarely found in properties around the area. Rooms have coffeemakers and hair dryers, and
a Continental breakfast with a few hot items is included. **Pros:** clean;
friendly; convenient location. **Cons:** just off the highway; not particularly serene or scenic. ✉ *630 S. Village Loop* ✉ *Box 2252, Benson
85602* ☎ *520/586–8800 or 888/263–2283* ⊕ *www.desertroseinnaz.com*
⏎ *62 rooms* ⚬ *In-room: a/c, refrigerator, Wi-Fi. In-hotel: pool, gym,
laundry facilities* ▤ *AE, D, DC, MC, V* ⑩ *CP.*

KARTCHNER CAVERNS STATE PARK

9 mi south of Benson on AZ 90.

GETTING HERE AND AROUND

Amateur cavers discovered Kartchner Caverns in 1974. From Exit 302
off Interstate 10, take AZ 90 for 9 mi.

EXPLORING

↻   The publicity that surrounded the official opening of **Kartchner Caverns**
Fodor'sChoice   in November 1999 was in marked contrast to the secrecy that shrouded
★   their discovery 25 years earlier and concealed their existence for 14
years. The two young spelunkers, Gary Tenen and Randy Tufts, who
stumbled into what is now considered one of the most spectacular
cave systems anywhere, played a fundamental role in its protection and
eventual development. Great precautions have been taken to protect
the wet-cave system—which comprises 13,000 feet of passages and
two chambers as long as football fields—from damage by light and
dryness.

The Discovery Center introduces visitors to the cave and its formations, and hour-long guided tours take small groups into the upper
cave. Spectacular formations include the longest soda straw stalactite
in the United States at 21 feet and 2 inches. The Big Room is viewed
on a separate tour: it holds the world's most extensive formation of
brushite moonmilk, the first reported occurrence of turnip shields, and
the first noted occurrence of birdsnest needle formations. Other funky
and fabulous formations include brilliant red flowstone, rippling multihued stalactites, delicate white helictites, translucent orange bacon,

and expansive mud flats. It's also the nursery roost for female cave myotis bats from April through September, during which time the lower cave is closed in an effort to foster the cave's unique ecosystem. Kartchner Caverns is a wet, "live" cave, meaning that water still rises up from the surface to increase the multicolor calcium carbonate formations already visible.

The total cavern size is 2.4 mi long, but the explored areas cover only 1,600 feet by 1,100 feet. The average relative humidity inside is 99%, so visitors are often graced with "cave kisses," water droplets from above. Because the climate outside the caves is so dry, it is estimated that if air got inside, it could deplete the moisture in only a few days, halting the growth of the speleothems that decorate its walls. To prevent this, there are 22 environmental monitoring stations that measure air and soil temperature, relative humidity, evaporation rates, air trace gases, and airflow inside the caverns. ■TIP➜ Tour reservations are required, and should be made several months in advance. If you're here and didn't make a reservation, you may be in luck: sometimes same-day reservations are available (call or arrive early for a shot at these). Hiking trails, picnic areas, and campsites are available on the park's 550 acres. ⊠ *AZ 90, 9 mi south of Exit 302 off I–10* ☎ *520/586–4100 information, 520/586–2283 tour reservations* ⊕ *www.pr.state.az.us* ✉ *$6 per vehicle up to 7 people, $2 each additional person; Rotunda/Throne Room tours $18.95, Big Room tours $22.95* ☉ *Daily 7:30–6; cave tours, by reservation, daily 8–4.*

SOUTHWEST ARIZONA

The turbulent history of the West is writ large in this now-sleepy part of Arizona. It's home to the Tohono O'odham Indian Reservation (the largest in the country after the Navajo Nation's) and towns such as Ajo, created—and almost undone—by the copper-mining industry, and Nogales, along the U.S.–Mexico border. Yuma, abutting the California border, was a major crossing point of the Colorado River as far back as the time of the conquistadors.

These days people mostly travel *through* Sells, Ajo, and Yuma en route to the closest beaches: during the school year, especially on warm weekends and semester breaks, the 130-mi route from Tucson to Ajo is busy with traffic headed southwest to Puerto Penasco (Rocky Point), Mexico, the closest access to the sea for Arizonans. All summer long, Interstate 8 takes heat-weary Tucsonans and Phoenicians to San Diego, California, and Yuma is the midpoint.

Natural attractions are a lure in this starkly scenic region: Organ Pipe Cactus National Monument provides trails for desert hikers, and Buenos Aires and Imperial wildlife refuges—homes to many unusual

8

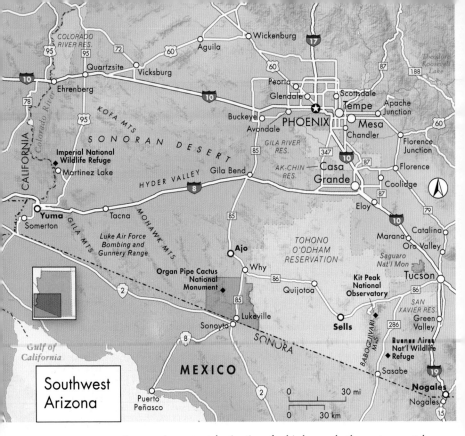

species—are important destinations for birders and other nature-watchers. Much of the time, however, your only companions will be the low-lying scrub and cactus and the mesquite, ironwood, and paloverde trees.

BUENOS AIRES NATIONAL WILDLIFE REFUGE

66 mi southwest of Tucson.

GETTING HERE AND AROUND
From Tucson, take AZ 86 west 22 mi to AZ 286; go south 40 mi to Milepost 8, and it's another 3 mi east to the preserve headquarters.

EXPLORING
Remote **Buenos Aires National Wildlife Refuge**, in the Altar Valley and encircled by seven mountain ranges, is the only place in the United States where the Sonoran–savanna grasslands that once spread over the entire region can still be seen. The fragile ecosystem was almost completely destroyed by overgrazing, and a program to restore native grasses is currently in progress. In 1985 the U.S. Fish and Wildlife Service purchased the Buenos Aires Ranch—now headquarters for the 115,000-acre preserve—to establish a reintroduction program for the endangered masked bobwhite quail. Bird-watchers consider Buenos

BORDER TOWN SAFETY: NOGALES, MEXICO

Nogales used to draw tourists and locals, who would park on the American side and walk across the border. Though shopping bargains and cheap bars are enticing, safety issues have changed in recent years.

⚠ **Drug-related violence in Mexico—especially near the U.S. border—has increased to the point that the U.S. government strongly discourages travel in and around Mexico border towns.**

Check ⊕ *www.state.gov/travel* for updates and details.

If you must cross, bring your passport, remain alert, and stay in the central area on Avenida Obregón, which begins a few blocks west of the border entrance and runs north–south.

Aires unique because it's the only place in the United States where they can see a "grand slam" (four species) of quail: Montezuma quail, Gambel's quail, scaled quail, and masked bobwhite. If it rains, the 100-acre Aguirre Lake, 1.5 mi north of the headquarters, attracts wading birds, shorebirds, and waterfowl—in all, more than 320 avian species have been spotted here. They share the turf with deer, antelope, coatimundi, badgers, bobcats, and mountain lions. Touring options include a 10-mi auto tour through the area, nature trails, a boardwalk through the marshes at Arivaca Cienega, and, by reservation only, guided tours on Saturday from December through March. ⊠ *AZ 286, Box 109, Sasabe* ☎ *520/823–4251* ⊕ *www.fws.gov/refuges* ☒ *Free* ☉ *Refuge headquarters and visitor center daily 7:30–4.*

WHERE TO STAY

$$$$ ⊡ **Rancho de la Osa.** This ranch, set on 250 eucalyptus-shaded acres near the Mexican border and Buenos Aires preserve, was built in 1889, and two adobe structures were added in the 1920s to accommodate guests. The rooms have modern plumbing and fixtures, wood-burning fireplaces, and porches with Adirondack chairs. Bread baked on the premises, salads made with ingredients grown in the garden, and water drawn from the well all contribute to the back-to-basics serenity. Rates include all meals and horseback riding, and guests are expected to dress for dinner. **Pros:** good riding; good food; tranquil. **Cons:** expensive; very isolated for those interested in touring the region. ⊠ *AZ 286* ☞ *Box 1, Sasabe 85633* ☎ *520/823–4257 or 800/872–6240* ⊕ *www.ranchodelaosa.com* ⟳ *18 rooms* ☖ *In-room: no TV. In-hotel: restaurant, bar, pool, bicycles, Wi-Fi hotspot, no kids under 6* ▭ *MC, V* ▯⊙▯ *FAP.*

KITT PEAK NATIONAL OBSERVATORY

70 mi northwest of Buenos Aires National Wildlife Refuge on AZ 286 to AZ 86; 56 mi southwest of Tucson.

GETTING HERE AND AROUND

To reach Kitt Peak from Tucson, take Interstate 10 to Interstate19 south, and then AZ 86. After 44 mi on AZ 86, turn left at AZ 386 junction and follow the winding mountain road 12 mi up to the observatory. In inclement weather, contact the highway department to confirm that the road is open. To get to Sells (for the nearest food and gas), from the base of the mountain it's 20 mi west on AZ 86.

EXPLORING

Funded by the National Science Foundation and managed by a group of more than 20 universities, **Kitt Peak National Observatory** is part of the Tohono O'odham Reservation. After much discussion back in the late 1950s, tribal leaders agreed to share a small section of their 4,400 square mi with the observatory's telescopes. Among these is the McMath, the world's largest solar telescope, which uses piped-in liquid coolant. From the visitors' gallery you can see into the telescope's light-path tunnel, which goes down hundreds of feet into the mountain. Kitt Peak scientists use these high-power telescopes to conduct vital solar research and observe distant galaxies.

The visitor center has exhibits on astronomy, information about the telescopes, and hour-long guided tours ($7.75 per person) that depart daily at 10, 11:30, and 1:30. Complimentary brochures enable you to take self-guided tours of the grounds, and there's a picnic area about 1.5 mi below the observatory. The observatory sells snacks and drinks, but there are no restaurants or gas stations within 20 mi of Kitt Peak. The observatory offers a nightly observing program ($48 per person) except from July 15 to September 1; reservations are necessary. ⊠ *AZ 386, Pan Tak* ☎ *520/318–8726, 520/318–7200 recorded message* ⊕ *www.noao. edu* ☞ *Free* ☉ *Visitor center daily 9–4.*

SELLS

32 mi southwest of Kitt Peak via AZ 386 to AZ 86.

The Tohono O'odham Reservation, the second-largest in the United States, covers 4,400 square mi between Tucson and Ajo, stretching south to the Mexican border and north almost to the city of Casa Grande. To the south of Kitt Peak, the 7,730-foot Baboquivari Peak is considered sacred by the Tohono O'odham as the home of their deity, I'itoi ("elder brother"). Less than halfway between Tucson and Ajo, Sells—the tribal capital of the Tohono O'odham—is a good place to stop for gas or a soft drink. Much of the time there's little to see or do in Sells, but in winter an annual rodeo and fair attract thousands of Native American visitors.

Kitt Peak National Observatory is open to visitors during the day, but it's easy to enjoy the night sky here.

GETTING HERE AND AROUND
If you're traveling east or west along AZ 86, take the exit for the Sells Hospital to explore this tiny town, which consists of a few stores, offices, and a school. The Papago Café sits at the highway exit. To get into town, drive south past the hospital, and go over the bridge.

EXPLORING
For traditional Indian and Mexican food like fry bread, tacos, and chili, try the **Papago Cafe** (⌧ *AZ 86, near Chevron Station* ☎ *520/383–3510*). At the Sells Shopping Center, the good-size market **Basha's Deli & Bakery** (⌧ *Topawa Rd.* ☎ *520/383–2546*) can supply all the makings for a picnic.

AJO

90 mi northwest of Sells on AZ 86.

"Ajo" (pronounced *ah*-ho) is Spanish for garlic, and some say the town got its name from the wild garlic that grows in the area. Others claim the word is a bastardization of the Indian word *au-auho,* referring to red paint derived from a local pigment.

For many years Ajo, like Bisbee, was a thriving Phelps Dodge Company town. Copper mining had been attempted in the area in the late 19th century, but it wasn't until the 1911 arrival of the Calumet & Arizona Mining Company that the region began to be developed profitably. Calumet and Phelps Dodge merged in 1935, and the huge pit mine produced millions of tons of copper until it closed in 1985. Nowadays Ajo is pretty sleepy; the town's population of 4,000 has a median age of 51, and most visitors are on their way to or from Rocky Point, Mexico.

At the center of town is a sparkling white Spanish-style plaza. The shops and restaurants that line the plaza's covered arcade today are rather modest. Unlike Bisbee, Ajo hasn't yet drawn an artistic crowd—or the upscale boutiques and eateries that tend to follow. Chain stores and fast-food haven't made a beeline here either—you'll find only one Dairy Queen and a Pizza Hut in this remote desert hamlet.

GETTING HERE AND AROUND

As you drive into Ajo on AZ 85, you'll see the small historical plaza, with a few shops, a pharmacy, and a library, immediately on your right. After jogging west for several blocks and changing its name three times, the highway turns north again, becoming 2nd Avenue and takes you out of town, past the Cabeza Prieta Wildlife Refuge and north to Gila Bend.

EXPLORING

The **Ajo Historical Society Museum** has collected a mélange of articles related to Ajo's past from local townspeople. The displays are rather disorganized, but the historical photographs and artifacts are interesting, and the museum is inside the territorial-style St. Catherine's Indian Mission, built around 1942. ⊠ *160 Mission St.* ☎ *520/387–7105* 🖼 *Donations requested* ☉ *Oct.–Apr., daily noon–4.*

The 860,000-acre **Cabeza Prieta National Wildlife Refuge**, about 10 minutes from Ajo, was established in 1939 as a preserve for endangered bighorn sheep and other Sonoran Desert wildlife. A free permit, essentially a "hold-harmless" agreement, is required to enter, and only those with four-wheel-drive or high-clearance vehicles, needed to traverse the rugged terrain, can obtain one from the refuge's visitor center. ⊠ *1611 N. 2nd Ave.,* ☎ *520/387–6483* ⊕ *www.fws.gov/refuges* 🖼 *Free* ☉ *Visitor center weekdays 7:30–4:30, refuge daily dawn–dusk.*

You get an expansive view of Ajo's ugly gash of an open-pit mine, almost 2 mi wide, from the **New Cornelia Open Pit Mine Lookout Point.** Some of the abandoned equipment remains in the pit, and mining operations are diagrammed at the volunteer-run visitors' shelter, where there's a 30-minute film about mining. The mine is about a mile southwest of the plaza; take La Mina Road or Estrella Road to Indian Village Road. ⊠ *Indian Village Rd.* ☎ *520/387–7742* 🖼 *Free* ☉ *Call for hrs.*

WHERE TO EAT AND STAY

$ ✕ **Ranch House Restaurant.** Carnivores will find plenty of good eatin'—
AMERICAN   like rib eyes, T-bones, pork chops, and the epitome of country-style cooking, chicken-fried steak—at this unassuming roadhouse decorated in (you guessed it) a cowboy theme. The lower-priced lunch menu emphasizes burgers, bratwursts, and sandwiches. Portions are generous, and the service is friendly. ⊠ *661 N. 2nd Ave.* ☎ *520/387–6226* ▤ *MC, V* ☉ *Closed weekends.*

$ 🏨 **Guest House Inn Bed & Breakfast.** Built in 1925 to accommodate visiting Phelps Dodge VIPs, this lodging is a favorite for birders: guests can head out early to nearby Organ Pipe National Monument or just sit on the patio and watch the quail, cactus wrens, and other warblers that fly in to visit. Rooms are furnished in various Southwestern styles, from light Santa Fe to rich Spanish colonial. **Pros:** pleasant hosts; well-preserved home. **Cons:** may be a little sedate for some. ⊠ *700 Guest House Rd.* ☎ *520/387–6133* ⊕ *www.guesthouseinn.biz* ⇆ *4 rooms* ⌂ *In-room: no phone, refrigerator, Wi-Fi* ⊟ *DC, MC, V* ⏏ *BP.*

ORGAN PIPE CACTUS NATIONAL MONUMENT

32 mi southwest of Ajo on AZ 86 to 85.

GETTING HERE

From Ajo, backtrack to Why and take AZ 85 south for 22 mi to reach the visitor center.

SAFETY AND PRECAUTIONS

Be aware that Organ Pipe has become an illegal border crossing hot spot. Migrant workers and drug traffickers cross from Mexico under cover of darkness. At this writing, much of Puerto Blanco Drive has been closed indefinitely to the public. A two-way road that only travels 5 of the 53 mi on Puerto Blanco Drive is open, but the rest of the road will remain closed due to continuing concerns over its proximity to the U.S.–Mexico border. Even so, park officials emphasize that tourists only occasionally have been the victims of isolated property crimes—primarily theft of personal items from parked cars. Visitors are advised by rangers to keep valuables locked and out of plain view and not to initiate contact with groups of strangers whom they may encounter on hiking trails.

EXPLORING

Organ Pipe Cactus National Monument, near Cabeza Prieta National Wildlife Refuge but much more accessible to visitors, is the largest habitat north of the border for organ-pipe cacti. These multiarmed cousins of the saguaro are fairly common in Mexico but rare in the United States. Because they tend to grow on south-facing slopes, you won't be able to see many of them unless you take one of the two scenic loop drives: the 21-mi **Ajo Mountain Drive** or the 53-mi **Puerto Blanco Drive,** both on winding, graded, one-way dirt roads.

A campground at the monument has 208 RV (no hookups) and tent sites. Facilities include a dump station with potable water, flush toilets, grills, and picnic tables. Ranger-led hikes are offered in winter and spring. ⊠ *10 Organ Pipe Dr., Ajo* ☎ *520/387–6849* ⊕ *www.nps.gov/orpi* ⊟ *$8 per vehicle* ⊙ *Visitor center daily 8–5.*

YUMA

232 mi northwest of Organ Pipe Cactus National Monument; 170 mi northwest of Ajo.

Today many people think of Yuma as a convenient stop between Phoenix or Tucson and San Diego—and this was equally true in the relatively recent past. It's difficult to imagine the lower Colorado River, now dammed and bridged, as either a barrier or a means of transportation, but until the early part of the 20th century this section of the great waterway was a force to contend with. Records show that since at least

1540 the Spanish were using Yuma (then the site of a Quechan Indian village) as a ford across a relatively shallow stretch of the Colorado.

Three centuries later, the advent of the shallow-draft steamboat made the settlement a point of entry for fortune seekers heading through the Gulf of California to mining sites in eastern Arizona. Fort Yuma was established in 1850 to guard against Indian attacks, and by 1873 the town was a county seat, a U.S. port of entry, and an army depot.

The steamboat shipping business, undermined by the completion of the Southern Pacific Railroad line in 1877, was finished off by the building of Laguna Dam in 1909. During World War II Yuma Proving Ground was used to train bomber pilots, and General Patton readied some of his desert war forces for battle at classified areas near the city. Many who served here during the war returned to Yuma to retire, and the city's economy now relies largely on tourism. The population swells during the winter months with retirees from cold climates who park their homes on wheels at one of the many RV communities. One fact may explain this: according to National Weather Service statistics, Yuma is the sunniest city in the United States.

GETTING HERE AND AROUND

AZ 8 runs through Yuma, which is approximately halfway between Casa Grande and the California coast. Most of the interesting historic sights are at the north end of town. Stop in at the Yuma Convention and Visitors Bureau and pick up a walking-tour guide to the historic downtown area. The town's largest shopping center, Yuma Palms, sits just to the east side of U.S. 8 (at the 16th Street exit). More than a half dozen modern hotels are a stone's throw from here.

Yuma is accessible by two commercial airlines: America West Express has direct flights to Yuma from Phoenix; Sky West, a United subsidiary, flies nonstop from Los Angeles to Yuma.

Yuma City Cab has the best taxi service in Yuma.

Amtrak trains run three times a week from Tucson west to Yuma.

ESSENTIALS

Visitor Info **Yuma Convention and Visitors Bureau** (⊠ 139 S. 4th Ave. ☎ 928/783–0071 or 800/293–0071 ⊕ www.visityuma.com ⊗ Weekdays 9–5, Sat. 9–4, Sun. noon–4).

Transportation Contacts **America West Express** (☎ 800/235–9292 ⊕ www. americawest.com). **Sky West** (☎ 435/634–3000 ⊕ www.skywest.com). **Yuma City Cab** (⊠ Yuma ☎ 928/782–4444). **Yuma train station** (⊠ 281 Gila St., Yuma). **Yuma International Airport (YUM)** (☎ 928/726–5882 ⊕ www. yumainternationalairport.com).

EXPLORING

Part of Fort Yuma, which is on the California side of the Colorado River and was later used as a school for Native American children, now serves as the small **Fort Yuma Quechan Indian Museum**. Historical photographs, archaeological items, and Quechan arts and crafts are on display. ⊠ CA 24 ☎ 760/572–0661 ☜ $1 ⊗ Daily 8–noon and 1–5.

On the other side of the river from Fort Yuma, the Civil War–period quartermaster depot resupplied army posts to the north and east and served as a distribution point for steamboat freight headed overland to Arizona forts. The 1853 home of riverboat captain G.A. Johnson is the depot's earliest building and the centerpiece of **Quartermaster Depot State Historic Park**. The residence also served as a weather bureau and home for customs agents, among other functions, and the guided tour through the house provides a complete history. Also on display are antique surreys and more "modern" modes of transportation like a 1931 Model A Ford pickup. You can visit a re-creation of the Commanding Officer's Quarters, complete with period furnishings. ⊠ *201 N. 4th Ave., between 1st St. and Colorado River Bridge* ☎ *928/329–0471* ⊕ *www. azstateparks.gov* ⊡ *$3* ☉ *Thurs.–Mon. 9–5.*

The adobe-style **Sanguinetti House Museum,** run by the Arizona Historical Society, was built around 1870 by merchant E.F. Sanguinetti; it exhibits artifacts from Yuma's territorial days and details the military presence in the area. If you're dining at the Garden Café this makes for an interesting stop, but it's not worth a visit on its own, especially if you plan on visiting the more popular Quartermaster Depot State Historic Park. ⊠ *240 S. Madison Ave.* ☎ *928/782–1841* ⊡ *$3* ☉ *Tues.–Sat. 10–4.*

☾ The most notorious tourist sight in town, **Yuma Territorial Prison**, now an Arizona state historic park, was built for the most part by the convicts who were incarcerated here from 1876 until 1909, when the prison outgrew its location. The hilly site on the Colorado River, chosen for security purposes, precluded further expansion.

Visitors gazing today at the tiny cells that held six inmates each, often in 115°F heat, are likely to be appalled, but the prison—dubbed the Country Club of the Colorado by locals—was considered a model of enlightenment by turn-of-the-20th-century standards: in an era when beatings were common, the only punishments meted out here were solitary confinement and assignment to a dark cell. The complex housed a hospital as well as Yuma's only public library, where the 25¢ that visitors paid for a prison tour financed the acquisition of new books.

The 3,069 prisoners who served time at what was then the territory's only prison included men and women from 21 different countries. They came from all social classes and were sent up for everything from armed robbery and murder to polygamy. R.L. McDonald, incarcerated for forgery, had been the superintendent of the Phoenix public school system. Chosen as the prison bookkeeper, he absconded with $130 of the inmates' money when he was released.

The mess hall opened as a museum in 1940, and the entire prison complex was designated a state historic park in 1961. ⊠ *1 Prison Hill Rd., near Exit 1 off I-8* ☎ *928/783–4771* ⊕ *www.azstateparks.gov* ⊡ *$5* ☉ *Daily 9–5.*

You can take a boat ride up the Colorado with **Yuma River Tours** (⊠ *1920 Arizona Ave.* ☎ *928/783–4400* ⊕ *www.yumarivertours.com*). Canoe, kayak, cruise on a stern-wheeler, or book 12- to 45-person jet-boat excursions through Smokey Knowlton, who has been exploring the area for more than 35 years.

8

Crested saguaros at Organ Pipe National Monument are found alongside the monument's namesake cacti and other succulent plants.

WHERE TO EAT

$
MEXICAN

✗ **Chretin's Mexican Food**. A Yuma institution, Chretin's opened as a dance hall in the 1930s, before it became one of the first Mexican restaurants in town in 1946. Don't be put off by the nondescript exterior or the entryway, which leads back past the kitchen and cashier's stand into three large dining areas. The food is all made on the premises, right down to the chips and tortillas. Try anything that features *machaca* (shredded spiced beef or chicken). ⊠ *505 E. 16th St.* ☎ *928/782–1291* ▭ *D, MC, V.*

$
CAFÉ

✗ **The Garden Café**. After a visit to the Sanguinetti House Museum, this adjoining café is a good place to stop for breakfast or lunch. This charming dining spot features lush gardens and aviaries on the outdoor patio, historical photos on the walls, and a menu of homemade salads, soups, and sandwiches. Favorites include the quiche, served with homemade fruit bread, and the tortilla soup. One of the best times to visit is Sunday brunch—complete with carne asada, tortillas, potatoes, scrambled eggs, a layered ham-and-egg strata, breakfast meats, fruit, and dessert. ⊠ *250 S. Madison Ave.* ☎ *928/783–1491* ▭ *AE, MC, V* ⊙ *Closed Mon. No dinner.*

¢
SOUTHWESTERN

✗ **Lutes Casino**. Packed with locals at lunchtime, this large, funky restaurant and bar claims to be the oldest pool hall and domino parlor in Arizona. It's a great place for a burger and a brew. The "Especial" combines a cheeseburger and a hot dog and adds a generous dollop of Lutes's "special sauce." ⊠ *221 S. Main St.* ☎ *928/782–2192* ⊕ *www.lutescasino.com* ▭ *MC, V.*

$$ ✕ **River City Grill.** This hip downtown restaurant is a favorite dining spot
AMERICAN for locals and visitors. It gets a bit loud on weekend nights, but the
★ camaraderie of diners is well worth it. Owners Nan and Tony Bain dish
out a medley of flavors drawing on Mediterranean, Pacific Rim, Indian,
and Caribbean influences. For starters you can sample everything from
Vietnamese spring rolls to curried mussels. Entrées include delicacies
like grilled wild salmon, rack of lamb, and such vegetarian dishes as
ricotta-and-spinach ravioli. ⊠ *600 W. 3rd St.* ☎ *928/782–7988* ⊕ *www.
rivercitygrill.com* ☰ *AE, D, DC, MC, V* ☉ *No lunch weekends.*

WHERE TO STAY

$ ⊞ **Best Western Coronado Motor Hotel.** This Spanish tile–roofed motor
hotel was built in 1938 and has been well cared for. Bob Hope used
to stay here during World War II, when he entertained the gunnery
troops training in Yuma. Yuma Landing Restaurant & Lounge is on-
site with an impressive collection of historical photos. The recently
updated rooms all have pillow-top beds, flat-screen TVs, refrigerators,
and microwaves. **Pros:** convenient to AZ 8, and a short walk from his-
toric downtown area; retro property; full breakfast at restaurant. **Cons:**
some highway noise in rooms. ⊠ *233 S. 4th Ave.* ☎ *928/783–4453 or
800/528–1234* ⊕ *www.bwcoronado.com* ⇗ *86 rooms* ⌂ *In-room: a/c,
refrigerator, DVD, Wi-Fi. In-hotel: restaurant, bar, 2 pools, gym, laun-
dry facilities, some pets allowed* ☰ *AE, D, DC, MC, V* ⦿| *BP.*

$$ ⊞ **Clarion Suites.** One wing of this sprawling hotel surrounds a well-man-
icured courtyard with a fountain; another faces the pool and Cabana
Club, where the complimentary breakfast and happy-hour drinks are
served. This is an all-suites property, and each accommodation has a
separate sitting area with a desk. **Pros:** spacious; quiet. **Cons:** unimpres-
sive location; no restaurant. ⊠ *2600 S. 4th Ave.* ☎ *928/726–4830 or
800/333–3333* ⊕ *www.clarionyuma.com* ⇗ *164 suites* ⌂ *In-room: a/c,
refrigerator. In-hotel: bar, pool, laundry facilities, some pets allowed,
Wi-Fi hotspot* ☰ *AE, D, DC, MC, V* ⦿| *BP.*

$$ ⊞ **Shilo Inn.** The full kitchens offered in the suites make this an excellent
☾ place for families to stay. Rooms are spacious and most have views of
the courtyard and pool. A sauna, steam room, and good-size fitness
center give this property more amenities than most in the area. **Pros:**
convenient to highway and across the street from the Yuma Palms
Shopping Center. **Cons:** higher priced than some newer hotels in the
area. ⊠ *1550 S. Castle Dome Rd.* ☎ *928/782–9511 or 800/222–2244*
⊕ *www.shiloinns.com* ⇗ *120 rooms, 15 suites* ⌂ *In-room: a/c, refrig-
erator, Wi-Fi. In-hotel: pool, gym, some pets allowed* ☰ *AE, D, DC,
MC, V* ⦿| *CP.*

SHOPPING

Art studios, antiques shops, and specialty boutiques have taken advan-
tage of downtown Yuma's face-lift. The retail outlet of the **Bard Date
Company** (⊠ *245 S. Main St.* ☎ *928/341–9966*) is a great place to sample
and purchase all grades of the high-fiber, fat-free fruit, including deli-
cious date shakes. **Colorado River Pottery** (⊠ *67 W. 2nd St.* ☎ *928/343–
0413*) features handcrafted bowls, vases, and dishes. **Prickly Pear** (⊠ *324
S. Main St.* ☎ *928/343–0390*) is packed with an assortment of gourmet

8

sauces, turquoise jewelry, imported dishes, hand-carved furniture, and wall art.

IMPERIAL NATIONAL WILDLIFE REFUGE

30 mi north of Yuma on U.S. 95.

GETTING HERE AND AROUND

From Yuma, take U.S. 95 north and follow the signs to the refuge. It's about a 40-minute drive, and between January and March look for army paratroopers taking practice jumps as you pass the Yuma Proving Ground.

EXPLORING

A guided tour is the best way to visit the 25,765-acre **Imperial National Wildlife Refuge,** created by backwaters formed when the Imperial Dam was built. Something of an anomaly, the refuge is home both to species indigenous to marshy rivers and to creatures that inhabit the adjacent Sonoran Desert—desert tortoises, coyotes, bobcats, and bighorn sheep. Mostly, though, this is a major bird habitat. Thousands of waterfowl and shorebirds live here year-round, and migrating flocks of swallows pass through in spring and fall. During those seasons, expect to see everything from pelicans and cormorants to Canada geese, snowy egrets, and some rarer species. Canoes can be rented at Martinez Lake Marina, 3.5 mi southeast of the refuge headquarters. It's best to visit from mid-October through May, when it's cooler and the ever-present mosquitoes are least active. Kids especially enjoy the 1.3-mi Painted Desert Nature Trail, which winds through the different levels of the Sonoran Desert. From an observation tower at the visitor center you can see the river, as well as the fields being planted with rye and millet, on which the migrating birds like to feed. Call ahead to arrange a guided tour. ⊠ *Martinez Lake Rd., Box 72217, Martinez Lake* ☎ *928/783–3371* ⊕ *refuges.fws.gov* ⊠ *Free* ☉ *Visitor center Apr.–Oct., weekdays 7:30–4; Nov.–Mar., weekdays 7:30–4, weekends 9–4.*

Northwest Arizona and Southeast Nevada

WORD OF MOUTH

"Check out the Hualapai mountains. They're very dry and cool with huge boulders and beautiful vistas and a gorgeous piney scent in the air. Lots of cool old cabins to rent as well. They're approximately 30 minutes' drive from Kingman."

—PDX

WELCOME TO NORTHWEST ARIZONA AND SOUTHEAST NEVADA

TOP REASONS TO GO

★ **Get wet:** Boating, fishing, and water adventure top the list of favorite activities on the cool Colorado River and the adjoining lakes of Havasu, Mohave, and Mead.

★ **Experience a slice of England:** Pass under on a boat or stroll over London Bridge in Lake Havasu City.

★ **Drive the open road:** Take a road trip on legendary Route 66 and cruise the longest remaining stretch of the Mother Road from Seligman to Kingman.

★ **Take a walk on the wild side:** For Vegas-style gambling and glitz spend some quality play time in the twin riverside cities of Laughlin, Nevada, and Bullhead City, Arizona.

★ **Hike Hualapai:** Take a break from the desert and climb the cool climes of Hualapai Mountain Park—the highest point in western Arizona.

Laughlin, Nevada's casinos are just over the Colorado River.

1 Northwest Arizona. Take a drive down memory lane on the longest remaining stretch of historic Route 66—roll down the windows and watch the sweeping desert views pass you by. Along the way, check out the funky little ghost towns of Oatman and Chloride and make a splash in the cool blue waterways of Lakes Mohave, Mead, and Havasu.

2 Southeast Nevada. Laughlin attracts laid-back gamblers and elite entertainers looking for all of the glitz and glamour of Las Vegas without the high prices and large crowds. Take a quick jaunt into Nevada for a look at the monumental Hoover Dam and a hand or two of blackjack in a riverside casino.

Rt. 66 is a classic American route for road trips.

GETTING ORIENTED

In the far northwestern corner of Arizona, the fast-growing communities of Lake Havasu and Laughlin/Bullhead City are good bases for outdoor recreation and gaming, respectively. Kingman, the Mohave County seat and a historic shipping center, is an ideal launch pad for exploring historic and quirky Route 66. The Colorado River flows out of the Grand Canyon to the north and then sweeps directly south, serving as the western border of the state of Arizona and supplying the lifeblood to the otherwise desolate desert region. Created from dams on the mighty Colorado River, Lakes Mead, Mohave, and Havasu provide a common link in the tristate area by offering some of the best water recreation around.

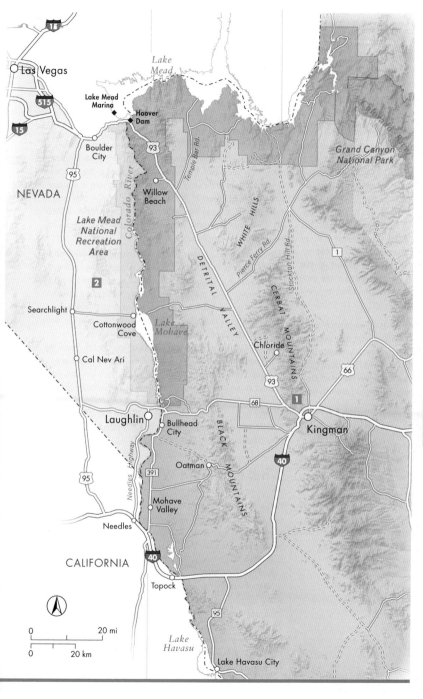

NORTHWEST ARIZONA AND SOUTHEAST NEVADA PLANNER

When to Go

Unlike many destinations, the communities in northwestern Arizona don't have distinct high and low seasons. The arid climate and clear winter skies attract "snowbirds," retirees flocking south to escape the harsh northern climes. On the flip side, the hot, sunny summer months attract sports enthusiasts looking to cavort in the cool, blue waterways—despite searing temperatures topping 120°F.

Lake Havasu City plays host to hordes of college revelers during spring break in March and Kingman fills up fast during the annual Route 66 Fun Run drive in May. Things simmer down a bit during the spring and fall months. Overall, expect fairly busy weekends during the summer months and sold-out rooms during sporting events and fishing tournaments.

Hualapai Mountain Park is the one part of northwestern Arizona that is high-altitude enough to get occasionally heavy snow in winter.

Getting Here and Around

Getting Here: Kingman and Laughlin/Bullhead City have very limited air service. Most visitors drive to this corner of the state—after all, the road to Kingman is the longest remaining stretch of Route 66. At first glance, the countryside can seem a bit stark and remote, but there are many surprises in this part of the world, including the strange-looking Joshua tree, the defining plant of the Mojave Desert. There are no traffic jams and navigation is as easy as travel in a one-stoplight town.

Getting Around: Historic Route 66 crosses east–west and curves north of Interstate 40, which provides the fastest path across the region. U.S. 93 is the main route for north–south travel. All of these roads are in excellent condition. On Interstate 40 high winds occasionally raise enough blowing dust to restrict visibility. In winter, ice may be present on Interstate 40 east of Kingman, as well as on sections of Route 66. When signage warns of ice ahead, heed the warnings and slow down. Most of the county roads are improved dirt roads, but washboard sections bounce you around a bit, so take your time and drive no faster than prudence dictates. ■TIP→ Fuel up while you're in this part of Arizona—all grades of gasoline can be as much as 30¢ to 50¢ per gallon less in Kingman and Bullhead City than in Laughlin, Nevada.

What to Do and Where to Do It

Three of North America's deserts—the Mojave, Sonoran, and Chihuahuan—converge along the sinuous shores of the mighty Colorado River as it winds along Arizona's western border into Mexico. With more than 1,000 mi of shoreline and three large reservoirs—Lake Mead, Lake Mohave, and Lake Havasu—Arizona's west coast offers warm weather and cool waters perfect for a wide array of year-round water sports including boating, kayaking, water-skiing, sailing, scuba diving, and fishing. For the best canoeing and kayaking, head to Topock Gorge on the Colorado River. Lake Havasu has the best swimming beaches and sailing. Fishermen will want to launch a boat on Lake Mead or Lake Mohave. Hualapai Mountain Park has great hiking.

Making the Most of Your Time

Kingman is an ideal base for exploring Lake Mead National Recreation Area, the ghost towns of Oatman and Chloride, and the forested Hualapai Mountain Park. You'll need at least a day to enjoy water sports on Lake Mead, whereas an hour or two is enough to explore the funky little ghost towns. Visitors to Lake Havasu should spend a night or two to get a real sense of this recreation hub, although you can get a quick taste by making a day trip from Kingman or Bullhead City. Water activities dominate the scene here, but in a shorter visit you can check out London Bridge, go on a birding expedition at Havasu National Wildlife Refuge, or a foray into the quaint shops in English Village. If gambling is on your list of things to do, you can just hop across the Colorado River to Laughlin and spend hours or days reveling in the glitz and glitter.

LOCAL FOOD AND LODGING

Mid-priced chain accommodations abound in Kingman and Lake Havasu, and to a lesser extent Bullhead City—though the casino resorts across the river in Laughlin are among the best values in the region. You'll also find a few historic hotels to break up the modern mix. Lake Havasu City has the swankiest resorts in the area, with the glittery but reasonably priced casinos in Laughlin also offering some upscale digs. Staying in a houseboat on Lake Havasu or Lake Mead puts a decidedly different twist on water recreation. Best of all, these floating rooms with a view can be maneuvered into countless coves and inlets, allowing for peaceful solitude rarely found on the busy beaches and popular waterways.

Dining in this remote corner of the state is quite casual, though also affordable. You're more likely to find a 1950s-inspired diner, a taqueria, or a family-owned café than a sophisticated, high-end eatery. For the most part you'll find home-cooked American favorites and "South of the Border" specialties. The best higher-end dining options are in Lake Havasu and across the Colorado River in Laughlin's casinos, where steak houses are particularly prolific.

WHAT IT COSTS

	¢	$	$$	$$$	$$$$
RESTAURANTS	under $8	$8–$12	$13–$20	$21–$30	over $30
HOTELS	under $70	$70–$120	$121–$175	$176–$250	over $250

Restaurant prices are per person for a main course at dinner. Hotel prices are for a standard double in high season, excluding taxes and service charges.

Festivals and Events

May Route 66 Fun Run. This three-day event is a 40-mi drive along the longest remaining section of the "Mother Road." ☎ 928/753–5001 ⊕ www.azrt66.com.

July Solar Egg Fry Contest. In Oatman, this yearly Independence Day celebration takes place at high noon. Accompanying the cook-off are Old West gunfights and other entertainment and food. ☎ 928/768–6222 ⊕ www.oatmangoldroad.org.

Sept. Andy Devine Days. The festival honors the film and television actor with a parade and rodeo. ☎ 928/753–6106 ⊕ www.kingmanrodeo.com.

Oct. London Bridge Days. Lake Havasu City heats up with a weeklong Renaissance festival, a parade, and British-themed contests. ☎ 928/453–3444 ⊕ www.golakehavasu.com.

What Time Is It?

Remember that Arizona, in the mountain time zone, does not observe daylight saving time, but the neighboring states of Nevada and California, both in the Pacific time zone, do. When scheduling interstate travel, double-check all times to avoid confusion and missed connections.

9

GET YOUR KICKS ON ROUTE 66

In 1938 the 2,400 mi of roadway connecting Chicago and Los Angeles was declared "continuously paved." U.S. Route 66 had been transformed from a ragged string of local lanes connecting isolated small towns into an "all-weather" highway that eased travel.

Above: A convertible is perfect for exploring the historic route. Top right: Colorful signs abound on the "Mother Road." Lower right: Gas pumps from the time when Rt. 66 was a major highway.

Just as the road crews changed what had been a string of rutty dirt roads into a paved roadbed, Route 66 changed the social landscape as communities adapted to the new road. The needs of travelers were met by new concepts, such as the gas station, the diner, and the motel. Nostalgic remnants from this retro road-tripping culture still exist along this stretch of the "Mother Road."

Most of old Route 66 has been replaced by the modern interstate system, but at Exit 139 from Interstate 40 you'll find yourself at the beginning of the longest remaining continuous stretch of the original Route 66. This 160-mi journey leads through Seligman, Peach Springs, Truxton, Valentine, Hackberry, Kingman, and Oatman, and on to the Colorado River near Topock.

BEST TIME TO GO

Although Route 66 is accessible year-round, spring and fall are the best times to explore roadside attractions or partake of nearby hikes.

FUN FACT

Route 66 is no longer an officially recognized U.S. highway—it hasn't appeared on maps or atlases since 1984, except for certain sections that have been designated as special historic routes.

BEST WAYS TO EXPLORE

SHOP FOR RETRO COLLECTIBLES IN OATMAN

The mother of all souvenir stops on the Mother Road is Oatman. You can get in the spirit of the Old West with the leather jackets, Western gun holsters, and moccasins offered at the **Leather Shop of Oatman** (⌧ *162 Main St.* ☎ *928/768–3833*). **Main Street Emporium** (⌧ *150 S. Main St.* ☎ *928/788–3298*) offers a wide array of handcrafted items including Western-themed wall art, handwoven blankets, and cholla cactus candles. Browse through a nice selection of Indian jewelry and Southwestern art at the **Ore House** (⌧ *194 Main St.* ☎ *928/768–3839*).

SIGN HERE

One of the joys of exploring Route 66 is admiring the vintage signage along the way. In Seligman, you can stop at **Delga-dillo's Snow Cap Drive-in** (⌧ *301 W Chino Ave., Seligman* ☎ *928/422–3291*) for a "small soda" and to view the old Coca-Cola and Burma Shave signs. In fact, the whole town is rife with old signs and cars. At the **General Store** (⌧ *11255 E Highway 66, Hackberry* ☎ *928/769–2605* ⊕ *hackberrygen-eralstore.com*) you can pose for pictures with vintage cars, kitschy signs, ancient gas pumps, and highway memorabilia while sipping sarsaparilla from a bottle of Route 66 Beer.

COOL OFF IN THE CAVERNS

Nestled among rolling, juniper-covered hills 60 mi east of Kingman, the full extent of **Grand Canyon Caverns** (⌧ *Rte. 66, Mile Marker 115, Peach Springs* ☎ *928/422–3223 or 928/422–4565* ⊕ *www.gccaverns.com* ⌧ *$14.95* ⊙ *Mar.–Oct., daily 8–6; Nov.–Feb., daily 10–4*), a massive dry cave, is still unknown. Daily tours include an elevator descent to the main floor of the caverns, 210 feet belowground. The 0.75-mi walking tour takes 45 minutes. For an additional fee, spelunkers can take the extended, two-hour tour (reservations required). In the rodeo arena behind the basic 48-room motel, restaurant, and curio shop, area cowboys often hold calf-roping competitions that are a hoot to watch, and free to boot.

QUICK BITES

Oatman Hotel (⌧ *181 Main St., Oatman* ☎ *928/768–4408*), an allegedly haunted landmark on Oatman's historic main drag, no longer rents rooms (years ago Carole Lombard and Clark Gable honeymooned here), but it does contain a fun little restaurant that's renowned for its juicy buffalo burgers and addictively filling "burro ears"—house-made potato chips served with tangy salsa.

Westside Lilo's Cafe (⌧ *415 W. Chino Ave., Seligman* ☎ *928/422–5456*),an unassuming roadhouse along Route 66 in Seligman, is a must for exceptionally well-prepared, hearty short-order cooking. The prodigious breakfast burritos, green-chile stew, hefty cheeseburgers, and famously massive cinnamon buns are a hit with regulars and tourists. One famous carrot cake "slice" is equal to three or four slices at most restaurants.

9

Updated by Andrew Collins

Northwestern Arizona and southeastern Nevada comprise a unique blend of deserts, mountains, and 1,000 mi of shoreline. Despite the superficial aridity of much of the landscape, the region bubbles with an abundance of springs and artesian wells. Without these water sources seeping from the rocks and sand, this wide-open region would never have developed into the major crossroads it is today.

The defining feature of the region is the Colorado River. Since the late Pleistocene epoch when Paleo-Indians first set foot in the river that was once described as "too thick to drink and too thin to plow," the Colorado has been a blessing and a barrier. Prehistoric traders from the Pacific Coast crossed the river at Willow Beach on their way to trade shells for pelts with the Hopi Indians and other Pueblo tribes farther east. When gold was discovered in California in 1848, entrepreneurs built ferries up and down the river to accommodate the miners drawn to the area by what Cortez called "a disease of the heart for which the only cure is gold." Prosperity followed, particularly for Kingman.

Every spring the snowmelt of the Rocky Mountain watershed of the Colorado River rushed through high basaltic canyons like water through a garden hose and washed away crops and livestock. Harnessing such a powerful river required no ordinary dam. In 1935, notched into the steep and narrow confines of Black Canyon on the border separating Arizona and Nevada, 726-foot high Hoover Dam took control of the Colorado River and turned its power into electricity and its floodwaters into the largest man-made reservoir in the United States: Lake Mead.

Today, thousands of vehicles travel through northwestern Arizona and southeastern Nevada every day. For many who view the area through the glass of their air-conditioned vehicles, the landscape is a daunting vision of distant mountains shimmering in the heat. But for those who pull over and step into the clean open air, the area offers an enchanting blend of past and present, earth and sky, river and wind.

NORTHWEST ARIZONA

Towns like Kingman hark back to the glory days of the old Route 66, and the ghost towns of Chloride and Oatman bear testament to the mining madness that once reigned in the region. Water-sports fans, or those who just want to laze on a houseboat, enjoy Lake Havasu, where you'll find the misplaced English icon, the London Bridge, and Lake Mead, one of the best fishing spots in the state.

KINGMAN

200 mi northwest of Phoenix, 149 mi west of Flagstaff via I–40.

The highway past Kingman may seem desolate, and the city itself doesn't have a ton of attractions, but the mountains that surround the area offer outdoor activities in abundance, especially along the Colorado River. Water sports play a big part in the area's recreation because about 1,000 mi of freshwater shoreline lie within the county along the Colorado River and around Lakes Havasu, Mohave, and Mead—all of which are within a one-hour drive of this major stopping point for fishing and boating aficionados. And for those interested in the region's mineral wealth, the nearby "ghost" towns of Chloride and Oatman offer a glimpse of the Old West.

GETTING HERE AND AROUND

Most visitors to the region arrive by car, which is by far the best way to explore Kingman and area sites. Additionally, Amtrak's *Southwest Chief* stops daily in Kingman.

ESSENTIALS

Transportation Contacts Kingman Cab (☏ *928/753–1222*). **Yellow Cab** (☏ *928/753–4444*).

EXPLORING

9

TOP ATTRACTIONS

Fodor'sChoice
★ You haven't truly hiked in northwestern Arizona until you've hiked in **Hualapai Mountain Park**. A 15-mi drive from town up Hualapai Mountain Road leads to the park's more than 2,300 wooded acres, with 16 mi of developed and undeveloped hiking trails, picnic areas, ATV trails, rustic cabins, and RV (full hookups) and tent areas. Along the park's trail system you'll find a striking variety of plant life such as prickly pear cactus and Arizona walnut. Abundant species of birds and mammals such as the piñon jay and the Abert squirrel live here, and pristine stands of unmarred aspen mark the higher elevations. Any of the trails can be hiked in about three hours. The **Hayden Peak Trail** is a branch of a 16-mi trail system, which links with many other trails at a high elevation. The popular **Aspen Peak Trail** is shorter, 2 mi one way. Trail maps are available at the park office. Keep in mind the terrain in the park ranges from 5,000 to 8,500 feet above sea level, and snow— sometimes heavy—is common in winter. ⊠ *6250 Hualapai Mountain Rd.* ☏ *928/681–5700, 877/757–0915 for cabin reservations* ⊕ *www. mcparks.com* ✉ *$5.*

WORTH NOTING

The **Powerhouse** building is a great first stop for visitors. **A Tourist Information and Visitor Center** (☎ 928/753–6106 or 866/427–7866 ⊕ www.kingmantourism.org), a converted 1907 electrical plant, has the usual brochures to acquaint you with local attractions. Pick up a walking tour map, which highlights 27 historic sights, including Locomotive Park—home to the 1928 steam locomotive Engine No. 3759. Inside the visitor center, the **Historic Route 66 Museum** (☎ 928/753–9889 💲 $4 includes admission to the Bonelli House and the Mohave Museum of History and Arts) provides a nostalgic look at the evolution of the famous route that started as a footpath followed by prehistoric Indians and evolved into a length of pavement that reached from Chicago, Illinois, to Santa Monica, California. The first weekend of May each year, the Historic Route 66 Association of Arizona holds the three-day **Route 66 Fun Run**, a 40-mi drive that attracts classic car buffs. Admission to the Historic Route 66 Museum also includes a visit to the nearby Mohave Museum of History and Arts and the Bonelli House. **Memory Lane,** also inside the Powerhouse, is a store crammed with kitschy souvenirs. ⊠ The Powerhouse, 120 W. Andy Devine Ave. ☉ Daily 9–5.

History buffs should check out the 1915 **Bonelli House,** an excellent example of Anglo-territorial architecture, featuring a facade of light-gray quarried stone and whitewashed wood accents, a very popular style in the early 1900s. It is one of more than 60 buildings in the Kingman business district listed on the National Register of Historic Places and contains period pieces including a large wall clock that was once the only clock in Kingman. ⊠ 430 E. Spring St. ☎ 928/753–1413 💲 $4 includes admission to Historic Route 66 Museum and the Mohave Museum of History and Arts ☉ Weekdays 11–3.

The **Mohave Museum of History and Arts** includes an Andy Devine Room with memorabilia from Devine's Hollywood years and, incongruously, a portrait collection of every president and first lady. The museum has an exceptional library collection of research materials related to the region. There's also an exhibit of carved Kingman turquoise, displays on Native American art and artifacts, and a diorama depicting the mid-19th-century expedition of Lt. Edward Beale, who led his camel-cavalry unit to the area in search of a wagon road along the 35th parallel. You can follow the White Cliffs Trail from downtown to see the deep ruts cut into the desert floor by the wagons that came to Kingman after Beale's time. ⊠ 400 W. Beale St. ☎ 928/753–3195 ⊕ www.mohavemuseum.org

ANDY DEVINE

Kingman's most famous citizen is Andy Devine (1905–77). The raspy-voiced Western character actor appeared in more than 400 films, most notably as the comic cowboy sidekick "Cookie" to Roy Rogers in 10 films. He also played "the Cheerful Soldier" in The Red Badge of Courage and was in several John Wayne flicks, including The Man Who Shot Liberty Valance (he played the hapless sheriff Linc Appleyard), Stagecoach, and Island in the Sky. On the last weekend of September each year, Kingman celebrates its favorite son with a rodeo (⊕ www.kingmanrodeo.com), parade, and community fair.

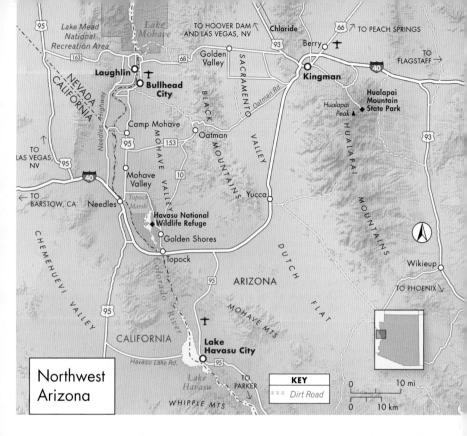

Northwest
Arizona

KEY
=== Dirt Road

0 ————— 10 mi
0 ————— 10 km

$4 *includes admission to Historic Route 66 Museum and the Bonelli House* ☉ *Weekdays 9–5, Sat. 1–5.*

OFF THE BEATEN PATH

Chloride. The ghost town of Chloride, Arizona's oldest silver-mining camp, takes its name from a type of silver ore mined here. During its heyday, from 1900 to 1920, some 75 mines operated in the area: silver, gold, lead, zinc, molybdenum, and even turquoise were mined here. Nearly 400 folks live in Chloride today; there is one restaurant, one saloon, a grocery store, an inn, and two RV parks. Sights include the old jail, Chloride Baptist Church, the Jim Fritz Museum, and the Purcell Galleries of Fine Art. Western artist Roy Purcell painted the large murals on the rocks on the east edge of town—10 feet high and almost 30 feet across, they depict a goddess figure, intertwined snakes, and Eastern and Native American symbols. To reach the murals, follow signs from the east end of Highway 125 along the unpaved road—it's a slow, twisting drive best attempted with four-wheel drive. Outdoors enthusiasts can take advantage of the miles of hiking trails and explore the mineral-rich hills with excellent rockhounding opportunities. Mock gunfights in the streets mark high noon on Saturday. On the last Saturday of June the entire town turns out for **Old Miner's Day**—the biggest event of the year featuring a parade, bazaar, bake sale, and family-friendly contests. The marked turnoff on Highway 125 for Chloride is about

12 mi north of Kingman on U.S. 93. For more information, contact the **Chloride Chamber of Commerce** (✉ *4940 Tennessee Ave. Chloride* ☎ *928/565–2204* ⊕ *www.chloridearizona.com*).

⚠ Give wide berth to abondoned mine entrances and shafts, which are often unstable and can cave in without warning. Experts believe there are more than 200,000 abandoned mines in Arizona, many in the rich mineral regions such as the one surrounding Chloride.

★ **Grand Canyon West Ranch.** Sprawling at the base of Spirit Mountain, this historic 106,000-acre working cattle ranch takes guests on an adventure to the Old West. Corriente cattle still roam the hills and their cowboy caretakers guide horseback tours and horse-drawn wagon rides through the rugged countryside. Tap Duncan (a member of the Hole-in-the-Wall Gang) lived here, and Andy Devine supposedly spent some time working here. The ranch now offers rustic cabins, home-cooked meals, horseback riding, wagon rides, and a helicopter tour of Grand Canyon West. Take U.S. 93 north from Kingman 40 mi and turn right onto Pearce Ferry Road. Follow the paved road for 27 mi, then turn right onto the unpaved Diamond Bar Ranch Road. The Grand Canyon West Ranch is 7 mi farther on the right side of the road. Located just 14 mi southwest of Grand Canyon West, the ranch is a popular stopping-off point for day-trippers seeking spectacular canyon views in this remote region. Call ahead to arrange your visit. ✉ *3750 E. Diamond Bar Ranch Rd., Meadview* ☎ *702/736–8787 or 800/359–8727* ⊕ *www.grandcanyonranch.com* ⚒ *Reservations essential.*

EN ROUTE Traveling north from Kingman, keep an eye out for the strange-looking namesakes of the **Joshua Tree Forest** (*Yucca brevifolia*). This native of the dry Mojave Desert isn't a tree, but actually a member of the lily family. Standing as tall as 40 feet, the alien-looking plant can be recognized by its gangly limbs ending in dense clumps of dark green, bayonet-shape leaves. Mormon emigrants traveling through the area in the mid-19th century named the towering plants after the biblical figure Joshua. From February through March, Joshua trees bloom in clusters of creamy white blossoms. The trees don't branch until after they bloom, and, because they rely on perfect conditions to flower, they don't bloom every year—you're most likely to see blossoms following a rainy December or January.

WHERE TO EAT

$ ✗ **El Palacio.** Set in a century-old building in the heart of Kingman's
MEXICAN historic downtown, this is a reliable choice for well-prepared Mexican favorites and Southwest specialties—and what many believe are the best chiles rellenos in the area. Other notable options include *machaca con huevos* (scrambled eggs with shredded beef and vegetables), carne asada tacos, pork tamales, and chicken mole poblano. A comprehensive drink menu includes a selection of Mexican beers, guava and banana margaritas, and fruity sangria. ✉ *401 E. Andy Devine Ave.* ☎ *928/718–0018* ⊕ *www.serranoent.com* ⊟ *AE, MC, V.*

¢ ✗ **Mr. D'z Route 66 Diner.** This popular spot serves up road food with a
AMERICAN '50s flair for breakfast, lunch, and dinner. (Even Oprah and Gayle King
☺ stopped here on their cross-country adventure in 2006.) The jukebox

Northwest Arizona is full of interesting pit stops off of Historic Route 66.

spins favorites, and tributes to Elvis and Marilyn Monroe adorn the walls in this old-fashioned diner decked out in bright turquoise and hot pink. Expect low prices and large servings of your favorite burgers and milk shakes, plus handcrafted root beer made on the premises. ✉ *105 E. Andy Devine Ave.* ☎ *928/718–0066* ▭ *AE, MC, V.*

WHERE TO STAY

$ ⊡ **Best Western–Kings Inn & Suites.** Conveniently located at the intersection of Interstate 40 and U.S. 93, this hotel has clean, spacious rooms and is a good base for visiting Hualapai Mountain Park, Laughlin, and the ghost towns of Chloride and Oatman. Furnishings are Southwest-inspired with tasteful, earthy color schemes and plush bedding as mid-priced motels go. The minisuites offer comfy beds and a sitting area. **Pros:** several restaurants are within walking distance; a great base for exploring the region; hot breakfast included. **Cons:** traffic can be heard from the highway. ✉ *2930 E. Andy Devine Ave.* ☎ *928/753–6101 or 800/750–6101* ⊕ *www.bestwesternarizona.com* ⇄ *101 rooms* ☖ *In-room: a/c, refrigerator (some), Wi-Fi. In-hotel: pool, gym, laundry facilities, Wi-Fi hotspot, some pets allowed* ▭ *AE, D, DC, MC, V* ⊧CP.

EN ROUTE

A worthwhile if hokey stop between Kingman and Bullhead City, the ghost town of **Oatman** lies along old Route 66. It's a straight shot across the Mojave Desert valley for a while, but then the road narrows and winds precipitously for about 15 mi through the Black Mountains. Oatman's main street is right out of the Old West; scenes from a number of films, including *How the West Was Won*, were shot here. It still has a remote, old-time feel: many of the natives carry sidearms, and they're not acting. You can wander into one of the three saloons or visit the shabbily endearing **Oatman Hotel,** where Clark Gable and Carole Lombard honeymooned in 1939 after they were secretly married in Kingman. Several times a day, resident actors entertain visitors with mock gunfights on the main drag.

Several curio shops and eclectic boutiques line the length of Main Street. The burros that often come in from nearby hills and meander down the street, however, are the town's real draw. A couple of stores sell carrots to folks who want to feed these "wild" beasts, which at last count numbered about a dozen and which leave plenty of evidence of their visits in the form of "road apples"—so watch your step. For information about the town and its attractions, contact the **Oatman Chamber of Commerce** (☏ 928/768–6222 ⊕ www.oatmangoldroad.org).

LAKE HAVASU CITY

60 mi southwest of Kingman on I-40 to AZ 95.

If there's an Arizona Riviera, this is it. Lake Havasu has more than 45 mi of lake shoreline—it's actually a dammed section of the Colorado River—and the area gets less than 4 inches of rain annually, which means it's almost always sunny. Spring, winter, and fall are the best times to visit; in summer, temperatures often exceed 100°F. You can rent everything from water skis to Jet Skis, small fishing boats to large houseboats. The lake area has about a dozen RV parks and campgrounds, more than 120 boat-in campsites, and hundreds of hotel and motel rooms. There are golf and tennis facilities, as well as fishing guides who'll help you find, and catch, the big ones. This city of about 56,000 has grown rapidly over the past couple of decades, and downtown has become steadily more upscale—at least compared with the rest of northwestern Arizona.

Learn about the purchase and reconstruction of London Bridge at the exhibit showcased at the Lake Havasu City Visitor Center, which is also a great place to pick up other information on area attractions.

GETTING HERE AND AROUND

You can explore downtown and the lakefront easily on foot, but most visitors arrive by car—the city lies about 25 mi south of Interstate 40 via AZ 95, and about 100 mi north of Interstate 10 via AZ 95. In town, call Arizona Road Runner Shuttle for local taxi service. River City Shuttle offers service from Lake Havasu to several Laughlin casinos as well as to McCarran Airport in Las Vegas.

ESSENTIALS

Transportation Contacts Arizona Road Runner Shuttle (☏ 928/854–9333 ⊕).**River City Shuttle** (☏ 928/854–5253 or 888/948-3427 ⊕ www.rivercityshuttle.com).

Visitor Info Lake Havasu City Visitor Center (✉ 420 English Village ☏ 928/855–5655 or 800/242-8278 ⊕ www.golakehavasu.com).

EXPLORING

Fodor's Choice
★
Remember the old nursery rhyme "London Bridge Is Falling Down"? Well, it was. In 1968, after about 150 years of constant use, the 294-foot-long landmark was sinking into the Thames. When Lake Havasu City founder Robert McCullough heard about this predicament, he actually set about buying **London Bridge**, having it disassembled, shipped 10,000 mi to northwestern Arizona, and rebuilt, stone by stone. The bridge was reconstructed on mounds of sand and took three years to complete. When it was finished, a mile-long channel was dredged under the bridge and water was diverted from Lake Havasu through the Bridgewater Channel. Today, the entire city is centered on this unusual attraction. At the east base of the bridge, a colorful re-creation of an **English Village** houses a few curio shops and restaurants and offers good views of the channel of cool blue water flowing under London Bridge. On the west side, you'll find a handful of more urbane restaurants as well as the hip Heat Hotel.

The **Lake Havasu Museum of History** takes an in-depth look at the history of the region with exhibits on the Chemehuevi Indians, London Bridge, Parker Dam, the mining industry, and historic steamboat operation. ⊠ *320 London Bridge Rd.* ☎ *928/854–4938* ⊕ *www.havasumuseum. com* ⊒ *$4* ⊙ *Tues.–Sat. 1–4.*

★ **Havasu National Wildlife Refuge** (⊠ *Exit 1 off I–40 at CA/AZ border, then follow signs to refuge entrance* ☎ *760/326–3853* ⊕ *www.fws.gov/ southwest/refuges/Arizona/havasu*), between Needles and Lake Havasu City, is a 37,515-acre refuge for wintering Canada geese and other waterfowl, such as the snowy egret and the great blue heron.

The largest surviving cottonwood-willow woodland in the region is part of the **Bill Williams River National Wildlife Refuge** (⊠ *AZ 95 between mileposts 160 and 161, 23 mi south of Lake Havasu City* ☎ *928/667–4144* ⊕ *www.fws.gov/southwest/refuges/arizona/billwill.html*). This 6,055-acre desert oasis is a favorite byway of neotropical migratory birds such as the flashy vermilion flycatcher and the brilliant summer tanager.

OFF THE
BEATEN
PATH
'Ahakhav Tribal Preserve. The 1,250-acre preserve, which includes a 3.5-acre park, is on the Colorado Indian Tribes Reservation and is a top spot in the area for bird-watching and hiking. Some 350 species of migratory and native birds live around the region or visit on their annual migrations. The best bird-watching is along the shoreline of the backwater area branching off the Colorado River. The 3-mi hiking trail has exercise stations along the way, and a trail extension will lead you to the tribal historical museum and gift shop. From AZ 95 in Parker, which is at the southern end of Lake Havasu, head west on Mohave Road for about 2 mi. When you reach the PARKER INDIAN RODEO ASSOCIATION sign, continue 0.5 mi farther and turn left at the TRIBAL PRESERVE sign at Rodeo Drive. ⊠ *25401 Rodeo Dr., Parker* ☎ *928/669–2664.*

SPORTS AND THE OUTDOORS

BACKCOUNTRY
EXPLORATION
Safari Tours (☎ *928/486–1891*) takes visitors on an adventurous 4½-hour tour of Bill Williams River National Wildlife Refuge, Parker Dam, and the Whipple Mountains for $55.

BOAT TOURS There is no white water on the Colorado River below Hoover Dam. Instead, the river and its lakes offer many opportunities to explore the gorges and marshes that line the shores. If you prefer to do it yourself, look into the canoe and kayak rentals available on Lakes Mead, Mohave, and Havasu. Raft adventures will take you through the Topock Gorge near Lake Havasu, or you can take a trip upriver from Willow Beach 12 mi to the base of Hoover Dam. Along the way, chances are good you'll see bighorn sheep moving along the steep basaltic cliffs. Expect to spend $35 to $65 for half a day, and twice that for a full-day adventure.

Blue Water Jet Boat Tours (✉ *501 English Village* ☎ *928/855–7171 or 888/855–7171* ⊕ *www.coloradoriverjetboattours.com*) takes guests on a 2½-hour narrated trip up the Colorado River to Topock Gorge in the climate-controlled *Starship 2010*. **Desert River Kayak** (✉ *1034 AZ 95, Bullhead City* ☎ *928/754–5320 or 888/529–2533* ⊕ *www.desertriveroutfitters.com*) has several launch sites for paddling trips which include a half-day trip along the Colorado River Heritage Trail and the all-day trip from Topock Gorge to the upper reaches of Lake Havasu. **Jerkwater Canoe Company, Inc.** (✉ *Topock* ☎ *928/768–7753 or 800/421–7803* ⊕ *www.jerkwatercanoe.com*) offers several one-day paddling trips including exploratory excursions of Topock Gorge and Black Canyon. **Western Arizona Canoe & Kayak Outfitter (WACKO)** (✉ *770 Winston Pl.* ☎ *928/715–6414 or 888/881–5038* ⊕ *www.azwacko.com*) gets the outdoor adventure going with paddling trips of Topock Gorge, Lake Havasu, and Bill Williams Wildlife Refuge.

GOLF **The Courses at London Bridge Golf Club** (✉ *2400 Clubhouse Dr.* ☎ *928/855–2719* ⊕ *www.londonbridgegc.com* 🏌 *Nassau Course: 6,036 yds. Par 71. Olde London Course: 6,618 yds. Par 71. Green Fee: $60*) comprises two beautifully laid-out 18-hole courses. Green fee is for either course. The Olde London course is championship caliber.

WATER SPORTS When construction of Parker Dam was completed in 1938, the reservoir it created to supply water to Southern California and Arizona became Lake Havasu. The lake is a 45-mi-long playground for water sports of all kinds. Whether it's waterskiing, jet skiing, powerboating, houseboating, swimming, fishing, or you name it, if water is required, it's happening on Lake Havasu.

Lake Havasu State Park (✉ *699 London Bridge Rd.* ☎ *928/855–2784* ⊕ *www.azstateparks.com* 🚗 *$10 per vehicle* ☉ *Sunrise–10* PM) is near the London Bridge and has an interpretive nature garden and a level 1.5-mi trail that's perfect for watching the sunset. With three boat ramps and 47 first-come, first-served campsites ($15 including day-use fee), it's an extremely popular spot in summer. On the eastern shore of the lake 15 mi south of Lake Havasu City is 2,000-acre **Cattail Cove State Park** (✉ *AZ 95, 15 mi south of Lake Havasu* ☎ *928/855–1223* ⊕ *www.azstateparks.com* 🚗 *$10 per vehicle* ☉ *Sunrise–10* PM). There are 61 first-come, first-served campsites ($19–$30) with access to electricity and water, and public restrooms with showers.

With a boat, you have more options: you can find a quiet, secluded cove or beach to swim or fish. If you have a need for speed, you can plane up and down the lake with or without a skier in tow.

If you don't have the equipment or the vessel necessary to enjoy your water sport, you can rent one from a number of reputable merchants. You can rent everything from Jet Skis to pontoon boats, by the day or by the week, at **Sand Point Marina and RV Park** (⊠ *7952 S. Sand Point Resort Rd.* ☎ *928/855–0549* ⊕ *www.sandpointresort.com*). **Arizona Water Sports** (⊠ *655 Kiowa Ave.* ☎ *928/453–5558 or 800/393–5558* ⊕ *www.arizonawatersports.com*) rents Jet Skis, jet boats, ski boats, and pontoon boats.

WHERE TO EAT

$
AMERICAN
✕ **Barley Brothers Brewery & Grill.** In the little Island Mall on the west side of London Bridge, Barley Brothers is most acclaimed for its micro-brewed ales on tap, especially JennaGrace Hefeweizen and the Kickstart Oatmeal Stout. The casual cooking is hearty and filling, including such tasty morsels as wood-fired shrimp flat bread and German sausage from the comprehensive appetizer menu. For dinner, the standard salads, rotis-serie chicken, burgers, and sandwiches are complemented by specials such as baby back ribs, Jamaican barbecue salmon, and savory porterhouse steaks. Barley Brothers is part of the Shugrue's regional restaurant family, as is popular Javelina Cantina across the street. ⊠ *1425 McCulloch Blvd.* ☎ *928/505–7837* ⊕ *www.barleybrothers.com* ▭ *AE, D, MC, V.*

$$$
AMERICAN
★
✕ **Cha-Bones.** Fiber-optic lighting, mod hanging lamps, and water sculp-tures create a contemporary vibe at this hip, elegant restaurant a short drive north of London Bridge. Steaks and seafood are the key draw, from 24-ounce porterhouse cuts to cioppino in a saffron-tomato broth, but also consider the barbecue ribs and linguine with chicken and poblano chiles—it's the best and most creative food in northwestern Arizona. There's also a long tapas list, including yam fries with honey-key-lime sauce and char-broiled lamb ribs with garlic and rosemary. ⊠ *25 112 London Bridge Rd.* ☎ *928/854–5554* ⊕ *www.chabones.com* ▭ *AE, D, MC, V.*

¢
MEXICAN
✕ **Chico's Tacos.** This always-hopping taqueria in the nondescript Basha's Shopping Center is worth seeking out. It may not be fancy, but this clean and comfortable short-order joint turns out the best Mexican food in town, including tacos, enchiladas, flautas, burritos, and fajitas served with chicken, grilled fish, carne asada, and other meat and veg-gie options. Six different salsas at the salsa bar add a bit of spice to the mix. ⊠ *1641 McCulloch Blvd.* ☎ *928/680–7010* ▭ *D, MC, V.*

$$
AMERICAN
✕ **Juicy's River Café.** This downtown locals' favorite is cozy and very popular—it fills up fast, especially for breakfast and on Sunday morn-ings. Their chicken-fried steak with biscuits and eggs is legendary. The varied menu of lunch and dinner standards includes burgers with bar-becue sauce and smoked bacon, meat loaf, pot roast Stroganoff, and homemade soups and desserts. Great service is paired with reasonable prices. ⊠ *25 N. Acoma Blvd.* ☎ *928/855–8429* ▭ *D, MC, V.*

$$$
AMERICAN
★
✕ **Shugrue's.** The Sedona Shugrue's is the original, but this branch is true to its excellent reputation. More relaxed than the original, this attrac-tive space set on a bluff overlooking London Bridge has one of the best wine lists in town plus consistently well-prepared steaks, seafood, and

9

On Lake Havasu, boaters combine recreation with a bit of English history as they pass under the London Bridge.

other American and international dishes. Highlights include flat bread with Havarti cheese, portabella mushrooms, and olive-tomato tapenade for a starter and blackened ahi tuna with grilled bok choy and lemon-soy butter as a main. The baked desserts are worth saving room for. Be sure to request a table with a bridge view. ✉ *1425 McCulloch Blvd.* ☎ *928/453–1400* ▭ *AE, D, MC, V.*

WHERE TO STAY

$ 🖼 **Havasu Springs Resort.** On a low peninsula reaching into Lake Havasu, this moderately priced resort comprises four motel buildings, each with different attributes. The closest accommodations to the lake are at the Marina Motel, which overlooks the inner harbor. For more sweeping views try the accommodations at the Lakeview Motel, which offers a panoramic vista of the surrounding desert. Those looking for a central location can book a room at the Poolside Motel. And for longer stays and larger families, Vista Suites features full kitchens, one- and two-bedroom suites, cozy yards, barbecue facilities, and excellent views of the lake and the outer harbor. In addition to standard hotel rooms, the resort also offers suites and apartments. **Pros:** comprehensive dining and recreation; friendly staff; nice lakeside beachfront. **Cons:** chair shortage at the pool; rooms are run-down; RV traffic. ✉ *2581 AZ 95, Parker* ☎ *928/667–3361* ⊕ *www.havasusprings.com* ✎ *38 rooms, 4 suites, 3 apartments* ⚑ *In-room: a/c, kitchen (some). In-hotel: restaurant, bar, golf course, tennis courts, beachfront, water sports, Internet terminal* ▭ *AE, D, MC, V.*

$$–$$$ 🖼 **Heat Hotel.** The hip rooms at this sleek, angular-looking boutique
★   hotel on the west side of London Bridge capture the see-and-be-seen

playfulness of Vegas, making it a hit with well-heeled, stylish visitors. Rooms have private balconies or patios overlooking Bridgewater Channel and are done in muted color schemes with soft Anichini linens, low-slung contemporary furniture, and plenty of creature comforts— flat-screen TVs, microwaves, and DVD/CD players. Although there's no pool, an outdoor bar facing the water has cushy private cabanas with daybeds—this area is a sea of tanned and toned bodies during busy periods. This is definitely the most interesting hotel in town. **Pros:** stylish and posh decor; steps from London Bridge and many restaurants; swanky bar and cabana area. **Cons:** Might be a bit too trendy and modern for some tastes. ⊠ *1420 McCulloch Blvd.* ☎ *928/854–2833 or 888/898–4328* ⊕ *www.heathotel.com* ⌁ *17 rooms, 8 suites* ⚲ *In-room: a/c, kitchen (some), DVD, Wi-Fi. In-hotel: bar, gym* ⊟ *AE, D, MC, V.*

$$–$$$ ⊞ **London Bridge Resort.** If you want to be close to the bridge, this hotel is a dependable choice. The decor is a strange mix of Tudor and Southwestern; other than that, studios are standard motel rooms with kitchenettes. The restaurant Martini Bay serves tapas and upscale but unimpressive American fare. The resort has a pair of nightspots popular with the under-30 crowd: Kokomo Havasu, a 10,000-square-foot nightclub with multiple dance floors, five bars, and an outdoor swimming pool; and Style Lounge, which presents rotating entertainment, from live bands to comedy nights to DJ dancing. **Pros:** great views of London Bridge; suites come with sleeper sofas for extra guests; nightlife and business center. **Cons:** limited availability during the busy summer months; sales pressure from the resort's time-share options; rooms need renovating. ⊠ *1477 Queen's Bay* ☎ *928/855–0888 or 800/624–7939* ⊕ *www.londonbridgeresort.com* ⌁ *4 studios, 72 1-bedroom suites, 46 2-bedroom suites* ⚲ *In-room: a/c, kitchen, DVD, Wi-Fi. In-hotel: 2 restaurants, room service, bars, golf course, pools, gym, beachfront, laundry facilities* ⊟ *AE, D, MC, V.*

HOUSEBOATS **Club Nautical Houseboats.** What houseboats lack in speed and maneuverability they make up for in comfort and shade. Club Nautical has some of the most luxurious boats on the lake and the crew makes certain that boaters get the best instruction and tips for their travel into cool blue waters. ⊠ *1000 McCulloch Blvd.* ☎ *800/843–9218* ⊕ *www. lakehavasuhouseboatrental.com.*

SOUTHEAST NEVADA

Updated by
Carrie Frasure

Laughlin, Nevada, and Bullhead City, Arizona, are separated by a unique state line: the Colorado River. It's an interesting juxtaposition of cities, with the casino lights of Laughlin sparkling across the river from Bullhead City. Sixty miles upstream, just southeast of Las Vegas, Boulder City is prim, languid, and full of historic neighborhoods, small businesses, parks, greenbelts—and not a single casino. Over the hill from town, enormous Hoover Dam blocks the Colorado River as it enters Black Canyon. Backed up behind the dam is incongruous, deep-blue Lake Mead, the focal point of water-based recreation for southern Nevada and northwestern Arizona and the major water supplier to seven Southwest states. The lake is ringed by miles of rugged desert country.

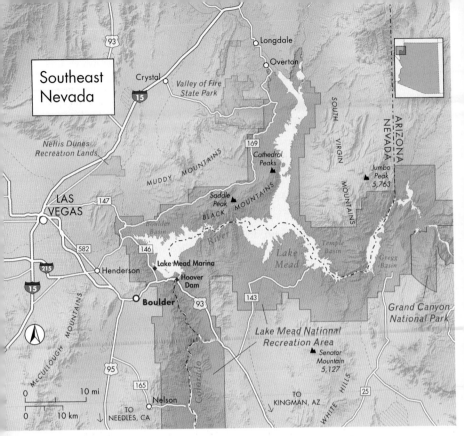

Southeast Nevada

Less than 0.5 mi downstream from the Hoover Dam and Lake Mead work continues on another engineering marvel—a bridge that will span the river canyon and link northwestern Arizona to southeastern Nevada, dramatically reducing traffic across Hoover Dam. At this writing, it's set for completion in late 2010 (⊕ *www.hooverdambypass.org*).

BULLHEAD CITY, ARIZONA, AND LAUGHLIN, NEVADA

35 mi northwest of Kingman on AZ 95 to I-40 to AZ 391.

Laughlin, Nevada, is separated from Arizona by the Colorado River. Its founder, Don Laughlin, bought an eight-room motel here in 1964 and basically built the town from scratch. By the early 1980s Laughlin's Riverside Hotel-Casino was drawing gamblers and river rats from northwestern Arizona, southeastern California, and even southern Nevada, and his success attracted other casino operators. Today Laughlin is the state's third major resort area, attracting more than 3 million visitors annually. The city fills up, especially in winter, with both retired travelers who spend at least part of winter in Arizona and a younger resort-loving crowd. The big picture windows overlooking the Colorado River lend a bright, airy, and open feeling unique to Laughlin casinos. Take a stroll along the river walk, then make the return trip by water taxi

($4 one way, $20 all day). Boating, using Jet Skis, fishing, and plain old wading are other options for enjoying the water.

TIMING

The state of Nevada is in the Pacific time zone, while Arizona is in the mountain time zone. Arizona does not observe daylight saving time, however. As a result, in summer Nevada and Arizona observe the same hours.

GETTING HERE AND AROUND

To get to Laughlin from Kingman, follow U.S. 93 for 35 mi.

Sun Country flies from several cities, including Seattle, Denver, Minneapolis–St. Paul, San Francisco, Phoenix, and Dallas–Fort Worth as well as various places in Mexico and the Caribbean.

Mills Tours, River City Shuttle, and Tri State Shuttle offer regular service from McCarran International Airport to Laughlin/Bullhead City. Reservations for all shuttle services are required.

Lucky Cab & Limo Company of Nevada services Laughlin and Bullhead City. For another approach in getting from casino to casino in Laughlin, hop aboard a water taxi with Americana River Ride or River Passage. Fares can be purchased at the casino dock ticket booths.

ESSENTIALS

Airline Sun Country Airlines (☎ 800/359-6786 ⊕ www.suncountry.com).

Airport Laughlin/Bullhead International Airport (☎ 928/754-2134).

Bus Contacts Mills Tours (☎ 877/454-3734). **River City Shuttle** (☎ 928/854-5253 or 888/948-3427 ⊕ www.rivercityshuttle.com). **Tri State Shuttle** (✉ 1528 Alta Vista Rd., Bullhead City ☎ 800/801-8687 ⊕ www.tristateshuttle.net).

Taxis Americana River Ride (☎ 928/754-3555). **Lucky Cab & Limo Company of Nevada** (☎ 702/298-2299). **River Passage** (☎ 702/299-0090 or 928/754-4391).

Visitor Info Laughlin Visitors Information Center (✉ 1555 Casino Dr. ☎ 702/298-3321 or 800/452-8445 ⊕ www.visitlaughlin.com).

EXPLORING

☼ Across the Laughlin Bridge, 0.25 mi to the north, the **Colorado River**
★ **Museum** displays the rich past of the tristate region where Nevada, Arizona, and California converge. There are artifacts from the Mojave tribe, models and photographs of steamboats that once plied the river, rock and fossil specimens, and the first telephone switchboard used in neighboring Bullhead City. ✉ *2201 Hwy. 68* ☎ *928/754-3399* 🖅 *$2* �

 Sept.–June, Tues.–Sat. 10–4.

Searchlight Museum. Searchlight was once the biggest boomtown in southern Nevada, and this modern, one-room exhibit inside the community center details the area's rich mining and railroad history. It also exposes the lives of its most famous couple, legendary silent-screen stars Rex Bell and Clara Bow. On the way to Laughlin from Las Vegas on U.S. 95, turn off at Cottonwood Cove Road, drive almost a mile to the end of town and turn left on Michael Wendell Way. ✉ *200 Michael Wendell Way, Searchlight* ☎ *702/297-1682* 🖅 *Free* ☼ *Weekdays 9–5, Sat. 9–1.*

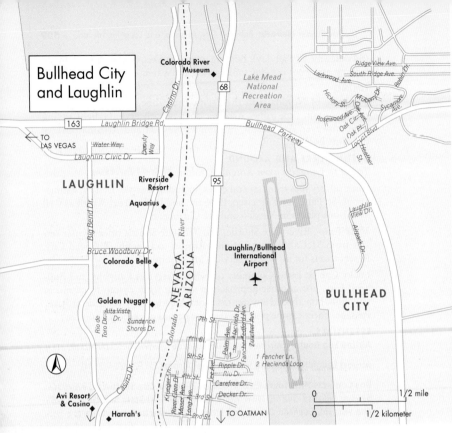

Bullhead City and Laughlin

Colorado River Museum

68

Lake Mead National Recreation Area

163   Laughlin Bridge Rd.

← TO LAS VEGAS

Water Way

Laughlin Civic Dr.

Bullhead Parkway

Ridge View Ave.
South Ridge Ave.
Larkwood Ave.
Hickory St.
Rosewood Ave.
Mulberry Dr.
Oak Ave.
Oak Cir.
Oak Pl.
Sycamore Ave.
Locust Blvd.
Heather St.

LAUGHLIN

Riverside Resort

95

Aquarius

Laughlin View Dr.

Big Bend Dr.

Bruce Woodbury Dr.

Colorado Belle

Laughlin/Bullhead International Airport

Airpark Dr.

Golden Nugget

Alta Vista Dr.

Rio de Toro Dr.

Sundance Shores Dr.

7th St.

6th St.

5th St.

4th St.

3rd St.

2nd St.

Palm Ave.
Hacienda Dr.
Fanchet Ave.
Zuckert Ave.
Ledford Ave.

Krueger Th.
River Glen Dr.
Mossel Ave.
Long Ave.
Joe Ave.
Ripple Dr.
Rio Dr.
Carefree Dr.
Decker Dr.

1 Fancher Ln.
2 Hacienda Loop

BULLHEAD CITY

Avi Resort & Casino

Harrah's

TO OATMAN

0   1/2 mile

0   1/2 kilometer

NEVADA / ARIZONA   Colorado River

OFF THE BEATEN PATH

Christmas Tree Pass, a dirt road located 14 mi south of Searchlight on U.S. 95, leads into the Lake Mead National Recreation Area and to an extensive petroglyph site in Grapevine Canyon. This side route runs 16 mi through a desert landscape sacred to several historical and modern native tribes. The pass cuts through the rough-cut Newberry Range near legendary Spirit Mountain. In addition to viewing the impressive collection of rock art etched on canyon boulders, you'll also get the chance to see desert wildflowers and blooming cacti in spring and early summer. The loop drive reconnects with U.S. 163 15 mi northwest of Laughlin.

WHERE TO EAT

$$
AMERICAN

✕ **Boiler Room Brew Pub.** Laughlin's only microbrewery pumps out 155,000 gallons of beer each year. Sample the handcrafted ales and stout, all of which pair nicely with the wood-fired specialty pizzas, gourmet hamburgers, and mesquite-grilled steaks. The pub is open daily for lunch and dinner. ⊠ Colorado Belle, 2100 S. Casino Dr., Laughlin ☎ 702/298–4000 or 866/352–3553 ⊕ www.coloradobelle.com ▤ AE, D, DC, MC, V.

$$
SEAFOOD
★

✕ **Joe's Crab Shack.** With a fun beachfront atmosphere and relaxing river views, this popular restaurant features fish-and-chips, seafood platters, Louisiana-style shrimp po'boy sandwiches, crab-stuffed shrimp, and heaping mounds of crab in a bucket. The seafood buffet, offered

Monday to Friday 11–3, is the best buffet around. ⊠ *Golden Nugget, 2300 S. Casino Dr., Laughlin* ☎ *702/298–7143* ⊕ *www.joescrabshack. com* ▤ *AE, D, DC, MC, V.*

$$$$ ✕ **The Range Steakhouse.** Old Las Vegas makes an appearance at this
STEAKHOUSE eclectic eatery featuring such tasty fare as herb-encrusted rack of lamb, surf and turf, and veal scaloppine. Riverfront views and an extensive wine list add to the elegant experience. ⊠ *Harrah's, 2900 S. Casino Dr., Laughlin* ☎ *702/298–6832* ⊕ *www.harrahslaughlin.com* ▤ *AE, D, DC, MC, V* ☉ *No lunch.*

WHERE TO STAY

At each resort you visit, visit guest services for a player's card. These casino programs quickly rack up points for cash and discounts.

¢ ▦ **Aquarius.** The old Flamingo Laughlin has shed its shabby image with extensive resort-wide renovations and a new name. The fully renovated guest lobby and casino feature 1,500 slot and video-poker machines, a poker room, and a sports book. The spacious rooms, which were completely gutted in 2008, have been refitted and dressed up in clean, bright colors. **Pros:** business center; a 3,000-seat outdoor amphitheater hosting big-name entertainers; Colorado River views. **Cons:** bland buffet; high hallway traffic. ⊠ *1900 S. Casino Dr., Laughlin* ☎ *702/298–5111 or 800/352–6464* ⊕ *www.aquariuscasinoresort.com* ⇆ *1,907 rooms, 82 suites* ⌂ *In-room: Wi-Fi. In-hotel: 4 restaurants, bars, tennis courts, pool, gym, laundry service, Wi-Fi hotspot, parking (paid)* ▤ *AE, D, DC, MC, V.*

¢ ▦ **Avi Resort & Casino.** The only tribally owned casino in Nevada is run
☺ by the Fort Mojave tribe. The 25,000-square-foot casino houses 1,038
★ slot and video-poker machines. The biggest draw, however, is the private white-sand beach where you can lounge or rent a watercraft from May through September. **Pros:** Sunday champagne brunch; eight-plex movie theater; KidQuest children's program. **Cons:** situated 10 mi south of the main drag; room refrigerators available on first-come, first-served basis (fee $10). ⊠ *10000 Aha Macav Pkwy., Laughlin* ☎ *702/535–5555 or 800/284–2946* ⊕ *www.avicasino.com* ⇆ *455 rooms, 29 spa suites* ⌂ *In-room: refrigerator (some), Wi-Fi. In-hotel: 6 restaurants, bar, golf course, pool, gym, beachfront, water sports, children's programs (ages 6 wks–12 yrs), laundry facilities* ▤ *AE, D, DC, MC, V.*

¢ ▦ **Colorado Belle.** This is a Nevada anomaly—a riverboat casino that's actually on a river. The 608-foot replica of a Mississippi paddle wheeler has nautical-themed rooms with views of the Colorado River. **Pros:** on-site market and gift shop; microbrewery; specialty candy shop. **Cons:** fee for in-room Wi-Fi ($9.99 for 24 hours); room refrigerators upon request for an additional fee ($7). ⊠ *2100 S. Casino Dr., Laughlin* ☎ *702/298–4000 or 866/352–3553* ⊕ *www.coloradobelle.com* ⇆ *1,119 rooms, 49 suites* ⌂ *In-room: kitchen (some), refrigerator (some), Wi-Fi. In-hotel: 5 restaurants, room service, bars, pools, gym, spa, beachfront, laundry service, Wi-Fi hotspot* ▤ *AE, D, DC, MC, V.*

¢ ▦ **Don Laughlin's Riverside Resort Hotel and Casino.** Town founder Don
☺ Laughlin still runs this northernmost joint himself. Check out the Loser's
★ Lounge, with its graphic homage to famous losers, such as the *Hindenburg*, the *Titanic*, and the like. And don't pass up Don's two free classic-

9

car showrooms, with more than 80 rods, roadsters, and tin lizzies. **Pros:** charter flights to the resort from all over the country; family destination features an arcade, bowling center, six-plex movie theater, and supervised playtime at Don's Kid Kastle. **Cons:** hotel fills up fast in summer; incidental fees for Wi-Fi ($8.99 for 24 hours) and in-room refrigerators ($8); rooms are basic and showing their age. ⊠ *1650 S. Casino Dr., Laughlin* ☎ *702/298–2535 or 800/227–3849* ⊕ *www.riversideresort. com* ☞ *1,400 rooms* ♿ *In-room: refrigerator (some), Wi-Fi. In-hotel: 6 restaurants, bar, pools, spa, children's programs (ages 3 mos–12 yrs), laundry facilities, Wi-Fi hotspot* ▤ *AE, D, DC, MC, V.*

¢–$ 🎰 **Harrah's.** This is the classiest joint in Laughlin: it comes with a private sand beach and two casinos (one is no-smoking). Big-name entertainers such as Gary Allan and Natalie Cole perform in the 3,000-seat Rio Vista Outdoor Amphitheater, and legendary artists such as Tony Orlando perform at the indoor Fiesta Showroom. There's a cocktail lounge in each of the casinos and another at the adults-only pool. Card fans might also want to check out the World Series of Poker–themed poker room. **Pros:** separate family and adult towers and pools; smoking and no-smoking casinos; air-charter flights from all over the United States directly to resort for player card members. **Cons:** pools fill up fast; long lines for guest services; incidental fees for Wi-Fi ($10.95 for 24 hours) and gym use ($5 per visit). ⊠ *2900 S. Casino Dr., Laughlin* ☎ *702/298–4600 or 800/427–7247* ⊕ *www.harrahslaughlin.com* ☞ *1,505 rooms* ♿ *In-room: Wi-Fi. In-hotel: 4 restaurants, room service, bars, pools, gym, spa, beachfront, water sports, laundry service, Wi-Fi hotspot* ▤ *AE, D, MC, V.*

BOULDER CITY

78 mi north of Laughlin on NV 163 and U.S. 95; 76 mi northwest of Kingman on U.S. 93.

In the early 1930s Boulder City was built by the federal government to house 5,000 construction workers on the Hoover Dam project. A strict moral code was enforced to ensure timely completion of the dam, and to this day, the model city is the only community in Nevada in which gambling is illegal. (Note that the two casinos at either end of Boulder City are just outside the city limits.) After the dam was completed, the town shrank but was kept alive by the management and maintenance crews of the dam and Lake Mead. Today it's a vibrant little Southwestern town.

GETTING HERE AND AROUND
It takes about two hours via U.S. 93 to get from Kingman to Boulder City.

ESSENTIALS
Visitor Info Boulder City Chamber of Commerce (⊠ *465 Nevada Way* ☎ *702/293–2034* ⊕ *www.bouldercitychamber.com* ⊙ *Weekdays 9–5*).

EXPLORING

★ Be sure to stop at the Dutch Colonial–style **Boulder Dam Hotel,** built in 1933. On the National Register of Historic Places, the 20-room bed-and-breakfast once was a favorite getaway for notables, including the man who became Pope Pius XII and actors Will Rogers, Bette Davis, and Shirley Temple. The **Boulder City/Hoover Dam Museum** (☎ 702/294–1988 ⊕ www.bcmha.org ☑ $2 ⊙ Mon.–Sat. 11–5, Sun. noon–5) occupies the first floor of the hotel. The museum has artifacts relating to the workers and construction of Boulder City and Hoover Dam. ⊠ 1305 Arizona St., Boulder City ☎ 702/293–3510 ⊕ www.boulderdamhotel.com.

HOOVER DAM

7 mi east of Boulder City via U.S. 93; 67 mi northwest of Kingman via U.S. 93.

GETTING HERE AND AROUND

Hoover Dam is about a 90-minute drive from Kingman via U.S. 93; it's about 15 minutes from Boulder City.

EXPLORING

In 1928 Congress authorized $175 million for construction of a dam on the Colorado River to control destructive floods, provide a steady water supply to seven Colorado River basin states, and generate electricity. Considered one of the seven wonders of the industrial world, the art deco **Hoover Dam** is 726 feet high (the equivalent of a 70-story building) and 660 feet thick (more than the length of two football fields) at the base. Construction required 4.4 million cubic yards of concrete—enough to build a two-lane highway from San Francisco to New York. Originally referred to as Boulder Dam, the structure was later officially named Hoover Dam in recognition of President Herbert Hoover's role in the project. Look for artist Oskar Hansen's plaza sculptures, which include the 30-foot-tall *Winged Figures of the Republic.*

Fodor's Choice
★

9

The self-paced **Powerplant Tour** allows you to see the power plant generators and other features. Guide staffers give talks every 15 minutes at each stopping point from 9 to 4:15 (early tours are less crowded). The more extensive **Hoover Dam Tour** gives visitors an up-close look at lesser-known parts of the dam. Guided tours begin at 9:30 and run every half hour until 3:30; it's not wheelchair accessible or for those under eight. Reservations are accepted for the Powerplant Tour, but Hoover Dam Tours are only offered on a first-come, first-served basis and are limited to 20 participants. Cameras, pagers, tote bags, and cell phones are subject to X-ray screening. January and February are the slowest months. The top of the dam is open to pedestrians during daylight hours only; approved vehicles can cross the dam 24/7. ⊠ U.S. 93 east of Boulder City ☎ 702/494–2517 or 866/730–9097 ⊕ www. usbr.gov/lc/hooverdam ☑ Hoover Dam Tour $30, Powerplant Tour $11, parking $7, visitor center $8 ⊙ Daily 9–5 ☞ Security, road, and Hoover Dam crossing information: ☎ 888/248–1259.

SPORTS AND THE OUTDOORS

RAFTING

Black Canyon, just below Hoover Dam, is the place for river running near Las Vegas. You can launch a raft here on the Colorado River year-round. On the Arizona side, the 11-mi run to Willow Beach, with its vertical canyon walls, bighorn sheep on the slopes, and feeder streams and waterfalls coming off the bluffs, is reminiscent of rafting the Grand Canyon. The water flows at roughly 5 mph, but some rapids, eddies, and whirlpools can cause difficulties, as can headwinds, especially for inexperienced rafters.

If you want to go paddling in Black Canyon on your own, you need to make mandatory arrangements with one of the registered outfitters. They provide permits ($12) and the National Park Service entrance fee ($3) as well as launch and retrieval services. You can get a list of outfitters at ☎ 702/494–2204, or go to the paddle-craft and rafting-tours section on the Bureau of Land Management's Web site (⊕ *www.usbr. gov/lc/hooverdam/*).

If you're interested in seeing the canyon on large motor-assisted rafts, **Black Canyon/Willow Beach River Adventures** (☎ *800/455–3490* ⊕ *black-canyonadventures.com*) launches every morning at 10.

For a more hands-on approach, try a guided kayak trip through Black Canyon with **Boulder City Outfitters** (☎ *702/293–1190 or 800/748–3702* ⊕ *www.bouldercityoutfitters.com*). Rates, which include permits, are $163 per person with a two-person minimum.

LAKE MEAD

★ *About 4 mi from Hoover Dam on U.S. 93, 67 mi northwest of Kingman.*

GETTING HERE AND AROUND

From Hoover Dam, travel west on U.S. 93 to its intersection with Lakeshore Drive to reach Alan Bible Visitors Center.

ESSENTIALS

Visitor Info Alan Bible Visitors Center (☎ 702/293–8990 ⊕ www.nps.gov/lame ☉ Daily 8:30–4:30).

EXPLORING

Lake Mead, which is actually the Colorado River backed up behind Hoover Dam, is the nation's largest man-made reservoir: it covers 225 square mi, is 110 mi long, and has an irregular shoreline that extends for 550 mi. You can get information about the lake's history, ecology, recreational opportunities, and the accommodations available along its shore at the Alan Bible Visitors Center. People come to Lake Mead to swim: **Boulder Beach** is the closest to Las Vegas, only a mile or so from the visitor center.

Angling and house boating are favorite pastimes; marinas strung along the Nevada shore rent houseboats, personal watercraft, and ski boats. At least 1 million fish are harvested from the lake every year including the popular striped and largemouth bass. It's stocked with rainbow trout on a weekly basis from late October through March. You can fish here

24 hours a day, year-round (except for posted closings). You must have a fishing license (details are on the National Park Service Web site), and if you plan to catch and keep trout, a separate trout stamp is required. Willow Beach is a favorite for anglers looking to catch rainbow trout; Cathedral Cove and Katherine are good for bass fishing. Divers can explore the murk beneath, including the remains of a B-29 Superfortress, which crashed into the Overton Arm of the lake in 1948. Other activities abound, including waterskiing, sailboarding, canoeing, kayaking, and snorkeling. ⊠ *601 Nevada Way, Boulder City* ☎ *702/293–8906* ⊕ *www. nps.gov/lame* ⊠ *$5 per vehicle, good for 5 days; lake-use fees $10 1st vessel, $5 additional vessel, good for 5 days.*

SPORTS AND THE OUTDOORS

BOATING

Echo Bay Resort and Marina, on the Overton Arm of the north side of the lake, has boat rentals, RV facilities, a gift shop, an open-air cocktail lounge, and a casual, nautical-themed restaurant. ■ TIP→ Make houseboat reservations at least six months in advance. ☎ *800/752–9669* ⊕ *www.sevencrown.com.*

Lake Mead Marina, located at Hemenway Harbor near Hoover Dam, has a general store, public beach, and a floating restaurant. The marina was moved in 2008 due to dropping water levels at Lake Mead. Boat rentals and personal watercraft are available through the Las Vegas Boat Harbor (☎ *702/293–1191 or 877/765–3745*). ⊠ *490 Horsepower Cove Rd. Boulder City,* ☎ *702/293–3484* ⊕ *www.boatinglakemead.com.*

CRUISES

At **Lake Mead Cruises** you can board the 300-passenger *Desert Princess*, an authentic Mississippi-style paddle wheeler that plies a portion of the lake; brunch and dinner cruises are available seasonally. Ninety-minute sightseeing cruises occur year-round. ⊠ *Hemenway Boat Harbor near Boulder Beach* ☎ *702/293–6180* ⊕ *www.lakemeadcruises.com* ⊠ *Prices start at $24; reservations required.*

SCUBA DIVING AND SNORKELING

The creation of Lake Mead flooded a huge expanse of land, and, as a result, deep-water sights abound for scuba divers. Wishing Well Cove has steep canyon drop-offs, caves, and clear water. Castle Cliffs and Virgin Basin both have expansive views of white gypsum reefs and submerged sandstone formations. In summer Lake Mead is like a bathtub, reaching 85°F on the surface and staying at about 80°F down to 50 feet below the surface. Divers can actually wear bathing suits rather than wet suits to do some of the shallower dives. But visibility—which averages 30 feet to 35 feet overall—is much better in the winter months before the late-spring surface-algae bloom obscures some of the deeper attractions from snorkelers. Be aware that Lake Mead's level has dropped because of low snowfall in the Rockies. This has had some effect on diving conditions; St. Thomas ghost town, for example, is now only partially submerged.

Outfitters American Cactus Divers ⊠ *3985 E. Sunset Rd., Suite B, Las Vegas* ☎ *702/433–3483* ⊕ *www.americancactusdivers.com).* **Desert Divers Supply** ⊠ *5720 E. Charleston Blvd., Las Vegas* ☎ *702/438–1000).*

Travel Smart Arizona

GETTING HERE AND AROUND

Most visitors to Arizona arrive either by car via one of the main east–west interstates, Interstate 40 or Interstate 10/8, or by air into the state's major airport in Phoenix. (Smaller but still significant numbers fly into Tucson.) Even visitors who fly in tend to rent cars; public transportation is limited and limiting, and this vast state is ideally suited for car touring. The state's highways are well maintained and have high speed limits (up to 75 MPH on interstates), so traveling even significant distances by car isn't a great challenge.

▋ AIR TRAVEL

Despite its high passenger volume, long lines at the check-in counters and security checkpoints at Phoenix Sky Harbor are usually not a problem, although during busy periods (spring break, holiday weekends, and so on) you should anticipate long waits and arrive at the airport 30 to 60 minutes earlier than you would otherwise. Because Phoenix is the hub for Southwest and US Airways, it has direct flights to most major U.S. cities and a number of international destinations elsewhere in North America (Calgary, Cancun, Edmonton, Guadalajara, Mexico City, Puerto Vallarta, San Jose [Costa Rica], Toronto, and Vancouver among them). Sample flying times from major cities are: one hour from Los Angeles, three hours from Chicago, and five hours from New York City.

AIRPORTS

Major gateways to Arizona include Phoenix Sky Harbor International (PHX), about 3 mi southeast of Phoenix city center, and Tucson International Airport (TUS), about 8.5 mi south of the central business area.

Phoenix Sky Harbor International Airport is one of the busiest airports in the world for takeoffs and landings but rarely suffers from congestion or lengthy lines. Its spacious, modern terminals are easily navigable, with plenty of dining options as well as free Wi-Fi. Sky Harbor's three passenger terminals are connected by inter-terminal buses that run regularly throughout the day.

Tucson International Airport has one terminal that has a smattering of restaurants and free Wi-Fi. Although it services far fewer passengers per day than Sky Harbor, it does offer nonstop flights to a number of major metropolitan areas around the western half of the country (Atlanta is the only eastern city with direct service).

Airport Info Phoenix Sky Harbor International (☎ 602/273–3300 ⊕ www.phxskyharbor. com). Tucson International Airport (☎ 520/573–8100 ⊕ www.tucsonairport.org).

FLIGHTS

Phoenix is a hub for Southwest Airlines and US Airways. These carriers offer direct flights in and out of Phoenix to most of the country's larger metro areas. The nation's other major airlines also fly into Phoenix and have a few flights into Tucson as well.

Among the smaller airlines, AirTran flies from Phoenix to Atlanta. Alaska Airlines has direct service from Phoenix to Portland and Seattle, and from Tucson to Seattle. Frontier connects Phoenix and Tucson with Denver. Hawaiian Airlines flies from Phoenix to Honolulu. Midwest Airlines connects Phoenix and Milwaukee. JetBlue has service from Phoenix to New York. Sun Country Airlines flies from Phoenix, Tucson, and (seasonally) the small airport in Bullhead City (across the river from Laughlin, NV) to Minneapolis. Canada's WestJet connects Phoenix with Edmonton, Calgary, and Winnipeg.

Within Arizona, US Airways Express/ Mesa Airlines (part of US Airways) flies from Phoenix to Flagstaff and Yuma. Great Lakes Aviation flies from Phoenix to Page and Show Low, as well as to Kingman and Prescott from both Ontario, CA, and Farmington, NM (where service continues on to Denver). Scenic Airlines flies from Las Vegas to the Grand Canyon.

Airline Contacts Alaska Airlines (☎ 800/252–7522 or 206/433–3100 ⊕ www.alaskaair.com). **American Airlines** (☎ 800/433–7300 ⊕ www.aa.com). **Continental Airlines** (☎ 800/523–3273 ⊕ www.continental.com). **Delta Airlines** (☎ 800/221–1212 ⊕ www.delta.com). **jetBlue** (☎ 800/538–2583 ⊕ www.jetblue.com). **Southwest Airlines** (☎ 800/435–9792 ⊕ www.southwest.com). **United Airlines** (☎ 800/864–8331 ⊕ www.united.com). **US Airways** (☎ 800/428–4322 ⊕ www.usairways.com).

Smaller Airlines AirTran (☎ 800/247–8726 or 678/254–7999 ⊕ www.airtran.com). **Frontier Airlines** (☎ 800/432–1359 ⊕ www.frontierairlines.com). **Great Lakes Aviation** (☎ 800/554–5111 ⊕ www.greatlakesav.com). **Hawaiian Airlines** (☎ 800/367–5320 ⊕ www.hawaiianair.com). **Midwest Airlines** (☎ 800/452–2022 ⊕ www.midwestexpress.com). **Scenic Airlines** (☎ 800/634–6801 ⊕ www.scenic.com). **Sun Country Airlines** (☎ 800/359–6786 ⊕ www.suncountry.com). **WestJet** (☎ 888/937–8538 ⊕ www.westjet.com).

▌ CAR TRAVEL

A car is a necessity in Arizona, as even bigger cities are challenging to get around in using public transportation. Distances are considerable, but you can make excellent time on long stretches of interstate and other four-lane highways with speed limits of up to 75 MPH (even rural two-lane highways often have speed limits of 65 MPH). In cities, freeway limits are between 55 MPH and 65 MPH. If you venture off major thoroughfares, slow down. Speed limits here generally are only 55 MPH, and for good reason. Many roadways have no shoulders; on many twisting and turning mountain roads speed limits dip to 25 MPH, and police officers often patrol heavily near entrances to small town centers, where speed limits often

drop precipitously. For the most part, the scenery you'll take in while driving makes it worth it.

At some point you will probably pass through one or more of the state's 22 Native American reservations. Roads and other areas within reservation boundaries are under the jurisdiction of reservation police and governed by separate rules and regulations. Observe all signs, and respect Native Americans' privacy. Be careful not to hit any animals, which often wander onto the roads; the penalties can be very high.

Note that in Phoenix certain lanes on interstates are restricted to carpools and multi-occupant vehicles. Seat belts are required at all times. Tickets can be given for failing to comply. Driving with a blood-alcohol level higher than 0.08 will result in arrest and seizure of your driver's license. Fines are severe. Radar detectors are legal in Arizona, as is driving while using handheld phones.

Always strap children under age five into approved child-safety seats. In Arizona children must wear seat belts regardless of where they're seated. In Arizona you may turn right at a red light after stopping if there's no oncoming traffic. When in doubt, wait for the green.

Information Arizona Department of Public Safety (☎ 602/223–2000, 602/223–2163 Highway Patrol ⊕ www.azdps.gov). **Arizona Department of Transportation** (☎ 511 Arizona road information from within Arizona, 888/411–7623 Arizona road information from outside state ⊕ www.az511.com).

GASOLINE

Gas stations, many of them open 24 hours, are widely available in larger towns and cities and along interstates. However, you'll encounter some mighty lonely and long stretches of highway in certain remote sections of Arizona; in these areas it's not uncommon to travel 50 or 60 mi between service stations. It's prudent to play it safe when exploring the far-flung corners of the state and keep your tank at least half full. Gas prices in Arizona are slightly higher than the national average but generally lower than in neighboring Nevada and California.

PARKING

Parking is plentiful and either free or very inexpensive in most Arizona towns, even Phoenix and Tucson. During very busy times, however, such as holidays, parking in smaller popular places like Sedona, Flagstaff, and Bisbee can prove a little challenging.

ROAD CONDITIONS

The highways in Arizona are well maintained, but there are some natural conditions to keep in mind.

Desert heat. Vehicles and passengers should be well equipped for searing summer heat in the low desert. If you're planning to drive through the desert, make sure you are well stocked with radiator coolant, and carry plenty of water, a good spare tire, a jack, a cell phone, and emergency supplies. If you get stranded, stay with your vehicle and wait for help to arrive.

Dust storms. These usually occur from May to mid-September, causing extremely low visibility. Dust storms are more common on the highways and interstates that traverse the open desert (Interstate 10 between Phoenix and Tucson, Interstate 10 between Benson and the New Mexico state line, and Interstate 8 between Casa Grande and Yuma). They also occur occasionally in northeastern Arizona around the Navajo and Hopi regions. If you're on the highway, pull as far off the road as possible, turn on your headlights to stay visible, and wait for the storm to subside.

Flash floods. Warnings about flash floods should not be taken lightly. Sudden downpours send torrents of water racing into low-lying areas so dry that they are unable to absorb such a huge quantity of water quickly. The result can be powerful walls of water suddenly descending upon these low-lying areas, devastating anything in their paths. If you see rain clouds or thunderstorms coming, stay away from dry riverbeds (also called arroyos or washes). If you find yourself in one, get out quickly. If you're with a car in a long gully, leave your car and climb out of the gully. You simply won't be able to outdrive a speeding wave. The idea is to get to higher ground immediately when it rains. Major highways are mostly floodproof, but some smaller roads dip through washes; most roads that traverse these low-lying areas will have flood warning signs, which should be seriously heeded during rainstorms. Washes filled with water should not be crossed until you can see the bottom. By all means, don't camp in these areas at any time, interesting as they may seem.

Fragile desert life. The dry and easily desecrated desert floor takes centuries to overcome human damage. Consequently, it's illegal for four-wheel-drive and all-terrain vehicles and motorcycles to travel off established roadways.

Winter snow and ice. First-timers to Arizona sometimes doubt the intensity and prevalence of icy and snowy winter weather in the state's higher elevations: the Interstate 40 corridor, Grand Canyon region, north-central and northeastern Arizona, as well as some high-elevation communities in eastern Arizona. It's not uncommon for Phoenix to enjoy dry weather and temperatures in the 50s and 60s, while Flagstaff—just 140 mi north—is getting heavy snow and high winds. The North Rim of the Grand Canyon is closed from late fall through spring due to snow. Always check on weather conditions before planning trips to northern and eastern Arizona from November through May.

ROADSIDE EMERGENCIES

In the event of a roadside emergency, call 911. Depending on the location, either the state police or the county sheriff's department will respond. Call the city or village police department if you encounter trouble within the limits of a municipality. Native American reservations have tribal police headquarters, and rangers assist travelers within U.S. Forest Service boundaries.

Information Automobile Association (*AAA* ⊕ *www.aaa.com*).

CAR RENTAL

Car-rental rates in Phoenix typically begin around $25 a day or $150 a week for an economy car with air-conditioning, automatic transmission, and unlimited mileage—rates vary according to supply and demand, tending to be lower in summer and higher in winter. This doesn't include taxes and fees on car rentals, which can range from about 15% to 50%, depending on pickup location. The base tax rate at Sky Harbor Airport is about 30%. When you add the daily fees (which are about $5 a day), taxes and fees can add up to almost half the cost of the car rental. You may be able to save by taking a cab to a retail location nearby to avoid the airport tax and additional daily fees. Taxes outside the airport are typically around 25% or less.

Check the Internet or local papers for discounts and deals. Local rental agencies also frequently offer lower rates.

Most agencies in Arizona won't rent to you if you're under the age of 21, and several major agencies will not rent to anyone under 25.

In Arizona the car-rental agency's insurance is primary; therefore, the company must pay for damage to third parties up to a preset legal limit, beyond which your own liability insurance kicks in.

Major Rental Agencies Alamo (🕾 *800/462–5266* ⊕ *www.alamo.com*). **Avis** (🕾 *800/331–1212* ⊕ *www.avis.com*). **Budget** (🕾 *800/527–0700* ⊕ *www.budget. com*). **Hertz** (🕾 *800/654–3131* ⊕ *www.hertz. com*). **National Car Rental** (🕾 *800/227–7368* ⊕ *www.nationalcar.com*).

❚ TRAIN TRAVEL

Amtrak's *Southwest Chief* operates daily between Los Angeles and Chicago, stopping in Needles, CA (near the Arizona border), Kingman, Williams Junction (from which bus transfers are available to the scenic Grand Canyon Railway), Flagstaff, Winslow, and Gallup, NM (near the state border). The *Sunset Limited* travels three times each week between Los Angeles and Orlando, with stops at Yuma, Maricopa (about 25 mi south of Phoenix), Tucson, and Benson. There's a connecting bus (a 2½-hour trip) between Flagstaff and Phoenix.

Train Info Amtrak (🕾 *800/872–7245* ⊕ *www. amtrak.com*).

ESSENTIALS

■ ACCOMMODATIONS

Arizona's hotels and motels run the gamut from world-class resorts to budget chains and from historic inns, bed-and-breakfasts, and mountain lodges to dude ranches, campgrounds, and RV parks. Make reservations well in advance for the high season—winter in the desert and summer in the high country. A few areas, such as Sedona and the Grand Canyon's South Rim, stay relatively busy year-round, so book as soon as you can. Tremendous bargains can be found off-season, especially in the Phoenix and Tucson areas in summer, when even the most exclusive establishments can cut their rates by half or more.

Phoenix and Tucson have the most variety of accommodations in the state, with Flagstaff offering the largest number in the northern part of the state. Lodgings in Sedona and in some of the smaller, more exclusive desert communities can be pricey, but there are inexpensive chains in or near just about every resort-oriented destination. That said, even the budget chains in these areas can have rates in the upper double-digits.

The Grand Canyon area is particularly pricey, but camping, cabins, and dorm-style resorts on or near the national park grounds offer lower rates. ■TIP➔ If you plan to stay at the Grand Canyon, make lodging reservations as far as a year in advance—especially if you're looking to visit in summer. You might have a more relaxing visit, and find better prices, in one of the gateway cities: Tusayan, Williams, and Flagstaff to the south, and Jacob Lake, Fredonia, and Kanab, Utah, to the north. Of all of these, Flagstaff has the best variety of lodging options in all price ranges.

The lodgings we list are the cream of the crop in each price category. We always list the facilities that are available, but we don't specify whether they cost extra;

when pricing accommodations, always ask what's included and what costs extra. Properties are assigned price categories based on the range from their least-expensive standard double room at high season (excluding holidays) to the most expensive. *See chapter Planners and city lodging sections for price charts.*

Most hotels and other lodgings require your credit-card details before they will confirm your reservation. If you don't feel comfortable e-mailing this information, ask if you can fax it (some places even prefer faxes). However you book, get confirmation in writing and have a copy handy when you check in.

Be sure you understand the hotel's cancellation policy. Some places allow you to cancel without any kind of penalty—even if you prepaid to secure a discounted rate—if you cancel at least 24 hours in advance. Others require you to cancel a week in advance or penalize you the cost of one night. Small inns and B&Bs are most likely to require you to cancel far in advance. Most hotels allow children under a certain age to stay in their parents' room at no extra charge, but others charge for them as extra adults; find out the cutoff age for discounts.

■TIP➔ Assume that hotels operate on the European Plan (EP, no meals) unless we specify that they use the Breakfast Plan (BP, with full breakfast), Continental Plan (CP, Continental breakfast), Full American Plan (FAP, all meals), or Modified American Plan (MAP, breakfast and dinner), or are all-inclusive (AI, all meals and most activities).

BED-AND-BREAKFASTS

Arizona is one of the better destinations in the country when it comes to B&Bs. You'll find luxurious Spanish colonial–style compounds and restored Victorian inns in the more upscale destinations, such as Tucson, Sedona, Flagstaff, and Prescott, as well as less-fancy lodges virtually everywhere. Check with the Arizona

Association of Bed and Breakfast Inns for details on its many members throughout the state. The Arizona Trails Reservation Service also has an extensive list of B&Bs and other lodgings, and can also help with vacation packages, guided tours, and golf vacations. Mi Casa Su Casa offers properties in a range of styles, from adobe haciendas in areas like Sedona and Tucson to pine cabins in the White Mountains.

Reservation Services Arizona Association of Bed and Breakfast Inns (☎ *No phone* ⊕ *www.arizona-bed-breakfast.com*). **Arizona Trails Reservation Service** (☎ *480/837-4284 or 888/799-4284* ⊕ *www.arizonatrails.com*). **Bed & Breakfast.com** (☎ *512/322-2710 or 800/462-2632* ⊕ *www.bedandbreakfast.com*) also sends out an online newsletter. **Bed & Breakfast Inns Online** (☎ *615/868-1946 or 800/215-7365* ⊕ *www.bbonline.com*). **BnB Finder.com** (☎ *212/432-7693 or 888/547-8226* ⊕ *www.bnbfinder.com*). **Mi Casa Su Casa** (☎ *480/990-0682 or 800/456-0682* ⊕ *www.azres.com*).

DUDE–GUEST RANCHES

Guest ranches afford visitors a close encounter with down-home cooking, activities, and culture. Most of the properties are situated around Tucson and Wickenburg, northwest of Phoenix. Some are resort-style compounds where guests are pampered, whereas smaller, family-run ranches expect *everyone* to join in the chores. Horseback riding and other outdoor recreational activities are emphasized. Many dude ranches are closed in summer. The Arizona Dude Ranch Association provides names and addresses of member ranches and their facilities and policies.

Information The Arizona Dude Ranch Association (☎ *520/823-4277* ⊕ *www.azdra.com*).

▌ COMMUNICATIONS

INTERNET

As in all major U.S. cities, high-speed Internet and Wi-Fi connections are ubiquitous at hotels throughout the state, even in remote areas (although sometimes there's a fee of $5 to $15 per day). There are also connections at cafés, restaurants, and other businesses. In more remote areas you'll find fewer ways to get online, but usually a local café or motel has Wi-Fi.

Contact Cybercafes (⊕ *www.cybercafes.com*).

▌ EATING OUT

Two distinct cultures—Native American and Sonoran—have had the greatest influence on native Arizona cuisine. Chiles, beans, corn, tortillas, and squash are common ingredients for those restaurants that specialize in regional cuisine (cactus is just as tasty but less common). Mom-and-pop *taquerias* are abundant, especially in the southern part of the state. In Phoenix, Tucson, Sedona, and increasingly Flagstaff, Bisbee, Prescott, Lake Havasu City, and some smaller but sophisticated parts of the state, you'll find hip, intriguing restaurants specializing in American and Southwestern cuisine, as well as some excellent restaurants specializing in such ethnic cuisines as Thai, Chinese, Japanese, and the like. *See chapter Planners and city dining sections for price charts.*

RESERVATIONS AND DRESS

Regardless of where you are, it's a good idea to make a reservation if you can. In some places (some of Scottsdale's top restaurants, for example) it's expected. We only mention them specifically when reservations are essential (there's no other way you'll ever get a table) or when they are not accepted. For popular restaurants, book as far ahead as you can (often 30 days), and reconfirm as soon as you arrive. (Large parties should always call ahead to check the reservations policy.) We mention dress only when men are required to wear a jacket or a jacket and tie.

Online reservation services, such as OpenTable and DinnerBroker, make it easy to book a table before you even leave home.

FOR INTERNATIONAL TRAVELERS

CURRENCY

The dollar is the basic unit of U.S. currency. It has 100 cents. Coins are the penny (1¢); the nickel (5¢), dime (10¢), quarter (25¢), half-dollar (50¢), and the very rare golden $1 coin and even rarer silver $1. Bills are denominated $1, $5, $10, $20, $50, and $100, all mostly green and identical in size; designs and background tints vary. You may come across a $2 bill, but the chances are slim.

CUSTOMS

Information U.S. Customs and Border Protection (⊕ www.cbp.gov).

DRIVING

Driving in the United States is on the right. Speed limits are posted in miles per hour (usually between 55 MPH and 70 MPH). Watch for lower limits in small towns and on back roads (usually 30 MPH to 40 MPH). Most states require front-seat passengers to wear seat belts; many states require children to sit in the back seat and to wear seat belts. In major cities rush hour is between 7 and 10 AM; afternoon rush hour is between 4 and 7 PM. To encourage carpooling, some freeways have special lanes, ordinarily marked with a diamond, for high-occupancy vehicles (HOV)—cars carrying two people or more.

Highways are well paved. Interstates—limited-access, multilane highways designated with an "I-" before the number—are fastest. Interstates with three-digit numbers circle urban areas, which may also have other limited-access expressways, freeways, and parkways. Tolls may be levied on limited-access highways. U.S. and state highways aren't necessarily limited-access, but may have several lanes.

ELECTRICITY

The U.S. standard is AC, 110 volts/60 cycles.

EMBASSIES

Contacts Australia (☎ 202/797-3000 ⊕ www.austemb.org). **Canada** (☎ 202/682-1740 ⊕ www.canadianembassy.org). **United Kingdom** (☎ 202/588-7800 ⊕ www.britainusa.com).

EMERGENCIES

For police, fire, or ambulance, dial 911 (0 in rural areas).

HOLIDAYS

New Year's Day (Jan. 1); Martin Luther King Day (3rd Mon. in Jan.); Presidents' Day (3rd Mon. in Feb.); Memorial Day (last Mon. in May); Independence Day (July 4); Labor Day (1st Mon. in Sept.); Columbus Day (2nd Mon. in Oct.); Thanksgiving Day (4th Thurs. in Nov.); Christmas Eve and Christmas Day (Dec. 24 and 25); and New Year's Eve (Dec. 31).

MAIL

You can buy stamps and aerograms and send letters and parcels in post offices. Stamp-dispensing machines can occasionally be found in airports, bus and train stations, office buildings, drugstores, and convenience stores. U.S. mailboxes are stout, dark blue steel bins; pickup schedules are posted inside the bin (pull down the handle to see them). Parcels weighing more than a pound must be mailed at a post office or at a private mailing center.

Within the United States a first-class letter weighing 1 ounce or less costs 44¢.

To receive mail on the road, have it sent c/o General Delivery at your destination's main post office (use the correct five-digit ZIP code). You must pick up mail in person within 30 days, with a driver's license or passport for identification.

Contacts DHL (☎ 800/225-5345 ⊕ www.dhl.com).**Federal Express** (☎ 800/463-3339 ⊕ www.fedex.com). **Mail Boxes, Etc./The UPS Store** (☎ 800/789-4623 ⊕ www.mbe.com). **United States Postal Service** (⊕ www.usps.com).

PASSPORTS AND VISAS

Visitor visas aren't necessary for citizens of Australia, Canada, the United Kingdom, or most citizens of European Union countries coming for tourism and staying for fewer than 90 days. If you require a visa, the cost is $100, and waiting time can be substantial, depending on where you live. Apply for a visa at the U.S. consulate in your place of residence; check the U.S. State Department's special Visa Web site for further information.

Visa Information Destination USA (⊕ www.unitedstatesvisas.gov).

PHONES

Numbers consist of a three-digit area code and a seven-digit local number. In Phoenix, the area code is 480, 623, or 602; other areas in the state use 520 or 928. Within many local calling areas you dial only the seven digits; in others you dial "1" first and all 10 digits—just as you would for calls between area-code regions. The same is true for calls to numbers prefixed by "800," "888," "866," and "877"—all toll-free. For calls to numbers prefixed by "900" you must pay—usually dearly.

For international calls, dial "011" followed by the country code and the local number. For help, dial "0" and ask for an overseas operator. Most phone books list country codes and U.S. area codes. The country code for Australia is 61, for New Zealand 64, for the United Kingdom 44. Calling Canada is the same as calling within the United States, whose country code, by the way, is 1.

For operator assistance, dial "0." For directory assistance, call 555–1212 or occasionally 411 (free at many public phones). You can reverse long-distance charges by calling "collect"; dial "0" instead of "1" before the 10-digit number.

Instructions are generally posted on pay phones. Usually you insert coins in a slot (usually 25¢–50¢ for local calls) and wait for a steady tone before dialing. On long-distance calls the operator tells you how much to insert; prepaid phone cards, widely available in various denominations, can be used from any phone. Follow the directions to activate the card (there's usually an access number, then an activation code), then dial your number.

CELL PHONES

The United States has several GSM (Global System for Mobile Communications) networks, so multiband mobiles from most countries (except for Japan) work here. Unfortunately, it's almost impossible to buy a pay-as-you-go mobile SIM card in the United States—which allows you to avoid roaming charges—without also buying a phone. That said, cell phones with pay-as-you-go plans are available for well under $100. The cheapest ones with decent national coverage are the GoPhone from Cingular and Virgin Mobile, which only offers pay-as-you-go service.

Contacts Cingular (☎ 888/333–6651 ⊕ www.cingular.com). **Virgin Mobile** (☎ No phone ⊕ www.virginmobileusa.com).

Contacts **DinnerBroker** (⊕ *www.dinnerbroker. com*). **OpenTable** (⊕ *www.opentable.com*).

WINES, BEER, AND SPIRITS

Although Arizona is not typically associated with viticulture, the region southeast of Tucson, stretching to the Mexico border, has several microclimates ideal for wine growing. The iron- and calcium-rich soil is similar to that of the Burgundy region in France, and, combined with the temperate weather and lower-key atmosphere, has enticed several independent and family-run wineries to open in the past few decades in the Elgin, Sonoita, and Nogales areas, with a somewhat more nascent crop of them having begun to develop in northern parts of the state, around Sedona and Verde Valley. Microbreweries have sprung up throughout the state in recent years, with a number of good ones in Phoenix, Tucson, and Flagstaff.

In Arizona you must be 21 to buy any alcohol. Bars and liquor stores are open daily, including Sunday, but must stop selling alcohol at 2 AM. In many municipalities, including Phoenix and Flagstaff, smoking is prohibited in restaurants and bars. You'll find beer, wine, and alcohol at most supermarkets. Possession and consumption of alcoholic beverages is illegal on Native American reservations.

Contact **Arizona Wine Growers Association** (⊕ *www.arizonawine.org*).

▎ HEALTH

ANIMAL BITES

Wherever you're walking in desert areas, particularly between April and October, keep a lookout for rattlesnakes. You're likely not to have any problems if you maintain distance from snakes that you see—they can strike only half of their length, so a 6-foot clearance should allow you to remain unharmed, especially if you don't provoke them. If you are bitten by a rattler, don't panic. Get to a hospital within two to three hours of the bite.

Try to keep the area that has been bitten below heart level, and stay calm, as increased heart rate can spread venom more quickly. Keep in mind that 30% to 40% of bites are dry bites, where the snake uses no venom (still, get thee to a hospital). Avoid night hikes without rangers, when snakes are on the prowl and less visible.

Scorpions and Gila monsters are really less of a concern, since they strike only when provoked. To avoid scorpion encounters, look before touching: never place your hands where you can't see, such as under rocks and in holes. Likewise, if you move a rock to sit down, make sure that scorpions haven't been exposed. Campers should shake out shoes in the morning, since scorpions like warm, moist places. If you're bitten, see a ranger about symptoms that may develop. Chances are good that you won't need to go to a hospital. Children are a different case, however: scorpion stings can be fatal for them. Always try to keep an eye on what they may be getting their hands into to avoid the scorpion's sting. Gila monsters are relatively rare and bites are even rarer, but bear in mind that the reptiles are most active between April and June. Should a member of your party be bitten, it is most important to release the Gila monster's jaws as soon as possible to minimize the amount of venom released. This can usually be achieved with a stick, an open flame, or immersion of the animal in water.

DEHYDRATION

This underestimated danger can be very serious, especially considering that one of the first major symptoms is the inability to swallow. It may be the easiest hazard to avoid, however; simply drink every 10–15 minutes, up to a gallon of water per day in summer.

HYPOTHERMIA

Temperatures in Arizona can vary widely from day to night—as much as 40°F. Be sure to bring enough warm clothing for hiking and camping, along with wet-weather gear. It's always a good idea to pack an extra set of clothes in a large, waterproof plastic bag that would stay dry in any situation. Exposure to the degree that body temperature dips below 95°F produces the following symptoms: chills, tiredness, then uncontrollable shivering and irrational behavior, with the victim not always recognizing that he or she is cold. If someone in your party is suffering from any of this, wrap him or her in blankets and/or a warm sleeping bag immediately and try to keep him or her awake. The fastest way to raise body temperature is through skin-to-skin contact in a sleeping bag. Drinking warm liquids also helps.

SUN EXPOSURE

Wear a hat and sunglasses and put on sunblock to protect against the burning Arizona sun. And watch out for heatstroke. Symptoms include headache, dizziness, and fatigue, which can turn into convulsions and unconsciousness and can lead to death. If someone in your party develops any of these conditions, have one person seek emergency help while others move the victim into the shade and wrap him or her in wet clothing (is a stream nearby?) to cool down.

▌HOURS OF OPERATION

Most museums in Arizona's larger cities are open daily. A few are closed Monday, and hours may vary between May and September (off-season in the major tourist centers of Phoenix and Tucson). Call ahead when planning a visit to lesser-known museums or attractions, whose hours may vary considerably. Major attractions are open daily.

Most retail stores are open 10 AM–6 PM, although stores in malls tend to stay open until 9 PM. Those in less-populated areas are likely to have shorter hours and may be closed Sunday. Shopping centers are often open Sunday noon–5 or later.

▌MONEY

Prices throughout this guide are given for adults. Substantially reduced fees are almost always available for children, students, and senior citizens.

CREDIT CARDS

Throughout this guide, the following abbreviations are used: **AE**, American Express; **D**, Discover; **DC**, Diners Club; **MC**, MasterCard; and **V**, Visa.

▌PACKING

Pack casual clothing and resort wear for a trip to Arizona. Stay cool in cotton fabrics and light colors. T-shirts, polo shirts, sundresses, and lightweight shorts, trousers, skirts, and blouses are useful year-round in all but the higher-elevation parts of the state, where cooler temperatures mandate warmer garb. Bring sun hats, swimsuits, sandals, and sunscreen—essential warm-weather items. Bring a sweater and a warm jacket in winter, necessary from November through April in the high country—anywhere around Flagstaff and in the White Mountains. And don't forget jeans and sneakers or sturdy walking shoes year-round.

SHIPPING SPORTING EQUIPMENT

If you're driving here, lugging your gear isn't much of a hassle. But travelers arriving by plane may find hauling bags of clubs, mountain bikes, and skis a bit daunting. Sports Express specializes in shipping gear. The service isn't cheap, but it is highly reliable and convenient.

Contact **Sports Express** (☎ *800/357–4174* ⊕ *www.sportsexpress.com*).

■ SAFETY

Arizona's track record in terms of crime is not unlike that of other U.S. states, if a little higher than average in Phoenix and Tucson. In these big cities you should take the same precautions you would anywhere—be aware of what's going on around you, stick to well-lighted areas, and quickly move away from any situation or people that might be threatening. In both of these cities it's easy to find yourself driving into a less-than-savory neighborhood with little notice; if you feel uneasy about your surroundings, turn around and go back the way you came.

■ **TIP→** Check the U.S. government travel advisory before you plan a trip to the Mexico border towns. Visitors should take extra precautions.

Contacts **Transportation Security Administration** (*TSA* ⊕ *www.tsa.gov*). **U.S. Department of State** (⊕ *travel.state.gov*).

■ TAXES

Arizona state sales tax (called a transaction privilege tax), which applies to all purchases except food in grocery stores, is 5.6%. Individual counties and municipalities then add their own sales taxes, which add another few percentage points. Phoenix and Tucson both levy city sales taxes of 2%, and Flagstaff taxes purchases at a rate of 1.72%. When added to county taxes, the total sales tax in Phoenix goes up to 8.3%; in Tucson, to 8.1%; and in Flagstaff, to 8.4%. Total sales taxes throughout the state range from 7.6% to 10.7%. Sales taxes do not apply on Indian reservations.

■ TIME

Arizona is in the mountain time zone, but Nevada, next door, is in the Pacific time zone. Arizona does not use daylight saving time, though, and as a result, from spring through fall Nevada and Arizona observe the same hours. ■ **TIP→** The Navajo Nation does observe daylight saving time, however, so it's always the same time on Navajo territory as in mountain time zone areas outside Arizona.

Information **Timeanddate.com** (⊕ *www.timeanddate.com/worldclock*) can help you figure out the correct time anywhere.

■ TIPPING

The customary tip for taxi drivers is 15%–20%, with a minimum of $2. Bellhops are usually given $2 per bag in luxury hotels, $1 per bag elsewhere. Hotel maids should be tipped $2 per day of your stay. A doorman who hails a cab can be tipped $1–$2. You should also tip your hotel concierge for services rendered; the size of the tip depends on the difficulty of your request, as well as the quality of the concierge's work. For an ordinary dinner reservation or tour arrangements, $3–$5 should do; if the concierge scores seats at a popular restaurant or show or performs unusual services (getting your laptop repaired, finding a good pet-sitter, etc.), $10 or more is appropriate.

Waiters should be tipped 15%–20%, though at higher-end restaurants a solid 20% is more the norm. Many restaurants add a gratuity to the bill for parties of six or more. Ask what the percentage is if the menu or bill doesn't state it. Tip $1 per drink you order at the bar, though if at an upscale establishment, those $15 martinis might warrant a $2 tip.

■ TOURS

ARCHAEOLOGY

The Archaeological Conservancy offers a number of tours covering significant sites around the country, including a few trips that involve sites in Arizona. Based in southwestern Colorado, Crow Canyon Archaeological Center has a few different trips that touch on portions of

Arizona. These vary year to year, but have included hiking in Carrizo Mountain Country, Hopi kachina and silver-jewelry workshops, backcountry archaeology in northeastern Arizona, and rock art in Arizona. Utah's Southwest Ed-Ventures, part of the Four Corners School of Outdoor Education, can work with you to customize your own trip through Arizona's Hopi and Navajo regions, and they also offer a number of scheduled group trips that touch on Arizona.

Contacts Archaeological Conservancy (☎ 505/266–1540 ⊕ www. americanarchaeology.org). **Crow Canyon Archaeological Center** (☎ 970/565–8975 or 800/422–8975 ⊕ www.crowcanyon.org). **Southwest Ed-Ventures** (☎ 435/587–2156 or 800/525–4456 ⊕ www.fourcornersschool.org/ southwest-ed-ventures).

BICYCLING

A number of companies offer extensive bike tours that cover parts of the Southwest. Backroads organizes a nine-day Utah and northern Arizona national parks journey, as well as biking and biking–hiking trips in southern Arizona's Sonoran Desert and Saguaro National Park. Scottsdale-based AOA Adventures offers a variety of bike trips throughout the state. Timberline Adventure has biking tours of Arizona's White Mountains. ■**TIP→** Most airlines accommodate bikes as luggage, provided they're dismantled and boxed.

Contacts AOA Adventures (☎ 480/945–2881 or 866/455–1601 ⊕ www.aoa-adventures.com). **Backroads** (☎ 510/527–1555 or 800/462–2848 ⊕ www.backroads.com). **Timberline Adventures** (☎ 303/368–4418 or 800/417–2453 ⊕ www.timbertours.com).

GOLF

Golfpac organizes golf vacations all over the world, Phoenix, Scottsdale, and Tucson being among its most popular destinations.

Contact Golfpac (☎ 888/848–8941 ⊕ www. golfpactravel.com).

HIKING

Scottsdale-based AOA Adventures offers multiday hiking and biking tours through some of the state's most dramatic scenery, from the Grand Canyon to Havasupai. Vermont-based Boundless Journeys has wonderful hiking tours that take in the Grand Canyon region as well as Bryce and Zion in Utah.

Contacts AOA Adventures (☎ 480/945–2881 or 866/455–1601 ⊕ www.aoa-adventures. com). **Boundless Journeys** (☎ 800/941–8010 ⊕ www.boundlessjourneys.com).

NATIVE AMERICAN HISTORY

You can explore a number of parts of the state important to indigenous peoples—Sedona, the Grand Canyon, Hopi Country, Antelope Canyon, Canyon de Chelly—on walking, float-trip, and jeep tours offered by Native American Journeys.

Contact Native American Journeys (☎ 928/284–4735 ⊕ www. nativeamericanjourneys.com).

NATURAL HISTORY

Consider booking a trip through Smithsonian Journeys if you're keen on experiencing the Grand Canyon with knowledgeable guides—they also have a "Canyons, Badlands, and Mesas" tour that includes Winslow, Petrified Forest, Sunset Crater, Meteor Crater, and Homolovi Ruins, in addition to the Grand Canyon. Victor Emanuel Nature Tours is another excellent tour operator, offering four different tours (three in summer, one in winter) that emphasize bird-watching throughout the state. Off the Beaten Path has a variety of tours in northern Arizona and elsewhere in the Southwest.

Contacts Off the Beaten Path (☎ 406/586–1311 or 800/445–2995 ⊕ www. offthebeatenpath.com). **Smithsonian Journeys** (☎ 202/357–4700 or 877/338–8687 ⊕ www.smithsonianjourneys.org). **Victor Emanuel Nature Tours** (☎ 512/328–5221 or 800/328–8368 ⊕ www.ventbird.com).

RIVER-RAFTING

Rafting on the Colorado River through the Grand Canyon is a once-in-a-life-time experience for many who try it. Numerous reliable companies offer rafting tours through the canyon, including Action Whitewater Adventures, OARS, Western River Expeditions, Wilderness River Adventures, and World Wide River Expeditions.

Contacts Action Whitewater Adventures (☎ 801/375–4111 or 800/453–1482 ⊕ www.riverguide.com). **OARS** (☎ 209/736–4677 or 800/346–6277 ⊕ www.oars.com). **Western River Expeditions** (☎ 801/942–6669 or 866/904–1160 ⊕ www.westernriver.com). **Wilderness River Adventures** (☎ 928/645–3296 or 800/992–8022 ⊕ www.riveradventures.com). **World Wide River Expeditions** (☎ 435/259–7515 or 800/231–2769 ⊕ www.worldwideriver.com).

▌ VISITOR INFORMATION

For local tourism information, see specific chapters and towns. Many of Arizona's Native American reservations have Web sites and helpful information. Some require permits for visiting certain areas.

Visitor Info Arizona Office of Tourism (☎ 602/364–3700 or 866/275–5816 ⊕ www.arizonaguide.com).

Native American Contacts Arizona Commission of Indian Affairs (☎ 602/542–3123 ⊕ www.indianaffairs.state.az.us). **Gila River Indian Community** (☎ 520/562–9500 ⊕ www.gric.nsn.us). **Inter Tribal Council of Arizona: Hopi Tribe** (☎ 928/734–2441 ⊕ www.itcaonline.com/tribes_hopi.html). **Navajo Nation Tourism Office** (☎ 928/810–8501 ⊕ www.discovernavajo.com). **Salt River Pima-Maricopa Indian Community** (☎ 480/850–8000 ⊕ www.saltriver.pima-maricopa.nsn.us). **Tohono O'odham Nation** (☎ 520/383–0211 ⊕ www.tonation-nsn.gov). **White Mountain Apache Nation** (☎ 928/338–4346 or 877/338–9628 ⊕ www.wmat.nsn.us).

INSPIRATION

Zane Grey's novels about the Wild West, Barbara Kingsolver's portraits of contemporary Tucson in *Pigs in Heaven*, and environmentalist Edward Abbey's *The Monkey Wrench Gang* all capture the spirit of Arizona. Many classic Westerns were shot around the state, including *How the West Was Won* (1962), *The Searchers* (1956), *Stagecoach* (1939), and *Gunfight at the O.K. Corral* (1957).

ONLINE RESOURCES

Information of particular interest to outdoorsy types can be found on the Web site for Arizona State Parks. At this writing, the state is facing a budget crisis and has decided to close some parks indefinitely. Several parks do remain open on a 5-day schedule, and others are being kept open through local funding. The site for the National Park Service has links to many of Arizona's parks and there are other Web sites devoted specifically to the Grand Canyon. The Great Outdoor Recreation Page is another font of information for hikers, skiers, and the like.

There is a handful of excellent general-interest sites related to travel in Arizona. A very good bet is the *Arizona Republic*–sponsored AzCentral.com, which provides news, reviews, and travel information on the entire state, with a particular emphasis on Phoenix. Alternative newsweeklies are another helpful resource, among them the Phoenix *New Times*. For the southern part of the state, look for *Tucson Weekly*. In Flagstaff and north-central Arizona, check out Flagstaff Live.

Contacts Arizona State Parks (⊕ www.azstateparks.com). **AzCentral.com** (⊕ www.azcentral.com).**The Canyon** (⊕ www.thecanyon.com). **Flagstaff Live!** (⊕ www.flaglive.com).The **Great Outdoor Recreation Page** (⊕ www.gorp.com). **National Park Service** (⊕ www.nps.gov). **Phoenix *New Times*** (⊕ www.phoenixnewtimes.com). ***Tucson Weekly*** (⊕ www.tucsonweekly.com).

INDEX

Shutterstock. 39 (top center), Nina B/Shutterstock. 39 (bottom center), robert van beets/iStockphoto. 39 (right), Walter Siegmund/wikipedia.org. 40 (left), Ashok Rodrigues/iStockphoto. 40 (top right), Daryl Faust/Shutterstock. 40 (bottom right), Eric Foltz/iStockphoto. Chapter 2: Phoenix, Scottsdale and Tempe: 41, Kerrick James. 42, John C. Russell/Four Seasons Hotels & Resorts. 43, Barbara Kraft/ Four Seasons Hotels & Resorts. 46, Royal Palms Resort and Spa. 47 (top), Sanctuary on Camelback Mountain, Scottsdale. 47 (bottom), InterContinental Hotels Group. 48, Starwood Hotels & Resorts. 49 (top), David Peeters/iStockphoto. 49 (bottom), The Boulders Resort & Golden Door Spa. 50 and 51 (top), Nicky HedayatZedeh. 51 (bottom), John Pozniak/wikipedia.org. 52, Kerrick James. 53, Wilde Meyer Gallery. 54, Paul Markow/Rancho de los Caballeros. 56 and 67, Kerrick James. 74, JW Marriott Desert Ridge Resort. 88-89, Royal Palms Resort and Spa. 112 (top), Reddie Henderson. 112 (bottom left), Arizona Grand Resort. 112 (bottom right), Sanctuary on Camelback Mountain, Scottsdale. 113 (top), The Westin Kierland Resort & Spa. 113 (bottom left), JW Marriott Desert Ridge Resort. 113 (bottom right), Barbara Kraft/Four Seasons Hotels & Resorts. 120, Wilde Meyer Gallery.123, Kerrick James. 126, Stuart Pearce/age fotostock. 139 (top), The Boulders Resort & Golden Door Spa. 139 (bottom), Mark Boisclair Photography. 145 and 149, Kerrick James. Chapter 3: Grand Canyon National Park: 151 and 153 (top and bottom), National Park Service. 156, Nickolay Stanev/Shutterstock. 161, poutnik/Shutterstock. 166, National Park Service. 181, Kerrick James. 188, Mark Lellouch/National Park Service. 190--91, Christophe Testi/Shutterstock. 192, Anton Foltin/Shutterstock. 193, Geir Olav Lyngfjell/Shutterstock. 194 (top and bottom) and 195 (top), Kerrick James. 195 (bottom), NPS. 196, Mark Lellouch/NPS. 197, Kerrick James.206, Kerrick James. Chapter 4: North-Central Arizona: 213, Kerrick James. 214, Tom Grundy/Shutterstock. 215 (top), sochigirl/Shutterstock. 215 (bottom), Tom Grundy/Shutterstock. 216, FloridaStock/Shutterstock. 218, David M. Schrader/Shutterstock. 225, Kerrick James. 230, Zack Frank/Shutterstock. 239 and 244, Kerrick James. 248, Lindy Drew. 257, Kerrick James. 258, LouLouPhotos/Shutterstock. Chapter 5: Northeast Arizona: 267, Kerrick James. 268 (left), Sourav and Joyeeta Chowdhury/Shutterstock. 268 (right), Katrina Brown/Shutterstock. 269 (top and bottom), Aramark Parks & Destinations. 272, Sylvain Grandadam/age fotostock. 273 (top), Library of Congress Prints and Photographs Division. 273 (bottom), SuperStock/age fotostock. 274, Frank Staub/ age fotostock. 275, Wolfgang Staudt/Wikimedia Commons. 276, Robcsee/Shutterstock. 282-83, 292, 301, 307, 310-11, and 314, CAN BALCIOGLU/Shutterstock. Chapter 6: Eastern Arizona: 321, Kerrick James. 322 (left), Jim Parkin/Shutterstock. 322 (right), George Burba/Shutterstock. 323 (top), Mike Norton/Shutterstock. 323 (bottom), Zack Frank/Shutterstock. 326, Jeffrey M. Frank/Shutterstock. 329, Raymond Forbes/age fotostock. 339, 344, 353, and 356, Kerrick James. 358, Sebastien Burel/Shutterstock. Chapter 7: Tucson: 361, 362, and 363 (top and bottom), Metropolitan Tucson Convention & Visitors Bureau. 366, Floris Slooff/Shutterstock. 367 (top), Miguel Malo/iStockphoto. 367 (bottom), stu_spivack/Flickr. 368, Jose Gil/Shutterstock. 369 and 370, Metropolitan Tucson Convention & Visitors Bureau. 376 and 389, Kerrick James. 400, Metropolitan Tucson Convention & Visitors Bureau. 408 (top), Loews Ventana Canyon. 408 (bottom left), Arizona Inn. 408 (bottom right), White Stallion Ranch. 411, 418, and 433, Metropolitan Tucson Convention & Visitors Bureau. Chapter 8: Southern Arizona: 437, Kerrick James. 438 (top), Kevin Cole/wikipedia.org. 438 (bottom), Mark Godfrey/The Nature Conservancy. 439 (top and bottom) and 441, Metropolitan Tucson Convention & Visitors Bureau. 442, Walter Bibikow/age fotostock. 443 (top), Nickolay Stanev/iStockphoto. 443 (bottom), Jlahorn/wikipedia.org. 444, White Stallion Ranch. 445, Norma Jean Gargasz/age fotostock. 446, Metropolitan Tucson Convention & Visitors Bureau. 455, Kerrick James. 462, Mark Godfrey/ The Nature Conservancy. 469, wikipedia.org. 476, Kerrick James. 481, Metropolitan Tucson Convention & Visitors Bureau. 486, Kerrick James. Chapter 9: Northwest Arizona and Southeast Nevada: 489, Kerrick James. 490 (left), cloki/Shutterstock. 490 (right), Bruce Grubbs/Shutterstock. 494, Heeb Christian/age fotostock. 495 (top) Kerrick James. 495 (bottom), jader alto/age fotostock. 496, Kerrick James. 501, Rolf Hicker Photography/Alamy. 506 and 515, Kerrick James.

NOTES

NOTES

ABOUT OUR WRITERS

John Blodgett is a regular contributor to *Fodor's Utah*, *Fodor's The Complete Guide to the National Parks of the West*, and other titles. He is based in Salt Lake City, Utah, but regularly travels the desert southwest in search of sun and solitude. He wrote the Native American Experience spotlight.

Andrew Collins, a former Fodor's editor, updated the Northeastern Arizona, Northwestern Arizona, Grand Canyon, and Travel Smart sections of this book. A resident of Oregon who travels several times a year throughout the Southwest, he has authored more than a dozen guidebooks and is the gay travel expert for the *New York Times* Web site, About.com. He also writes a syndicated weekly newspaper travel column, writes regularly about travel for FoxNews.com, and has contributed to *Travel & Leisure*, *New Mexico* magazine, *Sunset*, and dozens of other periodicals.

On hiatus from traveling the globe, JoBeth Jamison recently decided to spend more time trotting around her home state of Arizona. The thirtysomething Flagstaff native is a graduate of the University of Arizona. Currently, JoBeth resides in Sedona where she is the editor of *Sedona Magazine*. For this edition, JoBeth wrote spotlights on spas, golf, shopping and food.

Melissa Kim is a freelance writer who wrote "Arizona Landscape Adventures:" Author of a bicycling guide book and numerous articles on travel and recreation, her favorite Arizona experience is camping near the Grand Canyon's North Rim.

A Phoenix-based freelance writer and editor, Cara LaBrie left her native Arizona to report for newspapers across the country. She quickly learned that no place had Mexican food like the Valley, and eventually found the way back to her favorite salsas and enchiladas. Today she appreciates the striking desert sunsets more than she did in her childhood, and eagerly awaits the next out-of-state visitor she can take on a tour of her favorite local restaurants.

Tucson, North-Central, and Southern Arizona updater Mara Levin divides her time between travel writing, social work, and her role as mom to two daughters. A native of California, Mara now lives in Tucson, where the grass may not be greener but the mountains, tranquillity, and slower pace of desert life have their own appeal.